'Chinkin and Kaldor understand deeply and explain clearly the legal issues and distortions involved in justifications for international interventions into "new wars" and their aftermath. Their human security lens provides new creative focus to a burgeoning literature.'

Antonia Chayes,
Tufts University, USA

'An inspired collaboration between two leading world experts on the linkages between international law and war. *International Law and New Wars* is an outstanding contribution to scholarship, being the most comprehensive and authoritative treatment of this most important of all current global challenges. It seems to be the most significant book on international law published in the last decade.'

Richard Falk,
University of California, Santa Barbara, USA

'*International Law and New Wars* is a magisterial achievement of breath-taking power and originality. Chinkin and Kaldor lay out a realistic and achievable blueprint for peace and security in the twenty-first century.'

Anne-Marie Slaughter,
President and CEO, New America

INTERNATIONAL LAW AND NEW WARS

International Law and New Wars examines how international law fails to address the actual experience of what are known as 'new wars' - instances of armed conflict and violence in places such as Syria, Ukraine, Libya, Mali, the Democratic Republic of Congo and South Sudan. International law rests to a great extent on an outmoded concept of war drawn from the experiences of previous centuries. The book identifies different models for addressing contemporary forms of violence and shows how they are associated with different interpretations of international law. In some cases, this has dangerously weakened the legal restraints on war established after 1945. It emphasises the role of gender in understanding and responding to 'new wars', and puts forward a practical case for a 'second generation human security' and the implications this carries for international law.

CHRISTINE CHINKIN is Emerita Professor of International Law, Director of the Centre for Women, Peace and Security at the London School of Economics and William Cook overseas faculty member of the University of Michigan Law School. She is a leading expert on international law and human rights law, especially the international human rights of women.

MARY KALDOR is Professor of Global Governance and Director of the Civil Society and Human Security Research Unit at the London School of Economics. She has pioneered the concepts of new wars and global civil society. Her elaboration of the real-world implementation of human security has directly influenced European and national policies.

INTERNATIONAL LAW AND NEW WARS

CHRISTINE CHINKIN

MARY KALDOR

CAMBRIDGE
UNIVERSITY PRESS

CAMBRIDGE
UNIVERSITY PRESS

University Printing House, Cambridge CB2 8BS, United Kingdom

One Liberty Plaza, 20th Floor, New York, NY 10006, USA

477 Williamstown Road, Port Melbourne, VIC 3207, Australia

314-321, 3rd Floor, Plot 3, Splendor Forum, Jasola District Centre, New Delhi-110025, India

79 Anson Road, #06-04/06, Singapore 079906

Cambridge University Press is part of the University of Cambridge.

It furthers the University's mission by disseminating knowledge in the pursuit of education, learning and research at the highest international levels of excellence.

www.cambridge.org
Information on this title: www.cambridge.org/9781107171213
DOI: 10.1017/9781316759868

First published 2017

A catalogue record for this publication is available from the British Library

Library of Congress Cataloging in Publication data
Names: Chinkin, C. M., author. | Kaldor, Mary, author.
Title: International law and new wars / Christine Chinkin, Mary Kaldor.
Description: Cambridge [UK] ; New York : Cambridge University Press, 2017. | Includes bibliographical references and index.
Identifiers: LCCN 2016035546 | ISBN 9781107171213 (hardback) | ISBN 9781316622094 (Paperback)
Subjects: LCSH: War (International law) | Jurisdiction (International law) | Self-defense (International law) | Humanitarian law. | Reconciliation. | Peace-building. | Security, International. | BISAC: LAW / International.
Classification: LCC KZ6385 .C447 2016 | DDC 341.6–dc23 LC record available at https://lccn.loc.gov/2016035546

ISBN 978-1-107-17121-3 Hardback
ISBN 978-1-316-62209-4 Paperback

To Our Grandchildren

CONTENTS

FOREWORD

JAVIER SOLANA

It is a pleasure for me to write the foreword of this much-needed book. It has a special relevance for me since some of its ideas originated from the Human Security Study Group, present during my term as European Union High Representative for Common Foreign and Security Policy. I know very well the authors, Christine Chinkin and Mary Kaldor, who were the convenors of the group, and I witnessed their passion and dedication during those years and at their work at the LSE.

They have dedicated their time and efforts to the very commendable task of designing the best protection for human rights with the intention of applying their thoughtful work to alleviate suffering and help build long-lasting peace, which is, in a few words, the consequence of the application of the human security paradigm.

As a result of my years of experience in foreign policy and international organizations, I have become convinced that a new approach to conflict and post-conflict settings is urgently needed. In a globalized world the idea of human security, as opposed to the national security paradigm, is vital. The nature of conflict has changed fundamentally, and international law and practice have to adapt to it.

In this regard, the European Union has come a long way. Given its nature, the EU is not a state but a model of global governance. Its approach when acting externally has included emphasis on fundamental rights and the rule of law, and its operations have combined both civil and military elements. However, much remains to be done.

This book is unique in presenting the reality of the new warfare and the characteristics of the different security models, their causes and consequences. And it comes as a reminder for the whole international community. It is time to think again about the law of war. We should be honest and acknowledge that current approaches to conflict and post-conflict are not delivering as expected. The five-year war in Syria is one of the many examples we are witnessing. Actions based on current security models, although some according to international law, are not bringing stability and long-term peace. There is no doubt that the solution will have to come from the international legal system, but if this is not adapted to the new reality it will surely fail, as we are unfortunately seeing nowadays. Taking into account the logic of what is called 'new wars' – with actors, problems and dynamics different from those of modern wars – international law should give a response. If economic and political purposes are behind the main purpose of war, military action will not suffice to put an end to it or to make peace long-lasting.

Essential for scholars and thought-provoking for practitioners, this book is brilliant in elucidating the dilemmas of international law and how it might be adapted for addressing contemporary crisis. What is even more helpful, it offers a practical solution to security in an era of globalization. Although I was already familiar with the authors' ideas, reading this book has been an amazing discovery and an impulse to keep thinking about how to put these ideas into action, through concrete policies. I sincerely hope that the ideas put forth here will constitute a fundamental piece of a new international legal system.

ACKNOWLEDGEMENTS

This project has had a long gestation. It began with the work of the Human Security Study Group, which reported from 2003 onwards to Javier Solana, then European Union High Representative for Common Foreign and Security Policy, and continued with our collaboration in teaching and research at the LSE. In the course of writing the book, the world has changed dramatically and is still changing. This is partly why the project has taken us so long, as we have struggled to think through the implications of such changes. As far as possible we have endeavoured to include changes up to the end of 2016.

Many people and institutions have helped us in the long process of working on the book, and we are very grateful to them all. These include especially the European Research Council (ERC) for funding a five-year research programme that gave us the time to write this book. The UK Department for International Development (DFID) and the Open Society Foundation (OSF) also provided additional support. Others are Julian Perry Robinson, Iavor Rangelov, Henry Radice and Sabine Selchow, who read parts of the manuscript and suggested helpful sources and thoughts; Rebecca Sutton, Ruth Fitzharris and Domenika Spyratou, who helped bring the project to fruition; the students in our Human Security seminars at the LSE for their ideas and criticisms; and the anonymous reviewers at Cambridge University Press who provided very useful comments.

We would also like to thank our Departments at the LSE and both the Civil Society and Human Security Research Unit and the Centre for Women, Peace and Security for providing us with a stimulating and conducive environment for developing the ideas and concepts in this book.

Finally we thank each other for all we have learned from each other and for the fun in working together.

ABBREVIATIONS

ABM	Anti-Ballistic Missile Treaty
AFISMA	African-Led International Support Mission to Mali
AMISOM	African Union Mission in Somalia
ANZUS	Australia, New Zealand, United States Security Treaty
API	Additional Protocol I (to the 1949 Geneva Conventions)
AU	African Union
CCW	Convention on Prohibitions or Restrictions on the Use of Certain Conventional Weapons
CEDAW	Committee for the Elimination of Discrimination against Women
CESCR	Committee on Economic, Social and Cultural Rights
CIA	Central Intelligence Agency (USA)
CIS	Commonwealth of Independent States
CND	Campaign for Nuclear Disarmament
CPA	Coalition Provisional Authority
CSDP	Common Security and Defence Policy (EU)
CSSDCA	Conference on Security, Stability Development and Co-operation in Africa
DDR	Disarmament, Demobilisation and Reintegration
DDRR	Disarmament, Demobilisation, Rehabilitation and Reintegration
DPKO	Department of Peacekeeping Operations (UN)
DRC	Democratic Republic of the Congo
ECHR	European Convention on Human Rights
ECOMOG	Economic Community of West African States Monitoring Group
ECOWAS	Economic Community of West African States
ECtHR	European Court of Human Rights
ECtHR GC	European Court of Human Rights Grand Chamber
EU	European Union
EULEX	European Union Rule of Law Mission (Kosovo)
EUPM	European Police Mission (Bosnia)
FRY	Federal Republic of Yugoslavia
FSA	Free Syrian Army
GCTF	Global Counterterrorism Forum

GDP	Gross Domestic Product
GEST	Gender Expert Support Team (Darfur)
IAC	International Armed Conflict
IACtHR	Inter-American Court of Human Rights
IAEA	International Atomic Energy Agency
ICAN	International Campaign to Abolish Nuclear Weapons
ICBL	International Campaign to Ban Landmines
ICC	International Criminal Court
ICCPR	International Covenant on Civil and Political Rights
ICESCR	International Covenant on Economic, Social and Cultural Rights
ICISS	International Commission on Intervention and State Sovereignty
ICJ	International Court of Justice
ICRC	International Committee of the Red Cross
ICTR	International Criminal Tribunal for Rwanda
ICTY	International Criminal Tribunal for the Former Yugoslavia
IDP	Internally Displaced Persons
IGO	Inter-Governmental Organisation
IHL	International Humanitarian Law
ILC	International Law Commission
ILO	International Labour Organisation
INF	Intermediate-Range Nuclear Forces Treaty
IPTF	International Police Task Force (Bosnia)
IS	Islamic State
ISAF	International Security Assistance Force (Afghanistan)
JNA	Yugoslav National Army
KFOR	Kosovo Force
KLA	Kosovo Liberation Army
KPS	Kosovo Police Service
LAR	Lethal Autonomous Robotic ('killer robot')
LGBT	Lesbian, Gay, Bisexual and Transgender
LRA	Lord's Resistance Army (Uganda)
MAD	Mutual Assured Destruction
MINURSO	United Nations Mission for the Referendum in Western Sahara
MINUSMA	United Nations Multidimensional Integrated Stabilization Mission in Mali
MOD	Ministry of Defence (UK)
MONUSCO	United Nations Organization Stabilization Mission in the Democratic Republic of the Congo
NATO	North Atlantic Treaty Organisation
NIAC	Non-International Armed Conflict
NPT	Treaty on the Non-Proliferation of Nuclear Weapons; Non-Proliferation Treaty

OAS	Organisation of American States
OAU	Organisation of African Unity
OCHA	Office for the Coordination of Humanitarian Affairs (UN)
OHR	Office of the High Representative (Bosnia and Herzegovina)
ONUC	United Nations Operation in the Congo (Opération des Nations Unies au Congo)
OPCW	Organisation for the Prohibition of Chemical Weapons
OPT	Occupied Palestinian Territory
OSCE	Organisation for Security and Co-operation in Europe
NGO	Nongovernmental Organisation
PBC	Peacebuilding Commission (PBC)
PCIJ	Permanent Court of International Justice
RS	Republika Srpska
SADC	Southern African Development Community
SALT	Strategic Arms Limitation Talks
SCSL	Special Court for Sierra Leone
SEATO	Southeast Asia Treaty Organization
SOFA	Status of Forces Agreement
SORT	Strategic Offensive Reductions Treaty
SRSG	Special Representative of the Secretary-General
START	Strategic Arms Reduction Talks
UAV	Unmanned Aerial Vehicle (drone)
UDHR	Universal Declaration of Human Rights
UK	United Kingdom
UN	United Nations
UNAMI	United Nations Assistance Mission for Iraq
UNAMIR	United Nations Assistance Mission for Rwanda
UNAMSIL	United Nations Mission in Sierra Leone
UNDOF	United Nations Disengagement Observer Force
UNDP	United Nations Development Programme
UNEF	United Nations Emergency Force (Suez)
UN GA	United Nations General Assembly
UNFICYP	United Nations Peacekeeping Force in Cyprus
UN HRC	United Nations Human Rights Council
UNMIH	United Nations Mission in Haiti
UNMIK	United Nations Interim Administration Mission in Kosovo
UNMISET	United Nations Mission of Support in East Timor
UNMISS	United Nations Mission in South Sudan UNOCI United Nations Operation in Côte d'Ivoire
UNOHCHR	United Nations Office of the High Commissioner for Human Rights
UNPREDEP	United Nations Preventive Deployment Force (former Yugoslav Republic of Macedonia)

UNPROFOR	United Nations Protection Force
UN SC	United Nations Security Council
UN S-G	United Nations Secretary-General
UNTAC	United Nations Transitional Authority in Cambodia
UNTAES	United Nations Transitional Administration for Eastern Slavonia, Baranja and Western Sirmium
UNTAET	United Nations Transitional Administration in East Timor
UN Women	United Nations Entity for Gender Equality and the Empowerment of Women
USA	United States of America
US Africom	United States Africa Command
USSR	Union of Soviet Socialist Republics
WMD	Weapons of Mass Destruction

PART I

Conceptual Framework

1

Introduction

1.1 Introduction

This is a book about how international law related to the regulation of political violence fails to address the contemporary experience of what we call 'new wars' – bouts of armed violence in places such as Syria and Ukraine, Mali and Libya, the Democratic Republic of Congo and South Sudan, to name but a few of these zones of hostilities and insecurity at the time of writing. Contemporary international law, largely constructed in the nineteenth and twentieth centuries, rests to a great extent on outmoded conceptions of war drawn from the experience of European wars – inter-state clashes involving battles between regular armed forces, which we call 'old wars'.

In the twenty-first century, there have been efforts to adapt the international legal framework relating to the use of force, often in what we perceive as dangerous directions. Former US President George W. Bush talked about a 'new paradigm', which required 'new thinking' about international law,[1] while UK Prime Minister Tony Blair said that the 'rules of the game have changed'.[2] Whether we are talking about Bush's conception of 'pre-emptive self-defence' to justify the invasion of Iraq in 2003 or his depiction of detainees at Guantánamo Bay as 'illegal combatants', President Obama's justifications for targeted killings, President Putin's claim to be permitted to come to the defence of so-called Russian nationals in Ukraine or Georgia, or debates about the legality of

[1] 'Strengthen Alliances to Defeat Global Terrorism and Work to Prevent Attacks against Us and Our Friends', *The White House Archives*, 14 September 2001, http://georgewbush-whitehouse.archives.gov/nsc/nss/2002/nss3.html.

[2] 'Blair, in His Own Words', *BBC*, 5 August 2005, http://news.bbc.co.uk/1/hi/uk_politics/3750847.stm. Blair's comments followed the 7 July 2005 bombings on the London transport system.

airstrikes against the Islamic State (IS)[3] in Syria, attempts are made to stretch international law to accommodate current responses to 'new wars' in ways which, even if not widely accepted, tend to weaken the constraints on violence in international affairs agreed upon after the end of the Second World War. And indeed a similar argument may apply to some of the more well-meaning additions to international law relating to humanitarian interventions and/or peace agreements, put forward in international and regional institutions like the United Nations, the European Union or the African Union. In almost all of these cases, these purported adaptations of international law, we argue, are based on 'old war' assumptions.

We argue that war, both 'old' and 'new', needs to be reconceptualised as a humanitarian catastrophe. Despite the fact that the use of force in international relations was prohibited in the United Nations Charter adopted in 1945, the idea of war as a legitimate phenomenon has a powerful resonance, lingering on in the self-defence exception as well as in geo-political assumptions about the importance of military power and deeply rooted ideas of national (state) security. In the post–World War Two period, an important development has been the emergence of international human rights law, which offers a different perspective to how we understand 'new wars'. On this basis, we make the case for an alternative rights-based response to 'new wars', a second generation Human Security approach, as a practical rather than a utopian solution. We do not reject the reality that international law must – as it always has – develop and evolve, but we argue that such evolution must be based on a principled understanding of the realities of new wars and not on expedient responses to crisis.[4] We emphasise too the gender dimension of conflict and the critical role of gender in developing an alternative approach.

'War' is no longer a term used in modern international legal discourse[5] although it remains in popular discourse. By 'war' we refer to the collective use of force involving two or more actors. In international law terms, the

[3] This body is variously called Islamic State (IS), the Islamic State of Iraq and Syria (ISIS), the Islamic State of the Levant (ISIL), or, in Arabic, *Daesh*. Our use of IS does not in any way denote that we consider it as a state, or putative state.

[4] Charlesworth, Hilary 2002. 'International Law: A Discipline of Crisis', *Modern Law Review* 65: 377–392.

[5] The Covenant of the League of Nations, 1919, refers to 'war or the threat of war' and 'resort to war' (articles 11 and 12), while the United Nations (UN) Charter, 1945, refers to the use of force in international relations (article 2 (4)).

use of force refers to military force, or the use of armed force in conflict, governed by the laws of war. In contrast the (legitimate) use of force domestically refers to policing, which operates according to much tighter rules of engagement, at least in rights-based societies. Our argument that war is illegitimate does not imply that all uses of force are illegitimate. Rather it means that if force is used legitimately in the globalised arena, it must operate under similar sorts of constraints and with similar objectives as operate traditionally within rights-based societies.

We recognize that political developments are moving in the opposite direction. In 2016, the election of Donald Trump as President of the United States and the United Kingdom referendum vote to leave the European Union were both expressions of aspirations similar to those found in Russia or some east European countries, for a return to national sovereignty and the simplicities of geo-politics and polarisation around national and religious divisions. We take the view that these tendencies will only make things worse and exacerbate the various forms of violence to be found in 'new wars'. This is why a different and realistic understanding of security is all the more needed.

In this first chapter, we begin by describing what we mean by 'new wars'. We then discuss what has become known as the gap between legality and legitimacy. This has gained prominence as a consequence of challenges to international law as an inadequate tool to regulate contemporary forms of violence and recourse to arguments asserting the legitimacy of the use of force in preference to legal analysis. We then outline five different models or ways of responding to new wars and how they construct, interpret, adapt or stretch international law in accordance with their differing conceptions of legitimacy. These models then form the conceptual basis for analysis throughout the book. And in the concluding section, we outline the plan of the book.

1.2 New Wars

1.2.1 The Logic of New Wars

In a speech to the Academy of Military Science in January 2013, the Russian Chief of the General Staff, Valery Gerassimov, talked about the appearance of a new type of warfare, which he called 'non-linear war'. In an eerie anticipation of what was to happen in Crimea and Eastern Ukraine the following year, he argued that in 'the 21st century, we have seen a tendency towards blurring the lines between the state of war and peace. Wars are no longer declared and, having begun, proceed according to an unfamiliar template'. He went on to describe how 'a perfectly thriving state can, in a matter of months and even days ... sink into a web of chaos, humanitarian catastrophe, and civil war'. He said that 'frontal engagements of large formations of force ... are becoming a thing of the past' and that, instead, the use of special forces, exploitation of internal opposition 'as well as informational actions, devices and means' are the methods of contemporary warfare.[6]

In the literature about contemporary war, an array of terms has been used to make a similar point. The American military often use the term 'hybrid wars'.[7] Other terms include 'wars among the people',[8] 'wars of the third kind',[9] 'privatized wars',[10] 'post-modern wars'[11] as well as 'new wars'.[12] In this book, building upon earlier work by Mary Kaldor, we use the term 'new wars'. The advantage of the term is that it draws attention to the way that contemporary political violence is different from the predominant 'old war' conception that tends to underlie scholarly analysis, legal practice and policymaking.

The concept of 'new wars' has been criticised on the grounds that new wars are not 'new' and that they may not be 'war'.[13] We agree that 'new wars' are not necessarily empirically new; rather they are different from an idealised conception of 'old wars'. The aim is to elucidate different ways of understanding and analysing extreme political violence. It would be odd if all aspects of 'new wars' were empirically new, but it would be equally odd if there were no new features – the globalised aspects of new

[6] Gerassimov, Valery 2013. 'The Value of Science in Prediction', published in *Military-Industrial Kurier*, English version available at http://inmoscowsshadows.wordpress.com/2014/07/06/the-gerasimov-doctrine-and-russian-non-linear-war/.

[7] Hoffman, Frank 2007. *Conflict in the 21st Century: The Rise of Hybrid Wars*. Arlington, CA: Potomac Institute for Policy Studies.

[8] Smith, Rupert 2005. *The Utility of Force*. London: Alfred A. Knopf.

[9] Rice, Edward 1990. *Wars of the Third Kind: Conflict in Underdeveloped Countries*. Berkeley: University of California Press.

[10] Eppler, Erhard 2001. *Vom Gewaktmärkte zum Gewaltmarkt? Die Privatisierung und Kommerzialisierung der Gewalt*. Frankfurt: Suhrkmamp.

[11] Hables Gray, Chris 2007. *Post-Modern War: The New Politics of Conflict*. London: Routledge.

[12] Duffield, Mark 2001. *Global Governance and the New Wars: The Merging of Development and Security*. London: Zed Books; Kaldor, Mary 1999. *New and Old Wars: Organised Violence in a Global Era*. Cambridge: Polity Press, 3rd edn.; Munkler, Herfried 2005. *The New Wars*. Cambridge: Polity Press.

[13] These critiques are addressed in Kaldor, Mary 2013. 'In Defence of New Wars', *Stability Journal* 2:1–16.

wars, as we stress, are extremely important. For our purposes, however, the differences between 'old' and 'new wars' have to do with the logic and dynamics of these different types of wars rather than with their empirical characteristics. Indeed, the expression 'new wars' is a conceptual rather than descriptive categorisation.[14] We have some sympathy for the argument that new wars are not war since they can also be described as criminal enterprises, banditry, terrorism or massive violations of human rights; nevertheless they are fought in the name of political goals, and politics accordingly has to be part of the response.

The central argument is that new wars have a different logic from old wars. Clausewitz was the key theorist of 'old wars'. He defined war as 'an act of violence intended to compel our opponent to fulfil our will'.[15] From this definition, he derived the proposition that war is a clash of wills that tends to the extreme; the politicians want to achieve their political objective; the generals need to disarm the opponent; and the war releases hatred and passion among the people. If, however, we define war as 'an act of (organised) violence framed in political terms' then war might be understood either as a clash of wills or what we could describe as a mutual enterprise in which the various armed groups have more to gain from war itself, from fighting, than from winning or losing. In what follows, we elaborate this notion of a mutual enterprise, the way in which the various armed groups need the condition of war for economic and political purposes – war as a means of extracting resources or instrumentalising extremist identities. Where wars have more of the logic of a mutual enterprise than the logic of a contest of wills, they are likely to lead to persistence and spread, to be long, sporadic, difficult to end and difficult to contain geographically, in contrast to Clausewitzean wars that tend to the extreme. We argue that it is the failure to take into account the logic of new wars that, to a large extent, explains why most responses to new wars are so problematic.

1.2.2 The Characteristics of New Wars

We recognise that large-scale collective forms of violence – wars – all have their own unique histories, topographies[16] and trajectories, but

[14] A point made by Orly Stern.
[15] Von Clausewitz, Carl 1968. *On War*. London: Penguin Books, English edition, 5.
[16] For example, fighting in the urban areas of Ukraine differs greatly from the vast spaces of Northern Mali.

nevertheless we argue that there are some common features in 'new wars'. Accordingly, to elucidate this alternative logic of war, in this section we briefly describe how new wars differ from old wars in terms of goals and identities, actors, tactics and forms of finance, although these aspects interlink and are not easily discussed separately. We illustrate our discussion with examples drawn especially from the conflicts in Ukraine, Syria, Iraq and Mali.[17] However, the situation in these countries is fluid and constantly changing, so our examples are intended only as illustrative of particular points and not as an account of the course of the different conflicts.

Goals and Identities: New wars are largely fought in the name of identity – ethnic, religious or tribal – rather than for political ideas or geo-political goals. That is to say, the expressed goal of new wars is exclusive access to the state for those identified with a particular label.

Religious wars can be about ideas, such as the imposition of fundamentalist or extremist interpretations of Sharia law, or about identity, such as the right of representation in the name of a specific identity. The religious wars of seventeenth-century Europe between Protestants and Catholics were about ideas, dealing with the break-up of the Catholic Church's power, emerging secular power and the role of individuals; by contrast, the war in Northern Ireland from the late 1960s was about the identity and the rights of the different communities, defined by their religion, to political power. Other ascribed identities are ethnicity-based, such as the case of Hutus and Tutsis in Rwanda and Burundi, or both religion and ethnicity-based as in the case of Serbs, Croats and Muslims in the war in Bosnia.

Identity is fluid and changing; most human beings have multiple identities. War is an important mechanism through which identities are constructed and 'fixed', through the imposition of a binary 'us' and 'them'.[18] Even if previously they thought of themselves in terms of national identity, as 'Yugoslav' or 'Rwandan', people began to self-identify as Muslim or Tutsi because these were the identities that established them as the target once violence erupted. In neither of these cases nor, for example, in Northern Ireland could individuals change allegiance

[17] Mary Kaldor's original analysis of new wars was largely drawn from the wars around the breakup of the former Yugoslavia in the 1990s, although it also took into account wars in Africa and post-Soviet space. Its continued application to conflicts in 2016 attests to its durability.

[18] Kaldor, Mary 2013. 'Identity and War', *Global Policy* 4(4): 336–346.

by converting from one religion or ethnicity to another, as these became ascribed identities. Moreover, as several writers have observed, identities constructed in war, whether ethnic, religious or tribal, tend to be closely linked to gender and related to a (male) warrior mythology.[19]

In the era of decolonisation following World War II numerous conflicts were fought for the political goals of national liberation and sovereign independence. Some of these wars share features of new wars, indeed they could be viewed as the precursor of new wars. Post-independence, further conflict has broken out in many places, for instance, Rwanda, Burundi, Sudan, Ethiopia, Somalia, Sri Lanka, Libya, Yemen, which have often pitted against each other people of different ethnicities or tribal affiliations who were caught by the continuation of colonial boundaries.[20] In some instances these identities had been constructed by colonial powers who imposed classifications on what had previously been loose and inchoate groupings.[21]

An example of the identity-oriented goal of new wars in a post-colonial state is Mali. In Mali some of the northern nomadic Tuareg people (a term stemming from the French colonisers who divided and classified different groups in Northern Mali)[22] have made separatist claims virtually since the independence of the state in 1960 and have engaged in armed challenges against the government in the South on a number of occasions. In 2012 the violence took on a new intensity for two reasons; first, following the fall of Gaddafi in Libya, there was an influx of heavy weaponry into Mali and a return of migrant Tuareg who had been trained militarily by the Gaddafi government, and, second, they were backed by Islamist groups whose goal of imposing Sharia law

[19] Elshtain, Jean Bethke 1987. *Women and War.* University of Chicago Press.

[20] The legal principle of *uti possidetis* – the continuity of colonial boundaries – was upheld throughout decolonisation and accepted as customary international law; *Case Concerning the Frontier Dispute (Burkino Faso v. Mali),* 1986 ICJ Reports 554, judgment of 22 December 1986.

[21] The 1948 *Convention on the Prevention and Punishment of the Crime of Genocide* defines genocide in terms of intention to destroy a national, ethnical, racial or religious group. The International Criminal Tribunal for Rwanda thus had to determine whether Hutus and Tutsis are identified through ethnicity – this despite the fact that their earlier differentiation was based on lineage, and it was the Belgian colonisers who introduced distinction based on 'ethnicity'. See *Prosecutor v. Jean-Paul Akayesu*, Case No. ICTR-96-4-T, 2 September 1998; Convention on the Prevention and Punishment of the Crime of Genocide, 9 December 1948, United Nations Treaty Series, vol. 78, 277.

[22] See Grémont, Charles 2012. 'Villages and Crossroads: Changing Territorialities among the Tuareg of Northern Mali', in McDougall, James and Scheele, Judith (eds). *Saharan Frontiers: Space and Mobility in Northwest Africa.* Indiana University Press.

differed from their own. Much of the new separatist and religious ideology had been forged in exile by Tuareg (Tamachek) migrants in North Africa. This network of fighters controlled much of the North by March 2012. Following further instability and violence (both with respect to a coup against the Malian government and fighting between the various rebel groups) French troops entered the country at the request of the Malian government in January 2013. It should be noted that as in other cases of identity-based ideologies, the separatists never represented 'all' Tuareg. Moreover the main Tuareg separatist group, the MNLA (National Movement for the Liberation of Azawad–Northern Mali), remained distinct from the main jihadist factions; one of these, the Movement for Oneness and Justice in West Africa (MUJAO), expelled MNLA from Gao, and another, Al Qaeda in the Islamic Maghreb (AQIM), operated mainly in Timbuktu.

In a different manifestation of the genesis of new wars, in Ukraine, what began as a pro-democracy protest against the government[23] was manipulated and channelled into what appeared as sectarian conflict between ethnic Ukrainians and Russians.[24] Many of those who were engaged in the democracy movement explicitly rejected ethnic identities – the slogan 'I'm a drop in the ocean' was meant to symbolise the loss of traditional identities, and indeed the first person to die in the protests was neither Ukrainian nor Russian but Armenian.[25] After President Yanukovych fled from Ukraine in February 2014, following months of pro-democracy protests, pro-Russian separatists seized Crimea with the support of Russian forces. A referendum was quickly held in Crimea which resulted in a treaty being agreed between the Russian Federation and the Crimean Republic on the accession of the latter into the former. In effect Crimea was annexed by Russia.[26] A few months later, pro-Russian separatists seized administrative buildings in the Donetsk and

[23] This has been the case in several other new wars, e.g., Libya and Syria.

[24] For an account of the demographic shifts in Ukraine and the waves of violence against the different peoples see Snyder, Timothy 2010. *Bloodlands: Europe between Hitler and Stalin*. New York: Basic Books.

[25] See Forostyna, Oksana 2015. 'Poaching, Simmering and Boiling: The Declining Relevance of Identity Discourse in Ukraine', in Wilson, Andrew (ed.), *What Does Ukraine Think?* London: European Council on Foreign Relations, 25–33.

[26] In light of inaction in the Security Council because of the Russian veto, the General Assembly called upon states and international organisations not to recognise any change of status in Ukraine. UN GA Resolution 68/262, 1 April 2014 ('Territorial integrity of Ukraine') was adopted by 100 states in favour to 11 against, with 58 abstentions.

Luhansk regions of Eastern Ukraine. The consequence has been a conflict between Russian separatists, backed by Russia, and Ukraine. As Tim Judah, writing at the beginning of the war, reported: '[P]eople tell me that they don't believe war is coming and that Russians and Ukrainians are brothers. I remember the same brave talk, the same euphoria, and the same delusions before the Yugoslavs tipped their country into catastrophe in the 1990's'.[27] Language was already an issue in Ukraine, and one of the first acts of the Parliament after President Yanukovych fled the country was to pass an act downgrading the Russian language; even though it was vetoed by the new President, it provided another pretext for Russian actions in Crimea and Eastern Ukraine. As in the case of similar identity-based ideologies that characterise 'new wars', this ideology has a significant gender dimension: as illustration a rebel told Tim Judah that this was a conflict between the Russian world and the West where people no longer believe in families (what he meant was that people in the West tolerate gender equality and sexual minorities).[28] As long as the war continues, the narrative of a sectarian conflict between Ukrainians and Russians gains ground while the alternative narrative of the protestors (democracy versus the criminalised oligarchies of both Ukraine and Russia) is weakened; in other words sectarian identities are constructed through new wars.[29]

Actors: Old wars were fought by regular armed forces wearing uniforms and those recruited by the state through conscription or payment who were subject to national laws and military codes. In contrast, the participants in the new wars are often loose and fluid networks of state and non-state actors that cross borders. They include remnants or bits of the regular armed forces, paramilitary groups, warlords, jihadists, terrorists, mercenaries, private security contractors and criminal groups.

For example, the IS is a transnational network of fighters primarily from Iraq and Syria, but also from what might be described as a roll call of new wars – Chechnya, Gaza, Kosovo, Bosnia, Sudan, the Middle East,

[27] Judah, Tim. 'Ukraine: The Phony War?' *New York Review of Books*, 22 May 2014, www.nybooks.com/articles/2014/05/22/ukraine-phony-war/.

[28] Judah, Tim. 'Ukraine: What Putin Has Won', *The New York Review of Books*, 9 October 2014, www.nybooks.com/articles/2014/10/09/ukraine-what-putin-has-won/.

[29] Nevertheless, many of the pro-democracy protesters were Russian speakers, and the separatists have failed to mobilise support in other Russian-speaking regions. Indeed, the strongest support for military action against the separatists has come from the Russian-speaking neighbouring region of Dnipropetrovsk. See Hrystak, Yaroslav 2015, 'Rethinking Ukraine', in Wilson Andrew (ed.), *op. cit.*, 34–44.

as well as other parts of Europe and the United States. Arrayed against IS are a similar collection of networks. In Iraq they include the Kurdish *peshmerger*, various Shi'ia militias including the Mahdi army (previously a major enemy of the Western[30] occupation) and the Badr corps.[31] In Syria as well, IS faces networks of non-state actors. As of 2016, these included the Syrian Democratic Forces, an alliance of anti-Assad armed groups including Kurdish brigades as well as moderate rebels, and an array of Islamist militia including Jabhat Fatah al-Sham (Conquest of Syria Front) that changed its name from Jabhat al-Nusra and announced that it was severing ties with Al Qaeda. The Assad regime relies on similar types of armed groups and militias for use against the opposition including what are called the National Defense Forces (often recruited from regular soldiers and trained by the Iranian Revolutionary Guard), Hezbollah and Shabbiya (an Alawite militia).

Ukraine as of 2016 further illustrates the diversity of actors in new wars. The separatist forces include various armed groups generally attached to an individual, either the 'heads' of the so-called People's Republics of Donetsk and Luhansk, or adventurers like Igor Girkin (known as Igor Strelkov), a former colonel in the Russian Federal Security Service, a veteran of the conflicts in Bosnia, Transdiniester and Chechnya, a monarchist and supporter of the White anti-communist movement. Many such individuals have adopted *noms de guerre* drawn from superhero comics, for instance, after Alexander Bednov, killed on 1 January 2015, who was better known as Batman. Brigades include the Prizrak (Ghost) brigade headed by Alexei Mozgovoy, the Oplot (Stronghold) brigade led by Alexander Zakharchenko, a former mining engineer and head of the self-proclaimed Donetsk People's Republic, as well as the Vostok (East) brigade, Cossacks and military groups with names like Sparta and Somalia. Many of these groups include volunteers from other parts of the world, especially but not only, orthodox Christians from Russia, Serbia, Brazil and elsewhere.[32] They were supported initially with arms, money and information from Russia and subsequently by Russian volunteers known as 'holiday-makers'; this last is a reference to a

[30] By 'West' or 'Western' we refer to advanced capitalist countries, primarily the United States and its allies.

[31] Cockburn, Patrick. 'War against ISIS: US Strategy in Tatters as Militants March On', *Independent on Sunday*, 12 October 2014, www.independent.co.uk/voices/comment/war-against-isis-us-strategy-in-tatters-as-militants-march-on-9789230.html.

[32] International Crisis Group. 'Eastern Ukraine: A Dangerous Winter', *Crisis Group Europe Report* No. 235, 18 December 2014.

statement by Zakharchenko that 'several thousand Russian servicemen had spontaneously gone to Donetsk in their vacation time to fight alongside separatists bringing all their equipment with them'.[33] In Crimea, the Russian soldiers were known colloquially as 'little green men' since they wore green, unmarked uniforms and masks.

On the Ukrainian side, the regular forces, which were weak in the early stages of the conflict, have also been complemented by volunteer brigades. Some are veterans of the protests in Maidan (Nezalezhnosti) Square in late 2013 and 2014, supported by grassroots financing from civil society initiatives and small and medium businesses. Some are motivated by a far-right ideology like the ultra-conservative Right Sector or the notorious Azov brigade, whose members were shunned by the Maidan protestors because of their white supremacist and anti-democratic views. Others, like the Drepl brigade, were established by business oligarchs.[34]

As in old wars, the fighters are predominantly male with media reports depicting the leaders of such networks in ways that exemplify the construction of the physical and representational aspects of wartime masculinity. But on both sides, there have also been reports of women fighters. Some protestors from the Maidan formed a predominantly female self-defence unit known as Unit 39,[35] while in Eastern Ukraine there is reported to be a 25-member all-female battalion based in the town of Krasny Luch. Some have suggested that the women have been recruited on the Eastern side as human shields; a Kiev news agency reported Donetsk leaders as saying 'no one will shoot at the separatists if they are women'.[36] In Syria, Kurdish women make up a high proportion of Kurdish fighters including the commander of the resistance to IS in Kobane.

Means: In old wars, battle – the clash between opposing military forces – was the decisive encounter. The goals of the war were to be achieved through the military capture of territory and defeat of opposing

[33] *Ibid.* 15.

[34] Adrian, Karatuychky. 'Warlords and Armed Groups Threaten Ukraine's Rebuilding', *Washington Post,* 30 December 2014, www.washingtonpost.com/opinions/the-rise-of-warlords-threatens-ukraines-recovery/2014/12/30/a23b2d36-8f7b-11e4-a412-4b735edc7175_story.html?postshare=2981419988538209.

[35] Nemtsova, Anna 2014. 'Girls, Stop What You're Doing or Die', *Foreign Policy,* http://foreignpolicy.com/2014/05/23/girls-stop-what-youre-doing-or-die/.

[36] Sharma, Versha 2015. 'Meet the Female Fighters of Eastern Ukraine', *Vocativ,* www.vocativ.com/world/ukraine-world/meet-female-fighters-eastern-ukraine/.

forces. In new wars, by contrast, battles are rare and the main violence is directed towards civilians. The goals are to be achieved through the political control of territory; indeed, forced displacement is probably the most characteristic tactic of new wars. Typically, in new wars, armed groups take over areas where the state presence is weak and then use further violence as a form of intimidation. They often engage in highly visible atrocities – executions, torture, sexual violence, suicide bombings, planting landmines, looting, arson – as a way to generate fear and cause survivors to flee. Such violence spreads terror and is also targeted against those who disagree and those of a different identity. Social media and mass communications are widely used in new wars as an efficient way of spreading terror. IS, for instance, is highly skilled at communication techniques for propaganda and mobilisation and has a substantial social media presence that is used to propagate medieval notions of punishment and torture. In new wars, casualties (deaths) tend to be low compared with old wars, but displacement is extremely high.[37] Moreover most casualties are civilians even though it is often difficult to distinguish civilians and combatants.[38]

Mali is illustrative of the typical tactics of 'new wars'. There are reports of serious human rights violations in the North: 'summary executions, illegal arrests and forced disappearances, the use of children by armed groups, rape, forced marriages, destruction and looting of property'.[39] The United Nations Multidimensional Integrated Stabilization Mission in Mali (MINUSMA) personnel and property have also been subjected to attacks, including by improvised explosive devices, mortar shells and gunfire.[40] Destruction of historic and cultural buildings and symbols (such as the burning of historical manuscripts in Timbuktu[41] and devastation of ancient

[37] Rigterink, Anouk 2014. 'New Wars in Numbers: An Empirical Test of the 'New War' Thesis', *Security in Transition,* www.securityintransition.org/wp-content/uploads/2014/10/Rigterink.-New-Wars-in Numbers.pdf.

[38] See Chapter 6.

[39] Report of the Secretary-General on the situation in Mali, UN Doc. S/2013/189, 26 March 2013, para 16. This continues into 2016, when, despite the signing of the Agreement on Peace and Reconciliation in Mali in June 2016, the 'human rights situation continued to be of serious concern'. Report of the Secretary-General on the situation in Mali, UN Doc. S/2016/498, 31 May 2016, para 22.

[40] Report of the Secretary-General on the situation in Mali, UN Doc. S/2015/426, 11 June 2015, paras 21–22.

[41] In August 2016, Ahmad Al Faqi Al Mahdi pleaded guilty to charges of war crimes relating to the destruction of historical and religious monuments in Timbuktu before the International Criminal Court; *The Prosecutor v. Ahmad Al Faqi Al Mahdi,* ICC-01/12-01/15.

cultural sites in Iraq, Syria and elsewhere) is also used to demonstrate rejection of 'pagan' monuments and to frighten those of a different identity. IS moved into areas in Iraq or Syria where governance was weak and there was little resistance and established political control through systematic expulsion (or attacks on) those who do not accept their version of Islam. A 2014 report from the United Nations Office of the High Commissioner for Human Rights (OHCHR) and the United Nations Assistance Mission to Iraq[42] describes a 'staggering array' of killings, displacements and gross human rights violations against Sunnis who refuse to pledge allegiance to IS, members of the Iraqi security forces, Iraqi government personnel, prisoners and detainees from Shi'ia and other ethnic communities, including Turkmen, Shabak, Christians, Yezidi, Sabaeans, Kaka'e and Faili Kurds. The report details intentional destruction of religious sites such as mosques, churches and Yezidi shrines, and other buildings of cultural significance. It also includes reports of rape and sexual abuse and the active recruitment of children. The Report describes how Christians in Mosul were faced with the choice of conversion or death. The systematic killing of Yezidis has been widely reported, as has the beheading of Western journalists and aid workers. Sexual violence is also a way of targeting identity; IS is reported to have systematically recruited Yezidi girls as sexual slaves.[43] There have also been reports of mass killings of Iraqi army and air force cadets in Camp Speicher, allegedly in collaboration with Tikriti tribes, as well as mass executions of Syrian soldiers.[44]

In some cases new war networks establish some of the trappings of statehood – courts, taxation and public services. IS in particular tries to establish a state-like presence in the areas it controls in order to entrench their political position. They establish a bureaucracy, secure a monopoly of violence and provide public services such as water and electricity, bread and health care.[45]

[42] OHCHR and UNAMI, Report on the Protection of Civilians in Armed Conflict in Iraq: 6 July–10 September 2014, www.ohchr.org/Documents/Countries/IQ/UNAMI_OHCHR_POC_Report_FINAL_6July_10September2014.pdf.

[43] Callimachi, Rukmini. 'ISIS Enshrines a Theology of Rape', *New York Times*, 1 August 2015, www.nytimes.com/2015/08/14/world/middleeast/isis-enshrines-a-theology-of-rape.html?_r=0.

[44] Jiyad, Sajad 2014. 'Iraq's Response to the Challenge of Islamic State', *European Council on Foreign Relations*, www.ecfr.eu/content/entry/commentary_iraqs_response_to_the_challenge_of_the_islamic_state321.

[45] Turkmani, Rim 2015. 'ISIL, JAN and the War Economy in Syria', *Security in Transition*, www.securityintransition.org/wp-content/uploads/2015/08/ISIL-JAN-and-the-war-economy-in-Syria2.pdf.

In Crimea in early 2014, separatists seized administrative buildings, and, given the substantial presence of the Russian military and the decision by the Ukrainian government not to resist, political control was quite rapidly established. Human rights violations continued, especially against minorities, such as the Crimean Tatars, or against those who continued to claim a Ukrainian identity. In Eastern Ukraine too, where state institutions were very weak, separatists, with the support of foreign fighters, seized administrative buildings in the Donetsk and Luhansk regions, but they lacked coherence and sufficient local support to be able to extend their control to other areas.

The methods of exercising control of territory in Eastern Ukraine seem to follow the pattern of other new wars. The OHCHR reports widespread human rights violations including 'killings, abductions, ill-treatment, sexual violence, forced labour, ransom and extortion of money'.[46] The use of conventional forces by the Ukrainian Government, including the shelling and use of cluster munitions[47] in civilian areas and the subsequent large influx of Russian weapons and personnel, has greatly exacerbated the violence.

Forms of Finance: Old wars were financed by taxation and official state borrowing. They were typically associated with a war economy that was centralising, autarchic and totalising – involving all citizens. In particular, during the two World Wars, women were drawn into the paid labour force in large numbers. The economy of new wars is almost exactly the opposite. New war economies are decentralised and open to the global economy. Participation in military activity tends to be low, and unemployment tends to be high. Receipts from taxation are minimal or non-existent so the warring factions have to find other ways to finance their activities, ways which are usually directly related to violence. These methods of financing include looting and pillage; setting up checkpoints where assets such as televisions, cows and foreign currency are 'exchanged' for necessities; extortion and demands for protection money; 'taxation' and stealing of humanitarian aid; financial support from the diaspora; kidnapping and hostage-taking; and various kinds of

[46] Office of the United Nations High Commissioner for Human Rights. 'Report on the Human Rights Situation in Ukraine', 15 December 2014, www.ohchr.org/Documents/Countries/UA/OHCHR_eighth_report_on_Ukraine.pdf.

[47] OSCE Special Monitoring Mission to Ukraine. 'Civilians Killed and Wounded in Strike with Cluster Munitions in Izvestkova Street in Luhansk City', *Organization for Security and Co-operation in Europe,* 3 February 2016, www.osce.org/ukraine-smm/138906.

organised criminal activity, especially stealing, smuggling and trafficking valuable commodities such as oil, diamonds, antiquities, drugs and humans.

The economy of Ukraine has deteriorated precipitously since the conflict began,[48] as is typical of states where new wars are fought. In November 2014, the Ukraine government withdrew its institutions from the areas controlled by the rebels with devastating effects on the local populations already suffering from lack of services (medical services, water and electricity) due to widespread destruction. Much of the economy remains state controlled, so this decision meant the halting of payment of pensions and wages. People can only survive through relocating, through joining a militia or engaging in criminal activity. There are widespread reports of predatory economic activities, including seizure of property, extortion at checkpoints and ransom. Corruption in Ukraine was pervasive before the war began, and Ukraine was at the centre of various criminal networks, especially human trafficking and drug smuggling; indeed, the Maidan protests and the eagerness expressed for Ukraine to join the European Union had to do with a popular concern to tackle corruption. Despite anti-corruption efforts by civil society and (somewhat slowly) by the Poroshenko Government in Ukraine, the lawlessness in the East and the rise of armed groups only serve to entrench corruption and criminality in the whole of Ukraine, but especially in the East.

A similar situation pertains in Syria. In areas outside of government control, traditional sectors (agriculture, industry, tourism) have declined dramatically. Pensions and salaries have been halted, and access to humanitarian aid is precarious so that those who have not fled or do not receive remittances from abroad are forced to join a militia or engage in criminal activities to survive. The war has created a new class of war profiteers while everyone else has been greatly impoverished. At the same time, as in other new war situations, it is possible to identify numerous deals among the warring parties for economic purposes – for example,

[48] As stated in a March 2015 European Parliament Briefing Paper, 'Ukraine's economy has been ailing for years, and the current conflict has exacerbated the situation. Kyiv is now struggling to save its economy and its currency'. See Bentzen, Naja. 'Ukraine after Minsk II: The Next Level Hybrid Responses to Hybrid Threats?' *European Parliament Briefing Paper*, 16 March 2015, www.europarl.europa.eu/RegData/etudes/BRIE/2015/551328/EPRS_BRI(2015)551328_EN.pdf.

the sale of diesel by IS to all parties, or the exchange of water for electricity between government and rebel groups.[49]

As in the case of the methods of violence, men and women experience these economic aspects of 'new wars' differently. It is young men who are unemployed and often unable to marry who find themselves recruited into combatant groups or engaging in criminal activities. And it is, by and large, women who suffer the everyday consequences of loss of income, dependence on humanitarian assistance and, as in Ukraine, facing a 'heightened risk' of sexual violence (from armed groups), domestic violence by servicemen returning from conflict areas and of trafficking and resorting to prostitution as a means of survival.[50]

The Logic of Persistence and Spread: Taken together, these various aspects of new wars explain the tendency for their longevity and to spill over borders. Both for political reasons – the need to underpin extremist identity politics – and for economic reasons – the need to maintain access to resources – the various warring parties acquire a vested interest in continued violence. What becomes established is a predatory set of social relations that are difficult to contain in time and space. They are disseminated through identity politics, especially through vulnerable refugees and internally displaced persons and former combatants seeking a new role. Likewise, they spread through transnational criminalised networks, which are the vectors of various types of illicit (and violent) activity. Although new wars have many of the characteristics of civil wars,[51] they are not purely domestic; indeed, the distinction between 'inside' and 'outside' becomes blurred in new wars. This explains the emergence of 'bad neighbourhoods'[52] – the way in which new wars cluster in certain regions such as Central Africa, the Horn of Africa, Central Asia, the Balkans and, of course, the Middle East. But other regions cannot remain immune from their impact as the dramatic

[49] Turkmani, Rim with Ali, Ali A. K., Kaldor, Mary, and Bojicic-Dzelilovic, Vesna. 'Countering the Logic of the War Economy in Syria: Evidence from Three Local Areas', *Security in Transition,* 30 July 2015, www.securityintransition.org/wp-content/uploads/2015/08/Countering-war-economy-Syria2.pdf.

[50] Office of the United Nations High Commissioner for Human Rights. 'Report on the Human Rights Situation in Ukraine: 1 December 2014 to 15 February 2015', paras 61–63, www.wecf.eu/english/articles/2015/03/violence-against-women-in-ukraine.php. Another consequence is the high rate of child and forced marriage.

[51] See Kavylas, Stathis 2006. *The Logic of Violence in Civil War.* Cambridge University Press.

[52] See Weiner, Myron 1996. *Bad Neighbourhoods: An Enquiry into the Causes of Refugee Flows.* Cambridge, Mass.: MIT Press.

increase in the flow of migrants to Europe fromn the summer of 2015 vividly exemplifies.

New wars are difficult to end because few of the participants have an interest in winning; rather, they prefer the perpetuation of violence and/or disorder. When peace agreements are negotiated by the international community, the participants, typically leaders of the warring factions, are those with a vested interest in sustaining violence and entrenching their positions of power and the political economy of war from which they benefit. Indeed the promise of participation in peace talks, which offers a route to state power, increasingly becomes a motivation for engaging in violence, thereby contributing to the persistence of violence. This is why peace agreements, even when formally upheld by the international community, do not necessarily end the violence, particularly in regard to criminality and gender-based violence.[53] Women may have participated in the fighting, but they are rarely involved in peace processes and thus are excluded from positions of power and allocation of resources in post-conflict societies. As such, both the distinction between conflict and post-conflict and the distinctions between political, criminal and gender-based violence are blurred in new wars, and yet it is these distinctions that are so important for the application of international law as it is currently constituted. It is these tensions that are explored in the rest of this book.

1.3 Legality and Legitimacy

The Independent International Commission on Kosovo famously concluded that the 1999 bombing campaign undertaken by NATO against Yugoslavia was illegal but legitimate.[54] The war had, in the end, allowed Kosovar Albanians, who had been forcibly expelled or who had fled from Serbian persecution in Kosovo, to return, although often to destroyed villages and homes, but it was not authorised by resolution of the United Nations Security Council. Nor was it justified by the Genocide Convention as the expulsion and oppression of the Kosovar Albanians, even though they involved gross violations of human rights and crimes against humanity, did not amount to genocide.[55] One implication of this

[53] See Chapters 8 and 9.

[54] The Independent International Commission on Kosovo 2000. *Kosovo Report: Conflict, International Response, Lessons Learned.* Oxford University Press.

[55] The Convention on the Prevention and Punishment of the Crime of Genocide, *op. cit.* See further Chapter 5.

conclusion was that international law needs to be adapted to address today's realities and that a gap between legality and legitimacy greatly weakens the standing of international law. The finding of the Kosovo Commission has contributed to considerable debate about the legality and/or legitimacy of the use of force by states in particular incidents,[56] generally of the international legal system and of the desirability of the distinction.

One problem is what is understood as legitimacy. In the period before 1989, when an East–West nuclear confrontation was the worst threat that could be imagined, it was easier to establish a shared (albeit divided along those lines) framework for legitimacy since the common starting point was a geo-political 'old war' conception of international affairs.[57] In response to 'new wars' and globalisation, a range of competing conceptions of what is considered legitimate are now identified that are associated with different ways of addressing the gap between legality and legitimacy.

Legality – rules emanating from the accepted source of authority within a political unit – may either be compromised by illegitimacy or be reinforced by legitimacy. Legitimacy, as Max Weber in his original and seminal work expounded, has to do with beliefs and the idea that rules should be obeyed because it is right to do so.[58] Beliefs about the 'rightness' of particular rules are based on prevailing societal norms, grounded in religion or morality, for instance, a belief that responding to assist in a humanitarian crisis is the right thing to do. The concept of legitimacy is used to enhance the moral persuasiveness of international law by importing other values such as those of justice or equity. Conversely the centrality and universality of international law is undermined by assertions of its illegitimacy, either of the system as a whole or, more frequently, of particular rules.[59] 'Legitimacy', says Andrew Hurrell, 'refers

[56] Ian Clark points out that after a period when the concept was marginalised in international relations, it had become quite widely referred to from the early 1990s; Clark, Ian 2005. *Legitimacy in International Society*. Oxford University Press, 11–12.

[57] Ian Clark explains that the 'certainties' of the Cold War foreclosed discussions of legitimacy in international relations, while the post–Cold War order allowed for a 'harmony of international values' but also that 'political power' has brought about both 'hegemonic discourse' and divisions and uncertainties. Clark, Ian, *op. cit.*, chapter 8.

[58] Weber, Max 1978. *Economy and Society*. Berkeley: University of California Press.

[59] From different perspectives see Franck, Tom 1995. *Fairness in International Law and Institutions*. Oxford University Press; Tourme-Jouannet, Emmanuelle 2013. *What Is a Fair International Society?* French Studies in International Law, Hart Publishing.

to a particular kind of rule-following or obedience, distinguishable from purely self-interested or instrumental behaviour, on the one hand, and from straight-forward imposed or coercive rule, on the other'.[60] Legitimacy after a conflict may be imbued with the values and interests of the victor, suggesting that legitimacy is always contingent on power and domination. While a relationship between power and legitimacy must be acknowledged, Ian Clark offers a middle ground: 'Legitimacy constrains power, but also enables it; power suffuses legitimacy, but it does not empty it of normative content'.[61] Further, as Hurrell also acknowledges, the distinction between legitimacy and the calculation of interests can be hard to discern; indeed, legitimacy and self-interest may be entwined as when states regard the formation of and compliance with international institutions as in their self-interest.[62] And beliefs – the constituents of social legitimacy – also vary widely between participants within and across both domestic and international societies.[63] Governmental actors and civil society groups may have disparate views about what is legitimate action so that 'factors that may help to legitimise [action] in the eyes of non-state actors may help to delegitimise it in the eyes of state actors'.[64]

Efforts to unpack the meaning of the term by, *inter alia*, sociologists, political scientists, philosophers, anthropologists and lawyers include a variety of categories of legitimacy. In his original theory, Weber distinguished between legitimacy based on tradition and custom; legitimacy based on the charisma of individual leaders; and the bureaucratic-rational legitimacy that is characteristic of the modern period.[65] Legitimacy is also about the 'justification of authority'[66] as well as the acts those in authority perform.[67] In this regard, contemporary scholars often draw a distinction between procedural and substantive, or between input and output, legitimacy, distinctions that come close to that between legality

[60] Hurrell, Andrew 2007. *On Global Order: Power, Values, and the Constitution of International Society*. Oxford University Press, 78.

[61] Clark, Ian, *op. cit.*, 4.

[62] Bodansky, Daniel 2008. 'The Concept of Legitimacy in International Law', in Rüdiger Wulfrum and Volker Röben (eds.) *Legitimacy in International Law*. Berlin, Heidelberg and New York: Springer, 309–317, 312. See further Chapter 3.

[63] For an analysis from the perspective of the 'English school of international relations' see Clark, Ian, *op. cit.*

[64] Bodansky, Daniel, *op. cit.*, 314.

[65] Weber, Max, *op. cit.*

[66] Wulfrum, Rüdiger in Wulfrum, Rüdiger and Röben, Volker (eds.), *op. cit.*, 6.

[67] Coleman, Katharina 2007. *International Organisations and Peace Enforcement*. Cambridge University Press, chapter 1.

and legitimacy. Procedural or input legitimacy refers to the procedures through which an authority or a rule is established, for example, law-making procedures in a Parliamentary democracy, decisions of properly constituted judicial bodies or a UN Security Council resolution. Procedural and input legitimacy are more elusive in an international legal system lacking a constitution and legislative body. Substantive or output legitimacy refers to how an authority acts or a rule is implemented and whether this conforms to dominant beliefs. Substantive legitimacy is challenged when the subsequent acts of legally established international institutions are far removed from the initial understanding and language of the constitutive treaty. For instance, in the UK there is much discussion about the supposed illegitimacy of decisions of the European Court of Human Rights where the judges are perceived as going beyond the constitutive instrument, the European Convention on Human Rights.[68] Both compliance and enforcement are weakened by loss of legitimacy.[69] Tom Franck in his classic exposition of legitimacy in international law identifies four components of legitimacy that go beyond state consent and go to the quality, as well as the derivation, of the rule in question: the certainty and determinacy of a rule; its conformity with accepted forms and rituals; the conceptual coherence of the system as a whole; and adherence to right process and normative hierarchy.[70] Other objective indicators of legitimacy might be envisaged, such as those understood as constituting 'good governance' – procedural transparency, democratic decision-making, reasoned decisions, accountability and review mechanisms.[71] Where these are present they create the 'pull' factors towards compliance in a legal system lacking enforcement capability.

Within the international arena the power of symbolic legitimacy (or validation) should not be disregarded. Ian Hurd has pointed to the symbolic power of the United Nations Security Council (SC).[72] Despite

[68] Such criticism has even come from senior British Judges; for instance Lord Sumption has claimed that the European Court of Human Rights 'exceeds its legitimate powers, usurps the role of politicians and "undermines the democratic process"'; Bowcott, Owen. 'Senior Judge: European Court of Human Rights Undermining Democratic Process', *The Guardian*, 28 November 2013, www.theguardian.com/law/2013/nov/28/european-court-of-human-rights.

[69] See Chapter 3.

[70] Franck, Tom 1988. 'Legitimacy in the International System', *American Journal of International Law* 82: 705–759, 712.

[71] *Ibid.*

[72] Hurd, Ian 2002. 'Legitimacy, Power and the Symbolic Life of the UN Security Council', *Global Governance* 8: 35–51, 48.

its shortcomings as discussed in Chapter 2, the Security Council remains the global symbol of collective security, and the UN represents the hope of many whose security is threatened. SC authorisation of the use of 'all necessary means or measures'[73] thus bestows both legality and symbolic legitimation on the ensuing military operation. The NATO bombing campaign against the Federal Republic of Yugoslavia[74] in 1999 went ahead without SC authorisation after Russia and China indicated they would exercise their veto power;[75] NATO states and allies still sought the symbolic validation of a resolution endorsing the intervention but were unable to secure this. In turn, Russia (with Belarus and India) sought a condemnatory resolution, perhaps seeking thereby to counter a claim of legitimacy of the intervention.[76]

Similarly, before the 2003 invasion of Iraq, President Bush (apparently at the urging of Prime Minister Blair) sought an explicit SC vote and resolution authorising military action; if this had been achieved it would not only have secured the legality and procedural legitimacy of the intervention but would also have enhanced its symbolic legitimacy. In its absence, the intervening states had to justify their action through strained interpretations of earlier resolutions (thus still seeking that symbolic legitimacy), the threat of Weapons of Mass Destruction (WMD) in Iraq and humanitarianism. However, even if procedural legality of military action in Iraq had been secured through an appropriate UN SC resolution, questions of its moral and ethical legitimacy would not have been resolved.[77]

The Iraqi episode also illustrates the fluidity of legitimacy: proponents of the military action against Iraq claimed the SC itself had lost legitimacy through its failure to authorise it,[78] while those against such action

[73] This is the formula used by the Security Council in resolutions authorising military action under chapter VII of the UN Charter.

[74] In effect Serbia and Montenegro. The International Court of Justice determined that 'with effect from 4 February 2003' the FRY became 'Serbia and Montenegro'; *Legality of Use of Force (Serbia and Montenegro v. Belgium) Preliminary Objections,* 15 December 2004, ICJ Reports 279, para 1.

[75] UN Charter, article 27 (3).

[76] Greenwood, Christopher 2002. 'Humanitarian Intervention: The Case of Kosovo', *Finnish Yearbook of International Law* 13: 141–175, 152.

[77] See Craven, Matthew, Simpson, Gerry, Marks, Susan and Wilde, Ralph 2004. 'We Are Teachers of International Law', *Leiden Journal of International Law* 17: 363–374.

[78] Former US Secretary of State Colin Powell told the Security Council on 5 February 2003 that 'this body places itself in danger of irrelevance if it allows Iraq to continue to defy its will without responding effectively and immediately'. Cited in 'The United Nations and

considered that the Council had resisted power and by acting in accordance with UN Charter principles had enhanced its legitimacy.[79]

It may be argued that legitimacy can substitute for legality, but this exposes a gap between law and the values of at least some members of the international community, as well as posing questions about the legitimacy of the law itself if it is perceived as out of touch with the moral demands of international society. International law loses legitimacy in the eyes of local populations, or broader civil society,[80] when institutions fail to respond to certain practices. For instance, in Gaza the population knows that the violence and denial of basic services they experience are contrary to the 'implicit rules' of international society, as confirmed in numerous official reports.[81] But there is no response. This absence denies the 'constant nurturing' upon which the reciprocity of international law depends, and thus the law becomes 'unintelligible'[82] and irrelevant. When law becomes irrelevant or illegitimate, violent solutions are more likely to be sought and violence escalated.

International law can be described as a language through which states conduct their relations with other states and indeed with civil society,[83] including through institutions. It creates expectations as to behaviour and thus a predictability in international affairs. States and their military personnel are likely to require assurance that a particular course of action is legal, or at least not illegal. This explains why both George W. Bush and Vladimir Putin have been so anxious to justify their actions in legal terms – what the Russians describe as *Po Zakonu*, 'In accordance with

Iraq: Irrelevant, Illegitimate or Indispensable?' *The Economist*, 20 February 2003, www.economist.com/node/1592138.

79 'If the Security Council gave America its authority to attack Iraq, the war would become legal, but for many, perhaps most people, it would still be illegitimate. In the opinion of huge numbers of Africans, Arabs, Asians and Latin Americans, and not a few Europeans too, the Security Council would simply be acting as an instrument of American foreign policy'. *Ibid.*

80 It must be remembered that civil society, like governments, comprises peoples with widely disparate views and ideologies who thus do not necessarily share opinions as to what is legitimate behaviour.

81 See, for example, the annual reports of the UN Human Rights Council Special Rapporteur on the situation of human rights in the Palestinian territories occupied since 1967.

82 Brunnée, Jutta and Toope, Stephen 2010. *Legitimacy and Legality in International Law: An Interactional Account*. Cambridge University Press, 66.

83 Generally, when we refer to 'civil society' we do not only mean NGOs, but include grassroots groups, social movements, civic institutions and religious institutions, universities, public intellectuals etc. – that is, peoples concerned with the public interest.

law'.[84] In determining legality, decision-makers (and those affected by the decisions taken) are likely to start from some common notion of what constitutes the sources of law,[85] its content and its application to particular facts. Conclusions as to the legality or otherwise of certain actions may differ depending on such factors as the weight the decision-maker accords to different sources of law, diverse meanings given to acts or statements, the intelligence received, which facts he or she deems relevant, and the preferred interpretative techniques. Indeed, different claims about legality can be construed as competing efforts to establish legitimacy for a particular course of action. The gap between legality and legitimacy is an expression of the absence or the narrowness of shared understandings. In the twenty-first century, differing world views and differing conceptions of security help to explain the diversity of claims for legitimacy. How these claims play out according to different understandings about how to respond (or not) to 'new wars' is sketched through the different models of security we describe below and we explore throughout this book.

1.4 Models of Security

The term 'security' is yet another complex idea. On the one hand, it refers to an objective, a specific conception of 'safety'. The objective varies according to the referent (the nation, the region, the world, the community, the family, the individual) and how threats or risks, and now increasingly, 'challenges'[86] to 'safety' are defined (armed attack by a state or by terrorists, other types of violence and crime, disease, material deprivation of various kinds, disasters, natural and/or those caused through human activity). On the other hand, in everyday language, security often refers to a practice – the various institutions and agencies

84 See Reisinger, Heidi and Golts, Aleksandr 2014. 'Russia's Hybrid Warfare: Waging War below the Radar of Traditional Collective Defence', *Research Paper No. 105*. Rome: NATO Defense College.

85 Boyle, Alan and Chinkin, Christine 2007. *The Making of International Law*. Oxford University Press.

86 In both 2015 US National Security Strategy and the statement of the EU High Representative, Federica Mogherini to the June 2015 EU Summit, threats and risks are replaced by 'challenges and opportunities'. See 'National Security Strategy', The White House, February 2015, www.whitehouse.gov/sites/default/files/docs/2015_national_security_strategy.pdf; 'The European Union in a Changing Global Environment', *European Union External Action Service,* 2015, www.eeas.europa.eu/docs/strategic_review/eu-strategic-review_strategic_review_en.pdf.

responsible for providing security (armed forces, police, intelligence services) and the political authorities to whom they report (the state, international institutions etc.). These two aspects of security are very much interrelated. Security practices are supposed to respond to the prevailing understandings of what constitutes security as an objective (who is to be secured and what are the threats or risks to be secured against), but by the same token those prevailing conceptions are often shaped, indeed embedded, in specific security practices. Security is closely related to legitimacy. The most important task of political institutions is to provide safety; people accept institutions as legitimate if they believe that they do provide security. How that belief is constructed, in turn, may depend on the narrative associated with particular security measures.

In this book we use the concept of security models to illustrate the different ways that objectives and practices relate to each other. A security model is a stylised conception of security that combines a set of objectives and a set of practices that tend to reinforce each other. Each of the models offers a different response to 'new wars', and each has a different conception of legitimacy and interpretation of the legal regime – a specific way of addressing the gap between legality and legitimacy. We sketch out five such models even though each model contains what might be called sub-models and several are overlapping.

The first security model is called 'Geo-Politics'. This is the legacy of the Cold War. The dominant narrative is about great power contestation, and the dominant tools are deployment and use of regular military forces, economic sanctions and state-to state diplomacy. The objective is national security, and the threat is defined in terms of enemies, who are similar great powers, their allies and proxies. The practices include the deployment of military forces so as to deter a future war against a 'peer competitor' – Russia, China or the United States and other NATO states depending on the perspective. A Geo-Political intervention could be justified in terms of 'self-defence', 'counter-proliferation' (preventing the acquisition of WMD by 'rogue' states), preserving the security of the Global Commons, or energy transportation routes against a state enemy. It consists of classic war-fighting or the threat of classic war-fighting, including air strikes. Geo-Politics remains the dominant way of thinking about and structuring capabilities among the major states and accounts for the maintaining of nuclear arsenals and most defence spending.

In the Geo-Political model, 'new wars' tend to be invisible or irrelevant. They are outside or beyond the main confrontation. During the

Cold War, there were, of course, many conflicts that could be described as 'new wars', but they were dismissed as minor, as internal expressions of criminal rebellion, as limited or as situated within the wider geo-political framework. A recent and disturbing variant of the Geo-Political model is what has been described as 'guerrilla Geo-Politics'.[87] This applies to the so-called Gerassimov Doctrine where 'new wars' in Ukraine (and also Georgia) are viewed as means of pursuing geo-political objectives. In other words, an old war mentality is imposed on what are effectively new wars, and the war is clothed in terms of geo-political competition where the warring parties are assumed to be proxies. The main consequence is to exacerbate those conflicts and to enhance the sense of insecurity and polarisation that reinforces prevailing geo-political ideas; for instance, interventions in Crimea and Eastern Ukraine seem to have increased the domestic popularity of President Putin, which explains the self-reinforcing character of the model. Similarly 'proxy wars' fought in Syria and Yemen are cases where geo-political interests have greatly worsened violence at local levels.

The legal regime associated with the Geo-Political model is classic international law. The main justification for the use of force is self-defence, and International Humanitarian Law (IHL or the 'laws of war') provides a framework of rules for the way in which war may be legally fought. The regulation of weapons is relevant in so far as it constitutes a means of managing competition among the major powers and preventing the diffusion of weapons to smaller powers.

The second security model can be called the War on Terror. Even though President Obama abandoned the term, it remains useful because it emphasises the use of military means and the idea of war-based security. The objective of the War on Terror is the defeat of enemies, but, unlike the Geo-Political model, the enemies are non-state actors. 9/11 plays a foundational role in the concept, often compared to the role played by the 1941 Japanese attack on Pearl Harbor in the Geo-Political model. The War on Terror has arisen in response to what has been constructed as 'asymmetric threats' or 'new wars' (terrorism, insurgencies and various types of contemporary, largely non-state, violence). As in the Geo-Political model, the War on Terror is statist and unilateralist. Like Geo-Politics, the objective of the War on Terror is national (and sometimes global or regional) security but *vis-à-vis* the risk of terrorist attack

[87] Galeotti, Mark. 'How Far Will He Go?' *The European*, 9 September 2014, www.theeuropean-magazine.com/mark-galeotti/8970-putins-tactics-against-the-west.

rather than that of an armed attack by a foreign state. In so far as the practices of the War on Terror are believed to protect against the threat of terrorist attacks on the public in the US, European and other allied states, then terror and the War on Terror are self-reinforcing, helping to establish a mutual sense of threat that legitimises such security practices as mass surveillance at home and abroad, other human rights abuses and the use of drones to carry out targeted attacks abroad (but including on citizens).[88]

Two broad types of intervention within the framework of the War on Terror are distinguished. One is counter-insurgency – defeating insurgents and/or terrorists with military force. There are, of course, variants of counter-insurgency campaigns. Heavy handed tactics, such as those used by Russia in Chechnya, the Assad regime in Syria, the Americans in Vietnam, Iraq and Afghanistan, or Israel in Gaza in the winter of 2008–9 and the summer of 2014, include strikes on population centres where insurgents are said to be preparing their attacks, living or hiding. In contrast, the population security approach of the British in Malaya in the 1950s or of General Petraeus in Baghdad in 2007 aims to separate the insurgents from the general population and to protect the latter while attacking the former. However, it is usually the case that elements of both approaches are applied; thus British tactics in Malaya also included bombing campaigns and 'resettlement' programmes where the detainees suffered extreme conditions, while General Petreaus in Iraq ruthlessly attacked what he called the 'irreconcilables'. The second is what the Americans call counter-terror interventions – defeating suspected terrorists through intelligence and targeted killings, usually from the air (the drone campaign). The emerging counter-terror version of the War on Terror model of security involves a new set of practices: a shift from the military to a combination of intelligence agencies and private security contractors and the widespread use of new technologies for mass surveillance, cyber warfare and robotics.

Like guerrilla Geo-Politics, those engaged in the War on Terror participate in 'new wars', although in the case of the War on Terror, the express aim is defeating terrorists. Thus the primary preoccupation of the US in Afghanistan from 2001 onwards and in Syria since 2014 is the defeat of Islamic fighters (Al Qaeda, the Taliban and now IS) rather than dealing with, or ending, a new war; like Geo-Politics it imposes an old

[88] See Chapters 4 and 6.

war framework (especially the use of military force) on a new war situation, which merely exacerbates the violence and makes things worse for the population. In a circular fashion, the growth of terrorism has merely served to justify the War on Terror, which may well have led to an increase in mobilisation of and recruitment to extremist groups. Victories such as those by IS in Syria and Iraq in 2014–15 in turn generate further recruitment.

Proponents of the War on Terror seek to stretch existing international law in various ways. In terms of the use of force, the self-defence justification has been stretched to include anticipation of an unspecified future attack (in Iraq 2003) and as a response to an attack by non-state actors (military intervention in Afghanistan after 9/11), airstrikes in Iraq and Syria since 2014 and Libya in 2016; the conditions for self-defence – claims of proportionality and necessity – have also been stretched, as, for example, in the Israeli attacks on Gaza.[89] IHL[90] has been used selectively to legitimise the killings of terrorists who are treated as combatants, yet, at the same time, those detained as terrorists are described as 'illegal' (rather than as prisoners of war protected under IHL) to justify their treatment, in violation of IHL, in Guantánamo Bay, Bagram, Camp Bucca and other prisons elsewhere. Renditions transporting those suspected of terrorist activities to such prisons are also carried out.[91] Constraints imposed by occupation or human rights law are also discarded in the name of security against terrorist or insurgent action.[92] Within the War on Terror model there is little interest in the regulation of weapons,[93] or in *post-bellum* law.

The third security model is humanitarian intervention or the Responsibility to Protect. Interest in humanitarian intervention grew during the 1990s as a response to humanitarian tragedies in 'new wars' in places like Bosnia and Rwanda. The term 'Responsibility to Protect' was conceived by the International Commission on Intervention and Sovereignty[94] after the NATO intervention in Kosovo in 1999 as a way of recasting humanitarian intervention in terms of states' responsibility for their own citizens

[89] See Chapter 4. [90] See Chapter 6.

[91] *El-Masri v. The Former Yugoslav Republic of Macedonia*, ECtHR GC application no. 39630/09, 13 December 2012.

[92] See Chapter 8. [93] See Chapter 7.

[94] Report of the International Commission on Intervention and State Sovereignty 2001. *The Responsibility to Protect.* Ottawa: International Development Research Centre.

and the international community's responsibility to all people facing extreme human rights violations.[95]

In this model, there is a contradiction between the objective and the practice. The objective is the safety of individuals and communities in the case of genocide, crimes against humanity, war crimes and ethnic cleansing. The assumed practice in extreme cases and after other efforts have failed is that there will be military intervention by states and groups of states, often from the air.[96] Such interventions risk the lives of those they are they are supposed to be saving and may exacerbate violence on the ground. In both Kosovo and Libya the intervening forces 'won' in the sense of defeating governments who were responsible for massive violations of human rights, but they also entrenched armed groups and left a legacy of bitterness, polarisation and further violence. Thus it shares with the previous two models a preoccupation with 'enemies' and presupposes that 'old war' methods can be used to meet humanitarian objectives in new wars.

The Responsibility to Protect seeks a change in the international legal regime to allow the international authorisation of the use of force for humanitarian purposes. In the context of actual intervention, it assumes conformity with IHL and *post-bellum* law.

The fourth security model, the 'Liberal Peace', is associated with a body of what may be described as *post-bellum* law, or the law of peace.[97] It is also in keeping with efforts to regulate the weapons of new wars, sometimes known as humanitarian arms control.[98]

The Liberal Peace comprises a dramatic increase in multilateral interventions since the end of the Cold War: the expansion in the mandate and missions of multilateral interventions; the emerging security roles played by newly configured regional and global actors such as the United Nations, the Organisation for Security and Cooperation in Europe (OSCE), the European Union, the African Union, the Economic Community of West African states (ECOWAS), South African Development Community (SADC) and the Commonwealth of Independent States

[95] See Chapter 5.

[96] The Responsibility to Protect involves four pillars, only the last of which is military action. But discourse is engaged around this, even in cases where no such action is undertaken as in Syria from 2012 onwards. In reality there have been few examples of such military intervention; see further Chapter 5.

[97] Bell, Christine 2008. *On the Law of Peace: Peace Agreements and the Lex Pacificatoria.* Oxford University Press.

[98] See Chapter 7.

(CIS); and the construction of a narrative that is based on various key documents such as the *Agenda for Peace* published by the United Nations Secretary-General Boutros-Boutros Ghali in 1992, the *Report of the Panel on United Nations Peace Operations* (Brahimi Report) in 2000 and the *Report on High Level Peace Operations* in 2015.[99]

The difference between the Liberal Peace and the previous three models is the preoccupation with stability as opposed to enemies; in principle, security is achieved through establishing stability rather than by defeating an enemy. The objective in this case can be national, regional or global security. The Liberal Peace culture also involves a new set of actors: a range of international agencies, the deployment of peacekeeping forces, private contractors, NGOs and a variety of different (non-military) actions including reconstruction and state-building efforts. The Liberal Peace model is both statist and multilateralist. It is grounded in the liberal principles of democracy, the rule of law and human rights in the conviction that 'democracy provides the best chances of internal stability, as well as a peaceful international order'.[100]

The Liberal Peace model directly addresses new wars but clothes new wars in old war garb. The centre piece of the Liberal Peace is peacemaking, the peace process, resulting (if successful) in a peace agreement, which often takes the form of, or basis for, a domestic constitution. An agreement among the warring parties is the objective and is sometimes reached and given a legal veneer; however, it entrenches the positions of those responsible for extremist identity politics, violations of human rights and predatory economic activities. The security apparatus of the Liberal Peace is thus used to sustain the peace agreement. The consequence is to dampen overt clashes but not to end the mutual enterprise that constitutes new wars. Like the previous models, the Liberal Peace starts from old war assumptions, treating the warring parties as though they were states and presupposing that war consists of a clash of wills rather than a mutual enterprise. As we spell out in Chapter 9, the evidence suggests that the Liberal Peace has been relatively successful in ending open warfare in probably about half of cases, but, despite the

[99] United Nations Security Council. 'Report of the Panel on United Nations Peacekeeping Operations', UN Doc. A/55/305–S/2000/809, 21 August 2000; Report of the High-Level Independent Panel on Peace Operations on Uniting Our Strengths for Peace: Politics, Partnership and People, UN Doc. A/70/95–S/2015/446. 17 June 2015.

[100] Hay, Emily 2014. 'International(ized) Constitutions and Peacebuilding', *Leiden Journal of International Law* 27: 141–168, 149.

commitment to liberal values, is much less successful in ensuring the long-term safety of individuals and communities. It may involve sustaining corrupt regimes in the name of stability.[101]

The final model is what we term second generation Human Security. Human Security is about the safety of individuals and the communities in which they live. First generation Human Security involved a debate between broad and narrow versions. The broad version evolved from the development community and the idea that resources freed up from the end of the Cold War could be used for economic and social development. Threats to the safety of individuals and communities included the threat of material deprivation, and the emphasis was on prevention of new wars by strengthening state institutions and enhancing development. The narrow version was associated with the human rights movement and was about protecting people from the human rights violations that are central to new war tactics; thus the narrow version became associated with the Responsibility to Protect.

Second generation Human Security puts the emphasis on implementation. Human Security is what individuals enjoy in rights-based law-governed societies. Implementation is about extending this form of security globally. In contrast to the Responsibility to Protect, which is by definition top-down and, despite its reformulation as a responsibility, remains essentially about the right of states to intervene, Human Security is about the right to be protected and focuses on bottom-up efforts to provide security to individuals and how this might be assisted from outside. In contrast to Liberal Peace, which is about collective stability, Human Security focuses on the individual, men, women and their families and communities. In the context of new wars, Human Security involves locally negotiated ceasefires and/or locally protected safe areas, encompassing a range for political, economic and social initiatives as well as justice mechanisms. Outside assistance might involve humanitarian corridors; meaningful international guarantees for safe areas; mediation and monitoring; documentation and access to justice. In so far as international peacekeepers are deployed in Human Security roles, their rules of engagement would be more like policing than military action, even though a robust use of force might sometimes be required. Their goals would be protection of civilians, the

[101] Chayes, Sarah 2015. *Thieves of State: Why Corruption Threatens Global Security*. New York: W. W. Norton & Company.

saving of all lives and the arrest of those responsible for criminal acts rather than killing or defeating enemies.

All the models have a gendered dimension since security is a gendered concept.[102] The focus on individual (as opposed to state) security in the Human Security model, however, more readily allows for explicit recognition of this. The ways in which women experience insecurity differently from men, as well as the role of women as civil society activists, mediators or peacekeepers and, more broadly in challenging existing gender roles and reconstructing gender relations, are of key importance. In this model, protection and rebuilding, economic and social rights, as well as political and civil rights would all receive emphasis.

As we spell out in the final chapter, second generation Human Security would mean, in international law terms, representative and accountable international authority for the use of force, the recasting of war as a humanitarian catastrophe and a massive violation of human rights, the recasting of self-defence as scaled-up self-defence of individuals not states, and the application of human rights law, as well as IHL, to any use of force (or to put it another way, the use of force within the constraints of rights-based policing rather than military type rules of engagement). Such an approach would also need to involve large-scale disarmament. In other words, the only permissible use of force would be in cases of massive violations of human rights, but rules of engagement would be much tighter than for classic military force as they would have to conform to human rights.

Our argument is that Human Security is the only practical solution. The failure to take into account the logic of new wars and the persistence of old war thinking has undermined the potential of other models to achieve their security objectives. The first two models (Geo-Politics and the War on Terror) may (for a time) succeed in their own terms (reinforcing popular ideas of security within particular countries), but they only worsen the duration and violence of new wars. The second two models (the Responsibility to Protect and Liberal Peace) are unable to achieve their objectives of addressing new wars because of the old war assumptions that underlie their practices. Second generation Human Security is not about utopian ideas but concrete ways of addressing current predicaments. At the heart of the Human Security model is the

[102] Olonisakin, 'Fummi, Barnes, Karen and Ikpe, Elke 2011. *Women, Peace and Security: Translating Policy into Practice*. Routledge.

postulation that war as the use of force among collectivities is wholly illegitimate in both old and new guises.

1.5 Plan of the Book

This argument is developed through two parallel tracks. First, the book provides an introduction to the international legal regime relating to the regulation of violence, and second, it develops the different models in relation to various aspects of international law. Part I of the book sets out the conceptual foundations. Chapter 2 discusses the changing nature of sovereignty in a global era and shifting conceptions of 'right' authority to use force. It argues that a fundamental shift took place after 1945, when war was made unequivocally illegal for the first time. Sovereignty was always based on the classic distinction between the 'outside' (the world of anarchy with no single authority) and the 'inside' (the world of domestic order where the state is construed as the supreme power). Globalisation, which to some extent is a consequence of the prohibition on war, has involved a blurring of the inside and outside. The chapter describes how the authority to use force is interpreted according to different models of security and what these differing understandings of the inside/outside distinction imply for conceptions of sovereignty and world order.

Chapter 3 sets out the premise of the book that international law is a form of discourse that is not so very different from domestic law, especially in the context of globalisation. We adopt a constructivist understanding of this discourse whereby international law is underpinned by what Jutta Brunnée and Stephen Toope call 'shared understandings'[103] developed through state socialisation or among 'communities of practice', or what Jürgen Habermas calls 'reciprocal perspective-taking'.[104] We review the main theories of compliance with international law, followed by a discussion of the mechanisms for compliance – institutionalisation, enforcement, implementation and judicialisation. Our argument is that the different models of security depend on who is involved in the 'communities of practice', and thus they also involve different mixes of mechanisms of compliance.

[103] Brunnée, Jutta and Toope, Stephen, *op. cit.*, 15. See further Chapter 3.

[104] Habermas, Jürgen 2006. 'Interpreting the Fall of a Monument', in Bartholomew, Amy (ed.). *Empire's Law: The American Imperial Project and the 'War to Remake the World'*. London: Pluto Press, 44–51, 51.

Part II deals with the contemporary laws relating to the use of force (*jus ad bellum*). Chapter 4 is about the self-defence exception to the prohibition on the use of force. It focuses on how *jus ad bellum* – forged in old war terms – has been applied in in recent decades, notably the War on Terror. It shows how the concept of self-defence has been stretched in terms of interpretations of imminence, necessity and proportionality and by the assumption that attacks by non-state actors can constitute an armed attack and that states have the right to act in self-defence of their alleged nationals (non-state actors) in other countries. It concludes by suggesting that either more conservative interpretations of self-defence need to be upheld or else 'armed attack' needs to be reconceptualised as a crime against humanity and responded to as such.

Chapter 5 is about the use of force in response to massive violations of human rights and the Responsibility to Protect model. The chapter surveys the experiences of this type of intervention over recent decades. It argues that any intervention in the name of human rights must conform to human rights and that as currently conceived the Responsibility to Protect is more about the roles of the dominant powers than about the rights of those to be protected.

Part III is about the means and methods of warfare (*jus in bello* and weapons law). Chapter 6 is about how force is used in all these situations. It argues that IHL is based on 'old war' assumptions. It describes how this legal regime has been distorted, especially in the War on Terror. It also deals with the differing legal regimes applicable in conflict (*in bello*) and makes the argument, in particular, that the human rights regime has to be applied alongside IHL in 'new wars'.

Chapter 7 is about different legal regimes relating to weapons. It sets out three different but overlapping approaches: 'arms control' is about reducing the risks associated with the use, deployment and possession of particular weapons by states largely associated with the Geo-Political model; the humanitarian approach, which aims to alleviate suffering in war, is largely associated with the Liberal Peace; and the disarmament approach is based on the idea that the way to prevent war and the violence to individuals associated with war is to eliminate the means of fighting war. In the post–Cold War period, there have been significant initiatives in both the arms control and humanitarian approaches aimed primarily at weapons possessed by non-state actors. The chapter argues that for Human Security, the humanitarian approach needs to be complemented by disarmament.

Part IV is about *post-bellum* regimes. It comprises three chapters, which are largely about the Liberal Peace model. The chapters introduce the emerging body of what is known as *post-bellum* law. Chapter 8 discusses the misnomer 'post-conflict' and analyses models of so-called post-conflict governance. Chapter 9 discusses peacemaking, peacekeeping and peacebuilding; the chapter argues that the shortcoming of the Liberal Peace model has to do with the way it is underpinned by 'old war' assumptions, including the very notion of a *post-bellum* phase. It makes the argument that peace agreements often entrench power holders who have an interest in subverting peacemaking and peacebuilding efforts. Chapter 10 addresses transitional justice and the accountability of those engaged in these activities; it argues that international mechanisms of justice and accountability are often weakened by Geo-Political and War on Terror considerations, and this, in turn, diminishes the potential of such instruments in 'new war' contexts.

Part V is about the way forward. Chapter 11 is about second generation Human Security. It provides a brief history of the concept of Human Security and addresses the critiques. The distinctive element of second generation Human Security is the way it draws on a rights-based international legal regime and focuses on implementation. The final concluding chapter draws the various arguments together and outlines the elements of a legal regime that would need to be developed as part of the Human Security model. The chapter asks what human security requires of international law. Our objective is to reopen the debate about how to address contemporary seemingly pervasive manifestations of violence in ways that are not pre-determined by assumptions and habits inherited from the past.

2

Sovereignty and the Authority to Use Force

2.1 Introduction

Formal procedures always reflect and respond to past practices. Despite the flurry of law-making and institution-building over the last two decades, the current international legal system still fundamentally derives from the way statehood and state sovereignty were perceived in the immediate post–World War II period. This state-centric system is increasingly out of step with the changing nature of what might be called global politics as well as the changing nature of political violence: 'new wars', the role of and increased political activities by non-state actors (civil society, international governmental agencies, multinational corporations, as well as armed and extremist groups), growing interconnectedness at all levels, the communicative revolution, the importance and intransigence of transnational problems (climate change, poverty, pandemics, environmental degradation and air pollution, financial crisis, displacement and movement of peoples, war itself) not to mention prevailing norms and ideas. The dissonance between the formal rules of international society (and the ways of changing those formal rules) and everyday experience has given rise to questionings and claims for reinterpretations of the rules.

Some scholars suggest that the process of globalisation implies the beginning of the end of state sovereignty – a move towards a global constitution for the human community in which states are becoming an anachronism. Others argue that state sovereignty remains and should remain the lynchpin of the international legal system; a view that is associated with this latter position is the suspicion that the growth of global institutions is merely cover for empire – for expanding the power of dominant states.[1] We share the position articulated by Jean Cohen that

[1] For a discussion of these two positions, see Cohen, Jean 2012. *Globalization and Sovereignty*. Cambridge University Press.

different historical periods are characterised by 'shifting sovereignty regimes'.[2] State sovereignty continues, at least formally, to underpin the international legal system augmented by an emerging set of global rules and institutions, such as those that relate to individuals as subjects of law and including judicialisation. How we interpret the nature of the current sovereignty regime – the changing meaning and substance of sovereignty – depends, we suggest, on different understandings of world order, which are linked to our different models of security.

We make the argument that the most salient change in the nature of state sovereignty has to do with the role of organised violence. Sovereignty has always been associated with the authority to use force (*jus belli*) although it is only in the modern, post-Westphalian period[3] that the state has been considered the only institution with the authority to use force and thus holds the monopoly of legitimate organised violence. Moreover, the use of force by the state was supposed to be confined to law enforcement at home (regulated by the social contract, constitutionalism and the rule of law) and war abroad (regulated by international law principles of statehood and the use of force). Nowadays, the relationship between state sovereignty and the authority to use force is undergoing profound and complex challenges in light of far-reaching changes in the global context – changes that are only to some degree reflected in formal rules. How these changes are understood is closely linked, we argue, to our different models of security. Thus the interplay of these different models has and will have profound implications for the character of world order.

This chapter introduces some of the key concepts that shape thinking about international affairs – sovereignty, right authority and world order – and attempts to chart the different ways these concepts are changing in 'these global times'. The next part introduces the external and internal aspects of sovereignty and how these are linked specifically in relation to war. It then traces the evolution of the concept of sovereignty and draws attention to some of the ways in which globalisation has affected and continues to affect the distinction between the external and internal aspects

[2] *Ibid.*

[3] This refers to the 24 October 1648 Treaty of Westphalia, a peace treaty between the Holy Roman Emperor and the King of France and their respective allies. There is a large literature on the significance of the Treaty on the development of the European statehood, the concept of sovereignty and international law. For an overview see, for example, Fassbender, Bardo 2011. 'Westphalia, Peace of (1648)', in Wolfrum, Rudiger (ed.). *Max Planck Encyclopedia of Public International Law*. Vol. X. Oxford University Press.

of sovereignty and what this might imply for the international legal system. The third part of the chapter outlines the changing nature of what is known in just war theory as 'right authority' – ideas about who or what can legitimately authorise the use of force. It describes the shift from religious to secular authority in the seventeenth and eighteenth centuries, the shift from just war concepts to legal regulation of force in the nineteenth century, and from national (state) authority to international authority in the twentieth century. It then discusses current understandings of right authority and, in particular, the specific role of the United Nations Security Council (SC) in authorising the use of force and the problems of legitimation. The chapter concludes by outlining how different ideas about world order and the nature of state sovereignty are associated with the different models of security described in the previous chapter.

2.2 The Changing Nature of Sovereignty

2.2.1 The Great Divide

The modern concept of state sovereignty encapsulates what International Relations theorists call the Great Divide. As Hinsley explains in his classic text on sovereignty:

> Applied to the community, in the context of the internal structure of a political society, the concept of sovereignty has involved the belief that there is absolute political power within the community. Applied to the problems which arise in relations between political communities, its function has been to express the antithesis of this argument – the principle that internationally, over and above the collection of communities no supreme authority exists.[4]

Thus the 'Great Divide' consisted of a distinction between domestic order (civil society) peopled by individuals, norms, law and politics and an external state of nature or anarchy composed of autonomous states that pursue their national self-interest, where there is no single authority.[5]

The Great Divide was a distinction that had its origin in Greek and Roman ideas about the nature of political community and was later to be found both in classical Islamic thought and in the ideas of the European

[4] Hinsley, F. H. 1986. *Sovereignty*. Cambridge University Press, 2nd ed., 158.

[5] Clarke, Ian 1999. *Globalisation and International Relations Theory*. Oxford University Press; Walker, Rob 1992. *Inside/Outside: International Relations as Political Theory*. Cambridge University Press.

Enlightenment. Classical Islamic thought distinguished between the realm of Islam (*dar al-Islam*) and the realm of war (*dar al-harb*).[6] The realm of Islam was that of a community characterised by a political authority, whose authority derived from the rule of law (*Shari'a*) and a social contract (*Bay'a*); in contrast, the external realm of war referred to an arena of irrationality and ignorance where there was no overarching political authority and tribal conflict was endemic.[7]

This distinction between the realm of Islam and the realm of war was paralleled by the distinction in European Enlightenment thought between civil society (meaning at that time a legally ordered political community) and the state of nature.[8] Civil society, like the realm of Islam, was a political community with a single political authority, based on a rule of law and a social contract. The state of nature was an arena without any political authority, where human beings were more or less prone to violence, depending on the assumptions about human nature made by different Enlightenment thinkers. For a pessimist like Thomas Hobbes, who drew on his experience of the English civil war, it was 'warre, as is of every man, against every man' a condition of 'continual fear, and danger of violent death' in which 'the life of man is solitary, poor, nasty, brutish and short'.[9] For John Locke, violence arose when there was no way of arbitrating differences of interpretation of the law of nature (understood as God's will imprinted on human consciousness).[10] In other words, human beings are not purely selfish; they are moral beings who may disagree about the content of morality. These different assumptions about human nature gave rise to different versions of the social contract; for Hobbes, men (and he was talking about men) gave up their freedom in the state of nature in exchange for security; for Locke, the social contract was also about liberty and private property.[11]

6 See, for example, Kelsay, John 1993. *Islam and War: A Study in Comparative Ethics*. John Knox Press; Al-Fadl, Khaled Abou 1999. 'The Rules of Killing at War: An Enquiry into Classical Sources', *The Muslim World* 89(2): 144–57.

7 Ezzat, Heba Raouf and Kaldor, Mary 2005. 'Not Even a Tree: Delegitimizing Violence and the Prospects for Pre-Emptive Civility', in *Global Civil Society: 2006–2007*. Sage, 18–41, 28.

8 See Kaldor, Mary 2003. *Global Civil Society: An Answer to War*. Polity Press, chapter 2.

9 Hobbes, Thomas (1998; 1651). *Leviathan*. Gaskin, John Charles Addison (ed.). Oxford University Press, ch. xiii, para. 9.

10 Locke, John (1998; 1690). *Two Treatises of Government*. Laslett, Peter (ed.). Cambridge University Press.

11 Carole Pateman suggests that the social contract was 'fraternal'; it was brothers replacing fathers rather than a change in gender relations. See Pateman, Carole 1988. 'The Fraternal Social Contract', in Keane, John (ed.). *Civil Society and the State*. Verso.

Feminists suggest that the inside/outside is a gendered distinction in which the state is construed as a male subject combating other males abroad yet in control of the domestic arena, which might be either patriarchal and repressive or alternatively a freer and gentler arena.[12] One can draw a parallel between the outside/inside distinction, the external and internal aspects of sovereignty, and the public/private distinction in domestic law,[13] whereby the private domain remains largely unregulated. On this reading, sovereignty can be conceived as a 'shield' behind which states (and men) can preserve their privacy either to 'protect' domestic civil society or to seek to hide human rights violations and other atrocities.[14]

For some Enlightenment philosophers, external war was a necessary condition for domestic order. Theorists of civil society, for example, Adam Ferguson and Alexis De Tocqueville, feared the atomism and individualism of modern societies that were no longer held together through kinship relationships; for them war was a way of generating domestic social solidarity and instilling a sense of public duty.[15] This does not mean that they considered the international realm to be necessarily anarchic. Ferguson, for example, thought that European states, characterised by civil societies, fought wars in a more 'civilised' way, by which he meant in accordance with agreed international rules.[16]

A stronger version of this argument was taken up by Hegel, who believed the fundamental unit for study to be the nation-state as the 'political vehicle for the cultural and psychological aspirations of peoples'.[17] For Hegel, external sovereignty creates the basis of internal authority. Hegel argues that the state is established through crisis and war and that it is only through self-sacrifice that the citizen understands the

[12] MacKinnon, Catharine 1989. *Toward a Feminist Theory of the State*. Harvard University Press; Knop, Karen 1993. 'Re/Statements: Feminism and Sovereignty in International Law', *Transnational Law and Contemporary Problems* 3; Charlesworth, Hilary and Chinkin, Christine 2000. *The Boundaries of International Law: A Feminist Analysis*. Manchester University Press. This analogy between the state and the individual (male) person impacts upon the construction of the principles relating to the use of force, as discussed in the following chapters.

[13] Pateman, Carole 1988. *The Sexual Contract*. Stanford University Press.

[14] Henkin, Louis 1994. 'The Mythology of Sovereignty', in MacDonald, Ronald St. John (ed.). *Essays in Honour of Wang Tieya*. Martinus Nijhoff, 351–358, 351.

[15] Ferguson, Adam (1995; 1767). *An Essay on the History of the Civil Society*. Cambridge University Press; De Tocqueville, Alexis (2003; 1835). *Democracy in America and Two Essays on America*. Penguin Books.

[16] Ferguson, *op. cit.*, 193.

[17] Neff, Stephen C. 2003. 'A Short History of International Law', in Evans, Malcolm (ed.). *International Law*. Oxford University Press, 31–58, 47.

primacy of the state. Indeed, it is during war that the state acts as an individual and the role of the citizen is subsumed in the state. Thus it is through war rather than through any social contract that individual freedom and social solidarity are reconciled. War, says Hegel, is necessary to preserve the 'ethical health of peoples. . . . Just as the movement of the ocean prevents the corruption which would be the result of perpetual calm, so by war people escape the corruption which would be occasioned by a continuous or eternal peace'.[18] Hegel argues that 'sacrifice for the sake of the individuality of the state is the substantive relation of all the citizens, and is, thus, a universal duty'.[19]

A twentieth-century exponent of this argument was the Nazi legal theorist Carl Schmitt. The central proposition of Carl Schmitt's *The Concept of the Political (Der Begriff des Politischen)* is that 'the political' is defined by the friend-enemy distinction. As a constitutional lawyer, Schmitt was preoccupied with what lay beyond law. He was deeply critical of the positive law tradition of the nineteenth century while similarly unaccepting of the natural law argument – the idea that certain universalistic norms underpin law. For him, all law is 'situational', and his answer to the question of what lies beyond law had to do with political and historical circumstances. In particular, he argued that sovereignty was above the law and that sovereignty in turn is underpinned by the concept of the political. The first sentence of *The Concept of the Political* reads: 'The concept of the state presupposes the concept of the political'.[20] But what is the meaning of political? For Schmitt, it seems to derive from the notion of a political community defined by conflict.[21] In common with other theorists, Schmitt argued that different fields of human endeavour are characterised by binary distinctions: good and evil in the case of morality, beautiful and ugly in the case of aesthetics, profitable and unprofitable in the case of economics. In the case of politics, the defining binary distinction is the friend and enemy distinction, which has to include the 'real physical possibility of killing'.[22] Hence domestic order was intrinsically linked to external war, and in so far as

[18] Hegel, Georg Wilhelm Friedrich. (1996; 1896 [in English] and 1820 [in German]). *Philosophy of Right*. Dyde, Samuel Waters (trans.). Prometheus Books, 331.

[19] *Ibid.*, 334–335.

[20] Schmitt, Carl (1976; 1927). *The Concept of the Political*. Schwab, George (trans.). Rutgers University Press, 1.

[21] See Kaldor, Mary 2013. 'Identity and War', *Global Policy* 4(4): 336–346.

[22] Kaldor, *op. cit.* ('Identity in War').

international law was relevant, it was as the positive law made by states rather than through any assumption of universal morality.

Schmitt argued that in the nineteenth century wars were 'bracketed', that is to say, fought in a restrained way according to international rules. The claim for universal morality in the twentieth century, he argued, explained the devastating character of twentieth-century wars comparable to holy wars of an earlier era, as we discuss below. It has been observed that the Schmittian view of international law – that it is to be seen from the perspective of national interests – has been revived by some contemporary, primarily American international lawyers who consider international law to lack legitimacy when 'compared with the legitimacy of national democratic governance'.[23]

The alternative stream of thought that goes back to the Greek stoics is the cosmopolitan position in which domestic freedom is linked to international harmony rather than anarchy. The Roman law concept of *jus gentium* (law of nations) was the law applicable to all peoples as opposed to the *jus civile*, applicable only to Roman citizens. The former combined customary law of the local communities that lived around the Mediterranean and presupposed some shared universal norms.[24] Liberal political theorists from the seventeenth century onwards, who assumed a 'social contract' for the institution of government and the protection of individual rights along the lines put forward by John Locke, also envisaged the construction of a liberal international order linked to the rise of domestic civil society, in which force was increasingly limited to policing actions and the enforcement of justice. Many developed their own perpetual peace schemes.[25] One of the best known is Immanuel Kant's proposal, who drew

[23] Wulfrum, Rüdiger (2008). 'Legitimacy of International Law from a Legal Perspective: Some Introductory Considerations', in Wulfrum, Rüdiger and Röben, Volker (eds.). *Legitimacy in International Law*. Springer, 1–24, 2. Examples of this approach, or 'school' of international law, modernised through rational choice theory include Glennon, Michael 2010. *The Fog of Law: Pragmatism, Security, and International Law*. Stanford University Press; Goldsmith, Jack and Posner, Eric 2005. *The Limits of International Law*. Oxford University Press.

[24] Roman writers did not always distinguish the *jus gentium* and *jus naturale* – the universal law of nature, which derived from Greek philosophers. The only context in which the difference became pertinent was slavery, which was universally practiced in the ancient world but regarded by some as contrary to the laws of nature. Jolowicz, Herbert Felix and Nicholas, Barry 1972. *Historical Introduction to the Study of Roman Law*. Cambridge University Press, 3rd ed., 100–105.

[25] See Archibugi, Daniele 1992. 'Models of International Organisation in Perpetual Peace Projects', *Review of International Studies* 18(4): 295–317.

on Jean-Jacques Rousseau's description of the Abbé St Pierre's[26] scheme for perpetual peace. Kant took the view that the construction of civil society in the Enlightenment sense would be possible only if it were universalised. Indeed, while he argued that a republican constitution was a condition for perpetual peace, he also thought that a fully functioning civil society was not possible except in the framework of what we would now call a global civil society. According to Kant: 'The problem of establishing a perfect civil society is subordinate to the problem of a law-governed external relationship with other states, and cannot be solved unless the latter is also solved'.[27] War necessarily represented an infringement of civil freedom; it was expensive, destructive and uncertain. Indeed, Rousseau had suggested in his description of the Abbé St Pierre's scheme for peace through federation that war was the device through which rulers sustained their power, providing a 'pretext' for taxation and for obedience.[28] These thinkers were not necessarily utopian or determinist; Kant took the view that if a scheme for perpetual peace were not adopted either by chance or by deliberate action, a 'hell of evils' would overtake the world.[29]

The different schools of thought in International Relations originate in these different understandings of the relationship between domestic order and external anarchy. Classic realist thinking conceives the international arena in Hobbesian terms and denies the relevance of international law except as a tool for national interest. The English School of International Relations, deriving from the work of Hedley Bull and Martin Wight, suggests that even though there exists no single authority, states do constitute members of an international system based on agreed rules.[30] Among contemporary English School

[26] Rousseau, Jean-Jacques 1917. *A Lasting Peace through the Federation of Europe and the State of War*. Vaughan, Charles Edwyn (trans.). Constable and Company.

[27] Kant, Immanuel 1991. 'Idea for a Universal History with a Cosmopolitan Purpose', in *Kant's Political Writing*. Nisbet, H. B (trans.). Cambridge University Press, 41–53, 47.

[28] Rousseau, Jean-Jaques (1991; 1756). 'Abstract and Judgement of Saint-Pierre's Project for Perpetual Peace', in Hoffman, Stanley and Fidler, David P. (eds.). *Rousseau on International Relations*. Clarendon Press. The same point had been made by earlier thinkers on war and peace, especially Erasmus.

[29] Kant, *op. cit.*, 48. Jürgen Habermas has argued that a 'hell of evils' did indeed overtake the world. Habermas, Jürgen 1997. 'Kant's Idea of Perpetual Peace, with the Benefit of Two Hundred Years' Hindsight' in Bohman, James and Lutz-Bachmann, Matthias (eds.). *Perpetual Peace: Essays on Kant's Cosmopolitan Ideal*. MIT Press.

[30] Bull, Hedley 2012. *Anarchical Society: A Study of Order in World Politics*. Columbia University Press and Palgrave Macmillan, 4th ed.; Wight, Gabrielle and Porter, Brian (eds.) 1994. *International Theory: The Three Traditions*. Leicester University Press.

theorists, a distinction is drawn between pluralists, who assert norms of non-intervention, and solidarists, who argue that human rights norms do override sovereignty in some instances.[31]

In contrast to the realist conceptions of International Relations, whether we are talking about traditional realists, pluralists or solidarists, the Kantian position is often described as idealist or cosmopolitan. While there are overlaps with a solidarist view of International Relations, the cosmopolitan strand of thinking departs from the insistence on the pivotal significance of state sovereignty (though it does not deny some version of sovereignty) and gains increasing relevance in the context of the contemporary blurring of the Great Divide associated with the phenomenon known as globalisation. It is worth noting that the term 'cosmopolitan' should not be conflated with human or humanism;[32] cosmopolitanism celebrates the different ways of being human – hence it necessarily entails multiculturalism and pluralism. Indeed, one can argue that the Kantian position, as interpreted here, involves a deconstruction of the structural binaries between inside and outside or friend and enemy that underpin Western bases of power and that have been stressed in critical theories, including feminist and post-colonial theories.

2.2.2 The Evolution of Sovereignty

The term 'sovereignty' is said to have originated with Jean Bodin in his work *Six Livres de la République* published in 1576. It was taken up by Hugo Grotius in *De Jure Belli ac Pacis* (*The Laws of War and Peace*) published in 1625. According to Grotius: 'That power is called sovereign whose actions are not subject to the control of any other power so as to be annulled at the pleasure of any other human being'.[33] Along with the almost contemporary Spanish legal theorist, Vitoria (died 1546), Grotius argued that authority had to do, above all, with war-making: 'The acts of the sovereign executive power of a directly public kind are the making of peace and war and treaties and the imposition of taxes and other

[31] See Hurrell, Andrew 2008. *On Global Order: Power, Values and the Constitution of International Society*. Oxford University Press; Wheeler, Nicholas 2002. *Saving Strangers: Humanitarian Intervention in International Society*. Oxford University Press.

[32] See Appiah, Anthony 2000. *Cosmopolitanism: Ethics in a World of Strangers*. Norton.

[33] Grotius, Hugo (2003; 1625). *The Rights of War and Peace*. Campbell, Archibald Colin (trans.). Elibron Classics, 62.

exercises of authority over the persons and property of its subjects, which constitute the sovereignty of the state'.[34]

The concept of state sovereignty was 'invented by absolutist theorists in an absolutist age'.[35] It is associated with the rise of centralised authorities in Europe that were increasingly independent of international authorities, such as the Pope or the Holy Roman Emperor. 'It is a legal structure that came about to manage the disintegration of a community', earlier described as 'the world state of medieval Christendom'.[36] Despite their independence from each other, the establishment of domestic governance structures did depend in practice on recognition by others, although these were other states, or other forms of political entity such as city states, rather than higher authorities. It was Grotius who was one of the first to draw attention to the importance of international law, the 'law of nations', within which sovereignty, the 'oldest subject in international law',[37] is situated. States became accepted as the principal bearers of international legal personality, and conventional narratives of the modern international legal system emphasise the concept of statehood and states' sovereign rights and obligations in wartime and peace; the essentially internal concept of sovereignty thus became entwined with the notion of the 'sovereign state'. Indeed, Michael Walzer argues that the rights of states derive from the social contract within states in which individual rights are transmuted into state rights in exchange for protection against external encroachment and life and liberty at home.[38]

State sovereignty is not a 'fact' but the ascription of status that depends on conformity to the international framework of rules.[39] What has changed over time is those rules: the need for recognition,[40] the criteria

[34] *Ibid.*, 61.

[35] Keohane, Robert 2008. 'Discussion Following Presentations by Rudiger Wulfrum, Robert Keohane, Alain Pellet and Anthony D'Amato', in Wulfrum, and Röben (eds.), *op. cit.*, 93–108, 93.

[36] Abi-Saab, Georges 2008. 'The Security Council as Legislator and as Executive in Its Fight against Terrorism and against Proliferation of Weapons of Mass Destruction: The Question of Legitimacy', in Wulfrum and Röben (eds.), *op. cit.*, 109–131, 112.

[37] Henkin, Louis 1994. 'The Mythology of Sovereignty', in MacDonald, Ronald St. John (ed.). *Essays in Honour of Wang Tieya*. Martinus Nijhoff, 351–358.

[38] Walzer, Michael 2015. *Just and Unjust Wars: A Moral Argument with Historcal Illustrations*. Basic Books, 5th ed.

[39] Kratochwil, Friedrich 2012. 'Leaving Sovereignty Behind: An Inquiry into the Politics of Post-Modernity', in Falk, Richard, Juergensmayer, Mark and Popovski, Vesselin. *Legality and Legitimacy in Global Affairs*. Oxford University Press, 127–148, 134.

[40] Crawford points out that while sovereignty was 'merely the location of power within a particular territorial unit' there was no need for recognition by other external entities.

for recognition and the nature of the regimes that make up the international system. As Kratchowil points out, status was loosely connected to the capacity to act, or, as it is sometimes depicted, there is a link between *de jure* sovereignty (legal status) and *de facto* sovereignty (capacity to act).[41] In the early post-Westphalian period, status was linked to control of land and noble lineage. In the nineteenth century, control over peoples through the apparatus of the state and empire-building became more important, and, in the twentieth century, the notion of popular will – self-determination – became a salient criterion. In the late twentieth and early twenty-first century, human rights and the politics of nationalisms have become increasingly relevant, but often opposing, factors, which have 'transfigured "sovereignty"'.[42] The rules of international law have correspondingly shifted along with the changing substance of such claims.

Alongside other rules relating to sovereign states, for instance, diplomatic relations, treaty-making, acquisition of territory and jurisdiction, the laws relating to the use of force have shifted. In the post-Westphalian period, the international rules legitimated war-making by sovereigns. Indeed, the emergence of the modern state in Western Europe was closely associated with war-making: 'a state has a monopoly on violence within a bordered territory'. The border must precede the social contract (giving rise to internal sovereignty) as otherwise no-one would know to whom the contract applies. But the state must defend those borders, 'for it is here where communities meet, that the social contract has no force ... the sovereign function is necessarily, i.e., structurally, both law [internal] and war [external]'.[43] The state is thus described by Charles Tilly as a 'coercion-wielding institution'; Anthony Giddens has similarly called it a 'bordered power container'.[44] Grotius pointed out that war is not condemned according to the Law of Nations – a war that conforms to the Law of Nations 'is called just or perfect'.[45] The just war tradition remained the dominant framework for

Recognition had no place in international law until the middle of the eighteenth century. Crawford, James 2006. *The Creation of States in International Law*. Oxford University Press, 2nd ed., 12.

41 Kratochwil, *op. cit.*, 134. However, recognition may continue even where the capacity to act has been lost, as, for instance, with government in exile.

42 *Ibid.*, 135.

43 Kahn, Paul W. 2013. 'Imagining Warfare', *European Journal of International Law* 24: 199–226, 202–213.

44 Tilly, Charles 1992. *Coercion, Capital and European States: AD 990–1992*. Wiley-Blackwell; Giddens, Anthony 1985. *The Modern State and Violence*. Polity Press, 119.

legal analysis through the seventeenth and eighteenth centuries, although a shift was taking place on the ground; perfect (just) wars were distinguished from 'imperfect' (unjust) wars.[46] The former engaged certain rules and recognised practices, while the latter were 'excluded from the category of war altogether'. They were understood in different terms, such as reprisals. Individual self-defence was similarly understood as 'an inherent natural law right, distinct from war and exercisable by unjust parties as well as by just ones'.[47] These measures then perceived as short of war underwent different legal trajectories as they were further conceptualised in the twentieth century.[48]

From the seventeenth century onwards, wars between European states were interspersed with periods of peace, whose contours were established by post-war settlements. 'At the end of every war since the end of the eighteenth century', says Hinsley, 'the leading states made a concerted effort, each one more radical than the last, to reconstruct the system on lines that would enable them, or so they believed, to avoid a further war'.[49] To this end peace settlements were standardised during the seventeenth century. They sought compromise between the warring parties and were non-judgemental, typically encompassing cessation of military hostilities, title to captured property, freeing of prisoners of war and amnesty.[50] Earlier post-war settlements such as the 1648 Peace of Westphalia itself or the Peace of Utrecht, a complex of treaties signed between 1713 and 1714 that brought an end to the wars of Spanish succession, had made similar provision. These settlements could be considered as a sort of social contract among states that provided the basis for international legitimacy – an 'initial get-together' (to use Hannah Arendt's term for explaining legitimacy)[51] at an international level. But, as discussed below, and as continued in the post–World War II

[45] Grotius, *op. cit.*, 36.

[46] Neff, Stephen 2005. *War and the Law of Nations: A General History*. Cambridge University Press, 95 ff.

[47] *Ibid.*, 126.

[48] On self-defence see Chapter 4; reprisals were determined to be illegal by the UN General Assembly, Declaration on Principles of International Law concerning Friendly Relations and Co-operation among States in accordance with the Charter of the United Nations, UN GA Resolution 2625, 24 October 1970.

[49] Quoted in Ikenberry, John G. 2011. *Liberal Leviathan: The Origins, Crisis, and Transformation of the American World Order*. Princeton University Press, 11.

[50] Neff, *op. cit.* (*War and the Law of Nations*), 117.

[51] Arendt, Hannah 1972. *Crises of the Republic*. Harcourt Brace Jovanovich.

settlement, not all states were equal in these 'get-togethers', which were dominated by the great powers of the day.[52]

The nineteenth and early twentieth centuries were the high tide of state sovereignty and its manifestation – legal positivism. As expressed by the Permanent Court of International Justice (PCIJ) in the *Lotus* case, '[r]estrictions upon the independence of States cannot therefore be presumed'. In this laissez-faire era, states could only be in violation of international law if the accusing state could point to a positive principle prohibiting the action in question.[53] In this regard 'war reached its pinnacle of legal prestige'.[54] It was accepted as a regular instrument of policy whereby states each protected their own vital national interests. Accordingly, once war was declared, a set of legal principles came into play with respect to both the parties and third states that were bound by – and benefitted from – the rules of neutrality. This is what Schmitt meant by 'bracketed' wars.[55]

The victors against Napoleon and hence the major powers of the day (Austria, Russia, Britain and Prussia) convened in Vienna in 1815 to seek ways to manage Europe through maintaining the balance of power and their own interests, the so-called Concert of Europe. This hierarchical albeit informal arrangement – 'the first model of international government'[56] – was aimed at both ensuring that no single nation gained supremacy and maintaining stability in Europe.[57]

Especially in the nineteenth century after the 1815 settlement at Vienna, these periods of European peace allowed for the expansion of state power: territorially through overseas empire building (notably given legitimacy by the supposed 'civilising mission' of the 1885 Congress of Berlin)[58] and internally through the construction of the administrative state. Long periods of peace[59]

[52] Simpson, Gerry 2004. *Great Powers and Outlaw States: Unequal Sovereigns in the International Legal Order*. Cambridge University Press.

[53] *The Case of the SS Lotus (France v. Turkey)*, PCIJ Series A, No. 10, judgment of 7 September 1927, para. 44.

[54] Neff, *op. cit.* (*War and the Law of Nations*), 161.

[55] See Kaldor, *op. cit.* ('Identity and War').

[56] Mazower, Mark 2012. *Governing the World: The History of an Idea, 1815 to the Present*. Penguin Press.

[57] Simpson, *op. cit.*, chapter 4.

[58] 'Versions of the civilizing mission were used by all the actors who participated in imperial expansion'. Anghie, Anthony 2004. *Imperialism, Sovereignty, and the Making of International Law*. Cambridge University Press, 96.

[59] Uprisings and conflicts against colonial powers were disregarded as wars and thus as not disrupting the period of peace. They were perceived as being internal unrest and were responded to with extreme violence.

made possible growing interconnectedness in trade and communications, industrialisation and technological advances. Transnational groups emerged whose organised campaigning also sought the strengthening of international legal regulation. For example, the Anti-Slavery Society (founded in 1839 and originally called the British and Foreign Anti-Slavery Society) sought and campaigned for the worldwide abolition of slavery. In 1864 the actions of Henri Dunant, shocked by the humanitarian cost of the aftermath of war that he witnessed after the battle of Solferino (1859), led to the founding of the International Red Cross (International Committee of the Red Cross) and the commencement of the codification of the modern 'laws of war'.[60] At the end of the century, at The Hague Peace Conferences of 1899 and 1907, which were the first of what we now call global summit meetings, peace groups organised parallel sessions and even published a newsletter. They argued for peaceful methods for the settlement of disputes in place of war and hoped for the establishment of international adjudication, which transpired after World War I with the creation of the PCIJ,[61] even though the Court was not accorded compulsory jurisdiction because of the insistence on state sovereignty. It remains the case that jurisdiction of the successor International Court of Justice (ICJ) rests upon state consent.[62]

Thus the paradox of the growth of the modern state was that it contributed, on the one hand, to domestic prosperity and democratisation as well as growing interconnectedness, transnational civil society and increased inter-governmental agreements, and, on the other hand, to brutal colonialism, the genocide of American, African and Australian native tribes, and destructive wars: 'The state was simultaneously the vehicle for peace and war, for life and death. The logic of law pointed to individual well-being as the ground for legitimacy, while sovereign presence depended upon citizens being willing to kill and be killed'.[63] The

[60] This process began with the adoption of the *Convention for the Amelioration of the Condition of the Wounded in Armies in the Field*. Geneva, 22 August 1864. This was revised and replaced by new versions, culminating in the *Convention for the Amelioration of the Condition of the Wounded and Sick in Armed Forces in the Field*, 12 August 1949, 75 UNTS 31 (*Geneva Convention I*). See Chapter 6.

[61] *Covenant of the League of Nations*, 28 April 1919, article 14; *Statute of the Permanent Court of International Justice*, 16 December 1920, 6 LNTS 379, 390.

[62] *Statute of the International Court of Justice*, 26 June 1945, article 36.

[63] Kahn, *op. cit.*, 205; cf. 'The term "sovereignty", for example, has a long-standing and troubling history: from the times of Jean Bodin (1530–1596) and of Emerich de Vattel (1714–1767) up to the present, in the name of State sovereignty – unduly and inadvertently diverted from inter-State to intra-State relations – millions of human beings were sacrificed'.

militarism and nationalism that culminated in the wars and genocides of the twentieth century have to be explained in terms of the profound contradictions of state sovereignty.

Post-World War II

In the aftermath of two world wars, the establishment of the United Nations Organisation, preceded by the League of Nations in the inter-war period, formally reaffirmed the principle of sovereign equality of states in the UN Charter, article 2 (1). Although undermined by the privileged position of the five permanent members of the Security Council (UN Charter, articles 23 and 27), the principle of the sovereign equality of states was given expression through the one state/one vote basis of voting in the General Assembly (UN Charter article 18) and, after 1955, practical acceptance of the principle of universal membership of the Organisation. States are designated as equal, autonomous entities. Equality between sovereign states denotes a horizontal not a vertical relationship; no one sovereign state has authority over other states, which must respect each other's boundaries and refrain from interference in their domestic affairs.[64] Of course, power dynamics – economic, military and political inequality – undermine this formal position.

The principle of sovereign equality is upheld by corollary principles such as the prohibition of the use of force in international relations against the territorial integrity or political independence of another state (UN Charter, article 2 (4)) and the obligation to settle disputes peacefully (UN Charter, article 2 (3)). Unlike in the League Covenant, the principles for the maintenance of international peace and security were made applicable to non-members (article 2 (6)), and no provision was made for voluntary withdrawal from the Organisation.[65] State sovereignty was further entrenched by the end of colonialism: 'sovereignty was the watch-cry for the principle of self-determination'.[66] The League of Nations had

Jurisdictional Immunities of the State (Germany v. Italy: Greece intervening), 2012 ICJ Reports 99, judgment of 3 February 2012 (per dissenting opinion of Judge Trindade, para. 163).

[64] UN Charter, article 2 (7) prohibits UN intervention in matters within the domestic jurisdiction of states. 'No State or group of States has the right to intervene, directly or indirectly, for any reason whatever, in the internal or external affairs of any other State'; UN GA Resolution 2625, *op. cit.*

[65] UN Charter, articles 5 and 6 provide for suspension of membership and expulsion from the Organisation for persistent violation of the principles of the Charter.

[66] Henkin, Louis 1999. 'That "S" Word: Sovereignty, and Globalization, and Human Rights, Et Cetera', *Fordham Law Review* 68: 1–14, 1.

been established on the assumption of the continuation of colonial rule. This premise was continued, albeit in weakened form in the United Nations,[67] but which also included among its purposes the development of 'friendly relations among nations based on respect for the principle of equal rights and self-determination of peoples' (UN Charter, article 1 (2)). A major – if not the major – development in post-1945 international law has been the acceptance – and limitation – of the right to self-determination. Self-determination as expounded by both Woodrow Wilson and Lenin was perceived of as applicable to European peoples in the break-up of the Ottoman and Austro-Hungarian empires in the wake of World War I. Although the colonial territories of the defeated powers were placed under the League mandate system rather than being conferred as colonies, the League Covenant recognised the continuation of 'peoples not yet able to stand by themselves under the strenuous conditions of the modern world' (article 22).[68]

In addition, with the creation of new states by the peace settlement of 1919, thereby giving effect to some nationalist demands, a form of international protection was accorded to some individuals through the conclusion of treaties for the protection of national minorities. These minority treaties were limited. They applied only to those minorities identified by the treaties while others were not accorded such international recognition or protection (e.g., the Kurds). But, like the mandate system, they did provide for (limited) international supervision and redress, but through the advisory jurisdiction of the PCIJ rather than through individual rights themselves. Nevertheless, the jurisprudence of the PCIJ made an important contribution to the concept that individuals could have rights bestowed by treaty[69] and to the international legal understanding of equality.[70]

The year 1945 saw changes to both minority protection and the mandate system. Protection of national minorities was no longer given particular emphasis but was subsumed within the general notion of

67 Under the Trusteeship system; UN Charter, Ch. XI, articles 73 and 74.

68 On the history and application of the mandate system see Pedersen, Susan, *The Guardians: The League of Nations and the Crisis of Europe*. Oxford University Press, 2015.

69 *Polish Postal Service in Danzig*, PCIJ Series B No. 11, advisory opinion of 16 May 1925.

70 See, for example, *Minority Schools in Albania*, PCIJ Series A/B No. 64, advisory opinion of 6 April 1935, para. 64: 'Equality in law precludes discrimination of any kind; whereas equality in fact may involve the necessity of different treatment in order to attain a result which establishes an equilibrium between different situations'.

human rights.[71] The UN trusteeship system (which replaced the mandate system) recognised the obligation to promote the progressive development of each territory placed under the system 'towards self-government or independence as may be appropriate to the particular circumstances of each territory and its peoples and the freely expressed wishes of the peoples concerned'.[72] Although article 1 of both the International Covenant on Civil and Political Rights (ICCPR) and International Covenant on Economic, Social and Cultural Rights (ICESCR)[73] affirmed the right to self-determination, such claims of non-self-governing peoples were inspired by nationalist movements, in many cases rooted in the nineteenth century, anti-racism and anti-colonialism, rather than by human rights *per se*. Indeed, despite humanitarian antecedents to what might be termed the international human rights movement, it is argued that the latter did not fully emerge until after the achievement of self-determination for most colonised territories.[74] The achievement of self-determination did not guarantee the enjoyment of human rights for those in newly independent states, notwithstanding constitutional protections in many instances. Rather, the concept entrenched the sovereign equality of such states within their existing boundaries as determined by the colonial powers, the doctrine of *uti possidetis*.[75] The legal insistence on the territorial integrity of the newly independent sovereign states was upheld in practice as demonstrated by the lack of international support for Biafra, East Timor, Western Sahara and Bougainville as their claims were violently resisted by Nigeria, Indonesia, Morocco and Papua New Guinea, respectively. This legal resolve has been weakened in the wake of claims

[71] Article 27 of the *International Covenant on Civil and Political Rights* (ICCPR), 16 December 1966, United Nations Treaty Series, vol. 199, 171, is the only provision in the UN Covenants directed at minority protection. It is cast in terms of the right of individuals belonging to minorities not to 'be denied the right, in community with the other members of their group, to enjoy their own culture, to profess and practise their own religion, or to use their own language'. See also *Framework Convention for the Protection of National Minorities*, Strasbourg, 1 February 1995, European Treaty Series, No. 157.

[72] UN Charter, article 76.

[73] *International Covenant on Economic, Social and Cultural Rights* (ICESCR), 16 December 1966, United Nations Treaty Series, vol. 993, 3.

[74] Moyn, Samuel 2011. *The Last Utopia: Human Rights in History*. Belknap Press; for a rejoinder to this view see Alston, Philip 2013. 'Does the Past Matter? On the Origins of Human Rights', *Harvard Law Review* 126(7): 2043–2081.

[75] *Case Concerning the Frontier Dispute* (*Burkina Faso v. Mali*), 1986 ICJ Reports 554, 22 December 1986, para. 20: 'the principle of intangibility of frontiers inherited from colonization'.

for self-determination outside the European 'salt water' colonial context that have provided the justification for many of the 'new wars' of the 1990s and the early twenty-first century, in places like Sudan, the former Yugoslavia or the South Caucasus. Nevertheless, these claims tend to be based on group identities – nationalist or ethnic principles – rather than on human rights. The recognition of new states created out of the break-up of the former Yugoslavia and USSR in the 1990s, the separation of Eritrea from Ethiopia in 1991, the independence of Timor Leste in 2002 and of South Sudan in 2011 have all further undermined the grip of prior colonial history on the principle of territorial integrity.[76]

The principle of non-intervention in the domestic affairs of states in article 2 (7) of the UN Charter has parallels with the principle of non-intervention in family affairs, and like the latter, this is beginning to change. In the case of states, sovereignty was limited by the exception relating to the application of enforcement measures under UN Charter chapter VII. This embryonic notion of international governance is furthered by articles 24 and 25, giving primary responsibility for the maintenance of international peace and security to the SC and making Council decisions binding upon member states. While the significance was not fully recognised at the time, further constraints on state action were introduced by the stipulation of the promotion of respect for human rights as a purpose of the Organisation.[77] The development of normative human rights standards was progressed through the adoption of the Universal Declaration of Human Rights (1948), the Genocide Convention (1948) and the two International Covenants adopted by the General Assembly in 1966 (the ICCPR and ICESCR). The coming into force in 1976 of the ICCPR and ICESCR was an indication of the greater place of human rights, and accordingly constraints on state sovereignty, in at least the rhetoric of international affairs in the last quarter of the twentieth century, as well as in domestic affairs through their incorporation into national legal systems. As discussed

[76] Colonised territories – penetrated, exploited and subjected to violence – contrast with the masculine state. Liberation struggles against colonial rule and the quest for sovereignty by previously colonised peoples may be analogised to the fight for women's suffrage and equality, which were also resisted as disruptive to the existing hierarchical order.

[77] UN Charter, articles 1(3), 55 and 56. Article 68 allows for the setting up by the Economic and Social Council (ECOSOC) of a commission for the promotion of human rights. Without this institutional allocation of responsibility, the history of human rights within the UN might have been very different.

in Chapter 3 the development of individual complaints procedures meant that state actions could be directly challenged in international or regional judicial or quasi-judicial bodies.[78] That this inroad into sovereignty remains especially contested with respect to the status of women within the state is shown by the many reservations to the Convention on the Elimination of All Forms of Discrimination against Women[79] and the continued assertion of the 'domestic jurisdiction' exception. It has been argued that '[t]he fact that the international community is progressively moving from a sovereignty-centred to a value-oriented or individual-oriented system has left deep marks on its scope and meaning'.[80] The role of non-governmental organisations (NGOs), as they were now called, in pressing for their own inclusion[81] and for that of human rights in the post-war settlement could be said to have anticipated the growing salience of non-state actors in the spread of global norms in the current period.[82]

The above discussion demonstrates the fluidity of sovereignty. Nowadays sovereignty is often expressed in contingent or conditional terms,[83] for instance, in failed or weak state settings where state power

[78] For example, the *Convention for the Protection of Human Rights and Fundamental Freedoms* (European Convention on Human Rights or ECHR), 4 November 1950, as amended by Protocols Nos. 11 and 14, article 34; *Inter-American Convention on Human Rights*, 22 November 1969, article 44; *Protocol to the African Charter on Human and Peoples' Rights on the Establishment of the African Court on Human and Peoples' Rights*, 9 June 1998, articles 5 and 34; ICCPR, *op. cit.*, First Optional Protocol, 16 December 1966; ICESCR, *op. cit.* Optional Protocol, 18 June 2008.

[79] Connors, Jane 2012. 'Reservations', in Freeman, Marsha, Chinkin, Christine and Rudolf, Beate, *The UN Convention on the Elimination of All Forms of Discrimination against Women: A Commentary*. Oxford Commentaries on International Law.

[80] Tomuschat, Christian 1999. 'International Law: Ensuring the Survival of Mankind on the Eve of a New Century: General Course on Public International Law', in *Collected Courses of The Hague Academy of International Law* 281: 9–438, 25.

[81] UN Charter, article 71: 'The Economic and Social Council may make suitable arrangements for consultation with non-governmental organizations which are concerned with matters within its competence'.

[82] Keck, Margaret E. and Sikkink, Kathryn 1998. *Activists beyond Borders: Advocacy Networks in International Politics*. Cornell University Press; Finemore, Martha and Sikkink, Kathryn 1998. 'International Norm Dynamics and Political Change', *International Organization* 52: 887–917.

[83] 'There are two components to contingent sovereignty. The first is the extent to which a country enjoys sovereign rights and privileges, which has been described as the principle of *conditional sovereignty*. The second is the standards that may be used to distinguish among sovereign nations; call it *differentiated sovereignty*'; Council on Foreign Relations, 'UN Divided', Winter 2005–2006, www.cfr.org/international-organizations-and-alliances/un-divided/p9434.

is not operative in certain areas or where international rules relating to non-intervention are deemed not to apply to them,[84] or where the international community has taken responsibility for key elements of state provision.[85]

Global Governance, Global Civil Society and New Wars

The creation of international intergovernmental institutions had been underway since the nineteenth century, especially with respect to communications and transport. Within the Cold War framework, much like the inter-imperial framework of the nineteenth century, the post-war period witnessed a dramatic growth in interconnectedness at all levels – political, economic and cultural – and this had a profound impact on the actual character of states. Following the ICJ's opinion in 1949 that the UN is a subject of international law, enjoying objective international legal personality,[86] it has been accepted that the same is true of other international institutions. More and more international and regional inter-governmental institutions were established, generally based on inter-governmental agreements. Interconnectedness both reflected and facilitated the expansion in trade and the huge improvements in travel and communication. At the regional level greater economic and political integration has been pursued, notably in Europe but also elsewhere.[87]

Indeed, the establishment of what was to become the European Union had many parallels to the peace projects of Abbé St Pierre and Immanuel Kant, as discussed above. The founders of the European Economic Communities (now European Union) were determined to prevent another war on European territory. The method they adopted was gradual economic integration starting with the integration of the coal and steel industries of the protagonists of World War II and evolving into the present day European Union. The European Union can be considered a political experiment, a kind of model for global governance

[84] Elden, Stuart 2006. 'Contingent Sovereignty, Territorial Integrity and the Sanctity of Borders', *SIAS Review of International Affairs* 26: 11–24.

[85] The Independent International Commission on Kosovo 2000. *Kosovo Report: Conflict, International Response, Lessons Learned.* Oxford University Press, 271.

[86] *Reparation for Injuries Suffered in the Service of the United Nations, 1949* ICJ Reports 174, advisory opinion of 11 April 1949.

[87] Regional arrangements outside Europe include the African Union; the Economic Community of West African States; the Andean Community of Nations; South America's trade block, Mercosur; and the Caribbean Community, CARICOM.

rather than a new and larger nation-state; it is somewhere between a state and an intergovernmental organisation.[88] It involves the pooling of sovereignty and intensified interconnectedness in many aspects of economic and social life. Membership of international organisations constrains both internal and external state sovereignty. For instance, the supra-national European Union has direct law-making powers binding upon its member states and exclusive competence in some issues of foreign affairs. In 2015 demands made of the Greek government in return for an economic bailout were in opposition to the will of the Greek people as expressed in elections and a referendum. Although the façade of sovereignty was maintained through the adoption of the terms by the Greek parliament,[89] in this instance, sovereignty became highly contingent. The British vote to leave the European Union in a referendum in June 2016 (BREXIT) may mark a reversal of what had seemed up until then an inevitable process of increased interconnectedness and contingent sovereignty.

The EU is not the only intergovernmental organisation characterised by elements of supra-nationality. Some SC decisions, notably those with respect to sanctioned behaviours,[90] impact directly upon citizens of member states. International organisations may engage in international law-making without the direct consent of member states, thus undermining the nineteenth- and early twentieth- century voluntarist model of international law.[91] Under the World Trade Organisation compulsory dispute settlement has become accepted.[92] International bodies have exercised the full powers of a state (legislative, executive and judicial) in territories pending statehood.[93]

Associated with the emergence of an embryonic global governance (and of course a global market) is the emergence of global civil society,

[88] See Kaldor, Mary 2012. 'The EU as a New Form of Political Authority: The Example of the Common Security and Defence Policy', *Global Policy* 3(s.1): 79–86.

[89] Maltezou, Renee and Koutantou, Angeliki, 'Greek Parliament Approves Bailout Measures as Syriza Fragments', *Reuters*, 16 July 2015, www.reuters.com/article/2015/07/16/us-eurozone-greece-idUSKBN0P40EO20150716.

[90] See Chapter 3.

[91] Boyle, Alan and Chinkin, Christine 2007. *The Making of International Law*. Oxford University Press, chapter 3.

[92] As per the Dispute Settlement Understanding of the *Marrakesh Agreement Establishing the World Trade Organization*, 1994.

[93] The UN Interim Administration Mission in Kosovo (UNMIK), created pursuant to UN SC Resolution 1244, 10 June 1999; UN Transitional Administration in East Timor (UNTAET), created pursuant to UN SC Resolution 1272, 25 October 1999.

both in the Enlightenment sense of a legally constituted political authority based on legitimacy and in the contemporary sense of the growing importance of NGOs and social movements in influencing politics at a global level.[94] The English School of International Relations scholars tend to refer to world society to explain the growing role of non-state actors in upholding international norms.[95] The dramatic expansion of the internet, mobile telephony and social media underpins the proliferation of global networks at and across all levels of society. These emerging non-state political linkages are not necessarily benign or cosmopolitan. The growth of transnational fundamentalist and nationalist movements has been associated with the evolution of new wars.[96]

It is often argued that civil society in the contemporary sense needs a state; it needs to be protected by commitment to the rule of law that guarantees freedom of association and that, in turn, is influenced by and, indeed, constituted through civil associations. But it can also be argued that the emerging international framework of rules and institutions provides the conditions for civil society to function across borders so as to further strengthen that framework. What has been described as a 'partnership' between international governmental organisations and civil society serves to legitimise both;[97] the former's decisions and work may be better understood where there is effective engagement with the latter, who can benefit through working within the international machinery provided. Even though non-state actors are formally excluded from treaty-making, they have had an influence on a growing raft of treaties in such areas as weapons law (such as the Partial Test-Ban Treaty, Biological and Chemical

[94] 'Civil society groups must also be civically minded', which excludes from this discussion other non-state actors such as terrorists, criminal gangs and militia; Pfaffenholz, Thania, Kew, Darren and Wanis-St. John, Anthony, 'Civil Society and Peace Negotiations: Why, Whether and How They Could Be Involved', *Oslo Forum 06*, 67.

[95] Clarke, Ian 2007. *International Legitimacy and World Society*. Oxford University Press.

[96] See Kaldor, Mary and Muro, Diego 2003. 'Religious and Nationalist Militant Groups', in Anheier, Helmut, Glasius, Marlies and Kaldor, Mary (eds.). *Global Civil Society*. Oxford University Press, chapter 7.

[97] In August 2000, then-UN Secretary-General Kofi Annan stated: 'I believe these global policy networks, capable of bringing together Governments, civil society and the private sector, are the most promising partnerships of our globalizing age. They work for inclusion and reject hierarchy. They help set agendas and frame debates. They develop understanding and disseminate knowledge'; Secretary-General Kofi Annan's Opening Address to the Fifty-Third Annual Department of Public Information (DPI)/NGO Conference, August 2000, www.un.org/dpi/ngosection/annualconfs/53/sg-address.html.

Weapons Conventions and the Land Mines and Cluster Munitions Treaties),[98] international criminal law (the Rome Statute of the International Criminal Court) and human rights law.[99] They also play significant and influential roles in monitoring, supervision and implementation of such treaties, in participation in global summit meetings and in commencing and intervening in strategic litigation that challenges state power.

If bounded civil society was linked to the construction of modern rights-based states, then global civil society could be said to be linked to the construction of global governance. Particularly important in this respect is the human rights regime. In the 1970s and 1980s the human rights movements increasingly gave substance to the norms that underpin the growing body of international human rights law, directly contributing to the waves of democratisation that were then taking place in Latin America, Africa and Eastern Europe.[100]

Of course, critics argue that global civil society is dominated by the rich and powerful, primarily from the global North (including, for instance, Australia and Japan) and that it constitutes a false promise of democratisation and legitimisation that detracts from democracy at a national level.[101] Ken Anderson and David Rieff, for example, criticise the hubris of any notion of global politics. They argue that the idea of global civil society is a dangerous fallacy given the absence of representative institutions at a global level. They suggest that the various groups and organisations that call themselves 'global civil society' claim to represent world opinion and to substitute for the functioning of representative democracy at national levels and that this claim is profoundly anti-democratic. In particular, they suggest that global civil society becomes equated with a particular group of what might be described as cosmopolitan universalists, standard-bearers of 'environmentalism, feminism, human rights, economic regulation, sustainable development'.[102] These 'social movement missionaries' have arrogated to

[98] See Chapter 7. [99] Boyle and Chinkin, *op. cit.*, chapter 2.

[100] Keck and Sikkink, *op. cit.;* Kaldor, *op. cit.* (*Global Civil Society*).

[101] See, for example, Brown, Chris 2001. 'Cosmopolitanism, World Citizenship and Global Civil Society', *Critical Review of International Social and Political Philosophy* 3(1): 7–27; Chandler, David 2004. *Constructing Global Civil Society: Morality and Power in International Relations*. Palgrave Macmillan; Baker, Gideon and Chandler, David (eds.) 2005. *Global Civil Society: Contested Futures*. Routledge.

[102] Anderson, Kenneth and Rieff, David 2004. 'Global Civil Society: A Sceptical View', in Anheier, Helmut, Glasius, Marlies and Kaldor, Mary (eds.). *Global Civil Society 2004/5*. Sage.

themselves a supposed legitimacy that does not and cannot reflect the aspirations of individuals world-wide. Their influence on international law-making, such as the Landmines Treaty or the International Criminal Court, is also decried as that of the political lobbying of elite pressure groups that have no claim to democratic participation.[103] Others have suggested that global civil society is a way of legitimising the global market. Ronnie Lipschutz uses the Foucauldian term 'govermentality' to describe the activities of global NGOs, who ineffectively try to regulate the global market through campaigns about labour or environmental standards in the absence of state regulation.[104] They end up becoming part of the texture of globalisation, the way of thinking that allows for tacit acceptance of current global arrangements; they generate the 'mentality' of governance that underlies the exercise of power at a global level. They do not challenge the constitution of global power, only the way that power is distributed. Underlying this argument is the notion that globalisation is about the demise of state power and democracy at national levels and about the dominance of the market and the associated global inequalities.[105]

These arguments also seem to reflect a nostalgia for the primacy of the state. Yet the era of state dominance was also an era of terrible wars and totalitarianism,[106] when civil society only really functioned in small privileged parts of the world. Indeed, it could be argued that the existence

[103] Anderson, Kenneth 2000. 'The Ottawa Convention Banning Landmines, the Role of International Non-Governmental Organizations and the Idea of International Civil Society', *European Journal of International Law* 11: 91–120.

[104] Lipschutz, Ronnie D. 2005. 'Power, Politics and Global Civil Society', *Millennium: Journal of International Studies* 33(3): 747–769; see also Lipschutz, Ronnie D. and Rowe, James K. 2005. *Globalization, Governmentality, and Global Politics: Regulation for the Rest of Us?* Routledge.

[105] For a view on economic globalisation and markets from the global South see Oji, Elizabeth and Ozioko, M. V. C. 2011. 'Effect of Globalization on Sovereignty of States', *African Journals Online* 2, www.ajol.info/index.php/naujilj/article/download/82410/72564. See also Pahuja, Sundhya 2013, *Decolonising International Law: Development, Economic Growth and the Politics of Universality*. Cambridge University Press.

[106] Referring to the work of Ernst Casserer, Judge Cançado Trindade in the ICJ noted the 'twentieth century myth of the State' which was explained by 'the deleterious influence of traces of Machiavellian thinking (dismissal of, or indifference to, ethical considerations), of Hobbesian thinking (indissoluble links between the rulers and those ruled, with the subjection of the latter to the former), and of Hegelian thinking (the State as the supreme historical reality that has to preserve itself, the interests of which standing above anything, irrespective of any ethical considerations)'; *Germany v. Italy, op. cit.* (per dissenting opinion of Judge Cancado Trindade, para. 161).

of bounded civil society depended on a 'state of nature' elsewhere. Even if it were desirable, it is no longer possible to insulate civil society territorially since there are new communities and new loyalties that cross borders and new levels of authority assisted by new technologies

The underside of the emergence of global civil society is the spread of new wars. As elaborated in the previous chapter, new wars involve the spread of networks of extremist nationalist and religious groups often linked to transnational criminality. New wars tend to spread in areas where states are weak generally as a consequence of the opening up of authoritarian states to globalisation. If the emergence of global civil society represents 'inside' elements in the 'outside' – the spread of norms and politics in the international arena – then new wars could be said to constitute the 'outside' or anarchy and violence coming 'inside'. Instead of a territorial distinction between civil society (at home) and war (abroad) new wars and global civil society inhabit a shared 'globalised' space.

Summary

The erosion of the Great Divide through growing economic, cultural and social connectedness, the recognition that a wider range of actors exercise power on the international plane (individuals, international institutions, NGOs, criminal gangs, terrorists, multinational corporations), and that de-territorialised actions (for instance, in cyberspace) also affect power relations, have all led to multiple claims of the end of sovereignty, or at least its changed nature. For instance, Chayes and Chayes talk about the 'new sovereignty', the idea that:

> sovereignty no longer consists in the freedom of states to act independently in their perceived self-interest, but in membership in reasonably good standing in the regimes that make up the substance of international life. ... Sovereignty in the end is status – the vindication of a state's existence as a member of the international system.[107]

In reality this was always the case. The whole point of Westphalia is that it was a negotiated settlement: when neither of the sides in the bruising religious war (the 'Thirty Years War') could prevail, 'they sought a way out ... through a legal structure ... that would allow the co-existence of potentially antagonistic units'.[108] As we have noted, a

[107] Chayes, Abram and Chayes, Antonia Handler 1995. *The New Sovereignty: Compliance with International Regulatory Agreements.* Harvard University Press, 27.

[108] Abi-Saab, *op. cit.*, 112–113.

legal structure based upon absolutist forms of sovereignty within state borders assumes violence in protecting those borders from external threat – real or perceived – including especially from unwanted persons, as well as permitting repression at home. In the current epoch there are again arguments reminiscent of Kant for some form of global governance,[109] the constitutionalisation of the international order,[110] to recognise international law as offering multi-layered and integrated forms of governance constituting 'a common legal order for [humanity] as a whole'.[111] Such a legal order would not necessarily see the end of the Great Divide, but the difference between inside and outside would be conceived differently and serve the interests of peace and human rights; in Habermas' terms a constitutionalised international legal order would 'render[s] war as a legitimate means of resolving conflicts ... impossible, because there cannot be "external" conflicts within a globally inclusive commonwealth'.[112] Habermas argues that by uniting to form a 'large state body', sovereign states would promote their citizens to world citizens and submit themselves to a 'higher authority'. Others reject any such concept (apart from its current impracticability) by pointing to the inevitably non-democratic nature of any such a legal order,[113] or of the constituent members of such a higher authority,[114] or by arguing that sovereign equality represents a constraint on the most powerful states.[115] Yet, in the context of globalisation, it is difficult to go backwards (if indeed ideals of sovereign equality ever actually existed). As we develop throughout this book, the more likely alternative to a global legal order, where the inside of law and civil society becomes an integral part of the outside,

109 These ideas revert to those of Kant for a form of 'world federalism' or 'cosmopolitan constitution', that is 'a lawful federation under a commonly accepted international right'. See Brown, Garrett Wallace 2009. *Grounding Cosmopolitanism: From Kant to the Idea of a Cosmopolitan Constitution*. Edinburgh University Press, 91.

110 Dunoff, Jeffrey and Trachtman, Joel (eds.) 2009. *Ruling the World? Constitutionalism, International Law, and Global Governance*. Cambridge University Press.

111 Tomuschat, *op. cit.*

112 Habermas, Jürgen 2006. *The Divided West*. Cambridge: Polity Press.

113 See, for example, Delahunty, Robert J. and Yoo, John 2009. 'Kant, Habermas and Democratic Peace', *Chicago Journal of International Law* 10: 437–473.

114 For instance, the UN would be inherently unsuited to such a role given the non-democratic nature of the governing regimes of many of its member states, including two of the permanent SC members.

115 For a succinct discussion of the different views of constitutionalism and their critiques see von Bogdandy, Armin 2006. 'Constitutionalism in International Law: Comment on a Proposal from Germany', *Harvard International Law Journal* 47: 223–242.

is the nightmare spread of global anarchy within states as well as outside through persistent and spreading new wars.

This is not an argument for the end of sovereignty.[116] The state remains 'at the heart of the international legal system'.[117] However, the expansion of the numbers and powers of other actors means that the state is not the only form of authorised power, and nor should it be. The development of an embryonic system of global governance provides a check on state activities including the right to make war and to repress citizens. Civil society both depends on the extension of the system of global governance as a basis for its activities and, at the same time, helps to constitute the system, just as in the past the state and bounded civil society were mutually constitutive. It is true that, as yet, the enforcement of international standards sought by civil society is weak, although communicative action has proved important in opening up closed societies as in Eastern Europe, Latin America and the Middle East. In practice, enforcement or compliance, as discussed in the next chapter, depends both on a coercive apparatus and on the role of civil society as a site for constructing legitimacy. In the international arena, where the coercive apparatus is weak, the role of global civil society is all the more important both in underpinning regulatory procedures and in pressing for more effective forms of enforcement. Global civil society is certainly not representative and reflects power inequalities in and across societies as a whole just as is the case in domestic contexts, but its existence does give rise to a public debate at global levels (facilitated and augmented by social media) and a form of accountability based on public awareness.

In other words, the rules within which sovereignty is constituted are changing. In so far as these rules have to do with the prohibition of war and the promotion of human rights, sovereignty has been legally limited both internally and externally. As we argue in this book, different understandings of the rules are associated with different conceptions of sovereignty, which in turn are related to the different models of security set out in Chapter 1; the implications of current changes will depend on how those different understandings evolve.

[116] van Veen, Erwin 2007. 'The Valuable Tool of Sovereignty: Its Use in Situations of Competition and Interdependence', *Bruges Political Research Papers* 3.

[117] Higgins, Rosalyn 1993. *Problems and Process: International Law and How We Use It*. Oxford University Press, 39.

2.3 Right Authority and the Legitimate Use of Force

Authority is distinct from other concepts such as persuasion, coercion and power. In the words of Ramesh Thakur:

> Power is the capacity simply to enforce a particular form of behaviour. Authority signifies the capacity to create and enforce rights and obligations which are accepted as *legitimate* and binding by members of an all-inclusive society.[118]

The term *authority* is increasingly used to describe new forms of political institutions at both local and global levels, applied by scholars of international affairs and development studies.[119] However, it has a long trajectory in the major cultural traditions where 'right authority' is a crucial criterion for judging the legitimacy of the use of force. Or to put it another way, the use of force is deemed legitimate only if it is authorised by a recognised authority. The private use of force is prohibited except in individual self-defence defined in extremely constrained ways, or in culturally acceptable ways such as the chastisement of infants, or wives, or traditional responses to feuds.[120] With respect to political force, or the public use of force, all three monotheistic religions (Judaism, Christianity and Islam) traditionally drew a distinction between holy war (authorised by God or His representatives on earth) and just war (authorised by secular political authorities). Thus in Judaism a distinction is drawn between obligatory war and voluntary war. Obligatory war is the war that God ordered to kill all the Canaanites; since this is no longer applicable, the only wars are voluntary wars, which are circumscribed by rules about when they can be authorised and how they should be fought.[121] In classical Islamic thought, 'there is no theology ... of "holy war" in the sense of the

118 Thakur, Ramesh 2012. 'Law, Legitimacy and the United Nations' in Falk *et al.*, *op. cit.*, chapter 2, 47 (italics added).

119 Peters, Birgit and Schaffer, Johan Karlsson 2013. 'The Turn to Authority beyond States', *Transnational Legal Theory* 4(3): 315–35.

120 It is such variations regarding what constitutes acceptable force that is challenged by the universality of human rights. See for example the *Council of Europe Convention on Preventing and Combating Violence against Women and Domestic Violence* (The Istanbul Convention), 12 April 2011. Article 12(5) stipulates: 'Parties shall ensure that culture, custom, religion, tradition or so-called "honour" shall not be considered as justification for any acts of violence covered by the scope of this Convention'.

121 Solomon, Norman 2006. 'The Ethics of War: Judaism', in Sorabji, Richard and Rodin, David (eds.). *The Ethics of War: Shared Problems in Different Traditions.* Ashgate Publishing, 108–137.

concept as used in the Catholic faith since there was nothing along the lines of an institution of papal authority that could make determinations on the divine status of a war'.[122] A distinction is drawn between offensive wars to extend Islam (authorised by the Caliph in the Sunni tradition or by the 'hidden imam' in the Shi'ia tradition) and defensive wars authorised by political authorities. The term *jihad* refers to war fought for a legitimate cause and with legitimate means and is therefore close to just war in the Western tradition; it is a defensive war authorised by political authorities. In the Qur'an the word *jihad* is used to describe the struggle for the ultimate virtues of Islam, in the sense of testimony, as in Christian ethics; and the word used to describe military affairs is *qital*, which was governed by strict laws of war and imposes limitations on fighting. Thus, *jihad* is not necessarily a violent act; on the contrary, it is first and foremost a peaceful endeavour and struggle.[123] An International Law Association Committee Report concludes that

> Jihad, 'holy exertion', has to be in God and not just for God; in other words, it must be conducted within a divine framework and thus be in harmony with all the spiritual and ethical qualities that pertain to that framework; only on this condition will God guide the mujahideen along the appropriate paths, whether the exertion in question be conducted in the realm of outward warfare, moral and social endeavour, intellectual and scholarly effort, or, at its most profound, spiritual struggle against that greatest enemy, one's own congenital egotism.[124]

In the medieval Western (Christian) tradition, just war was distinguished from holy war in that it was authorised by secular authorities, and both the justification for war and the conduct of war were restrained by a set of rules based on canon law as well as the chivalric code. Holy war, by contrast, could be authorised by religious authorities and was waged against non-Christians. This is why the Crusades were so bloody: when the Crusaders sacked Jerusalem, some 65,000 'heathens' were killed. It was not because the wars were fought against non-Europeans; rather, the Crusaders believed themselves to be fighting a holy cause (or on holy authority), which was therefore not restrained by what was then understood as *in bello* rules. Interestingly, Angeliki Laiou describes how the Eastern Church never developed a concept of holy war; on the contrary, a

[122] International Law Association, Committee on Islamic Law and International Law, *The Hague Conference Report*, 2010, 12.

[123] Al-Fadl, *op. cit.*

[124] *Ibid.*, 15.

just war was purely defensive with the goal of peace and not the eradication of the enemy. She explains this difference in socio-economic terms. In the West, aristocrats were a fighting class who extended their wealth through violence. In the Byzantine Empire, the aristocracy were administrators for whom peace made economic sense.[125]

In most traditions, internal rebellions against a rightful authority are condemned. But whereas in the Islamic tradition restraints on war applied even more stringently because internal rebellions involved conflicts among Muslims, in the Western tradition the opposite was the case. Luther's views on the German peasants' revolt (1524–1525) have been widely quoted: 'No matter how just their complaints, a peasants' victory would mean lawlessness, disorder, bloodshed and suffering'. Thus, the rebels should be treated not as soldiers but as criminals, and Luther urged the nobility to employ their armies to 'stab, kill and strangle' the peasants as though they were rabid beasts.[126] International lawyers barely concerned themselves with civil wars before the nineteenth century.[127] It was only when such instances began to come onto the legal agenda, for instance, the American civil war, that rebels began to be accorded some of the protections of the rules of war.[128]

In the Islamic tradition, by contrast, binding regulations applied to wars between Muslims provided the rebels were considered to have a plausible reason for fighting based on a valid interpretation of the Islamic sources (*Ta'wil*). Thus, tribal reasons or greed were not plausible. The rebels also had to be sufficiently well-organised and powerful (*Shawka*):

> As the jurists put it, without the requirement of Shawka, anarchy and lawlessness will spread. . . . They contend that without the requirement of Shawka, every corrupt person will invent or fabricate a Ta'wil and claim to be a Baghii (a legitimate rebel).[129]

[125] Laiou, Angeliki 2006. 'The Just War of Eastern Christians and the Holy War of Crusaders', in Sorabji and Rodin, *op. cit.*, 30–43. A highly influential thinker was St. Basil of Caesarea, who punished soldiers who killed in war with three years' abstention from communion.

[126] Kelsay, *op. cit.*, 79. [127] Neff, *op. cit.*, 16 (*War and the Law of Nations*).

[128] General Orders No. 100 (Lieber Code), 24 April 1863, articles 149 ff.: see especially article 152: 'When humanity induces the adoption of the rules of regular war to ward rebels, whether the adoption is partial or entire, it does in no way whatever imply a partial or complete acknowledgement of their government, if they have set up one, or of them, as an independent and sovereign power. Neutrals have no right to make the adoption of the rules of war by the assailed government toward rebels the ground of their own acknowledgment of the revolted people as an independent power'.

[129] Al-Fadl *op. cit.*, 148.

Of course, in the Western tradition, there was always a republican stream of thought, of which Jean-Jacques Rousseau was the most famous exponent, which had a much more citizen-based conception of justice. In this tradition, law comes before war, and citizens have a duty to disobey and resist invasion, occupation and tyranny.[130]

In the Western transition to modernity, scholars influential in framing international law such as Vitoria (1483–1546) and Grotius (1583–1645) were responsible for the 'dethroning of religion'[131] whereby religious authority was no longer the right authority for the use of force. Vitoria recognised the power to wage war as a sovereign (non-Papal) prerogative. He made the point that a universal natural law deriving from secular sources applies to all people, including non-Christians such as the indigenous peoples whom the Spaniards came up against in their colonial enterprises.[132] Likewise, for Grotius, a just or perfect war was one fought by a sovereign authority, which also had just cause: 'Wars undertaken by public authority are attended with certain effects of right, and have the sanction of public opinion in their favour. But they are not the less criminal when made without just cause'.[133]

The significance of the Peace of Westphalia was not, as is often assumed, the birth of the modern state and the establishment of the modern conception of sovereignty. According to Ian Clarke, the earlier Peace of Augsburg in 1555 had established the basic template of state sovereignty. Rather, the significance of Westphalia had to do with the secularisation of legitimacy. The basis of legitimacy shifted 'from a predominantly moral/theological one to one rooted in conceptions of legality'.[134] This shift was, of course, linked to the growing authority of the state in relation to both religious authorities and private wars. Indeed, it was associated with the emergence of what might be described as the modern state and the establishment of a monopoly of legitimate violence.

[130] Nabulsi, Karma 2006. 'Conceptions of Justice in War: From Grotius to Modern Times', in Sorabji and Rodin, *op. cit.*, 44–60.

[131] Johnson, James Turner 1981. *Just War Tradition and the Restraint of War: A Moral and Historical Inquiry*. Princeton University Press.

[132] However, he also brought Christian principles into this secular system of international law; hence the non-Christian native peoples could not be sovereign. The use of force against them was justified by Vitoria on the grounds that international law (as formulated by the Europeans) included a right to travel to distant lands. Therefore 'any Indian attempt to resist Spanish penetration would amount to an act of war, which would justify Spanish retaliation'. Cited in Anghie, *op. cit.*, 22 ff. On Vitoria's analysis non-Christians could not – were 'inherently incapable' – of waging a just war.

[133] Grotius, *op. cit.*, 74. [134] Clarke, *op. cit.*, 49 (*Legitimacy in International Society*).

It can be argued that the current period since the end of World War II is as momentous for notions of authority as was the period prior to Westphalia.

2.3.1 Collective Security and the UN Security Council

The United Nations Charter signalled a fundamental break with classic notions of state sovereignty as it pertained to the use of force in international relations. It marked a potential shift from national to international authority, to legal and institutional regulation, as significant as the shift from religious to secular authority in the Peace of Westphalia. Under the UN Charter regime, except in the case of self-defence, armed force could only be used if authorised by the UN Security Council 'to maintain or restore international peace and security'.[135] States were still entitled to use force internally, even though this has been increasingly constrained by the emerging human rights regime and recognition by the SC that violations of human rights can constitute a threat to international peace and security.[136]

Legal steps were first undertaken to reduce war and subsequently to prohibit it after the cataclysm of World War I.[137] The Covenant of the League of Nations made any war, or threat of war, a matter of concern to all members of the League, and State parties had agreed to seek other peaceful means of resolving disputes likely to lead to rupture.[138] In 1928 States party to the Kellogg-Briand Pact condemned 'recourse to war ... and renounce[d] it, as an instrument of national policy in their relations with one another'.[139] Failure by the League to take firm action

[135] UN Charter, articles 39 and 42.

[136] Kress notes that related questions of whether a state may use force against internal violent challenge to governmental authority and whether the government can seek external assistance against such challenge are addressed primarily in terms of human rights; Kress, Claus 2014. 'Major Post-Westphalian Shifts and Some Important Neo-Westphalian Hesitations in the State Practice on the International Law on the Use of Force', *Journal on the Use of Force and International Law* 1: 11–54.

[137] However, article 1 of the *Convention (III) Relative to the Opening of Hostilities*, The Hague, 18 October 1907, requires contracting powers to 'recognize that hostilities between themselves must not commence without previous and explicit warning, in the form either of a declaration of war, giving reasons, or of an ultimatum with conditional declaration of war'.

[138] *Covenant of the League of Nations*, 28 April 1919, articles 11 and 12.

[139] *General Treaty for Renunciation of War as an Instrument of National Policy* (Pact of Paris), 27 August 1928, article 1.

against Italy in Abyssinia (Ethiopia), Japan in Manchuria and aggressive action by Nazi Germany leading to the outbreak of World War II signified the need for a stronger legal commitment against the use of force. The London Charter, the decree issued on 8 August 1945 that set down the laws and procedures by which the Nuremberg trials were to be conducted, included crimes against peace (article 6), 'namely, planning, preparation, initiation or waging of a war of aggression, or a war in violation of international treaties' within the jurisdiction of the Nuremburg Tribunal. This – not genocide – was the focus of the war crimes trials. Later in the same year the drafters of the UN Charter 'determined to save succeeding generations from the scourge of war',[140] and the primary purpose of the post-1945 legal order as set out in article 1 of the UN Charter was the maintenance of 'international peace and security'.

The UN Charter scheme for state security is upheld by three central legal pillars. First is the obligation on states to settle their disputes in such a way that international peace and security are not endangered;[141] second is the prohibition of the threat or use of force against the territorial integrity and political independence of any state[142]; and third is the collective security system whereby the SC is accorded the primary responsibility for the maintenance of international peace and security.[143] UN chapter VI on peaceful methods of dispute resolution such as mediation tends to be given less importance in assessments of the Council than Chapter VII, which deals with coercive measures.

UN Charter chapter VII provides that in response to a 'threat to the peace, breach of the peace, or act of aggression' (article 39), the SC can authorise economic[144] and military measures (articles 41 and 42) to restore 'international peace and security'. Under the Charter design, states were to make available to the Council 'armed forces, assistance, and facilities' for its own military force (article 43). Such forces have never materialised; through over sixty years of practice it is now accepted that the SC can authorise states or a regional organisation to use force in pursuit of Charter objectives,[145] or work in partnership with them. Regional arrangements are provided for in chapter VIII but are made subordinate to the Council by the requirement that any enforcement

[140] UN Charter, article 39. [141] UN Charter, article 2 (3) and chapter VI.
[142] *Ibid.*, article 2 (4). [143] *Ibid.*, article 24. [144] On sanctions see Chapter 3.
[145] For the SC's evolving interpretation of 'threat to international peace and security' see Chapter 5.

action they undertake must be with its authorisation, although in practice such action has also received subsequent endorsement.[146]

Under the Charter vision of collective security there was in effect a return to the just war concepts of 'just authority' and of 'just cause' secured through military means.[147] In the words of the International Commission on Intervention and State Sovereignty (ICISS) 'The authority of the UN is underpinned not by coercive power, but by its role as the applicator of legitimacy'.[148] Security Council–authorised action is – as with just war – a form of law enforcement, but is not triggered by a violation of international law, but by the threat or actuality of a dangerous political situation. In this sense it is reminiscent of the powers asserted by the Great Powers under the Concert of Europe.[149] But unlike that system, other states (including non-member states) are required to comply with the SC's decisions,[150] amounting to 'an express prohibition against neutrality in UN enforcement actions'.[151] Nor is Council-authorised enforcement action required to be defensive. In this respect, international law enforcement presupposes military force in contrast to domestic law enforcement that is based on policing. Thus it reinforces the reliance of states on military structures for security.

As is well recognised – and demonstrated by the many instances of armed conflict that have erupted since 1945 – this legal framework has not been entirely successful in its purpose of 'sav[ing] succeeding generations from the scourge of war'. One reason for this reality is the Council's geo-political composition, which is reminiscent of the Great Power 'legalised hegemony' of the Concert of Europe.[152] The permanent members (the United States, the Soviet Union – now Russia – China, France and the United Kingdom) dominate decision-making and are able to exercise their veto power on non-procedural matters,[153] and, especially during the Cold War, this has stymied coordinated international

[146] See Chapter 5 (actions by ECOWAS in Liberia and Sierra Leone).

[147] Heathcote, *op. cit.*, 35.

[148] Report of the International Commission on Intervention and State Sovereignty 2001. *The Responsibility to Protect*. International Development Research Centre (ICISS Report), para. 6.9.

[149] Neff, *op. cit.*, 323–324 (*War and the Law of Nations*).

[150] UN Charter, article 2 (6) (non-members); article 25 (members).

[151] Neff, *op. cit.*, 325 (*War and the Law of Nations*).

[152] Simpson, *op. cit.*, 68: 'the existence within an international society of a powerful elite of states whose superior status is recognised by minor powers as a political fact giving rise to the existence of certain constitutional privileges'.

[153] UN Charter, article 27 (3).

action.[154] Even after the relaxing of Cold War tensions, the use or threat of the veto impedes principled decision-making. A second reason is that the SC lacks an independent capacity to act and is dependent on the readiness of key states to contribute resources to actions that it has authorised. In numerous cases the willingness to ensure adequate resources to allow effective and efficient performance of the Council's mandate has been lacking. A third and perhaps most important reason is that threats to international peace and security were envisaged in a classic state-centric framework, as an attack (or apprehended attack) by one state against another state. Contemporary forms of violence rarely fit this framework and nor is the type of enforcement envisaged in the Charter appropriate in these new settings. General economic sanctions and the use of classic war-fighting military force are forms of collective enforcement that affect innocent victims caught up in violent situations. Indeed, as will be discussed in subsequent chapters, this type of enforcement often exacerbates civilian insecurity and may contribute to the escalation of violence.

2.3.2 The Legitimacy of the Security Council

The end of the Cold War ushered in high hopes for the future of Council-authorised collective action. Indeed, the 1991 Gulf War appeared to conform to classic conceptions of threats to international peace and security, representing a collective response to an invasion by one sovereign state (Iraq) against another (Kuwait).[155] But as it turned out, the experience of the conflicts in the Balkans and in Africa was to be much more typical of the kinds of political violence to which the 'international community' was asked to respond.[156] Four significant developments in the SC's role took place in the following two decades. First, the Council began to authorise military intervention in response to a much wider range of issues. As discussed in Chapter 5, it interpreted threats to international peace and security broadly to encompass *inter alia*

[154] For an overview of enforcement action prior to the end of the Cold War see Wills, Siobhán 2009. *Protecting Civilians: The Obligations of Peacekeepers*. Oxford University Press, 6–19.

[155] UN SC Resolution 678, 29 November 1990 (Iraq-Kuwait), para. 2 authorised 'Member States cooperating with the Government of Kuwait' to use 'all necessary means' to end Iraq's occupation of Kuwait.

[156] Kaldor, Mary 2012. *New and Old Wars: Organized Violence in a Global Era*. Polity Press, 3rd ed.

humanitarian suffering and a military coup against a democratically elected government, essentially authorising the use of force without state consent in what international law terms a non-international conflict – that is to say, internal affairs.[157] The adoption of the concept of a 'Responsibility to Protect' by the General Assembly in 2005[158] provided the basis for the SC's authorisation of intervention in Libya in 2011, explicitly based on the concept and without the Libyan government's consent.[159] Secondly, the Council introduced a number of innovations in the mechanisms for dealing with political violence, often under pressure from campaigning groups, which focussed on both individual protection and individual responsibility. Protective devices included the idea of humanitarian corridors, no-fly zones and safe havens; individual responsibility was addressed through targeted or smart sanctions,[160] as well as through the establishment of the *ad hoc* international criminal tribunals for the former Yugoslavia and Rwanda, a hybrid tribunal in Sierra Leone and other domestic criminal law institutions *inter alia* in Timor Leste and Cambodia. The Council has thus engaged the language of accountability, justice and the rule of law,[161] not directly provided for in the Charter with respect to its functions.[162] And thirdly, the SC became much more visible politically, made possible by twenty-four-hour news availability and social media coverage. This was especially true in the run-up to the 2003 Iraq war, when the Council refused to authorise an American intervention and when US Secretary of State Colin Powell's presentation to it of the case for war was broadcast across the world.

The fourth development has been the adoption of what have been termed 'legislative measures', resolutions imposing legally binding

157 See Chapter 5.

158 UN GA Resolution 60/1, 24 October 2005 ('World Summit Outcome Document'); UN SC Resolution 2150, 16 April 2014 reaffirms paras. 138 and 139 of the World Summit Outcome Document.

159 UN SC Resolution 1973, 17 March 2011.

160 A significant step in this regard was the adoption of UN SC Resolution 1267, 15 October 1999, imposing sanctions targeted at the Taliban and Osama bin Laden and those associated with him.

161 See Chapter 10.

162 In a 2014 statement, the Council President stated: 'The Security Council reaffirms . . . its continued recognition of the need for universal adherence to and implementation of the rule of law, as well as emphasis on the vital importance it attaches to promoting justice and the rule of law as an indispensable element for peaceful coexistence and the prevention of armed conflict'; Statement by the President of the Security Council 2014/5, 21 February 2014.

obligations upon individuals and states.[163] The former involve such sanctioning measures as freezing of assets and travel bans; the latter requires states to adopt legislation to prevent the financing of terrorist activities[164] and to adopt and enforce measures against the proliferation of weapons of mass destruction to non-state actors.[165] These resolutions both replicate treaty provisions, thus making them binding upon states that have chosen not to become parties to the relevant treaty, and filling gaps in the treaties.[166] However, there have been positive consequences in that more states have become parties to the Financing of Terrorism Convention.[167]

States are required to report to and are subject to scrutiny by a range of Council committees, including sanctions committees and the counter-terrorism committee. The largely unreviewable SC intrusion into areas traditionally regarded as within a state's domestic jurisdiction has been a major factor in the blurring of the line between international and domestic law. This has lessened individuals' protections against arbitrary actions (e.g., being listed by the Council as a terrorist suspect or Al Qaeda associate) and has raised tensions between a US-dominated international legal order and the European legal order,[168] between the SC and regional human rights bodies[169]

163 Legislation 'signifies the enactment of prospective, general and abstract rules of conduct that bind all the subjects in the unlimited future, whenever the contingencies they provide for obtain'. Abi-Saab, *op. cit.*, 117.

164 Commencing with UN SC Resolution 1373, 28 September 2001, which was adopted in the wake of the terrorist attacks of 11 September 2001.

165 Commencing with UN SC Resolution 1540, 28 April 2004.

166 This expansion of SC power was immediately remarked upon; see, for example, Szasz, Paul 2002. 'The Security Council Starts Legislating', *American Journal of International Law* 96: 900–905; Alvarez, Jose 2003. 'Hegemonic International Law Revisited', *American Journal of International Law* 97: 873–888; Talmon, Stefan 2005. 'The Security Council as World Legislature', *American Journal of International Law* 99: 175–193.

167 *International Convention for the Suppression of the Financing of Terrorism*, UN GA Resolution 54/109, 9 December 1999.

168 Most notably through the Kadi case; *Yassin Abdullah Kadi and Al Barakaat International Foundation v. Council of the European Union and Commission of the European Communities*, Case C-402/05 P and C-415/05, [2008] ECR I-06351. See De Búrca, Grainne 2010. 'The European Court of Justice and the International Legal Order after Kadi', *Harvard International Law Journal* 51, 1; Kokott, Juliane and Sobotta, Christoph 2012. 'The Kadi Case – Constitutional Core Values and International Law – Finding the Balance?' *European Journal of International Law* 23: 1015–1024.

169 *Nada v. Switzerland*, ECtHR GC, application no. 10593/08, judgment of 12 September 2012; *Al-Dulimi and Montana Management Inc. v. Switzerland*, ECtHR application no. 5809/08, judgment of 21 June 2016.

and between states of nationality or residence of targeted individuals and third states that have suffered financial disadvantage through the enforcement of sanctions on other states. In response the Council has progressively introduced some process safeguards such as through the establishment of an ombudsperson[170] to whom listed persons can submit a request to be delisted. The ombudsperson can make a recommendation to the sanctions committee. However, recommendations are not necessarily acted upon, and the ombudsperson does not have jurisdiction over all sanctions regimes. The adequacy of this process with respect to human rights norms has been criticised by, for instance, the UN Human Rights Council special rapporteur on counter-terrorism, who concluded that 'the mandate of the Ombudsperson still does not meet the structural due process requirement of objective independence from the [Sanctions] Committee'.[171] His proposal that the position be renamed the Office of the Independent Designations Adjudicator to entrench the independence of its position from the Council has not been implemented.

These developments have enhanced the SC's role and visibility, but they have also weakened its legitimacy. In the words of Jean Cohen, they 'are Janus-faced: while in some instances they prevent or help rectify humanitarian disasters and protect human rights, in others they lead to the evisceration of the rule of law and constitutionalism on all levels of the international political system, and undermine the foundational Charter principles of sovereign equality and human rights'.[172] Many commentators have noted that the SC's authority suffers from a perception of profound lack of legitimacy,[173] and that this loss of legitimacy has acquired prominence precisely at a time when the Council has

[170] UN SC Resolution 1730, 19 December 2006, states the UN SC's commitment 'to ensuring that fair and clear procedures exist for placing individuals and entities on sanctions lists and for removing them, as well as for granting humanitarian exemptions'; UN SC Resolution 1904, 17 December 2009 creates the ombudsperson. The detailed mandate of the ombudsperson is set out in Annex II of the resolution; see also UN SC Resolution 1989, 17 June 2011; UN SC Resolution 2083, 17 December 2012; UN SC Resolution 2161, 17 June 2014.

[171] 'Promotion and Protection of Human Rights and Fundamental Freedoms While Countering Terrorism', Report to the UN GA 67/396, 26 September 2012.

[172] Cohen, *op. cit.*

[173] See generally de Wet, Erika 2004. *The Chapter VII Powers of the United Nations Security Council*. Hart Publishing; Wheatley, Steven 2006. 'The Security Council, Democratic Legitimacy and Regime Change in Iraq', *European Journal of International Law* 17(3): 531–551.

emphasised accountability and the rule of law for others.[174] Thakur, for instance, identifies a quadruple legitimacy deficit – performance, representational, procedural and accountability. In performance terms, as will be discussed in subsequent chapters, the SC has either failed to act in a timely fashion as in the case of the 1994 Rwandan genocide or in Darfur in western Sudan, or else the mandated means have not been appropriate for the protection of civilians as, we will argue, was the case in Bosnia and Libya. Moreover, the Council is charged with double standards, for example, for authorising intervention in Libya but not in other humanitarian tragedies such as Chechnya or Syria, or failing to sanction Israel for breaches of international law such as those arising from its construction of the wall in the Occupied Palestinian Territory, as advised by the ICJ,[175] while imposing sanctions on other states. A related critique is the inconsistency of its members or of the SC acting as a whole. For instance, in the context of nuclear non-proliferation it is argued that the Council's nuclear weapon states (in practice the P5) disregard their obligations under article VI of the 1968 Nuclear Non-Proliferation Treaty (NPT), as endorsed by the ICJ,[176] while castigating and sanctioning other nuclear weapon states, non-parties to the NPT, for testing nuclear weapons.[177] Since North Korea is not a party to the 1996 Comprehensive Nuclear Test Ban Treaty (which in any case is not in force) and withdrew from the NPT in January 2003,[178] it is not breaking any treaty obligation in testing, although it is in violation of resolutions adopted by the SC. The Council states that such testing constitutes a challenge to the NPT and has demanded that North Korea return to the treaty regime. It has not similarly sanctioned the nuclear programmes of other states, for instance, Israel, Pakistan and India, raising the accusation of

174 Caron identifies five challenges to the legitimacy of SC grouped under the headings of 'perception of dominance of the Security Council by a few states' and 'perception of unfairness surrounding the veto'; Caron, David 1993. 'The Legitimacy of the Collective Authority of the Security Council', *American Journal of International Law* 87: 552–588.

175 *Legal Consequences of the Construction of a Wall in the Occupied Palestinian Territory*, 2004 ICJ Reports 136, advisory opinion of 9 July 2004.

176 *Legality of the Threat or Use of Nuclear Weapons*, 1996 ICJ Reports 226, advisory opinion of 8 July 1996, paras. 102–103.

177 UN SC Resolution 2094, 7 March 2013.

178 *Treaty on the Non-Proliferation of Nuclear Weapons* ('NPT'), 1 July 1968, article X provides for withdrawal in the exercise of national sovereignty, 'if a state decides that extraordinary events, related to the subject matter of this Treaty, have jeopardized the supreme interests of its country'.

selectivity.[179] The SC procedures lack transparency, with the major decision-making taking place outside the formal sessions, in which pre-agreed positions are reiterated. Such positions are largely those agreed by the permanent members, with non-permanent members complaining of exclusion. The vast majority of resolutions are also sponsored by permanent members; the corollary of this is that it is the permanent members who carry the burden of membership and perform the bulk of the work. The SC is not open to civil society, except through the Arria formula,[180] and other persons (for instance, the special representatives of the Secretary-General, special rapporteurs of the Human Rights Council) attend by invitation. The SC is not formally accountable to the General Assembly and thus is accountable politically only to the member states. Although the ICTY appellate chamber has asserted that the Council must act within the purposes and principles of the Charter,[181] the ICJ has rejected any such power of review.[182] The Council remains essentially not subject to review by any institutional body. Other tribunals have generally sought to avoid confrontation by failing to find any conflict between states' obligations under SC resolutions and other obligations under international law, such as human rights obligations necessitating such review.[183] However, this compromise position is becoming tenuous.[184] Eyal Benvenisti argues strongly that the substance and processes of decision-making by the Council (along with other international institutions) should be subject to legal constraints in the same ways as domestic decision-makers in accordance with the rule of law.[185] In his terms, sovereigns are the

[179] UN SC Resolution 1172, 6 June 1998 condemns tests by India and Pakistan and 'urges' them to become parties to the NPT.

[180] Arria-formula meetings were initiated in 1992. They allow SC members to have an informal exchange of views with people whom they consider it would be beneficial to hear. Meetings are informal and confidential. See UN Secretariat 2002. 'Background Note on the "Arria-Formula" Meetings of the Security Council Members', *UN SC Working Methods Handbook*, www.un.org/en/sc/about/methods/bgarriaformula.shtml.

[181] *Prosecutor v. Dusko Tadic*, ICTY IT-94-AR72, 2 October 1995, para. 28.

[182] *Case Concerning Questions of Interpretation and Application of the 1971 Montreal Convention Arising from the Aerial Incident at Lockerbie* (*Libyan Arab Jamahiriya v. United Kingdom*) (Preliminary Objections), 1998 ICJ Reports 9, judgment of 27 February 1998.

[183] *Al-Jedda v. the United Kingdom*, ECtHR GC application no. 27021/08, judgment of 7 July 2011; Kadi case, *op. cit.*

[184] *Al- Dullimi and Montana Management Inc. v. Switzerland*. ECtHR GC, application no. 5809/08, judgment of 21 June 2016.

[185] Benvenisti, Eyal 2014.*The Law of Global Governance*. Brill, Nijhof.

'trustees of humanity'[186] and must be accountable for their exercise of power. Erica de Wet has added a further dimension to non-reviewability of SC decisions, what she terms their lack of contestability, whereby decisions of the Council can be terminated only by the Council.[187] She acknowledges that if this were not the case, member states would be able to make their own determinations as to when the aim of SC decisions had been achieved, opening the way for further uncertainty and differing conclusions depending on states' interests. Nevertheless, this means that in practice 'an open-ended Security Council decision remains incontestable, as long as it has the support of one permanent member'.[188] This has particular applicability to economic sanctions, for instance, those applied against Iraq in 1990[189] in response to the invasion of Kuwait. By 2000 it was evident that even the application of the humanitarian exception to the sanctions regime was not safeguarding the lives and health of Iraqi people, in particular children.[190] Yet affected individuals, or their representatives, could not challenge the sanctions regime.

The Council's geo-political composition, the lack of any accountability to local populations or to global public opinion, and the intrusive and non-transparent legislative measures adopted in the wake of 9/11 have greatly weakened the UN in the eyes of many. The ICISS (the body that proposed the Responsibility to Protect) recognised this reality and linked it to both the need for reformed membership and a code of restraint in the exercise of the veto in situations of humanitarian crisis.[191] Similar issues were raised in the context of the UN reform process embarked upon by then Secretary-General Kofi Annan in the early years of the millennium. Despite suggestions for reform, the proposals for strengthening the UN in the 2005 Outcome Document supported only 'early reform of the Security Council . . . in order to make it more broadly representative, efficient and transparent and thus to further enhance its effectiveness and the legitimacy and implementation of its decisions'.[192]

[186] Benvenisti, Eyal 2013. 'Sovereignty as Trusteeship for Humanity — Historical Antecedents and Their Impact on International Law', *American Journal of International Law* 107: 295–333.

[187] de Wet, *op. cit.*, 140. de Wet also considers the legitimacy defects of lack of transparency, participation and efficiency.

[188] *Ibid.*, 141. [189] UN SC Resolution 661, 6 August 1990.

[190] Gordon, Joy 2010. *Invisible War: The United States and the Iraq Sanctions.* Harvard University Press.

[191] ICISS report, *op. cit.*, paras. 6.19–6.21.

[192] World Summit Outcome Document, *op. cit.*, paras. 152, 153.

A decade later the process for reform is ongoing in the UN GA Intergovernmental Negotiations on Security Council Reform, which involves extensive government submissions and discussions through an 'inclusive and transparent' process.[193]

Thus, since the middle of the last century, a profoundly important shift has taken place in the authority to use force. States no longer have the unilateral right to authorise the use of the force despite certain exceptions to be discussed in subsequent chapters: 'Right authority' has shifted from the state to the SC. But the Council is itself composed of states, and a privileged position is reserved for those powers that were considered the Great Powers in the aftermath of World War II. Moreover, it lacks accountability either to citizens or to legal processes. The paradox is that the shift to international authority for the use of force is hugely weakened by its lack of legitimacy.

2.4 Alternative Conceptions of World Order and the Transformation of Sovereignty

The term 'globalisation' is hotly contested. But what scholars who study globalisation share is a preoccupation with what this phenomenon means for the future of the state and the concept of sovereignty. Those who equate globalisation with the spread of a global market tend to assume that states are losing their autonomy and becoming less powerful; sovereignty in the sense of supreme power has been undermined.[194] Some enthusiasts welcome this trend, while others seek its reversal. Those who understand globalisation as increased interconnectedness in all fields (for e.g., political, cultural, social, economic, civil) or as a fundamental change in global consciousness (our awareness of a single human community) suggest that a transformation is underway in which states increasingly become one node in a global framework of governance, though there are, of course, differences about the significance of the node.[195] For example,

[193] Letter from the President of the General Assembly, *Intergovernmental Negotiations on the Question of Equitable Representation on and Increase in the Membership of the Security Council and Related Matters*, 15 July 2015, www.centerforunreform.org/sites/default/files/PGA%20Letter%20to%20MS%20IGN%20%2B.pdf.

[194] Ohmae, Kenichi 1990. *The Borderless World: Power and Strategy in the Interlinked Economy*. Collins; or Friedman, Thomas 2000. *The Lexus and the Olive Tree*. Harper Collins; Hirst, Paul, Thompson, Grahame and Bromley, Simon 1999. *Globalization in Question: The International Economy and the Possibilities of Governance*. Polity Press.

Anne-Marie Slaughter suggests that states are becoming disaggregated, whereby parts of governments are increasingly tied into networks that perform many of the governance functions formerly performed by states. In the case of the judiciary, for example, she suggests that a combination of constitutional cross-fertilisation, the increasing relevance of international law for national courts, the growing importance of human rights law, and increased transnational litigation are all components of an emerging judicial network. Other transnational institutions that reduce the monopoly of power of states include banks, multinational corporations, the internet and sporting bodies such as the International Olympic Committee or FIFA. Globalisation, Slaughter suggests, involves three shifts: from national to global, from government to governance and from unitary to disaggregated states.[196]

Our argument is that the changing character of sovereignty is closely bound up with the authority to use force. States remain the legal repositories of sovereignty; they are independent legal persons under international law, and they are the primary players in the making of international law, including the responsibility to negotiate international treaties and participate in institutional decision-making. Despite some albeit limited, legal recognition of the rights and duties of other actors such as international governmental organisations, multinational corporations and NGOs, militias, paramilitary groups and individuals, the supremacy of states in the international legal system has still not been seriously challenged. The state is still formally perceived as a unitary entity, and there remains a single model of statehood, but with some *de facto* limitations of sovereignty for 'failed' or 'rogue' states. This has had a number of consequences in contemporary international governance: for example, in shaping the international regulatory framework, limiting participation in international fora, excluding non-state actors from its ambit and constraining doctrinal and institutional change. Although the actions of non-state actors impact upon decision-making with respect to the use of force – both against them as in the War on Terror and ostensibly at least in their protection as in the Responsibility to Protect and Human Security – the law relating to the use of force remains

[195] Held, David, McGrew, Anthony, Goldblatt, David and Perraton, Jonathan 1999. *Global Transformations: Politics, Economics and Culture*. Polity Press; Shaw, Martin 2000. *Theory of the Global State: Globality as an Unfinished Revolution*. Cambridge University Press; Scholte, Jan Art 2000. *Globalization: A Critical Introduction*. Palgrave Macmillan.

[196] Slaughter, Anne-Marie 2004. *A New World Order*. Princeton University Press.

centred around states.[197] The primacy of state sovereignty as embodied in the requirement of consent weakens the international legal system, for instance, through the absence of compulsory jurisdiction before the ICJ and the scarcity of other adequate enforcement mechanisms.

But the absolutist character of sovereignty is increasingly constrained in the context of globalisation and through the multiple roles played by non-state actors. We argue that states are adapting to these changes in different ways and that a key determinant is how the authority to use force – and against whom – is interpreted. In what follows, we outline how the different models of security described in the previous chapter are associated with different conceptions of sovereignty and thus of world order.

The *Geo-Political* Model

The first model is a traditional idea of state sovereignty associated with what Robert Cooper calls the 'modern' state.[198] These are states which retain the monopoly of force both domestically and internationally and possess a capacity to use force unilaterally in an international context in pursuance of what they perceive as their national interest. These states may act unilaterally in self-defence, or through organisations such as the United Nations, NATO, the Organization of American States or the Commonwealth of Independent States,[199] but still insist that they operate within the framework of international law. Whereas in the past such states would have assumed that the use of force to further national interest was legitimate, since World War ll, interventions that are undertaken tend to be couched in legalistic language. They strongly defend the norm of non-intervention, as least as concerns other states, and envisage a world order peopled by states with Great Powers acting as guarantors. Russia, China and India are perhaps the classic exponents of the Geo-Political conception, upholding the concept of territorial integrity and the right to use force internally and, in some cases, externally according to what is considered to be in their national interest – Georgia, Ukraine, Syria, for example, in the case of Russia[200] and the land and maritime claims in the South China Sea in the case of China. This could be

[197] For analysis of the extent to which rules relating to the use of force have shifted from the Westphalian system; see Kress, *op. cit.*

[198] Cooper, Robert 1996. *The Post-Modern State and the World Order*. Demos.

[199] Regional arrangements are provided for in the UN Charter, chapter VIII.

[200] Or outside the neighbourhood, as in the case of Russian intervention in Syria in 2015.

described as a classic realist conception of international order, even though it formally accepts an international law framework.[201] Sovereignty remains situated in the classic distinction between 'inside' and outside' even though the 'outside' is somewhat constrained by international law as it developed after World War II.

The *War on Terror* Model

Although the United States, supported by realist scholars such as Morganthau,[202] has for a long time articulated the Geo-Political model, for example, in the Monroe Doctrine, there has always been a strand of thinking linked to ideas of American exceptionalism. Thus both World War ll and the Cold War were framed not as Geo-Political conflict but as struggles for human rights and democracy. The neo-conservative thinkers who came to the fore in the aftermath of 9/11 espoused the idea that force could be used against the acts of non-state actors (as well as those of states) for democratic transformation, and this, in their conception, is legitimate. Thus the model underlying the War on Terror is one in which American state sovereignty can be combined with intervention in other states, proxy wars, the construction of military bases overseas and the current drone campaign. The American model does not reject international law or argue that morality trumps law; rather it justifies this model, as will be discussed in subsequent chapters, in terms of a legal framework, which involves a stretching of the concept of self-defence and a strange reinterpretation of parts of international humanitarian law. This model involves a conception of world order based on uni-polar hegemony that operates within a framework of rules laid down and/or interpreted by the global hegemon. According to Habermas, the revolutionary claim of the neo-conservatives is that if 'the regime of international law fails, then the hegemonic imposition of a global liberal order is justified even by means that are hostile to international law'.[203]

The language of exceptionalism fits the Schmittian idea that sovereignty is the monopoly to decide on the exception; hence rules can be overridden or interpreted selectively and flexibly in exceptional times, such as those associated with the global threat presented by terrorists.

201 Kingsbury, Benedict 1997. 'A Grotian Tradition of Theory and Practice? Grotius, Law, and Moral Skepticism in the Thought of Hedley Bull', *Quinnipac Law Review* 17: 3–34.

202 Morganthau, Hans 1965. *Politics among Nations: The Struggle for Power and Peace*. McGraw-Hill, 6th ed.

203 Habermas *op. cit.*, 45, fn 25.

While most associated with US policy, other states too claim the justifications of the War on Terror when it is expedient for them to do so.

The *Liberal Peace* Model

This model is multilateralist but state centric, placing the emphasis on the norm of non-intervention. Peace is understood as peace between states, or quasi- states as in the case of conflicting groups – that is to say, the warring parties in a conflict are treated as legitimate actors using force for political purposes as though they were states at least in waiting. It is a collective concept that trumps human rights and/or justice. This model is associated with peacemaking through peace agreements, peacebuilding and peacekeeping. It is favoured by what Robert Cooper calls 'post-modern' states[204] or what Ian Clarke calls globalising states.[205] These are states that maintain their monopoly of force domestically but do not have the capacity or the will to use force externally, except in the context of multilateral missions. These states are usually linked to regional or international institutions – the European Union, the African Union, the Organization of American States, as well as the United Nations and a range of other organisations. These are states with an interest in global security because they cannot guarantee national security unilaterally. They understand that their role is increasingly as members of an international system where they can influence the rules but cannot act as they please. This model draws implicitly on the pluralist strand of English School thinking of International Relations, assuming a denser framework of rules than the Geo-Political model. In this model, state sovereignty remains the pivot of the international system, in conjunction with global governance institutions, but that sovereignty is exercised in a framework that precludes the international use of force except when authorised by the SC.

The *Responsibility to Protect* Model

The Responsibility to Protect model emphasises the obligations of sovereignty, the shift 'from *sovereignty as control* to *sovereignty as responsibility* in both internal functions and external duties'.[206] The state's primary responsibility is to ensure the security of its citizens. If it fails

[204] Cooper, *op. cit.*
[205] *Ibid.*; Clarke, *op. cit.* (*Globalisation and International Relations Theory*).
[206] ICISS Report, *op. cit.*, para. 2. 14.

to do so, that sovereignty becomes contingent, and, in extreme instances, the responsibility shifts to the international community. It is accordingly also multilateralist but less state-centric than the Liberal Peace because the norm of non-intervention can be overridden by SC authorisation in cases where states fail to protect their populations, notably against cases of genocide, ethnic cleansing and massive violations of human rights (crimes against humanity). In this model the Council's role is more significant than in the Liberal Peace model. Indeed, Orford suggests that the Responsibility to Protect model is the way that the UN acquires executive power.[207] Thus it is a model of multi-polar hegemony based on a framework of international law that echoes notions of just war. Responsibility to Protect might be said to correspond to the solidarist strand of English school thinking, and, indeed, it is a concept that is embraced by scholars who define themselves in these terms.

The *Human Security* Model

Human Security is the Kantian cosmopolitan model where peace is combined with human rights. It is also multilateralist and has considerable overlaps with both the Liberal Peace and the Responsibility to Protect models, but in the Human Security model multilateral institutions are much more accountable to global civil society than in the Liberal Peace model. In contrast to the Liberal Peace, state sovereignty is conditional on human rights, but, in contrast to the Responsibility to Protect, law enforcement is based on human rights rather than just war assumptions.

These different conceptions are summarised in Table 2.1.

All these models except for Human Security assume that war is a legitimate phenomenon and that states are the only actors that can decide either unilaterally or collectively when military force can be used. They differ as to the rules about how and when classic military force is used apply in the international arena. As expounded in the previous chapter, there is a distinction between the use of force in the international arena, which involves war, the use of military force against a collective enemy and the use of force domestically, which is considered policing against individual criminals (in the case of a rights-based society) or against individual dissidents (in the case of repressive societies). Parallel to this distinction is another between the external instrument of peace and

[207] Orford, Anne 2011. *International Authority and the Responsibility to Protect*. Cambridge University Press.

Table 2.1 *Security Models and World Order*

	Authority to Use Force	Rules governing the Use of Force	World Order	Underlying Philosophical Assumption
Geo-Politics	Unilateralist in case of self-defence	*Jus ad bellum* self-defence; collective enforcement action if SC vote secured	Multi-polar (Great Powers)	Classical Realism
War on Terror	Unilateralist (although support through 'coalitions of the willing')	'Just War' externally but intervention in other internal situations	Uni-polar hegemony	Schmittian exceptionalism
Liberal Peace	Multilateralist	Treats 'new wars' as 'old wars'	Multi-polar and multilateralist	Pluralist realism
Responsibility to Protect	Multilateralist	Just War and Human Rights	Multi-polar hegemony	Solidarist Realism
Human Security	Multilateralist	Human Rights	Global Governance	Cosmopolitanism

diplomacy (between collective entities-states) and politics and justice (within states). Only the Geo-Political model sustains these distinctions. The War on Terror, Liberal Peace and Responsibility to Protect models all bring the 'outside inside' in different ways. The War on Terror uses the instrument of war for policing purposes – the 'inside' of other states, whether to impose democracy or to kill terrorists. The Liberal Peace model uses the external instrument of diplomacy and peacemaking in new war contexts that are both inside and outside. Responsibility to Protect also uses the instrument of war for internal purposes, specifically human rights violations. Only the Human Security model brings the 'inside' 'outside', as will be developed in Chapter 11, using methods more akin to policing for dealing with violations of human rights, including armed attacks. In the remainder of this book, we will make the argument that the use of classic 'outside' instruments in response to new wars tends to intensify their violence and duration; this is the basis for the practical case for a Human Security approach.

2.5 Conclusion

In this chapter, we have argued that we are living through a period of fundamental change in the nature of state sovereignty that is exemplified in the changing relationship of the state to the use of force in both procedural and substantive terms. Sovereignty, as we explain, was an expression of the 'Great Divide' between the inside and the outside. The use of force internally was constrained by law and constitutionalism (even if this was instrumentalised for tyrannical purposes) and externally by just war criteria expressed in diverse cultures and emerging international law. In procedural terms, there are profound contradictions between notions of sovereign equality and human rights, between the prohibition of war and the various exceptions, and between the shift of formal authority from the national to the international and the geopolitical composition of the Security Council. In substantive terms, there are contradictions between the growing interconnectedness and disaggregation of states associated with the emergence of global governance, global civil society and globalising states, on the one hand, and, on the other, new forms of political violence associated with the use of force by powerful states acting unilaterally or through coalitions, the spread of physical insecurity in weak or failing states, the increasing attacks by networks of extremist non-state actors, and the legitimacy deficit of the United Nations, especially of the SC. The populist attempt to reclaim closed concepts of national sovereignty, as proposed by Donald Trump or the proponents of BREXIT in the United Kingdom, cannot reverse the process of globalisation; rather they are likely to bring the outside of war and anarchy inside.

Such contradictions do offer openings for agency. But how that agency is exercised is different for different actors. With the prohibition on war contained in the UN Charter, the Great Divide has been eroded, and law and constitutionalism have become increasingly important outside and as the inside is increasingly integrated both practically and legally in the wider international framework. While the Geo-Political model adheres to a classic concept of sovereignty, each of the other models involves a blurring of inside and outside though in different directions that are expressed in different understandings of international law. These will be spelled out throughout the remainder of this book.

The next chapter elaborates what is understood by international law, and later chapters investigate the different directions in which international law is changing according to the different models we have outlined. In other words, we are in the midst of a far-reaching debate about the direction of international law and the shape of world order. This book explores the different strands of that debate as it relates to war and violence.

3

The Relevance of International Law

3.1 Introduction

The basis for the binding nature of international law[1] has long occupied international lawyers,[2] while scholars of international relations and political science have become concerned with the impact of international law upon state behaviour, in particular whether states comply with its norms, even against their interests. These questions have mirrored shifting understandings of security, as discussed through the models in Chapters 1 and 2. During the Cold War, prevailing realist views perceived the state as a unitary and monolithic entity. These proponents of the Geo-Political model rejected the relevance of international law, arguing that states were single-minded in pursuing their interests; security was understood largely in terms of national security supported by military power and, in particular, the concept of deterrence. Deterrence was maintained through the possession of nuclear weapons by the five permanent members of the UN Security Council (SC) and defensive alliances whereby non-nuclear states were perceived to shelter under the nuclear umbrella of the nuclear weapon states.[3]

[1] International law comprises treaties, customary international law and general principles of law; *Statute of the International Court of Justice*, 26 June 1945, article 38 (1). There is also a significant body of what is often referred to as 'soft law', e.g., non-binding UN General Assembly and Human Rights Council resolutions, codes of conduct and guidelines.

[2] The two rival doctrines for the basis of states' legal obligations derive from the 'natural rights' of states and state consent ('voluntarism'); see, for example, Clapham, Andrew 2012. *Brierly's Law of Nations*. Oxford University Press, 7th ed., 47. See also Lauterpacht, Hersch and Waldock, C. H. M. (eds.) 1958. *The Basis of Obligation in International Law and Other Papers by the Late James Leslie Brierly*. Oxford University Press.

[3] In the words of the 1996 ICJ: 'In order to be effective, the policy of deterrence, by which those States possessing or under the umbrella of nuclear weapons seek to discourage military aggression by demonstrating that it will serve no purpose, necessitates that the intention to use nuclear weapons be credible'. *Legality of the Threat or Use of ('Nuclear Weapons')*, ICJ Reports 226, advisory opinion of 8 July 1996, para. 48.

Following the termination of the Cold War, the 'new world order' saw a plethora of writing on compliance and a growing mutual interest between the disciplines of international law and international relations.[4] But just as international relations theorists were increasingly taking note of international law and seeking empirical evidence of, and explanations for, its impact on state behaviour,[5] scepticism was emerging within its ranks. Martti Koskenniemi expressed the now famous insight that international law sways between Apology (for its basis in the acts of the powerful) and Utopia (for its potential as an instrument of the powerless).[6] International legal argument can and does provide support for both positions. It has been raised to both support and deny humanitarian action (in defence of state sovereignty), as a tool of Empire, and also of resistance in national jurisdictions against state behaviour (for instance, in human rights cases brought against abuses conducted by the military in places such as Iraq and Afghanistan) and by governments to justify those same behaviours. Recourse to formalism and process has been seen as one response, even by the most committed sceptics; as Amy Bartholomew points out, even the Bush Administration couched its defence of practices such as the prison at Guantánamo Bay in (self-defined) legalistic language, while asserting the law as a binding obligation for those it deemed hostile.[7] Similarly the Russian annexation of Crimea in 2014 has been framed by President Putin in legalistic language.

In the preceding chapters we have outlined some of the key concepts and tenets of international law – sovereignty, statehood, the prohibition

[4] See, for example, Slaughter Burley, Anne-Marie 1993. 'International Law and International Relations Theory: A Dual Agenda', *American Journal of International Law* 87 (2): 205–239; Slaughter, Anne-Marie 1995. 'International Law in a World of Liberal States', *European Journal of International Law* 6: 503–538.

[5] International lawyers too have turned to empiricism; its role as a tool for transnational problem-solving has motivated what has been termed a 'new realist' methodology of international law that advocates scholarship based on empirical evidence on how law is used and applied by the relevant actors. See, for example, Lang, Andrew 2015, 'New Legal Realism, Empiricism, and Scientism: The Relative Objectivity of Law and Social Science', *Leiden Journal of International Law* 28(2): 231–254, and the other four articles in a special series of *Leiden Journal of International Law* 28(2); for critique see Klabbers, Jan 2015. 'Whatever Happened to Gramsci? Some Reflections on New Legal Realism', *Leiden Journal of International Law* 28(3): 469–478.

[6] Koskenniemi, Martti 2006. *From Apology to Utopia: The Structure of International Legal Argument.* Cambridge University Press, rev. ed.

[7] Bartholomew, Amy 2012. 'Defending Legality in the Age of Empire's Law', in Falk, Richard, Juergensmayer, Mark and Popovski, Vesselin. *Legality and Legitimacy in Global Affairs.* Oxford University Press, 92–126.

of the use of force and the obligation of the peaceful settlement of disputes in the United Nations Charter – and these and others are developed in subsequent chapters. Throughout we interpret international law as a discourse – a set of narratives and practices – that bind together what international relations theorists call international society. This discourse is based on and shaped by what Jutta Brunnée and Stephen Toope call 'shared understandings'[8] developed through state socialisation, or among 'communities of practice', or through the various networks described by Anne-Marie Slaughter that operate between professional experts, for example, diplomats, international officials, international non-governmental organisations (NGOs), foreign policy experts and international lawyers.[9]

The concept of 'shared understandings' might assume a homogenous international society, which, of course, is not the case. Historically and geographically different societies elaborated their own systems of rules regulating their relations with other political groups, but these were largely discounted as international law emerged as an essentially European construct. The turn to history[10] in recent accounts of international law has demonstrated its complicity in silencing and reconstructing the subaltern, supporting assertions of title to colonised territories and legalising colonial exploitation of peoples and resources.[11] There are many writings that elucidate and celebrate other traditions of international law[12] and seek the proper acknowledgement of their contribution to the discipline. Other critiques demonstrate its structural

[8] Brunnée, Jutta and Toope, Stephen 2010. *Legitimacy and Legality in International Law: An Interactional Account.* Cambridge University Press, 15.

[9] Slaughter, Anne-Marie 2013. 'Filling Power Vacuums in the New Global Legal Order', *Boston College International and Comparative Law Review* 54(3): 919–936.

[10] For an account of this trend see Galindo, George Rodrigo Bandeira 2005. '*Martti Koskenniemi and the Historiographical Turn in International Law*', *European Journal of International Law* 16(3): 539–559, reviewing Koskenniemi, Martti 2001. *The Gentle Civilizer of Nations: The Rise and Fall of International Law 1870–1960.* Cambridge University Press.

[11] See, for example, Anghie, Anthony 2004. *Imperialism, Sovereignty, and the Making of International Law.* Cambridge University Press.

[12] See, for example, the *Asian Journal of International Law,* which commenced publication in 2011; Gathi, James 2012. 'Africa and the History of International Law', in Fassbender, Bardo *et al.* (eds.). *The Oxford Handbook of the History of International Law.* Oxford University Press (this volume is an important compendium of many other traditions of international law). See also International Law Association, Committee on Islamic Law and International Law, *The Hague Conference Report,* 2010 and *Sophia Conference Report,* 2012.

biases,[13] including its inherent male bias and role in creating and maintaining gender hierarchies to the detriment of half the world's population.[14] It might be thought that such diversity undermines any prospect of 'shared understandings'. However, Toope and Brunée argue, optimistically, that 'communities of practice can actually have impact without deeply-shared substantive values . . . as mutual engagement increases, it may be possible for even adversaries to learn from each other'.[15]

A similar version of this standpoint is put forward by Jürgen Habermas. For him, international law does not derive from a given universal morality – the law of nature – but from what he calls 'reciprocal perspective taking'. Habermas argues that

> The "reason" of modern international law does not consist of universal "values" that one can own like goods and distribute and export throughout the world. "Values" – including those that that have a chance of winning global recognition – don't come from thin air. They gain their binding force only within normative orders and practices of particular forms of cultural life.[16]

Thus while international law admittedly draws on a European tradition of thought, the extent to which it is assimilated depends on how far it resonates within the cultures and interpretations of other societies. The 'reciprocal perspective taking' to which Habermas refers is speeded up and intensified in an era of growing interconnectedness.

We also recognise law as a narrative that allows 'the sanctity of the legal text to be challenged. . . . Law as narrative is a reference to the possibility of law as one telling among many rather than presenting law as an objective and universal standard'.[17] Such learning, as Brunée and Toope envisage, must be sought through seeking alternative narratives

13 The contribution made by critical legal scholars is well summarised in Cass, Deborah 1996. 'Navigating the Newstream: Recent Critical Scholarship in International Law', *Nordic Journal of International Law* 65(3): 341–383.

14 Charlesworth, Hilary and Chinkin, Christine 2000. *The Boundaries of International Law: A Feminist Analysis*. Manchester University Press; Kouvo, Sari and Pearson, Zoe (eds.) 2011. *Feminist Perspectives on Contemporary International Law: Between Resistance and Compliance*. Hart Publishing.

15 Brunnée and Toope, *op. cit.*, 87.

16 Habermas, Jürgen 2006. 'Interpreting the Fall of a Monument', in Bartholomew, Amy (ed.). *Empire's Law: The American Imperial Project and the "War to Remake the World"*. Pluto Press, 44–51, 51.

17 Heathcote, Gina 2012. *The Law on the Use of Force: A Feminist Analysis*. Routledge, 15.

from those who are marginalised by the state-based and European-based hegemony of international law, through cross-cultural exchanges that rest on mutual communication in an attempt to bridge the cultural gaps that inhibit acceptance of and compliance with international standards. The necessities of common dealings in the globalised world impel the expansion of communities of practice and narratives of international law.

It can be argued that it is the composition of those 'communities of practice' – the power relations that underpin the shared discourse – that explains the continuum between Apology and Utopia and, in particular, shapes the different conceptions of law associated with our different security models. Thus, for the Geo-Politics model, the main participants in the discourse are states, and particularly what are known as 'Great Powers', while the War on Terror model is linked to American military dominance and the formation of 'coalitions of the willing'. The Responsibility to Protect and Liberal Peace models express the discourse of international institutions, wider groupings of states ('like-minded states') and policies at least rhetorically directed towards peoples, while civil society participation, especially at the local level, is important for the Human Security model.

Institutionalisation, enforcement, judicialisation and internalisation are all expressions of the discourse of international law, promoting coherence and helping to underpin the discourse, but also fostering fragmentation and exposing differences. Indeed, the mix of these processes differs according to our security models. But ultimately, we argue, compliance does not depend on them; rather it depends on an amalgam of expediency, shared objectives and belief in the legitimacy of those objectives and a willingness to work for their achievement.

The prime subjects of international law – states – are not the same as those of domestic law. The primacy of states accounts for what is often considered the main way domestic law differs from international law, in that the former is embedded in a much more extensive web of enforcement and judicialisation. But, as is often observed, in reality the regimes are not so different: international law now encompasses a broader range of subjects, and norms of domestic law may be observed even where enforcement is lax, or, on the contrary, violated despite enforcement. Compliance depends on the acceptance of the legitimacy of the authority from which the laws emanate and of the values that underpin the law and are produced and reproduced by similar sorts of 'communities of practice' – legislators, lawyers, regulators, commentators, NGOs, think tanks and other such bodies. And this is even true of undemocratic societies where, to be sure, power and coercion play a much more important role in enforcement but nevertheless compliance cannot entirely be guaranteed through force except in a situation of permanent terror; there has to be some 'shared understandings'. As Brooks puts it:

> For years, legal scholars who focussed on domestic legal issues dismissed International Law as 'not really law' but something else: unenforceable moral directive, for example, or mere politics. In other words, the claim that international law is really a matter of social norms, not law. To-day, however, domestic law experts are beginning to recognise the powerful role social norms often play in guiding, buttressing, and sometimes undermining domestic law.[18]

Moreover international and domestic law are becoming more and more interwoven. On the one hand, instruments of judicialisation and enforcement are being developed at the international level to the extent that there is a concern about their proliferation and the ensuing impact on the coherence of the international legal system.[19] Further, domestic bodies, including the legislative, executive and judiciary, must give effect to principles of international law in a growing number of circumstances so that the classic divide between 'monist' and 'dualist' states[20] is weakening and being replaced by a fluid synergy between the two.[21] Failure to take account of international law at the domestic level may incur state responsibility for the commission of an internationally wrongful act, and international law does not allow incompatibility with national law as a justification for non-compliance.[22] On the other hand 'communities of practice' that rely on and must take account of both domestic

[18] Brooks, Rosa Ehrenreich 2003. 'The New Imperialism: Violence, Norms, and the "Rule of Law"', *Michigan Law Review* 101(7): 2275–2340, 2287.

[19] See Kingsbury, Benedict 1999. 'Foreword: Is the Proliferation of International Courts and Tribunals a Systemic Problem?' *NYU Journal of International Law and Politics* 31(679), and other articles in the 1999 Symposium on the Proliferation of International Courts and Tribunals, *NYU Journal of International Law and Politics* 31; International Law Commission 2006, 'Conclusions of the Work of the Study Group on the Fragmentation of International Law: Difficulties Arising from the Diversification and Expansion of International Law', *Yearbook of the International Law Commission* 2, part 2.

[20] Crawford, James 2012. *Brownlie's Principles of Public International Law*. Oxford University Press, 48–50.

[21] Nijman, Janne and Nollkaemper, Andre (eds.) 2007. *New Perspectives on the Divide between National and International Law*. Oxford University Press.

[22] International Law Commission, *Articles on the Responsibility of States for Internationally Wrongful Acts*, annex of UN GA Resolution. 56/83, 12 December 2001, especially articles 1–4.

and international law increasingly cross state boundaries and include multinational companies, farmers and other workers affected by international directives, human rights activists, international administrations, inter-agency policing, diaspora lobbying groups or even criminal networks.

In this chapter, we review the main theories of compliance with international law, followed by a discussion of the mechanisms for compliance –institutionalisation, enforcement, implementation and judicialisation. Compliance decreases where belief in the legitimacy of the system declines, or in the context of violence where it is thought to be out of touch with contemporary realities. While the laws of war remain based in the assumption of 'old wars', this disconnect will continue to the detriment of human security. In the final section we reflect on how different understandings of legalisation, enforcement and compliance are challenged by, yet underpin, the diverse models of security and the gap between legitimacy and legality that we describe in Chapter 1 – differences that help to explain the fluidity and uncertainty of the period we are living through.

3.2 Theories of Compliance

Compliance denotes the acceptance of an obligation and adopting behaviour in accordance with it.[23] Philippe Sands has explained that non-compliant behaviour may arise through a failure 'to give effect to substantive norms', to 'fulfil procedural requirements' or to fulfil an obligation arising out of institutional membership.[24] Compliance need not necessarily denote uniform behaviour by states and other actors. Obligations may be differentiated, requiring different levels of performance from, for instance, developing and developed states. This is the case with a number of environmental treaties, but is not generally the case with human rights obligations,[25] subject to the margin of

[23] For an overview see Raustiala, Kal and Slaughter, Anne-Marie 2012. 'International Law, International Relations and Compliance', in Carlsnaes, Walter and Risse, Thomas and Simmons, Beth (eds.). *Handbook of International Relations*. Sage, 2nd ed., chapter 8.

[24] Sands, Philippe 2003. *International Environmental Law*. Cambridge University Press, 172.

[25] The *International Covenant on Economic, Social and Cultural Rights* (ICESCR), 16 December 1966, United Nations Treaty Series, vol. 993, 3, article 2 may indicate subjective determination ('appropriate means', 'available resources'); article 2 (3) suggests some leeway for developing states: 'Developing countries, … may determine to what extent they would guarantee the economic rights recognized in the present Covenant to non-nationals'. The Committee on Economic, Social and Cultural Rights (CESCR) has,

appreciation.[26] While compliance is sought, non-compliance with international obligations does not necessarily impact upon peoples' experiences on the ground; non-compliance with procedural or institutional human rights requirements such as failing to report in a timely fashion does not of itself mean a failure of human rights implementation. The language of non-compliance emerges from international relations rather than international law; for instance, the Vienna Convention on the Law of Treaties speaks not of non-compliance but of 'material breach',[27] the Geneva Conventions of 'grave breaches'[28] and human rights tribunals typically of 'violations'. The concept of compliance emerged explicitly in international regulatory regimes in the 1980s, notably those relating to the environment, giving rise to debate about the relationship between breach and non-compliance.[29]

An obligation may be legal, social or moral. Compliance with an obligation of international law assumes recognition of the latter's binding nature, and thus compliance derives its meaning and utility from different theories of law.[30] However, there can be no simple binary distinction between compliance and non-compliance or between law and non-law,[31] as international practice in law-making and application is fluid, variable and contextual.[32] Accordingly concepts of compliance depend upon understandings of the relations

however, emphasised that while the standard may vary according to resources, the required conduct is common; CESCR 5th session 1990. 'General Comment No. 3: The Nature of States Parties' Obligations', ICESR article 2 para. 1.

[26] The doctrine of the margin of appreciation has been especially evolved by the European Court of Human Rights and has been much discussed; see, e.g., Shany, Yuval 2005. 'Toward a General Margin of Appreciation Doctrine in International Law?' *European Journal of International Law* 16: 907–940.

[27] *Vienna Convention on the Law of Treaties*, 23 May 1969, UNTS vol. 1155 p. 331, article 60.

[28] E.g., *Convention Relative to the Protection of Civilian Persons in Time of War*, 12 August 1949, 75 UNTS 287 (*Geneva Convention IV)*, article 147; *Protocol Additional to the Geneva Conventions of 12 August 1949, and Relating to the Protection of Victims of International Armed Conflicts*, 8 June 1977, 1125 UNTS (Additional Protocol I), article 85.

[29] Koskenniemi, Martti 1992. 'Breach of a Treaty or Non-Compliance? Reflections on the Enforcement of the Montreal Protocol', *Yearbook of International Environmental Law* 3: 123–162.

[30] Kingsbury, Benedict 1998. 'The Concept of Compliance as a Function of Competing Conceptions of International Law', *Michigan Journal of International Law* 19: 345–372 ('The Concept of Compliance').

[31] Shelton, Dinah (ed.) 2000. *Commitment and Compliance: The Role of Non-Binding Norms in the International Legal System*. Oxford University Press.

[32] Kingsbury, *op. cit.*, 346 ('The Concept of Compliance').

between *inter alia* law, behaviour, objectives and justice. Compliance must also be distinguished from processes of implementation and enforcement. Implementation may be understood narrowly as the incorporation of international law into national law or practice,[33] although a state (or other actor) can comply with an international legal obligation without having taken steps formally to implement that obligation. It may be that implementation is not required because the relevant behaviour is already in conformity (intentionally or through coincidence) or that no formal implementation procedures are required. Enforcement denotes some external, top-down sanctioning process and lies at the core of John Austin's positivist understanding of law.[34] Seeing international law through different lenses, for instance, as international legal process,[35] as 'a continuing process of authoritative decisions'[36] or as a framework of norms subject to competing interpretations through which international and transnational relations are conducted,[37] makes the lack of effective enforcement mechanisms less important. Similarly, compliance and effectiveness should not be conflated; compliance with norms of international law does not necessarily achieve the sought-after goals.[38] Nevertheless new processes and techniques for compliance, implementation and enforcement are being developed, in conjunction with institutionalisation and judicialisation, which reflect both different understandings of international law and the disparities of power entrenched within the legal system. The discussion will also consider

[33] The development of National Action Plans is a way of implementing international obligations; e.g., UK Foreign and Commonwealth Office 2014. 'United Kingdom National Action Plan on Women, Peace and Security: 2014–2017'.

[34] The so-called 'command' theory of law: 'sovereign command made effective by the application of [threat] of sanction'; Higgins, Rosalyn 1993. *Problems and Process: International Law and How We Use It*. Oxford University Press, 13.

[35] International law is seen as a process of examining 'the role of law in constraining decision-makers and affecting the course of international affairs'; Ratner, Steven and Slaughter, Anne-Marie 1999. 'Appraising the Methods of International Law: A Prospectus for Readers', *American Journal of International Law* 93: 291–302, 294.

[36] Higgins, *op. cit.*, 12.

[37] Howse, Robert and Teitel, Ruti 2010. 'Beyond Compliance: Rethinking Why International Law Really Matters', *NYU School of Law, Public Law and Legal Theory Research Paper Series Working Paper No. 10-08*.

[38] E.g., Shany analyses the relationship between compliance with the decisions of international courts and effectiveness in achieving the objectives of dispute resolution, norm enhancement, legitimation and regime support; Shany, Yuval 2014. *Assessing the Effectiveness of International Courts*. Oxford University Press, especially chapters 5 and 6.

how they are affected by the strengthening of norms relating to individuals as opposed to states.

A widely cited international law text of the late 1960s and 1970s was Professor Louis Henkin's *How Nations Behave* with its descriptive but unexplained assertion that 'it is probably the case that *almost all nations observe almost all principles of international law and almost all of their obligations almost all of the time*'.[39] Despite this optimism about compliance with international law, in the realist model of international law which prevailed during the Cold War, law is seen primarily as a set of aspirations, which may sometimes admit of compliance where it is in the self-interest of states to do so. This model assumes no effective enforcement, and during the Cold War the veto power pre-empted the possibility of SC-imposed sanctions.[40] It is encapsulated by the verdict of Dean Acheson at the time of the 1963 Cuba Missile crisis that 'law simply does not deal with such questions of ultimate power – power that comes close to the sources of sovereignty. . . . The survival of states is not a matter of law'.[41] Despite such opinions in President Kennedy's executive committee, legal argument was engaged, not least to ensure international support.[42]

An important theory of international law from the same period, the New Haven School of Law and Policy, also departed from rule-based positivism, seeing international law as 'a process of decision-making by which various actors in the world community clarify and implement their common interests in accordance with their expectations of appropriate processes and of effectiveness in controlling behaviour'.[43] However, its classification of 'values' that human society seeks to protect and promote (power, enlightenment, wealth, well-being, skill, affection, respect and rectitude)[44] facilitated the 'pursuit of an imposed higher

[39] Emphasis in the original.

[40] UN Charter, article 27 (3). Until 1989 the SC had decided upon measures under UN Charter article 41 on only two occasions.

[41] 1963 Proceedings, *American Society of International Law* 57, 14.

[42] Chayes, Abram 1974. *The Cuban Missile Crisis: International Crises and the Role of Law*. Oxford University Press. Slaughter notes a series of studies that were undertaken during the Cold War under the auspices of the American Society of International Law that elucidate the role of international law in 'shaping or facilitating' decision-making, despite the prominence of realist thought; Raustiala and Slaughter, *op. cit.*, 540.

[43] Ratner and Slaughter, *op. cit.*, 294.

[44] Wiessner, Siegfried and Willard, Andrew 1999. 'Policy-Oriented Jurisprudence and Human Rights Abuses in Internal Conflict: Toward a World Public Order of Human Dignity', *American Journal of International Law* 93: 316–333, 318.

norm, the defence and maintenance of (American) liberal democracy as a bulwark against the spread of communism'.[45] Nevertheless the New Haven methodology was espoused by some, without necessarily accepting the associated political stance.

Following the end of the Cold War, compliance theories (and practices) proliferated, along with international law-making, further institutionalisation and international judicial tribunals, as discussed below. For instance, Antonia and Abram Chayes were proponents of a state- and institutional management–based model whereby compliance is based on interests in membership of international organisations and the leverage that can thus be exercised upon actors.[46] Sovereignty has shifted to become a consideration of status; states 'measure their power and prestige less by their degree of autonomy' than by the extent of their participation in institutions.[47] Compliance is induced not through coercive measures but through the benefits of regime interaction, of being a member 'in reasonably good standing' in the institutions of international life.[48] This form of managerialism has been described as a 'rationalist, interest based account of state behaviour' in that it does not purport to determine any basis for legal obligation, only that state conduct is regarded as more 'compelling' when it conforms with legal and institutional rules.[49]

A further instrumentalist model, reminiscent of the realists, is the rational choice theory of compliance,[50] which regards the state as a unitary actor and state decision-making as based upon economic realities and achieving optimum benefit.[51] International law tracks the interests of the powerful. In this instance there is again little place for law (unless state interests coincide with legal obligations) and no place for enforcement. There is an assumption that targeted actors perceive their interests

[45] Scobbie, Iain 2003. 'Some Common Heresies about International Law: Sundry Theoretical perspectives', in Evans, Malcolm (ed.). *International Law*. Oxford University Press, 59–87, 68.

[46] Chayes, Abram and Chayes, Antonia Handler 1995. *The New Sovereignty: Compliance with International Regulatory Agreements*. Harvard University Press. See further Chapter 2.

[47] Alvarez, Jose 2007. 'Legal Perspectives', in Weiss, Thomas and Daws, Sam (eds.). *The Oxford Handbook on The United Nations*. Oxford University Press, 58–81, 70.

[48] Chayes and Chayes, *op. cit.*, 28.

[49] Brunnée and Toope, *op. cit.*,104.

[50] Guzman, Andrew 2008. *How International Law Works: A Rational Choice Theory*. Oxford University Press.

[51] Goldsmith, Jack and Posner, Eric 2005. *The Limits of International Law*. Oxford University Press.

solely in objective rational terms, which removes from the equation the apparently irrational (and often manipulated) behaviour and messy attributes of nationalism, historical attachment to land, religious fervour, domestic political calculations or even humanitarianism. It also takes no account of the reality that states – both the powerful and less powerful – choose to incur costs through joining international institutions and entering into international agreements. The powerful seek the legitimacy of institutional membership while for the less powerful institutional membership and compliance with international law may be attractive as a means of safeguarding their broader security concerns, even if in particular instances this is apparently contrary to their immediate interests. As Raustiala asks: 'If these institutions do not constrain states – if they are simply formalistic, moralistic and unable to influence the realities of international life – what are [presumably rational states] doing?'[52] Within the model of rational, self-interested states, Andrew Guzman recognises this reality that 'international law matters' to states through his emphasis on states' concern for the reputational implications of non-compliance. He argues that a country's reputation for reliability has value in its relations with other countries and that reputational loss (for instance, through reneging on international commitments) must be salvaged 'by demonstrating a pattern of compliance with international law'.[53]

A further model is that of Ryan Goodman and Derek Jinks, who have over time developed a theory of 'state socialization'[54] whereby states' identities, interests and organisational attributes are shaped by global regimes. They discuss three influences on state behaviour: persuasion (carrots), coercion (sticks) and 'acculturation' – a general process through which actors 'adopt the beliefs and behavioural patterns of the surrounding culture',[55] which may encompass law compliant behaviour.

[52] Raustiala, Kal. 2006. 'Refining the Limits of International Law', *UCLA School of Law Research Paper No. 06-02.*

[53] Guzman, Andrew 2015. 'A Compliance-Based Theory of International Law', www.law.berkeley.edu/files/guzmanComplianceandIL.doc.

[54] Goodman, Ryan and Jinks, Derek 2004. 'How to Influence States: State Socialization and International Human Rights Law', *Duke Law Journal* 54(3): 621–703; Goodman, Ryan and Jinks, Derek 2008. 'Incomplete Internationalization and Compliance with Human Rights Law', *European Journal of International Law* 19: 725–748; Goodman, Ryan and Jinks, Derek 2013. *Promoting Human Rights through International Law.* Oxford University Press.

[55] *Ibid.*, 626 ('How to Influence States').

Deviance from the prevailing cultural norms incurs 'social costs' while conformity confers substantial affective returns ('cognitive comfort').[56] This too assumes a homogenous culture and progress towards compliance allowing non-conforming 'outliers and time-dependent complexities [to be] thus conveniently relegated to the periphery'.[57]

The so-called 'interaction theory of international law', proposed by Stephen Toope and Jutta Brunnée,[58] applies constructivist theories of international relations[59] to international law. They argue that legal norms arise in the context of social norms based on shared understandings and that the internal features of law are crucial to law's ability to promote compliance.[60] Such 'shared understandings' must exist between 'communities of practice', such as diplomatic circles, those working in human rights, the environment or women's organisations.[61] These are formed across state boundaries and 'mediate between states, individuals and human agency on the one hand and social structures and systems on the other'.[62] Toope and Brunnée see formal law-making through the negotiation and entry into force of a treaty as a good first step in building legality but argue that this is not sufficient. They evoke the necessity for international law to carry out its 'hard work', towards achieving the requisite shared understanding that includes resolving ambiguities and disagreements of principle.[63] This 'hard work'[64] builds up the legality elements of law, thereby enhancing obligation and inducing compliance.[65] An example is the

[56] *Ibid.*, 645.

[57] Mushkat, Roda 2009. 'Incomplete Internalization and Compliance with Human Rights Law: A Reply to Ryan Goodman and Derek Jinks', *European Journal of International Law* 20(2): 437–442, 441.

[58] Brunnée and Toope, *op. cit.*, 15.

[59] 'Early constructivist scholars emphasised mechanisms that drew on the normative power of rules and the importance of shared knowledge and discourse in shaping identity and interests'; Raustiala and Slaughter, *op. cit.*, 540.

[60] Toope and Brunnée draw upon the insights of Lon Fuller and the internal features of law relate to the 'criteria of legality', as understood by Fuller; Brunnée and Toope, *op. cit.*, 20–55.

[61] 'An international legal community can exist only through a practice that sustains shared basic shared understandings and, most importantly a practice that sustains shared understandings of legality'; Brunnée and Toope, *op. cit.*, 70.

[62] *Ibid.*, 116. [63] *Ibid.*, 72. [64] *Ibid.*, 9.

[65] Discussing the reaction of international lawyers to the 2003 Iraq war, Simpson argues that Toope and Brunnee's understanding of the 'reinvigoration of international society through confidence building among estranged allies and institutional renewal' is a view similarly espoused by the UN reform bodies, e.g., Report of the UN Secretary-General's High-Level

development of international criminal law in the decades following the end of the Cold War. A first step was importing the basic idea of individual criminal responsibility for crimes against humanity into the statutes of the *ad hoc* international criminal tribunals, followed by the 1998 Rome Statute of the International Criminal Court (ICC). But these formal law-making instruments must be supplemented by 'shared understandings' between the multiple stakeholders (including governments, legal personnel, civil society) and accumulated around multiple issues such as the nature of the crimes, appropriate process, who should be charged for what crimes and what sentences should be passed, before it can be confidently assumed that there is indeed 'interactional international law'.[66] In 2016, with some crisis of confidence in the international criminal tribunals generated by a number of acquittals by the appeals chamber of the ICTY, the length of proceedings before the ICC, budgetary constraints and allegations about inappropriate judicial behaviour emanating from within the courts, such an assertion remains uncertain.[67]

State compliance with international obligations has particular resonance in such contexts as the legal protection of human rights, environmental standards, investment and regulation of weapons, all areas largely regulated by international agreements and where individuals look to international standards as constraints upon state behaviour. Guzman indeed argues that these are the areas to which international law scholars should direct their focus as international law is less likely to affect state behaviour where the stakes are high, such as the rules relating to the use of force.[68] In what has been described as 'path-breaking' quantitative work,[69] Oona Hathaway argued that international agreements have both an instrumental (creation of legal obligation intended to have particular effects) and expressive (of the state's position) function, and that

Panel on Threats, Challenges and Change, *A More Secure World: Our Shared Responsibility*, UN Doc. A/59/565, 2 December 2004; Report of the Secretary-General, *In Larger Freedom; Towards Development, Security and Human Rights for All*, UN Doc. A/59/2005, 21 March 2005; Simpson, Gerry 2007. *Law, War and Crime*. Polity Press, 55–56.

66 Toope and Brunnee, *op. cit.*, 73. 67 See Chapter 10.

68 Guzman, *op. cit.* Guzman includes arms agreements in his subjects where stakes are high and international law yields little benefit but concedes that it may have more influence where large stake issues are approached from the perspective of compliance involving, for instance, monitoring and verification measures.

69 Simmons, Beth 2010. 'Treaty Compliance and Violation', *Annual Review of Political Science* 13: 273–296, 289. Simmons also indicates some ways in which Hathaway's work is problematic.

compliance must be understood in light of both these functions.[70] By the expressive function states send a message to other members of the international community; for instance, by entering into a human rights treaty a state makes a public declaration that its government is committed to human rights.[71] Other scholars have also noted the 'powerful role' of international agreements in signalling a state's policy stances, which constrain its domestic political choices.[72] The expressive and instrumental functions work largely in unison with each other where there is effective monitoring and enforcement, but where this is not the case they may be in opposition and the expressed message of commitment to the goals of the treaty undermined by non-compliance. Crucially, little or ineffective monitoring means that non-compliance will not be exposed, and 'countries that join the treaty will enjoy the expressive benefits of joining the treaty, regardless of whether they actually comply with the treaty's requirements' and at little cost or risk of adverse consequences. Hathaway controversially found that states parties to human rights treaties (for instance, the Convention against Torture or the Genocide Convention) were as likely to commit the prohibited acts as non-parties, but later researchers have made more positive quantitative findings about the consequences of treaty ratification.[73]

A number of theorists have argued the importance of domestic policy in evaluating compliance with international law, and a significant repeated element in compliance theories is internalisation. For instance, the pursuit of social legitimacy is described by Goodman and Jinks as 'deeply internalized'.[74] To international lawyers, internalisation signifies the relationship between international law and national law. It may denote formal incorporation of international law into the constitutions and laws of states, its application by national judges and implementation by the executive. It may also indicate a more informal penetration of international norms into the actions and policies of government agencies, for instance, through National Action Plans, and of NGOs, multinational corporations, networks and individuals through a variety of social, political and legal processes. An important characteristic of globalisation is

[70] Hathaway, Oona 2002. 'Do Human Rights Treaties Make a Difference?' *Yale Law Journal* 111(8): 1935–2042.

[71] *Ibid.*, 2005–2006.

[72] Raustiala, *op. cit.*, 42.

[73] For an overview of the political science quantitative research into the effects of treaty ratification see Simmons, *op. cit.*, 288–292.

[74] Goodman and Jinks, *op. cit.*, 645 ('How to Influence States').

the spread of shared procedures within and across borders: 'Politics may have once stopped at the water's edge but today domestic interest groups and transnational interest groups lobby hard about foreign policy'.[75]

A state's international obligations both further domestic political goals and influence domestic actors, who in turn use them in seeking to affect their state's behaviour.[76] Hathaway, for instance, assumed that non-compliance with states' human rights obligations would attract little attention outside the formal monitoring arrangements. This may not be the case, especially where NGOs and lawyers use states' treaty obligations to challenge their behaviour in domestic courts. It should also be remembered that treaties incur obligations in addition to the prohibition of the act in question. For instance, by entering into the Torture Convention the United Kingdom expressed its view of the unacceptability of torture and willingness to undertake not to commit it. But the Convention imposes other obligations, including not to resort to evidence obtained through torture, but this was established only after lengthy litigation in the UK courts at the instance of those seeking to hold the United Kingdom to its treaty obligations.[77] This illustrates Simmons' 'primary finding' that treaties have their most consistent impact where domestic stakeholders (construed broadly) have both the motive and the means to demand compliance.[78]

Harold Koh focuses on the process of internalisation to understand 'obedience to' (rather than compliance with) international law. He contends that internalisation of international norms into domestic legal systems is 'pivotal' in a shift in behaviour from habitual conformity to obedience to international law, even when it is inconvenient or against the state's interests to do so.[79] His argument is based in transnational legal process, which he terms a 'fourth historical strand on compliance theory' (the other strands being variants upon rational self-interest, Kantian liberalism and constructivism).[80] Koh sees such norm internalisation as developing through three stages. First, one or more transnational actors provoke interactions with one another. Second, these interactions generate an interpretation or elucidation of the applicable global norm. Third, by so doing, the moving party seeks to

[75] Raustiala, *op. cit.*, 54. [76] *Ibid.*, 38.

[77] *A and Others v. Secretary of State for the Home Department* (No. 2), [2005] UKHL 71.

[78] Simmons, *op. cit.*, 291.

[79] Koh, Harold 1996–1997. 'Why Do Nations Obey International Law?' *Yale Law Journal* 106: 2599–2659, 2603.

[80] *Ibid.*, 2632–2633. Simpson summarises the literature on compliance through identification of reciprocal sanctions, coalitions of like-minded states and self-identifications of states as bases for compliance; Simpson, *op. cit.*, 55–56 (*Law, War and Crime*).

internalise the norm into the other party's internal normative system. This process, which is 'normative, dynamic and constitutive', generates the norm that will then guide future interactions. Eventually, 'repeated participation in the process will help reconstitute the interests and even the identities of the participants in the process'.[81] Such internalisation provides for fluidity and pluralist legal orders. It is a far cry from the rigidity of monist/dualist categorisation, as discussed in traditional international law texts.[82] The dividing line between international law (the law of the 'outside') and national law (the law of the 'inside') has become blurred, flexible and contingent.

However, while this account of internalisation of international norms may explain a process that is sometimes only implicitly undertaken by states (and the other actors recognised by Koh), there may also be internal resistance to incorporation of established or emerging international law. Some judges in national courts explicitly refuse to internalise global norms, preferring to maintain a strict division between domestic law and international law.[83] Such positions may also stem from disagreement as to the operation of the separation of powers between the branches of government, or between the central and state governments in a federal state and the proper role of the judiciary, whether national or international. Alternatively, shared interpretations of international law norms may be rejected with a preference for unilateral reinterpretation.[84] Disputes over what behaviour is required to constitute compliance with an international obligation may be subject to some form of authoritative international dispute resolution process, as, for instance, when individuals can pursue their complaint to a regional human rights court, or between members of the World Trade Organization, but this remains the exception in the international order. In any case, rulings by international courts may be rejected by domestic bodies that may consider the

[81] *Ibid.*, 2646.

[82] The distinction has always been more theoretical than applied in practice. A former Judge of the ICJ has stated that he has almost nothing to say about those theories because he does not find them useful. Keith, Kenneth 2013. '"International Law Is Part of the Law of the Land": True or False?' *Leiden Journal of International Law* 26(2): 351–368, 357.

[83] E.g., former Justice Scalia of the US Supreme Court rejected the use of international and foreign norms by the majority Justices (i.e., internalisation of such norms) to determine a national consensus about the use of the death penalty against juveniles; *Roper v. Simmons*, [2005] USSC 03–633.

[84] For example, the interpretation by the US administration of President G. W. Bush of the Geneva Conventions as not applying to terrorist suspects detained at Guantánamo Bay.

international body to have exceeded its authority or to lack democratic legitimacy.[85] Internalisation may provide the pivot between international obligation and compliance, but it may also construct a barrier behind which state sovereignty and unilateralism continue to flourish. Hostility in the United Kingdom towards some decisions of the European Court of Human Rights (and misinformation about the Convention and Court in the popular press) shows the fragility of internalisation of international obligations, even after more than sixty years since ratification. Are these counter-examples, remnants of the past or signposts to the future?

It has also been argued that what has become a 'central pre-occupation' with theories of compliance with international law is unhelpful and even counter-productive in that it detracts from the understanding of legal norms and the importance of their interpretation in the complex realities of multiple legal regimes and institutions. Robert Howse and Ruti Teitel provide a number of examples across human rights, trade, investment and international criminal law of what they term 'ultracompliance': the influence of international norms in what are often unexpected or unintended ways.[86] This expanded discourse of international law may create expectations that law can resolve 'enduring human problems' (such as post-conflict reconstruction) where politics, economics and morality have failed. Rather than expecting too much of law, or asking whether there has been (or is likely to be) compliance with international law, they urge that inquiry should be into 'those properties of "law" that it possesses which make international law distinctive as a mode of discourse in international order, and *then* to see the effects of international law through such an understanding'. Rules do not have stable and fixed meanings but shift through interpretation and multiple forms of discourse.

3.3 Institutions and Networks

The international legal scene was transformed throughout the twentieth century through the growth of what might be seen as some of the trappings of global governance – international institutions[87] that in

[85] See, for instance, the criticism of the European Court of Human Rights by Lord Sumption, Justice of the UK Supreme Court; Lord Sumption, 'The Limits of Law', *27th Sultan Azlan Shah Lecture,* 20 November 2013, www.supremecourt.uk/docs/speech-131120.pdf.

[86] Howse and Teitel, *op. cit.*

[87] Raustiala, Kal 2012. 'Institutional Proliferation and the International Legal Order', in Dunoff, Jeffrey and Pollack, Mark (eds.). *Interdisciplinary Perspectives on International Law and International Relations: The State of the Art.* Cambridge University Press.

various and diverse ways have exercised legislative, executive, judicial and quasi-judicial powers.[88] In the previous chapter, we briefly outlined the lure of global governance and discussed some of the implications for state sovereignty. The next sections focus on international institutionalisation as a mechanism for compliance and enforcement.

The year 1918 has been denoted as the beginning of the epoch of international institutions.[89] The number of regional and global intergovernmental institutions continued to grow in the inter-war years and during the Cold War in such diverse fields as international economic regulation, communications, labour, health, agriculture, fisheries, trade, refugees, maritime and aviation. As international organisations are functional extensions of states, it was in their self-interest to achieve mutually beneficial cooperation by acting through such institutions, thereby reducing transactional costs, promoting package deals and enhancing transparency.[90]

That the UN would enjoy nearly universal membership was accepted after the resolution of disputes over admission to membership in the 1950s.[91] But political division was entrenched through a particular form of Cold War institution – military alliances formed for the purpose of collective self-defence.[92] Institutions with some security agenda have further multiplied in the decades since the end of the Cold War, and tensions persist between the way in which some such institutions formally remain as expressions of the legal norms of an earlier era (e.g., NATO) and others which have emerged (or been reconfigured) with a greater emphasis on human rights–based norms (for example, the Organisation for Security and Co-operation in Europe,[93] the European

88 See, for example, Klabbers, 2015. *Introduction to International Organizations Law*. Cambridge University Press, 3rd ed.

89 Kennedy, David 1987. 'The Move to Institutions', *Cardozo Law Review* 8: 841–988, 844. For the continuity between the League of Nations and the United Nations Organisation see Mazower, Mark 2009. *No Enchanted Palace: The End of Empire and the Ideological Origins of the United Nations* Princeton University Press.

90 Raustiala, *op. cit.*, 13.

91 Following the advisory opinions of the 1948 ICJ: *Conditions of Admission of a State to Membership in the United Nations (Article 4 of the Charter)*, 1948 ICJ Reports 57, advisory opinion of 28 May 1948; *Competence of the General Assembly for the Admission of a State to the United Nations*, 1950 ICJ Reports 4, advisory opinion of 3 March 1950.

92 See Chapter 4.

93 The OSCE replaced the Conference on Security and Co-operation in Europe (CSCE) in January 1995, following the end of the Cold War.

Union[94] or the African Union[95]). In the particular case of collective self-defence institutions, some have fallen out of existence (Warsaw Pact), while others have sought to reinvent themselves (NATO acting in the name of humanitarianism in 1999 and 2011, and developing crisis management tools). The UN somewhat uneasily brings together both political power structures and individuals' rights: on the one hand, the 1945 power structure remains in place within the SC, and, on the other, human rights institutions have proliferated within the UN in a way that was not envisaged in 1945.

In line with the greater receptivity of international relations scholars to public international law, it is now more accepted that institutions furnish spaces and opportunities for engagement with and around legal norms.[96] International law is the framework for treaty-based institutions through which they are constructed and operate. Alongside policy development, providing a forum for generating discussion, conducting negotiations and carrying out operations, institutions contribute to law-making through their practice, conclusion of treaties and adoption of 'soft law' instruments such as guidelines, resolutions and codes of conduct.[97] Institutions thus represent a way of entrenching the legal norms expressed in treaties and interpreting those treaties;[98] by the 1980s 'political scientists came to recognize that legal rules do, in fact, foster compliance with regime norms by providing channels for dispute-settlement, signalling and triggering retaliatory actions, and requiring states to furnish information regarding compliance'.[99] They also shape the processes through which actors are socialised, thereby influencing the internalisation and dissemination of norms and ideas.[100]

94 The European Union replaced the European Communities in 1993. The *Charter of Fundamental Rights of the European Union* was proclaimed on 7 December 2000 and became legally binding on the EU with the coming into force of the *Treaty of Lisbon* in December 2009.

95 The African Union replaced the Organisation of African Unity in 2001.

96 E.g., to develop the shared understanding and communities of practice; Brunnée and Toope, *op. cit.*, 100.

97 Alvarez, José 2005. *International Organizations as Law-makers*. Oxford University Press.

98 Arato, Julian 2013. 'Treaty Interpretation and Constitutional Transformation: Informal Change in International Organizations', *Yale Journal of International Law* 38(2): 289–357.

99 So-called 'regime theory' – 'the study of principles, norms, rules, and decision making procedures that converge in given issue areas'; Koh, *op. cit.*, 2625.

100 Hafner-Burton, Emilie and Victor, David and Lupu, Yonatan 2012. 'Political Science Research on International Law: The State of the Field', *American Journal of International Law* 106: 47–97, 59.

They both limit states' autonomy and promote international legitimacy for states' actions;[101] for instance, states make considerable efforts to gain a mandate from an international (or regional) organisation before undertaking a military intervention.[102] Without such a mandate, the intervention is more likely to be regarded as wrongful, or even as aggression. These functions reflect those that pervade compliance theories – co-operation, legitimation, effectiveness and the sharing of ideas.

International institutions can provide an important meeting place for global civil society and state authorities. Although civil society bodies interacted with governments through conferences and institutions prior to the United Nations,[103] the inclusion of consultative status at the behest of NGOs in the Charter[104] has opened the way for wider participation, especially in the human rights institutions. Partnership between institutions and civil society (between 'top-down' and 'bottom-up') is of mutual benefit in enhancing legitimacy; consultation and inclusivity allow institutions a positive response to claims of democratic deficit, while NGOs can profit from the international standing of the institution and of having their documents recognised within the institution.[105] Nevertheless this should not be over-stated; states remain the 'gatekeepers' to institutions and their processes, and NGOs themselves are not necessarily democratic or 'bottom-up' institutions.[106]

Alongside treaty-based institutions are the myriad of looser informal transnational networks formed between government units, defined by Slaughter as 'a pattern of regular and purposive relations among like government units working across the borders that divide countries from one another and which demarcate the "domestic" [inside] from the "international" [outside] sphere'.[107] There are also governmental networks (such as the G8, now G7 and G20), networks of officially appointed experts, for instance, regulators, judges, ombudspersons and law enforcement bodies, as well as private bodies such as bankers and

[101] Lewis, Patricia and Thakur, Ramesh 2004. 'Arms Control, Disarmament and the United Nations', *Strengthening Disarmament and Security* 1: 17–28.
[102] Coleman, Katharina 2007. *International Organisations and Peace Enforcement: The Politics of International Legitimacy*. Cambridge University Press, 3.
[103] Willetts, Peter 2011. *Non-Governmental Organisations in World Politics: The Construction of Global Governance*. Routledge, 6–7.
[104] UN Charter, article 71. [105] See further Boyle and Chinkin, *op. cit.*, chapter 2.
[106] See Chapter 2. [107] Slaughter, Anne-Marie 2004. *A New World Order*. Princeton, 14.

airline alliances.[108] These allow for interactions between states and private parties (public–private partnerships)[109] and civil society. Their multiple functions include information generating and sharing, enforcement and harmonisation.[110] Some are 'open' networks, allowing many different parties to participate in multiple ways,[111] others are closed. The US Government is reported as increasingly using such informal processes for significant foreign policy purposes. An active network is the Global Counterterrorism Forum (GCTF), founded with the objective of helping 'countries around the world to enhance their capacities – and especially those of their civilian institutions – to meet the terrorist threats within their borders and regions'.[112] Co-chaired by the United States and Turkey, it seeks to reduce recruitment by terrorist groups and increase capabilities for dealing with terrorist threats, including through strengthening criminal justice and other rule of law institutions. Membership comprises twenty-nine founding states and the EU. The existence of networks in turn leads to new forms of international law-making through the formation of common approaches and policies that are expressed in declarations and codes of good practice. The GCTF has, for example, adopted codes of good practice on effective responses to foreign fighting forces, on denying the benefits of ransom following kidnappings and on education and countering violent extremism. Such documents are not formally binding as sources of international law but create a framework for common action and expectations of compliance and implementation.[113] Their outputs may even be accepted as having obligatory force. The significance of IGOs and NGOs as new actors on the international scene is now widely accepted, as is

[108] Slaughter, Anne-Marie 2013. 'Filling Power Vacuums in the New Global Legal Order', *Boston College International and Comparative Law Review* 54(3): 919–936, 929.

[109] Including in the context of the National Security Strategy; Slaughter, Anne-Marie 2012. 'International Law and International Relations Theory: Twenty Years Later', in Dunoff and Pollack, *op. cit.*, 619.

[110] Slaughter, *op. cit.*, 51–52 (*A New World Order*)

[111] Slaughter, *op. cit.*, 930 ('Filling Power Vacuums').

[112] Crook John (ed.) 2013. 'United States Promotes Informal Multilateral Counterterrorism Mechanism', *American Journal of International Law* 107: 437–438.

[113] E.g., the assertion that 'rape and other forms of serious sexual violence in armed conflict are war crimes and also constitute grave breaches of the Geneva Conventions and their first Protocol'. G8 UK, *Declaration on Preventing Sexual Violence in Conflict*, 11 April 2013, para. 4.

acknowledgement that 'the sources of law and interpretive tools to understand them, will also have to change'.[114]

On the one hand, the law facilitates such networks and sets the parameters of their operations, and their legitimacy is heightened by the checks and balances that surround democratic governmental structures.[115] On the other hand, they operate outside the formal constraints of legally defined participation and law.[116] Civil society protests that erupt in response to meetings of the G7 or G20 (and the corresponding heightened provision of and expenditure on security) suggest these networks lack legitimacy in the view of at least some sectors of civil society and highlight the difficulties in obtaining any consensus around legitimacy in controversial situations. They create new forms of insecurity as yet little regulated. They are used to resist state power but in some instances also engage in violence and other forms of intimidation. Crucially, such networks are separated from the power of the state in that their expertise and authority neither derive from, nor are dependent on, statehood. Martti Koskenniemi explains how power has shifted 'from the hands of states to global systems of knowledge and expertise'.[117] In this sense international law could become irrelevant, or simply a useful 'vocabulary for articulating alternative preferences and for carrying out (strategic) manoeuvres in order to limit the powers of global executive classes and expert groups'. BEXIT is seen as a reversal of this trend.

The distinction between networks and institutions represents a distinction between informality and formality. While informal networks proliferate in response to changing circumstances, formal institutions are much slower to develop or change.[118] Networks can provide a flexible and innovative approach to cross-border challenges and problems, but they lack transparency and accountability and they escape the formal

[114] Simma, Bruno and Paulus, Andreas 1999. 'The Responsibility of Individuals for Human Rights Abuses in Internal Conflicts: A Positivist View', *American Journal of International Law* 93(2): 302–316, 306.

[115] Slaughter, *op. cit.* (*A New World Order*).

[116] Chimni, B. S. 2004. 'International Institutions Today: An Imperial Global State in the Making', *European Journal of International Law* 15: 1–37, 18.

[117] Koskenniemi, Martti 2010. 'What Use for Sovereignty Today?' *Asian Journal of International Law* 1: 61–70.

[118] For a discussion of the development and change of UN institutions with respect to women see Charlesworth, Hilary and Chinkin, Christine 2013. 'The New United Nations "Gender Architecture": A Room with a View?' 17 *Max Planck Yearbook of United Nations Law* 17: 1–60.

framework of rule-making. The extent to which institutions are able to 'catch up' with networks may be a critical factor in compliance.

3.4 Processes for Implementation and Enforcement

States, institutions and civil society actors have evolved multiple processes for securing implementation and enforcement of international obligations. They encompass methods that are more akin to 'inside' domestic legal procedures, for instance, courts and tribunals, as well as those 'outside' political and diplomatic processes peculiar to international law. The latter include top-down mandates, action and inaction, and engage a range of techniques, ranging from 'light touch' intervention to coercive measures, from 'carrots to sticks': *inter alia*, persuasion and encouragement, facilitation, review, inspection, verification, coercion, inducement, co-operation, peer pressure, 'naming and shaming', technical and financial assistance, inter-governmental co-operation and accountability. Reciprocity and reputation (as an aspect of self-interest)[119] are seen as key to international enforcement mechanisms.[120] Goodman and Jinks have argued for the systematic incorporation of compliance theories into the design of international institutional processes, but these have rather evolved and multiplied, often in an unsystematic, *ad hoc* and overlapping fashion.

This section examines some of the concrete ways in which institutions seek to further compliance with the international rules. Recourse to any such process rests upon a variety of factors: geo-politics, the continued dominance of states in international affairs and the requirement in many instances for state consent, civil society activism, finding an actor to commence action (for example, table a resolution, bring a matter to the attention of the SC or other institution, commence litigation, coordinate activities), costs (transactional, political, personal) and institutional rivalry. Similar factors and determination of the state's interest also determine whether there will be compliance with the ruling of a judicial or quasi-judicial body. Many such processes are located within the political institutions, but another post–Cold War trend has been the proliferation of courts and tribunals where accountability is sought through judicial processes, as discussed in the next section.

[119] Guzman, Andrew 2006. 'Reputation and International Law', *Georgia Journal of International and Comparative Law* 34: 379–391.

[120] Simmons, *op. cit.*, 275.

3.4.1 *Legalisation and Judicialisation*

Domestic legal systems are characterised by the existence of agencies for the enforcement of law, including through adjudication and effective implementation of court orders. There has been a strongly held view dating back to the 1899 Hague Peace Conference and supported by what today would be termed civil society groups that determination of international disputes through adjudicative methods would enhance peace and stability. From that time on there have been moves for the institution of international judicial processes. The first successes were through the institutionalisation of arbitration in 1899/1907,[121] followed by the establishment of the Central American Court in 1907[122] and the Permanent Court of International Justice (PCIJ) in 1920.[123] In 1945 the International Court of Justice (ICJ) succeeded the PCIJ in almost identical form and jurisdiction, which is limited to disputes between states.[124]

However, both World Courts were, and remain, limited by the lack of compulsory jurisdiction and the requirement of state consent. Although other judicial and quasi-judicial bodies were created during the Cold War (e.g., European Court of Human Rights, Inter-American Court of Human Rights), since its termination there has been what has been described as the judicialisation of international affairs[125] through a proliferation of international courts and tribunals,[126] including the African Court of Justice, the International Tribunal for the Law of the Sea, *ad hoc* international criminal tribunals, the International Criminal Court (ICC) and the World Trade Organization dispute settlement body.[127] This has led to the emergence of new professionals (the international judge and counsel)[128] and advanced the evolution of

[121] *Convention for the Pacific Settlement of International Disputes*, The Hague, 29 July 1899, articles 20–29; *Convention for the Pacific Settlement of International Disputes*, The Hague, 18 October 1907, articles 41–50.

[122] *Convention for the Establishment of the Central American Court of Justice*, Washington, 20 December 1907.

[123] *Statute of the Permanent Court of International Justice*, 16 December 1920.

[124] *Statute of the International Court of Justice*, 1945, article 34 (1).

[125] Abbott, Kenneth *et al.* 2000. 'The Concept of Legalization', *International Organization* 54: 401–419.

[126] 1999 Symposium on the Proliferation of International Courts and Tribunals, *NYU Journal of International Law and Policy* 31: 679–993.

[127] Mackenzie, Ruth *et al.* (eds.) 2010. *Manual on International Courts and Tribunals*. Oxford University Press, 2nd ed.

[128] Alvarez, Jose 2003. 'The New Dispute Settlers: (Half) Truths and Consequences', *Texas International Law Journal* 38: 405–444, 407; Terris, Daniel and Romano, Cesare and

distinct sub-disciplines of international law (for instance, international criminal law, international human rights law, international trade law). This may have lessened the effectiveness of those special regimes not characterised by adjudication (for instance, weapons law,[129] international humanitarian law) and the overall judicialisation of the discipline, but, alternatively it may offer an example to be emulated. Judicialisation provides for legal accountability for behaviour that violates international norms, of states at the ICJ, the regional human rights and economic courts and inter-state arbitral tribunals and of individuals in domestic courts, and at the international criminal tribunals and the permanent ICC. However, the behaviour of international organisations has not been made subject to judicial scrutiny, and widespread immunity persists for violations by such bodies and their personnel.[130] Compliance in the context of judicialisation is generally taken to refer to conformity with the decisions of judicial tribunals;[131] where there is such compliance it remains unclear whether it more broadly makes international law more effective in protecting security (international, national or human).

Legalisation and judicialisation go hand in hand. Legalisation denotes the framing of behavioural norms into legal obligation, within the international legal system through the adoption of treaties, customary international law and the activities of international institutions, notably the SC.[132] Legalisation in the context of dispute resolution represents a turn away from bargaining and a delegation of decision-making to third-party tribunals that apply general legal principles.[133] These tribunals also contribute to the evolution of international law even as they purportedly apply it. For example, the Special Tribunal for Lebanon is a criminal tribunal created by the SC for the trial of those responsible for the 'terrorist crime' of assassinating the former Lebanese Prime Minister Rafiq Hariri on

Leigh Swigart, 2007. *The International Judge: An Inquiry into the Men and Women Who Decide the World's Cases*. Oxford University Press.

129 Possession of nuclear or other weapons of mass destruction is not subject to the jurisdiction of the ICC.

130 Reinisch, August 2000. *International Organisations before National Courts*. Cambridge University Press.

131 Shany, *op. cit.*, especially chapter 6 (*Assessing the Effectiveness of International Courts*).

132 See Chapter 2.

133 Keohane, Robert O. and Moravcsik, Andrew and Slaughter, Anne-Marie 2000. 'Legalized Dispute Resolution: Interstate and Transnational', *International Organization* 54: 457–488.

14 February 2005. It is empowered to apply 'the provisions of the Lebanese Criminal Code relating to the prosecution and punishment of acts of terrorism'.[134] However, attempts to define terrorism in an international treaty, or even a UN General Assembly resolution, have been unsuccessful, and there is no accepted international law definition. The Tribunal therefore created its own definition drawing on a range of sources, which may well become a widely accepted applicable norm.[135]

3.4.2 *Coercive Measures*

The use of force and economic sanctions are the main forms of coercive enforcement of international norms. As discussed in Chapter 2, the use of force is prohibited in international law, but military action may be authorised by the SC as an appropriate enforcement measure in response to a threat to international peace and security as in the case of the Iraqi invasion of Kuwait (1990),[136] as a response to genocide, massive violations of human rights or ethnic cleansing,[137] or as peacekeeping forces to uphold peace agreements.[138]

UN Charter article 41 provides for the authorisation of economic and other measures short of the use of armed force in situations deemed to constitute a threat to the peace, breach of the peace or an act of aggression.[139] Member states agree to accept and carry out such decisions (UN Charter, article 25). The use or threat of the veto by permanent SC members during the Cold War meant that sanctions were rarely imposed; in contrast since 1989 the Council has mandated sanctions on many occasions, including as a response to violations of human rights and international humanitarian law, terrorist threats and development of nuclear capabilities. The SC has prescribed listing of parties to conflict that are credibly suspected of rape or other sexual

[134] UN SC Resolution 1757, 30 May 2007, *Statute of the Special Tribunal for Lebanon*, articles 1 and 2. The Tribunal was established pursuant to UN SC Resolution 1664, 29 March 2006.

[135] Interlocutory Decision on the Applicable Law: Terrorism, Conspiracy, Homicide, Perpetration, Cumulative Charging, Case No. STL-11-01/I, 16 February 2011.

[136] UN SC Resolution 678, 28 November 1990. [137] See Chapter 5.

[138] See Chapter 9. [139] UN Charter, article 39.

violence as a precursor to actions, 'including, as appropriate, measures in accordance with the procedures of the relevant sanctions committees'.[140] Sanctions typically comprise a mix of economic and political measures; since the widely reported adverse consequences of the long-term sanctions against Iraq on the civilian population,[141] targeted (or smart) sanctions have been favoured, which are directed against particular persons or groups, and against particular activities, typically comprising diverse financial measures, travel bans, arms embargoes and no-fly zones. Collective sanctions are also imposed by other institutions, for instance, the World Bank, and regional organisations.[142] Institutional sanctions may restrict rights of membership[143] or expel or suspend a state from the organisation, as has been the case at different times for Greece,[144] Turkey[145] and Russia[146] from the Council of Europe; Libya from the Human Rights Council in 2011;[147] Cuba from the Organization of American States (OAS) in 1962 following the Castro revolution;[148] and Syria from the Arab

[140] UN SC Resolution 1960, 16 December 2010, on women and peace and security; see also UN SC Resolution 1612, 26 July 2005, which opened the way for targeted sanctions over individuals recruiting or targeting children in armed conflict.

[141] Gordon, Joy 2010. *Invisible War: The United States and the Iraq Sanctions*. Harvard University Press.

[142] For example, the EU has imposed a range of measures against Russia in response to the latter's annexation of the Crimea and actions against the territorial integrity of Ukraine; see 'Fact Sheet on EU Restrictive Measures', *EU Newsroom*, 29 April 2014, http://europa.eu/newsroom/highlights/special-coverage/eu_sanctions/index_en.htm.

[143] Chayes and Chayes, *op. cit.*, 71–72.

[144] Following the military junta, a draft resolution for the suspension of Greece was circulated in the Council of Europe Committee of Ministers, but the Greek government pre-empted its adoption by withdrawing from the Council; *HC Deb*, 16 December 1969 vol. 793 cc1137–43. Greece returned to membership in 1974 following the fall of the regime.

[145] Following the military coup in 1980 until 1984 after democratic elections; 'Withdrawal, expulsion and suspension of a member state of the Council of Europe', *Centre Virtuelle de la Connaissance sur L'Europe*, 11 September 2012, www.cvce.eu/content/publication/2006/1/9/f9b31f98-f1a1-407c-97ad-7e92363117fd/publishable_en.pdf.

[146] Russia's policies on Chechnya led to its suspension from the Assembly from 2000 to 2001; *ibid.*

[147] Following a resolution from the UN Human Rights Council recommending such a step the General Assembly adopted UN GA Resolution 65/265, 3 March 2011 ('Suspension of the Rights of Membership of the Libyan Arab Jamahiriya in the Human Rights Council').

[148] At the insistence of the United States, Cuba was suspended on 21 January 1962 until the OAS 39th General Assembly in June 2009 when members voted unanimously to lift suspension. Cuba has declined to rejoin. Lee, Brianna. 'The Organization of American

League in 2011.[149] Suspension from membership is a two-edged sword – it deprives the suspended member of the benefits of membership but also denies the other members the authority of the institution with respect to its further acts. A state that is thus excluded may consider itself free from further institutional constraints to the detriment of the security of its citizens.

As the leading protagonist in the War on Terror and a permanent member of the SC, the United States has sought compliance with its assertions of legality ('you're either with us or against us in the fight against terror'),[150] attempting to change the rules in its favour and seeking enforcement of its demands, where possible through SC sanctions, and where it has been unable to secure a Council vote, through unilateral sanctions and threats of withdrawal of benefits. Following especially SC Resolution 1267, 15 October 1999, imposing sanctions against the Taliban, Osama Bin Laden and his associates, and Resolution 1383, 28 September 2001, imposing sanctions against 'persons who commit, or attempt to commit, terrorist acts or participate in or facilitate the commission of terrorist acts', implementation of SC sanctions requires complex national legislation, involving criminalising the specified activities, regulating the behaviour of banks and other financial institutions with respect to named (and other potential) individuals and imposing immigration and border controls. As discussed in Chapter 2, state implementation is overseen by SC Sanctions Committees and Counter-Terrorism Committee, which make decisions with respect to such issues as to what constitutes prohibited goods or activities, exemptions, whether national legislation is adequate and the targets of sanctions.

Economic and other measures against a state, organisation or non-state actors may be imposed for a number of objectives, including inducing behavioural change, punishment for failure to comply with international norms or minimising access to resources (e.g.,

States', *Council on Foreign Relations*, 13 April 2012, www.cfr.org/latin-america-and-the-caribbean/organization-american-states/p27945#p6.

149 At an emergency session of its twenty-two member states in Cairo the Arab League agreed to exclude Syria over its failure to stop the violence and until it implements the terms of an earlier agreed peace deal. Batty, David and Shenker, Jack, 'Syria Suspended from Arab League', *The Guardian*, 12 November 2011, www.theguardian.com/world/2011/nov/12/syria-suspended-arab-league.

150 'Bush Says It Is Time for Action', *CNN*, 6 November 2001, http://edition.cnn.com/2001/US/11/06/ret.bush.coalition/index.html.

financial resources, weapons or personal freedom). They may also be imposed in a spirit of desperation: something needs to be seen to be done. Compliance with sanctions has two aspects: compliance by all states and non-state bodies with the terms of the sanctions, and compliance by the sanctioned state with the underlying norms of law in question. With respect to the first, it may be that compliance is simply not appropriate for states that must bear major economic and political losses by virtue of a SC resolution for which they have not been able to vote. To maximise the likelihood of compliance, all states (or at least a sufficient number) must perceive the sanctions as appropriate, legitimate and fair. Regardless of their legal justification, if the imposition of sanctions is not so considered, compliance will be less forceful and may cease if sufficient states consider their duration to be excessive. Regarding the second, there is unlikely to be compliance, or attitudinal change, if the sanctioned state does not accept the legitimacy of the SC action.

The imposition of sanctions often assumes a positivist approach to the violation of a rule (or rules) of international law and a belief that the punishment and shaming of wrongdoing actors will induce changed behaviour. This assumption is open to question; it may not be punishment that leads to compliance but the likelihood of sanctions being imposed. If a wrongdoing state knows that it can rely upon support within the Council, or that proposed sanctions against it will be vetoed, it is more likely to continue its behaviour. The same is true of the reputational costs of sanctions, which may be limited if they are not widely upheld by the international community.[151] This both weakens the normative order and fosters a climate of non-compliance. It is also worth remembering that for those without a stake in the established international legal order – states that see themselves as disadvantaged by the existing order, marginalised groups, rebels challenging the internal authority of the state – sanctions will be perceived as tools of the powerful and have little or no effect on attitudinal change.

The impact of sanctions on national or human security may also be problematic. During the period of sanctions on Iraq, the Committee on Economic, Social and Cultural Rights (CESCR) commented on the adverse impact of sanctions on Covenant rights.[152] It noted especially

[151] Simmons, *op. cit.*, 276.

[152] CESCR, General Comment No. 8, The Relationship between Economic Sanctions and Respect for, Social and Cultural Rights, UN Doc. E/C.12/1997/8, 12 December 1997. The Committee noted that during the 1990s sanctions had been imposed against South

that sanctions cause 'significant disruption in the distribution of food, pharmaceuticals and sanitation supplies, jeopardize the quality of food and the availability of clean drinking water, severely interfere with the functioning of basic health and education systems, and undermine the right to work'. The suffering thus inflicted on the population, especially vulnerable groups, contributes to human insecurity. To redress it, the Committee recommended that human rights – including economic, social and cultural rights – be taken into account in the design of a sanctions regime, that the effect of sanctions is monitored and that steps are taken to 'respond to any disproportionate suffering experienced by vulnerable groups within the targeted country'. The impact of sanctions on security goes beyond lack of access to essential services. The CESCR continued to describe the 'unintended consequences' of sanctions, which include:

> reinforcement of the power of oppressive élites, the emergence, almost invariably, of a black market and the generation of huge windfall profits for the privileged élites which manage it, enhancement of the control of the governing élites over the population at large, and restriction of opportunities to seek asylum or to manifest political opposition.

The economic instability caused by sanctions and the ensuing social disability can also impact especially adversely on women's rights. With respect to sanctions imposed against Burma (Myanmar), researchers reported on the 'substantial decline in women's participation in the workforce and the deterioration of their overall status in society, both essential components to maintaining economic independence, self-empowerment, and personal autonomy'.[153] While initiation by the SC of smart sanctions to some extent took such concerns into account, they do not address the inequalities and use of coercive power that may be accompaniment to sanctions.[154]

In another illustration of how sanctions may in fact undermine security, the rationale for an arms embargo is that it reduces violence. But it

Africa, Iraq/Kuwait, parts of the former Yugoslavia, Somalia, the Libyan Arab Jamahiriya, Liberia, Haiti, Angola, Rwanda and the Sudan.

153 Drury, A. Cooper and Peksun, Dursun 2014. 'Women and Economic Statecraft: The Negative Impact International Economic Sanctions Visit on Women', *European Journal of International Relations* 20(2): 463–490, 464.

154 Bianchi, Andrea 2006. 'Assessing the Effectiveness of the UN Security Council's Anti-terrorism Measures: The Quest for Legitimacy and Cohesion', *European Journal of International Law* 17(5): 881–919, 882.

fails to take into account the availability of arms through the black market or that one side is likely to have greater access to the weapons already available in the country and thus exacerbates inequality and may enhance violence. For instance, the arms embargo imposed by the SC on Yugoslavia[155] denied the Bosnian Muslims access to arms, which compromised their ability to defend themselves, while the Serbs had possession of the arms of the former Yugoslav National Army. Arms for the Bosnian Muslims (and further arms for the Bosnian Serbs) were obtained in defiance of the sanctions. Similarly, in 2012 and 2013, the Syrian opposition made known their need for weaponry for fighting against well-armed government forces.[156] In 2011 the EU imposed an embargo on Syria on all military equipment that might be used for repression of the population,[157] operating against all parties. Regional arms embargoes, of course, are likely to be at odds with the policies of other regional institutions or individual states. Inevitably all parties to the conflict in Syria had access to arms from other, non-EU states, which were transported through the EU.[158] The EU arms embargo was lifted in May 2013 in light of disagreements about the supply of arms to non-government forces (although other trade restrictions remained in place). The rise of IS in 2014 illustrates graphically the dangers of arms coming into the possession of forces other than those to whom they have been supplied.

In addition to economic measures imposed by an international or regional institution, unilateral counter-measures may be taken by an 'injured state' in response to a prior international wrong in order to 'induce that [wrongdoing] state to comply with its obligations'.[159] The counter-measures that an injured state may adopt are limited in the first

155 UN SC Resolution 713, 25 September 1991.

156 Schmitt, Mike 2014. 'Legitimacy Versus Legality Redux: Arming the Syrian Rebels', *Journal of National Security Law and Policy* 7: 139–159; Ruys, Tom 2014. 'Of Arms, Funding and "Nonlethal Assistance" – Issues Surrounding Third-State Intervention in the Syrian Civil War', *Chinese Journal of International Law* 13: 13–53.

157 EU Council Decision 2011/273/CFSP, 9 May 2011 and EU Council Regulation No. 442/2011, 9 May 2011 (concerning restrictive measures against Syria); the embargo was subsequently refined, EU Council Regulation No. 36/2012, 18 January 2012 and EU Council Regulation No, 509/2012, 15 June 2012.

158 EU Council Decision 2012/420/CFSP, 23 July 2012 authorised EU member states to inspect vessels in their territories bound for Syria where there was reason to suspect the transport of sanctioned items.

159 International Law Commission, *op. cit.*, article 49 (*Articles on Responsibility of States for Internationally Wrongful Acts*).

instance to non-performance of prior international obligations owed to it by the wrongdoing state (such as financial obligations or interference with air travel over its own air space). Certain obligations are not subject to non-performance as counter-measures, including the prohibition against the use of force, fundamental human rights, humanitarian obligations prohibiting reprisals and peremptory norms of international law. Counter-measures must also be proportionate to the injury suffered.

It is perhaps in relation to coercive measures that international law differs most from domestic law. In domestic law, enforcement depends on due process against an identified (legal) person. Whether coercive measures are approved by the SC is largely determined by geo-political considerations, in particular the interests of the five permanent members. Collective sanctions can be critiqued along similar lines to critiques of war – namely, that sanctions also severely harm individuals who are not responsible for the violations of law that are being punished. But even in the case of targeted sanctions, questions arise since the problem is that states determine the responsibility of particular individuals for non-compliance with the law, without any form of due process or legal redress. This is especially grave in the case of targeted killings, discussed further in Chapter 6.

In this sense, coercive measures aimed at compliance are not very different from coercive measures undertaken in pursuit of geo-political interests. For example, North Korea is currently and Iran has been subject to sanctions[160] because their nuclear programmes are deemed a threat to peace and security. Iran is not a member of the Nuclear Non-Proliferation Treaty while North Korea has withdrawn. Yet despite the commitment in the Treaty[161] to reduce the arsenals of the nuclear powers, there is no question of their programmes being targeted. This highlights the perception of double standards in enforcement and the notion that international law is merely an instrument of the powerful.

3.4.3 Non-Coercive Measures

International law has also developed a number of non-coercive possibilities for the monitoring of state behaviour in order to determine

[160] Following the Joint Comprehensive Plan of Action, UN Doc. S/2015/544, 14 July 2015, the UN SC provided for the termination of sanctions against Iran, subject to verifications. UN SC Resolution 2231, 20 July 2015.

[161] *Treaty on the Non-Proliferation of Nuclear Weapons* ('NPT'), 1 July 1968, article VI. See Chapter 7.

compliance and to induce or facilitate compliant behaviour, punish and make reparation for non-compliant behaviour. Different techniques are associated with the different legal regimes, contributing to the perception of a fragmented system. Human Rights law[162] possesses the greatest range of enforcement bodies and processes: *inter alia* reporting to the UN human rights treaty bodies;[163] inquiry; inter-state complaints; individual complaints; visitation; expert evaluation by special rapporteurs and working groups; and technical assistance. With the exception of inter-state and individual complaints before the regional human rights courts, the outcome of all processes is recommendatory, and 'constructive dialogue' is preferred to a punitive approach.[164] Such institutionalised mechanisms have become part of what might be termed the 'human rights industry' engaging peer review, human rights experts, institutional bureaucrats and civil society. Their impact is variable, making this a ripe area for quantitative and qualitative analysis; since formal compliance with the relevant procedures does not necessarily inculcate a human rights mentality, nor ensure protection of human rights in reality, such analysis must take account of resistance by, and the ongoing commitment of, human rights defenders – in the broadest sense of the term.

International Humanitarian Law (IHL)[165] lags behind human rights in terms of monitoring and enforcement. There is no regular system of state reporting[166] or individual complaints. Reciprocity has been seen as the main mechanism for compliance with IHL, but this has been in the context of traditional forms of 'old wars'.[167] Reciprocity has less leverage with respect to human rights abuses and in asymmetrical warfare such as in 'new wars', where those fighting have no stake in compliance. In both cases this is to the detriment of the civilian population.[168] In a blurring of IHL and international criminal

[162] See Chapter 6.

[163] UN GA Resolution 68/268, 9 April 2014, strengthening and enhancing the effective functioning of the human rights treaty body system.

[164] 'The work of the [Human Rights] Council shall be guided by the principles of universality, impartiality, objectivity and non-selectivity, constructive international dialogue and cooperation'; UN GA Resolution. 60/251, 3 April 2006.

[165] See Chapter 6.

[166] Reports are required from countries on the SC's agenda, as well as reports from the Secretary-General.

[167] Empirical studies on war, fighting, peace and security, cited in Simmons, *op. cit.*, 280–282.

[168] Lamp, Nicholas 2011. 'Conceptions of War and Paradigms of Compliance: The 'New War' Challenge to International Humanitarian Law', *Journal of Conflict and Security Law* 16(2): 225–262.

law, attention has been given to the prosecution of international crimes in the international, hybrid and national criminal tribunals as part of the concept of transitional justice.[169] Successive SC resolutions on the protection of civilians, in particular those on children in armed conflict and on women and peace and security, have urged measures for enhanced compliance, including training in IHL, human rights and gender and sexual violence, inclusion of prohibitions in military manuals, clear orders through chains of command, disciplinary measures, vetting of military personnel, the establishment of specialist institutional posts and disciplinary measures.[170] Implementation of these measures remains limited.[171]

Fact-finding has become another widely used method of seeking compliance in different areas of international law. The IHL fact-finding-process provided for by article 90 of Protocol I to the Geneva Conventions has never been used, but the Security Council,[172] General Assembly[173] and Human Rights Council[174] have all mandated *ad hoc* commissions of inquiry with respect to alleged violations of both human rights and international humanitarian law.[175] Independent fact-finding bodies have also been established by the UN

[169] See Chapter 10.

[170] Including the Special Representative to the Secretary General (SRSG) on Children and Armed Conflict, established pursuant to UN GA Resolution 51/77, 12 December 1996 and the SRSG on Sexual Violence in Armed Conflict, established pursuant to UN SC Resolution 1888, 30 September 2009.

[171] E.g., UN SC Resolution 2242, 13 October 2015 recognizes the 'need for far greater implementation of the women, peace and security agenda' and its deep concern at under performance of many of its specifics.

[172] E.g., UN SC Resolution 1564, 18 September 2004 requesting the UN Secretary General, para. 12 to 'rapidly establish an international commission of inquiry in order immediately to investigate reports of violations of international humanitarian law and human rights law in Darfur by all parties, to determine also whether or not acts of genocide have occurred'.

[173] Indeed, UN GA Resolution 46/59, 9 December 1991, (Declaration on Fact-Finding by the United Nations in the Field of the Maintenance of International Peace and Security), para. 7 states that 'Fact-finding missions may be undertaken by the Security Council, the General Assembly and the Secretary-General'.

[174] E.g., with respect to Darfur, Libya, Syria and Gaza.

[175] Guidelines have been worked upon in an attempt to promote greater commonalities; e.g., with respect to international institutions, Bassiouni, Cherif and Abraham, Christina (eds.) 2013. *Siracusa Guidelines for International, Regional and National Fact-Finding Bodies*. Intersentia; with respect to NGO fact-finding, The Raoul Wallenberg Institute and International Bar Association 2015, *Guidelines on International Fact-Finding Visits and Reports* (the London-Lund Guidelines), rev. ed.

Secretary-General,[176] regional organisations[177] and NGOs.[178] There are a number of ostensible objectives for fact-finding missions: seeking to expose wrongdoing and induce compliance with the legal standards, thus changing behaviours; allowing for further investigations into disputed facts;[179] perhaps laying the ground for subsequent criminal prosecutions (the creation of both the ICTY and ICTR was preceded by a SC-mandated fact-finding mission, as was referral of the situation in Darfur to the ICC by the Council); contributing to international peace and security; providing a process through which victims' voices can be heard and recorded.[180] In recent times greater efforts have been made to ensure that these include women's voices and that gender considerations are adequately investigated and addressed.[181] The plethora of fact-finding missions since the early 1990s suggests that this has become an institutional response where some response is needed. The establishment of a permanent fact-finding mechanism has been proposed but without apparent strong support from states.[182]

Fact-finding by technical experts and reporting lie at the core of the verification, on-site inspection and safeguard techniques,[183] which have

[176] E.g., Report of the Secretary-General's Panel of Experts on Accountability in Sri Lanka, 31 March 2011, www.un.org/News/dh/infocus/Sri_Lanka/POE_Report_Full.pdf.

[177] E.g., Council of the EU, Report of the Independent International Fact-Finding Mission on the Conflict in Georgia, 30 September 2009, www.ceiig.ch/Report.html.

[178] E.g., International Bar Association, Human Rights Institute.

[179] The UN Fact-Finding Mission to Gaza included in its recommendations that both the Government of Israel and the Palestinian authorities establish domestic-based investigative procedure; Report of the United Nations Fact Finding Mission on the Gaza Conflict, 25 September 2009, www2.ohchr.org/english/bodies/hrcouncil/docs/12session/A-HRC-12-48.pdf.

[180] Chinkin, Christine 2010. 'UN Human Rights Council Fact-Finding Missions: Lessons from Gaza', in Arsanjani, Mahnoosh *et al.* (eds.). *Looking to the Future: Essays on International Law in Honor of W. Michael Reisman*. Martinus Nijhoff, chapter 26, 497.

[181] Coomeraswamy, Radhika 2015. *Preventing Conflict, Transforming Justice Securing the Peace: Global Study on the Implementation of United Nations Security Council Resolution 1325*, 113.

[182] Cassese, Antonio 2012. 'Fostering Increased Conformity with International Standards: Monitoring and Institutional Fact-Finding', in Cassesse, Antonio (ed.). *Realizing Utopia: The Future of International Law*. Oxford University Press, 295–303.

[183] *Statute of the International Atomic Energy Authority* (IAEA), 23 October 1956, articles III and XII set out the framework for safeguards and provide for the conclusion of safeguard agreements; under the NPT Treaty, *op. cit.*, article III non-nuclear weapon states undertake to accept IAEA safeguards and to conclude safeguard agreements with the IAEA. The safeguard system is strengthened by the *Protocol Additional to*

been most fully provided for to ensure compliance with weapons regulation. Inter-state complaint has been merged with inspection through provision for a 'challenge inspection' whereby a state party concerned about another state's compliance may request that an inspection team be sent to that other state.[184] In this instance, states parties 'have committed themselves to the principle of 'anytime, anywhere' inspections with no right of refusal'.[185] The SC has mandated both weapons inspectors and sanctions, for instance, in the cases of Iraq following the 1991 conflict,[186] Iran and North Korea. Civil society demands for institutional transparency and accountability generated the creation of fact-finding with respect to actions of the international financial institutions, commencing with the World Bank in 1993 and followed by other multilateral development banks. Compliance in this instance is with respect to the various institutions' own constitutive documents, policies and procedures, not for instance member states' international environmental or human rights obligations, except in so far as such safeguards are incorporated into the policies and practices of those institutions. They have provided a tool for public accountability by allowing adversely affected persons and NGOs to challenge behaviours.[187]

The language of compliance has been incorporated into intergovernmental cooperative processes such as compliance committees, meetings or conferences of states parties, review conferences or specially established bodies such as the Organisation for the Prohibition of Chemical Weapons.[188] In international environmental law institutional techniques for addressing non-compliance reflect the management model extolled by Chayes and Chayes.[189] The Vienna Convention for the

Agreements between States and the IAEA for the Application of Safeguards, 1 September 1997, INFCIRC/540 (Corr.).

184 *Chemical Weapons Convention*, 3 September 1992, article IX, para. 8, www.opcw.org/chemical-weapons-convention/.

185 *Ibid.*

186 UN SC Resolution 687, 3 April 1991, para. 9; UN SC Resolution 1441, 8 November 2002, para. 5.

187 For differences and similarities between the approaches of the various financial institutions see Bissell, Richard E. and Nanwani, Suresh 2009. 'Multilateral Development Bank Accountability Mechanisms: Developments and Challenges', *Manchester Journal of International Economic Law* 6: 2–55.

188 Established under the *Chemical Weapons Convention*, *op. cit.*, article VIII.

189 Fitzmaurice, Malgosia and Redgwell, Catherine 2000. 'Environmental Non-Compliance Procedures and International Law', *Netherlands Yearbook of International Law* 31: 35–65.

Protection of the Ozone Layer (1986) and the 1987 Montreal Protocol[190] were innovative in their introduction of processes involving all state parties to determine and respond to non-compliance in ways that have not been taken up in human rights or IHL treaties.[191] Inter-state complaints mechanisms are yet another cross-cutting device, under specific human rights[192] or other treaties,[193] or under the Charter with respect to the maintenance of international peace and security.[194]

3.5 Conclusion: Continuing Questions

In this chapter we have argued that international law is a discourse or medium through which states and increasingly global civil society manage their relations. As a formal set of rules and procedures, the effectiveness of international law depends by and large on the acceptance of the utility of those rules and procedures. This acceptance may derive from self-interest, for example, membership in international fora and reciprocity, as well as a belief in shared norms. The different interpretations of international law associated with our models are an expression of divergent views as to the normative standards.

The array of processes and mechanisms for enforcement of international law are significant not necessarily in compelling enforcement, but in upholding the norms and 'shared understandings' that underpin the law. It may be, for example, that more coercive instruments such as sanctions or conditionality clauses attached to trade agreements produce a counter-reaction, while monitoring, reporting and membership in institutions contribute to an increasingly thick discourse about what

[190] *Montreal Protocol on Substances that Deplete the Ozone Layer*, 16 September 1987.

[191] There is a large literature on compliance with international environmental law; see Bodansky, Daniel and Brunnee, Jutta and Hey, Ellen (eds.) 2007. *The Oxford Handbook of International Environmental Law*. Oxford University Press.

[192] The right of inter-state complaint is provided for in certain UN human rights treaties, e.g. the ICCPR, *op. cit.*, article 41. It has never been activated in the UN human rights treaty system but has been activated under the ECHR, *op. cit.*, article 33.

[193] E.g., the *Convention on the Prohibition of the Development, Production and Stockpiling of Bacteriological (Biological) and Toxin Weapons and on Their Destruction* 10 April 1972 (*Biological Weapons Convention*), allows any state party that considers another state party to be acting in violation of the Convention to bring a complaint to the SC; the Board of Governors of the IAEA shall report non-compliance with the Statute of the IAEA determined by inspectors to the SC and General Assembly.

[194] E.g., any state can bring a dispute or situation to the SC 'which might lead to international friction'; UN Charter, article 34, 35.

constitutes the law. Despite the array of techniques now garnered to induce compliance or redress non-compliance, compliance and enforcement of international norms still rest upon attitudes towards law and the social/political/economic benefits of conformity with law, as well as on political will and the willingness to invest resources in institutions and mechanisms. Methods such as the world-travelling notion advanced by Isabelle Gunning[195] or the cross-cultural dialogue advocated by Abdullah An-Naim[196] that rest on mutual communication in an attempt to achieve understandings of the root problems may in the long term be more effective than coercion. However, resistance to participating in such dialogue may negate such optimism.

In terms of our models of security, we have argued that the legal discourse that is the expression of each model reflects the combination of actors or 'communities of practice'; different combinations of compliance techniques are an expression of different versions of international law inherent in the different models of security. They uphold different combinations of 'shared understandings'. Thus in the Geo-Political and War on Terror models the primary actors remain those states with a 'Great Power' mentality that are more likely to utilise 'outside' techniques, namely, coercive measures applied in what are often instrumental ways. For the Liberal Peace and Responsibility to Protect models, the primary actors are international institutions and multilateralist states; for them institutionalisation is of central significance. In the Human Security model, civil society actors are more salient, which is one reason why judicialisation, the typical 'inside' technique, is more important.

International law has its 'dark side';[197] it entrenches power differentials, it legitimates violence and it can be used as a cover both for the defence of the *status quo* and for various forms of oppression. Legalisation allows for behaviour that does not fall foul of its prohibitions – manipulation of facts and manipulation of law, for

[195] Gunning, Isabelle 1991–1992. 'Arrogant Perception, World Travelling and Multicultural Feminism: The Case of Female Genital Surgeries', *Columbia Human Rights Law Review* 23: 189–248.

[196] An-Na'im, Abdullahi Ahmed 1995. 'State Responsibility to Change Religious and Customary Laws', in Cook, Rebecca (ed.) 1995. *Human Rights of Women: National and International Perspectives*. University of Pennsylvania Press, chapter 7, 178–181.

[197] Kennedy, David 2005. *The Dark Sides of Virtue: Reassessing International Humanitarianism*. Princeton University Press.

instance, of the definition of torture,[198] in order to deny that status to such acts as water-boarding.[199]

In the immediate aftermath of the Cold War international law increasingly became part of a wider public debate at least in liberal states and within civil society, and this created pressures for restraining its darker side and for promoting human rights. At the state level it seemed possible before 9/11 to identify a trend towards a greater role for human rights – in the growing importance of legislation in relation to individual rights, in the construction of international institutions in which human rights are central, in the proliferation of mechanisms for compliance with human rights as well as in the growing share of international judicial instruments relating to human rights. It is this combination of rules and processes that has been described as 'humanity's law'.[200] The reversion to Geo-Politics and the development of the War on Terror model in the twenty-first century seems to have revived the dark side.

Nevertheless, the very existence of international law as a discourse of empowerment through which the most vulnerable can in principle participate offers the possibility of resistance, as illustrated by the use of social media, for instance, to bear witness to human rights violations and abusive power, to promote solidarity and to gather evidence.[201] By unpacking the ways in which this discourse is interpreted in the law relating to the international use of force in the following chapters, we hope to be able to identify openings for different understandings.

198 *UN Convention against Torture and Other Cruel, Inhuman or Degrading Treatment or Punishment*, 10 December 1984, article 1.

199 Sands, Philippe 2008. *Torture Team: Deception, Cruelty and the Compromise of Law*. Allen Lane; Cole, David 2009. *Torture Memos: Rationalizing the Unthinkable*. New Press.

200 Teitel, Ruti 2011. *Humanity's Law*. Oxford University Press.

201 Public debate, of course, also gives rise to other types of pressure, for example, nationalism and anti-migrant views.

PART II

Jus ad Bellum

4

Self-Defence as a Justification for War: The Geo-Political and War on Terror Models

4.1 Introduction

Article 2 (4) of the United Nations Charter prohibits the threat or use of force in international relations, a prohibition that is accepted as customary international law.[1] However, at the San Francisco Conference (1945) middle-level states were unwilling to give up their 'inherent' right to use force in self-defence. Article 51 of the Charter therefore allows a short-term limitation[2] to article 2 (4) whereby a state may have recourse to individual or collective self-defence 'if an armed attack occurs . . . until the Security Council has taken measures necessary to maintain international peace and security'. The affirmation of a right to self-defence undermines the absolute nature of the prohibition against unauthorised use of force in article 2 (4). Unsurprisingly, therefore, states have sought to bring almost any unilateral use of force within the legal ambit of self-defence, so much so that as early as 1970 Professor Franck famously asked: 'Who killed article 2 (4)?'[3] In the twenty-first century, article 2(4) is widely understood as being in a state of 'grave weakness', even 'on the brink of clinical death or in intensive care'.[4]

[1] In the *Nicaragua* case neither party challenged the customary international law status of UN Charter, article 2(4); *Military and Paramilitary Activities in and against Nicaragua (Nicaragua v. United States of America)*, (Merits) 1986 ICJ Reports 14, judgment of 27 June 1986, para. 188 (*'Nicaragua'*). For an overview of contemporary international law relating to the use of force see Crawford, James 2012. *Brownlie's Principles of Public International Law*, Oxford University Press, 8th ed., chapter 33.

[2] Jean D'Aspremont notes that UN Charter, article 51 does not derogate from article 2(4) but imposes a temporary limitation upon it; D'Aspremont, Jean 2014. Mapping the Concepts behind the Contemporary Liberalization of the Use of Force in International Law, *University of Pennsylvania Journal of International Law* 31: 1089–1149.

[3] Franck, Thomas 1970. 'Who Killed Article 2(4)? or: Changing Norms Governing the Use of Force by States', *American Journal of International Law* 64: 809–837. For a reply to this question see Henkin, Louis 1971. 'Editorial Comment, The Reports of the Death of Article 2(4) Are Greatly Exaggerated', *American Journal of International Law* 65: 544–547.

[4] D'Aspremont, *op. cit.*

The self-defence exception has taken on a new significance by its use to justify the unilateral use of force by states, notably by the United States in the 'War on Terror' and by Russia in its military operations in Georgia, Crimea and Ukraine. The former embodies a war of global reach. While President Obama dropped the terminology of War on Terror and embraced collective action more than his predecessor, he continued a 'global campaign to degrade and ultimately defeat [IS] in Iraq and Syria, including by working to disrupt the flow of foreign fighters to those countries, while keeping pressure on Al Qaeda,[5] through military (and other) means. The latter reverts to claims relating to territorial spheres of influence, that is, military actions in the territories of the defunct Soviet Union.

To justify this deterritorialised war 'of global reach' and the reversion to claims of self-defence common throughout the Cold War, the notion of self-defence has been increasingly stretched and adapted through broad interpretations about what counts as an armed attack by and against whom, and what is meant by imminence, necessity and proportionality. Through such interpretations, the concept of self-defence has been used, on the one hand, to justify the US-led wars in Afghanistan and Iraq as well as the continuing drone campaign and, on the other, Russian military operations in Georgia and the Ukraine. In addition, armed conflicts in Syria since 2012[6] and Iraq since 2014 have raised other questions around the meaning and scope of the right to self-defence, which remain unresolved.

The legal status of such claimed exceptions to the prohibition of the use of force remains uncertain as state practice is often inconclusive and continues to be driven by political as well as legal considerations. What is striking is that claims made by the liberal democracies for a more elastic interpretation of the permissibility of the use of force are echoed by powerful, non-liberal states.[7] The same is true of theorists from both realist and liberal traditions who make an intellectual case for the liberalisation of the use of force and its implications.[8] This chapter discusses these tensions in the contemporary law of self-defence. It examines how the traditional realist-based model of self-defence (defence of the state against armed attack by other states) has shifted through new or revised

[5] US National Security Strategy, 2015.

[6] For different views as to when armed conflict in Syria commenced see Chapter 6.

[7] Krisch, Nico 2014. 'Crimea and the Limits of International Law', *EJIL Talk*, 10 March 2014, www.ejiltalk.org/crimea-and-the-limits-of-international-law/.

[8] D'Aspremont, *op. cit.*

claimed legal justifications for the use of force, including both the War on Terror model of security and the Geo-Political model.[9] President Obama has assumed the methods of war in continuing what he describes as '[o]ur systematic effort to dismantle terrorist organizations'.[10] Simultaneously with extended – 'perverted'[11] – claims for self-defence both in the case of Russian actions in neighbouring states and in the War on Terror, other justifications for the use of force are put forward, in particular those relying on humanitarian arguments, thereby causing the blurring of the models. Nevertheless we discuss arguments arising from the realist Geo-Political and War on Terror models in this chapter, and those more explicitly relating to the humanitarian model in the following chapter.

This chapter starts with a brief overview of the evolution of the concept of self-defence. We then analyse the conditions for self-defence and how they have been stretched as a justification for recent wars.[12] In the final section, drawing on the work of David Rodin,[13] we discuss how self-defence might be reinterpreted so as to strengthen the prohibition on war and enhance human security. Self-defence is premised on the idea that the state is a subject analogous to the individual human being. We suggest that such an analogy is misleading, especially in the context of transnational inter-connection and communication, and that it is better to interpret the state as a collectivity of individual human beings. If this is the case, an armed attack can be reconceptualised as a massive violation of human rights – the response to such an attack then raises similar questions as in the case of humanitarian intervention.

4.2 Background: From Just War to the UN Charter

Before the UN Charter made the *jus ad bellum* universally applicable, justifications for going to war were more developed in the Western tradition than in other traditions.[14] Richard Sorabji says that in most

[9] Crook, John R. (ed.) 2013. 'President Obama Outlines Shifts in U.S. Counterterrorism Policy', *American Journal of International Law* 107: 674–679.

[10] *Ibid.* [11] D'Aspremont, *op. cit.*, 1116.

[12] The chapter does not address the application of self-defence to incidents of cyber warfare, although we recognise that such forms of warfare may entail violent consequences for populations. On the principles of the *jus ad bellum* relating to cyber warfare see Schmitt, Michael 2013. *Tallinn Manual on the International Law Applicable to Cyber Warfare*. Cambridge University Press.

[13] Rodin, David 2002. *War and Self-Defense*. Clarendon Press.

[14] In his dissenting opinion in the *Legality of the Threat or Use of Nuclear Weapons*, 1996 ICJ Reports 226, advisory opinion of 8 July 1996 (*'Nuclear Weapons'*), Judge

other traditions, much more emphasis is placed on the *jus in bello*, the means used to fight wars, although, as discussed in Chapter 2, right authority is critical in all traditions.[15] Saint Augustine of Hippo[16] is generally considered the father of the institution of just war in the Western tradition.[17] He believed a just war was about redressing harm or avenging an injury. It was a reactive doctrine with the goals of peace, law enforcement and the restoration of order. There was, however, an important difference between a punitive approach, which was adopted by many medieval and later Western scholars, for instance, Grotius, and a defensive approach, which was more common in the Byzantine Empire. The latter was more limited and excluded the eradication of the enemy.[18] Drawing on the Western tradition, contemporary scholars typically point to five *ad bellum* criteria for a war to be considered just: just cause, last resort, right authority, proportionality (that the war does not cause more harms than the good achieved by victory) and reasonable prospect of success. Some authors also add right intention and the goal of peace.[19]

The notion of going to war to bring about religious conversion, which was prevalent in the early period of Islam and in the medieval period in Western Europe, was largely dismissed once authority passed from religious to secular authorities. In the eighteenth and nineteenth centuries, the influence of just war thinking lessened and war as an institution was

Weeramantry considered the example of Buddhism: 'According to Buddhism there is nothing that can be called a "just war" – which is only a false term coined and put into circulation to justify and excuse hatred, cruelty, violence and massacre. Who decides what is just and unjust? The mighty and the victorious are "just", and the weak and the defeated are "unjust". Our war is always "just" and your war is always "unjust". Buddhism does not accept this position'; *Nuclear Weapons* case (per dissenting opinion of Judge Weeramantry, para. 481), citing Rahula, Walpola 1959. *What the Buddha Taught*. One World Publications, 84.

15 Sorabji, Richard 2006. 'Just War from Its Ancient Origins to the Conquistadors Debate and Its Modern Relevance', in Sorabji, Richard and Rodin, David (eds.) *The Ethics of War: Shared Problems in Different Traditions*. Ashgate Publishing, chapter 1.

16 Prior to the conversion of the Emperor Constantine to Christianity, Christians were pacifist. It was St. Augustine, who lived during that period, who originated the justifications for war in Christianity.

17 For a defence of 'just war' as a long-standing Christian tradition made by a contemporary 'Augustinian Christian' see Biggar, Nigel 2013. *In Defence of War*. Oxford University Press.

18 See Laiou, Angeliki 2006. 'The Just War of Eastern Christians and the Holy War of the Crusaders', in Sorabji and Rodin (eds.) *op. cit.*, 30–43.

19 Johnson, James Turner 1981. *Just War Tradition and the Restraint of War: A Moral and Historical Inquiry*. Princeton University Press.

'largely cut off from its natural-law roots'.[20] Just cause was increasingly reduced to *raison d'état* in Europe; war came to be regarded 'as a means – and a highly imperfect one at that – of settling disputes between two [or more] sovereigns who recognised no common judge'[21] and recourse to force was seen as a tool in the political rivalries of nineteenth-century Europe.[22] But by the mid-twentieth century, as the physical and human costs of wars mounted, the dominant justifications came to be focussed on defensive wars against aggression, even though there was always a significant stream of thought concerned with what we call nowadays humanitarian intervention, as discussed in Chapter 5.

While war was recognised as a legal instrument of state politics, self-defence was of little legal significance: in the nineteenth century it had only 'a shadowy and peripheral role'.[23] However, in order to avoid the constraints of the legal state of (declared) 'war', such as rules appertaining to neutrality, states claimed their coercive actions to fall within other legal categories, for instance, a reprisal ('an act of war taking place in time of peace' and thus law enforcement)[24] or actions taken of necessity. In this regard the incident that became the classic exposition of the criteria for legally justified self-defence was not perceived as occurring during a war and was thus technically irrelevant to the laws of war. The facts of the *Caroline* case[25] arose during a rebellion in Canada in 1837. Rebels (i.e., non-state actors) attacked British ships as they sailed through Canadian waters. The *Caroline* was an American ship carrying supplies for the rebels. The British responded by seizing the *Caroline* from American waters and sending her over Niagara Falls, with loss of life. In determining the legality of the British actions, diplomatic correspondence followed between the Americans and British. For the former, Secretary of State Webster asserted that 'to show a necessity of self-defence, [action must be] instant, overwhelming, leaving no choice of means, and no moment for deliberation'. The British concurred with this formulation and necessity and instantaneous action

[20] Neff, Stephen C. 2005. *War and the Law of Nations: A General History*. Cambridge University Press, 167.

[21] Bugnion, François 2002. 'Just Wars, Wars of Aggression and International Humanitarian Law', *International Review of the Red Cross* 84 (847): 523–546.

[22] Neff, *op. cit.* [23] *Ibid.*, 241. [24] *Ibid.*

[25] Exchange of letters between US Secretary of State Daniel Webster and Lord Ashburton, Foreign Secretary of Great Britain, relating to the case of the *SS Caroline*, 1837 ('*Caroline*').

subsequently became accepted as the defining customary international law criteria for self-defence.

Although some states had reserved the right to self-defence under the Kellogg-Briand Pact,[26] self-defence took on a greater legal significance when, as previously discussed, the founders of the United Nations, who aimed 'to save succeeding generations from the scourge of war',[27] agreed on the self-defence limitation. Although there is some resonance with the earlier concept of just war, the legality of the use of force in contemporary international law does not depend upon the justness of the cause, but on whether it is a purely defensive response to aggression.

As self-defence is the only exception to the prohibition of the use of force other than UN Security Council (SC) authorisation under UN Charter, chapter VII, it is unsurprising that states argue that particular exercises of force fall within the exception, thereby seeking to expand the meaning of the wording of article 51 and the scope of legal coercive action. It is equally unsurprising that such claims are resisted by other states. Thus there are a number of controversies and a lack of clarity over the scope of both article 2 (4) and the self-defence exception. Claims and counter-claims are bolstered through differing theoretical approaches to international law. Some prefer a positivist approach, arguing that states are bound only by what they have agreed to – to the precise wording of the UN Charter or by what can be proved to constitute a principle of customary international law.[28] This approach warrants a restrictive interpretation of both articles. Others favour a purposive, policy-oriented interpretation of the Charter. In their view the Charter was drafted in a different era, and the changed

[26] *Treaty between the United States and Other Powers Providing for the Renunciation of War as an Instrument of National Policy,* Paris, 27 August 1928, ('Kellogg-Briand Pact'). Secretary Kellogg proclaimed that 'It seemed to [him] incomprehensible that anybody could say that any nation would sign a treaty which could be construed as taking away the right of self-defense if a country was attacked. That is an inherent right of every sovereign, as it is of every individual, and it is implicit in every treaty'. Hearings Before the Committee on Foreign Relations United States Senate Seventieth Congress on The General Pact for the Renunciation of War signed at Paris August 27, 1928, 7 and 11 December, 1928. See Crawford, James 2012. *Brownlie's Principles of Public International Law.* Oxford University Press, 8th ed.

[27] UN Charter, preamble.

[28] The ICJ has held that there is a 'natural' or 'inherent' right of self-defence of a customary nature, 'even if its present content has been confirmed and influenced by the Charter'. This customary right exists independently of the UN Charter and the substantive rules are not identical in content. *Nicaragua, op. cit.*, paras. 175–177.

nature of conflict (notably the threat of nuclear confrontation and contemporary threats of terrorist attacks) and development of other rules of international law mean that its provisions should not be understood literally. A constitutional instrument, such as the UN Charter, was never intended to be a 'suicide pact'.[29] They argue that an expansive interpretation, coupled with a generous assumption of evolving custom, would allow force to be legally used in response to modern challenges and threats to security.

In the absence of any compulsory, authoritative arbiter of the situation, whether particular incidents of the use of force can be understood as coming within the self-defence limitation – and thus potentially contributing to changing meanings of the concept – largely rests upon the response of other states, including as recorded in (political) resolutions of the SC or General Assembly (GA). In addition, the International Court of Justice (ICJ) has given some guidance on how the right of self-defence should be construed. However, the scope of the right to self-defence, while evolving, remains contested. Some of the controversial aspects are discussed below.[30]

4.3 Conditions for Self-Defence

UN Charter, article 51 sets out the conditions for a claim of self-defence:

> Nothing in the present Charter shall impair the inherent right of individual or collective self-defence if an armed attack occurs against a Member of the United Nations, until the Security Council has taken measures necessary to maintain international peace and security. Measures taken by Members in the exercise of this right of self-defence shall be immediately reported to the Security Council and shall not in any way affect the authority and responsibility of the Security Council under the present Charter to take at any time such action as it deems necessary in order to maintain or restore international peace and security.

[29] Reisman, Michael 2000. 'Unilateral Action and the Transformations of the World Constitutive Process: The Special Problem of Humanitarian Intervention', *European Journal of International Law* 11: 3–18; Reisman, Michael 1993. 'The Constitutional Crisis in the United Nations', *American Journal of International Law* 87: 83–100, 89. For a critical view of Reisman's argument see Hathaway, James C. 2000. 'America, Defender of Democratic Legitimacy?' *European Journal of International Law* 11: 121–134, 126–127.

[30] For a full discussion see Gray, Christine 2008. *International Law and the Use of Force*. Oxford University Press, 3rd ed., chapter 4.

Article 51 shifts the decision to use force from the collectivity (the SC) to the individual state; by so doing, in line with many writers from Grotius onwards, it 'embeds a model of sovereignty drawn from the interpersonal self-defence rights'.[31] This analogy with domestic law is seen as fundamental to the international legal order of sovereign states. In the words of Michael Walzer:

> Our primary perceptions and judgments of aggression are the products of analogical reasoning. When the analogy is made explicit, as it is among lawyers, the world of states takes the shape of a political society the characterisation of which is entirely accessible through such notions as crime and punishment, self-defense, enforcement and so on.[32]

It is worth noting that common law notions of self-defence have gendered connotations. Making the analogy of the state with the individual and of self-defence as expressed in article 51 of the Charter with common law notions of self-defence reproduces the way in which the latter is biased towards the male subject of law.[33] The focus on a single act of aggression (armed attack) 'replicates the public, one-off and aggressive nature of attacks envisaged in inter-personal relations' to which violence in self-defence is a justifiable response. Accordingly, 'through the explicit linkage with the legal features of interpersonal self-defence, Article 51 is given a sexed meaning that draws on Western canons of masculinity to define danger, violence and aggression'.[34]

4.3.1 *'If an Armed Attack Occurs . . .'*

At the time of the adoption of the Charter, in light of the experience of World War II, the main threat to international peace and security was envisaged as a threat of armed attack by one state against another state. Accordingly, self-defence is provided for 'if an armed attack occurs'.[35] This does not correlate precisely with article 2(4), which prohibits 'the threat or use of force', indicating that some such

[31] Heathcote, Gina 2012. *The Law on the Use of Force: A Feminist Analysis*. Routledge, 79.

[32] Walzer, Michael 2006. *Just and Unjust Wars*. Basic Books, 4th ed., 58, cited in Heathcote, *op. cit.*, 80.

[33] Charlesworth, Hilary and Chinkin, Christine 2000. *The Boundaries of International Law: A Feminist Analysis*. Manchester University Press, chapter 5.

[34] Heathcote, *op. cit.*, 79.

[35] This is provided for under UN Charter, article 51 and customary international law; see *Oil Platforms (Islamic Republic of Iran v. United States of America)*, 2003 ICJ Reports, judgment of 6 November 2003, para. 51 ('*Oil Platforms*').

incidents may not justify force in self-defence. Nor is it configured in the same terms as the trigger for SC response under chapter VII of the Charter: 'breach of the peace, threat to the peace or act of aggression'.[36] Nevertheless armed force that cannot be justified as self-defence may constitute aggression.[37] The first question is therefore what constitutes an armed attack. Unlike aggression, there has been no negotiated definition. Authorities suggest that 'to be deemed an armed attack, an operation must have a minimum "scale and effects"'.[38] In the *Oil Platforms* case the ICJ stated the need to distinguish 'the most grave forms of the use of force (those constituting an armed attack) from other less grave forms'.[39] While there must be cross-border forcible action to constitute an armed attack, minor localised border skirmishes are unlikely to be accepted as such, even if they involve loss of life,[40] although 'a cumulative series of minor attacks may constitute an armed attack'.[41] A consequence of excluding small-scale violence from the concept of 'armed attack' is to rule out the right to self-defence and to minimise the threat of escalation of violence; contrariwise it has been argued that so doing is 'conceptually confused, inconsistent with customary practice and undesirable as a matter of policy. ... The better view is that any deliberate projection of lethal force onto the territory of another state ... will normally trigger the application of Article 2(4)'.[42]

Events in the Crimea in 2014 raise the question whether of an armed attack has occurred where there is an undoubted military presence but no use of direct force. Russian troops were legally present in the Crimea in accordance with the terms of a 1997 Treaty (extended

[36] UN Charter, article 39.

[37] UN GA Resolution 3314 (XXIX), Definition of Aggression; International Criminal Court, Review Conference, RC/Res.6; The crime of aggression, adopted at the 13th plenary meeting, Kampala, 11 June 2010. An 'understanding' adopted at the Kampala Conference confirmed the definition of aggression adopted there was 'for the purpose of the [Rome] Statute only'. This was intended to ensure that the crime of aggression and aggression under the *jus ad bellum* remained distinct.

[38] Council of the EU, Report of the Independent International Fact-Finding Mission on the Conflict in Georgia ('Report on Georgia'), 30 September 2009, vol. 2, 245, www.ceiig.ch/Report.html.

[39] *Oil Platforms*, *op. cit.*, para. 51.

[40] Eritrea-Ethiopia Claims Commission, Partial Award on the *Jus ad Bellum*: Ethiopia's Claims 1-8,19 December 2005, paras. 11–12.

[41] *Oil Platforms*, *op. cit.*, para. 62.

[42] Tom, Ruys 2014. 'The Meaning of "Force" and the Boundaries of the Jus ad Bellum: Are "Minimal" Uses of Force excluded from UN Charter Article 2(4)?' *American Journal of International Law* 108: 159–210.

in 2010) agreed between Russia and Ukraine.[43] But the Treaty imposed restrictions on those foreign troops; major troop movements required prior consultation, and numbers could not be unilaterally increased. Russia did not comply with these terms. The 1974 GA definition of aggression provides that '[t]he use of armed forces of one State which are within the territory of another State with the agreement of the receiving State, in contravention of the conditions provided for in the agreement' qualifies as an act of aggression. But, as stated earlier, not every act of aggression constitutes an armed attack, triggering the right to self-defence; is it an armed attack when no shot has been fired? The indisputable show of considerable force made possible the referendum providing for Crimea's secession from Ukraine,[44] which ensured that the 'scale and effects' of the action were grave: annexation of the territory of a sovereign state.[45] As has been pertinently pointed out, the implications for the UN Charter if these events did not constitute an armed attack would be that 'Ukraine could not lawfully use force against Russian troops to protect territory that undisputedly is part of Ukraine'[46] The affair seemed rife with Cold War assumptions about the use of force by a regional hegemon in its own backyard.[47] On the other hand, the presence of the Russian military did involve violations of human rights on a considerable scale: this included holding a referendum without proper procedures and under military pressure; discrimination against ethnic Ukrainians and Crimean Tartars; infringement of property rights; and control over

[43] *Partition Treaty on the Status and Conditions of the Black Sea Fleet*, 28 May 1997. The Treaty was denounced by the State Duma in March 2014 during the Crimean crisis: 'Putin Submits Proposals on Denouncing Some Russia-Ukraine Agreements on Black Sea Fleet', *ITAR-TASS News*, 28 March 2014, http://tass.ru/en/russia/725725.

[44] On the issue of the secession of Crimea from Ukraine see Kress, Claus 2014. 'Major Post-Westphalian Shifts and Some Important Neo-Westphalian Hesitations in the State Practice on the International Law on the Use of Force', *Journal on the Use of Force and International Law* 1: 11–54, 38; Marxsen, Christian, 'Crimea's Declaration of Independence', *EJIL Talk*, 18 March 2014, www.ejiltalk.org/crimeas-declaration-of-independence/.

[45] UN GA Resolution 25/2625, 24 October 1970, Declaration on Principles of International Law Concerning Friendly Relations and Co-operation among States in Accordance with the Charter of the United Nations, provides that 'No territorial acquisition resulting from the threat or use of force shall be recognized as legal'. It is argued that the hastily conducted referendum does not change this situation.

[46] Deeks, Ashley. 'Here's What International Law Says about Russia's Intervention in Ukraine', *New Republic*, 2 March 2014, www.newrepublic.com/article/116819/international-law-russias-ukraine-intervention.

[47] Krisch, *op. cit.*

media and information.[48]Indeed, it could be argued that the debate about whether the annexation of Crimea constituted an armed attack obscured the more important practical debate about how to respond to violations of human rights.

In other scenarios the ICJ has been reluctant to recognise all forms of even coercive intervention by a state into another state as an armed attack. In the *Nicaragua* case the Court found that sending armed bands into the territory of another state could constitute an armed attack if it was of sufficient scale and effects. Assisting rebel forces (e.g., through the provision of weapons or logistical support) is not in the opinion of the Court an armed attack,[49] although it may constitute a threat or use of force, or illegal intervention. In the Court's view the appropriate legal response to wrongful intervention is not military force in self-defence but the imposition of non-forcible counter-measures. However, these may be practically impossible for a weaker state to impose against a more powerful one[50] in the same way as power disparities in gender relations may make it impossible for the weaker party (usually the woman) to seek sanctions against perpetrators of violence. This approach allows for instability and insecurity in the target state and the wider region, as experienced in the conflicts in Central America in the 1980s and demonstrated by the *Nicaragua* case.

4.3.2 Collective Self-Defence, Consent and Invitation

A further complexity is added where the armed attack is against a state other than the one responding, that is, where states A and B seek to react in self-defence to an attack on C, even though they have neither suffered nor anticipate any attack against themselves. The attacked state, C, has the right to collective self-defence, to seek assistance from

[48] See, for example, 'Rights in Retreat: Abuses in Crimea', *Human Rights Watch,* 17 November 2014, www.hrw.org/report/2014/11/17/rights-retreat/abuses-crimea; 'Report on the Human Rights Situation in Ukraine', *UN Office of the High Commissioner for Human Rights*, 14 May 2015, www.ohchr.org/Documents/Countries/UA/10thOHCHRreportUkraine.pdf.

[49] On the legality of providing arms to rebels against oppressive regimes see 'Aggression and the Use of Force in International Law', Proceedings of the Annual Meeting of the American Society of International Law, vol. 108 (2014).

[50] *Nicaragua, op. cit*, para. 195; on non-forcible counter-measures see International Law Commission, *op. cit.*, articles 49–54 ('Responsibility of States for Internationally Wrongful Acts').

other states, as Kuwait did following the invasion by Iraq in 1990. In Resolution 678 (29 November 1990) the SC authorised 'States cooperating with the Government of Kuwait ... to use all necessary means' against Iraq.[51] Kuwait's right of collective self-defence meant that this authorisation was not strictly necessary. Nevertheless, SC approval added legitimacy to the collective military action against Iraq and provided the opportunity for the invocation of Council powers under UN Charter, chapter VII in the changed political environment of 1990, giving rise to the optimism of a New (post–Cold War) World Order.

Defensive alliances have long been part of the European landscape and were instrumental in the advance to war in 1914[52] and 1939. Part of the Cold War landscape was the conclusion of collective self-defence arrangements committing states to respond to an attack on one of their members, such as NATO,[53] SEATO[54] and ANZUS[55] (all protecting the security of US allies against possible communist attack) and the Warsaw Pact,[56] with membership of the Eastern European states. The Gulf Cooperation Council Peninsula Shield Force was formed towards the end of the Cold War in 1984 in light of the regional instability engendered by the Iran-Iraq war, which broke out in 1980. Some collective self-defence institutions have disappeared (Warsaw Pact), while others have changed their role (NATO acting in the name of humanitarianism in 1999 with the concerns for human security expressed in Chapter 5).

Despite this network of alliances, the right of collective self-defence has been little used in practice, as states tend to avoid military participation in conflicts between other states.[57] This hesitation is perhaps indicative of some unease with the concept of collective self-defence, which moves away from the domestic law analogy and is thus less readily embraced. Only in exceptional circumstances under domestic law can a person justify the use of force in response to an attack on another person, and the recognised collective response is through law enforcement agencies. However, the concept of collective institutional action (or 'solidarity') has re-emerged in the context of counter-terrorism. NATO invoked article 5

[51] UN SC Resolution 678, 29 November 1990 (on Iraq-Kuwait).
[52] MacMillan, Margaret 2013. *The War That Ended Peace: The Road to 1914*. Profile Books.
[53] *North Atlantic Treaty*, Washington, D.C., 4 April 1949.
[54] *Southeast Asia Collective Defense Treaty*, Manila, 8 September 1954.
[55] *Australia, New Zealand, United States Security Treaty*, San Francisco, 1 September 1951.
[56] *Treaty of Friendship, Co-operation, and Mutual Assistance*, Warsaw, 14 May 1955.
[57] Gray, *op. cit*, 167.

of the North Atlantic Treaty[58] for the only time in the wake of the terrorist attacks of 11 September 2011;[59] article 222 of the Treaty on the Functioning of the European Union (2010) provides for joint action if a Member State is the object of a terrorist attack;[60] and during the so-called 'Arab Spring' the Peninsula Shield force was invoked by Bahrain in response to internal riots and protests. Formal collective defence institutions have been supplemented by more informal coalitions, such as the coalition of the willing against Afghanistan in 2001[61] and the coalition of states fighting against IS since 2014. The *ad hoc* formation of a coalition of willing states has been described as the 'antithesis of the maintenance of order by the international community'.[62] It dispenses with the need for SC authorisation while claiming the legitimacy associated with multilateralism.

There are also concerns about the potential misuse of the right to collective self-defence. A state might launch an attack against another, purporting to be acting in collective self-defence of that state against an anticipated attack by another state. The case brought by Nicaragua in 1984 against the United States in the ICJ arose out of the widespread violence in Central America in the 1980s, in the Cold War context. The United States claimed that its military actions against Nicaragua were in

[58] *The North Atlantic Treaty*, *op. cit.*, article 5: 'The Parties agree that an armed attack against one or more of them ... shall be considered an attack against them all and consequently they agree that, if such an armed attack occurs, each of them, in exercise of the right of individual or collective self-defence recognised by Article 51 of the Charter of the United Nations, will assist the Party or Parties so attacked by taking forthwith, individually and in concert with the other Parties, such action as it deems necessary, including the use of armed force, to restore and maintain the security of the North Atlantic area'.

[59] UN SC Resolution 1368, 12 September 2001 and UN SC Resolution 1373, 28 September 2001 adopted in response to the 9/11 terrorist attacks reaffirmed the 'inherent right of individual or collective self-defence' but did not explicitly authorise the use of force as had been the case with UN SC Resolution 678, 29 November 1990, with respect to Kuwait.

[60] Article 222 provides that 'The Union and its Member States shall act jointly in a spirit of solidarity if a Member State is the object of a terrorist attack or the victim of a natural or man-made disaster. The Union shall mobilise all the instruments at its disposal, including the military resources made available by the Member States, to: (a) prevent the terrorist threat in the territory of the Member States; protect democratic institutions and the civilian population from any terrorist attack; assist a Member State in its territory, at the request of its political authorities, in the event of a terrorist attack'.

[61] The United States did not draw upon NATO's invocation of article 5 and the ensuing attack on Afghanistan was not carried out under NATO's auspices but by a 'coalition of the willing' brought together by the United States.

[62] D'Aspremont, *op. cit.*, 1147.

collective self-defence of El Salvador, which was subject to armed attack by the Sandanista (left-wing) government in Nicaragua. The ICJ took a restrictive approach, which it reaffirmed in the *Oil Platforms* case, and determined that there are two conditions to the exercise of the right to collective self-defence: the victim state must declare that it has been attacked and must request assistance.[63] While this provides protection against wrongful claims of self-defence, especially for weaker states, it may delay assistance in an appropriate case until too late.

In 2014 the 'newly formed' Government of Iraq[64] sought the assistance of the United States in resisting violent armed attacks by the forces of IS.[65] IS forces had come from Syria[66] and had succeeded in occupying considerable areas across Iraq and Syria, thereby effectively dismantling the border between the two states. Iraq's request to the United States 'to lead international efforts to strike IS sites ... with our express consent'[67] is a widely accepted example of collective self-defence, which accords with the conditions stipulated by the ICJ (even though the issue of whether self-defence can be claimed against non-state actors as discussed below has hardly been raised). At an International Conference on Peace and Security in Iraq in September 2014, participants[68] determined that IS constitutes a threat to the international community and underscored the need to remove it from

[63] *Nicaragua, op. cit.*, paras. 195–196; *Oil Platforms, op. cit.*, para. 51.

[64] Statement by the President of the Security Council, UN Doc. S/PRST/2014/20, 19 September 2014. Marc Weller argues that it is the fact of the recently held elections in Iraq that gave the government the legitimacy to seek such assistance against armed forces taking over part of its territory; Weller, Marc 2015. 'Striking ISIL: Aspects of the Law on the Use of Force', *American Society of International Law Insights* 19(5).

[65] For a full analysis of the legal issues involved see Deeks, Ashley 2012. '"Unwilling or Unable": Toward an Normative Framework for Extra-Territorial Self-Defense', *Virginia Journal of International Law* 52: 483–550; as they are applied in Syria, Arimatsu, Louise and Schmitt, Michael 2014. 'Attacking "Islamic State" and the Khorasan Group: Surveying the International Law Landscape', *Columbia Journal of Transnational Law Bulletin* 54: 1–29.

[66] As Samantha Power stated: 'Iraq has made clear that it is facing a serious threat of continuing attacks from IS coming out of safe havens in Syria'. See Letter from Samantha Power, US Ambassador to the UN, to the UN Secretary-General, Ban Ki-moon, 23 September 2014.

[67] Letter from the Permanent Representative of Iraq to the UN, 20 September 2014; UN Doc. S/2014/691, 22 September 2014.

[68] Bahrain, Belgium, Canada, China, the Czech Republic, Denmark, Egypt, France, Germany, Iraq, Italy, Japan, Jordan, Kuwait, Lebanon, the Netherlands, Norway, Oman, Qatar, Russia, Saudi Arabia, Spain, Turkey, United Arab Emirates, United Kingdom, United States of America, Arab League, EU and UN.

the regions where it had established control 'by any means necessary, including appropriate military assistance, in line with the needs expressed by the Iraqi authorities, in accordance with international law'.[69] The SC's welcoming of this Conference[70] implicitly approved the military assistance that has been provided by a number of states to Iraqi forces. In June 2015 at a ministerial meeting a 'small group of the coalition to counter Da'esh [IS]' reiterated this resolve.[71]

The United States (and some other states) have also carried out airstrikes in Syria, which had not requested such assistance. Use of force in Syria violates that state's territorial integrity and is therefore contrary to UN Charter article 2 (4), unless it can be justified. In a letter to the SC, the US ambassador to the UN, Samantha Power, asserted the inherent right of the United States to both individual and collective self-defence, since 'IS and other terrorist groups in Syria are a threat not only to Iraq, but also to many other countries, including the United States and our partners in the region and beyond'.[72] Neither IS nor 'other terrorist groups' (notably Khorasan, said by the Americans to be an 'al-Qaeda affiliated terrorist group') has launched an armed attack against the United States (although individual terror attacks may be claimed by IS), so the claim of individual self-defence must rest on questions of imminence, as discussed below. With respect to collective self-defence, the question is whether a request for assistance in self-defence by one state (Iraq) can justify the use of force in another state (Syria). Ambassador Power asserted that this was the case because the governing regime in Syria was 'unwilling or unable to prevent the use of its territory for such attacks'.[73]

The language of 'unwilling or unable' is used elsewhere in international law, for instance in the Rome Statute of the International Criminal Court (ICC) to make a case admissible although it is being investigated or prosecuted by a state with jurisdiction.[74] Although it is

[69] International Conference on Peace and Security in Iraq, Paris, 15 September 2014.

[70] Statement by the President of the Security Council, UN Doc. 2014/20, 19 September 2014. The SC also urged 'the international community, in accordance with international law to further strengthen and expand support for the Government of Iraq as it fights IS and associated armed groups'.

[71] Ministerial Meeting of the Small Group of the Global Coalition to Counter Da'esh – Declaration of the Co-Chairs, Paris, 2 June 2015 ('Ministerial Meeting').

[72] Letter from Samantha Power, *op. cit.* [73] *Ibid.*

[74] *Rome Statute of the International Criminal Court,* adopted 17 July 1998, article 17.

not self-evidently applicable to the use of force in self-defence, it appears to have been accepted by UN Secretary-General Ban Ki-moon:

> I am aware that today's strikes were not carried out at the direct request of the Syrian Government, but I note that the Government was informed beforehand. I also note that the strikes took place in areas no longer under the effective control of that Government. I think it is undeniable – and the subject of broad international consensus – that these extremist groups pose an immediate threat to international peace and security.[75]

Of course, the language of a 'threat to international peace and security' is that of SC competence to authorize force under UN Charter, chapter VII, not that for triggering self-defence under article 51. No SC action has been authorised. Marc Weller argued that it is the attack that triggers the right to self-defence against the perpetrators of the attack, but that if 'there is no actual or imminent use of force amounting to an armed attack, the doctrine of "unwilling or unable" cannot furnish a legal justification for the use of force in self-defence'. Self-defence is applicable only where an immediate armed response is needed, which 'implies that the territorial state would not forestall or terminate the imminent threat or attack – if it did, the criterion of necessity would not be met. Hence, there is no additional need to prove that the territorial state is unwilling or unable to act'. He concluded that 'the infrastructure of IS in Syria is sufficiently closely intertwined with its ongoing operations in Iraq to justify extending the application of the right to self-defense to Syria'.[76] However, this position accepts the collapse of the border between Iraq and Syria, (an illustration of the way that the 'new wars' paradigm muddies legal interpretation).[77] Further, the transference of the language of 'unwilling or unable' to justifications for the use of force in collective self-defence 'shields the state using force against terrorists from responsibility for forceful incursions on the territory of another state',[78] and this argument thus constitutes yet another reinterpretation and thus extension of the right to self-defence in the War on Terror.

Following the spate of terrorist attacks by IS, including those 'in Sousse, on 10 October 2015, in Ankara, on 31 October 2015, over Sinaï, on 12 November 2015, in Beirut and on 13 November 2015 in Paris',[79]

[75] UN Secretary General Ban Ki-moon. 'Remarks at the Climate Summit Press Conference' (including comments on Syria), *UN News Centre*, 23 September 2014, www.un.org/apps/news/infocus/sgspeeches/statments_full.asp?statID=2356#.VoAe8oeJndk.

[76] Weller, *op. cit.* [77] See Chapter 1. [78] Heathcote, *op. cit.*, 100.

[79] UN SC Resolution 2249, 20 November 2015.

the arguments in favour of military strikes in Syria as self-defence became stronger. For instance, James Stavridis, the former commander of NATO in Europe, argued that NATO should invoke article 5;[80] retaliatory airstrikes by France were described by the foreign minister, Laurent Fabius, as an act of 'self-defence';[81] David Cameron told the United Kingdom Parliament that the violence meant 'working with our allies to strike against those who pose a direct threat to the safety of British people around the world'.[82] The then prime minister argued the case for airstrikes against IS in Syria to be 'founded on the right of self-defence as it is recognised in Article 51 of the UN Charter'.[83] He asserted this to be supported by UN SC Resolution 2249 of 20 November 2015, which calls upon 'Member States that have the capacity to do so to take all necessary measures, in compliance with international law, ... on the territory under the control of ISIL also known as Da'esh, in Syria and Iraq, to redouble and coordinate their efforts to prevent and suppress terrorist acts committed specifically by ISIL'. Military action was to be carried out in conjunction with political and diplomatic efforts at settlement and humanitarian assistance. While Resolution 2249 neither directly upholds self-defence nor unequivocally authorises military action, the case for self-defence has not apparently been questioned.

Whether a request for intervention has been genuinely made and, if so, whether it has emanated from a legitimate authority within the state in question must always be context-specific. Another factor is whether the alleged attack derives from another state, or from within (but often with suggestions of external support), merging claims of self-defence with those for internal self-determination or democratic choice. During the Cold War both the United States and the Soviet Union made geo-political claims of such requests from governments seeking to shore up their power against ideologically opposed

[80] 'NATO's Turn to Attack', *Foreign Policy*, 14 November 2015.

[81] 'France launches 'massive' airstrike on Isis stronghold of Raqqa', *The Guardian*, 16 November 2015. www.theguardian.com/world/2015/nov/16/france-launches-massive-airstrike-on-isis-stronghold-in-syria-after-paris-attack.

[82] Prime Minister's statement on Paris attacks and G20 Summit, www.gov.uk/government/speeches/prime-ministers-statement-on-paris-attacks-and-g20-summit.

[83] Memorandum to the Foreign Affairs Select Committee. Prime Minister's Response to the Foreign Affairs Select Committee's Second Report of Session 2015–16: The Extension of Offensive British Military Operations to Syria, November 2015 at www.parliament.uk/documents/commons-committees/foreign-affairs/PM-Response-to-FAC-Report-Extension-of-Offensive-British-Military-Operations-to-Syria.pdf.

challenge: for instance, with respect to the Dominican Republic (1965) and Granada (1983) in the case of the United States and Hungary (1956), Czechoslovakia (1968) and Afghanistan (1979) in the case of the Soviet Union. In similar terms, in 2014 President Putin claimed that Ukrainian President Viktor Yanukovych had requested military assistance; however, it was doubtful whether he remained in a position to give a valid request.[84] Nor does international law allow a sub-state entity, such as Crimea, to seek external intervention. Putin's actions with respect to Ukraine have been made subject to sanctions by the United States and EU.[85]

The legal basis for Russia's intervention in Syria is also said to be 'intervention by invitation', even though the Russian government has not made a formal statement to this effect. However, two questions arise that militate the validity of this claim. First, can the government of Syria that is being supported by Russia be considered the legitimate authority; even though it is still the government, large parts of the country are no longer under its authority or control. Further, can a government that is committing gross violations of human rights against its own people request assistance from another government, even though the objective is ostensibly to defeat an extremist group, IS, in opposition to that government? Second, related and perhaps more importantly, Russia is violating the principle of distinction, an 'intransgressible principle'[86] of International Humanitarian Law as discussed in Chapter 6, in particular, through air strikes on hospitals and other civilian targets. The commission of war crimes falls under the *ius in bello*, but it seems that consent to intervention must be vitiated by such

84 The United States responded that '[a]fter Yanukovych fled Ukraine, even his own Party of Regions turned against him, voting to confirm his withdrawal from office and to support the new government. Ukraine's new government was approved by the democratically elected Ukrainian Parliament, ... which will shepherd the country toward democratic elections on May 25th – elections that will allow all Ukrainians to have a voice in the future of their country'. See US Department of State, 'President Putin's Fiction: 10 False Claims about Ukraine', 5 March 2014, www.state.gov/r/pa/prs/ps/2014/03/222988.htm.

85 As reported by the EU newsroom, 'The Council of the European Union on 3 March 2014 condemned the clear violation of Ukrainian sovereignty and territorial integrity by acts of aggression by the Russian armed forces as well as the authorisation given by the Federation Council of Russia on 1 March for the use of the armed forces on the territory of Ukraine'. Sanctions followed on 17 March 2014. See 'EU Sanctions against Russia over Ukraine Crisis', *European Union Newsroom*, 12 December 2014. http://europa.eu/newsroom/highlights/special-coverage/eu_sanctions/index_en.htm.

86 *Nuclear Weapons, op. cit..*, Advisory Opinion, para. 79.

acts. This raises similar issues of consent to those discussed with respect to targeted killing later in this chapter.

Despite reports of heavy civilian casualties and a humanitarian catastrophe, the military intervention by Saudi Arabia in Yemen has not been subject to sanctions by the United States or EU.[87] Saudi Arabia's actions are in response to a request from the deposed President Abd Rabbuh Mansur Hadi for external assistance in self-defence against internal uprising.[88] President Hadi acceded to power following Arab Spring uprisings in 2012 and an election where he was the only candidate; his term of office was due to expire in February 2014 but had been extended for a year without further polling.[89] His authority as the legitimate head of state and thus as able to seek assistance against internal rebellion is seen by some as debateable, although supported by the SC.[90] Saudi Arabia's military action appears to be in support of protecting its borders and maintaining a regional hegemony against Shi'ite rebels backed by Iran, echoing those Cold War interventions described above. It is backed in its military action by the Gulf Cooperation Council, thus giving it the veneer of collective action.

4.3.3 *Imminence: Anticipatory Self-Defence*

The risk of escalating violence under the cover of self-defence is theoretically limited by the legal requirements that such action be imminent, necessary and proportionate. However, determining any precise and

[87] The White House issued a statement of support for Saudi Arabia and condemned 'ongoing military actions taken by the Houthis against the elected government of Yemen'; Statement by NSC Spokesperson Bernadette Meehan on the Situation in Yemen, *White House Briefing Room,* 25 March 2015, www.whitehouse.gov/the-press-office/2015/03/25/statement-nsc-spokesperson-bernadette-meehan-situation-yemen.

[88] In a letter transmitted to the SC, President Hadi stated that he had 'requested from the Cooperation Council for the Arab States of the Gulf and the League of Arab States to immediately provide support, by all necessary means and measures, including military intervention, to protect Yemen and its people from the continuing aggression by the Houthis'; UN SC Resolution 2216, 14 April 2015.

[89] Dyke, Joe, 'Is the Saudi War on Yemen Legal?' *IRIN Middle East,* 3 April 2015, www.irinnews.org/report/101320/is-the-saudi-war-on-yemen-legal; see also Weizmann, Nathalie, 'International Law on the Saudi-Led Military Operations in Yemen', *Just Security,* 27 March 2015, www.justsecurity.org/21524/international-law-saudi-operation-storm-resolve-yemen.

[90] The SC reaffirmed 'the legitimacy of the President of Yemen, Abdo Rabbo Mansour Hadi' and condemned 'the ongoing unilateral actions taken by the Houthis'; UN SC Resolution 2201, 15 February 2015; UN SC Resolution 2216, 14 April 2015.

agreed content to these conditions is problematic. The issue of imminence arises in relation to the notion of anticipatory self-defence. The wording of article 51 is clear: the right to self-defence arises 'if an armed attack occurs'. A restrictive approach would therefore prohibit any defensive action until this has taken place. But this interpretation is 'hotly contested by writers and in state practice'.[91] It is argued that it would punish the victim and favour the aggressor, supporting a strong argument that a state cannot be expected to wait until an anticipated attack eventuates. This position carries further weight in the context of nuclear weapons and other weapons of mass destruction (WMDs) or fears of terrorist activity. In addition to the interpretive issue is the practical question of what evidence is required to justify such a first strike and who is to make that evaluation. The state that fears that it may become subject to an attack may not be able to make an objective assessment and may act prematurely out of fear, suspicion, on the basis of unreliable intelligence or in bad faith.

In 2002 the unresolved debate with respect to anticipatory self-defence took on a further twist. In that year the US National Security Strategy addressed the threats of WMD and terrorism. It asserted that international law had long 'recognized that nations need not suffer an attack before they can lawfully take action to defend themselves against forces that present an imminent danger of attack', but that the concept of imminence must be adapted to address contemporary threats.[92] It set the stage for the 2003 invasion of Iraq by setting out a claimed right to act unilaterally 'to exercise our right of self-defence by acting pre-emptively against such terrorists, to prevent them from doing harm' to the United States – the people and the country.[93] The core difference between this claim and that to take anticipatory action in self-defence is one of degree: what may be termed pre-emptive self-defence[94] applies to the military response to some potential future attack, even if the timing and place of such an attack are uncertain, rather than to one that is imminently

[91] Harris, David and Sivakumaran, Sandesh 2015. *Cases and Materials on International Law*. Sweet and Maxwell, 8th ed., 760.

[92] 'National Security Strategy', *The White House*, 17 September 2002, 15, www.state.gov/documents/organization/63562.pdf.

[93] *Ibid.*, 6.

[94] In this chapter we use anticipatory self-defence to indicate awareness of some imminence of attack and pre-emptive where there is no apparent immediate threat. Walzer and others use 'anticipatory' to signify pre-emptive action, while 'pre-emptive' refers to preventive action. See Walzer, *op. cit.*

anticipated. 'Imminence' in the terms of the *Caroline* case means 'instant, overwhelming, leaving no choice of means and no moment for deliberation'.[95] In her 2002 Wriston Lecture at the Manhattan Institute, Condoleeza Rice commented on the 2002 National Security Strategy's call for a new concept of imminence: 'some threats are so potentially catastrophic – and can arrive with so little warning, by means that are untraceable – that they cannot be contained . . . new technology requires new thinking about when a threat actually becomes 'imminent'.[96]

Thus the argument for pre-emptive self-defence in the case of the 2003 invasion of Iraq is based on a subjective determination that there is a latent threat caused by the nature of the target state as a 'rogue state', as seeking to develop a nuclear capacity, or as possessing (and thus potentially using) WMDs.[97] The failure to locate any WMDs in Iraq following the 2003 invasion highlighted the dangers of such claims. A broad interpretation of article 51 allowing for pre-emptive self-defence was not supported by other states, with the United Kingdom, for instance, preferring to base its claim for the legality of the invasion of Iraq on the interpretation of earlier SC resolutions.[98] Nor has it since gained ground with states, commentators or the ICJ. In his report *In Larger Freedom* the UN Secretary-General considered that 'Imminent threats are fully covered by article 51' and that '[l]awyers have long recognized that this covers an imminent attack as well as one that has already happened'. Beyond that, however, only the SC has the responsibility to authorize the use of preventive force.[99] The GA in its 2005 Millennium Outcome Document also failed to endorse any notion of pre-emptive self-defence, instead reaffirming 'that the relevant provisions of the Charter are

95 *Caroline, op. cit.*

96 Rice, Condoleeza. 'A Balance of Power that Favours Freedom', *2002 Manhattan Institute Wriston Lecture,* 1 October 2002, www.manhattan-institute.org/html/wl2002.htm.

97 Lee Feinstein and Anne-Marie Slaughter argued that the Bush administration did not go far enough and that there should be a 'duty to prevent 'rogue' states acquiring such weapons'. See Feinstein, Lee and Slaughter, Anne-Marie. 'A Duty to Prevent', *Foreign Affairs,* January/February 2004, www.foreignaffairs.com/articles/59540/lee-feinstein-and-anne-marie-slaughter/a-duty-to-prevent.

98 Legal advice given by the Attorney General, Lord Goldsmith, to the prime minister on 17 March 2003 and published on 28 April 2005. See 'Full Text: Written Answer on Iraq Advice', *BBC News,* 28 April 2005, http://news.bbc.co.uk/1/hi/uk_politics/vote_2005/frontpage/4492195.stm.

99 Report of the Secretary-General of the United Nations for decision by Heads of State and Government in September 2005, *In Larger Freedom: Towards Development, Security and Human Rights for All,* UN Doc. A/59/2005, 21 March 2005, paras. 124–125.

sufficient to address the full range of threats to international peace and security'.[100] However, in rejecting the notion of pre-emptive self-defence, these statements appear to accept the less radical concept of anticipatory self-defence. The ICJ has not clarified the question. In a case brought by the Democratic Republic of the Congo against Uganda, the Court asserted that the use of force in self-defence applies only 'within the strict confines' of article 51, which 'does not allow the use of force by a State to protect perceived security interests beyond these parameters'.[101] The Court noted that there are other means to protect security interests 'including, in particular, recourse to the Security Council',[102] a view that is weakened by the political and practical limitations on effective SC response as discussed in Chapter 2.

Despite this first overwhelming rejection of pre-emptive self-defence, in 2006 President George W. Bush reiterated that the doctrine of self-defence needs to be revised and rewritten, including that the requirement that a threat needs to be imminent should be revisited. While this too has not achieved widespread acceptance, a first stage in law-making is articulating what may be perceived as a problem to be addressed. In the decentralised international legal system, lacking a legislative body and compulsory adjudication, the claims of the powerful to change law in accordance with their wishes may carry significant weight, and their practice prove hard to resist. On the other hand, divisions between powerful players may inhibit any movement for legal change.[103] As discussed above, the United States has raised individual self-defence as a basis for their airstrikes in Syria despite there having been no armed attack against it. President Obama stated that IS will 'ultimately' pose a threat outside the Middle East, to the United States, Europe and 'far-flung countries like Australia'.[104] Former Prime Minister Cameron made a similar assessment that IS 'represents a major threat to us, here at home',[105] and that we should not 'wait until an attack takes place here: we should act in advance, recognising that there are inherent risks in any course'.[106] In a further extension of the concept of 'armed attack' the

[100] UN GA Res. 60/1, 24 October 2005 (2005 World Summit Outcome), para. 79.

[101] *Armed Activities on the Territory of the Congo* (*Democratic Republic of the Congo v. Uganda*), 2005 ICJ Reports 168, judgment of 19 December 2005 ('*Uganda*'), para. 148.

[102] *Ibid.* [103] Boyle and Chinkin. *op. cit.* [104] Arimatsu and Schmitt, *op. cit.*

[105] *Ibid.*

[106] Memorandum to the Foreign Affairs Select Committee. Prime Minister's Response to the Foreign Affairs Select Committee's Second Report of Session 2015–16: The Extension of Offensive British Military Operations to Syria, November 2015, www.parliament.uk/

threat is also seen as coming from radicalised fighters returning home to the United Kingdom. What is factually uncertain at the time of writing is whether an armed attack is 'imminent' such that a right to anticipatory self-defence has arisen, or whether military action against IS in Syria represents acceptance in practice of earlier – pre-emptive – action. Or, as discussed above, there is a growing preference for the rationale that the host state is 'unwilling or unable' to take effective action against non-state actors on its territory.

While former President Bush may have considered that taking action in Iraq in 2003 in advance of any anticipated imminent attack would enhance security, it must be asked 'whose security'? There is an argument for considering that it would increase the security of Israel and that of other states in the region who might have been under threat from Saddam Hussein, but it is harder to see how it enhanced the security of the United States or United Kingdom. In the event, regional security has been undermined by the violence in Iraq and the subsequent emergence of IS.[107] It must also be remembered that if pre-emptive self-defence is accepted, other states (including those with nuclear capabilities) would be able to act similarly. This would generate instability and uncertainty: who would have the right to determine the existence of a potential threat? What would be the protection against exaggerated claims for pre-emptive self-defence?[108]

4.3.4 *Necessity and Proportionality*

It is equally difficult to give a precise content to the two other conditions for self-defence – the concepts of necessity and proportionality.[109] Necessity presupposes that all other possibilities have been exhausted before recourse to force. The threshold is high: the International Law Commission Articles on State Responsibility allow necessity to preclude wrongfulness only if the

documents/commons-committees/foreign-affairs/PM-Response-to-FAC-Report-Extension-of-Offensive-British-Military-Operations-to-Syria.pdf.

107 While the emergence of IS cannot be solely attributed to the invasion of Iraq in 2003, the Report of the Independent International Commission of Inquiry on the Syrian Arab Republic states that its 'origins lie in the establishment of Al-Qaeda in Iraq (AQI) by Abu Musab Al-Zarqawi in 2004'. Report of the Independent International Commission of Inquiry on the Syrian Arab Republic, *Rule of Terror: Living under ISIS in Syria*, 14 November 2014, para. 6.

108 Byers, Michael 2005. *War Law (New World Order)*. Atlantic Books, 75–81.

109 'The submission of the exercise of the right of self-defence to the conditions of necessity and proportionality is a rule of customary international law'. *Nuclear Weapons, op. cit.*, para. 41; reiterated in *Oil Platforms, op. cit.*, 76.

act (a) 'is the only way for the State to safeguard an essential interest against a grave and imminent peril and (b) does not seriously impair an essential interest of the State or States towards which the obligation exists, or of the international community as a whole'.[110] Article 21 of the Articles reiterates the right of self-defence,[111] but does not elaborate any further the meaning of necessity as a condition for self-defence. It could be argued that recourse to force in the name of self-defence of itself impairs an essential interest of the international community as a whole, the right to security, an argument that has greater strength if 'international community'[112] is understood as including individuals.

Necessity also has a temporal element. States may be unwilling to undertake time-consuming steps and to wait to see if a forceful response is in fact necessary. For example, in August 1990 the SC imposed economic and other sanctions on Iraq in response to its military action against Kuwait.[113] In November 1990, before there had been time to see if they would be effective, 'Member States cooperating with the Government of Kuwait' were authorised by the Council 'to use all necessary means' (i.e., military force) in January 1991 if Iraq had not withdrawn from Kuwait before that date.[114] Similarly, the United States determined that Al Qaeda, which was being sheltered by the unrecognised Taliban regime in Afghanistan, was responsible for the attacks on 11 September 2001. The United States demanded that Osama Bin Laden be handed over. When this did not happen it led the coalition of the willing to take military action against Afghanistan, claiming the action to be a lawful exercise of self-defence. This action commenced on 7 October 2001 before the United States had had time to determine whether the hand-over of Bin Laden could be negotiated.[115] The military response could be

[110] International Law Commission *op. cit.*, article 25 ('Responsibility of States for Internationally Wrongful Acts').

[111] Article 21 stipulates: 'The wrongfulness of an act of a State is precluded if the act constitutes a lawful measure of self-defence taken in conformity with the Charter of the United Nations'.

[112] The 'international community' is a much used but undefined concept; it may apply to the community of states, the international institutional community such as the UN, or be a broader concept encompassing civil society and individuals. There is a large literature, e.g., Mosler, Hermann 1974. 'The International Society as a Legal Community', *RCADI* 140 IV, 17; Kolb, Robert 2002. 'Quelques réflexions sur la communauté internationale', *African Yearbook of International Law* 10: 431–451.

[113] UN SC Resolution 661, 6 August 1990.

[114] UN SC Resolution 678, *op. cit.*

[115] Thomas Barfield reports that an assembly of three hundred clergy called by Mullah Omar after 9/11, to ask whether he should protect his guest (Al Qaeda), concluded that

understood as a reprisal (prohibited under the GA Declaration on the Principles of Friendly Relations)[116] or as pre-emptive action against further attacks. However, the international community widely accepted the US action against Afghanistan as legal self-defence.

Proportionality in the *jus ad bellum* is another slippery concept. Vaughan Lowe has asked whether 'the degree of force [is] to be calibrated against the scale of violence that would – might – occur if the threat against which the state is defending itself were to be realised? Or is proportionality to be measured against the force necessary to prevent – or to respond – to the attack?'[117] In the *Nicaragua* case the ICJ favoured the second approach, thereby limiting forceful action in self-defence to what is needed to reply to an attack.[118] This is consistent with the approach of Professor Ago in the International Law Commission, who determined that the concept of proportionality 'was that which was proportionate to repelling the attack, and not a requirement of symmetry between the mode of the initial attack and the mode of response'.[119]

It is evident that a determination of legality would differ according to which approach to proportionality is preferred. This has particular application in the context of terrorist attacks. For example, at the outset of Operation Cast Lead – Israel's military action against the Gaza Strip in December 2008 through January 2009 – the state's permanent representative at the UN, Gabriela Shalev, sent identical letters to the UN Secretary-General and the President of the SC stating:

> I am writing this urgent letter in order to inform you that after a long period of utmost restraint, the Government of Israel has decided to exercise, as of this morning, its right to self-defence. Israel is taking the necessary military action in order to protect its citizens from the ongoing terrorist attacks originating from the Gaza Strip and carried out by Hamas and other terrorist organizations.[120]

'because a guest should not cause his host problems Bin Laden should be asked to leave Afghanistan voluntarily as soon as possible'; Barfield, Thomas 2010. *Afghanistan: A Cultural and Political History*. Princeton University Press, 269. Nevertheless the air attacks began two days later.

116 UN GA Resolution 2625, *op. cit.*, 'States have a duty to refrain from acts of reprisal involving the use of force'.

117 Lowe, Vaughan 2007. *International Law*. Clarendon Press.

118 *Nicaragua*, *op. cit.*

119 Cited in *Nuclear Weapons*, *op. cit.* (per dissenting opinion Judge Higgins, para. 5).

120 UNSC, *Identical Letters Dated 27 December 2008 from the Permanent Representative of Israel to the United Nations Addressed to the Secretary-General and to the President of the Security Council*, U.N. Doc. S/2008/816, 27 December 2008.

The military operation involved a week-long air attack, a ground invasion (with continuing air cover) and shelling of the coast by the Israeli navy. Statistical data of casualties differ as does determination of the proportion of civilian casualties, not least because of the problems of definition and identification of individuals as civilians.[121] In September 2009, the UN Fact-Finding Mission to Gaza (Goldstone Report) reported that NGOs estimated the overall number of Palestinian deaths as between 1,387 and 1,417; the Gaza authorities put the number at 1,444 and the Israeli Government at 1,166. There was also extensive damage to civilian and social infrastructure. The Government of Israel also stated that three Israeli civilians and one soldier were killed in southern Israel by rocket and mortar attacks launched by Palestinian armed groups, and nine Israeli soldiers were killed during the fighting inside the Gaza strip, four as a result of friendly fire.[122]

As is apparent from the letters submitted by the Israeli permanent representative to the UN, Israel justified this military action as legal self-defence against ongoing terrorist attacks from Gaza. The Goldstone Report found that more than 8,000 rockets and mortars had been launched from Gaza into southern Israel since April 2001, that they had caused relatively few fatalities and physical injuries among the residents of southern Israel and that property damage was also not extensive.[123] As well as rockets failing to strike persons and property, casualties are reduced by the warning systems and protective bomb shelters within Israel. What, of course, must not be underestimated is the deep insecurity and fear that these attacks cause to the affected populations, as well as psychological trauma. Israel unarguably has the right to defend itself against armed attacks, but was Operation Cast Lead a proportionate exercise of this right? The Goldstone Report does not address this question as its mandate referred only to the conduct of the military operation (*jus in bello* and human rights), not its initial lawfulness (*jus ad bellum*). The answer may depend on the basis for determining proportionality; if the criterion is quantitative assessment of harm, it appears disproportionate, if, however, it is the intensity of action necessary to prevent further attacks, then it may appear proportionate.

[121] See Chapter 6.

[122] UN Fact-Finding Mission to Gaza, UN Doc. A/HRC/12/48, 25 September 2009, paras. 29–31.

[123] *Ibid.*, paras. 1597–1598.

That the latter is not necessarily borne out by the facts is suggested by the reality that the ceasefire negotiated in June 2008 was more successful in lowering the level of violence than the military action. In any event the assessment cannot be made in these simplistic and militaristic terms but should also factor in the context, including the occupation, the economic blockade of Gaza, Hamas control in Gaza and the stalled peace process.

It could also take into account the broader impact of the conflict on both populations, but 'assessment of overall civilian harm and deaths ... do[es] not form part of the proportionality *jus ad bellum* equation ... because to a degree, these are the expected consequences of the use of force'.[124] Certain harms are excluded from any determination of proportionality, such as 'long term civilian casualties resulting from starvation or disease', displacement, refugee flows[125] and disruption to children's education contributing to continued poverty and unemployment. The particular impact of such harms on women 'represents an unacknowledged gendered consequence of force', even force in self-defence.[126] Heathcote uses feminist analysis to argue for the reconfiguration of the requirements of proportionality and necessity to take account of women's experiences of conflict in a way that would contribute to de-gendering article 51.[127] She points to Judith Gardam's suggestion that the principles of necessity and proportionality could offer real constraints to the use of force by states if they were 'refined and developed to produce the outcomes ostensibly claimed by their presence'.[128] These outcomes should include the impact of military force on the populations of both the targeted state and of the state purportedly acting in self-defence. Such an understanding would move the principles beyond an assessment that takes into account solely the contingencies of the conflict and the state's military capabilities.

4.4 Armed Attack by or against Whom?

4.4.1 Self-Defence in Response to Attacks against Nationals

The use of force in defence of nationals is a version of both self-defence (attacks on the nationals of a state constitutes an armed attack

[124] Heathcote, *op. cit.*, 90.

[125] Gardam, Judith 1992. 'Proportionality as a Restraint on the Use of Force', *Australian Yearbook of International Law* 20: 161–174.

[126] Heathcote, *op. cit.*, 91. [127] *Ibid.*, 92. [128] *Ibid.*, 93.

on the state) and of humanitarian intervention, as discussed in Chapter 5. There has been a long history of powerful states intervening in weaker ones on this basis, although only on a few occasions since World War II.[129] Incidents during the Cold War, for instance, by Belgium in the Congo (1960), the United States in Grenada (1983) and Panama (1989) and Israel at Entebbe (1976) have all been extensively discussed.[130]

The claim has become another example of the stretching of self-defence in the twenty-first century as President Putin has claimed that Russia's actions in Georgia in 2008 and in the Crimea in 2014 were for the protection of Russian nationals against armed attacks. In both cases, Russian troops were already deployed in the area, as peacekeepers in Georgia and as military deployment in Crimea. Putin's legal justification with respect to the Crimea was expressed in a letter to the Federal Council, the upper house of Parliament that has the constitutional right to approve deployment of Russian armed forces outside the territory of the Federation. He noted 'the extraordinary situation in Ukraine, the threat to the lives of citizens of the Russian Federation. Our compatriots, the personnel of the military contingent of the Armed Forces of the Russian Federation deployed on the territory of Ukraine'.[131] Putin has argued that the Federal Council's authorisation also covers the deployment of Russian troops in Eastern Ukraine, although he has said 'I hope very much I do not have to take advantage of this right.'[132] Nevertheless, despite denials, the evidence that Russian soldiers and special forces are operating in the region is rather compelling.[133] In explaining to the Duma Russia's actions with respect to the Crimea, President Putin emphasised that attempts had been made in Ukraine 'to deprive Russians of their historical memory, even of their language and to subject them to forced assimilation' and that the rights of ethnic minorities – Russians – had been violated. He continued that when 'residents of Crimea and Sevastopol turned to Russia for help in defending their rights and lives', Russia could not ignore their plea: 'we could not abandon Crimea and its residents in distress. This

[129] Gray, *op. cit.* [130] *Ibid.*

[131] Quoted in International Crisis Group, 'Ukraine: Running Out of Time', *International Crisis Group Europe*, Report No. 231, 14 May 2014, 20.

[132] *Ibid.*

[133] See, for example, 'Ukraine: Mounting Evidence of War Crimes and Russian Involvement', *Amnesty International*, 7 September 2014, www.amnesty.org/en/news/ukraine-mounting-evidence-war-crimes-and-russian-involvement-2014-09-05.

would have been betrayal on our part'.[134] On 27 March 2014 the GA called upon states not to recognise any change in the status of the Autonomous Republic of Crimea and to refrain from actions or dealings that might be interpreted as such.[135]

A further twist is the process of 'passportisation'[136] in both Georgia and Ukraine. The issuance of Russian passports designated people as Russian who were therefore to be defended by Russia.[137] Leaving aside whether Russian nationality for these people is 'real and effective'[138] and even if it is accepted that an attack on nationals validates intervention for their defence,[139] there must be evidence of such attacks and the requirement of proportionality must be fulfilled. However, there has been no credible evidence of such violence against ethnic Russians in Ukraine (including Crimea) or of any such attacks being imminent.[140]

4.4.2 Armed Attack by Non-State Actors

In contemporary political violence, neither the attackers nor the defenders are necessarily states. The classic case is the terrorist attacks on New York and Washington, D.C., on 11 September 2001; similarly, the 'public brutality and indoctrination'[141] committed by IS in Syria and Iraq demonstrate the ongoing capabilities of non-state actors for extreme violence.

134 'Address by President of the Russian Federation', *The Kremlin*, Moscow, 18 March 2014, http://en.kremlin.ru/events/president/news/20603.

135 UN GA Resolution 262/68, 27 March 2014 (Territorial integrity of Ukraine).

136 Green, James 2014. 'The Annexation of Crimea: Russia, Passportisation and the Protection of Nationals Revisited', *Journal on the Use of Force and International Law* 1: 3–10.

137 An estimated 143,000 Russian passports were issued to Ukrainians in the last two weeks of February 2014. *Ibid.*, 3, 8.

138 *Nottebohm Case* (second phase) (*Liechtenstein v. Guatemala*), 1995 ICJ Reports 4, judgment of 6 April 1955, para. 22.

139 Christine Gray notes that there are few adherents to the doctrine but that claims for intervention on behalf of nationals are rarely the sole asserted basis for legality; this renders it difficult to ascertain the level of acceptance or rejection of this ground. Gray, *op. cit.*

140 According to the US Department of State: 'Outside of Russian press and Russian state television, there are no credible reports of any ethnic Russians being under threat. ... Ethnic Russians and Russian speakers have filed petitions attesting that their communities have not experienced threats'. US Department of State, *op. cit.* ('President Putin's Fiction').

141 Report of the Independent International Commission of Inquiry on the Syrian Arab Republic, *op. cit.*, para. 1.

While flying civilian planes into the World Trade Center and the Pentagon indisputably constituted attacks of a high threshold of violence, they were carried out by non-state actors. Article 51 does not explicitly say that the armed attack must emanate from a state, although the UN Charter regulates relations between sovereign states and is predicated upon that basis. This starting point is also explicit in the GA's 1974 definition of aggression, which states that 'aggression is the use of armed force by a State'.[142] The definition of the crime of aggression by the Review Conference of the ICC similarly states that 'an "act of aggression" means the use of armed force by a State against another State'.[143] However, the African Union has adopted a definition that encompasses the use of armed force 'by a State, a group of States, an organization of States or non-State actor(s) ... against the sovereignty, political independence, territorial integrity and human security of the population of a State Party to this Pact'.[144] The inclusion of aggression as a crime subject to the jurisdiction of the ICC constitutes the criminalisation of war.[145] This approach assumes that aggression can be committed by an individual responsible for its 'planning, preparation, initiation or execution'.[146] However, the individual must be linked to the state, for it applies to a person 'in a position effectively to exercise control over or to direct the political or military action of a State',[147] not apparently to the same acts of a non-state military or terrorist group.

The ICJ has not directly considered whether there is a right of self-defence against the acts of non-state actors, but by indicating that the inherent right of self-defence arises in the case of armed attack by one state against another state has apparently adopted a restrictive, state-based approach.[148] The majority in the case of *Armed Activities on the Territory of the Congo* (involving claims by the DRC against Uganda) did not determine 'whether and under what conditions contemporary international law provides for a right of self-defence against attacks by irregular forces'. Judges Simma and Kooijmans, however, directly addressed the

[142] UN GA Resolution 3314 (XXIX), 14 December 1974, Annex: Definition of Aggression.

[143] The Crime of Aggression, RC/Res. 6, 11 June 2010, Annex I, article 8 (2) *bis*.

[144] African Union Non-Aggression and Common Defence Pact, Abuja, 31 January 2005.

[145] Simpson, Gerry 2008. '"Stop Calling It Aggression": War as Crime', *Current Legal Problems* 61: 191–228.

[146] The Crime of Aggression, RC/Res. 6, 11 June 2010, Annex I, article 8(1) *bis*.

[147] *Ibid.*, Annex II, article 8, Elements, (2).

[148] *Legal Consequences of the Construction of a Wall in the Occupied Palestinian Territory*, 2004 ICJ Reports, advisory opinion of 9 July 2004 ('*Wall*'), para. 139.

issue; Judge Simma considered that SC Resolutions 1368 and 1373 (adopted in the aftermath of 11 September 2001) 'cannot but be read as affirmations . . . that large scale attacks can qualify as "armed attacks"' within the terms of article 51, and both he and Judge Kooijmans considered that armed attacks by non-state actors should be subject to the same tests as those committed by states.[149] Judge Buergenthal in the *Wall* case thought likewise, noting that

> In its resolution 1368 (2001), adopted only one day after the 11 September 2001 attacks on the United States, the SC invokes the right of self-defence in calling on the international community to combat terrorism. In neither of these resolutions did the SC limit their application to terrorist attacks by State actors only, nor was an assumption to that effect implicit in these resolutions.[150]

The ICJ's majority position has not been uncritically accepted, not least through concern about its consequences. For instance, the unwillingness of the majority in the ICJ to affirm a right to self-defence against an attack by non-state actors might encourage states to use non-uniformed armed rebels who are indistinguishable from the local population to carry out their illegal aggressive plans.[151] Jensen argues that in this way states could 'orchestrate large scale armed violence without creating a right to self-defense for their victims and simultaneously increasing the survivability of their attackers by clothing them in the protection of civilians'.[152] However, it can be countered that states would remain responsible for any illegal act attributable to them in accordance with the International Law Commission's Articles on State Responsibility, giving rise at least to non-forcible counter-measures in response. In the *Wall* case Judge Buergenthal considered that the Court had failed to address not only the question of a right to self-defence against the acts of non-state actors, but more broadly that of Israel's right to self-defence from continuous terrorist attacks, or the extent to which the wall 'is a necessary and proportionate response to these attacks'.[153] Such an analysis would seek to weigh the impact of the wall on the Palestinians' right to self-determination and human rights against Israel's right to security, and of Israelis to human security. On the one hand, the construction of a wall is less harmful to human security than a

[149] *Uganda, op. cit.* [150] *Wall, op. cit.*, declaration of Judge Buergenthal.

[151] Jensen, Eric Talbot 2007. 'The ICJ's "Uganda Wall": A Barrier to the Principle of Distinction and an Entry Point for Lawfare', *Denver Journal of International Law and Policy* 35(2): 241–274, 267.

[152] *Ibid.* [153] *Wall, op. cit.*, declaration of Judge Buergenthal.

military assault such as took place in Operation Cast Lead in 2008–2009, Operation Pillar of Defense in November 2012 or Operation Protective Edge in the summer of 2014; on the other hand, the wall has divided communities, cut Palestinians off from their sources of livelihood and limited their freedom of movement in harmful ways.

An international body that has taken a different approach from that of the ICJ is the International Fact-Finding Mission into the conflict in Georgia that was constituted by the EU after the Russian intervention in South Ossetia in August 2008. In an extremely detailed report it directly addressed the issue of non-state actors and asserted that UN Charter articles 2(4) and 51 both apply to the acts of non-state entities (in this instance South Ossetia and Abkhazia).[154] The consequence of this conclusion is that the actions of such entities may both constitute a wrongful use of force or an armed attack and that they may act legally in self-defence. Consequentially other actors (in this instance Russia) may claim to be acting in collective self-defence of those entities, an expansive interpretation with the potential for escalation of violence.[155]

Other states as well as the United States have used force in response to armed attacks by non-state actors, including Israel in Lebanon in 2006 and Turkey's incursions into northern Iraq in 2008 against Kurdistan Worker's Party (PKK) bases situated there. Kress notes that the lack of international criticism of Turkey 'cannot be ignored'.[156] After careful consideration of the relevant state practice and commentaries, he concludes that despite the ICJ's contrary position, since 11 September 2011 there exists a right of self-defence against armed attacks committed by non-state actors.[157] However, the parameters of this have not been determined; any such use of force must be subject to the requirements of necessity and proportionality, which, as discussed above, are especially difficult to apply in the context of terrorism.

If self-defence against an armed attack by a non-state actor is accepted as justifiable, the next question is: who is the legitimate target of such coercive response? In Afghanistan, the military action of the coalition of the willing was not directed solely at Al Qaeda but also at the Taliban, the then (unrecognised) government in Afghanistan, justified on the grounds that it had harboured the terrorists. In international law terms, providing a safe place for terrorist activity initiated from its territory amounts to a direct internationally wrongful act, attributable

[154] Report on Georgia, *op. cit.* [155] *Ibid.* [156] Kress, *op. cit.* [157] *Ibid.*

to the state. But it is not clear whether there is a right to self-defence against a state simply for the harbouring of terrorists. In the *Nicaragua* case the ICJ required a state to exercise 'effective control' over non-state groups in order for their acts to be attributable to the state.[158] President Bashar al-Assad in Syria cannot be said to be 'harbouring' IS, but nor, of course, is he in 'effective control' of the territories captured by their forces. He has been engaged in civil war in Syria since 2012. Nevertheless, as discussed above, the United States claims that its actions in bombing IS bases in Syria are in individual and collective self-defence that is justified by Syria's inability or unwillingness to control IS. This claim conflates internal conflict, consent, individual and collective self-defence, and collapses state boundaries to justify widespread military action in the war on terror. Crawford has suggested that a nuanced approach would be to accept that the right to self-defence applies only with respect to the acts of states, but to seek relaxation of this 'effective control' test, thereby making the acts of non-state actors more readily attributable to the state.[159] However, he also suggests that 'it may be better to leave the use of force against non-state actors to the Security Council'.[160] The claim of self-defence may be stronger against a 'failed' state that is unable or unwilling to control the acts of non-state bodies on its territory, as indicated by Judges Kooijmans and Simma in the *Armed Activities* case, discussed above. It is unclear whether the Taliban in 2001 were able to exercise 'effective control' over the use of their territory for these ends, or to respond to the United States' demands to surrender Osama Bin Laden. Following the defeat of the Taliban, continued strikes against Al Qaeda were justified by the consent of the newly elected government and the presence of a multilateral force (ISAF) mandated by SC resolution.[161]

158 The ICJ affirmed this principle in *Application of the Convention on the Prevention and Punishment of the Crime of Genocide* (*Bosnia and Herzegovina v. Serbia and Montenegro*), 2007 ICJ Reports, judgment of 26 February 2007, paras. 399–407.

159 It has been remarked that this involves the fiction that the harbouring state has launched an 'armed attack' against the target state; Comments by Dr. Michal Kowalski at a Conference in honour of Krzysztof Skubiszewski (Minister, Judge, Professor, Embassy of the Republic of Poland) in London, 14 November 2013.

160 See Crawford, *op. cit.* 773.

161 UN SC Resolution 1386, 20 December 2001: '*Authorizes*, as envisaged in Annex 1 to the Bonn Agreement, the establishment for 6 months of an International Security Assistance Force to assist the Afghan Interim Authority in the maintenance of security in Kabul and its surrounding areas'.

4.4.3 *Targeted Killings*

The other aspect of the use of force in counter-terror operations is the use of 'targeted killings' that have come into prominence since the beginning of the twenty-first century. They can take many forms, although particular publicity has been given to killing by unmanned aerial vehicles, or drones. Philip Alston, the former special rapporteur on extrajudicial, summary or arbitrary executions, a special procedure of the UN Human Rights Council, has identified the following distinguishing features of targeted killings:[162] they involve premeditated lethal force, intentionally directed at an identified individual by a state agent or an organised armed group. There is a possibility (often a high possibility) that other non-targeted people, including undoubtedly civilians, will be also killed. Targeted killings may take place outside the targeting state's own territory, as, for example, with the killing by Israeli agents of a Hamas leader in a hotel in Dubai, United States drone attacks in Pakistan, Yemen and Afghanistan and, of course, the killing of Osama Bin Laden in Pakistan. Unmanned aerial attacks are favoured by those states with the requisite technology: they are relatively cheap and safe from the perspective of the attacking state, certainly in comparison with interventions by ground forces. As well as the high casualty rate, living under the threat of drone attacks is debilitating, can be destructive of traditional ways of life and undermine community coherence;[163] it can also promote radicalisation and the desire for revenge attacks.

The drone campaign greatly intensified during President Obama's administration. Such attacks are shrouded in secrecy, giving rise to a lack of detailed knowledge about the incidence, location, targets of individual attacks and civilian deaths and casualties.[164] The legality of drone attacks is contested and has been the subject of a number of UN

[162] 'The [current] Special Rapporteur does not use the expression "targeted killing" herein because its meaning and significance differ according to the legal regime applicable in specific factual circumstances'. Report of the Special Rapporteur on the Promotion and Protection of Human Rights and Fundamental Freedoms while Countering Terrorism, UN Doc. A/68/389, 18 September 2013, para. 24 ('Report of the Special Rapporteur').

[163] Tribal Maliks from North Waziristan in Pakistan have asserted that drone strikes 'had fractured their existing tribal structures, and destroyed their way of life'. Further the strikes had 'given rise to a desire, particularly among young men, to seek revenge for the drone strikes, thus radicalizing a new generation'. Reported in UN OHCHR, 'Statement of the Special Rapporteur following Meetings in Pakistan', 14 March 2013, www.ohchr.org/EN/NewsEvents/Pages/DisplayNews.aspx?LangID=E&NewsID=13146.

[164] 'The single greatest obstacle to an evaluation of the civilian impact of drone strikes is lack of transparency, which makes it extremely difficult to assess claims of precision targeting objectively'; Report of the Special Rapporteur, *op. cit.*, para. 41.

reports from different perspectives; different conclusions are reached according to analysis under the *jus in bello*, human rights law or refugee law, contributing to the lack of legal certainty and human insecurity.

The use of targeted killings also raises questions under the *jus ad bellum*.[165] In justification of targeted killing in the territory of another state, the US State Department has asserted that since the United States 'is in an armed conflict with Al-Qaeda, as well as with the Taliban and associated forces, in response to the horrific 9/11 attacks, [. . . it] may use force consistent with its inherent right to self-defense'.[166] As discussed above, claims of self-defence in response to terrorist acts highlight legal uncertainties with respect to when the right arises, against whom and the application of the principles of proportionality and necessity. For instance, bearing in mind that there is no international legal definition of terrorism, what acts constitute an armed attack giving rise to self-defence, and what is the threshold of violence to constitute an armed attack for the purpose of self-defence? The asserted right of self-defence in the ongoing war against Al Qaeda (and associated suspected terrorist armed groups) extends it spatially and territorially. Former Prime Minister Cameron's use of the self-defence justification for the killing of two UK citizens, Reyaad Khan and Ruhul Amin, by drones in Syria in August 2015[167] puts international law as interpreted within the framework of the War on Terror above the claims of UK criminal law – bringing the 'outside' 'inside'.[168] This is a one-sided application of the War on Terror since those who commit terrorist acts within the United Kingdom are rightly subjected to criminal procedures.

In a 2013 statement President Obama averred that US counter-terrorism was no longer to be defined by a 'boundless "global war on terror," but rather as a series of persistent, targeted efforts to dismantle specific networks of violent extremists that threaten America'.[169]

[165] Aronsson, Marie 2014. 'Remote Law-Making? American Drone Strikes and the Development of *Jus Ad Bellum*', *Journal on the Use of Force and International Law* 1: 273–298 discusses the precedent setting effect of US use of drone strikes for the development of international law.

[166] Koh, Harold. 'The Obama Administration and International Law', *Speech at the American Society of International Law (ASIL) Proceedings*, 25 March 2010, www.state.gov/s/l/releases/remarks/139119.htm.

[167] MacAskill, Ewan. 'Drone Killing of British Citizens in Syria Marks Major Departure for the UK', *The Guardian*, 7 September 2015, www.theguardian.com/world/2015/sep/07/drone-british-citizens-syria-uk-david-cameron.

[168] See Chapter 2. [169] Crook, *op. cit.*, 674.

Although he reaffirmed the US right to self-defence in what he termed 'a just war, – war waged proportionately, in last resort and in self-defence', Obama also asserted that drone attacks would not be undertaken where there is the ability to capture and detain individuals: 'our preference is always to detain, interrogate and prosecute'.[170] But strikes will be undertaken against 'terrorists who pose a continuing and imminent threat to the American people, and where there are no other governments capable of effectively addressing the threats'.[171] While the objective of constraining drone attacks is welcomed, the speech lacks precision and specificity as to what constitutes 'a continuing and imminent threat' and how the capability of other governments to address effectively threats is to be judged. Nor did President Obama indicate any deference to the requirement of reporting to the SC.

Justifications based on self-defence are not necessary where the state in which the attack takes place has consented, thus precluding the wrongfulness of the intervention.[172] This is said to be the case with respect to states such as Pakistan, Yemen and Somalia. But as with 'invitation' what does consent mean? There has been little debate about the validity of 'consent'[173] in the context of what are described as 'weak' or 'failing' states and many uncertainties. Is tacit or implied consent sufficient? What does 'consent' mean where states do not have effective control over all their territory? Consultation is not the same as consent; Pakistan is said to have been 'consulted' when a US commando operation killed Osama Bin Laden in a suburban house near Abbotsville, but, apparently, the government was not actually informed of the details for fear that the information would leak and the attack would be foiled. Even if consent has been given for the killing of an identified person on the territory of another state, that state remains bound by its own human rights obligations, unless it has formally derogated from them to the extent that it is legally able to do so.[174] A state cannot abdicate its own responsibilities to

170 *Ibid.*, 676. 171 *Ibid.*

172 Article 20 of the ILC Articles on State Responsibility states: 'Valid consent by a State to the commission of a given act by another State precludes the wrongfulness of that act in relation to the former State to the extent that the act remains within the limits of that consent'. International Law Commission, *op. cit.*, Annex, article 20.

173 But see Ashley, Deeks 2013. 'Consent to the Use of Force and International Law Supremacy', *Harvard International Law Journal* 54: 1–60.

174 ICCPR, *op. cit.*, article 4; *European Convention for the Protection of Human Rights and Fundamental Freedoms* (European Convention on Human Rights, as amended) (ECHR), art. 15.

those within its territory by allowing another state to attack them or otherwise violate their human rights, for instance, through wrongful arrest or rendition.[175]

4.4.4 *Recasting Self-Defence: The 'Bethlehem Principles'*

In light of the uncertainties surrounding the scope of self-defence, in particular its applicability in response to terrorist attacks by non-state actors, the desirability of a draft 'Declaratory Resolution on Self-defence' has been raised.[176] While no such instrument has been forthcoming, the former advisor to the UK Foreign and Commonwealth Office, Daniel Bethlehem, has put forward a set of what he has called 'Principles Governing Self-defence against Non-State Actors'.[177] They have been formulated after discussions with foreign ministries, defence ministries and legal military advisors. Drawing upon these discussions, Bethlehem maintains that his objective is to bridge the gap between academic discourse and the operational needs of states and to bring some clarity and precision to when states may use force in the territory of another state against an armed attack by a non-state entity. Among the sixteen principles articulated by Bethlehem are the following:

> that armed attack includes 'a series of attacks that indicate a concerted pattern of continuing armed activity';
>
> that those acting 'in concert' with perpetrators of an armed attack include those providing material support essential to the attacks;
>
> that imminence is to be determined by reference to all relevant circumstances, including the nature and immediacy of the attack, the probability of the attack, whether the anticipated attack is part of a pattern of armed activity and its likely scale and the likelihood of other opportunities to take effective action in self-defence that may cause less collateral harm;
>
> that action against a non-state actor in the territory of another state must be with the consent of that state, but that such consent is not required if

[175] The European Court of Human Rights has found violations of the ECHR with respect to illegal detention and acts of rendition; *El-Masri v. The Former Yugoslav Republic of Macedonia*, ECtHR GC Appl. No. 39630/09; *Al Nashiri v. Poland and Husayn (Abu Zubaydah) v. Poland*, 24 July 2014, ECtHR, application no. 7511/13, 13 December 2012.

[176] Ronzitti, Natalino 2006. 'The Expanding Law of Self-Defence', *Journal of Conflict and Security Law* 11(3): 343–359.

[177] Bethlehem, Daniel 2012. 'Self-Defense against an Imminent or Actual Armed Attack by Nonstate Actors', *American Journal of International Law* 106: 770–777.

> that state is 'colluding' with the non-state actor, or is otherwise unwilling to restrain its activities;
>
> that consent is further dispensed with where there is 'a strong, reasonable and objective basis for concluding that the seeking of consent would be likely to materially undermine the effectiveness of action in self-defence-... or would increase the risk of armed attack, vulnerability to future attacks';
>
> that seeking consent provides the third state with an opportunity to agree 'a reasonable and effective plan of action', and failure to do so 'may support a conclusion' of collusion with the non-state actors[.] That consent may be 'strategic or operational, generic, *ad hoc*, express or implied'.
>
> Finally, the Principles are said to be without prejudice to the UN Charter, and also to the right of self-defence 'that may operate in other circumstances in which a state or its imperative interests may be the target of imminent or actual attack'.[178]

The Principles warrant – and have received – careful analysis. They have been subject to some considerable and wide-ranging criticism. They appear to conflate the *jus ad bellum* and *jus in bello* (when force may be used and against whom).[179] In fact, they express the inter-relation between all the different ways in which the concept of self-defence has been reinterpreted and stretched since the end of the Cold War, and more particularly since the onset of the War on Terror. Throughout, Bethlehem claims that legitimate action depends upon there being a 'reasonable and objective basis', but there is, of course, no independent authoritative body able to make such a determination. In reality it depends upon the subjective interpretation by the state concerned, which is likely to be biased and may be misleading. For instance, before the military action against Iraq in 2003 Secretary of State Powell purported to present 'reasonable and objective' evidence of Iraq's possession of WMDs, which turned out to be false. What is the basis for deciding that a state is 'unwilling' to curtail terrorist activities on its territory? Many of the criteria lack precision. What constitutes 'vulnerability to future attack'? Who has the final word as to whether some other course of action is 'reasonable and effective'? Some statements are excessively

[178] *Ibid.*

[179] Rona, Gabor and Wala, Raha 2013. 'No Thank You to a Radical Rewrite of the Jus Ad Bellum', *American Journal of International Law* 107: 386–390.

'terse': 'The term 'armed attack' includes both discrete attacks and a series of attacks that indicate a pattern of continuing armed activity';[180] 'self-defense must be proportionate to the threat that is faced'. The assertion that they are without prejudice to the UN Charter presents them as within the framework of existing international law, and as such legitimate. However, the suggestion of a right to self-defence 'in other circumstances', including that a state's 'imperative interests' may be the target of imminent or actual attack go well beyond the wording of UN Charter, article 51 –'if an armed attack occurs'. Defining state consent as encompassing 'strategic or operational, generic, *ad hoc,* express or implied' consent expands the concept of 'valid' consent as understood in other areas of international law (for instance, treaty law) and as such could contribute to the fragmentation of international law.[181] In sum, the Principles seek to legitimate an extensive interpretation of self-defence in order to address 'the realities of contemporary threats'. They reinforce the political stance of the United States and other Western powers; indeed, they seem to 'uniquely benefit' the US practice of targeted killings.[182] The Principles do not, of course, constitute international law, but once articulated such ideas tend to develop a life of their own. In terms of security, they seem likely to escalate violence by allowing for subjective determination of the imminence of an armed attack by the state using force. They assume military action and enable, rather than constrain, violence.

4.5 Reinterpreting the Right to Self-Defence

The lack of clarity about the legal parameters of article 51 and the customary right of self-defence undermines the prohibition on the use of force, allowing claims and counter-claims to be made in an ever growing range of scenarios, to the detriment of those whose security is undermined by the violence and denied the protection of legal certainty. Extending the scope of legitimate coercive action by states and non-state

[180] This does not clarify what the proportionality and necessity tests must be assessed against, that is, whether it is against the series of attacks or just the last attack; Wilmshurst, Elizabeth and Wood, Michael 2013. 'Self-Defense against Nonstate Actors: Reflections on the "Bethlehem Principles"', *American Journal of International Law* 107: 390–395, 394.

[181] O'Connell, Mary Ellen 2013. 'Dangerous Departures from the Law of Self-Defense', *American Journal of International Law* 107: 380–387, 383.

[182] *Ibid.*, 384.

actors puts more people at risk. Labelling coercive action 'aggression' or an 'armed attack' allows supposedly defensive violence in response, thereby legitimating further violence.[183] This has particular resonance in the context of the War on Terror and also has wider implications. The normalisation of the use of military force has laid the ground for a resurgence of its use within the Geo-Political and War on Terror models. Nevertheless, there are also clear indications that the dangers of such expansionism are recognised by states, the ICJ and commentators, who seek to promote the 'de-escalation of tension and probably the use of non-forcible countermeasures and criminal law processes, rather than employment of the inter-state framework on the use of force'.[184]

Alongside the legal complexities of article 51, David Rodin has drawn attention to the conceptual difficulties associated with the notion of a state's right to self-defence.[185] There is general agreement about the existence of an individual right to self-defence within domestic criminal laws: it is generally agreed that killing can be justified, to use the words of Grotius, 'if a man were attacked in the night, or in a secret place, where no assistance can be procured'.[186] Of course, the defender should try to avoid killing the aggressor, but the life of the defender has greater weight because of the culpability of the attacker. The right of a state, however, to life – existence – and thus to self-defence is much more ambiguous. The ICJ opined in 1996 that it could not definitively conclude 'whether the threat or use of nuclear weapons would be lawful or unlawful in an extreme circumstance of self-defence in which the very survival of a State would be at stake'.[187] This conclusion was adopted by the President's casting vote. But what do these chilling words really mean? What constitutes the 'survival of a state'?

According to Rodin, the right of a state to self-defence is generally justified in one of two ways. It is either treated as a scaling up of individual self-defence, that is to say, self-defence of a collectivity of individuals, or as an analogy whereby the state rather than the individual human being is the subject. The problem with the first approach, says Rodin, is the moral asymmetry between individual

183 Megret, Frederic 2002. 'War? Legal Semantics and the Move to Violence', *European Journal of International Law* 13(2): 361–399

184 Brunnée and Toope, *op. cit.*, 308.

185 Rodin, *op. cit.*

186 Grotius, Hugo (2003; 1625). *The Rights of War and Peace*. Campbell, Archibald Colin (trans.). Bel Air, CA: Elibron Classics, 56.

187 *Nuclear Weapons*, *op. cit.*, para. 105.

soldiers and civilians. If the individual right of self-defence rests on the culpability of the attacker, can it be right to kill soldiers and civilians on the attacker's side who are not actually responsible for the attack? 'There is a gap in the moral explanation between a right to act against an aggressive state and the right to act against the persons who are its soldiery – a conceptual lacuna between the two levels of war'.[188] In just war theory, 'the enemy soldier though his war may well be criminal, is nevertheless as blameless as oneself'.[189]

Of course, if a group of people are brutally attacked, they must have a right to be protected or to protect themselves, something that is germane to the concerns of this book. But how is that different from a crime against humanity – genocide or massive violations of human rights? Does it have to be defined in terms of a state's right to self-defence?

The war in Bosnia-Herzegovina (1992–1995) well illustrates this dilemma. The war was fought by a combination of remnants of the Yugoslav army and territorial defence forces and paramilitary groups composed of local and foreign volunteers, those protecting their homes, criminals and fanatics. Those who favoured international intervention claimed that this was a war of aggression by Serbia and Croatia against Bosnia-Herzegovina, in which case the Bosnian government had a right to self-defence and there was a collective case for third party intervention (collective self-defence). Those who were against intervention claimed that this was a civil war among Bosnian Serbs, Croats and Muslims, not an attack by a foreign state, in which case the right of self-defence did not apply.[190] Yet the moral case for intervention derived surely not from notions of self-defence but from the rights of the victims. This was a war involving genocide[191] and ethnic cleansing, massacres, large-scale population displacement, siege and starvation, detention camps and widespread atrocities, including mass rape and other forms of torture. Did it matter whether these crimes and violations of human rights were inflicted by Serbs from Serbia or Bosnian Serbs, by regular forces or paramilitary groups, or whether Bosnia-Herzegovina was an independent state or part of Yugoslavia?

[188] Rodin, *op. cit.*, 164. [189] *Ibid.*, 166.

[190] But as discussed above in the context of Yemen (2015) in some instances claims of self-defence are made by a government in response to internal attack.

[191] The International Court of Justice and the International Criminal Tribunal for the former Yugoslavia (ICTY) have determined that genocide was committed in Srebrenica; *Bosnia and Herzegovina v. Serbia and Montenegro, op. cit.*, para. 278ff; *Prosecutor v. Radovan Karadžić* (IT-95-5/18), judgment of 24 March 2016.

The problem with the second approach is what constitutes the subject of the state. What, for instance, constitutes the United Kingdom or the United States or the Bosnian state as in the case of the war in Bosnia-Herzegovina? There are several possible answers. The state could represent a common way of life, a community, a set of shared values, a social contract or vehicle for self-determination; it could represent a state apparatus necessary to keep everyday life functioning; or it might be the entity that is legally recognised as sovereign on a specific territory. Each of these ideas is problematic in different ways. First of all, they imply an exclusive and constructed conception of what constitutes the state. If the state constitutes a community or set of shared values, does this exclude other communities, and does it presuppose that other communities do not share the same values? Does the recourse to war to defend community or shared values involve an attack on other communities and shared values? If the state is conceived as an expression of a social contract and the ability of individuals to determine their own futures, does this mean that undemocratic states such as Saudi Arabia, China or North Korea do not have a right to self-defence? If by the state, we mean the state apparatus, does this justify the destruction of the state apparatuses of other countries as was the case in Iraq and Afghanistan? And if it is a legally recognised entity, what about competing claims as was the case in the Bosnian war?

Secondly, in a global era, the state is no longer the unique repository of any of these conceptions. Why is the community of the state privileged over the town, or region, or even horizontal communities of shared belief, for example, that cross state boundaries? Is it just an accident of history – the Peace of Westphalia? Nowadays, the social contract at national levels is increasingly supplemented by social contracts at regional and global levels, presenting the argument that regional and global institutions such as the UN or the EU could also claim the right of self-defence. To argue that international institutions can claim a right of self-defence would open up even more possibilities for expansive interpretations. The same problem applies to the idea that the state represents an apparatus within a given territory necessary for securing everyday life. In today's world, the state apparatus is so linked into numerous agreements, networks and other apparatuses of governance, that it is difficult to argue that the state has a unique right to self-defence. Likewise, if a state is the legally recognised repository of sovereignty, how do we deal with conflicts over legal recognition? But if the uniqueness of the state is abandoned, does this not open up a kind of free for all? In the contemporary context where authority is fragmented, where the national social contract is increasingly supplemented by other agreements at local, regional and international levels, and where cultural communities are often horizontal and transnational, it is increasingly difficult to define the subject to be defended. As Rodin puts it: 'Our lives are embedded within an indefinite number of common lives, many of which criss-cross national boundaries, each of which possess an ongoing character and each of which constitutes a value for those who participate in it'.[192]

A further problem is whether the recourse to war actually defends the subject – the state – or rather also undermines ideas of community, self-determination and even the state apparatus. In rejecting the UK Government's derogation from article 5 of the ECHR following the 9/11 attacks,[193] Lord Hoffman in the House of Lords rejected the notion that there was a 'public emergency threatening the life of the nation':

> This is a nation which has been tested in adversity, which has survived physical destruction and catastrophic loss of life. I do not underestimate the ability of fanatical groups of terrorists to kill and destroy, but they do not threaten the life of the nation. Whether we would survive Hitler hung in the balance, but there is no doubt that we shall survive Al-Qaeda. The Spanish people have not said that what happened in Madrid, hideous crime as it was, threatened the life of their nation. Their legendary pride would not allow it. Terrorist violence, serious as it is, does not threaten our institutions of government or our existence as a civil community. ...
>
> The real threat to the life of the nation, in the sense of a people living in accordance with its traditional laws and political values, comes not from terrorism but from laws such as these. That is the true measure of what terrorism may achieve. It is for Parliament to decide whether to give the terrorists such a victory.[194]

What is required is a reinterpretation of the right to self-defence that strengthens the prohibition against any use of force. One way would be to define the right to self-defence conservatively along the lines that were originally assumed at the time of the signing of UN Charter. Accordingly, self-defence should apply only to an attack by a foreign state, and the

[192] Rodin, *op. cit.*, 159

[193] Derogation (within limits) is permitted under the ECHR, article 15 'in time of war or other public emergency threatening the life of the nation'. See ECHR, *op. cit.*, article 15.

[194] *A (FC) and Others (FC) v. Secretary of State for the Home Department*, [2004] UKHL 56, paras. 96–97 (per Lord Hoffmann).

requirements of imminence, necessity and proportionality should also be conservatively defined and applied. Proportionality should be understood in a way that minimises the harms suffered by the population and thus as imposing real constraints upon the use of force. This conservative approach could be modified by taking into account the gendered nature of self-defence. Because the principles of self-defence, like the concept of self-defence itself, have entered international law through the domestic law analogy, they fail to take account of their gendered nature. Gina Heathcote argues in her excellent feminist critique of the use of force that they should be re-scripted, possibly 'through empirical accounts of the impact of military behaviour on civilian communities'. This would be a minimalist approach that takes account of the political importance to states of the right to self-defence and the 'difficulty ... of conceiving of an international legal order that is not predicated on the human subject of domestic legal systems'.[195]

Another, bolder, approach would be, in line with Rodin's argument, to suggest that to base self-defence on the notion of the state as individual subject is anachronistic in a world where old wars, between states, are rare, and where the character of states and state sovereignty is changing. The implication is that the very term 'armed attack' needs to be reconceptualised as a crime against humanity. If this were the case, the relevant approach would be rights-based law enforcement as in domestic situations. The individual right of self-defence would still apply as would the right of a third party to defend another person but in the same way as it applies within the domestic context. A large-scale attack constitutes a scaling up of self-defence and might require robust forms of law enforcement, but as we argue in subsequent chapters this is very different from recourse to war.

A similar argument can be made from a feminist perspective. Heathcote also suggests a rejection of the analogy between international and domestic law and the need to challenge the continued viability of states' right to self-defence: 'This strategy would accommodate the consideration that the armed attack requirement, on the one hand, is too narrow in that it is not inclusive of threats to women's security while, on the other hand, acknowledging the broader claim that any move towards increased forms of justified force ultimately undermine women's security'.[196]

[195] Heathcote, *op. cit.*, 106. [196] *Ibid.*, 107.

4.6 Conclusion

The only exception to the prohibition against the use of force in international relations contained in the Charter of the United Nations was the right to self-defence, although, of course, force could be authorised by the SC under chapter VII as long as it is in keeping with the principles of the Charter. At the time, this referred to the defence of a state against an attack by another state. In the twenty-first century setting, the interpretation of the right to self-defence has been stretched to cover responses to attacks by non-state actors (9/11, IS) defence of non-state entities (South Ossetia), protection of nationals abroad (Georgia, Ukraine), protection against internal attacks (Yemen) as well as in anticipation (pre-emption) of external attacks (Iraq and Afghanistan). Indeed, the way that Western air strikes on IS targets in Iraq and from 2014 onwards in Syria have been justified seem to suggest that stretched notions of imminence, necessity and proportionality and the assumption that self-defence can be claimed against non-state actors are being regularly assimilated into and normalised within legal discourse.

At the same time, the very concept of a state's right to self-defence has been called into question in the context of a blurring of the difference between what is external ('outside') and what is internal ('inside'), as well as the increasing consciousness of belonging to a single human community. If a state is defined as a subject in the same way as an individual is a subject, it is unclear what constitutes the subject in a world of overlapping jurisdictions and cultures. If a state is defined as a collective group of people, then it is difficult to understand why the right of self-defence is any different from a right of defence against genocide or massive violations of human rights, or, in the case of third-party support, humanitarian intervention. When the state is defined as the subject it preserves the sharp distinction between outside (international law) and inside (domestic law). But where the distinction is blurred it allows for the application of outside methods – military force – to problems that might be better addressed as 'inside' problems.

War is ultimately about the security of a collective group of people versus another collective group, even when cast in other terms. In contrast, human security is about the security of individuals (men, women and children). In protecting individuals, the lives of other individuals must be taken into account. This is the case in domestic policing, which is constrained by the demands of human rights law. Had the bombers of 9/11 been American citizens sheltered by other American citizens, could the Bush Administration have attacked an American city where they lived or were trained? And could it have killed or sanctioned their associates and presumed associates[197] rather than trying first to arrest them and bring them before a court of law? At the time perhaps not, but the normalisation of the War on Terror has meant that even American and British citizens have now become targets of drone attacks. Of course, if a group of people is attacked with the weapons of war, it may well be necessary to use physical force. There should surely have been more robust protection of the men and boys of Srebrenica or the Tutsis and moderate Hutus of Rwanda. But how that force is used and whether there can be a difference between a war approach and a human rights approach are critical questions. These are the subject of the following chapters.

[197] UN SC Resolution 1267, 15 October 1999, that first imposed sanctions on Osama Bin Laden and the Taliban refers to 'his associates', an imprecise term for the imposition of sanctions.

5

The Humanitarian Model for Recourse to Force

5.1 Introduction

The UN Charter is rooted in the geo-political context of 1945. The changed – and changing – context since that time, particularly of political violence and technology as well as growing human rights awareness, has given rise to claims for exceptions to the prohibition on the use of force unauthorised by the United Nations Security Council (SC) in addition to that of self-defence. One of the most significant – and contested – is the claim to use force in the name of humanitarianism, previously widely labelled as 'humanitarian intervention', recast as the Responsibility to Protect. Like other attempts to expand the scope of recognised exception, this too has been brought within the rubric of self-defence, although today claims are made more explicitly in the name of humanitarianism. Politically, states – especially Western states – generally see it as desirable first to seek SC authorisation for any use of armed force, but, if this is not forthcoming, to justify it through a range of arguments, including the legality, or at least legitimacy,[1] of force in response to widespread violations of human rights, thereby seeking to secure acceptance of their actions both with other states and with civil society at home and abroad.

This chapter examines the evolution of humanitarian intervention and its contemporary guise in the Responsibility to Protect. Our fundamental argument is similar to that raised in the previous chapter in relation to the concept of self-defence. It concerns the contradiction between *jus ad bellum* and *jus in bello,* between the humanitarian justification for the use of force and the methods of war. If war is understood as a humanitarian catastrophe, can it be right to use methods that violate humanitarian norms in the name of humanitarianism? This is not to say that we oppose humanitarian intervention; the problem, up to now, as we demonstrate in this chapter, is that the goals of humanitarian intervention have been

[1] See discussion of legitimacy in Chapter 1.

combined with the means and methods of war. Moreover, war in the name of humanitarianism tends to be conducted and authorised by the dominant powers giving rise to concerns that their interests matter more than the rights of those for whose protection they purportedly act. The challenge for the Human Security model, which we elaborate in later chapters, is how to develop ways to protect people from gross violations of human rights while at the same time conforming to human rights.

In the next section, we describe the re-emergence of the idea of humanitarian intervention in the 1990s. The subsequent section explains the way that humanitarian intervention was recast as the Responsibility to Protect in the early 2000s and discusses its actual practice. In the final section, we reflect on the implications of these developments for the fulfilment of humanitarian norms in situations of extreme violence.

5.2 Humanitarian Intervention

5.2.1 An Exception to the Prohibition against the Use of Force: 1945–1989?

There has always been a significant stream of thought within the just war tradition that considers humanitarian intervention as a just cause for war.[2] In particular, Hugo Grotius, who is often considered the source of this notion of humanity, asserted that '[If a ruler] should inflict upon his subjects such treatment as no one is warranted in inflicting, the exercise of a right vested in human nature is not precluded'.[3] The term 'humanitarian intervention' was used in the nineteenth century to justify interventions by European powers to express solidarity with vulnerable co-religionists, protecting (mainly Christian) people oppressed by the Ottoman Empire. The first instance was the intervention in Greece in 1827, which was to lead to Greek independence in 1830, followed by interventions in Syria to protect the Druze from massacre.[4] Despite possible humanitarian impulses other considerations cannot be excluded, for instance, France's imperial designs in the Middle East, which culminated in its becoming the mandatory power in Syria following World War I.

[2] Similar generalised sentiments can be traced much further back, including in the work of Aristotle; Massingham, Eve 2010. 'Military Intervention for Humanitarian Purposes: Does the Responsibility to Protect Doctrine Advance the Legality of the Use of Force for Humanitarian Ends?', *International Review of the Red Cross* 91(876): 803.

[3] Quoted in Teitel, Ruti 2011. *Humanity's Law*. Oxford University Press, 111.

[4] Bass, Gary 2008. *Freedom's Battle: The Origins of Humanitarian Intervention*. Knopf.

The UN Charter does not allow for a humanitarian exception to the prohibition of the use of force, nor is there any other such general treaty provision.[5] Accordingly the only legal basis for this exception must be customary international law or SC resolution. Customary law requires both uniform state practice and a legal intent to comply with the law (*opinio juris*).[6] The Cold War saw a plethora of interventions, in particular by the Soviet Union (e.g., Hungary 1956, Czechoslovakia, 1968, Afghanistan 1979), the United States (e.g., the Dominican Republic 1965, Grenada 1983, Panama 1989) and Western European states (e.g., Belgium in the Congo 1960, 1964; France in the Central African Republic 1979) where humanitarian justifications were sometimes put forward, typically in conjunction with other justifications,[7] by intervening governments. However, these can be largely discounted as incidents of humanitarian intervention, as the facts do not bear them out.[8] In these and other incidents, an argument based on the need to rescue nationals of the intervening state from situations of danger and/or human rights abuses combined humanitarian motives with claims of self-defence, whereby nationals are equated to the state. For instance, in defending the rescue by Israeli forces of Jewish passengers who had been detained at Entebbe airport after the hijacking of their plane in 1976, Israel argued for self-defence of its nationals.[9]

During the Cold War period, ideology played a significant role in justification. In the case of both the Soviet Union and United States, assumptions of regional hegemony were paramount while Western European states intervened in their previous colonial possessions, perhaps seeking continued influence there. During this period there were also several interventions which could have been characterised as

[5] However, the *Constitutive Act of the African Union*, Lomé, Togo, 11 July, 2000, article 4 (h) provides 'the right of the Union to intervene in a Member State pursuant to a decision of the Assembly in respect of grave circumstances, namely: war crimes, genocide and crimes against humanity'.

[6] The ICJ set out the requirements of customary international law in the *North Sea Continental Shelf Cases* (Federal Republic of German/Denmark; Federal Republic of Germany/The Netherlands), 1969 ICJ Reports 3, judgment of 20 February 1969, para. 37; *Legality of the Threat or Use of Nuclear Weapons*, 1996 ICJ Reports 226, advisory opinion of 8 July 1996, paras. 64–73.

[7] E.g., request by the host government for assistance in self-defence; see Chapter 4.

[8] For details see Chesterman, Simon 2001. *Just War or Just Peace? Humanitarian Intervention and International Law*. Oxford University Press, chapter 2.

[9] Gray, Christine 2008. *International Law and the Use of Force*. Oxford University Press, 3rd ed., 32. See further Chapter 4.

humanitarian interventions, in which a repressive and murderous regime was replaced through military action by a neighbouring state. Three incidents from this time especially generated academic debate as to the emergence of a right of humanitarian intervention under customary international law that cannot be readily dismissed.[10] These were the intervention in East Pakistan by India, which led to the creation of Bangladesh (1971); the intervention against the Khmer Rouge in Kampuchea (Cambodia) by Vietnam (1978); and the overthrow of Idi Amin in Uganda by Tanzania (1979). However, in each instance the state in question relied upon self-defence rather than asserting that it exercised a right of humanitarian intervention, thus undermining the requisite *opinio juris.*[11] Humanitarian considerations lessened international condemnation of such acts, which also received a degree of popular local approval, but there was little support for a customary international law right of humanitarian intervention. Any such claim pits humanitarianism against state sovereignty: while the former is endorsed as a purpose of the UN (UN Charter, article 1 (3)), the latter is enshrined as a core principle in accordance with which states must act (UN Charter, article 2). The equation of sovereignty with the recognised government of a state has meant that only a government can request assistance in the case of insurgency against it.[12] Since in many cases it is government action that is complained against as violating human rights, demands for intervention on humanitarian grounds disrupt the traditional international law indifference to, and prohibition of, intervention in the internal acts of a government. Gray comments that '[t]he basic principle of the right of a government to invite a third state to use force and the absence of any such right for an opposition may be accepted in theory, but its application in practice has not been simple'.[13]

The idea of humanitarian intervention gained further ground in the 1970s and 1980s with the growth of humanitarian non-governmental organisations (NGOs) and human rights groups struggling to address the

[10] Lillich, Richard (ed.) 1973. *Humanitarian Intervention and the United Nations.* University Press of Virginia.

[11] Wheeler, Nicholas 2000. *Saving Strangers: Humanitarian Intervention in International Society.* Oxford University Press.

[12] E.g., the request by the government of Bahrain for assistance from neighbouring countries through the Gulf Cooperation Council against protesters in the context of the Arab Spring in 2012.

[13] Gray, *op. cit.,* 81.

consequences of the erupting forms of violence, especially against civilian populations in Africa and elsewhere. The modern concept is often credited to Bernard Kouchner, the founder of Médecins sans Frontières and later Foreign Minister of France. In the late 1980s Kouchner, together with his colleague, the lawyer Mario Bettani, launched the idea of a *Devoir d'Ingérence* (Duty to Interfere), which later became a *Droit d'Ingérence* (Right/Law of Interference).

Kouchner became French Minister of Humanitarian Action in 1988, and in the same year the United Nations General Assembly (GA) passed a resolution which reaffirmed the sovereignty of states but also recognised that the 'international community makes an important contribution to the sustenance and protection' of victims in emergency situations.[14] The focus, at that time, was material assistance. Failure to provide humanitarian assistance 'constitutes a threat to life and human dignity'. The resolution stressed the 'important contribution' of 'intergovernmental and non-governmental organisations working with strictly humanitarian motives'. Subsequently, the GA praised the UN Secretary-General for continuing consultations on facilitating the delivery of emergency food and medical supplies, including through the establishment of 'relief corridors'.[15]

The GA was affirming the importance of 'humanitarian assistance', inviting states in need of assistance to facilitate its delivery and appealing to other states to support those organisations offering such assistance. It did not recommend non-consensual intervention or military action in support of humanitarian goals. Similarly the International Court of Justice (ICJ) in the *Nicaragua* case had accepted a definition of humanitarian assistance as 'the provision of food, clothing, medicine, ... it does not include the provision of weapons, weapons systems, ammunition, or other equipment, vehicles, or material which can be used to inflict serious bodily harm or death'.[16] The Court gave no support to the concept of forceful humanitarian intervention. However, humanitarian relief for civilian populations is likely to be essential throughout a conflict, and, as became apparent, for instance, in Bosnia, safe delivery of assistance often depends upon negotiation with hostile forces for a temporary ceasefire, safe

[14] UN GA Resolution 43/131, 8 December 1988.

[15] UN GA Resolution 45/100, 14 December 1990, para. 6.

[16] *Military and Paramilitary Activities in and against Nicaragua* (*Nicaragua v. United States of America*), (Merits) 1986 ICJ Reports 14, judgment of 27 June 1986 ('*Nicaragua*'), para. 97.

passage, as well as military support and escort. Humanitarian packages also become a target for attack as their contents are sought for the fighting forces and contribute to the war economy. In 'new war' contexts, humanitarianism, military intervention and politicisation were becoming increasingly hard to keep distinct and called into question earlier assumptions about the need to combine the imperatives of 'humanity, neutrality, impartiality and independence in order to ensure the continued provision of humanitarian assistance, the safety of civilians receiving assistance and the security of humanitarian personnel'.[17]

5.2.2 *Security Council Authorisation for Military Intervention on Humanitarian Grounds*

In the aftermath of the Cold War, humanitarianism and human rights became much more prominent in international discourse. Starting with the establishment of a safe haven in northern Iraq in 1991, and culminating in the NATO air strikes in Yugoslavia in 1999, the presumption that there is a right to use armed force in support of humanitarian objectives became much more widely accepted, especially in some Western and international elite circles. In this way the just war notion of a just cause was making a reappearance. According to Kofi Annan, then UN Secretary-General:

> This developing international norm in favour of intervention to protect civilians from wholesale slaughter will no doubt continue to pose profound challenges to the international community.
>
> Any such evolution in our understanding of state sovereignty and individual sovereignty will, in some quarters, be met with distrust, scepticism, even hostility. But it is an evolution we should welcome.
>
> Why? Because despite its limitations and imperfections, it is testimony to a humanity that cares more, not less, for the suffering in its midst, and a humanity that will do more, and not less, to end it.
>
> It is a hopeful sign at the end of the twentieth century.[18]

[17] E.g., in UN SC Resolution 2100, 25 April 2013 (with respect to Mali); see further Holmes, John 2013. *The Politics of Humanity: The Reality of Relief Aid*. Head of Zeus.

[18] UN Secretary General's Report to the United Nations General Assembly, 20 September 1999. Text available at 'Secretary General Presents His Annual Report to the General Assembly', *UN Press Release*, 20 September 1999, www.un.org/press/en/1999/19990920.sgsm7136.html.

Northern Iraq (1991)

The first practical application of what Kouchner described as *the Droit d'Ingérence* was in Iraq in 1991 at a time when Kouchner himself was French Minister for Humanitarian Affairs. Inspired by the 'magnitude of the human suffering' of the Iraqi civilian population, in particular that of the Kurdish population in the aftermath of Iraq's defeat by the coalition forces, the SC insisted that 'Iraq allow immediate access by international humanitarian organizations to all those in need of assistance in all parts of Iraq'.[19] Resolution 688 was not adopted under UN Charter, chapter VII and did not actually mandate the use of force (or 'all necessary means'); nevertheless Operation Provide Comfort involved the deployment of more than 20,000 troops to protect what was in effect a safe haven for the Kurds in northern Iraq. The resolution was couched in terms of the threat to 'international peace and security' posed by refugees and by the situation in the area. The term 'haven' was used in preference to 'enclaves' at the insistence of the British Ambassador to the UN, Sir David Hannay, on the grounds that 'enclaves' suggested a redrawing of territorial boundaries.[20] Nevertheless, while reaffirming Iraqi sovereignty, the resolution did create a precedent in that it demanded that Iraq 'immediately end this repression' and 'ensure that the human and political rights of all Iraqi citizens are respected'.

Bosnia-Herzegovina (1992–1995)

The war in Bosnia-Herzegovina generated heated debate about humanitarian assistance and intervention and their place alongside repeated attempts at negotiating an end to conflict. The war led to widespread civil society mobilisation across Europe as local volunteer groups in different countries organised the collection and delivery of humanitarian assistance and, through links established with local peace and human rights groups in the former Yugoslavia, put forward a range of proposals for addressing the conflict.[21] Pressure from the media and civil society led to a series of SC resolutions authorising interventions for the

[19] UN SC Resolution 688, 5 April 1991.

[20] Gardiner D., Brown J., 'UK Urges Kurdish Enclave, *Financial Times*, 9 April 1991; Dickie, John 2004. *The New Mandarins: How British Foreign Policy Works*. I. B. Tauris, 208.

[21] For a more detailed exposition of the role of civil society, See Kaldor, Mary 2001. 'A Decade of Humanitarian Intervention: 1991–2000', in Anheier, Helmut, Glasius, Marlies and Kaldor, Mary (eds.) *Global Civil Society 2001*. Oxford University Press, chapter 5.

protection of the population by the international community on humanitarian grounds: the protection of aid convoys and the establishment of humanitarian corridors and safe havens, as well as more coercive action such as the imposition of sanctions, a no-fly zone, creation of the *ad hoc* international criminal tribunal for prosecution of crimes committed in the former Yugoslavia during the war, and international territorial administrations for the divided cities of Sarajevo and Mostar. However, the Rules of Engagement allowed troops only to use force in self-defence of its own personnel.[22] These interventions failed to stop the violence – sniper fire, siege, ethnic cleansing, detention, rape camps and fighting – and neither did the rounds of peace talks. Towards the end of the war, UN-protected safe havens fell to the Bosnian Serbs; in the case of Srebrenica this led to the genocide of some 8,000 men and boys.[23] Finally, in August-September 1995, NATO forces that had earlier provided air support to UNPROFOR and carried out some limited air strikes entered into a sustained bombing campaign of Bosnian Serb military targets (Operation Deliberate Force). An agreement was finally reached at Dayton in November 1995, thereby formally ending the conflict.[24]

It is worth noting that throughout the war, there was a contradiction between what was happening in the high-level peace processes and the humanitarian actions on the ground. From the beginning, the former took the form of talks about how to carve up Bosnia into ethnically clean territories. The assumption that this was acceptable actually contributed to ethnic cleansing. For example, the Vance-Owen Plan of January 1993 divided Bosnia-Herzegovina into ten cantons, nine of which were based on the domination of one or other of the ethnic groups (and the open city of Sarajevo). The plan was rejected by the Bosnian Serb Assembly in May 1993 (and also by the United States), but not before it had provided the legitimation for the Croats to ethnically cleanse the regions they were awarded under the plan. This marked the beginning of the Croat-Muslim conflict. (It was said that HVO, the initials of the Croat militia, stood for 'Hvala Vance Owen' – 'Thank you Vance Owen'.) Under pressure from the Americans, a Muslim-Croat ceasefire was negotiated in

22 It was estimated that 35,000 troops were required to fulfil the mandate but only 7,600 were deployed. See Findlay, Trevor, 2002. *The Use of Force in UN Peace Operations.* SIPRI. Oxford University Press.

23 *Application of the Convention on the Prevention and Punishment of the Crime of Genocide* (*Bosnia and Herzegovina v. Serbia and Montenegro*), 2007 ICJ Reports, judgment of 26 February 2007, para. 297.

24 See Chapter 9.

the spring of 1994; essentially, the Washington Agreement, as the ceasefire agreement was known, established a Bosnian-Croat federation partitioned into even smaller ethnically dominated cantons. Similarly, Florence Hartmann has revealed in a book, published in 2015, how the international negotiators came to the conclusion that an agreement was possible only if the eastern Muslim enclaves –Srebrenica, Zepa and Goradze – were ceded to the Serbs.[25] The negotiators presumably did not anticipate the subsequent massacre in Srebrenica, but accepting the notion of partition on ethnic lines in a mixed society meant a tacit political approval of ethnic cleansing, a sort of legitimation of Serb (and Croat) behaviour.

This meant that humanitarian initiatives could not counter ethnic cleansing; indeed, humanitarian efforts were, in effect, mopping up the consequences of a deliberate strategy of ethnic cleansing. This tacit endorsement of ethnic partition culminated in the Dayton agreement of 1995 – an explicit legitimation of ethnic partition discussed further in Chapter 9. Without high-level political support, humanitarian initiatives were bound to face serious obstacles. For some commentators, the long period of conflict with heavy civilian casualties discredited the notion of humanitarian intervention, even when UN authorised. They were seen as offering no more than a 'band-aid' to the besieged populations, keeping them alive through negotiations with the Serbs for safe passage of essential provisions but not relieving the violence, and serving as a smokescreen for the lack of effective action. Others argued that the problem was that the intervention was too weak; insufficient troops were provided, and therefore the Rules of Engagement (allowing for the use of force only in self-defence of the peacekeepers) were inadequate.[26] This second argument was reinforced by the perceived success of Operation Deliberate Force following the fall of Srebrenica when NATO forces carried out air strikes against Serb targets.[27] This is credited with hastening the end of the war

[25] Hartmann, Florence 2015. *L'affaire Srebrenica: Le Sang De La Realpolitik* (The Srebenica Affair: The Blood of Realpolitik). Don Quichotte Éditions. See also Vulliamy, Ed and Hartmann, Florence, 'How Britain and America Decided to Abandon Srebrenica to Its Fate', *The Guardian,* 4 July 2015, www.theguardian.com/world/2015/jul/04/how-britain-and-us-abandoned-srebrenica-massacre-1995.

[26] See Kaldor, Mary 2007. 'A Decade of Humanitarian Intervention', in Kaldor, Mary, *Human Security: Reflections on Globalisation and Intervention*. Polity Press.

[27] NATO forces had been previously providing support to UNPROFOR and policing the no-fly zones over Bosnia. The decision to undertake airstrikes was 'made by NATO only' without UN SC authorisation; Holbrooke, Richard 1999. *To End a War*. Modern Library, 72.

and enabling the peace negotiations at Dayton. The belief that bombing contributed to Dayton may also have influenced NATO's decision to undertake airstrikes against human rights abuses that came to the fore in Kosovo in 1999.[28] However, another equally plausible explanation for these negotiations is that ethnic partition had been achieved on the ground, and the warring parties sought legitimation for their positions. Both the negotiations and the air strikes were based on the 'old war' assumption that the warring parties were legitimate political actors and that the wars were a contest of wills. By contrast, the humanitarian initiatives were an early response to an understanding of war as a massive violation of human rights.

Somalia (1992)

The SC decision to authorise intervention in Somalia in 1992 may well have been a reaction to the debate in the early months of the war in Bosnia. SC Resolution 794, which was adopted unanimously on 2 December 1992, was widely considered to break new ground. Even though Resolution 688 had referred to the threat to 'international peace and security', Resolution 794 was the first resolution to authorise, under chapter VII of the UN Charter, 'all necessary means' to relieve human suffering through the establishment of a 'secure environment for humanitarian relief'. The focus remained on humanitarian assistance, but was supported by an unrestricted military mandate. In 1992 Somalia was a 'collapsed' or 'failed' state without a government; the resolution was thus adopted without state consent. Many states that had opposed Resolution 688, particularly in Africa supported Resolution 794. For Kouchner, it was a triumph: 'a fantastic step forward, a new legal base for the international *Droit d'Ingérence*'. The headline in *Liberation* the next day was 'L'humanitaire s'en va t'en guerre'.[29] But the Somali intervention ended in fiasco when Somali militia attacked and killed a number of Pakistani UN peacekeepers and succeeded on 3–4 October 1993 in shooting down two American helicopters, killing eighteen American soldiers and wounding seventy-five in the ensuing battle. The bodies of the American soldiers were paraded publicly in front of jeering crowds and international television cameras.

[28] '[I]t seems that the NATO's operational and humanitarian success in 1995 set it up for the intervention, and also some tough surprises, in Kosovo in 1999'. Owen, Robert 'Operation Deliberate Force: A Case Study on Humanitarian Constraints in Aerospace Warfare', at http://carrcenter.hks.harvard.edu/files/carrcenter/files/owen2001.pdf, 68.

[29] 'L'Humanitaire s'en va t'en Guerre', *Liberation*, 3 December 1992.

Rwanda (1994)

The debacle in Somalia had ripple-on effects. The *USS Harlan County* bringing US troops to Haiti was prevented from landing by violence in Port-au-Prince on 11–12 October 1993 and was followed by the withdrawal of members of a UN human rights observer mission, to the cries of 'Haiti! Somalia! Haiti! Somalia! . . . Aidid! Aidid!'[30] President Clinton issued Presidential Decision Directive 25 in May 1994, which strictly limited American participation in future peacekeeping operations. It was invoked precisely as pressure mounted from NGOs and the media to intervene to stop the horrifying genocide of Tutsis and Hutus believed to be tolerant towards the Tutsis that was taking place in Rwanda between April and June 1994. Between 500,000 and 1 million people were killed in 100 days. There was in April 1994 a small UN force of 1,500 troops in Rwanda, the United Nations Assistance Mission to Rwanda (UNAMIR), to monitor the ceasefire and implementation of the 1993 Arusha Peace Agreement.[31] The mandate was limited and in particular did not include recovery of arms.[32] Despite warnings from the Force Commander, General Dallaire, and proposals to seize weapons and create safe havens, the SC took the decision to prepare for withdrawal and to scale down the UN force.[33] UNAMIR was not able to provide protection to civilians who sought it from them,[34] although through the personal courage of some UN personnel the lives of some civilians and political leaders were saved.[35]

Later, when it was clear that Dallaire's warnings should have been taken seriously, the Secretary-General proposed an intervention force of

30 Cain, Kenneth, Postlewait, Heidi and Thomson, Andrew 2004. *Emergency Sex and Other Desperate Measures: A True Story from Hell on Earth*. Miramax Books, 170.

31 UN SC Resolution 872, 5 October 1993. The *Arusha Peace Agreement*, 4 August 1993 was concluded between different Rwandese groups with the objective of ending civil war in Rwanda.

32 Report of the Independent Inquiry into the Actions of the United Nations during the 1994 Genocide in Rwanda, UN Doc. S/1999/1257, 16 December 1999, 8 ('Rwanda Report').

33 By UN SC Resolution 912, 21 April 1994, UNAMIR was scaled down from 2,548 personnel to 270.

34 For example, 'About 2000 people had sought refuge at ETO, believing that the UNAMIR troops would be able to protect them. . . . [A]fter the expatriates in ETO had been evacuated by French troops, the Belgian contingent at ETO left the school, leaving behind men, women and children many of whom were massacred by the waiting soldiers and militia'. Rwanda Report, *op. cit.*, 19.

35 *Ibid.*, 30.

5,500 personnel. Belatedly the SC increased the size of UNAMIR and imposed an arms embargo on Rwanda.[36] Several African forces were prepared to take part, but they needed American logistical support, which was not forthcoming. The UN Independent Inquiry into the UN's actions in Rwanda later concluded that the overwhelming reason for the failure of the UN to prevent the genocide was 'a lack of resources and a lack of will to take on the commitment' to do so.[37] Indeed, the Clinton Administration actively mobilised against those governments, NGOs and media that wanted to describe what was happening in Rwanda as 'genocide' for fear that this would oblige it to act under the 1948 Genocide Convention.[38] At the end of August 1994, a French intervention force was dispatched. But by this time the genocide was over, and the Rwandan Patriotic Front had largely succeeded in overthrowing the extremists. The French intervention was suspect because of French support for the previous regime; all it was able to achieve was to provide safe havens for fleeing Hutus, many of whom were former militiamen engaged in the genocide. The destabilisation caused by the dispersal of these people across the region, and their pursuit by the Rwandan Government, was a contributing factor to the deadly conflicts in the Great Lakes region of Africa, notably the Democratic Republic of Congo (DRC) in the late 1990s, in which millions of civilians died, were raped or mutilated.

Haiti (1994)

Another significant military intervention during this period, Operation Uphold Democracy in Haiti, shifted the discourse towards protection of democracy. In response to the escalation of 'politically motivated violence' following a military coup against the elected government, the SC had authorised the establishment of a UN Mission in Haiti (UNMIH) in September 1993.[39] The events of October 1993 described above obstructed the Mission from deploying.[40] However, in July 1994 the SC authorised the use of 'all necessary means' to restore democracy in Haiti.[41] President Clinton saw it more widely as a mix of self-interest and humanitarianism, stating that the purpose was 'to protect our

[36] UN SC Resolution 918, 17 May 1994. [37] Rwanda Report, *op. cit.*, 30.

[38] *Convention on the Prevention and Punishment of the Crime of Genocide*, 9 December 1948, United Nations Treaty Series, vol. 78, 277; Wheeler, *op. cit.*, 224–225.

[39] UN SC Resolution 867, 23 September 1993.

[40] UN SC Resolution 873, 13 October 1993. [41] UN SC Resolution 940, 31 July 1994.

interests, to stop the brutal atrocities that threaten Haitians, to secure our borders and to preserve stability and democracy on our continent'.[42] But however expressed, this and a similar resolution with respect to Sierra Leone in 1997[43] brought a new dimension to post–Cold War military intervention: regime change in the name of democracy. In both Haiti and Sierra Leone the SC deemed the overthrow of a democratically elected government to constitute a threat to international peace and security.[44]

In Iraq (1991), Bosnia, Somalia and Haiti, military intervention for humanitarian or democratisation purposes was authorised by the SC in exercise of its primary responsibility for the maintenance of international peace and security.[45] In effect the SC had expanded its competence through broadening its understanding of such threats to encompass humanitarian emergencies. In two further instances the SC subsequently endorsed military intervention by a regional organisation that had not been authorised in advance. Both cases involved action undertaken at the behest of the Economic Community of West African States (ECOWAS), in Liberia in 1990–1992[46] and in Sierra Leone in 1997.[47] The SC's retroactive approval of these military interventions is indicative of the continuing willingness to encourage regional responses to conflict and human rights violations.[48] However, it left unanswered the claim that unauthorised military intervention could be legally undertaken if carried out for humanitarian purposes, that is, that right authority (the SC) could be displaced by just cause. Such an argument also meant allowing SC-authorised action to be understood as state practice for the purpose of customary international law with respect to unauthorised action. This set the UN Charter framework for collective security against claims for unilateral protection of human rights.

[42] Quoted in Weiss, Thomas 2012. *Humanitarian Intervention*. Polity Press,184.

[43] UN SC Resolution 1132, 8 October 1997.

[44] This acceptance of regime change may have paved the way for supporting justifications for the legality of interventions in Afghanistan (2001), Iraq (2003) and Libya (2011).

[45] UN Charter, article 24.

[46] UN SC Resolution 788, 19 November 1992: 'Commends ECOWAS for its efforts to restore peace, security and stability in Liberia'.

[47] UN SC Resolution 1162, 17 April 1998: 'Commends the Economic Community of West African States (ECOWAS) and its Military Observer Group (ECOMOG), deployed in Sierra Leone, on the important role they are playing in support of the objectives related to the restoration of peace and security'.

[48] 'Regional and subregional organizations are becoming more prominent features in the global peace and security landscape, as had been foreseen in the drafting of Chapter VIII of the Charter 70 years ago'. Report of the High-Level Independent Panel on Peace Operations on Uniting our Strengths for Peace: Politics, Partnership and People ('Report of the Independent Panel'), UN Doc. A/70/95–S/2015/446, 17 June 2015, para. 55.

5.2.3 Unauthorised Military Intervention on Humanitarian Grounds

The decade – and debate – culminated in the NATO intervention in Kosovo in March 1999. The British Prime Minister, Tony Blair, used the occasion of NATO's fiftieth anniversary, which took place during the air strikes, to enunciate a new 'Doctrine of International Community' that linked markets, political ideology, security and the use of force: 'We are all internationalists now whether we like it or not', Blair told an audience in Chicago. 'We cannot refuse to participate in global markets if we want to prosper. We cannot ignore new political ideas in other countries if we want to innovate. We cannot turn our backs on conflicts and the violation of human rights in other countries if we still want to be secure'.[49]

In 1989 Kosovo's autonomous status within the Yugoslav Republic of Serbia was repealed by Slobodan Milošević, then President of Serbia, and a period of non-violent resistance and parallel administration was undertaken by Kosovar Albanians against Serbian oppression. Towards the end of the 1990s, after the omission of Kosovo from the Dayton peace process in 1995 and after the opening up of weapons caches in Albania, a small group financed by the Diaspora, calling itself the Kosovo Liberation Army (KLA), commenced a series of armed attacks against Kosovar Serbs, to which Serb forces reacted with great brutality. By 1998 armed conflict between the Serbian forces on one side and the KLA and other Kosovo Albanian armed groups on the other had come to be characterised as 'a continuing grave humanitarian situation throughout Kosovo and [an] impending humanitarian catastrophe'.[50] In contrast to the Western powers favouring armed intervention, Russia and the People's Republic of China indicated that they would veto a SC resolution authorising such intervention. Following the failure of negotiations at Rambouillet to conclude a peace agreement,[51] in March 1999 NATO went ahead with a bombing campaign in Kosovo and Serbia without SC authorisation.

In the wake of the NATO military action, claims for the conformity of intervention for humanitarian purposes with international law, despite the prohibition of the use of force, were made strenuously and also resisted. Opinions among states and commentators were

[49] 'The Blair Doctrine', *PBS Newshour*, 22 April 1999, www.pbs.org/newshour/bb/international-jan-june99-blair_doctrine4-23/.

[50] UN SC Resolution 1203, 24 October 1998.

[51] Weller, Marc 1999. 'The Rambouillet Conference on Kosovo', *International Affairs* 75(2): 211–251.

divided.[52] Members of the UK Government, for example, although stopping short of asserting a broader right of humanitarian intervention, claimed that where there was 'overwhelming humanitarian necessity, ... in light of all the circumstances, a limited use of force is justifiable as the only way to avert a humanitarian catastrophe'.[53] In its pleadings before the ICJ in a case brought by Serbia against all NATO member states alleging the illegality of the action, Belgium argued that it was an instance of humanitarian intervention and as such was compatible with UN Charter article 2 (4) as it was not against the territorial integrity or political independence of Serbia.[54] SC Resolution 1244 of 10 June 1999, adopted after the end of the bombing campaign, did not explicitly endorse the action (as had resolutions with respect to ECOWAS action in Liberia and Sierra Leone), although it did decide 'that a political solution to the Kosovo crisis shall be based on the general principles in annex 1' (adopted on 6 May during the bombing campaign) 'as further elaborated in the principles in annex 2' (adopted 2 June, also during the bombing).

Among commentators a third line was taken between those who considered the action to have been contrary to the UN Charter and those who accepted its legality in accordance with a new principle of customary international law. This refinement was to indicate an emergent rule of customary international law; thus the action was deemed to have been only slightly illegal, or illegal but legitimate in that the intentions of the NATO states were disinterested and humanitarian. Further, despite accelerated ethnic cleansing under cover of the bombing, in the end all the Kosovo Albanians were able to return to their homes.[55] Evidently this position is motivated by a concern that the foundational principles of international law should uphold a moral position: 'an interpretation of international law which would forbid intervention to prevent something as terrible as the holocaust ... would be contrary to the principles upon

52 For a range of views see Kosovo: House of Commons Foreign Affairs Committee 4th Report, June 2000, summarised with contributions in 2000 *International and Comparative Law Quarterly* 49: 876–943.

53 Cited in UK Parliament, Select Committee on Foreign Affairs, Fourth Report, International Law, para. 124, www.parliament.the-stationeryoffice.co.uk/pa/cm199900/cmselect/cmfaff/28/2813.htm.

54 *Legality of Use of Force* (*Serbia and Montenegro v Belgium*) (Provisional Measures), 1999 ICJ Reports, 10 May 1999, pleadings of Belgium.

55 The Independent International Commission on Kosovo 2000. *Kosovo Report: Conflict, International Response, Lessons Learned.* Oxford University Press, 119.

which modern international law is based'.[56] A reversion from legal analysis to claims of morality and ethical response – legitimacy – is evocative of the language and reasoning of just war. On the one hand it is supported for its supposed responsiveness to popular opinion and refusal to allow legal formalism to inhibit humanitarian action; on the other it is criticised for its subjectivity and undermining of the rule of international law.

The difficulty, however, with any concept of humanitarian intervention is the problem that Rodin has elucidated with respect to a state's right of self-defence that we discussed in Chapter 4. It is the contradiction between the *jus ad bellum* and *jus in bello*. Can it be right to use the methods of war to protect people when this also involves the killing of, and injury to, other non-combatants? Can there be a right to kill civilians to save other civilians?[57] Is collective enforcement an appropriate tool against brutal oppressors since it also involves attacking the victims of those oppressors? After the initial deployment of the OSCE Verification Mission and its removal prior to the commencement of the bombing campaign,[58] what played little part in the debates is the language of individual – human – security and whether there were ways of protecting the security of one population (the Kosovar Albanians) without endangering that of other populations (Kosovar Serbs, other minorities in Kosovo and the population in Serbia) by the exercise of military force. This language could have been addressed much earlier by offering support to the peaceful resistance to Serbian authority through the parallel administration headed by Ibrahim Rugova. The need to secure Milošević's participation at Dayton in 1995 contributed to the Western powers failure

[56] Memorandum submitted by Christopher Greenwood QC, UK Parliament, Select Committee on Foreign Affairs, Minutes of Evidence, 22 November 1999, www.publications.parliament.uk/pa/cm199900/cmselect/cmfaff/28/0020802.htm.

[57] The Constitutional Court of Germany found the Air Security Law of 2005 that authorised the Government to shoot down a civilian aircraft that had been hijacked and could be used in a terrorist attack to be contrary to the Basic Law. The Court found that deliberate killing, even in such a situation, would violate human dignity; Beltrán de Felipe, Miguel and Rodríguez de Santiago, José María 2007. 'Shooting Down Hijacked Airplanes? Sorry, We're Humanists: A Comment on the German Constitutional Court Decision of 2.15.2006, Regarding the *Luftsicherheitsgesetz* (2005 Air Security Act)', www.unodc.org/tldb/pdf/EssayCivilAviation1.pdf.

[58] UN SC Resolution 1203, 24 October 1998. Much of the Resolution addresses the safety and security of diplomatic personnel, members of the OSCE Verification Mission, and international and non-governmental humanitarian personnel in the FRY rather than that of civilians.

to respond to this act of internal self-determination by the Kosovar Albanians; support when it came was top-down, militaristic and without reference to this alternative narrative.[59]

Humanitarianism was both the asserted reason for the NATO airstrikes in Kosovo and imposed the *jus in bello* constraints upon it.[60] But it was not so easy to apply humanitarian principles in practice. NATO relied on airstrikes without ground troops. NATO did not succeed, in the initial stages, in knocking out the Yugoslav air-defence system: this is why NATO aircraft continued to fly at 15,000 feet. Effectively this meant that the risks to NATO forces were given priority over the risks to the civilian population. It is understandable that, given the need for popular support, NATO states were unwilling to risk the lives of NATO pilots in a war that had no direct national interest, but this stance was incompatible with the human security of those on the ground and may have increased the number of deaths and injuries. Although 'NATO made substantial efforts to avoid civilian casualties',[61] because of the insistence that aircraft fly above 15,000 feet, pilots could not see what was happening below them and were dependent on intelligence from numerous, often badly coordinated, sources. Consequently, repeated mistakes were made, as became embarrassingly clear for the duration of the air strikes. Low points included the bombing of refugees inside Kosovo and the Chinese Embassy in Belgrade. Some 1,400 people were killed or injured in so-called collateral damage.[62] Cluster bombs continued to detonate for some time after the end of the bombing.[63] Huge damage was done to civilian infrastructure and industrial facilities with environmental, health and social consequences. Historic sites were destroyed, in Novi Sad, for example; a building housing a TV transmitter was blown up, killing journalists inside, and targets were hit

[59] Heathcote notes that this failure to listen to an alternative narrative resonates with Western failure to accommodate diversity and is exposed by feminist theory; Heathcote, Gina 2012. *The Law on the Use of Force: A Feminist Analysis*. Routledge, 172.

[60] Owen, Robert C. 2001. 'Operation Deliberate Force: a Case Study on Humanitarian Constraints in Aerospace Warfare', *Carr Centre*, http://carrcenter.hks.harvard.edu/files/carrcenter/files/owen2001.pdf. On the *jus in bello* see Chapter 6.

[61] *Kosovo Report*, *op. cit.*, 94. [62] *Ibid.*

[63] See, e.g., the facts of *Behrami v France*, ECHR GC application no. 71412/01, 2 May 2007: 'On 11 March 2000 eight boys were playing in the hills in the municipality of Mitrovica. . . . At around midday, the group came upon a number of undetonated cluster bomb units ("CBUs") which had been dropped during the bombardment by NATO in 1999 and the children began playing with the CBUs. Believing it was safe, one of the children threw a CBU in the air: it detonated and killed Gadaf Behrami. Bekim Behrami was also seriously injured and taken to hospital in Pristina'.

in Montenegro, whose government had refused to participate on the Serb side in the war in Kosovo. There also may have been long-term, health and environmental consequences of the use of depleted uranium by NATO, although this remains unclear.[64]

Far from halting the oppression of Kosovar Albanians, the Serb forces accelerated the process of forced displacement under the cover of the bombing. After 24 March 1999, when the bombing began, some 10,000 people were killed in the cleansing operation, including children, and more than a million were forced to leave Kosovo, fleeing especially to Macedonia and Montenegro. Displacement – and lack of secure shelters – enhanced the possibility of illness and violence. When NATO ground forces entered the territory in June, only 600,000 people were left in Kosovo, and, of these, 400,000 were internally displaced.[65] Moreover, a process of reverse ethnic cleansing followed SC Resolution 1244 of 10 June 1999 and the entry of NATO troops. From the summer of 1999 onwards and despite the deployment of a military (KFOR) and civilian security force (UNMIK Police), abductions and murderous attacks against the Serbian population remaining in Kosovo and members of other minorities (primarily Roma and Ashkali), as well as against those Albanians suspected of collaboration, erupted and became the over-riding security concern:[66] 'Numerous crimes were committed both against Serbs who had stayed in the region and against Kosovar Albanians (and other minorities) suspected of having been "traitors" or "collaborators", or who fell victim to internal rivalries within the KLA'.[67]

[64] Immediately following the conflict the UN Environmental Programme (UNEP) carried out the 'first ever international assessment of the environmental impact of depleted uranium (DU) when used in a real conflict situation'. It concluded that there was present only low-level radioactivity and no immediate cause for concern regarding toxicity, but nevertheless urged precaution and the need for monitoring, especially of groundwater. This is echoed in a 2012 UNGA Resolution that recalled scientific uncertainties about the long-term environmental impacts of depleted uranium and requested further research on the issue. The resolution supports a precautionary approach, albeit in restrained terms, but nevertheless the United States, United Kingdom, France and Israel voted against it. UN GA Resolution, 67/36, 4 January 2013 (Effects of the use of armaments and ammunitions containing depleted uranium).

[65] These estimates are taken from the *Kosovo Report*, 88–92.

[66] Report of the Secretary General on the United Nations Interim Administration in Kosovo, UN Doc S/1999/1250, 23 December 1999, paras. 15–9; Kosovo Human Rights Advisory Panel, *S.C. v. UNMIK*, Case No. 02/09, 6 December 2012, paras. 14–15.

[67] Council of Europe Parliamentary Assembly, Committee on Legal Affairs and Human Rights, 'Inhuman Treatment of People and Illicit Trafficking in Human Organs in Kosovo', AS/Jur (46, 12 December 2010, para. 4).

Some 160,000 Serbs left the country. A further major outbreak of violence against the Serbs in Kosovo erupted in March 2004, which the UN Mission in Kosovo[68]and KFOR were unable immediately to contain. The violence resulted in nineteen deaths, nearly 1,000 people being injured and nearly 2,000 people displaced. Hundreds of houses primarily belonging to Kosovar Serbs were burned, as were Serbian Orthodox churches and monasteries. This was followed by another exodus from Kosovo of numbers of Kosovar Serbs. Today, the Serbs who remain mostly live in isolated enclaves or in the northern city of Mitrovica, and tension between Serbs and Albanians in Kosovo continues. When the UN is perceived to have failed in its first task – stopping the killing, looting and violence – the mission loses credibility and is undermined in its ability to carry out other tasks.

It can be argued that the political consequences of this type of bombing were also counterproductive. Despite the insistence of NATO spokespersons that there is a big difference between killing by mistake and killing deliberately, this difference was not obvious to the victims of the bombing. Who determines whether the killing of civilians counts as a 'massacre' or as 'collateral damage'?[69] Likewise, the insistence of Western leaders that the bombing was directed against the regime and not against Serbs was not at all evident to those who experienced its effects. The air strikes mobilised Serbian national sentiment, allowing Milošević to crack down on NGOs and independent media during the war and thus to minimise domestic constraints against his activities in Kosovo, thereby permitting the sense of victimhood to overshadow any sense of responsibility for the wars.[70] Together with the influx of refugees, the air strikes polarised opinion in both the Former Yugoslav Republic of Macedonia and in Montenegro, accentuating domestic tensions and the risk of the further spread of violence. They also polarised international opinion: for many in the East and South, the claim that this was a war for human rights was viewed as a cover for the pursuit of Western imperial interests in the Balkans. In sum, the Kosovo conflict illustrated three challenges of humanitarian intervention that are often discounted: downplaying the

[68] UNMIK, mandated by UN SC Resolution 1244, 10 June 1999.

[69] See Chapter 6 for discussion of international humanitarian law.

[70] Milošević was indicted by the ICTY on 27 May 1999 during the NATO bombing campaign for genocide, crimes against humanity, grave breaches of the Geneva Conventions and violations of the laws or customs of war; *Prosecutor v. Slobodan Milosevic,* Case No. IT-01-51-I.

difficulties of halting violations of human rights by the use of force; inadequate preparation for the post-conflict situation; and the impact of perceived public opinion on constraining decisions to deploy troops.[71]

Kosovo elicited renewed concern about the legality of unilateral intervention. Consent even for SC-authorised missions was sought. For instance, a few months later, in September 1999, the SC put pressure on the Indonesian government to 'request' an intervention in response to the continuing violence, deteriorating security situation and 'systematic, widespread and flagrant violations of international humanitarian and human rights law' in East Timor, following the referendum held in August 1999.[72] The British intervention in Sierra Leone in 2000 similarly was in line with the Blair doctrine discussed above and had the consent of the Government and the United Nations mission.[73]

In both the cases of Afghanistan (2001) and Iraq (2003), humanitarian justifications were used by intervening states in addition to those relating to self-defence, discussed in Chapter 4. In Afghanistan, the Taliban's human rights abuses meant that the fall of Kabul in late 2003 was (rightly) celebrated as a humanitarian victory. Laura Bush and Cherie Blair, for example, both emphasised the importance of the intervention for women's rights, although this instrumentalisation contrasted with earlier disregard of such violations. In the case of Iraq, many of those who favoured intervention were so-called liberal interventionists, for instance, the columnist Christopher Hitchens and the human rights scholar and politician Michael Ignatieff, who used pro-human rights and democracy arguments.[74] These arguments became much more prevalent after the failure to locate weapons of mass destruction. In the cases of both Afghanistan and Iraq, the continued presence of US-led forces following the transfer of power to the local government was cast as being at their request.[75]

[71] Wertheim, Stephen 2010. 'A Solution from Hell: The United States and the Rise of Humanitarian Interventionism, 1991–2003', *Journal of Genocide Research* 12(3–4): 149–172.

[72] UN SC Resolution 1264, 15 September 1999.

[73] The United Nations Mission in Sierra Leone (UNAMSIL) had been established by UN SC Resolution 1270, 22 October 1999. It was an early resolution to authorise 'the necessary action ... within its capabilities and areas of deployment, to afford protection to civilians under imminent threat of physical violence, taking into account the responsibilities of the Government of Sierra Leone and ECOMOG'. See further Chapter 9.

[74] See, e.g., Ignatieff, Michael 2003. 'Friends Disunited', *The Guardian*, 24 March 2003, www.theguardian.com/politics/2003/mar/24/iraq.world; Hitchens, Christopher 2003. *The Long Short War: The Postponed Liberation of Iraq*. Penguin Books.

[75] *Agreement on Provisional Arrangements in Afghanistan Pending the Re-establishment of Permanent Government Institutions* ('Bonn Agreement'), December 2001, Annex I, para. 3:

5.3 The Responsibility to Protect

5.3.1 The Concept of the Responsibility to Protect

Following the Kosovo war and against the backdrop of failure to prevent the massive numbers of civilian deaths in Rwanda and Bosnia, the absence of a formal exception to the UN Charter prohibition of the use of force based on humanitarian intervention and continued disagreement about its legality led to the establishment of the International Commission on Intervention and State Sovereignty (ICISS). This body of experts articulated the notion of a responsibility to protect,[76] thereby shifting the language back to the legal concept of state (sovereign) responsibility[77] and that of the broader international community. The Responsibility to Protect rests on three pillars. First, the state has the primary responsibility to protect its own population against genocide, ethnic cleansing, war crimes and crimes against humanity.[78] Second, in an extension of the traditional notion of state responsibility, the international community bears the responsibility to assist states to discharge this responsibility. Third, if a state is failing to discharge its responsibility, the international community must be ready to act collectively in accordance with the UN Charter. The ICISS also set out criteria for intervention that were drawn from the just war tradition: there must be just cause; right authority (ideally the UN Security Council, but in the Commission's view an intervention supported by 'an overwhelming majority' of the General Assembly would also have legitimacy); right intention; the intervention must be as a 'last resort'; it must be proportionate (the scale of the

'the participants in the UN Talks on Afghanistan request the United Nations Security Council to consider authorizing the early deployment to Afghanistan of a United Nations mandated force'; UN SC Resolution 1546, 8 June 2004: 'Notes that the presence of the multinational force in Iraq is at the request of the incoming Interim Government of Iraq'.

[76] Report of the International Commission on Intervention and State Sovereignty 2001. *The Responsibility to Protect.* Ottawa: International Development Research Centre ('ICISS Report').

[77] The concept of 'sovereignty as responsibility' had been developed in a book by Francis Deng, Special Representative of the Secretary-General on Internally Displaced Persons and Others; Deng, Francis *et al.* 1996. *Sovereignty as Responsibility: Conflict Management in Africa.* Brookings Institution.

[78] This pillar was emphasised by then Prime Minister David Cameron in his memorandum to the Foreign Affairs Select Committee about extending airstrikes in Syria, 26 November 2015; 'Full Text of David Cameron's memorandum on Syria Airstrikes', *The Guardian*, 26 November 2015, www.theguardian.com/politics/2015/nov/26/full-text-of-david-camerons-memorandum-on-syria-airstrikes.

operation must be the minimum necessary to secure the defined human protection objective); and there must be a reasonable prospect of success.

The concept of a Responsibility to Protect was formally adopted by the GA in 2005, although responsibility remained with states and it did not (could not) specifically authorise international intervention except on a case-by-case basis through the SC.[79] After appointment as Secretary-General in January 2007, Ban Ki-moon said that 'he will spare no effort to operationalize Responsibility to Protect'.[80] He appointed special advisors on the topic[81] and established a Responsibility to Protect Fund supported by Sweden, the United Kingdom and Australia. Annually since 2009,[82] the GA has considered the Secretary-General's reports on aspects of implementation of the Responsibility to Protect and has held informal interactive dialogues on the subject. The reports have *inter alia* examined how the Responsibility to Protect can be operationalised in a timely and decisive manner,[83] emphasised the tools available to states, including for prevention of violations of human rights, and the linkage between the three pillars.[84]

The Responsibility to Protect is often equated with military intervention. However, it is a continuum of obligation: to prevent, react, reconstruct. Military intervention is the last resort, and the concept encompasses the responsibility to prevent and the responsibility to rebuild.[85] The responsibility to prevent is not new: since 1948, the

[79] Outcome Document of the High-Level Plenary Meeting of the 60th Session of the UN General Assembly, 14–16 September 2005, paras. 138–140.

[80] Secretary-General, Ban Ki-moon, address to the Summit of the African Union, Addis Ababa, UN Doc. SG/SM/11396-AFR/1651, 31 January 2008.

[81] The Joint Office of the Special Adviser on the Prevention of Genocide and Special Adviser Responsible for the Conceptual, Political and Institutional Development of the Responsibility to Protect, Secretary-General, Ban Ki-moon, address to the Summit of the African Union, Addis Ababa, UN Doc. SG/SM/11396-AFR/1651, 31 January 2008.

[82] Report of the Secretary-General, Implementing the Responsibility to Protect, UN Doc. A/63/677, 12 January 2009, was the first comprehensive report presented to the General Assembly on the Responsibility to Protect. It has been followed by further annual reports since then.

[83] Report of the Secretary-General, Responsibility to Protect: Timely and Decisive Response, 25 July 2012, UN Doc. A/66/874–S/2012/578, 25 July 2012.

[84] Report of the Secretary-General, Responsibility to Protect: State Responsibility and Prevention, UN Doc. A/67/929–S/2013/399, 9 July 2013.

[85] The major problem with the responsibility to rebuild is how it equates with regime change. We consider the issue of post-conflict rebuilding in our discussion of transitional justice (Chapter 9) but note here that the experience of the reverse ethnic cleansing against the Kosovo Serbs after June 1999 illustrates its importance.

Genocide Convention has required states (including non-parties to the Convention)[86] to 'prevent and punish' genocide; the obligation to prevent genocide has been described by the ICJ as 'normative and compelling'.[87] The ICJ found Serbia in violation of this obligation with respect to the genocide in Srebrenica.[88] The Court also noted that there was 'persuasive evidence' that Uganda had failed to prevent conflict in the Ituri district in the DRC that resulted in 'some 10,000 deaths and the displacement of some 50,000 people'. However, Uganda's culpability appears to go beyond failing to prevent these deaths; the Court also noted that Uganda had incited ethnic violence there and referred to a report that found that instead of trying to calm the situation, '[Ugandan troops] preferred to benefit from the situation and support alternately one side or the other according to their political and financial interests'.[89]

Successive UN reports have highlighted the importance of prevention of conflict, for instance, Secretary-General Boutros-Boutros Ghali in his Agenda for Peace (1992 and Supplement 1995) and in July 2015 the High Level Independent Panel on Peace Operations headed by Ramos Horta.[90] There has been little positive reaction. Prime Minister Blair's assertion that the choice in Kosovo in 1998–1999 was between doing nothing and military intervention was too simplistic; more measures aimed at prevention of atrocities might have been sought. Certainly, ever since 1990, the conflict in Kosovo was waiting to happen, and much more could have been done in terms of prevention during the 1990s. In 1998, an OSCE Verification Mission had placed unarmed personnel in the territory, both to act as ceasefire observers and to deter the commission of further atrocities.[91] An air verification mission over Kosovo was also agreed at the same time, agreed to by the permanent Council of the OSCE[92] and

[86] '[T]he principles underlying the Convention are principles which are recognized by civilized nations as binding on States, even without any conventional obligation'. *Reservations to the Convention* on *Genocide,* 1951 ICJ Reports 15, 23, advisory opinion of 28 May 1951.

[87] *Application of the Convention on the Prevention and Punishment of the Crime of Genocide* (Bosnia and Herzegovina v. Serbia and Montenegro), 2007 ICJ Reports, judgment of 26 February 2007, para. 427.

[88] *Ibid.*, paras. 425–438.

[89] *Armed Activities on the Territory of the Congo* (Democratic Republic of the Congo v. Uganda), 2005 ICJ Reports 168, judgment of 19 December 2005 ('*Uganda*'), para. 209.

[90] Report of the High-Level Independent Panel, *op. cit.*, para. 62ff.

[91] Known as 'clockwork oranges' because of their uniforms, they were, however, widely considered ineffective.

[92] OSCE. 'Kosovo Verification Mission (closed)', www.osce.org/node/44552.

endorsed by SC Resolution 1203, 24 October 1998. At this late stage such measures were evidently insufficient; moreover, the observers were removed before the March 1999 bombing campaign commenced. Attempts at making such preventive mechanisms more holistic and effective should be explored.[93]

Some also argue that the United Nations Preventive Deployment Force (UNPREDEP) established by the SC in March 1995 to prevent the spread of the conflict in Bosnia-Herzegovina to Macedonia[94] was an instance of a successful deployment of UN peacekeeping forces in the prevention of conflict and violence against civilians.[95] The operation was prematurely shut down on February 28, 1999, after Macedonia recognised Taiwan in return for financial support and China vetoed the renewal of UNPREDEP's mandate. Conflict in Macedonia broke out in 2001 largely as a spillover from Kosovo. Approximately 20 percent of the population is Albanian, and this number was swelled by the influx of refugees from Kosovo in 1999–2000. The justification for the conflict had to do with the unequal treatment of Albanians in relation to education, public service and citizenship in the aftermath of the break-up of the former Yugoslavia. An offshoot of the KLA, the National Liberation Army of Macedonia (NLA), exploited these grievances. It is not clear whether UNPREDEP could have prevented the conflict since its mandate was to monitor developments on the border and to prevent Serb incursions; however, while deployed its presence was probably a deterrent to internal violence.

5.3.2 *Protection of Civilians in Armed Conflict*

The emphasis of the Responsibility to Protect is on responses to serious human rights abuses in the form of war crimes, crimes against humanity, genocide and ethnic cleansing. Alongside the evolution of the Responsibility to Protect the SC has adopted since 1999 a succession of thematic resolutions on the protection of civilians in armed conflict.[96] Since 2006 these resolutions have also affirmed the basic principles of the

93 Bellamy, Alex and Griffin, Stuart 2002. 'OSCE Peacekeeping: Lessons from the Kosovo Verification Mission', *European Security* 11: 1–26.

94 UN SC Resolution 983, 31 March 1995.

95 Sokalski, Henry 2003. *An Ounce of Prevention: Macedonia and the UN Experience in Preventive Diplomacy*. US Institute of Peace Press.

96 The first such resolution was UN SC Resolution 1265, 17 September 1999. It follows the Report of the Secretary-General, Causes of Conflict and the Promotion of Durable Peace and Sustainable Development in Africa, UN Doc. S/1998/318, 13 April 1998 and Report

responsibility to protect.[97] They also demand humanitarian access in crisis zones and indicate the Council's preparedness to act in cases where civilians are deliberately targeted.[98] In its thematic resolutions on the protection of civilians, the SC has made general reference to the need for protection of women and children[99] and has also adopted resolutions specifically on their protection. Following the presentation of Graça Machel's definitive report on children in armed conflict to the GA in 1996,[100] the Assembly recommended that the Secretary-General appoint a Special Representative (SR-SG) on the impact of armed conflict on children.[101] The Special Representative has made annual reports to the SC, which since 1999 has adopted regular resolutions on the basis of the reports.[102] These Resolutions emphasise the importance of bringing those who recruit and abuse children in armed conflict[103] to justice and demand special protective measures for children.

With respect to women, the SC responded later and more slowly in adopting institutional measures.[104] In October 2000 the SC adopted its first Resolution on Women and Peace and Security,[105] recasting gendered violence in terms of a threat to international peace and security. SC

of the Secretary-General, Protection for Humanitarian Assistance to Refugees and Others in Conflict Situations, UN Doc. S/1998/883, 22 September 1998.

97 UN SC Resolution 1674, 28 April 2006: '*Reaffirming* that parties to armed conflict bear the primary responsibility to take all feasible steps to ensure the protection of affected civilians'; UN SC Resolution 2286, 3 May 2016: '*Reaffirming* the primary responsibility of States to protect the population throughout their whole territory.'

98 UN SC Resolution 1674, 28 April 2006, and UN SC Resolution 1894, 11 November 2009.

99 E.g., UN SC Resolution 1265, 17 September 1999: 'Noting that civilians account for the vast majority of casualties in armed conflicts and are increasingly targeted by combatants and armed elements, gravely concerned by the hardships borne by civilians during armed conflict, in particular as a result of acts of violence directed against them, especially women, children and other vulnerable groups'.

100 Machel, Graça 1996. 'The Impact of Armed Conflict on Children', UN Doc. A/51/306, 26 August 1996.

101 UN GA Resolution 51/77, 20 February 1997.

102 UN SC Resolution 1261, 30 August 1999; UN SC Resolution 2225, 18 June 2015. See also Machel, Graca 2009. 'Study: 10 Year Strategic Review, Children and Conflict in a Changing World', UNICEF.

103 UN SC Resolution 2068, 19 September 2012 stresses that it does not legally determine whether situations referred to in the Secretary-General's report are or are not armed conflicts under the Geneva Conventions, 'nor does it prejudge the legal status of the non-State parties involved in these situations'.

104 Hudson, Natalie 2009. *Gender, Human Security and the United Nations: Security Language as a Political Framework for Women*. Routledge.

105 UN SC Resolution 1325, 13 October 2000.

Resolution 1325 has been followed by other resolutions on women and peace and security.[106] SC Resolution 1325 and its follow-up resolutions are based upon four pillars: prevention, protection, participation, and relief and recovery, which are similar to those underpinning the Responsibility to Protect. Despite recognition in SC Resolution 1325 of the important role of women in the prevention and resolution of conflicts, in peacebuilding and of the need to implement international law that protects the rights of women and girls during and after conflict, there is emphasis on the obligations of all parties to armed conflict to protect women and girls from all forms of sexual violence.[107] This is furthered by the appointment of the Special Representative of the Secretary-General on Sexual Violence in Conflict, pursuant to SC Resolution 1888 in 2009. While recognition of the systematic nature of sexual violence in conflict, especially committed against women, and the need to address it is to be welcomed, there are also reasons for caution. Linkage with the SC's responsibility for international peace and security reinforces the assumption of military means as most appropriate for the protection of women; appointment of the SR-SG under SC Resolution 1888 limits the mandate to conflicts on the Council's agenda with the risk of discounting other conflicts (although the special representative has in fact addressed a broader range of conflict-affected situations); and focus on sexual violence can cast women solely in terms of their sexual identities, as victims, and deny their agency. This is exacerbated by the reality that states have taken little heed of the need for inclusion of women, for instance, in peace processes, and the strictures of Resolution 1325 in this regard remain largely ignored.[108] The SC's recognition therefore in 2013 that women and girls are subject to 'the full range of threats and human rights violations and abuses' and its expressed intention to 'include provisions on the promotion of gender equality and the empowerment of women in conflict and post-conflict situations'[109] are welcome.

There remains a disconnect between, and compartmentalisation of, the relevant legal regimes. The children in armed conflict, women's peace and

[106] UN SC Resolution 1820, 19 June 2008; UN SC Resolution 1888, 30 September 2009; UN SC Resolution 1889, UN SC Resolution 1960, 16 December 2010; UN SC Resolution 2106, 24 June 2013; UN SC Resolution 2122, 18 October 2013; UN SC Resolution 2242, 13 October 2015.

[107] See especially UN SC Resolution 1820, 19 June 2008.

[108] See Chapter 9.

[109] UN SC Resolution 2122, 18 October 2013. In 2015 the SC welcomed similar language with respect to women's empowerment in the Sustainable Development Goals; UN SC Resolution 2242, 13 October 2015.

security and Responsibility to Protect agendas are not necessarily operationalised as complementary and mutually reinforcing, even though they all engage the language of the Responsibility to Protect.[110] The former are essentially about the *jus in bello* while the Responsibility to Protect is a justification for the use of force – *jus ad bellum*. Although the SC in its thematic resolutions relating to both women and children affirms its primary responsibility for the maintenance of international peace and security,[111] it has not acted under UN Charter chapter VII nor linked these resolutions to the *jus ad bellum*. They do not provide a basis for intervention, or for the use of 'all necessary means' to put an end to extreme and violent acts against women and children without specific SC authorisation.

Indeed, there has been debate between women's human rights advocates as to the desirability of military intervention in situations of violations of their rights.[112] On the one hand this would accord status to such violations, recognising their pervasiveness and extreme nature in some situations, such as that of the Taliban regime in Afghanistan prior to 2001, or currently in IS held regions in Syria and Iraq, where sexual slavery has been introduced,[113] and moving them from the protected private sphere of domestic jurisdiction to the public arena where intervention is permissible.[114] On the other hand, upholding the military

[110] E.g. UN SC Resolution 2068, 19 September 2012 (children): '*Stressing* the primary role of Governments in providing protection and relief to all children affected by armed conflict'; UN SC Resolution 2122, 18 October 2013 (women, peace and security): '*Recognizing* that States bear the primary responsibility to respect and ensure the human rights of all persons within their territory and subject to their jurisdiction as provided for by international law, and *reaffirming* that parties to armed conflict bear the primary responsibility to ensure the protection of civilians'.

[111] E.g., UN SC Resolution 2068, 19 September 2012 (children): '*Reiterating* its primary responsibility for the maintenance of international peace and security and, in this connection, its commitment to address the widespread impact of armed conflict on children'; UN SC Resolution 2122, 18 October 2013 (women andpeace and security): 'primary responsibility of the Security Council under the Charter for the maintenance of international peace and security'.

[112] Engle, Karen 2007. 'Calling in the Troops: The Uneasy Relationship Among Women's Rights, Human Rights and Humanitarian Intervention', *Harvard Human Rights Journal* 20: 189–226.

[113] For a fascinating and horrifying account of IS practices, particularly in relation to people who are *al harb* (of war), notably the Yazidis, see Yehoshuam Y., Green, R. and Agron A. 2015, 'Sex Slavery in the Islamic State – Practices, Social Media Discourse, and Justifications; Jabhat Al-Nusra: ISIS Is Taking Our Women as Sex Slaves Too', Middle East Media Research Institute.

[114] For a feminist analysis of humanitarian intervention by analogy with domestic law relating to domestic violence see Heathcote, *op. cit.*, chapter 5.

model of intervention preserves the hierarchical and gendered structures of militarised power,[115] as well as the adverse consequences for civilians, including women, of military action.[116]

5.3.3 The Responsibility to Protect in Action

Debates around whether the legal criteria for recourse to force on humanitarian grounds have changed, or are changing, have continued after the formulation of the Responsibility to Protect. They are shaped by instances where there has, or has not, been intervention, some of which are discussed below. All such situations are highly political, and they highlight the similarly political nature of the concept. Despite the institutional endorsements and amplification, the Responsibility to Protect remains a political, rather than a legal, concept. It 'is not and does not purport to be a new norm of international law, while basing its arguments on the existing body of such laws'.[117] Practice following the articulation of the concept is inconsistent, as is seen in the instances discussed below.

Darfur (2003 Onwards)

One early focus of debate was Darfur where a wave of violence began in February 2003 when a rebel group called the Darfur Liberation Front seized the town of Gulu. This was the beginning of an extremely complicated conflict, in which a government-led counter-insurgency campaign that included regular soldiers using disproportionate military force, militias (often known as *janjawijd*) composed of nomadic groups without access to land, bandits, outlaws and criminals (some deliberately released from prison) were all pitted against rebel groups largely composed of sedentary farmers and intellectuals. The former were construed as 'Arab' and the latter as 'African', although anthropologists have shown that both groups were highly mixed.

[115] See the many contributions in Sjoberg, Laura (ed.) 2010. *Gender and International Security*. Routledge; Nicole Detraz 2012. *International Security and Gender*. Polity.

[116] E.g., the impact of military action in Afghanistan; Kouvo, Sari 2011. 'Taking Women Seriously: Conflict, State-building and Gender in Afghanistan', in Kouvo, Sari and Pearson, Zoe (eds.). *Feminist Perspectives on Contemporary International Law: Between Resistance and Compliance*. Hart Publishing, 159–176.

[117] Pommier, Bruno 2011. 'The Use of Force to Protect Civilians and Humanitarian Action: The Case of Libya and Beyond', *International Review of the Red Cross* 93(884): 1063–1083, 1066.

The debate turned on whether the conflict was more accurately described as 'genocide' or as a civil war. A massive campaign in the United States, involving celebrities, argued that what was happening was a genocide, based on the assumption that military intervention is legal only when it is undertaken to prevent genocide, as defined in the Genocide Convention.[118] Among the achievements of the campaign was a resolution passed by the US Congress on 22 July 2004 declaring that 'the atrocities unfolding in Darfur, Sudan, are genocide'. The resolution urged calling the atrocities 'by their rightful name: "genocide"'.[119] To prove that the Darfur conflict was genocide it was necessary to exaggerate civilian deaths and to demonstrate the intent to destroy the group, based on their racial or ethnic identity – hence the emphasis on Arab and African identities. In contrast, the Commission of Inquiry in Darfur established by the SC[120] concluded that 'the Government of the Sudan has not pursued a policy of genocide' as the crucial element of genocidal intent appeared to be missing. The Commission emphasised that this did not detract from the gravity of the offences in Darfur, where massive atrocities amounting to crimes against humanity against the civilian population had been 'perpetrated on a very large scale', without punishment.[121]

Those who opposed military intervention argued that the Darfur conflict was a civil war (in which there should be no intervention) and that the best approach was a negotiated settlement. Critics such as Mamdani claimed that shrill calls for military intervention and the one-sided application of international criminal law, as in the indictment by the International Criminal Court (ICC)[122] of Omar Al-Bashir, the President of Sudan, were really a justification for a new imperialism: 'More than anything else, the "Responsibility to Protect" is a right to

[118] Genocide Convention, *op. cit.*, article 2: 'genocide means any of the following acts committed with intent to destroy, in whole or in part, a national, ethnical, racial or religious group, as such: (a) Killing members of the group; (b) Causing serious bodily or mental harm to members of the group; (c) Deliberately inflicting on the group conditions of life calculated to bring about its physical destruction in whole or in part; (d) Imposing measures intended to prevent births within the group; (e) Forcibly transferring children of the group to another group.'

[119] H.Con.Res. 467 (108th): Declaring genocide in Darfur, Sudan, 22 July 2004.

[120] UN SC Resolution 1564, 18 September 2004.

[121] Report of the International Commission of Inquiry on Darfur to the United Nations Secretary-General, Pursuant to Security Council Resolution 1564 of 18 September 2004, Geneva, 25 January 2005, paras. 640–642.

[122] The 'situation in Darfur' was referred to the ICC by UN SC Resolution 1593, 31 March 2005.

punish without being held accountable – a clarion call for the recolonisation of "failed states" in Africa. In its present form, the call for justice is really a slogan that masks a big power agenda to recolonise Africa'.[123]

The problem is that while extreme violence was evident in Darfur, it is not easily characterised as either genocide or civil war. Legal definitions and constraints allow narrow distinctions to be made that bring the law into disrepute and do not reflect the realities for the victims. Rwanda was 'clearly' genocide (but still meaningful intervention was withheld), while Darfur is more controversial. Despite the Prosecutor of the ICC requesting that the warrant for arrest against Bashir include genocide, the ICC pre-trial chamber at first did not include this charge;[124] just over a year later a second arrest warrant did so.[125] In any event, like other contemporary conflicts, the situation in Darfur involves ethnic cleansing and massive human rights violations. These constitute good enough reasons for outside intervention, in some form. It is difficult to describe the conflict as a civil war as it involves many external actors and is typical of contemporary 'new wars' that are rendering unworkable the international law distinction between international armed conflict and non-international armed conflict.[126] Numerous attempts to reach a negotiated agreement have failed.[127] The long time it took to authorise a substantial mission and the practical obstacles to protecting civilians are among the reasons for the continued suffering of the people of Darfur. Only a small African Union (AU) force was deployed to Darfur in 2004,[128] and a

[123] Mamdani, Mahmoud 2009. *Saviours and Survivors: Darfur, Politics, and the War on Terror*. Verso, 300. See further Chapter 11.

[124] The Situation in Darfur, *Prosecutor v. Omar Hassan Ahmad al Bashir*, Warrant of Arrest of Omar Hassan Ahmad al Bashir, Pre-trial chamber I, ICC-02/05-01/09, 4 March 2009.

[125] The Situation in Darfur, *Prosecutor v. Omar Hassan Ahmad al Bashir*, Second Warrant of Arrest of Omar Hassan Ahmad al Bashir, Pre-trial chamber I, ICC-02/05-01/09, 12 July 2010.

[126] See Chapter 6.

[127] The situation was made more complex by the ongoing negotiations between the Government of Sudan and the Sudan People's Liberation Movement/Sudan People's Liberation Army that culminated in the *Comprehensive Peace Agreement*, 2005, which formally brought to an end the war with South Sudan.

[128] The African Union decided that among the tasks of the African Mission in Sudan (AMIS) from October 2004 was the protection of 'civilians whom it encounters under imminent threat and in the immediate vicinity, within resources and capability, it being understood that the protection of the civilian population is the responsibility of the [Government of Sudan]'. Communique, Peace and Security Council, 17th Meeting, Addis Ababa, Ethiopia, 20 October 2004, PSC/PR/Comm (XVII), para. 6.

larger hybrid UN/AU force was only agreed in July 2007[129] and has been plagued with difficulties, including inadequate resources and obstruction from the Government of Sudan. The real problem has been that the terms of the debate have left no room for a serious analysis about how to protect people: whether military intervention actually helps or makes things worse, and what sort of justice and outside help are required. As Iavor Rangelov has put it:

> The Save Darfur movement, in particular has prioritised political will over other important questions such as ideas, instruments and capabilities for resolving conflict. Publicising the plight of civilians in Darfur was useful in eliciting global debate about the need to respond but not at the expense of a debate about the means to respond and the efforts needed to mobilise the range of international and local actors with stakes in a sustainable solution to Darfur.[130]

Libya (2011)

In contrast to Darfur, SC-authorised military intervention was forthcoming in Libya in 2011. The NATO intervention was hailed as the first legally mandated Responsibility to Protect operation: 'the first time the [Security] Council had authorised the use of force for human protection purposes against the wishes of a functioning state'.[131] United Nations SC Resolution 1970 of 26 February 2011 referred 'the situation' in Libya to the ICC, established air corridors and imposed sanctions. As violence escalated, SC Resolution 1973 was adopted on 17 March, just weeks later. It called on member states and regional organisations to 'take all necessary measures ... to protect civilians and civilian populated areas under threat of attack in the Libyan Arab Jamahiriya, including Benghazi, while excluding a foreign occupation force of any form on any part of Libyan territory'.[132] The Resolution has been described as a 'sort of amalgam between "humanitarian" objectives and other political considerations

[129] UN SC Resolution 1769, 31 July 2007 authorised the establishment of an AU/UN Hybrid operation in Darfur (UNAMID) *inter alia* to support the implementation of the Darfur Peace Agreement and to protect civilians.

[130] Rangelov, Iavor 2013. 'The Role of Transnational Civil Society', in Lupel, Adam and Verdeja, Ernesto (eds.). *Responding to Genocide: The Politics of International Action*. International Peace Institute, Lynn Riener.

[131] Bellamy, Alex and Williams, Paul 2011. 'The New Politics of Protection? Côte d'Ivoire, Libya and the Responsibility to Protect', *International Affairs* 87(4): 825–850.

[132] UN SC Resolution, 17 March 2011.

such as "the legitimate demands of the Libyan people"'.[133] As such, tension was inevitable, in particular with respect to the demand of the anti-Gaddafi forces for regime change, a goal supported by some of those government leaders instrumental in securing the resolution. Essentially, NATO extended its regional reach and entered the war on the side of the anti-Gaddafi forces, as it had in practice supported the KLA in 1999 against the Serbian forces in Kosovo. Indeed, British and French special forces were on the ground in civilian clothes advising and training the rebels.

The resolution was adopted just in time to prevent Gaddafi's forces from overrunning the eastern town of Benghazi, which anti-Gaddafi protestors had liberated. As in Kosovo, however, NATO relied mainly on air strikes. NATO and partner aircraft conducted some 24,200 sorties including more than 9,000 strike sorties. In addition, the United States used Predator and Reaper remotely piloted aircraft between April and September 2011. NATO claims to have destroyed some 5,900 military targets including more than 400 military and command control centres. The initial targets were air defences and heavy weaponry in the vicinity of rebel strongholds, but gradually the range of targets was extended to include command centres and military convoys in the open desert.

In the end the action led to regime change as Gaddafi was overthrown, but, as we explore in the final section, the record on the humanitarian and security consequences of the intervention is very problematic. It raises the question of whether such an SC-authorised military intervention should be considered a Responsibility to Protect operation, an intervention aimed at regime change or some amalgam of the two.

Côte d'Ivoire (2011)

March 2011 was the high spot for the authorisation of military intervention in the language of the Responsibility to Protect as contemporaneously with the intervention in Libya, the SC also addressed the escalation of violence and violations of human rights, international humanitarian law and refugee law in Côte d'Ivoire. Against a complex background of social division and conflict, in 2004 the SC mandated the United Nations Operation in Côte d'Ivoire (UNOCI) with an extensive civilian and peacekeeping mandate.[134]

[133] Pommier, *op. cit.*

[134] UN SC Resolution 1528, 27 February 2004.

Violence again erupted in the context of presidential elections in 2010. The Constitutional Court determined that there had been massive electoral fraud, discounted several thousand votes for the contender, Alassane Ouattara, and thereby in effect secured victory for the incumbent President, Laurent Gbagbo. Further violence ensued, and following the position of ECOWAS and the AU (but not that of the Constitutional Court), the SC urged recognition of Ouattara as properly elected.[135] This decision shifted the political ground. It legitimised economic measures against Gbagbo and his supporters, and, as no longer the legitimate government, made his consent to the deployment of UN and French peacekeepers legally irrelevant.[136] Attempts at a negotiated solution followed amidst concerns about the security of civilians and the potential for mass atrocities. The situation on the ground worsened, and in March 2011 the SC stressed UNOCI's mandate to protect civilians. Again employing the language of the Responsibility to Protect, the SC reaffirmed the primary responsibility of the state to protect its citizens and authorised UNOCI 'to use all necessary means . . . to protect civilians under imminent threat of physical violence, within its capabilities and its areas of deployment, including to prevent the use of heavy weapons against the civilian population'.[137] Military action by UNOCI and French troops enabled Ouattara to be installed as President. In October the prosecutor of the ICC filed an application to investigate the situation in Côte D'Ivoire relating to the post-electoral violence.[138] Laurent and his wife, Simone Gbabgo (also a politician), have been indicted by the ICC. The trial of the former has commenced[139] but the latter is not in the custody of the Court.[140]

As in Libya, this raises questions about the extent to which authorisation of intervention for civilian protection legitimates regime change, although in this instance Ouattara had been declared by the regional and international bodies (but not the local judicial body) as the electoral victor. The formula 'all necessary means' warrants the use of force, but the general objective of civilian protection does not clarify its level and scope. In particular, there was disagreement, even among those states

[135] UN SC Resolution 1962, 20 December 2010. [136] Bellamy and Williams, *op. cit.*, 833.

[137] UN SC Resolution 1975, 30 March 2011.

[138] *Investigation into the Situation in the Republic of Côte d'Ivoire*, ICC-02/11, 3 October 2011.

[139] *The Prosecutor v. Laurent Gbagbo and Charles Blé Goudé*, ICC-02/11-01/15 and ICC-02/11-01/12.

[140] *The Prosecutor v. Simone Gbagbo*, ICC-02/11-01/12.

that had voted for it, about whether SC Resolution 1975 extended UNOCI's mandate or simply reiterated SC Resolution 1962. The United Kingdom, for instance, considered that it did 'not alter' UNOCI's already 'robust mandate . . . under which the Operation is already authorized to use all necessary means to protect civilians'. India stressed that peacekeepers 'cannot be made instruments of regime change', and the Russian Foreign Minister stated that 'We are looking into the legality of this situation [taking the side of Ouattara against Gbagbo] because the peacekeepers were authorised to remain neutral, nothing more'.[141]

In Libya and Côte D'Ivoire, the attitude of other states in the region was influential in achieving the relevant resolutions for authorising intervention. Both of these authorisations of force in terms of the Responsibility to Protect were actively supported by regional states beyond a Euro-American preserve. Russia and China abstained from (rather than vetoed) the vote for Resolution 1973 (as did Brazil, India and Germany) and voted in favour of Resolution 1975 (Côte d'Ivoire). Critically, Resolution 1973 (Libya) was pushed for by the Arab League, and the AU and ECOWAS were both active in the post-election crisis in Côte d'Ivoire. Bellamy and Williams underscore the significance of the attitude of regional arrangements as a critical determinant of SC action, not only in securing action but also in what they term their 'emerging role as "gatekeepers" – influencing which issues get debated in the Council, how they are framed and the range of possible Council responses'.[142]

Mali (2012)

In Libya and Côte D'Ivoire the SC made explicit reference to the Responsibility to Protect in authorising (or extending the mandate for) intervention. Subsequently the concept has been side-lined. For instance, the response to violence in Mali in 2012 was a mix of unilateral, regional and UN intervention, justified on a slew of grounds that draw upon the different security models. Mali in 2012 was described as experiencing 'a crisis of governance that encompasses endemic corruption, weak State capacity to deliver basic services and the low level of legitimacy of State institutions and the political system'.[143] Violent conflict involving

[141] Cited in Bellamy and Williams, *op. cit.*, 835. [142] *Ibid.*

[143] Report of the Secretary-General on the Situation in Mali ('Report on Mali'), UN Doc. S/2013/189, 26 March 2013, para. 34

insurgent groups (assisted by armed men arriving from Libya after the fall of the Gaddafi regime) broke out in early 2012, seeking autonomy for the Tuareg people in the north of the country. In response to the government's mishandling of this crisis – and in consequence of its weakened state – a military faction overthrew the Government, and, following this, the National Movement for the Liberation of Azawad (northern Mali) declared a separate state for the Tuareg people. Armed Islamist groups (with links to Al Qaeda) participated in the violence, reportedly imposing a brutal and extreme interpretation of Islamic law in areas where they gained control. By July those seeking autonomy for the Tuareg had lost control to the Islamist groups. The conflict exacerbated an already serious food shortage in the Sahel region, sparking a humanitarian crisis.[144] Throughout the violence widespread human rights abuses were reported, including extra-judicial killings, rapes, use of child soldiers and widespread population displacement, as well as looting of food, hospitals, government buildings and destruction of World Heritage archaeological sites in Timbuktu. Amnesty International reported that 'All parties to the conflict are believed to be committing human rights violations and abuses'.[145]

Following a severe deterioration of the security situation in early January 2013, France militarily intervened in 'Operation Serval' to assist the government of Mali retake the north of the country. The intervention did not receive prior SC authorisation, although the Council subsequently 'welcomed the swift action by the French forces, at the request of the transitional authorities of Mali'.[146] The situation in Mali was not presented as an application of the Responsibility to Protect; rather, an array of justifications was put forward by François Hollande, President of France, to justify French intervention. He asserted that France's assistance had been sought by the government ('transitional authorities');[147]

[144] 'More than 4.3 million Malians were in need of assistance in 2012 because of the food and nutrition crisis. Despite good harvests in late 2012, approximately 747,000 people were in need of immediate food assistance and an additional 1.3 million were at risk of food insecurity'. *Ibid.*, para. 12.

[145] Amnesty International. 'Mali: Five Months of Crisis: Armed Rebellion and Military Coup', *Amnesty International Publications,* 16 May 2012. The SC also noted 'widespread abuses of human rights by terrorist, extremist and armed groups in the north of Mali' and condemned 'the reports of retaliatory attacks, including those based on ethnicity and those allegedly perpetrated by members of the Malian Defence and Security Forces against civilians'. UN SC Resolution 2100, 25 April 2013.

[146] UN SC Resolution 2100, 25 April 2013. [147] *Ibid.*

that it was supporting the Malian army; that Mali's existence as a state was under threat; that there was the need to protect the local population and some 6,000 French citizens living in Mali (and there were known French hostages in Mali). The intervention was also seen as contributing to the War on Terror, with the French Foreign Minister contending that unless the terrorists were stopped, 'the whole of Mali will fall into their hands threatening all of Africa, and even Europe', thus also implicating self-defence.[148] France received considerable support, including backing from the United States and EU. More significantly, as in Libya and Côte D'Ivoire there was political support from the region through the AU and ECOWAS and military assistance from an African-led International Support Mission in Mali (AFISMA). The military action had some significant successes and liberated major population centres in the north of Mali, although violence and insecurity continue through the activities of armed groups and terrorists, criminal networks kidnappings, hostage taking and human rights violations.[149]Multiple steps have been taken by the regional bodies and the UN to promote security in Mali and maintain its territorial integrity. The SC mandated the establishment of the United Nations Multidimensional Integrated Stabilization Mission in Mali (MINUSMA) to stabilise key population centres and support the reestablishment of state authority throughout the country. Following the signing of the Agreement on Peace and Reconciliation in Mali in 2015 MINUSMA's 'strategic priority' is to support its implementation. MINUSMA's mandate is also to 'protect, without prejudice to the primary responsibility of the Malian authorities, … civilians under threat of physical violence … and to take robust and active steps' to this end, as well as to protect United Nations personnel. [150] MINUSMA is authorised to use all necessary means to carry out its mandate 'within its capabilities and its areas of deployment' and French troops are authorised to use all necessary means to intervene in support of MINUSMA 'when under imminent and serious threat upon request of the Secretary-General'. In addition to this blend of military and political support, there have been moves towards accountability through the transitional authorities'

[148] 'France Confirms Mali Military Intervention', *BBC News*, 11 January 2013, www.bbc.co.uk/news/world-africa-20991719.

[149] Report of the Secretary-General on the situation in Mali, UN Doc. S/2016/498, 31 May 2016, para 22.

[150] UN SC Resolution 2295, 29 June 2016. MINUSMA's mandate was extended until 30 June 2017 and its force size increased. For protection of civilians by peacekeepers see Chapter 9.

referral of the 'situation in Mali since January 2012' to the ICC on 13 July 2012[151] and SC sanctions through the listing of key individuals and groups on the Al Qaeda sanctions list.[152]

The French approach in Mali and in the Central African Republic has been described as a new doctrine, a 'self-consciously benign form of armed interventionism based on international authority and local consent'.[153] It constitutes a 'broader agenda' and practice on how a state can 'do' international security at a time when the United States is withdrawing its ground forces (but continuing targeted aerial attacks) and China is wielding its economic power in Africa but is not taking responsibility for security. It is said to be a measured response to Islamist extremism and sectarianism in northern Africa, from the Horn to the Sahel and Maghreb.[154] The 'Hollande' doctrine in Africa has been described as encompassing the following characteristics: (i) it aims to supply humanitarian security assistance in states where law and order has broken down; (ii) it operates with UN backing, or at least acquiescence, and preferably with the support of African regional or sub-regional organisations; (iii) it seeks prior consent from local parties who most closely share Western values and interests; and (iv) it has defined and limited objectives, with the aim of handing over to (authorised) regional peacekeepers.[155] However, at the same time it seeks to re-establish French influence in areas traditionally within its sphere of influence (former colonial powers) in Africa.

5.4 The Responsibility to Protect/Humanitarian Intervention: Does It Uphold Humanitarian Norms?

5.4.1 Evidence of Humanitarian Crisis

The distinct views as to the nature of the violence in Darfur discussed above indicate the difficulty of gathering reliable information about the facts in any given situation of violence and the interpretation of those facts. The setting up of a Commission of Inquiry is one response to the

[151] In September 2016 the ICC sentenced Ahmad al-Faqi al-Mahdi (who had pleaded guilty) to imprisonment for destroying historic sites and shrines in Timbuktu; *The Prosecutor v. Ahmad Al Faqi Al Mahdi*, ICC-01/12-01/15.

[152] In accordance with UN SC Resolution 1267, 15 October 1999 and UN SC Resolution 1989, 17 June 2011.

[153] Tisdall, Simon. 'France in the Central African Republic Is Latest Use of 'Hollande Doctrine'', *The Guardian*, 5 December 2013, www.theguardian.com/commentisfree/2013/dec/05/france-central-african-republic-hollande-doctrine.

[154] *Ibid.* [155] *Ibid.*

information gap (or overload in the days of social networking and twenty-four-hour news), and this has been done by the SC, the UN Human Rights Council and the GA.[156] This may be proactive, done before any further measures are undertaken, as was the case with Darfur and by the SC before the establishment of the *ad hoc* international criminal tribunals with respect to atrocities in the former Yugoslavia and genocide in Rwanda. With respect to Libya, SC Resolution 1970 was adopted the day after the UN Human Rights Council had decided upon an international commission of inquiry to investigate alleged human rights abuses in Libya and 'to establish the facts and circumstances of such violations and of the crimes perpetrated, and where possible identify those responsible'.[157] This action by the UN human rights body may have spurred the SC into action. An independent fact-finding body can provide impartial and expert advice as to the situation and recommend appropriate action, although there must always be caution in accepting the findings of a fact-finding mission.[158] However, it may contribute to delay before any action is taken, during which time the humanitarian situation may worsen and the need for civilian protection increase. Mandating a commission of inquiry may also serve to suggest that something is being done (e.g., by the SC) when in fact there is no political will to take stronger action. For instance, by 2016, the Commission of Inquiry on Syria has issued multiple reports confirming violations of international humanitarian law and human rights by government forces, pro-government militia and non-state armed forces.[159] Nevertheless no chapter VII action has been authorised by the SC, which has only been able to condemn the use of chemical weapons[160] make demands for safe delivery of humanitarian assistance, and call for compliance with international humanitarian and human rights law and for a political solution.[161]

[156] See Chapter 3.

[157] Report of the Human Rights Council on its Fifteenth Special Session, UN Doc. A/HRC/RES/S-15/1, 25 February 2011.

[158] This may be especially the case if the fact-finding mission has been denied entry into the relevant location.

[159] Report of the Independent International Commission of Inquiry on the Syrian Arab Republic, UN Doc. A/HRC/31/68, 11 February 2016; see also Report of the Independent International Commission of Inquiry on the Syrian Arab Republic: "They came to destroy": ISIS Crimes Against the Yazidis, UN Doc. A/HRC/32/CRP.2, 15 June, 2016.

[160] UN SC Resolution 2118, 27 September 2013.

[161] UN SC Resolution 2258, 22 December 2015.

5.4.2 *Scope of Humanitarian Crisis*

Another limitation is that the triggers for intervention under the Responsibility to Protect are inadequate. They do not, for instance, include mass starvation or poverty. Humanitarian organisations have the right to offer humanitarian aid to states without this being regarded as intervention, but whether there is any obligation upon the state to receive humanitarian assistance remains contested. Article 70 of Protocol I to the Geneva Conventions provides that in international armed conflict 'humanitarian and impartial relief actions that are conducted without any adverse distinction shall be undertaken, subject to the agreement of the Parties. . . . Offers of such relief shall not be regarded as interference in the armed conflict or as unfriendly acts'. With respect to non-international armed conflict, Protocol II, article 18 provides that:

> If the civilian population is suffering undue hardship owing to a lack of the supplies essential for its survival, such as foodstuffs and medical supplies, relief actions for the civilian population which are of an exclusively humanitarian and impartial nature and which are conducted without any adverse distinction shall be undertaken subject to the consent of the High Contracting Party concerned.

In both cases consent of the parties concerned is required. It has been argued that 'Consent must be given when the necessary requirements are fulfilled' and that failure to give consent 'would be equivalent to a violation of the rule prohibiting the use of starvation as a method of combat'[162] It could thus constitute a war crime, or crime against humanity.

In non-conflict situations, the position is more uncertain. In 2008 the restrictions imposed by Myanmar on delivery of foreign assistance following the devastation caused by Cyclone Nargis caused concern. The International Law Commission (ILC)[163] adopted in 2016 Draft Articles for the Protection of Persons in the Event of Disasters.[164] The

[162] Rottensteiner, Christa 1999. 'The Denial of Humanitarian Assistance as a Crime under International Law', *International Review of the Red Cross* 81(835): 555–582.

[163] The ILC is charged by the GA with the 'codification and progressive development of international law'. UN Charter, article 13 (a); UN GA Resolution 174 (II), 21 November 1947.

[164] Draft Articles for the Protection of Persons in the Event of Disasters, adopted by the International Law Commission at its sixty-eighth session, in 2016, and submitted to the General Assembly as a part of the Commission's report covering the work of that session, UN Doc. A/71/10, para. 48.

rapporteur, Eduardo Valencia-Ospina, implicitly engaged the language of the Responsibility to Protect and human security by emphasising principles of humanity and human dignity, as well as the responsibility of the affected state to protect its citizens. He noted that 'the principle of humanity [is] a long-standing principle of international law' and 'a meeting point between international humanitarian law and international human rights law'.[165] While the consent of the affected state is required, its absolute sovereignty is lessened by its human rights obligations. In debate it was pointed out that the proposed draft articles are for the protection of persons, not of states. Among the draft articles adopted are ones imposing a duty on an affected state to seek assistance if the disaster exceeds its national response capacity (article 11) and that it must not arbitrarily withhold consent to external assistance (article 13 (2)). However, the very act of drafting these articles reinforces the legal distinction between conflict (to which IHL applies)[166] and 'disasters';[167] we argue that war is a disaster, a humanitarian catastrophe, to which an 'adequate and effective response . . . that meets the essential needs of the persons concerned' is required. The duty to mitigate the effects of disaster should also be made applicable to conflict. It is contrary to the concept of humanity that states should have lesser duties in the case of conflict than in natural disasters.

Nor does the concept of the Responsibility to Protect address the structural causes of genocide, crimes against humanity and ethnic cleansing, but rather accepts their occurrence and is reactive. Intervention as a response to crisis tends to constitute a late and hurried response; nor does crisis take account of the structural forms of everyday violence.[168] There is a reluctance to address structural, that is to say socio-economic, causes of violence that are supported by the interests of the powerful.[169]

[165] ILC, Report on the Work of its Sixty-second Session (3 May–4 June and 5 July–6 August 2010), Third Report on the Protection of Persons in the Event of Disasters, UN Doc. GAOR A/65/10, para. 304.

[166] Article 18(2) of the Draft Articles specifies that they do not apply where IHL is applicable.

[167] '"Disaster" means a calamitous event or series of events resulting in widespread loss of life, great human suffering and distress, mass displacement, or large-scale material or environmental damage, thereby seriously disrupting the functioning of society'. *Ibid.*, article 3.

[168] Charlesworth, Hilary 2002. 'International Law: A Discipline of Crisis', *Modern Law Review* 65: 377–392.

[169] Marks, Susan 2011. 'Human Rights and Root Causes', *Modern Law Review* 74: 57–78.

5.4.3 Double Standards

The Responsibility to Protect does not resolve the problem of what intervention is possible (or should be undertaken or can legally be undertaken) where no political agreement can be reached for action and human rights violations continue, as in Syria. Since the end of the Cold War there have been other humanitarian tragedies which have failed to elicit an international response giving rise to charges of double standards. These include in Europe the violence against the Kurds in Turkey (continuing as of 2016) and in Chechnya in 1994–1996, and in Asia the war in Sri Lanka in 1983–2009 and continuing violence in Myanmar. Despite the fact that these wars involved widespread violations of human rights, outside involvement was minimal.

Another instance is the Gaza Strip. In Gaza 80 percent of the population live below the poverty line, and living conditions are bleak in a society dominated by poverty, unemployment and military assault. The situation is a result of political choices – political and economic embargo of Gaza by the EU and United States after the election of Hamas, supported by the UN as a member of the Quartet[170] – and an unwillingness (or inability) to prevent rocket and other violent attacks on Israelis by Palestinians. The embargo is effectively a collective punishment on Palestinian voters and has created a severe humanitarian situation. In the words of the former Special Rapporteur on Human Rights in the Occupied Territories: 'This is difficult to understand'. Israel, which is in breach of SC and General Assembly resolutions, escapes economic sanctions while the people living under occupation have been subjected to 'possibly the most rigorous form of international sanctions' of modern times.[171] Where the people have no state to protect them – as is the case in occupation – the international community has an even stronger responsibility to protect, including to ensure the occupier's compliance with the laws of occupation. But in this instance the international community is not exercising any Responsibility to Protect but is rather contributing to the denial of rights of the Palestinian people.

The lack of SC response to the brutal crackdown by President Assad of Syria on pro-democracy activists, and the failure to prevent or stop the

[170] The Quartet is a group of states and organisations established to play a key role in the Middle East peace process. It comprises the United States, Russia, the UN and EU.

[171] Report of the Special Rapporteur on the Situation of Human Rights in the Palestinian Territories Occupied since 1967, UN Doc. A/HRC /4/17, 29 January 2007.

ensuing deadly violence, is often contrasted with the intervention in Libya, where, it was argued, the lure of oil was a significant factor. Throughout 2012, Russia's stance prevented any SC measures, such as imposition of an arms embargo, sanctions or referral to the ICC of the 'situation in Syria', which would encompass actions by both government and non-government forces. Instead the Council reaffirmed its support for a political solution as set out in the six-point proposal made by the Joint Special Envoy of the UN.[172] Nor has the GA indicated any willingness to substitute itself for the SC, for instance, by invoking the Uniting for Peace resolution adopted in 1950[173] in response to the blocking of SC action in Korea because of the Soviet veto. Despite this formal inaction, the high level of ongoing foreign involvement in Syria from both states and non-state actors, including Al Qaeda affiliates and Jihadists, makes the classification of the conflict complex and is a reminder that intervention is not a Western preserve but has diverse objectives and sources. As of 2016 there are, of course, interventions by both Russia and the West; the former is aimed at shoring up the Assad regime and the latter at defeating IS from the air. Both indicate the priority of Geo-Politics and the War on Terror over any concept of humanitarianism.

The ICISS were aware of the likelihood of double standards, warning that no action would be taken against permanent members of the SC or their supporters and that a needed humanitarian action could be held hostage by unrelated interests of one of the permanent members[174] – a prescient view of what has occurred in Syria. Nevertheless, the Commission had 'absolutely no doubt' that the central role of the SC in responding to questions of military intervention in cases of humanitarian need should be retained. The GA also reasserted the authority of the SC.[175] The ICISS supported a proposal for a 'Code of Conduct' whereby permanent members would mutually agree not to exercise their right to veto in a situation of humanitarian need that did not impact upon their national interest.[176] No such approach – or other approach to SC reform – has materialised.

[172] UN SC Resolution 2042, 14 April 2012, annex.

[173] UN GA Resolution 377 A (V), 3 November 1950. The ICISS suggested that a recommendatory vote by the GA for interventionary action would carry considerable 'moral and political support'. ICISS Report, *op. cit.*, 48.

[174] *Ibid.*, 49.

[175] Outcome Document of the High-Level Plenary Meeting of the 60th Session of the UN General Assembly, 14–16 September 2005, para. 139.

[176] ICISS Report, *op. cit.*, para. 6.21.

5.4.4 *The Responsibility of Great Powers?*

In geo-political terms, acceptance of the Responsibility to Protect impacts upon the global allocation of power. In principle, it entrenches the shift from national to multinational authority to use force. However, the SC remains a top-down geo-political body, dominated by the permanent members and its exercise of power in authorising non-military sanctions and 'all necessary measures' remains unchallenged, thereby raising the issues of SC legitimacy, as discussed in Chapter 1.

Some critics of the Responsibility to Protect, drawing on a Hobbesian or Schmittian perspective, argue that it can be understood as a way in which the SC establishes executive power by claiming the right to act in exceptional circumstances. This is the position of Anne Orford, for example, who suggests that this is a continuation of the way in which the UN has acquired executive power since the era of Dag Hammarskjöld as UN Secretary-General[177] – power that is normalised and thus rendered invisible.[178]

The way in which great powers influence the SC can be seen, for instance, in its response to events in Haiti in 2004. Jean-Baptiste Aristide (who had been supported by the United States in 1994 and been re-elected in 2000) was overthrown and expelled from Haiti. The relevant SC resolution speaks of the 'resignation' of Aristide and the 'appeal' of the newly installed President to the UN for assistance and authorises 'the immediate deployment of a Multinational Interim Force . . . [t]o contribute to a secure and stable environment in the Haitian capital . . . in order to support Haitian President Alexandre's request for international assistance to support the constitutional political process under way in Haiti'.[179] In contrast, in a petition to the Inter-American Commission of Human Rights, Haitian human rights groups alleged a 'long-term, systematic plan' that undermined the 'democratically elected Haitian government through a development-assistance embargo' and supported armed opposition groups in overthrowing the democratically elected Haitian government and replacing it with a government with no constitutional or electoral legitimacy.[180] The petition

[177] Orford, Anne 2011. *International Authority and the Responsibility to Protect*. Cambridge University Press.

[178] Orford, Anne 2012. 'In Praise of Description', *Leiden Journal of International Law* 25(3): 609–625.

[179] UN SC Resolution 1529, 29 February 2004.

[180] Complaint Regarding Violations of the Right to Participate in Representative Government, submitted to the Inter-American Court on Human Rights, 2 February 2006, www.teledyol.net/IJDH/IACHRPet_v.pdf.

was brought against the United States and Dominican Republic. Events can thus be construed in two ways: the official narrative of SC-authorised assistance in restoring constitutional order to Haiti, providing humanitarian support and promoting human rights; and the alternative narrative of the forced removal of a government that challenged Washington's imperial interests and of ensuing terror in Haiti unleashed and supported by MINUSTAH (United Nations Stabilization Mission in Haiti).[181] This latter view is supported by accusations of MINUSTAH standing by and failing to intervene to protect civilians from attack.[182] What is unarguable is the SC authority to bestow legality upon such action and the lack of any process for review.

Some argue that humanitarianism was deliberately developed as a counterpart to the US neo-conservatives' desire to wage war in the late 1990s and that it is no accident that neo-conservatism and humanitarian intervention arose concurrently. Both seek transformative intervention, and humanitarianism provides the smokescreen for a neo-conservative ideology. On this analysis the Responsibility to Protect is a deliberate shift to create the normative framework for multilateral intervention rather than one to legalise humanitarian intervention as an exception to UN Charter article 2 (4). Its enabling of force rather than constraints upon its use undermines the legitimacy of the argument.[183]

Humanitarian Intervention and the Responsibility to Protect are discussed in the literature predominantly through the lens of Western states: it is their interventions, or failures to intervene, that shape the law and the doctrine. Non-Western states are visible primarily as sites for intervention, when it suits the agenda of Western states to do so. The doctrines reinforce the binary distinction of protector/protected, casting the latter as victims and lacking agency. Yet it should be noted that the dominant Western powers are not the only proponents of humanitarian intervention. In the Cold War era it was non-Western states – India, Vietnam and Tanzania – that intervened to put an end to human rights abuses in their neighbouring states. While their actions were not justified in such terms, they undoubtedly had humanitarian benefits for the local populations. In the post–Cold War era, African states concerned about

181 Miéville, China 2008. 'Multilateralism as Terror: International Law, Haiti and Imperialism', *Finnish Yearbook of International Law* 16: 63–92.

182 Wills, Siobhán 2009. *Protecting Civilians: The Obligations of Peacekeepers*. Oxford University Press, 69.

183 Wertheim, *op. cit.*

the failure of the Organisation of African Unity to prevent extreme abuses such as those in the Central African Empire (later the Central African Republic) and Rwanda replaced it with the AU and established an African peace and security architecture that 'sought seriously to address the mammoth crises bedevilling Africa'.[184] The right to intervene is entrenched in article 4 of the Constitutive Act of the African Union.[185] This provides 'the right of the Union to intervene in a Member State pursuant to a decision of the Assembly in respect of grave circumstances, namely: war crimes, genocide and crimes against humanity' and 'the right of Member States to request intervention from the Union in order to restore peace and security',[186] a so-called doctrine of 'non-indifference' to atrocity.[187] It provides a statutory basis for intervention, removing any need to justify intervention on moral and ethical grounds: under the AU the right to intervene is not 'a euphemism for humanitarian intervention but ... a normative commitment of AU States to prevent mass atrocity crimes on the continent'.[188]

As with the Responsibility to Protect, prevention is important, through, for instance, a turn towards human security. Regional and sub-regional forces have been deployed to conflict zones in Africa, including Sierra Leone, Liberia, Darfur, South Sudan, Lesotho, Mali, Côte D'Ivoire and the Central African Republic, either separately or in conjunction with UN-mandated forces. This is an aspect of seeking African solutions to violence on the continent, relieves pressure on international forces and through the deployment of ground forces moves away from reliance on air strikes. However, allegations of abuses, corruption and unprofessional conduct by members of African – as well as other – forces, in both UN and regional missions, have tainted this initiative. A report submitted to the Africa Union on African peace missions in

184 Abass, Ademola 2010. 'African Peace and Security Architecture and Protection of Human Security', in Abass, Ademola (ed.). *Protecting Human Security in Africa*. Oxford University Press, chapter 11, 249.

185 Kioko, Ben 2003. 'The Right of Intervention under the African Union's Constitutive Act: From Non-Interference to Non-Intervention', *International Review of the Red Cross* 85 (852): 807–825.

186 The relationship of this provision with the UN Charter prohibitions on the use of force and provision for regional arrangements under UN Charter, chapter VIII is controversial.

187 Kioko, *op. cit.*, 819.

188 Kuwali, Dan 2009. 'The End of Humanitarian Intervention: Evaluation of the African Union's Right of Intervention', *African Journal on Conflict Resolution* 9: 41–62, 58.

2016 suggests that political engagement is more important than coercive action in protecting civilians.[189]

In addition to questions about the normativity of the Responsibility to Protect and its practical implementation remains the ethical question as to whether the SC, or a regional organisation, has any right to ask member states to send troops into dangerous places at the risk to their own lives. UN forces were discredited in Bosnia and Rwanda because they lacked the mandate to use force to protect those who were being massacred; the Responsibility to Protect explicitly authorises 'all necessary' means to do this. The use of aerial bombing missions minimises the threat to such forces, but may be ineffective in preventing further violence on the ground. On the other hand, must they remain in situations where they themselves are attacked and killed? Is there a difference if their task is to protect the delivery of humanitarian assistance to beleaguered populations from when it is to protect them from violence and death? But humanitarian assistance is targeted for its contribution to the war economy, making its delivery itself a dangerous activity. What is clear is that forces seeking to provide protection must be properly equipped, resourced and supported in their mission,[190] otherwise their inadequacies may endanger unnecessarily their own lives and contribute to disaster for the population. In the words of a UN medical doctor in Srebrenica: 'But for me there's only one lesson … If blue-helmeted UN peacekeepers show up in your town or village and offer to protect you, run. Or else get weapons. Your lives are worth so much less than theirs. I learned that the day we were evacuated from Haiti'.[191]

5.4.5 *Protection of Civilians*

Despite the reiteration that parties to conflict 'bear the primary responsibility to take all feasible steps to ensure the protection of civilians',[192] the political decision to authorise force to protect civilians can obscure the existing legal obligations under international humanitarian law to

[189] *African Politics: African Peace* http://fletcher.tufts.edu/African-Peace-Missions/Report.

[190] The UK Supreme Court has held that the positive obligations under ECHR article 2 (right to life) apply to troops serving abroad, for instance, with respect to the provision of adequate equipment; *Smith v. MOD*, [2013] UKSC 41, 19 June 2013.

[191] Cain, Postlewait and Thomson, *op. cit.*, 252.

[192] For example, UN SC Resolution 1674, 28 April 2006 and UN SC Resolution 1894, 11 November 2009.

minimise civilian casualties.[193] Once NATO forces intervened, the situation in Libya was clearly framed as an international armed conflict; therefore NATO forces were required to comply with the rules of international humanitarian law. The ICRC sent many memoranda to all forces involved – the Libyan government, the rebels and NATO – reminding them of their IHL obligations and setting out their application to the situation.[194] NATO claimed to the Commission of Inquiry on Libya that it had 'utilized a standard of zero expectation of death or injury to civilians in its campaign, and that no targets had been struck if there had been any reason to believe civilians would be killed or injured'. The Commission accepted there had been a demonstrable determination to avoid civilian casualties but nevertheless that there was evidence of some loss of civilian life, which required investigation.[195]

Because NATO controlled the air space and because of improvements in precision targeting over the past decade, there is no doubt that NATO was much more successful at minimising civilian casualties from air strikes than during the Kosovo war (the requirement of IHL), but this is still not the same as protecting civilians (the mandate of SC Resolution 1973). The air strikes were, of course, aimed at destroying Gaddafi's capacity to attack peaceful protests, and undoubtedly the destruction of aircraft and other heavy equipment has meant fewer casualties compared with what Assad is able to continue doing in Syria. But as the aim of the operation shifted from the protection of civilians to support for the rebels (and hence regime change), then inevitably civilians were bound to be caught up in the crossfire. Further, despite the mandate to protect civilians, this was not understood in an even-handed way: 'it was never considered a possibility to carry out the coalition's mission to protect civilians in the case of civilians threatened by the actions of the armed opposition'.[196]

At the time of writing there are no casualty figures for the war in Libya; estimates vary from 2,000 to 100,000. But because this was a war, many civilians and fighters died as a result of the fighting. Is it legitimate to kill soldiers or civilians who are not responsible for carrying out humanitarian atrocities in order to protect the victims and sometimes the victims themselves? In the end Gaddafi was overthrown, but the fighting has

[193] See Chapter 6. [194] Pommier, *op. cit.*, 1072.

[195] Report of the Special Rapporteur on the Promotion and Protection of Human Rights and Fundamental Freedoms while Countering Terrorism, UN Doc. A/68/389, 18 September 2013, para. 36.

[196] Pommier, *op. cit.*, 1078.

empowered armed militias, there is a growing threat of IS-related terrorist groups and the long-term prospects for the end of violence are still difficult to assess.

The fundamental issue is how to conceptualise a humanitarian intervention. If it is conceptualised as an armed conflict, then IHL applies. But is a response to a humanitarian catastrophe the same as an armed conflict? Surely, if the language of humanity is being used, the rules of engagement should be based on human rights rather than IHL and should be more like the rules of engagement in domestic policing. The aim is not to defeat the adversary in a conflict but to protect people and arrest criminals responsible for violations of human rights. In both Kosovo and Libya, the intervention was treated as a war in which there were bound to be civilian casualties even if the intervening force sought to minimise them. The means of intervention, air strikes, were not compatible with the aim of protecting civilians.

5.4.6 Legality and Legitimacy Revisited?

We consider that the unauthorised Kosovo intervention was illegal under existing international law while those in Libya and Côte d'Ivoire were legal, at least in terms of right authority and process as they were authorised by the SC. The intervention in Mali was unauthorised but subsequently 'welcomed' by the SC and hence endorsed. SC resolutions are negotiated instruments, and their terms may be ambiguous and open to differing interpretations; the extent to which the military actions in Libya and Côte d'Ivoire went outside the terms of the mandate, and hence compromised their legality, is less clear. There is a case for their legitimacy in all cases;[197] in Kosovo, the Serbian oppression of the Kosovar Albanians was halted, all military, police and paramilitary forces from the FRY were required to withdraw from Kosovo[198] and refugees were able to return; in Libya a brutal dictator was overthrown, and referral of the 'situation in Libya' to the ICC has resulted in criminal charges against Gaddafi's son and a colonel in the

[197] Chinkin, Christine 2012. 'Rethinking Legality/Legitimacy after the Iraq War', in Falk, Richard, Juergensmayer, Mark and Popovski, Vesselin. *Legality and Legitimacy in Global Affairs*. Oxford University Press, 219–247. See also discussion in Chapter 1.

[198] UN SC Resolution 1244, 10 June 1999. Somewhat inconsistently the resolution also reaffirmed the 'commitment of all Member States to the sovereignty and territorial integrity of the Federal Republic of Yugoslavia'.

Libyan army;[199] in Côte d'Ivoire, Bellamy and Williams conclude that 'the course set by UNOCI's leadership and the UN Secretariat helped to stabilize the situation and minimize casualties'.[200] In Mali presidential elections have taken place and a new government sworn in.

In practice, the picture is more mixed. In Kosovo there was new displacement and further civilian deaths that the deployment of the international civil and security presences was unable to prevent. In Libya human rights violations and extreme factional violence and terrorist groups continue to destabilise the country, and the violence has spilled over into Mali. Libya has become the departure point for mass migration across the Mediterranean Sea through people smuggling, contributing to the deaths of thousands of desperate people. In Côte d'Ivoire there was intervention into complex internal politics, and there is no certainty that such intervention will not do more harm. In Mali, despite intervention, violent terrorist activity continues, the security situation is still deteriorating and insecurity, especially in the north, prevails.[201] Transnational organised crime and terrorism continue, and there is an ongoing food and humanitarian crisis.[202] A resident of Gao in the north of Mali put it graphically: 'We are still scared. . . . We sit outside because we are too are afraid to sit indoors, and when we do, we don't even want to close the door in case it makes it harder to get out'.[203] Bellamy and Williams conclude that a human protection agenda inevitably engages international actors 'in messy and complicated national and international politics'[204] requiring ill-informed peacekeepers to reach judgements about how to interpret their mandate and balance contradictory elements within it.

Different actors will assess legitimacy differently.[205] Thus those that prioritise immediate goals such as regime change are more likely to interpret these various interventions as legitimate. Those who start from

199 *Prosecutor v. Saif Al-Islam Gaddafi* and *Prosecutor v. Abdullah Al-Senussi*, ICC-01/11-01/11. The situation was referred by UN SC Resolution 1970, 26 February 2011. See further Chapter 11.

200 Bellamy and Williams, *op. cit.*, 838.

201 International Crisis Group. 'Mali', *Crisis Watch Database*, 1 November 2013, www.crisisgroup.org/en/publication-type/crisiswatch/crisiswatch-database.aspx?CountryIDs=%7B00784553-1A92-4A05-8825–9235786CF9BC%7D.

202 UN SC Resolution 2227, 29 June 2015.

203 Hirsch, Afua. 'Mali's Fight with Militants Is Far from Over', *The Guardian*, 17 October 2013, www.theguardian.com/world/2013/oct/17/mali-fights-militants-far-from-over.

204 Bellamy and Williams, *op. cit.*, 837.

205 For a discussion of the legitimacy of humanitarian intervention from a feminist perspective see Heathcote, *op. cit.*, chapter 5.

a human rights perspective will have a much more complex and nuanced interpretation of legitimacy. We suggest that any assessment of legitimacy needs to take into account the factors enumerated above – credible evidence of a humanitarian crisis, the role and agendas of the Great Powers and the SC and the extent to which the means are tailored to the ends. Legality is a much narrower concept and therefore easier to assess, although made harder by the extended claims discussed throughout this book. Upholding the international rule of law is a factor inducing human security, but the formal rules need to be underpinned by the broader concept of legitimacy. That this is not the case, at least from a human rights or human security perspective, should be of deep concern.

5.5 Conclusion

The Responsibility to Protect is the expression of an apparently global concern (as demonstrated by its endorsement by the GA) to respond to massive violations of human rights. At the same time, it remains within a state-centric, top-down framework, enhancing the power of the SC permanent members without any increase in their accountability, using the methods of war in ways that fundamentally contradict its ultimate objectives and privileging the lives of those engaged in such operations over the lives of those they are supposed to protect.

Throughout the discussion it is apparent that there is no clear agreement on what constitutes 'protection', and the concept differs under different legal regimes with very little cohesion. As will be seen in Chapter 6, under international humanitarian law it is essentially limited to protection from illegal targeting, and the *jus ad bellum* Responsibility to Protect also assumes this position, although the responsibility to reconstruct may go further. Similarly, under occupation law the occupier must ensure food, medical supplies, religious support and other basics to the population.[206] Human rights law requires protection from wrongful intervention with dignity, life, bodily integrity and liberty; it also imposes positive obligations such as the provision of security and an adequate standard of living.[207] Among the objectives of international criminal law are deterrence, the delivery of justice and the enhancement of international peace and security, but, as discussed in Chapter 10, there are many flaws in

[206] *Convention Relative to the Protection of Civilian Persons in Time of War*, 12 August 1949, 75 UNTS 287 (*Geneva Convention IV*), Section III.

[207] ICCPR, article 9; ICESCR, articles 9, 11.

achieving accountability and justice. SC resolutions mandating missions for the protection of civilians do not usually determine what measures should be undertaken, essentially leaving it to the mission in question.[208]

At its best, 'protection' should be understood widely and should incorporate preventing or putting an end to specific patterns of abuse; alleviating their immediate effects, such as responsive measures, including protection through advocacy and negotiations with relevant actors (including civil society); seeking interventions at higher levels, naming and shaming; protection activities aimed at restoring dignity, reparations, restitution and rehabilitation, including accessible and available access to law enforcement and justice, accountability and an end to impunity, appropriate and effective mechanisms for fair restitution of property; creating and running institutions for health care and rehabilitation (including psychological care) for victims; fostering an environment conducive to guaranteeing human rights and equality; preventing violations of human rights; stopping ongoing violations; preventing violations; and repairing, restoring and rehabilitating victims and their families.[209] A gender perspective should be integrated into all policies and practices of protection so as to promote and effectively implement policies of equality between women and men and the empowerment of women.

A problem with the Responsibility to Protect, despite the way it was originally framed, is that the focus is on the much narrower conception of protection linked to the use of force, understood as war. We know that wars always involve human tragedies and have long-term consequences for the way power and resources are allocated and exercised in the aftermath. If we start from the assumption of individual as opposed to collective rights, then the question arises as to whether it is possible to protect individuals in contexts of deep insecurity (genocide, e.g., or massive violations of human rights) without a response that also undermines the security of large numbers of people. Can war, which of its nature is collective on both sides, be used to protect individual rights? Is there a middle way between the disastrous failures of Srebrenica and Rwanda and the excesses of Kosovo and Libya? This question is at the heart of our concern with human security.

[208] See Chapter 9.

[209] This draws heavily on – with some adaptations – the Report of the UN High Commissioner for Human Rights, Outcome of the Expert Consultation on the Issue of Protecting the Human Rights of Civilians in Armed Conflict, UN Doc. A/HRC/11/31, 4 June 2009, para. 31.

PART III

Jus in Bello

6

How Force Is Used

6.1 Introduction

Changing manifestations of political violence have presented a challenge to the international rules governing the conduct of war – the *jus in bello*, the 'laws of war' or international humanitarian law (IHL), as well as to those regulating recourse to force, as discussed in Chapters 4 and 5. This was especially the case during the Administration of President George W. Bush, following the terrorist attacks of 11 September 2011. Indeed, claims were made to bypass the *jus in bello* entirely. For instance, US Attorney General Alberto Gonzales famously asserted that the Third Geneva Convention's strict limitations on questioning of enemy prisoners had become obsolete in situations of contemporary conflict[1] and described some of the Geneva provisions as 'quaint'.[2] The Administration argued that the Geneva Conventions applied to 'traditional' wars and therefore needed to be revised in the light of a 'new war paradigm'. While the Administration's view was backed by some judges,[3] lawyers and academic commentators,[4] others in the State Department and the US military disagreed.[5]

1 *Convention Relative to the Protection of Prisoners of War*, 12 August 1949, 75 UNTS 135 (*Geneva Convention III*).

2 Memo from Alberto Gonzalez to President Bush, 'Application of the Geneva Convention on Prisoners of War to the Conflict with al Qaeda and the Taliban', 25 January 2002, www2.gwu.edu/~nsarchiv/torturingdemocracy/documents/; Sands, Philippe 2008. *Torture Team: Deception, Cruelty and the Compromise of Law*. Allen Lane.

3 E.g., 'War is a challenge to law, and the law must adjust . . . prior frameworks are ill-suited to the bitter wine of this new warfare'. *Al-Bihani v. Obama* (2010) 590 F. 3rd 866, 882 (DC Circ.), Brown J. concurring.

4 E.g., Yoo, John. 'Commentary: Behind the 'Torture Memos', UC Berkley News, 4 January 2005, www.berkeley.edu/news/media/releases/2005/01/05_johnyoo.shtml.

5 Memo from Colin Powell to Alberto Gonzalez, 'Draft Decision Memorandum for the President on the Applicability of the Geneva Convention to the Conflict in Afghanistan', 26 January 2002, http://nsarchive.gwu.edu/torturingdemocracy/documents/20020126.pdf.

In particular, the concept of an 'unlawful combatant' or 'enemy combatant',[6] renamed by the Obama Administration as an 'alien belligerent', the establishment of special military commissions to try some detainees and the failure to charge others, and the practice of torture were all justified in terms both of a 'supreme emergency' that overrides existing law and of a new kind of enemy 'that doesn't share our values' and as such is not deserving of humane treatment.[7] In effect the Bush administration was challenging the legitimacy of the law itself and thus rejecting its 'pull' factor towards compliance.[8]

Paradoxically, we share the view that the laws of war are inadequate in the new global context. While we reject many of the assertions of the Bush Administration, notably those relating to the practice of torture and detention without charge, we accept that questions as to the relevance of the laws of war remain. The rules regulating violent conduct between states are integral to the Geo-Political model but do not fit and are only uneasily applied in the other conflict models; even if formally applied their ineffectiveness weakens their purported humanitarian purpose in all contemporary forms of violence. Further, while theoretically restraining the worst violence of war, they allow for the legitimation of what is not prohibited. Newer bodies of law, particularly human rights law and international criminal law, do, at least in theory, fill some of the gaps in IHL but also expose other gaps. The challenge is how to strengthen, co-ordinate and implement these bodies of law in order to enhance security in general, rather than simply rejecting earlier bodies of law. We argue that war must be understood as a violation of human rights, in which case human rights law should be the predominant legal regime. Nevertheless the specific protections of IHL have been built up over many years and, despite the overall problematic nature of IHL in 'new

Powell warned that opting out of the Geneva Conventions 'will reverse over a century of U.S. policy . . . and undermine the prosecutions of the law of war for our troops'.

[6] 'An "enemy combatant" is defined as "an individual who was part of or supporting Taliban or al-Qaida forces, or associated forces that are engaged in hostilities against the United States or its coalition partners. This includes any person who has committed a belligerent act or has directly supported hostilities in aid of enemy armed forces" (see the Memorandum of 14 July 2006 on Implementation of Combatant Status Review Tribunal Procedures for Enemy Combatants Detained at US Naval Base Guantánamo Bay)'. Cited *Boumediene and Others v. Bosnia and Herzegovina,* ECtHR appl. no. 38703/2006 and others, judgment of 18 November 2008, para. 41.

[7] See Brahimi, Alia 2010. *Jihad and Just War and the War on Terror*. Oxford University Press.

[8] See Chapters 1 and 3.

wars', should be clarified and retained. The significance of international criminal law as complementary to both bodies of law, despite its uneven application, is beyond question.

This chapter starts with a recapitulation of the *jus in bello* tradition. It then summarises the basic principles of contemporary IHL, and their inadequacies for regulating new wars. It also considers its continued applicability to all sides in these supposedly 'just' conflicts, as well as in those undertaken for humanitarian purposes – the supposed convergence between the *jus ad bellum* and *jus in bello*. It finally considers the interaction between IHL and human rights law in situations of armed conflict.

6.2 The *Jus in Bello* Tradition

Rules about how war is to be conducted are to be found in all traditions and have a long genealogy. They were incorporated into international law much earlier than the rules governing either the recourse to war or human rights.

Certain principles are repeated across the *jus in bello* rules in all traditions. In the words of a former Judge of the International Court of Justice (ICJ), 'the concept is of ancient origin, with a lineage stretching back at least three millennia[.] . . . It is deep-rooted in many cultures – Hindu, Buddhist, Chinese, Christian, Islamic and traditional African'.[9] Such principles typically include rules relating to the exclusion of certain people and property from the violence of conflict. For instance, in the Mahabarat – the story of one of the greatest battles in history between the Pandava brothers and the Kauravas that is at the core of the Hindu tradition – a long list of categories of persons to be excluded from warfare is given. It covers 'women and children, the aged, Brahmans and ascetics, those from whom one has received food, drivers, transporters, drummers, conch players, foragers, camp-followers, doormen, menials or servants in charge of menials, artisans such as miners, those who are beginning a sacrifice, seeking deliverance or undertaking religiously motivated fast to death'.[10] The Jewish and Islamic traditions also include

[9] *Legality of the Threat or Use of Nuclear Weapons*, 1996 ICJ Reports 226, advisory opinion of 8 July 1996 (per dissenting opinion Judge Weeramantry, para. 478).

[10] Allen, Nick 2010. 'Just War in the Mahabharata', in Sorabji, Richard and Rodin, David (eds.). *The Ethics of War: Shared Problems in Different Traditions*. Ashgate Publishing, 138–150, 139.

environmental factors as necessary to sustain civilian life. Thus in Deuteronomy 20:19, God commanded the Jews not to cut down fruit trees: 'When thou shalt besiege a citie a long time, in making warre against it to take it, thou shalt not destroy the trees thereof, by forcing an axe against them: for thou mayest eate of them, and thou shalt not cut them downe (for the tree of the field is man's life) to employ them in the siege'. This injunction was further developed in the Islamic tradition. The famous and often quoted opinion of Abu Bakr, the first Caliph, instructed Muslims as follows:

> Do not mutilate; do not kill little children or old men or women; do not cut off the heads of palm trees or burn them; do not cut down the fruit trees; do not slaughter a sheep or a cow or a camel except for food, and if you pass by the monasteries of believers who devoted themselves to worship ... leave them to what they chose to do.[11]

In 1339 the Emperor Codalago ordered commanders to 'restrict the killing of innocents and to absolutely forbid the torching of shrines and temples'.[12] In African warfare too, humanitarian traditions were in some areas 'highly developed systems of etiquette, conventions and rules'.[13] Such rules were accepted in order to preserve civil society's *status quo* and to minimise the destruction of warfare.[14] The rules were also part of the formalisation of war as a legitimate phenomenon.

These rules were not only ethical norms; they were codified at an early stage, in Roman Law, in Shari'a law in the classical Islamic period, in canon law and in the chivalric code in medieval Europe. A body of customary international law had begun to be built up, accepted by the European founding fathers of international law. For instance, Vitoria (1483–1546) considered non-combatant immunity as a principle of the laws of war, and Grotius (1583–1645) too enumerates all those whose lives should be spared, including the innocent, women, children and the aged, those whose occupations are religious or concerned with letters, farmers, merchants or prisoners of war.[15] In 1621, King Gustavus

[11] Ezzat, Heba Raouf and Kaldor, Mary 2005. 'Not Even a Tree: Delegitimizing Violence and the Prospects for Pre-Emptive Civility', in *Global Civil Society: 2006–2007*. Sage.

[12] Sellers, Patricia Viseur 1999. 'The Cultural Value of Sexual Violence', *American Society of International Law Proceedings* 93, 312.

[13] *Nuclear Weapons, op. cit.* (per dissenting opinion Judge Weeramantry, para. 480).

[14] Sellers, *op. cit.*, 312.

[15] Grotius, Hugo 2012 *On the Law of War and Peace* (edited and annotated by Steven Neff) Cambridge University Press, book III, chapter 11.

Adolphus of Sweden signed the 150 Articles of War. Limitations on the conduct of warfare were accepted in the post-Westphalian period. For instance, in 1785 the Treaty of Amity between the United States and Prussia – primarily a commercial treaty – included provisions to be applied if either party was at war with another party and by both sides if they were ever to go to war with each other:

> And all women & children, scholars of every faculty, cultivators of the earth, artizans, manufacturers and fishermen unarmed and inhabiting unfortified towns, villages or places, & in general all others whose occupations are for the common subsistence & benefit of mankind, shall be allowed to continue their respective employments, & shall not be molested in their persons, nor shall their houses or goods be burnt, or otherwise destroyed, nor their fields wasted by the armed force of the enemy, into whose power, by the events of war, they may happen to fall; . . . And all merchant and trading vessels employed in exchanging the products of different places, & thereby rendering the necessaries, conveniencies & comforts of human life more easy to be obtained, . . . shall be allowed to pass free & unmolested.[16]

Further, 'to prevent the destruction of prisoners of war . . . by crouding them into close & noxious places' the parties agreed that they would not behave in this way but would place them 'in wholesome situations', officers in 'comfortable quarters' and 'common men' in 'cantonments, open & extensive enough for air & exercise'.[17]

6.3 Codification of International Humanitarian Law: Geneva and Hague Law

In the late nineteenth century the incorporation of these *jus in bello* traditions into conventional international law gathered pace.[18] In the American Civil War, Abraham Lincoln commissioned Francis Lieber, a Professor at Columbia University, to draw up a 'Code of War for the Government of the Armies of the United States in the Field'.[19] In Europe, during the same period, Henri Dunant founded the International

[16] *Treaty of Amity and Commerce between his Majesty the King of Prussia, and the United States of America*, The Hague, 10 September 1785, article 23.

[17] *Ibid.*, article 24.

[18] For an overview of the 'period of solid codification of the acts constituting a war crime and for which an individual could be held criminally liable', see *Kononov v. Latvia*, ECtHR GC, application no. 36376/04, judgment of 17 May 2010, paras. 206–217.

[19] General Orders No. 100 (Lieber Code), 24 April 1863.

Committee of the Red Cross (ICRC), following his own experience at the Battle of Solferino in 1859, and this led to a series of Geneva Conventions (1864, 1906, 1929), eventually (1949) comprising four treaties[20] and three additional protocols (1977[21] and 2005[22]). These dealt largely with the treatment of those *hors de combat*, providing protection for the sick and wounded after battle on land and at sea, prisoners of war and, only after 1949, despite earlier efforts, civilians. The Hague Peace Conference of 1899 added 'Hague Law' to Geneva law. The Hague Regulations, annexed to the Second Hague Convention of 1899[23] (and to the Fourth Hague Convention in 1907), addressed the laws and customs of war, including those applicable during military occupation, restraining the powers of the occupier with respect to the inhabitants of occupied territory. In particular 'Family honour and rights, the lives of persons, and private property, as well as religious convictions and practice, must be respected'.[24] In addition, the St Petersburg Conference of 1868 and The Hague Conferences of 1899 and 1907 addressed the issue of weapons which were not to be used in wars in order to avoid 'uselessly aggravat[ing] the sufferings of disabled men or render their death inevitable'.[25] Weapons law has been continued through both Hague and Geneva law (especially Additional Protocol I) and through specialist sectoral treaties.[26]

By and large the rules of *jus in bello* applied to wars between mutually recognised authorities, usually states, that were declared. For legal

[20] *Convention for the Amelioration of the Condition of the Wounded and Sick in Armed Forces in the Field; Convention for the Amelioration of the Condition of Wounded, Sick and Shipwrecked Members of Armed Forces at Sea; Convention relative to the Treatment of Prisoners of War; Convention relative to the Protection of Civilian Persons in Time of War (Geneva Conventions I–V)*, all of 12 August 1949.

[21] *Protocol Additional to the Geneva Conventions of 12 August 1949, and relating to the Protection of Victims of International Armed Conflicts (Additional Protocol I)*, 8 June 1977; *Protocol Additional to the Geneva Conventions of 12 August 1949, and relating to the Protection of Victims of Non-International Armed Conflicts (Additional Protocol II)*, 8 June 1977.

[22] *Protocol Additional to the Geneva Conventions of 12 August 1949, and relating to the Adoption of an Additional Distinctive Emblem (Protocol III)*, 8 December 2005.

[23] *Hague Convention (II) respecting the Laws and Customs of War on Land* and its annex: *Regulations concerning the Laws and Customs of War on Land*, 29 July 1899, 32 Stat. 1803, 1 Bevans 247.

[24] *Hague Convention (IV) Laws and Customs of War on Land and its annex*: 18 October 1907, 36 Stat. 2277, 1 Bevans 631.

[25] Declaration Renouncing the Use, in Time of War, of Explosive Projectiles under 400 Grammes Weight. Saint Petersburg, 29 November/11 December 1868.

[26] See Chapter 7.

purposes, the term war 'referred to declared hostilities between two or more states, or very occasionally to civil conflicts in which an insurgent group had gained control over sufficient territory to be recognised as having belligerent status'.[27] The primary purpose of such a declaration was to activate the laws applicable to war, including those relating to the status of neutrality relevant to non-combatant states.[28] The Lieber Code, however, applied to a civil war, although Lincoln recognised the rebels as belligerents and applied the law as relating to international armed conflict.[29] As outlined in Chapter 2, rebellions against rightful authority did not count as wars, and so the international rules did not apply domestically where national laws applied or in the colonies, where rebellions were responded to extremely harshly by colonial powers in accordance with colonial laws.[30] The Islamic tradition allowed for internal conflicts with a stringent application of the rules, namely, that the rebels had to be sufficiently well-organised and to have a legitimate grievance.

In order to avoid claims that the laws of war do not apply in the absence of a declaration of war, the 1949 Geneva Conventions and Additional Protocol I apply to international armed conflict (IAC), as well as to a declared war[31] and Geneva Conventions, common article 3 and Additional Protocol II apply to armed conflict not of an international character (NIAC).[32] The former (IAC) takes place between two or more of the parties to the Geneva Conventions (i.e., between states) and is a matter of fact. There is no indication as to the

[27] Dworkin, Anthony 2005. 'Military Necessity and Due Process: The Place of Human Rights in the War on Terror', in Wippman, David H. and Evangelista, Matthew (eds.). *New Wars, New Laws? Applying Laws of War in 21st Century Conflicts.* Transnational Publishers, chapter 3, 57.

[28] See Neff, Steven 2005. *War and the Law of Nations: A General History.* Cambridge University Press.

[29] Under traditional international law rebels or insurgents that were recognised by the government as belligerents were deemed a state actor with the attendant rights and privileges under international law. This has apparently now become outdated; Clapham, Andrew 2006. 'Human Rights Obligations of Non-State Actors in Conflict Situations', *International Review of the Red Cross* 88 (863): 491–523, 492.

[30] The application of human rights law in the colonies was addressed in the European Convention on Human Rights, 1950, article 56 (originally article 63); see Moor, Louise and Simpson, Brian 2005. 'Ghosts of Colonialism in the European Convention on Human Rights', *British Yearbook of International Law* 76: 121–194.

[31] *Geneva Conventions I–V, op. cit.*, common article 2.

[32] For a detailed account of NIAC see Sivakumaran, Sandesh 2012. *The Law of Non-International Armed Conflict.* Oxford University Press.

required level of intensity. In the context of armed attack the ICJ has determined the need to distinguish 'the most grave forms of the use of force (those constituting an armed attack) from other less grave forms'.[33] But the purpose of determining the existence of an IAC differs from that of an armed attack. The former is to make applicable humanitarian constraints upon the violence, while the latter allows for escalation through triggering the right to self-defence (see Chapter 4). Accordingly, there are good policy arguments for requiring a higher threshold of violence for an 'armed attack' than for an international armed conflict, a position supported by the ICRC that considers IHL to apply to 'any dispute between two States involving the use of their armed forces. Neither the duration of the conflict, nor its intensity, play a role'.[34]

NIAC is not defined except negatively in article 3, common to the Geneva Conventions – armed conflict not of an international character. The scope of Additional Protocol II is limited. It applies only to conflict between the forces of a state party and dissident groups or organised forces 'under responsible command' and exercising control over territory such as 'to enable them to carry out sustained and concerted military operations'. It excludes 'internal disturbances and tensions, such as riots, isolated and sporadic acts of violence'.[35] In short, Protocol II is narrower than common article 3 and applies only to intense, protracted conflicts[36] 'that in fact approximate to traditional conceptions of inter-State warfare, namely where an organised force exercises military control over a part of the territory of a State Party'.[37] In response to the wars of liberation that had accompanied decolonisation, apartheid and the occupation of Palestinian territories, Protocol I, article 1 (4) deems 'armed conflicts in which peoples are fighting against colonial domination and alien occupation and against racist regimes in the exercise of their right of self-determination' to constitute IACs. The regime for protection of those *hors de combat* in an IAC is much greater than that in a NIAC; prior to the adoption of Additional Protocol II in 1977, only common article 3 was

[33] See *Oil Platforms* (Islamic Republic of Iran v. United States of America), 2003 ICJ Reports, judgment of 6 November 2003 ('*Oil Platforms*'), para. 51.

[34] ICRC Commentary to Additional Protocol I, para. 62.

[35] *Additional Protocol II*, *op. cit.*, article 1 (2).

[36] For the many factors that go to determining intensity see, e.g., *Prosecutor v. Ramush Haradinaj, Idriz Balaj and Lahi Brahimaj*, IT-04-84*bis*-T, 29 November 2012, para. 394.

[37] Stewart, James 2003. 'Towards a Single Definition of Armed Conflict in International Humanitarian Law: A Critique of Internationalized Armed Conflict', *International Review of the Red Cross* 85(850): 313–350.

applicable in the latter. Classification of conflict and thus determination of the applicable law remains contested. Further, since not all states are parties to the Additional Protocols,[38] the obligations of states within an alliance such as NATO, or an informal coalition of the willing, will differ. While the jurisprudence of the international criminal tribunals has brought the two regimes closer together, not all of their rulings are accepted as customary international law,[39] contributing to the uncertainties as to both the appropriate legal regime and the substantive content of the applicable rules.

6.4 The Basic Principles of IHL

6.4.1 Principle of Humanity

While many of the rules relating to warfare are highly detailed and technical, The Hague Convention on the Laws of War incorporated as a residual protection the basic principle of humanity that 'the inhabitants and the belligerents remain under the protection and the rule of the principles of the law of nations, as they result from the usages established among civilized peoples, from the laws of humanity, and the dictates of the public conscience'.[40] This so-called Martens clause (named after the Russian delegate to the 1899 Hague Peace Conference who proposed the clause) signifies that in addition to those principles set out in the codified laws of war, there exists a body of general principles of humanity: it has been described as 'encapsulating in its short phraseology the entire philosophy of the law of war'.[41] It has been incorporated in modern form in Additional Protocol I[42] and also in effect has been amplified by the provision of fundamental guarantees of humane treatment in both

[38] There is universal acceptance of the 1949 Geneva Conventions; 173 states are parties to Additional Protocol I, and 167 states are parties to Additional Protocol II. As of December 2016 174 states are parties to Additional Protocol I or II.

[39] See Jenckaerts, Jean-Marie and Doswald-Beck, Louise 2005. *Customary International Humanitarian Law*. Cambridge University Press; ICRC database www.icrc.org/customary-ihl/eng/docs/home. Not all the conclusions of the ICRC with respect to custom are accepted by all states.

[40] *Hague Convention (IV), op. cit.*, preamble.

[41] *Nuclear Weapons, op. cit.*, dissenting opinion Judge Weeramantry, 486.

[42] *Additional Protocol I, op. cit.*, article 1 (2): 'In cases not covered by this Protocol or by other international agreements, civilians and combatants remain under the protection and authority of the principles of international law derived from established custom, from the principles of humanity and from the dictates of public conscience'.

Protocols.[43] It has been argued that the clause 'safeguards' customary international law and ensures that exclusion from a treaty does not necessarily mean exclusion from the law.[44] In the advisory opinion on the *Threat or Use of Nuclear Weapons* the majority in the ICJ referred to the Martens clause and 'elementary considerations' of humanity as 'fundamental rules . . . to be observed by all States'[45] and pointed to the former as an 'affirmation' that IHL applies to nuclear weapons.[46] Nevertheless the Court did not go on to outlaw definitively nuclear weapons.[47]

6.4.2 The Principles of Distinction, Proportionality and 'Unnecessary Suffering'

Some 'cardinal' principles predominate in IHL. The first is the principle of discrimination, or distinction, which distinguishes between combatants and those who are *hors de combat* – between *inter alia* civilians, the wounded, prisoners of war, religious actors, journalists and military personnel, and between civilian property and military targets. Before 1949 there was no Convention specifically addressing the position of civilians in armed conflict, although the International Law Association prepared a Draft Convention for the Protection of Civilian Populations against New Engines of War in 1938.[48] It defined civilians negatively as 'those not enlisted in any branch of the combatant services nor for the time being employed or occupied in any belligerent establishment'. It sought to limit aerial bombardment and further the establishment of safety zones for civilians. This forward-looking non-governmental initiative was not adopted by states.

The principle of distinction means that 'The civilian population as such, as well as individual civilians, shall not be the object of attack',[49] but must be protected in an IAC as innocent individuals who do no harm to the enemy cause.[50] A corollary is combatant immunity for the killing or

[43] *Ibid.*, article 75; Additional Protocol II, *op. cit.*, article 4.

[44] Meron, Theodor 2000. 'The Martens Clause, Principles of Humanity and the Dictates of Public Conscience', *American Journal of International Law* 94: 78–89, 87.

[45] *Nuclear Weapons, op. cit.*, para. 79. [46] *Ibid.*, para. 87. [47] *Ibid.*, para. 95.

[48] *Draft Convention for the Protection of Civilian Populations against New Engines of War*, Amsterdam, 1938, www.icrc.org/applic/ihl/ihl.nsf/Treaty.xsp?action=openDocument&documentId=29DF95181E9CC0FDC12563CD002D6A9B.

[49] *Additional Protocol I, op. cit.*, article 51 (2).

[50] 'The cardinal principles contained in the texts constituting the fabric of humanitarian law are the following. The first is aimed at the protection of the civilian population and

wounding of a combatant of the other side, in accordance with the laws of war. The principle of distinction does not apply in a NIAC where there is no acceptance of lawful killing by a combatant (who is after all a rebel against the government) and thus no entitlement to prisoner of war status.[51] Instead, civilians in a NIAC shall not be the object of attack 'unless and for such time as they take a direct part in hostilities'.[52] Those who do not take a direct part in hostilities, or who have ceased to do so, are to be treated humanely.[53]

The second and closely linked principle is known in the Western tradition as 'proportionality', or 'necessity', and 'double effect'. The idea behind these concepts is that killing or harming enemy civilians can be justifiable if it is an unavoidable side effect of an attack on a military target, which is necessary in order to win the war, if it is unintentional, and if the harm done is proportionate to the harm that might be done if the military target were not destroyed or captured. *Jus in bello* proportionality must be distinguished from *ad bellum* proportionality (and human rights proportionality). *Ad bellum* proportionality refers to the criteria for recourse to war itself, that the harm inflicted by the war should be less than the benefit achieved by fighting the war; *jus in bello* proportionality refers to the application of minimal force, no more than is necessary to achieve a particular military goal.[54] If civilians are unintentionally killed in a military action that is necessary and proportionate, then that is counted as 'double effect' or in today's jargon, 'collateral damage'. Additional Protocol I thus defines a (prohibited) indiscriminate attack as one that 'may be expected to cause incidental loss of civilian life, . . . which would be excessive in relation to the concrete and direct military advantage anticipated'[55] and requires an attack to be cancelled or suspended 'if it becomes apparent . . . that the attack may be expected to cause incidental loss of civilian life, . . . which would be excessive in relation to the concrete and direct military advantage anticipated'.[56] The military advantage may not always be apparent, for instance, in

civilian objects and establishes the distinction between combatants and non-combatants'; *Nuclear Weapons, op. cit.*, para. 78.

51 However, following the end of hostilities, 'the authorities in power shall endeavour to grant the broadest possible amnesty to persons who have participated in the armed conflict'. *Additional Protocol II, op. cit.*, article 6(5).

52 *Ibid.*, article 13.

53 *Ibid.*, article 4.

54 Johnson, James Turner 1981. *Just War Tradition and the Restraint of War: A Moral and Historical Inquiry*. Princeton University Press.

55 *Additional Protocol I, op. cit.*, article 51 (5) (b).

56 *Ibid.*, article 57 (2)(b).

attacks in residential areas.[57] In similar vein is the requirement to take precautionary measures in attacks to avoid, or at least mimimise, 'incidental loss of civilian life, injury to civilians and damage to civilian objects'.[58]

A further principle, which integrates weapons law,[59] is the prohibition of 'unnecessary suffering' or useless aggravation of the suffering of combatants. Here too these concepts are understood as 'harm[s] greater than that unavoidable to achieve legitimate military objectives'.[60] It is clear that despite expressions of the principles of humanity, military necessity imbues IHL and enjoys priority throughout the application of even these cardinal principles.

6.4.3 *Enforcement of IHL*

At the time of the adoption of the 1949 Geneva Conventions, and even the 1977 Additional Protocols, there was no international criminal tribunal. Accordingly enforcement could only be through national courts. In the context of international armed conflict, states parties are required to legislate to provide for jurisdiction and penal sanctions for what are termed 'grave breaches' of each of the Conventions and Protocol I.[61] This makes criminal proceedings dependent on the ability and willingness of national law enforcement bodies to exercise their powers and assert jurisdiction. Since the 1990s grave breaches have also been made subject to the jurisdiction of the International Criminal Tribunal for the former Yugoslavia (ICTY) and the International Criminal Court (ICC).[62] This has brought the IAC/NIAC distinction into modern international criminal law, a position reinforced by the inclusion of only violations of Geneva Conventions common article 3 within the jurisdiction of the International Criminal Tribunal for Rwanda (ICTR) and Special Court for Sierra Leone (SCSL),[63] thereby deeming

57 Report of the Independent Commission of Inquiry Established Pursuant to Human Rights Council Resolution S-21/1 UN Doc. A/HRC/29/52A 24 June 2015, para. 40 (with respect to Gaza, 2014) ('Independent Inquiry on Gaza').

58 *Additional Protocol I*, *op. cit.*, article 57 (Precautions in Attack). See Independent Inquiry on Gaza, paras. 41–43.

59 See Chapter 7. 60 *Nuclear Weapons, op. cit.*, para. 78.

61 *Geneva Convention I*, *op. cit.*, article 49; *Geneva Convention II*, article 50; *Geneva Convention III*, article 129; *Geneva Convention IV*, article 146; *Additional Protocol I*, article 85.

62 Statute of the ICTY, article 2; *Rome Statute of the ICC*, article 8 (2).

63 Statute of the ICTR, article 4; Statute of the Special Court for Sierra Leone, article 3.

violence in those states to constitute NIAC. The *ad hoc* international criminal tribunals have sought to lessen the substantive impact of the distinction.[64]

The concept of a 'grave breach' is not without difficulties. First, it creates a hierarchy of violations and allows the assumption that non-grave breaches are not subject to any penal sanction. This has, however, also been lessened by the concept and listing of 'other serious violations' of IHL.[65] Second, grave breaches are itemised[66] allowing arguments that omissions are not deemed to come within the category, for example, rape and sexual violence, and therefore are not subject to the obligations to enact appropriate legislation and bring alleged perpetrators before their courts.[67] The open-ended category of 'wilfully causing great suffering or serious injury to body or health', while evidently pertinent, is no guarantee of an interpretation that brings such violations within the category of grave breaches. The recognition by the G8 in 2013 that rape and sexual violence constitute grave breaches with ensuing legal obligations is a significant step towards removing this uncertainty[68] but is not applicable to all states.[69] Third, The Hague and Geneva Conventions are intended to regulate the behaviour of combatants in the field rather than form the basis of criminal prosecutions. The language does not entirely map onto criminal law. For instance, key crimes are not defined (e.g., torture, rape, murder, enforced prostitution), requiring the tribunals to craft their

[64] E.g., 'internal strife is now governed to a large extent by the rules and principles which had traditionally only applied to international conflicts'. Cassesse, Antonio 1999. Memorandum to Members of the Preparatory Committee on the Establishment of the International Criminal Court, 'Definition of Crimes and General Principles of Criminal Law as Reflected in the International Tribunal's Jurisprudence', 22 March 1996; Moir, Lindsay 2009. 'Grave Breaches and Internal Armed Conflicts', *Journal of International Criminal Justice* 7(4): 763–787.

[65] E.g., Statute of the Special Court for Sierra Leone, article 4.

[66] E.g., *Geneva Convention IV*, *op. cit.*, article 147: 'wilful killing, torture or inhuman treatment, including biological experiments, wilfully causing great suffering or serious injury to body or health, unlawful deportation or transfer or unlawful confinement of a protected person, compelling a protected person to serve in the forces of a hostile Power, or wilfully depriving a protected person of the rights of fair and regular trial prescribed in the present Convention, taking of hostages and extensive destruction and appropriation of property, not justified by military necessity and carried out unlawfully and wantonly'.

[67] E.g., *Ibid.*, article 146.

[68] G8 UK, *Declaration on Preventing Sexual Violence in Conflict*, 11 April 2013, para. 4.

[69] However, UN SC Resolution 2106, 24 June 2013, recognised the Declaration and the commitments therein.

own definitions, which has sometimes caused inconsistency between them.[70]

6.5 The Challenges of IHL

6.5.1 Classification of Conflicts

IHL presents a number of challenges to lawyers seeking to determine its parameters and to those seeking to apply it in the 'fog of war'. These include clarification of the applicability of the laws of war since contemporary forms of political violence do not easily fit the definitions of international and non-international armed conflict. This distinction has long been considered 'difficult to justify',[71] as well as to apply.[72] 'Classic' international wars between states are infrequent nowadays and rarely declared, although military actions involving NATO states against Serbia (1999) and coalitions against Iraq (1991 and 2003) and Afghanistan (2001), Russia in Georgia (2008) and Ukraine (2014 onwards) and some African conflicts (Ethiopia and Eritrea) have somewhat changed the picture.

NIAC is frequently equated with internal conflict, but in new wars violence crosses often porous borders in diverse ways that make it difficult to determine what counts as internal or external. Leaders of fighting forces move into neighbouring states, to shelter from government operations or to continue their violent acts from a new base. Rebel factions receive assistance and arms from governments and other non-state groups. For example, was the war which took place on the territory of the Democratic Republic of Congo (DRC) and involved some eight African states, as well as numerous non-state armed forces, an international or a non-international war? The ICJ answered this question by determining with respect to Uganda that its

70 For instance, the ICTR and ICTY developed differing definitions of rape, until the ICTR Appeal Chamber resolved the difference; *Prosecutor v. Gacumbitsi*, ICTR-2001-64-A, judgment of 7 July 2006, paras. 147–157. The Elements of Crimes, ICC-ASP/1/3 (part II-B), 9 September 2002, provides definitions of crimes within the jurisdiction of the ICC, allowing for greater certainty

71 Warbrick, Colin and Rowe, Peter 1996. 'The International Criminal Tribunal for Yugoslavia: The Decision of the Appeals Chamber on the Interlocutory Appeal on Jurisdiction in the Tadic Case', *International and Comparative Law Quarterly* 45(3): 691–701, 698.

72 It has been considered fully in recent studies, e.g., ICRC, *Interpretive Guidance on the Notion of Direct Participation in Hostilities under International Humanitarian Law*, adopted by the Assembly of the ICRC, 26 February 2009; Wilmshurst, Elizabeth (ed.) 2012. *International Law and the Classification of Conflicts*. Oxford University Press.

military intervention in the DRC constituted an illegal use of force under UN Charter article 2 (4), and there was thus an IAC in which Ugandan forces committed violations of international humanitarian law for which it bore international responsibility.[73] In the *Lubanga* case the ICC trial chamber considered that although there was no doubt that Uganda had intervened in the DRC and was occupying Ituri (a province in northeast DRC), the conflict in which Lubanga's militia was a party was not 'a difference arising between two states' but protracted violence involving multiple non-state armed groups. It accordingly did not fit within the Geneva Conventions' common article 2 and remained a NIAC.[74] The difficulty of classification is demonstrated by the fact that the pre-trial chamber had determined this situation – occupation by a state of the territory of another state, in which territory a conflict is being fought between various non-state groups[75] – to constitute an IAC. However – and to add to the complexity – the trial chamber acknowledged that there could be an IAC between Uganda and the DRC contemporaneous with a NIAC between non-state groups. Recognition that an IAC and NIAC can occur concurrently within the same territorial space adds to the complexities of determining which legal regime applies to which fighters.

The war in Bosnia-Herzegovina (1992–1995) raises similar problems: was it an international war between Croatia, Serbia and Bosnia or an internal war inside the former Yugoslavia, or inside Bosnia? In the first case before it, the ICTY determined that a situation that appeared *prima facie* to be internal to a state would nevertheless be international if the forces of one side were under the 'overall' control of a foreign state:

> given that the Bosnian Serb armed forces constituted a 'military organization', the control of the Federal Republic of Yugoslavia (FRY) authorities over these armed forces required by international law for considering the armed conflict to be international was *overall control* going beyond the mere financing and equipping of such forces and involving also participation in the planning and supervision of military operations.[76]

[73] *Armed Activities on the Territory of the Congo* (Democratic Republic of the Congo v. Uganda), 2005 ICJ Reports 168, judgment of 19 December 2005 ('*Uganda*'), para. 168.

[74] *Situation in the Democratic Republic of the Congo in the case of Prosecutor v. Thomas Lubanga Dyilo* (*The Lubanga Case*), ICC-01/04-01/06, 14 March 2012, para. 563.

[75] Akande, Dapo. 'ICC Delivers Its First Judgment: The Lubanga Case and Classification of Conflicts in Situations of Occupation', *EJIL Talk*, 16 March 2012, www.ejiltalk.org/icc-delivers-its-first-judgment-the-lubanga-case/.

[76] *Prosecutor v. Dusko Tadic*, IT-94-1-A, 15 July 1999, para. 145 ('*Tadic*'). The ICJ has rejected the 'overall' control test in favour of the narrower requirement of 'complete

However, the appeal chamber also envisaged that if circumstances changed – that is, if the Bosnian Serbs could no longer be considered organs of the FRY – the classification of the conflict would change.[77] In *Blaskic* the ICTY Trial Chamber accepted that an apparently non-international conflict may be 'deemed' international 'where the troops of another State intervene in the conflict or even where some participants in the internal armed conflict act on behalf of this other State'.[78] It determined that the presence of some three to five thousand regular Croatian military forces in Bosnia, albeit in areas outside the conflict zone, characterised the conflict as international because this 'inevitably also had an impact on the conduct of the conflict in that zone'.[79] This ruling made military intervention the determining factor in internationalising the conflict (rather than overall control of irregular forces) but does not clarify the level of intervention required.

A strict dichotomy between IAC and NIAC is too simplistic for the complexities of new wars, involving networks of state and non-state players operating across territories irrespective of formal boundaries. It has to some extent been redressed by the techniques of internationalising internal conflict. However, the jurisprudence lacks 'a principled basis for distinguishing internationalized armed conflicts from those "international in character alongside an internal armed conflict."'[80] Since an international armed conflict must be between 'high contracting parties' to the Geneva Conventions (common article 2) a conflict between a state and non-state actors is excluded, even if fought across state borders. Thus conflict between Israel and Hezbollah or Hamas, or between the United States and Al Qaeda, cannot qualify as an IAC, although the Israeli Supreme Court, various UN organisations, humanitarian and human rights bodies and others have held otherwise.[81] It seems counter-intuitive to describe the 'global' War on Terror as a NIAC (or a series of such conflicts), the only possible label under common article 2 of the Geneva Conventions; rather it may be described as a 'non-international conflict

dependence'; *Application of the Convention on the Prevention and Punishment of the Crime of Genocide* (Bosnia and Herzegovina v. Serbia and Montenegro), 2007 ICJ Reports, 43, judgment of 26 February 2007, paras. 402–407.

[77] *Tadic*, *op. cit.*, para. 87.

[78] *Prosecutor v, Blaskic*, IT-95-14, judgment of 3 March 2000, para. 76.

[79] *Ibid.*, para. 94. [80] Stewart, *op. cit.*, 330.

[81] Report: Part One, The Public Commission to Examine the Maritime Incident of 31 May 2010 (The Turkel Commission), January 2010, para. 41.

fought in a global battlefield'.[82] The Islamic State (IS) asserts state-like structures in areas under its control (territory, a top-down ruling structure, monopoly of violence),[83] but this characterisation is widely rejected and IS is not, of course, a high contracting party to the Geneva Conventions. A further category of transnational conflict – a 'conflict without borders' – might be considered, with determination of the ensuing consequences for applicable law. Another, and opposite suggestion, is to abandon the classification altogether and require states to apply the stricter rules appertaining to IAC in all situations where they 'utilize their armed forces as state agents to apply sovereign force, including counter-insurgencies'.[84] It is contended that such an approach would ensure application of the 'most detailed and robust' protective regime and bring certainty and clarity to the currently confused situation. Of course, states are likely to resist such a proposal as it would deny them the manipulation that they currently enjoy with respect to classification of conflicts. And there are other concerns about this approach since classifying forms of violence as an IAC gives them a legitimate status.

6.5.2 The Threshold Violence for NIAC

A further challenge is elucidation of the threshold of violence needed for the existence of a NIAC under the Geneva Conventions, common article 3 and/or Additional Protocol II. In legal terms this seeks to resolve when IHL becomes complementary to or displaces human rights law. This is not easily applied to factual situations, especially as governments resist recognising a NIAC, thereby incurring (admittedly limited) obligations under IHL and according some status to those fighting against government authority. The situation in Libya in 2011 and in Syria in 2012 highlights this difficulty. In both countries protests erupted against human rights violations committed by repressive and brutal dictatorships. A government has the right – even duty – to maintain public order

[82] Dworkin, *op. cit.*, 55.

[83] Wood, Graeme 2015. 'What ISIS Really Wants', *The Atlantic*, March 2015, www.theatlantic.com/magazine/archive/2015/03/what-isis-really-wants/384980/; Turkmani, Rim 2015. 'ISIL, JAN and the War Economy in Syria', *Security in Transition*, www.securityintransition.org/wp-content/uploads/2015/08/ISIL-JAN-and-the-war-economy-in-Syria2.pdf.

[84] Jensen, Eric Talbot 2013. 'Reunifying the Law of Armed Conflict in COIN Operations through a Sovereign Agency Theory', in Banks, William. *Counterinsurgency Law: New Directions in Asymmetric Warfare*. Oxford University Press, chapter 3, 46.

and internal security but must comply with its obligations under international human rights law.[85] These may involve balancing such rights as those to freedom of expression, association and movement with the government's right (duty) to maintain order. At some point, in both countries each government's violent response to protests and demonstrations moved beyond public disorder and led to armed rebellion. When does such escalation amount to a NIAC and the applicability of international humanitarian law? The language of the UN Security Council (SC) resolutions may be indicative of classification but is not always conclusive, as illustrated by resolutions responding to the unfolding violence in Libya and Syria from 2011 onwards.

SC Resolution 1970 (adopted February 2011) with respect to Libya refers to 'violence', 'attack' and 'repression of demonstrators'. The Council urges the government to respect human rights and international humanitarian law. The latter might suggest the existence of an armed conflict, but a broader understanding of IHL than Hague and Geneva law includes crimes against humanity, which can occur outside conflict.[86] SC Resolution 1973 (adopted less than three weeks later) more explicitly indicates escalation to armed conflict. It reaffirms the primary responsibility of 'parties to armed conflict' to take steps to ensure civilian protection, references SC Resolution 1738, 23 December 2006, on the protection of civilians in armed conflict and demands a 'ceasefire'. Since it also authorises 'all necessary means to protect civilians', the Council might have considered it politic to indicate that a threshold of violence had been met, although the responsibility to protect applies to crimes against humanity as well as to war crimes.[87]

In contrast, in Resolutions 2042, 14 April 2012, and 2043, 21 April 2012, with respect to Syria, the SC refers to 'armed violence', 'government troops and heavy weapons', but condemns only violations of human rights. There is no reference to IHL, and the objective is 'cessation of violence' rather than the term more readily associated with conflict, 'ceasefire'. The SC's failure to take any active steps to protect civilians encouraged the adoption of resolutions by the UN General Assembly

[85] If the conditions are satisfied, the government may derogate from its human rights obligations under a treaty which permits derogation. It cannot derogate from its obligations under customary international law. On derogation under the ICCPR see UN Human Rights Committee, CCPR General Comment 29, States of Emergency (article 4), UN Doc. CCPR/C/21/Rev.1/Add.11, 31 August 2001.

[86] *Rome Statute of the ICC*, 1998, article 7.

[87] See Chapter 5.

(GA) in 2012, which describe the escalation of violence and refer to the use of heavy weapons and indiscriminate shelling by the Syrian authorities but again does not invoke violations of IHL, only gross violations of human rights.[88] Such language evades labelling the conflict as an IAC or NIAC engaging the laws of war. Similarly in September 2013, the SC condemned the killing of civilians by chemical weapons and supported the agreement for their destruction, but did not categorise the conflict.[89] Yet in July 2012, the ICRC had determined there to be a NIAC in Syria, thus making IHL applicable.[90] In its third report, released in August 2012, the Commission of Inquiry mandated by the UN Human Rights Council in August 2011[91] for the first time applied IHL, determining that 'the intensity and duration of the conflict combined with the increased organisational capabilities of anti-Government armed groups' warranted this classification.[92]

The threshold requirement of a level of organisation of armed groups opposing governmental forces may delay the determination of a NIAC, even in the face of sustained violence with heavy weapons by government forces. The level of government force is not *per se* determinative of the existence of a NIAC. Fragmentation between armed opposition groups may be another factor that militates against classification as a NIAC. Asymmetry between attacks by governmental forces and those by separate non-governmental forces has made problematic the requirements of intensity and organisation, seemingly assuming coordination between armed groups. But can there be armed conflict 'if the combined effect of force exerted by a number of armed groups' against a state is of sufficient intensity, even if they do not exhibit organised leadership or any coordination between them?[93] Anthony Dworkin has suggested a broad functional approach to the problem: that a NIAC can be any bout of organised violence that is not a classic inter-state war, since the aim of Geneva Conventions common article 3 is to require that persons taking no active part in hostilities be treated humanely, but this too requires a degree of organisation.[94] One must also ask whether

[88] UN GA Resolution 66/253 A, 16 February 2012; UN GA Resolution 66/253 B, 3 August 2012.
[89] UN SC Resolution 2118, 27 September 2013.
[90] 'Syria in Civil War, Red Cross Says', *BBC News*, 15 July 2012, www.bbc.co.uk/news/world-middle-east-18849362.
[91] UN HRC Resolution S-17/1, 22 August 2011 (Situation of Human Rights in the Syrian Arab Republic).
[92] UN Doc. A/HRC/21/50, 2012, para. 12.
[93] Chatham House, Classification Workshop (13–14 March 2013).
[94] Cf. *Additional Protocol II, op. cit.*, article 13 (Protection of the Civilian Population).

categorisation of a conflict as a NIAC offers more protection and security to civilians than reliance on human rights law, as discussed below.

6.5.3 Interpreting IHL: Distinction, Necessity and Proportionality

The elasticity and imprecision of the concepts of distinction, necessity, proportionality and double effect, as well as differences of opinion as to how these concepts should be understood and weighed against the military advantage sought, present further challenges to the effectiveness of IHL. It has been remarked that 'as law has become an ever-more important yardstick for legitimacy . . . the legal categories used to make those distinctions have become far too spongy to permit clear resolution – or become spongy enough to undergird the experience of self-confident outrage by parties on all sides of a conflict'.[95]

First is the distinction between combatants and civilians, which is central to IHL and indeed to international criminal law, where crimes against humanity must be 'directed against any civilian population'.[96] The distinction has always been beset with interpretive and practical difficulties. While central to what is permissible and impermissible in conflict, it has been incapable of certain application.[97] The 'new wars', fought by networks of state and non-state actors, present particular problems. For the purpose of determining who is entitled to prisoner of war status (captured combatants), Geneva law defines combatants primarily as regular armed forces of the state and militias and voluntary corps forming part of the state's armed forces. Other militias and fighting groups are entitled to Geneva protections provided they 'came under responsible command, distinguished themselves from civilians, carried their weapons openly, and themselves observed the laws and customs of war'.[98] The definition is extended by Additional Protocol I,[99] article 43 to

[95] Kennedy, David 2012. 'Lawfare and Warfare', in Crawford, James and Koskenniemi, Martti (eds.). *The Cambridge Companion to International Law*. Cambridge University Press, chapter 7, 165.

[96] *Rome Statute of the ICC*, article 7(1).

[97] Kinsella shows how the binary of civilian/combatant is 'enabled by, and occurs through, the regulation of sex and sex difference', itself supporting other binaries such as civilised/barbarian, just/unjust, Christian/non-Christian, innocent/guilty. Kinsella, Helen 2005. 'Gendering Grotius: Sex and Sex Difference in the Laws of War', *Political Theory* 34:161–191.

[98] *Geneva Convention III*, *op. cit.*, article 4; see also Dworkin, *op. cit.*, 57, see footnote 23.

[99] The extended definition is not applicable to status as a prisoner of war, which is determined by *Geneva III*, article 4.

include 'all organized armed forces, groups and units which are under a command responsible to that Party, ... even if that Party is represented by a government or an authority not recognized by an adverse Party. Such armed forces shall be subject to an internal disciplinary system'. All such forces are entitled to 'participate directly in hostilities' and thus to combatant immunity. These definitions rest primarily on a soldier's status as a member of an organised fighting force and are applicable regardless of an individual soldier's actual functions or tasks. Armed insurgencies, terrorist activities, sectarian killings, colonial revolts and other similar forms of violence to a large extent fall outside these criteria and thus the remit of IHL, unless those involved are under a responsible command and clearly distinguishable from non-combatants.[100]

Yet very often violence is undertaken by loosely coordinated networks without a single command system, and although militias, para-military groups, mercenaries and even criminal gangs often wear distinctive clothing and dress themselves up in sometimes weird costumes before they engage in violence (ski goggles, women's clothing, Ray-Ban sunglasses or Adidas shoes, to take a few examples!), this does not necessarily count as objective, or self-identification, as a soldier. Where state and non-state actors operate together, it is often the case that a division of labour is arranged whereby the non-state combatants undertake tasks that are clearly forbidden under the Geneva Conventions, precisely to avoid the responsibility of the state. A typical pattern, observed in the Balkan wars[101] but also reproduced in East Timor and in African conflicts, is that regular forces shell a village from a distance, thereby creating panic and then non-state groups are sent in to kill, rape, rob and force people from their homes. It is noteworthy too that in Abu Ghraib (Iraq), some of the most heinous cases of torture were undertaken by private contractors who may have supposed themselves to be less tightly bound by the Conventions (or to have been unaware of them). Despite being addressed in US official reports, Clapham concludes that 'from a human rights perspective [and also that of IHL], the response to the participation in abuse by private contractors has been rather feeble'. He notes that such companies have apparently suffered no disadvantage, nor have any incentive to improve their procedures.[102]

[100] *Ibid.*, article 4(2).

[101] Final Report of the Commission of Experts established pursuant to Security Council Resolution 780 (1992), 27 May 1994, UN Doc. S/1994/674, paras. 110–150.

[102] Clapham, *op. cit.*, 519.

Since the definitions of combatant are included in Geneva Convention III and Additional Protocol I, applicable to IAC, they do not apply in a NIAC.[103] Nevertheless, the concept of a NIAC was intended to provide some protections for 'persons taking no active part in the hostilities', that is, civilians caught up in fighting of this kind. Accordingly, in a NIAC civilians are protected 'unless and for such time as they take a direct part in hostilities'.[104] This is another ambiguous term, creating uncertainties as to how it applies to civilians who have temporarily taken up arms. For example, in February 2012 the ICRC was trying to negotiate safe passage for women and children out of the city of Homs in Syria. But the women were understandably unwilling to leave behind men, who were civilians but who had taken up arms to defend their families in the face of Government attacks. The Free Syrian Army (FSA) included defecting soldiers, but the bulk of the FSA in Homs was composed of volunteers – civilians directly participating in hostilities. Should the men, as civilians, have also been escorted out of Homs? Or should the women have been seen as taking a 'direct part in hostilities'?

How do we deal with situations where women and children play an active supporting role? In the first decision before the ICC, the Court had to determine whether conscripted children had taken an 'active' part in hostilities and thus could be identified as child soldiers, giving rise to conviction for their recruitment under the ICC Statute.[105] Such participation in hostilities could be direct (fighting in battles, killing the enemy) or indirect. In addressing 'indirect' participation, the Court determined the decisive factor to be whether 'the support provided by the child to the combatants exposed him or her to a real danger by becoming a potential target' – a somewhat circular argument. The supporting tasks required of children included providing escorts and bodyguards, cooking and other domestic work. Although the Tribunal offered no definitive definition of the concept of the 'use [of children] to participate actively in the hostilities', leaving it to a case by case determination, these roles were evidently included. However, sexual violence (directed primarily at girl soldiers but committed by male child soldiers as well as adults) was excluded. This

[103] The UK Supreme Court has held that military attacks by a non-state armed group against any or all state or inter-governmental organisation armed forces in the context of a non-international armed conflict can constitute 'terrorism' within the statutory definition; *R. v. Gul*, [2013] UKSC 64, 23 October 2013.

[104] *Additional Protocol II*, *op. cit.*, article 13(3).

[105] *Rome Statute of the ICC*, article 8(b)(xxvi); 8(e)(vii).

position was rejected by Judge Odio-Bentio who considered sexual violence was thus rendered invisible, including the fact that it is often committed by a side's own forces.[106]

The high civilian casualty figures in recent conflicts underscore the difficulty of distinguishing combatants and non-combatants. When fighters live or hide in cities among civilians as in Gaza[107] or indeed use civilians as human shields, as, for instance, in Sri Lanka[108] how is it possible to target them without killing civilians? This is the classic problem of counter-insurgency or what is known as asymmetric warfare. Counter-insurgency 'includes armed conflict and warfare, but its elements require careful calibration and refinement of issues not traditionally at the center of IHL, including modification of the principles of distinction and proportionality'.[109] Counter-insurgency objectives may be claimed as justification for attacks on civilians. For instance, Milošević claimed that attacks by Serbian forces in Kosovo against Kosovar Albanians were counter-insurgency not ethnic cleansing; Serb forces were merely trying to root out members of the Kosovo Liberation Army. In Chechnya, massive population displacement and killing has taken place as a result of Russian attempts to defeat the insurgency. The European Court of Human Rights (ECtHR) accepted 'that the situation that existed in Chechnya at the relevant time called for exceptional measures by the State ... to suppress the illegal armed insurgency. ... [T]hose measures could presumably include the deployment of army units equipped with combat weapons, including military aviation and artillery'.[110]

106 *The Lubanga Case, op. cit.*, separate and dissenting opinion, Judge Odio Benito, para. 16.

107 The Report of the UN Fact-Finding Mission on the Gaza Conflict found the presence of Palestinian armed fighters in urban residential areas during the military operations to be established, although it was unable to form an opinion 'on the exact nature or the intensity of their combat activities in urban residential areas that would have placed the civilian population and civilian objects at risk of attack'. The Mission found no evidence that 'Palestinian combatants mingled with the civilian population with the intention of shielding themselves from attack', although it recognised that they did not dress distinctively; Report of the United Nations Fact-Finding Mission on the Gaza Conflict, UN A/HRC/12/48, 25 September 2009, para. 483 ('UN Fact-Finding Mission on Gaza').

108 E.g., the Report of the Secretary-General's Panel of Experts on Accountability in Sri Lanka, 31 March 2011, www.un.org/News/dh/infocus/Sri_Lanka/POE_Report_Full.pdf, found credible allegations that the LTTE had used civilians as human buffers.

109 Banks, William 2013. *Counterinsurgency Law: New Directions in Asymmetric Warfare.* Oxford University Press, xi.

110 *Isayeva v. Russian Federation*, ECtHR application no. 57950/00, judgment of 24 February 2005, para. 180. The Court, however, applied human rights law; see below.

In response to the insurgency that erupted in Iraq following the invasion and occupation in 2003, American attacks on Fallujah in 2004 resulted in 150,000 displaced persons as well as large numbers (unknown) of civilian casualties. Likewise, the Israelis counted many civilians in Lebanon in 2006 as Hezbollah resistance fighters and, in Operation Cast Lead (2008–2009), as terrorists. Accordingly, Palestinian figures for deaths of combatants and civilians were in the order of more than 900 civilians out of around 1,400 deaths, while the Israelis claimed 1,166 Palestinians killed, out of which 709 were Hamas terror operatives, 295 'uninvolved Palestinians' and the remainder Palestinian 'men that have not yet been attributed to any organization'.[111] There was also disagreement about whether the approximately 254 Palestinian police officers who were killed mostly in the opening hours of Operation Cast Lead could be categorised as civilians.[112] When Israeli soldiers landed on the Turkish vessel *Mavi Marmara* in May 2010 to prevent it from proceeding to Gaza, they were confronted by members of a Turkish activist group, the IHH (Foundation for Human Rights and Freedoms and Humanitarian Relief). These resisted the landing, including with various improvised weapons such as iron rods, chairs and other objects. Other people on the ship were passengers who did not participate in what was described as resistance that was 'planned, and extremely violent'.[113] In order to comply with the principle of distinction every Israeli soldier had to 'to differentiate between those persons who were direct participants in hostilities and those who were not',[114] a demanding legal standard in the confused and dangerous situation on board the vessel. Both IHL and human rights law recognise a 'reasonable belief' standard in this regard.

In 2016, Russian and Syrian bombing of civilians in eastern Aleppo, including the alleged destruction of hospitals and buildings of historic importance, has called into question the principle of distinction. According to a *Guardian* report 'Russia has been directly and repeatedly accused of war crimes at the UN security council in an unusually blunt session, as hopes of any form of ceasefire were flattened by the scale and ferocity of the Syrian regime's assault on eastern Aleppo. The war crimes accusations centred on the widespread use of bunker-busting and

[111] There was also disagreement as to casualty figures collected by the United Nations, Israel, the State of Palestine and non-governmental organisations with respect to the conflict in the summer of 2014; see Independent Inquiry on Gaza, *op. cit.*

[112] UN Fact-Finding Mission on Gaza, *op. cit.*, paras. 352–360; for the opposite view see Margulies, Peter 2013. 'Valor's Vices: Against a State Duty to Risk Armed Forces in Armed Conflict', in Banks, William, *op. cit.*, 87, 93.

[113] The Turkel Commission, *op. cit.*, Report: Part 1, para. 199.

[114] *Ibid.*, para. 216.

incendiary bombs on the 275,000 civilians living in the rebel-held east of the city, weapons that Moscow's accusers say were dropped by Russian aircraft.'[115] Likewise Saudi air strikes in Yemen illustrate these points only too tragically; 'The ongoing attacks from the ground and the air have continued to inflict heavy casualties, caused extensive damage to public and private infrastructure and frequently impeded the rapid passage of humanitarian relief for civilians in need'.[116] Other core principles of IHL pose problems in practice. For instance, the precautionary principle inhibits the advantage of surprise attacks and thus endangers military forces. Accordingly, it is limited by proportionality. It must be determined, on the one hand, whether 'the military advantage of surprise would be undermined by giving a warning' and, on the other, whether the injury to civilians in the latter by not giving a warning is excessive in relation to the military advantage of a surprise attack.[117] But even if warnings are given, they may offer little protection from violence in closely packed urban areas. In Gaza in Operation Cast Lead the Israeli forces dropped leaflets, made telephone calls and used loudspeakers to warn of attacks. However, Gaza offers little space for safety and lack of transport and the closed borders allowed no escape. The warnings may have constituted formal compliance with the requirements of Protocol I, article 57, but the context made them ineffective in preventing civilian casualties. Warnings may also be construed by the population as threats, or intimidation.

Application of the principles of distinction and proportionality is especially problematic with respect to new technology, or to weapons that were deliberately excluded from the prohibitions of the Geneva Conventions and Protocols, as was the case with nuclear weapons. In its advisory opinion the majority of the ICJ acknowledged that the threat or use of such weapons should be compatible with the principles and rules of international humanitarian law.[118] Dissenting judges found this scenario difficult to conceive of: nuclear weapons are by their very nature indiscriminate and almost certainly disproportionate. But:

> [i]t seems difficult, with any due regard to the consistency that must underlie any credible legal system, to contemplate that all these hard-

[115] 'Russia Accused of War Crimes in Syria at UN Security Council Session', *The Guardian*, 26 September 2016.
[116] Report of the United Nations High Commissioner for Human Rights, *Situation of Human Rights in Yemen*, UN Doc. A/HRC/33/38, 4 August 2016, para. 12.
[117] UN Fact-Finding Mission on Gaza, *op. cit.*, para. 529.
[118] *Nuclear Weapons, op. cit.* para. 87, 105.D.

> won principles should bend aside in their course and pass the nuclear weapon by, leaving that unparalleled agency of destruction free to achieve on a magnified scale the very evils which these principles were designed to prevent.[119]

Nevertheless, this was not enough in the eyes of the majority (with the Presidential casting vote) to make their use or threat of use *per se* illegal. New technologies exacerbate the legal conundrums, as is the case with 'killer robots' and unmanned aerial vehicles, as discussed below. It is not only in the context of Weapons of Mass Destruction that application of the principles generates differences of opinion. For instance, the Palmer Report into the Israeli action in 2010 against the flotilla seeking to break the economic blockade of Gaza found that the blockade was not of itself disproportionate, as its impact on the overall humanitarian crisis in Gaza was slight.[120] However, the use of force in boarding and over-powering passengers on the *Mavi Marmara* was unacceptable,[121]that is, disproportionate to the level of force needed to secure the military objective. The finding that the blockade was a proportionate response to Israel's security concerns differed from that of the Turkish inquiry into the incident, illustrating the fact that the concepts of 'necessity' and 'proportionality' are notoriously hard to define and allow for considerable leeway.[122] Assessment of what is 'excessive' injury to civilians against the anticipated military advantage is comparing like with unlike; it entails 'a mental process of pondering dissimilar considerations – to wit, civilian losses and military advantage – and is not an exact science'.[123]

6.5.4 *Critiques of IHL*

The discussion of the scope and interpretation of IHL has suggested various inadequacies in the legal regime that undermine its effectiveness in providing an operating code for those engaged in armed conflict and protective guarantees for those caught up in conflict. This is especially the case with contemporary forms of political violence, 'new wars'. The

119 *Nuclear Weapons, op. cit.*, dissenting opinion Judge Weeramantry, p. 518.

120 Report of the Secretary-General's Panel of Inquiry on 31 May, 2010 Flotilla Incident, September 2011, paras. 72, 77.

121 *Ibid.*, para. 134.

122 Different findings again were made by the Turkel Commission, *op. cit.*

123 Dinstein, Yoram 2005. 'Collateral Damage and the Principle of Proportionality', in Wippman, David and Evangelista, Matthew (eds.). *New Wars, New Laws?* Transnational Publishers, 211–224, 215.

fundamental problem is that IHL is based on the assumption that wars will happen, and its primary objective is to mitigate their worst aspects and in so doing tacitly endorses their legitimacy. IHL does not seek to judge the lawfulness of conflict but to prohibit a range of actions during war. This presents a number of problems.

The Hierarchy of Lives

First, despite the commitment to the principle of humanity, IHL introduces a hierarchy of lives – something that is much more visible in the current era of global awareness.[124]

Suppose we assume a war between Country X and Country Y. On X's side, lives are valued in the following order. First come X's civilians, then come X's soldiers, then come Y's civilians, and finally Y's soldiers. 'Double effect' implies minimising all killing, but deliberate killing of Y's soldiers is permissible if necessary to achieve victory or to save the lives of X's soldiers and civilians. Unintentional killing of Y's civilians is permissible if necessary to achieve military advantage, or to save the lives of X's soldiers and civilians. The last is controversial, and not everyone agrees about whether it is permissible to risk the lives of Y's civilians to save those of X's soldiers; during the Second World War, Pierre Mendès France, who flew on Allied bombing missions, deliberately took the risk of flying low so as to be more accurate and to save civilian lives. Walzer has argued that the attacker has a duty to risk the lives of its own forces to reduce the deaths of civilians on the other side.[125] This protective view is at odds with the practice of some Western military as demonstrated by the high flights over Kosovo and Serbia in 1999 and the level of protection accorded to troops in a variety of conflict contexts compared with civilians. Anyone visiting a war zone, where international troops are deployed, whether Afghanistan, Mali or Iraq, cannot fail to be struck by the way that the troops inhabit protected enclaves and only venture out in armoured vehicles wearing protective clothing.[126]

[124] Butler, Judith 2009. *Frames of War: When Is Life Grievable?* Verso Books, provides a full and critical account of the role of the media in constructing and normalising such hierarchies.

[125] Walzer, Michael 2015. *Just and Unjust Wars: A Moral Argument with Historical Illustrations.* Basic Books, 5th ed., 157 ff.

[126] See Andersson, Ruben and Weigand, Florian 2015. 'Intervention at Risk: The Vicious Cycle of Distance and Danger in Mali and Afghanistan', *Journal of Intervention and Statebuilding* 9(4): 519–541.

Judith Gardam makes a similar point in relation to gender. She argues that the priority given to military necessity constructs a gender hierarchy that discounts the interests of women (primarily civilians) in favour of those of combatants (primarily males). She asserts:

> Far from being a neutral yardstick, military necessity in fact incorporates a hierarchy of values. It assumes [makes natural] that the military victory of the State is pre-eminent. From this flows the seemingly logical value judgment that the life of the combatant is more important than that of the civilian, even more so if that civilian belongs to the enemy 'State'. . . . The military resists strongly the notion that combatants should assume risks to protect the civilian population. But their position is not immune to challenge. It assumes that war is inevitable.[127]

Of course, all of us do have an implicit hierarchy of lives, although this hierarchy is not necessarily defined in territorial terms. Our communities, to whom we feel loyal, may cross borders and be defined in terms of family, ethnicity, religion, class or politics. The influence of diasporas in 'new wars' rests upon such ties (even 'imagined' ties)[128] as do loyalties in conflict based on membership of tribe or clans, rather than to the state. The British suicide bomber of 7 July 2005 in his farewell video talked about his community as the Muslim Umma rather than his local community in Leeds or the community of British citizens. But this kind of hierarchy, whether national, religious or on any other basis, runs counter to the concept of humanity as expressed in the Martens clause and, indeed, legitimates such practices as racial and religious profiling.

Legalising Killing

IHL implicitly legitimises what is not prohibited, namely, the killing of enemy soldiers and in certain circumstances, enemy civilians. It is the means by which they do this that is prohibited. Soldiers who fight according to the rules of war cannot be held criminally liable for acts of war, which are not prohibited, and, are entitled to be treated as prisoners of war, if captured. Further, the principle of humanitarianism is subordinated to military necessity, and proportionality and unnecessary suffering are measured against military advantage, thereby legalising and legitimating violence that complies with this undemanding test.

[127] Gardam, Judith 1997. 'Women and the Law of Armed Conflict: Why the Silence?' *International and Comparative Law Quarterly* 46: 55–80, 72.

[128] Anderson, Benedict 2006. *Imagined Communities: Reflections on the Origin and Spread of Nationalism*, Verso, rev. ed.

There is no question that contemporary Western armies, such as American, British, Israeli and NATO forces, try to apply the principle of distinction and to minimise civilian casualties and lawyers advise on targeting through military action. Indeed, they claim that, because of new technologies allowing for precision targeting, attacks from the air or from the ground are much more accurate and discriminate than ever before. Donald Rumsfeld claimed during the Iraq War: 'We are doing everything humanly possible to avoid collateral damage'.[129] By historical standards, 'collateral damage' in Kosovo, Afghanistan, Iraq or even Lebanon has been relatively low. But what is low by the standards of war is high by the standards of human rights. In Afghanistan and Iraq, the numbers of civilians killed is far higher by a multiple of hundreds than the number killed in the September 11 attacks. And even by the standards of war the principle of proportionality is in tension, but not necessarily conflicting, with US military doctrine that 'favors the overwhelming use of force in order to achieve decisive victory quickly and at minimum cost in terms of US casualties'.[130]

A similar problem arises in the Israeli-Palestinian conflict. Palestinian rocket attacks and those by suicide bombers, deliberately and indiscriminately targeting Israeli civilians, cause terror in Israel and may constitute crimes against humanity.[131] The Palestinian groups – Hamas, Islamic Jihad or the Al Aqsa Brigades – are all included in the State Department's list of international terrorist groups. On the other hand, the Israeli security forces, who as state actors are considered a legitimate fighting force and who are tasked with minimising civilian casualties, have killed far more Palestinians, mostly civilians, and including children. Or to take yet another example, in the 2006 war in Lebanon, the Israelis killed some 1,200 Lebanese civilians; estimates of combatants killed vary from 500 (Israeli Defence Forces estimate) to 74 Hezbollah fighters (Hezbollah

[129] Quoted in Crawford, Neta C. 2003. 'Just War Theory and the US Counterterror War', *Perspectives on Politics*, 5–25.

[130] Roberts, Adam 2003. 'The Laws of War in the War on Terror', in Borch, Fred and Wilson, Paul S. *International Law and the War on Terror, International Law Studies* 79: 175–230, 184.

[131] 'The absence of any possible military advantage resulting from rockets that cannot be directed at a military objective, coupled with statements by Palestinian armed groups, strongly suggest that the primary purpose of the rocket attacks was to spread terror among the civilian population, in violation of international humanitarian law.' Independent Inquiry on Gaza, *op. cit.*, para. 34; see also Fact-Finding Mission on Gaza, *op. cit.*, para. 1724.

estimates) and 46 Lebanese soldiers (Lebanese figures).[132] Some 44 Israeli civilians died and some 119 members of the Israeli Defence Forces.

The problem is the changing perception of war. What appears to Americans or Israelis as relatively low collateral damage in a just war against terrorism can equally be presented as large-scale human rights violations and denial of human security. An illustration of this is the 2012 acquittal by the ICTY Appeals Chamber of Ante Gotovina, Croatian operational commander of Operation Storm in the southern portion of the Krajina. Gotovina was indicted and convicted by the Trial Chamber as a participant in a joint criminal enterprise for murder as crimes against humanity and violations of the laws and customs of war committed during the military action against Serbs in the Krajina region of Croatia in 1995. Part of the indictment related to the allegation that artillery attacks on towns were directed at the civilian population. As dissenting Judge Agius noted: 'it was undisputed that over 900 artillery projectiles fell on Knin in the course of one and half days in the absence of any resistance from the town itself'.[133] The Trial Chamber adopted what was called an 'impact analysis', holding that any strike more than 200 metres from a legitimate military target was evidence of unlawful, indiscriminate targeting, and thus illegal killing of civilians. The Appeals Chamber rejected this methodology as it could not 'exclude the possibility that all of the impact sites considered in the Trial Judgment were the result of shelling aimed at targets that the Trial Chamber considered to be legitimate. The fact that a relatively large number of shells fell more than 200 metres from fixed artillery targets could be consistent with a much broader range of error'.[134] The ruling has been much criticised for allowing leniency in the determination of legitimate – military – targets and thus for the justifiable killing of a greater number of civilians and lessening the scope of command responsibility.

It must be remembered that as treaties, The Hague and Geneva Conventions were negotiated by states who were concerned primarily to protect their own interests rather than motivated by humanitarian

[132] For these estimates see Kaldor, Mary and Schmeder, Genevieve, 'Human Insecurity in Lebanon: Consequences of War and Prospects for Peace' in Martin, Mary and Kaldor, Mary 2009. *The European Union and Human Security: External Interventions and Missions*. Routledge.

[133] *Prosecutor v. Gotovina*, IT-06–90-A, 16 November 2012, (per dissenting opinion of Judge Agius, para. 18).

[134] *Ibid.*, para. 65.

concerns.[135] It has been noted, for example, that the only means and methods of warfare that were unequivocally banned by The Hague Conventions were those with little military utility while other technologies (such as aerial warfare) were allowed to develop legally apace.[136] While it has been argued that the Martens clause redresses such legitimation of violence,[137] 'one searches in vain for a single instance of the use of this clause by a tribunal, statesman, belligerent or jurist to confer tangible protection on real persons'.[138] Civil society may be more receptive to its ideals; for instance, the preamble to the Landmines Convention, the adoption of which may be largely attributed to civil society and 'like-minded' states (see Chapter 7), stresses 'the role of public conscience in furthering the principles of humanity as evidenced by the call for a total ban of anti-personnel mines'.

The problem is also one of law. Killing of civilians is legal under IHL provided there is proportionality between a permissible (military) objective and the means sought to achieve it. Fighting war according to the legal rules normalises violence and creates its own legitimacy as 'Sovereign conduct that complies with the law will appear more legitimate than that which violates it'.[139] Further, law influences public perceptions of rightfulness and accordingly stops people from questioning the social and political power structures that support war.[140] But from the point of view of the victims it makes no difference whether they were legally killed in a war, or as a result of repression, or whether the killing was intentional or unintentional, or according to the rules of an international, or non-international armed conflict. And they are in no position to challenge the entire structure of war-making. The effects of legalisation, through the adoption of further treaties and recognition of rules of customary international law, contribute to the phenomenon of war, in particular those wars engaged in by NATO, the United States or other regular Western forces, being fought in conjunction with sophisticated military lawyers who advise on legal targeting and ensure strict

[135] The invitation from Czar Nicholas II to the 1899 Hague Peace Conference has been described as a 'peace rescript [that] had been conceived in fear, brought forth in deceit and swaddled in humanitarian ideals'. Cited Jochnick, Chris and Normand, Roger 1994. 'The Legitimation of Violence: A Critical History of the Laws of War', *Harvard International Law Journal* 35: 49–90, 70, fn. 87.

[136] *Ibid.*, 68.

[137] E.g. *Nuclear Weapons, op. cit.* (per dissenting opinion of Judge Weeramantry, para. 486 ff).

[138] Jochnick and Normand, *op. cit.*, 74. [139] *Ibid.*, 57. [140] *Ibid.*, 58.

compliance with the letter of the law. This protects them from claims of violations of the laws of war, but with often harsh results for civilians. Such 'lawfare' presents law as a 'vocabulary for the exercise of legitimate power and justifiable death',[141] as in the *Gotovina* case above.

The 'Moral Equivalence' of Combatants

The humanitarian impulse of international humanitarian law means that no judgment is made in the *jus in bello* with respect to the legality or legitimacy of recourse to force, the subject of the *jus ad bellum*. This means that the rules apply to all combatants whether fighting in a legal (or just) conflict, or not. Accordingly, those who are aggressors, or fighting in an 'unjust' conflict, are also entitled to the protections of the laws of war (e.g., in an IAC, prisoner of war status, if captured, and combatant immunity for killings in accordance with the laws of war). In the context of contemporary forms of violence, this equivalence has been questioned.[142] First, it accords some status to, for instance, those fighting in an 'unjust' cause, such as the Taliban, although it does not accord any such status to terrorist tactics.[143] *Jus ad bellum* and *jus in bello* remain distinct legal regimes despite a tendency to their convergence through labels such as terrorism. Second, it has become difficult to establish what constitutes an IAC or NIAC (as opposed to other forms of violence) and thus who counts as an enemy soldier. The global extension of the theatre of war in the War on Terror has removed territorial limits and allowed claims of ongoing conflict against the determination of the sovereign power in whose territory it is taking place.[144] Third, it has been argued that some uses of force are inherently just, such as self-defence against aggression or terrorism, and that those it is waged against (aggressors, terrorists) should not have the benefit of the laws of war, especially where they do not themselves comply with these laws.[145] This argument has

[141] Kennedy, *op. cit.*, 162.

[142] Weiler, J. H. H. and Deshman, Abby 2014. 'Far Be It from Thee to Slay the Righteous with the Wicked: An Historical and Historiographical Sketch of the Bellicose Debate Concerning the Distinction between *Jus ad Bellum* and *Jus in Bello*', *European Journal of International Law* 24: 25–62, provides an analysis of how contemporary events at different times have shaped the debate around the interaction between these two bodies of law.

[143] Terrorist tactics, or 'Acts or threats of violence the primary purpose of which is to spread terror among the civilian population are prohibited'; *Additional Protocol I*, *op. cit.*, article 51(2); *Additional Protocol II*, *op. cit.*, article 13(2).

[144] See further discussion in the context of unmanned aerial warfare, below.

[145] McMahan, Jeff 2009. *Killing in War*. Clarendon Press.

greater traction in light of the atrocities committed by IS; conversely despite the atrocities committed by the Assad regime, his governmental status assumes applicability of IHL to him. Nevertheless, the challenge to the probity of the 'moral equivalence' of combatants, central to IHL, has been contested on empirical, practical and philosophic grounds,[146] but the debate itself demonstrates unease with the existing rules of war.

The Applicability of IHL to Non-State Actors

Fourth, it has always been problematic how non-state actors that are not competent to become parties to treaties are bound by the laws of war.[147] Nevertheless common article 3 is explicit ('each party to the conflict shall be bound'), and Additional Protocol II assumes this to be the case, applying its 'wide range of duties to both sides fighting in the internal armed conflict'.[148] Various institutions have taken the same approach. For instance, the Sierra Leone Special Court Appeals Chamber has accepted that 'it is well settled that *all* parties to an armed conflict, whether states or non-state actors are bound by international humanitarian law, even though only states may become parties to international treaties'.[149] The Appeal Chamber added that all parties are also bound by customary international law. In practical terms, UN Human Rights Council special procedures – fact-finding missions and special rapporteurs – investigate violations of human rights and IHL by all parties.[150] Armed groups sometimes also accept the constraints of all or part of IHL through unilateral declarations, agreement, codes of conduct or even internal regulation, perhaps determining that this heightens their legitimacy and enhances support for their cause.[151] However, there will

[146] E.g., Rodin, David and Shue, Henry (eds.) 2008. *Just and Unjust Warrior: The Moral and Legal Status of Soldiers*. Oxford University Press; Roberts, Adam 2008. 'The Equal Application of the Laws of War: A Principle under Pressure', *International Review of the Red Cross* 90(872): 931–962.

[147] Clapham, *op. cit.* [148] *Ibid.*, 497.

[149] *Prosecutor v. Sam Hinga Norman*, SCSL-2004-14-AR72(E)), 31 May 2004, Decision on preliminary motion based on lack of jurisdiction (child recruitment), para. 22 (footnotes omitted, italics in original).

[150] E.g., Report of the Independent International Commission of Inquiry on the Syrian Arab Republic, A/HRC/30/48, 13 August 2015 details allegations of violations by all parties; the UN Fact-Finding Mission on Gaza considered 'any actions by all parties' including Palestinian Armed Groups; UN Fact-Finding Mission on Gaza *op. cit.*, paras. 151–152.

[151] Sivakumaran, Sandesh 2011. 'Lessons for the Law of Armed Conflict from Commitments of Armed Groups: Identification of Legitimate Targets and Prisoners of War', *International Review of the Red Cross* 93(882): 463–482.

remain some uncertainty as to the applicability of the laws of war to non-state fighting groups in some instances. As has been discussed, Protocol II has a high threshold, and common article 3 assumes a degree of organisation and control of territory on the part of non-state actors, which may not always be the case, for instance, with respect to unorganised networks and loosely associated groups. Further, it is unlikely that many armed groups fighting in 'new wars' have learned about, or are even aware of, the laws of war. Common article 1 of the Geneva Conventions requires states to 'ensure respect' for the Conventions, and regular armed forces in many states will have access to training sessions and to military manuals; it is doubtful whether this is the case with the networks of non-state actors in new wars. And even if they know of the laws of war, they may well feel they lack legitimacy as instruments concluded by states to which they have had no input, and indeed they are fighting against state authority.

The Legality of 'New Wars'

Finally and more fundamentally, the very basis of IHL is in conflict with the aims and objective of 'new wars'.[152] It has been argued more generally that the traditional rules of IHL cannot be made applicable or effective in new wars.[153] IHL seeks to minimise the harm caused to civilians through conflict; new wars are characterised by deliberate targeting of civilians, often through ethnic cleansing of territory, terrorist actions and insurgency. Such objectives deny any legitimate 'military target', which should shift the balance towards civilian protection, but this is, of course, undermined by the ethos of new wars.

Paradoxically, the Bush Administration used many of the same arguments about the inadequacies of IHL. On the one hand, the Administration claimed that the War on Terror was a war – in contrast to critics who have argued for a law enforcement approach towards terrorists – and that therefore the killing of terrorists and their detention for indefinite periods is legal. According to the former Attorney General Gonzales:

> [T]he brutal attacks of September 11th were not only crimes but acts of war. Since at least that day, the United States has been at war with Al Qaeda. While Al Qaeda may not be a traditional armed force of a single

[152] See Chapter 1.

[153] Lamp, Nicolas 2011. 'Conceptions of War and Paradigms of Compliance: The "New War" Challenge to International Humanitarian Law', *Journal of Conflict and Security Law* 16(2):225–262, 241.

> nation-state, Al Qaeda is clearly a foreign enemy force. It has central direction, training and financing and has members in dozens of countries around the world who are committed to taking up arms against us. It has political goals in mind. Al Qaeda has attacked not only one of our largest cities killing thousands of civilians, but has also attacked our embassies, our warships, and our government buildings. While different in some respects from traditional conflicts with nation states, our conflict with Al Qaeda is clearly a war.[154]

At the same time, members of the Bush Administration assert that this 'new war paradigm' does not fit the understandings of war enshrined in IHL and that this has justified their declaring prisoners to fall within the category of 'unlawful combatants'[155] and the establishment of military commissions to try them. Or to put it another way, the war on terror does not fit into the Geneva Conventions. Thus according to Lieutenant Colonel Lietzau:

> The Geneva Conventions speak to the circumstances of 'international armed conflict' and 'internal armed conflict' or 'conflict not of an international character'. But this new era of terrorist activity ill fits either category. It is likely that attacks will be perpetrated by an organisation like Al Qaeda – an entity that crosses international borders – excepting the conflict from designation as an 'internal armed conflict'. Yet neither is the war on terrorism a war between nations; there are no clashes of armies, navies and air forces. Rather this a war prosecuted against nebulous networks of secret cells – not found on maps – with no capitals to destroy. The 'international' category is accordingly inapt. Moreover despite their acute effect, the sporadic incidence of terrorist attacks calls into question the 'ongoing nature' of any such armed attack.[156]

Accordingly captured Al Qaeda members are not to be afforded the protections of prisoner of war status – those who kill are not to be considered legitimate soldiers with combatant immunity. The United States also failed to submit the determination of status to a tribunal as provided for by Geneva Convention IV, article 5 and Additional Protocol I, article 45. However, all persons in the power of a party to a conflict

[154] 'Introduction', in Wippman and Evangelista, *op. cit.*, 14.

[155] This has long been a contested term. Roberts notes that US military manuals use the terms 'unprivileged belligerents', 'detainees', 'unlawful combatants' and 'illegal combatants' apparently interchangeably to denote those who are regarded as not belonging to the armed forces of a party to the conflict and thus as not having the right to engage in hostilities; Roberts, *op. cit.*, 214.

[156] Lietzau, William 2005. 'Combating Terrorism: The Consequences of Moving from Law Enforcement to War', in Wippman and Evangelista, *op. cit.*, 31–51, 42.

have the right to be treated 'humanely',[157] as is apparently accepted by the United States.[158]

But even if the Geneva Conventions are problematic in a context of 'new wars', it would be a mistake to conclude that their specific humanitarian protections can be neglected. IHL has been of critical importance in protecting certain categories of people, not only prisoners of war and civilians, but also medical personnel, diplomats, journalists, religious leaders and others, as well as restraining certain methods of warfare. State practice and policy confirms the importance of observance of the laws of war even in counter-terrorist or insurgency actions. For instance, in the context of counter-insurgency in Malaya in the late 1940s and early 1950s, Sir Robert Thompson argued that it is imperative that the government comply with the law. He acknowledged the strong temptation not to do so (legal processes are cumbersome, legal safeguards are inappropriate in such conflicts and terrorists 'deserve to be treated as an outlaw anyway'), but this is both morally wrong and will eventually create more problems for a government than it resolves.[159] The importance of law is also stressed in the 2010 US Counter-Insurgency Manual, which General David Petraeus was instrumental in producing.[160]

Two further issues require particular consideration. First is whether there should be a new law-making process for the revision of IHL, either in its entirety or at least in the form of a Protocol addressing its inadequacies. The disadvantages of such a process are evident; it would be lengthy, controversial and either risk lessening rather than enhancing legal protections for those *hors de combat* or result in a treaty unacceptable to the United States and other major powers. The refusal of three of the permanent members of the SC – the United States, Russia and China – to become parties to the ICC Statute is a salutary reminder of the pitfalls of treaty-making. In any case it is debateable whether core issues are inherently capable of being reduced to legal form. The fact that there has been no successful outcome to negotiations for a comprehensive ban on nuclear weapons or on a definition of terrorism serves as a warning. But without such a process there is a danger that the practices of powerful states – not just the United States and its NATO allies, but others such as Russia, China and India – will become entrenched as

157 *Additional Protocol I*, *op. cit.*, articles 45, 75; *Additional Protocol II*, *op. cit.*, article 4.

158 Roberts, *op. cit.*, 218. 159 *Ibid.*, 188.

160 US Counter-Insurgency Manual, 2010, http://usacac.army.mil/cac2/Repository/Materials/COIN-FM3-24.pdf. See especially 'Appendix D: Legal Considerations'.

customary international law.[161] Second is to give further attention to an approach that seeks other legal regimes, complementary to IHL, that build on humanitarian principles but that are more consistent with the prohibition on war. This is what we consider below.

6.6 Human Rights Law and IHL as Complementary Regimes

6.6.1 Human Rights Law

Since 1945, the protection of civilians has also become the subject of other bodies of international law: human rights law, international criminal law and more specific regimes such as those appertaining to refugees,[162] internally displaced persons (IDPs)[163] and in recognition that 'the preservation of the cultural heritage is of great importance for all peoples of the world', for the protection of cultural property.[164] This section considers human rights law and its relationship with IHL.

International human rights law is much younger than IHL although its legal antecedents[165] include the humanitarian protections accorded to the specific groups of people accorded protection under IHL, and notionally at least the Martens clause. Other earlier humanitarian initiatives include the abolition of slavery; the accordance of rights to workers through the establishment of the International Labour Organisation (ILO); the guarantee of religious and other rights to identified minorities in the political reshaping of Europe following the Concert of Europe and more especially in the Minority Treaties after World War I; as well as those apparently protected by the inter-war mandate system; and children.[166] But these advances should not be understood in terms of

161 This should not be over-stated; international law is created by all states; Byers, Michael 2005. *War Law*. Atlantic Books, 11.

162 *Convention Relating to the Status of Refugees*, Geneva, 1951; *Protocol Relating to the Status of Refugees*, Geneva, 1967; see especially Hathaway, James and Foster, Michelle 2014. *The Law of Refugee Status*. Cambridge University Press, 2nd ed.

163 Guiding Principles on Internal Displacement, UN Doc. E/CN.4/1998/53/Add. 2, 11 February 1998.

164 *Convention for the Protection of Cultural Property in the Event of Armed Conflict with Regulations for the Execution of the Convention*, 1954. In September 2016, the ICC delivered sentence in the first case before it concerning the destruction of cultural property in Mali; *The Prosecutor v. Ahmad Al Faqi Al Mahdi*, ICC-01/12-01/15.

165 Henkin, Louis 1989. 'International Law: Politics, Values and Functions', *Hague Recueil*, 216, 208; Tomuschat, Christian 2014. *Human Rights between Idealism and Realism*. Oxford University Press, 3rd ed.

166 Geneva Declaration of the Rights of the Child, 26 September 1924.

contemporary human rights; they were often based on other motives, were developed piecemeal and were not necessarily based on an assumption of human equality (although this did apply to the campaign to abolish slavery, it has also been observed that it also 'served the British nationalist aspiration of asserting superiority over the United States, its upstart former colony').[167]

Some scholars suggest that World War II was the moment when the notion of human consciousness captured the public imagination.[168] During the war ideas of human rights were raised, for instance, in the campaign by novelist H. G. Wells for the Rights of Man and in the 'Four Freedoms' speech by President Franklin Roosevelt.[169] Both the Holocaust and the dropping of atomic bombs on Hiroshima and Nagasaki have been interpreted as global events, as humanitarian catastrophes not assolely Jewish and Romany or Japanese catastrophes. Thus the real foundations of international human rights law are to be found in the post–World War II developments, and, in particular, in the commitment made in the Preamble to the UN Charter to 'reaffirm faith in fundamental human rights'.[170] Since then, there has been a dramatic growth in international human rights law and procedures for the implementation of this law within global and regional institutions. Alongside the imposition of individual criminal responsibility for the commission of crimes against humanity (as well as for crimes against peace and war crimes) that was made at Nuremburg[171] and Tokyo,[172] there was a need to assert that individuals also have legal rights, such as those to equality, to be free from arbitrary killings and other harms and to be free from want. Collectively individuals have the right to existence. These rights were articulated by the GA in its Resolution on the Affirmation of the Principles of International Law recognised by the Charter of the Nuremburg Tribunal[173] and adoption on 9 December 1948 of the Genocide

[167] MacFarlane, Neil and Khong, Yuen Foong 2006. *Human Security and the UN: A Critical History*. Indiana University Press, 47.

[168] Robertson, Roland 1992. *Globalization, Social Theory and Global Culture*. Sage.

[169] Bergers, Jan Herman 1992. 'The Road to San Francisco: The Revival of the Human Rights Idea in the Twentieth Century', *Human Rights Quarterly* 14: 447–477.

[170] Promoting respect for human rights and fundamental freedoms is a principle of the United Nations under UN Charter, article 1(3), and further provided for under articles 55 and 56.

[171] *Charter of the International Military Tribunal*, 8 August 1945, article 6.

[172] *Charter of the International Military Tribunal for the Far East*, 19 January 1946, article 5.

[173] UN GA Resolution 95(1), 11 December 1946.

Convention[174] and, a day later, of the Universal Declaration of Human Rights (UDHR).[175] At the time, this appeared to only involve minimal normative change; the UDHR was a non-binding resolution, and attempts at drafting a binding treaty rapidly became mired in Cold War political obstacles. It was not until 1966 that the two treaties – the International Covenant on Civil and Political Rights (ICCPR) and the International Covenant on Economic Social and Cultural Rights (ICESCR) – were agreed. Although the Genocide Convention came into force in 1951, no permanent penal tribunal as envisaged by article VI was established.

Until 1976 when both the ICCPR and ICESCR came into force human rights were primarily a European exercise through the adoption of the European Convention for the Protection of Human Rights and Fundamental Freedoms (ECHR) in 1950 and creation of the European Court of Human Rights (ECtHR) in 1959 subsequent to the Convention coming into force in 1953. But from the late 1970s onwards[176] this framework of law gave rise to the emergence of campaigning human rights groups, especially in Latin America[177] and Eastern Europe, who, in turn, pushed for its strengthening and application.[178] The UDHR has been reinforced and expanded through its incorporation into national constitutions and the many human rights instruments subsequently concluded under the auspices of international and regional institutions. Most remarkable has been the growing acceptance of the right of individuals to commence legal proceedings against their own states for violations of their rights and the prospect (at least at the regional level) of a binding determination of state responsibility for those breaches of international law.[179]

Following the collapse of the Soviet Union and the fall of the Berlin Wall and in the triumphalism of the 'New World Order', human rights

[174] *Convention on the Prevention and Punishment of the Crime of Genocide*, 9 December 1948, United Nations Treaty Series, vol. 78, 277.

[175] UN GA Resolution 217 A (III), 10 December 1948.

[176] Moyn, Samuel 2010. *The Last Utopia Human Rights in History*. Harvard University Press.

[177] *The Inter-American Convention on Human Rights,* 114 UNTS 123, was signed on 22 November 1969.

[178] Further impetus came from the newly independent states, from the South, especially with respect to challenging racist and colonial policies in southern Africa and which led to the 1503 procedure of the Commission on Human Rights; Steiner, Henry and Alston, Philip and Goodman, Ryan 2007. *International Human Rights in Context: Law Politics Morals*. Oxford University Press, 3rd ed., 754.

[179] See Chapter 3.

came to the forefront in international politics in the 1990s as the meta-theory of the day, or *Last Utopia*.[180] Democracy, human rights and the rule of law became the mantra for peace processes, for transition to democracy and for foreign policy. They were not just about individual well-being but about international stability. The Vienna World Conference on Human Rights in 1993 asserted its belief that efforts towards 'universal respect for, and observance of, human rights . . . contribute to the stability and well-being necessary for peaceful and friendly relations among nations, and to improved conditions for peace and security as well as social and economic development'.[181] Human rights were declared to be 'universal, indivisible and interdependent and interrelated'.[182] However, even as the Conference convened, events in Bosnia, Somalia and Rwanda were unfolding that would challenge this optimism about the contribution of human rights. Looking back from the second decade of the twenty-first century, the terrorist attacks of 11 September 2001, global neo-liberal economics, religious and other extremisms, as well as human rights scepticism in places like the United States and the United Kingdom have all tempered the impact of human rights as a force for promoting security.[183]

6.6.2 Human Rights Law and IHL Compared

Human rights law thus now co-exists alongside IHL. There are differences between the two regimes. Human rights law is universal, regulating state behaviour with respect to all individuals (including refugees, asylum seekers, migrants) within a state's own territory and subject to its jurisdiction (which may involve extraterritorial application, as discussed below), 'without distinction on the basis race, colour, sex, language, religion, political or other opinion, national or social origin, property, birth or other status'.[184] It reallocates power between the state and the individual. Violation of human rights gives rise to state responsibility for which reparation should be made. Traditionally non-state actors do not have obligations under human rights law, although the state may be

[180] Moyn, *op. cit.*
[181] Vienna Declaration and Programme of Action, A/CONF.157/23, 12 July 1993, I, para. 5.
[182] *Ibid.*, para. 6.
[183] Charlesworth, Hilary, Chinkin, Christine and Wright, Shelley 2005. 'Feminist Approaches to International Law: Reflections from Another Century', in Buss, Doris and Manji, Ambreena (eds.). *International Law: Modern Feminist Approaches*. Hart Publishing, 17–47.
[184] Universal Declaration of Human Rights, 10 December 1948, article 2.

liable for failure to exercise due diligence to prevent, investigate, prosecute and punish human rights violations committed by non-state actors.[185] Further, as is the case with IHL, non-state bodies may accept human rights obligations. For instance, as a UN body the international territorial administration in Kosovo, UNMIK, was not legally bound by human rights treaties. Nevertheless, by regulation UNMIK allows individuals to make complaints against it for violation of the UDHR and six human rights treaties.[186] Further, the SC, UN Human Rights Council special procedures and other bodies have assumed the applicability of human rights to non-state bodies, including fighting forces.[187] Human rights law is applicable at all times, unless there has been a formal derogation within the terms of the relevant treaty (where such derogation is permissible). Derogation is allowed under the ICCPR, article 4, 'in time of public emergency that threatens the life of the nation', and the ECHR, article 15, 'in time of war or other public emergency threatening the life of the nation'. Certain specified absolute rights cannot be derogated. Core human rights are absolute and not limited by concepts such as military necessity, while other rights may be subject to restrictions necessary to protect other imperatives such as public safety, order, health and safety[188] or national security.[189] Proportionality under human rights law is more restrictive, limited with respect to non-absolute rights to pursuit of a legitimate goal and 'the permissible level of force based on the threat posed by the suspect to others'.[190] For instance, a law enforcement officer must use the minimum force against a person resisting arrest necessary to make the arrest.

In contrast to human rights law, the starting point of the laws of war is that in international armed conflict actions that would otherwise be illegal are acceptable, for example, the killing of combatants and destruction of enemy property. Combatants have a 'right to participate directly

[185] *Velasquez-Rodrigues v. Honduras*, 29 July, 1988, IACHR (Ser. C) No. 4.

[186] UNMIK Regulation No. 2006/12 of 23 March 2006 (on the establishment of the Human Rights Advisory Panel in Kosovo).

[187] Andrew Clapham cites an International Law Institute resolution (1999): 'All parties to armed conflict in which non-State entities are parties, irrespective of their legal status . . . have the obligation to respect international humanitarian law as well as fundamental rights'. Clapham, *op. cit.*, 505.

[188] E.g., ICCPR, article 18 (3) (freedom of religion), 19 (freedom of expression), 21 (public assembly), 22 (freedom of association).

[189] E.g., ICCPR, article 19 (3) (b) (freedom of expression).

[190] Alston, Philip, Report of the Special Rapporteur on Extrajudicial, Summary or Arbitrary Executions, Study of Targeted Killings, A/HRC/14/24/Add.6, 28 May 2010, para. 32.

in hostilities',[191] and one of IHL's guiding principles is the paramount importance of military necessity. Distinction is at the heart of IHL in that certain people have a defined legal status, such as prisoner of war or protected person under article 4 of the Fourth Geneva Convention, which gives rise to particular rights and obligations. The applicability of IHL only in an international or non-international armed conflict necessarily entails that it is not aimed at enhancing long-term security or human well-being as is the case with human rights law. Its objective is limited to mitigating the horrors of violent conflict in different ways for people depending upon their legal status (e.g., for all persons including combatants not to be subject to unnecessary suffering, for civilians not to be the subject of targeted or indiscriminate attack). Compliance with IHL – and an absence of large-scale atrocities – during conflict may facilitate post-conflict reconciliation and sustainable peace.[192]

IHL obligations are owed between states, and one of the strongest factors inducing compliance is the principle of reciprocity, although failure by one party to comply with its obligations does not entitle the other party to suspend its own.[193] Human rights law has impacted upon IHL: the cruelty of internal conflicts and the influence of universal human rights standards are among the reasons given by former President of the ICTY, Antonio Cassese, for the growing convergence between the law applicable in international and non-international armed conflict.[194] Similarities between IHL and human rights law, for example, the acceptance of peremptory norms from which no derogation may be made such as the prohibition of torture and arbitrary deprivation of life, are made especially visible through the lens of international criminal law. Despite this commonality it cannot, however, be presumed that such peremptory norms are understood the same way in both legal regimes. The ICTY rejected the definition of torture set out in article 1 of the Torture Convention, considering it inappropriate in armed conflict to require the involvement of a public

[191] *Additional Protocol I*, *op. cit.*, article 43 (2). There is no equivalent provision in *Additional Protocol II* and states may prosecute participants for treason, or for engaging in conflict.

[192] The importance of international criminal law as a post-conflict mechanism for accountability is discussed further in Chapter 10.

[193] See also the *Vienna Convention on the Law of Treaties*, 23 May 1969, article 60(5).

[194] Other reasons are the increase in the number of civil conflicts and the increasing interdependence of states; Cassesse, *op. cit.*

official in an act of torture. The ICC Statute adopted the same approach with respect to torture as a crime against humanity.[195]

6.6.3 *Applicability of Human Rights Law in Armed Conflict*

The traditional position was that IHL applies in cases of international or non-international armed conflict, while human rights law applies in peace. This position is now more flexible, in particular the extent to which human rights law applies in an IAC, and when IHL comes into play alongside human rights in a NIAC, and the relationship between the two in counter-insurgency operations, including during a military occupation. In 1968 the GA adopted a resolution on Respect for Human Rights in Armed Conflicts,[196] which nevertheless made no explicit mention of the applicability of the human rights treaties during conflict (the ICCPR and ICESCR were not yet then in force). Since that time a number of bodies have sought to clarify the applicability of human rights law in armed conflict alongside IHL. Although the contentious jurisdiction of the ICJ is limited to determining disputes between states, this Court has made a number of important statements on the issue. In its advisory opinion on the *Legality of the Threat or Use of Nuclear Weapons*, the International Court observed:

> that the protection of the International Covenant on Civil and Political Rights does not cease in times of war, except by operation of Article 4 of the Covenant whereby certain provisions may be derogated from in a time of national emergency. Respect for the right to life is not, however, such a provision. In principle, the right not arbitrarily to be deprived of one's life applies also in hostilities. The test of what is an arbitrary deprivation of life, however, then falls to be determined by the applicable *lex specialis*, namely, the law applicable in armed conflict which is designed to regulate the conduct of hostilities.[197]

Accordingly, human rights law does not cease to apply during armed conflict; rather the two regimes are mutually reinforcing and complementary. But determining whether there has been a violation of the human rights guarantee of the right to life requires recourse to the

195 *Rome Statute of the ICC*, article 7(2)(e): '"Torture" means the intentional infliction of severe pain or suffering, whether physical or mental, upon a person in the custody or under the control of the accused'.

196 UN GA Resolution 2444, (XXIII), 19 December 1968.

197 *Nuclear Weapons*, para. 25.

principles of IHL, for example, the principle of distinction. The Court repeated this dictum in its Advisory Opinion on the *Legal Consequences of the Construction of a Wall in the Occupied Palestinian Territory* and added that in some situations the two may apply simultaneously:[198] thus some issues may be exclusively matters of IHL, others exclusively of human rights law and still others may be matters of both branches of international law. While it may be assumed that the more specific and detailed law is the *lex specialis*, [199] the Court did not elucidate any process for determination which of these three possibilities is the appropriate one for any given situation. An expert group convened by the office for the High Commissioner of Human Rights has suggested that the more stable a situation is (perhaps as in the Palestinian Occupied Territories) the more human rights law would be applicable, while instability and little effective control would make IHL more 'applicable to supplement human rights law'. The group acknowledged that such an approach would not be easy and would raise 'complex legal questions'.[200] Legal uncertainty reduces the effectiveness of legal protection and engenders instability and insecurity.

This position has been echoed by UN human rights bodies. The UN Human Rights Committee has confirmed the applicability of the ICCPR in armed conflict to which the rules of international humanitarian law were applicable.[201] The UN Human Rights Council too has acknowledged human rights law and international humanitarian law to be complementary and mutually reinforcing and that measures should be taken to guarantee and monitor the implementation of human rights in respect of civilian populations in situations of armed conflict.[202] The

198 The *Wall* case, *op. cit.*, para. 105.

199 Criddle has argued for a 'relational theory' of *lex specialis*: 'whenever a state uses force against ... people over whom it has asserted control, HRL's stricter proportionality standard constitutes the applicable *lex specialis*. Conversely, when states use force against those beyond their domain of asserted control, IHL proportionality applies'. Criddle, Evan J. 2013. 'Proportionality in Counter-insurgency: Reconciling Human Rights and Humanitarian Law', in Banks, *op. cit.*, 37.

200 Outcome of the Expert Consultation on the Issue of Protecting the Human Rights of Civilians in Armed Conflict, A/HRC/11/31, 4 June 2009, para. 14 (Expert Consultation on Civilians).

201 Human Rights Committee, General Comment No. 31, The Nature of the General Legal Obligation Imposed on States Parties to the Covenant, 29 March 2004, UN Doc. CCPR/C/21/Rev.1/Add.13, para.11: 'As implied in General Comment 29, the Covenant applies also in situations of armed conflict to which the rules of international humanitarian law are applicable'.

202 Expert Consultation on Civilians, *op. cit.*, para. 5.

European and Inter-American human rights courts have both applied the relevant human rights conventions in situations of internal violence and insecurity, for instance, in Northern Ireland, Chechnya, Turkey, Cyprus, Peru, Guatemala and elsewhere in the Americas. The European Court has asserted the applicability of the ECHR to situations of extreme violence and highlighted the need for civilian protection under the right to life. Thus the Court has subjected Russian military operations in Chechnya to a high level of scrutiny, for instance, in Katyr-Yurt on 4–7 February 2000 where there was heavy aerial bombing. Civilians were killed trying to flee. The Court concluded that even accepting that the operation had a legitimate aim (to suppress illegal armed insurgency) and that military action with heavy weaponry was justified, it did not accept that 'it was planned and executed with the requisite care for the lives of the civilian population'.[203] The Court made no reference to IHL (which is not within its jurisdiction) but described the situation as one of conflict and drew upon concepts familiar to IHL: indiscriminate killing, protection of civilians, necessity and precaution. In its analysis, however, the primary aim was to 'protect lives from unlawful violence' and thus it concluded that the 'massive use of indiscriminate weapons . . . cannot be considered compatible with the standard of care prerequisite to an operation of this kind involving the use of lethal force by State agents'. This human rights approach was not subjugated to military necessity.

Cases, such as those regarding Chechnya, uphold states' human rights obligations to its own citizens, in the case of a NIAC. More complex is whether they are also owed to the citizens of other states situated outside the territory of the member state as in the contexts of international armed conflict – invasion or military occupation. This is determined by the jurisdictional provision in the relevant treaty. The obligation upon states party to the ECHR is spelled out in article 1: to secure the Convention rights to all persons 'within their jurisdiction'. The interpretation of 'within their jurisdiction' is therefore crucial to determining the Convention's territorial scope.

In some early cases arising out of the Turkish military action in Cyprus in 1974, the European Commission on Human Rights concluded that acts of Turkish soldiers in killing civilians, raping, carrying out acts of torture of civilians who were arbitrarily held in detention, causing displacement of civilians from their homes and families and confiscating

[203] *Isayeva v. Russian Federation, op. cit.*, para. 200.This was the first of many judgments the Court has issued with respect to the conflict in Chechnya.

homes, farms and livestock all constituted violations of the Convention.[204] The applicable principle was that authorised state agents (for example, military forces) 'not only remain under [the state's] jurisdiction when abroad but bring any other person . . . "within the jurisdiction" of that state, to the extent they exercise authority over such persons'. Killing, raping and harming civilians in northern Cyprus constituted an exercise of authority by the Turkish military for which violations Turkey was responsible. In subsequent cases brought after the assertion of the Turkish Republic of Northern Cyprus in 1983, Turkey claimed that the local administration and not its soldiers were responsible for continued human rights violations. The Court, however, considered that the continued presence of large numbers of Turkish troops meant that Turkey could be deemed still to be in effective control of the area and as such remained responsible for securing ECHR rights there.[205]

This strong position was undermined in *Banković v. Belgium* where the Court denied the European Convention's applicability to military actions committed in Serbia. In that case, six Yugoslav nationals living in Belgrade brought proceedings against the European member states of NATO with respect to NATO's campaign of air strikes against what was then the Federal Republic of Yugoslavia (now two states – Serbia and Montenegro) during the Kosovo conflict, alleging violation of a number of rights, including the right to life. The European Court determined that there was no jurisdictional link between the victims of the acts complained of and the NATO states – the latter did not exercise administrative control over the territory, and the military actions (aerial bombing) did not bring the victims within the Convention's ambit. The Court held that the Convention was an instrument of European public order that was not designed to be applied throughout the world, even with respect to the conduct of State parties. This position has been undermined in subsequent cases where the Court has held the Convention to be applicable in Iraq, a state evidently outside the public order of Europe, for the protection of Iraqi civilians.[206] The ECtHR has received applications arising out of the military actions by Russia in Crimea and

[204] *Cyprus v. Turkey*, 4 EHRR 482, 10 July 1976. 10 July 1976, 4 EHRR 482.
[205] *Cyprus v. Turkey*, 35 EHRR 731, 10 May 2001, and *Loizidou v. Turkey* (Preliminary Objections), 20 EHRR 99, 23 March 1995.
[206] E.g., *Al-Skeini v. UK*, ECtHR GC application no. 55721/07, 7 July 2011; *Hassan v. UK*, ECtHR GC application no. 29750/09, 16 September 2014. As these cases have arisen in the context of occupation rather than active conflict they are discussed in Chapter 8.

eastern Ukraine, both from the Ukrainian government[207] and from more than a hundred individuals. If found admissible, these cases will require the Court to determine further a state's extraterritorial obligations under the ECHR with respect to those affected by its military actions. Such litigation can be viewed from diverse perspectives, either as a form of resistance to unbridled governmental power, holding governments to the obligations they have undertaken, or as an adverse form of 'lawfare', restricting a state's options and weakening its fighting capabilities. It has been suggested it goes further and is 'about more than just delegitimising a state's right to defend itself; it is about the abuse of the law and our judicial systems to undermine the very principles they stand for: the rule of law, the sanctity of innocent human life, and the right to free speech'.[208] Unsurprisingly, the incorporation of human rights into decisions about war in this broad sense is controversial and is rejected by some judges[209] and military commentators.[210] Further, even within an alliance states have not all accepted the same legal obligations (for instance, the United States is not a party to the ECHR) and thus may favour different tactics.

What does it mean to apply human rights in conflict? Surely conflict of itself constitutes a violation of human rights. Does not the attempt to apply human rights in conflict contradict the illegality (in human rights terms) and illegitimacy of conflict itself. Indeed, it can be argued that given there is a fundamental contradiction between human rights and war, that making human rights law applicable in warfare gives a comforting – but false – reassurance that conflict has been humanised and thus rendered more acceptable,[211] thereby opening up human rights law to similar critiques as those that are made of IHL.

207 *Ukraine v. Russia*, ECtHR application no. 20958/14, lodged on 13 March 2014; *Ukraine v. Russia II*, ECtHR application no. 43800/14, lodged on 13 June 2014. 'See also *Georgia v. Russia* (No. II) ECtHR, application no. 38263/08, arising out of the August 2008 conflict in South Ossetia.

208 Goldstein, Brooke 2010. '*Lawfare*: Real Threat or Illusion?' Speech on 5 November 2010, Princeton Club, New York City.

209 *Smith v. MOD*, [2013] UKSC 41, para. 131, per Lord Mance, dissenting; see Chapter 8 for discussion of this case.

210 Hansen, Michelle 2007. 'Preventing the Emasculation of Warfare: Halting the Expansion of Human Rights Law into Armed Conflict', *Military Law Review* 194: 1–65.

211 Verdirame, Guglielmo 2008. 'Human Rights in Wartime: A Framework for Analysis', *European Human Rights Law Review* 6: 689–705.

6.6.4 *Dilemmas of Multiple Regimes*

The bodies of international law that protect individuals in the midst of violence include IHL, human rights, international criminal law and refugee law. Other legal regimes may also be relevant depending on the circumstance, for instance, the law of the sea[212] or one of the many treaties against diverse terrorist acts. While these are all distinct from the *jus ad bellum* (discussed in Part II), claims that seek to extend the permissibility of violence tend to confuse the distinction. Multiple legal regimes allow for 'blurred boundaries between regimes and their appropriate triggers and selective application for purposes of political impact, not analytical clarity or administrative order and accountability'.[213] The current debates about the use of targeted killings (as defined in Chapter 4) illustrate these dilemmas of multiple applicable legal regimes and the different questions that must be asked according to the preferred legal regime, IHL, human rights or international criminal law.[214] Different answers with respect to the legality of targeted killings are given depending upon which regime is applied. Targeted killings of alleged terrorists on the territory of another state also cause deaths of other civilians, 'residential houses, vehicles, worshippers in mosques, mourners in funeral processions and even rescue workers . . . residential houses are burnt into ashes along with vehicles and cattle heads'.[215] Sites of such killings are often in the poorest rural areas, far from any conventional scene of war. The understanding of targeted killings and the questions around their legality under the *jus ad bellum* have been discussed in Chapter 4. Turning to the *jus in bello*, if we accept the United States' State Department's assertion of the use of force in self-defence, IHL is applicable, as conceded by the Department when Harold Koh argued that the targeted strikes are in accordance the principle of distinction and IHL proportionality.[216] In his 2013 statement about the shift in US counter-terrorism policy, President Obama implicitly agreed to the importance of the principle of distinction, avowing that 'before any strike is taken, there must be a near certainty that no civilians will be killed or injured – the

[212] E.g., Zoli, Corri 2013. 'The Gaza Freedom Flotilla: Politicizing Maritime Law in Asymmetric Contexts', in Banks, *op. cit.*, 178.

[213] *Ibid.*, 182. [214] For a detailed analysis of these questions see Alston, *op. cit.*

[215] Peshawar High Court, judgment of 11 April 2013.

[216] 'The Obama Administration and International Law', speech by Harold Hongju Koh, Legal Advisor, US Dept. of State, 25 March 2010.

highest standard we can set'. He also expressed a preference for a law enforcement model.[217]

President Obama also admitted 'the hard fact' that American drone strikes have killed civilians, 'a risk that exists in every war'. The legality of such killings therefore still remains to be considered and a number of questions to be clarified. First, is the conflict international or non-international? The United States is not in conflict with Pakistan or Yemen (except through some notion of a 'shadow war' whereby attacks ostensibly carried out by the forces of the target state are in fact carried out clandestinely by US military forces, with the consent of the former),[218] and since Al Qaeda is not a high contracting party to the Geneva Conventions it seems that conflict with it should not be designated an international armed conflict. It must therefore be a NIAC, a somewhat strange way of categorising the 'global war on terror'. As discussed above, however, there has been some acceptance of conflicts involving non-state actors (Hamas, Hezbollah) as international armed conflict, thereby incurring the heavier obligations upon participants and, theoretically at least, greater protections for non-combatants. If it is indeed an international armed conflict, is the targeted person a combatant and therefore a legal target? If not, assuming a NIAC, the question must again be asked whether the targeted individual is directly participating in hostilities. If this is not the case, the person cannot be legally targeted. Deaths of other civilians must be proportionate to the military advantage to be achieved by the targeted killing, and all feasible measures must have been taken to prevent those deaths. It has been argued that drone attacks in Pakistan are 'signature strikes'[219] and as such disproportionate.[220]

It must also be asked whether the so-called war against Al Qaeda is of a sufficient intensity and protracted nature to constitute a

[217] Crook, John R. 2013. 'President Obama Outlines Shifts in U.S. Counterterrorism Policy', *American Journal of International Law* 107(3): 674–674, 676.

[218] Chesney, Robert 2013. 'The Use of Force Regime and Unconventional Threats: Anwar Al-Awlaki as a Case Study', in Banks, *op. cit.*, chapter 9, 170.

[219] 'The term "signature strike" is used to distinguish strikes conducted against individuals who "match a pre-identified 'signature' of behavior that the U.S. links to militant activity," rather than targeting a specific person'. Greenfield, Danya. 'The Case against Drone Strikes on People Who Only 'Act' like Terrorists', *The Atlantic,* 19 August 2013, www.theatlantic.com/international/archive/2013/08/the-case-against-drone-strikes-on-people-who-only-act-like-terrorists/278744/.

[220] Peshawar High Court, judgment of 11 April 2013.

non-international armed conflict. If not, it can only be a situation of occasional, admittedly extreme, violence, to which human rights law applies. Further, as discussed above, human rights law continues to apply in armed conflict. If the terrorist act is treated as a crime (potentially a crime against humanity), a law enforcement model compatible with human rights must comply with human rights standards, for instance, ICCPR, articles 6 (the right to life) and 14 (the right to a fair trial). Force under human rights law must be strictly and directly necessary to defend a person from unlawful violence, to save life.[221] Lethal force pursuant to a lawful arrest can be applied only if the person resists arrest and 'it proves strictly necessary to use firearms'.[222] The Turkel Commission set out what it regarded as the basic principles with respect to the use of force in compliance with the human rights requirements of necessity and proportionality:

> (i) application of non-violent means before resorting to the use of force and firearms; (ii) use of force and firearms only if other means are ineffective or without promise of achieving the intended result; (iii) use of warnings before using firearms unless it places personnel at risk or is inappropriate or pointless in the circumstances; (iv) intentional lethal use of firearms only when strictly unavoidable to protect life; (v) providing law enforcement personnel with self-defense equipment; and (vi) use of less-lethal incapacitating weapons to restrain the use of deadly force.[223]

Excessive force may amount to an arbitrary deprivation of life.

In any case under human rights law there must be an effective and impartial independent investigation into the killing: 'a legal prohibition of arbitrary killing by the agents of the State would be ineffective, in practice, if there existed no procedure for reviewing the lawfulness of the use of lethal force by State authorities'.[224] This is a higher standard than

[221] United Nations Basic Principles on the Use of Force and Firearms by Law Enforcement Officials, 7 September 1990, by the Eighth United Nations Congress on the Prevention of Crime and the Treatment of Offenders.

[222] Statement by Ben Emmerson, UN Special Rapporteur on Counter-Terrorism and Human Rights concerning the launch of an inquiry into the civilian impact, and human rights implications of the use of drones and other forms of targeted killing for the purpose of counter-terrorism and counter-insurgency ('Emerson Statement'), UNOHCHR, News Release, January 2013, www.ohchr.org/Documents/Issues/Terrorism/SRCTBenEmmersonQC.24January12.pdf.

[223] The Turkel Commission, Report: Part 1, para. 189.

[224] *MCann and Others v. United Kingdom*, ECtHR GC application no. 18984/91, judgment of 27 September 1995, para. 161.

is required under IHL, where, after all, killing of combatants in the enemy side is accepted as the purpose of conflict.[225]

On the one hand, terrorism is increasingly becoming the focus of domestic policing and intelligence. On the other hand, those same methods applied abroad are used for targeted killing rather than arrest and trial. Targeting killing in general and the drone campaign in particular raise questions about the blurring of war and policing, about the meaning of 'consent' and the adequacy of existing legal regimes to address contemporary problems of violence.[226] In the words of the former UN Special Rapporteur on Counter-terrorism and Human Rights:

> The exponential rise in the use of drone technology in a variety of military and non-military contexts represents a real challenge to the framework of established international law and it is both right as a matter of principle, and inevitable as a matter of political reality, that the international community should now be focussing attention on the standards applicable to this technological development, particularly its deployment in counterterrorism and counter-insurgency initiatives, and attempt to reach a consensus on the legality of its use, and the standards and safeguards which should apply to it.[227]

The mistaken killing of American citizens including two hostages has raised questions about the degree of scrutiny and investigation prior to drone attacks. President Obama's justification that this is a consequence of the 'fog of war' only serves to highlight the blurring of war and policing.[228]

Differences between the legal regimes add to the complexities: the 'individualistic approach to targeting (through assassination) highlights the tensions between the human rights concentration on the individual and the traditional group-based focus of conflict and the combatant'.[229]

[225] However, the language in UN SC Resolution 2286, 3 May 2016: Protection of Civilians is closer to that of human rights with respect to investigation under IHL: '*Strongly urges* States to conduct, in an independent manner, full, prompt, impartial and effective investigation within their jurisdiction of violations of international humanitarian law.'

[226] Bigo, Didier 2000. 'When Two Became One: Internal and External Securitisations in Europe'. In Kelstrop, M. and Williams, M. (eds.). *International Relations Theory and the Politics of European Integration, Power, Security and Community*. Routledge, 171–204.

[227] Emerson statement, *op. cit.*

[228] Fredericks, Bob and Feuerherd, Ben, 'American, Italian al Qaeda Hostages Killed in Drone Strikes', *New York Post*, 23 April 2015, http://nypost.com/2015/04/23/obama-says-he-takes-full-responsibility-for-al-qaida-hostage-deaths.

[229] Watkin, Kenneth 2005. 'Humans in the Cross-Hairs: Targeting, Assassination and Extra-legal Killing in Contemporary Armed Conflict', in Wippman and Evangelista (eds.), *op. cit.*, 137–179, 147.

In terms of security it may be argued that targeted killings are a 'clean' use of force, without risk to the protagonists and minimising that to surrounding civilian areas in accordance with the IHL cardinal principle of distinction. But intelligence is subjective, may lack clarity, be wrong, lack verification or be misunderstood, targets may be missed, and such attacks promote insecurity and fear in surrounding populations. The secrecy with which such attacks are undertaken heightens anxiety and offers no proof as to the involvement of targets in terrorist activities, even assuming that such participation justifies the killings. The disconnect between those planning the attacks who remain within the security of their environment and those subject to them removes physical and psychological constraints on the use of violence: it may be equated more with a game on a PlayStation than the killing of a real person. Precisely because they make it easier to kill without a risk to the targeting state's forces, 'policy makers and commanders will be tempted to interpret the legal limitations on who can be killed and under what circumstances, too expansively'.[230] They 'substantially lower the threshold for waging war in general' and in particular for waging war in urban areas[231] – traditionally a time of danger for attacking forces. The secrecy maintained by governments around the legal rationale for their use of targeted killings and the scope of and occasion for the deployment of predator drones undermine transparency, certainty and accountability.

In its lengthy and detailed Second Report, the Turkel Commission, appointed by Israel following the *Mavi Marmara* incident, examined the 'procedures for examining and investigating complaints and claims of violations of international humanitarian law' with the objective of improving investigative mechanisms within Israel, and elsewhere.[232] It based its analysis on existing IHL and human rights laws and a comparison between such mechanisms in Israel and within other countries. Looking forward, it recommended that the human rights obligation to carry out an effective, impartial and independent investigation into deaths in suspicious circumstances be made applicable to alleged violations of international humanitarian law. There are already steps in this direction. The ECtHR has held that the investigative obligation under ECtHR, article 2 applies 'in difficult security conditions including in a

[230] Alston, *op. cit.*, para. 80.

[231] Wippman, David and Evangelista, Matthew 2005. 'Introduction: Do New Wars Call for New Laws?' in Wippman and Evangelista (eds.). *op. cit.*, chapter 1, 6.

[232] The Turkel Commission, Report: Part II, 31.

context of armed conflict ... even in difficult security conditions, all reasonable steps must be taken to ensure that an effective, independent investigation is conducted into alleged breaches of the right to life'.[233] The Human Rights Advisory Panel in Kosovo has extended this to the acts of UNMIK, a UN territorial administration.[234] *Ad hoc* UN fact-finding missions have been mandated to investigate violations of international humanitarian law, including those committed by non-state actors. The Turkel Commission recommended that the obligation to commence such an investigation arises '*inter alia*, to exceptional or unexpected events and incidents such as civilian casualties that were not anticipated when the attack was planned that do not, *prima facie*, give rise to a reasonable suspicion of a war crime'.[235] Information about such events may be partial and circumstantial and could emanate from any plausible source, including NGOs. The special rapporteur on counter-terrorism has gone somewhat further in proposing that the principle of transparency be applied to fact-finding missions in 'any case where there are grounds to believe that civilians may have been killed or injured'. We agree with his view that such an obligation should become 'an inherent part of the State's legal obligations of accountability under international humanitarian law and international human rights law'.[236]

While we welcome President Obama's commitment to oversight of what he terms 'lethal action', the past expansion of the territorial scope of the conflict has added to global insecurity, and there is no certainty that his promised concentration on 'specific networks of violent extremists that threaten America' will in fact lessen that insecurity.[237] Terrorist attacks in, *inter alia,* Boston, Madrid, London, Mumbai, Nairobi, Somalia, Kenya, Mali, Beirut, Turkey, northern Nigeria, Iraq, Syria, Sousse, Paris and Brussels indicate the continuance of such violence. Anger at drone attacks may well add to global recruitment of terrorists. It now seems impossible to consider issues of intervention (both under the *jus*

233 *Al-Skeini v. UK*, *op. cit.*, para. 164.

234 *S.C. v. UNMIK*, Case No. 02/09, 6 December 2012, para. 102. See Chapter 10.

235 'Some form of an examination is required when ... the information is only partial or circumstantial, and there is a need to ascertain the circumstances of the event (in this Report this type of examination will be referred to as a 'fact–finding assessment')'; The Turkel Commission, *op. cit.*, Report: Part II, para. X.

236 Report of the Special Rapporteur on the Promotion and Protection of Human Rights and Fundamental Freedoms while Countering Terrorism, UN Doc. A/68/389, 18 September 2013, para. 45.

237 Crook., *op. cit.*

ad bellum and *jus in bello*) without reference to the War on Terror (even if no longer labelled as such), which has undermined any assumption about the primacy of human rights in national or international policy-making with respect to rogue or outlaw territories. It has also flattened the identities of those living within such territories – whether innocent or not. Those labelled as terrorists, or as suspected terrorists, or as living in areas from where terrorist attacks emanate, have lost their claims to other identities such as prisoners of war, protected civilians within occupied territories, children, legal or illegal immigrants, asylum seekers, nationals of a particular state or of the home state, even as individuals entitled to basic civil and political, economic and social rights. These are all labels around which legal regimes have been carefully constructed for the security of individuals and which had been assumed to have permanent, progressive effect, but which have now been revealed as contingent and readily displaced. Our task is to recapture these regimes and the responsibility to ensure their effectiveness.

6.7. Conclusion

In this chapter, we have argued that the cardinal principles of IHL do not fit contemporary forms of war. The threshold requirement and the principles of distinction, necessity and proportionality are very difficult to apply in 'new wars'. Moreover, in an era of global consciousness, the hierarchy of lives introduced by IHL and the legitimisation of violence implied by IHL, are increasingly unacceptable. It can, of course, be argued that 'new wars', which involve non-state actors and deliberately target civilians, are illegitimate not only in human rights terms but also in relation to IHL. Yet the current trends for legalisation, especially in relation to the War on Terror, in some ways exacerbate the difficulties by allowing for legality without consideration of the insecurity thereby invoked.

Nevertheless, and despite the shortcomings of IHL, the body of IHL that has been constructed out of centuries of experience contains many specific safeguards for different categories of persons living in insecure places. Our argument is that although IHL is becoming anachronistic, it should not be dispensed with. But it needs to complemented by other regimes, in particular international criminal law and human rights law. This is not, of course, the whole argument since although international criminal law offers potentially a way to significantly enhance security, it is a somewhat heavy, reactive doctrine, and its capacity for enforcement is very weak. Likewise, human rights law has as its objective the enhancement of human dignity and thus also human security but, despite the evolving human rights jurisprudence, legal uncertainties about its extraterritorial applicability remain. Further, it also lacks capacity for enforcement and implementation, and as discussed in Chapter 3, positive decisions from human rights courts do not necessarily equate with compliance.

War is illegal from a human rights perspective since attacks on enemies, even when they comply with IHL, can be construed as violations of human rights. Many contemporary conflicts are low-level, protracted and sporadic. Periods and places of 'war' and 'peace' are often difficult to distinguish. The continued designation of an armed conflict, whether an IAC or a NIAC, seems to apply in practice not so much based on a threshold of violence but on whether the violence is framed in political terms. In Kosovo the armed conflict was deemed to be over from the end of the NATO bombing in 1999, and the violence subsequently committed against the Kosovo Serb population is subject to domestic, not international, criminal law. Or to take another example, thousands of people have died in the Mexican drug wars, but because they are not framed in political terms they are regarded as victims of criminality and human rights violations rather than war. The same is true of the murders and disappearances of the hundreds of women in the Mexican *maquilas*.[238] From the perspective of those experiencing insecurity, these legal distinctions have little relevance. It is of little import to the victim of a violent governmental response or a brutal attack by a non-state actor, whether it is deemed to be a violation of human rights or of one of the regimes of international humanitarian law.

IHL in contrast to human rights law starts from the presumption of a state of war. But what sort of war? Law traditionally addresses the problems of the past, and the kind of war to which IHL primarily refers is a classic international war between states. Contemporary forms of violence do not conform to this conception. Two alternative ways of resolving the dilemmas of multiple legal regimes have been proposed. One, proposed by Anthony Dworkin, is to categorise these new forms of violence as Non-International Armed Conflict. Contemporary forms of violence are simultaneously local and global rather than either internal or

[238] Report on Mexico produced by the Committee on the Elimination of Discrimination against Women under article 8 of the Optional Protocol to the Convention, and reply from the Government of Mexico, CEDAW/C/2005/OP8/Mexico, 27 January 2005.

international. Such a categorisation would mean that those caught up in the violence but not directly participating have the protection of IHL, but such a conflict, in contrast to an IAC, may not be considered legitimate. This is more or less the same argument as the Bush Administration used. However, unlike the Bush Administration, neither American forces nor terrorists would be considered lawful belligerents, and such an approach would assume that human rights law applies as well as the domestic law of the territory where violence is taking place or the domestic law of those engaged in violence. The other approach is to categorise these new types of violence as either crimes or repression subject to human rights and domestic law norms.

In the previous chapter, we argued that the self-defence exception to the prohibition on war should be reconceptualised as the collective individual right to life. If that is the case, there is a clear linkage between the existence of that right and how it is exercised. In defending themselves or in calling on third parties to assist, those who use force must conform with human rights as well as IHL, and this prescribes much tighter rules about how such force can be used.

This chapter focussed on the protections afforded to people. The next chapter will discuss law relating to weapons, the means used in applying force.

7

Weapons

7.1 Introduction

The possession of weapons has traditionally been seen as a hallmark of state sovereignty, a corollary of the state monopoly over the legitimate use of force. The International Court of Justice (ICJ) has summed up this aspect of state sovereignty: 'in international law there are no rules, other than such rules as may be accepted by the State concerned, by treaty or otherwise, whereby the level of armaments of a sovereign State can be limited, and this principle is valid for all States without exception'.[1] Similarly, and more recently, the UN General Assembly (GA) has affirmed 'the right of all States to manufacture, import, export, transfer and retain conventional arms for self-defence and security needs, and in order to participate in peace support operations'.[2]

In the aftermath of the Cold War, the world has been flooded with easily transportable, conventional lethal weapons such as AK 47s, Kalashnikovs, Qassam missiles, surface-to-air missiles. Their easy obtainability by non-state groups – those rebelling against governmental authority, militia, terrorists, criminal gangs, war lords and individuals – has been a contributing factor to the violence of new wars. It has made difficult disarmament in the wake of a ceasefire, with former fighters reluctant to dispose of their weapons and their continued accessibility furthering lasting criminal violence, including gender-based violence. Fears of the availability of weapons of mass destruction (WMDs) have been heightened post 9/11.

The long history of constructing rules relating to the institution of war also includes efforts to regulate, reduce and/or eliminate weapons used in

[1] *Military and Paramilitary Activities in and against Nicaragua* (Nicaragua v. United States of America), (Merits) 1986 ICJ Reports 14, judgment of 27 June 1986, para. 269 ('*Nicaragua*').

[2] UN GA Resolution. 61/89, 6 December 2006.

war – efforts that gathered pace in the late nineteenth century and have subsequently continued. Perhaps more than in any other field of international law, various treaties and regulatory frameworks introduced in recent years can be said to constitute a response to the 'new wars'. Commentators have noted a shift from the preoccupation with weapons possessed by states towards controlling the acquisition of weapons by the actors in 'new wars', both in the name of the War on Terror and in the name of Liberal Peace or Human Security. Critical scholars argue that these initiatives have not only neglected disarmament in general but actually condone what is in effect the vast bulk of weapons and weapons trade in the hands of powerful states and weapons dealers. In particular, they suggest, treaties designed to eliminate weapons that cause unnecessary and indiscriminate suffering like land mines or cluster munitions end up legitimising weapons perceived as precise or discriminate such as Unmanned Aerial Vehicles (UAVs or drones), while efforts to regulate the arms trade focus on the shadow or illicit trade to non-state actors while permitting large-scale sales of conventional weapons to regimes which abuse human rights such as Saudi Arabia, Syria or China.[3]

It is true that all forms of prohibition can have the effect of legitimising what is not prohibited, and that it is impossible to talk about 'good' and 'bad' weapons. Nevertheless, we argue in this chapter that the humanitarian achievements in the post–Cold War period in the field of weapons law are indeed significant but that they need to be complemented by disarmament. In particular the Human Security model is necessarily associated with disarmament.

In developing this argument, we start with a brief background to international efforts to regulate weapons and show how they can be broadly grouped into the three approaches – arms control, which is associated with the Geo-Political and War on Terror models; humanitarian, which is associated with Responsibility to Protect and Liberal Peace; and disarmament, which, we argue, is critical for the Human Security model. The next section focuses on post – Cold War arms control with subsections on bilateral arms control, and non-proliferation and counter-proliferation. This is followed by a section on humanitarian approaches with subsections on international humanitarian law, land mines and cluster munitions, the Arms Trade Treaty, arms embargoes and on the possibilities for legal regulation of autonomous or semi-autonomous

[3] Cooper, Neil and Mutimer, David 2011. 'Arms Control for the 21st Century: Controlling the Means of Violence', *Contemporary Security Policy* 32(1): 3–19.

weapons. The final section is about disarmament. In the conclusion we discuss the way that law in this area is changing and what this implies for the interplay of our models of security. One short chapter cannot possibly do justice to the range and content of international regulation in this field; rather we have selected certain examples to illustrate these points.

7.2 The International Legal Regulation of Weapons

There have been many historical examples of the prohibition or regulation of certain types of weapons. Poison gas was prohibited in war by ancient Hindus according to the Law of Manu, by the Saracens based on their reading of the Koran,[4] and mentioned by Hugo Grotius, along with assassination and espionage, as unacceptable in war.[5] The Second Lateran Council of the Catholic Church, attended by more than a thousand clerics, prohibited the use of crossbows against Christians in 1139, and this injunction was to be repeated at the Fourth Lateran Council in 1215. And in seventeenth- and eighteenth-century Japan, firearms were virtually eliminated.[6]

Attempts to regulate various weapons through international agreement became increasingly salient in the late nineteenth century and continued throughout the twentieth century along with the development of the Laws of War[7] so that there is now a sizeable number of relevant international and regional treaties. It is possible to discern three distinct, but blurring, lines of approach. The first is what can be described as the 'arms control' approach. The term 'arms control' was developed by strategic theorists in the 1950s such as Thomas Schelling and Morton Halperin drawing on notions of rationality as a way of managing the arms race. Classic arms control dating from that time 'focussed primarily (if not exclusively) on nuclear deterrence between the superpowers [and] assumed that rational actors had a mutual interest in the avoidance of nuclear destruction and . . . aimed to achieve strategic and crisis stability

[4] Robinson, Julian Perry 2007. 'Mass Destruction, Chemical Weapons and Human Security', unpublished paper in possession of authors.

[5] Grotius, Hugo 1625. *The Law of War and Peace*, Book 3, Chapter 4, XV.

[6] Cooper, Neil 2013. 'The Post – Cold War Arms Paradox: Humanitarian Arms Control, NGOs and the Strategic Complexes of the Liberal Peace', in Smith, Jackie and Verdeja, Ernesto (eds.) *Globalization, Social Movements and Peace-keeping*. Syracuse University Press, 21–46.

[7] See Chapter 6.

partly through the design of force structures but also through negotiations underpinned by a commitment to mutual vulnerability and the principles of parity'.[8] Tortuous reasoning about Mutual Assured Destruction (MAD) was designed to preserve the idea of a nuclear confrontation while minimising the possibility of it actually happening. It assumed that states behaved in ways that were considered rational and involved esoteric calculations about numbers of warheads and missiles on each side of the Cold War divide and what constituted 'parity'. The approach was deeply embedded in the strategic cultures of the nuclear powers and involved an epistemic community of arms control experts.

Today the term 'arms control' is loosely used to cover all forms of weapons regulation. But for our purposes it is useful to retain a more limited definition that refers to the way in which the regulation of weapons helps, as Keith Krause puts it, 'to preserve, if not reinforce, the geopolitical hierarchy of global politics, and the relative military advantages of particular states'.[9] Arms control, described as 'a stable set of self-restraining measures applied by states to the military equipment used by their own state forces',[10] assumes continued possession of weapons and therefore legitimises them. A recent trend has seen the more powerful states seek to apply the concept to the military objectives and programmes of others,[11] thereby delegitimising actions of the latter while retaining control over their own. This is another sense through which sovereignty itself becomes contingent.[12] Thus arms control includes not only bilateral negotiations among the superpowers on nuclear weapons but also the various non-proliferation and counter-proliferation initiatives designed to prevent weapons from getting into the hands of those (both states and non-state actors) who are perceived as maverick or rogue and who might challenge the dominance or threaten the security of the leading powers.

The second approach can be called the humanitarian approach. This relates to efforts through the *jus in bello* to mitigate the consequences of war, first for combatants (e.g., the prohibition of poisonous gases) and

[8] Cooper and Mutimer, *op. cit.*, 8.

[9] Krause, Keith 2011. 'Leashing the Dogs of War: Arms Control from Sovereignty to Governmentality', *Contemporary Security Policy* 32(1): 2–39, 22.

[10] Anthony, Ian 2009. 'Weapons of Mass Destruction: Reduction of Stockpiles and Non-Proliferation', in Giegerich, Thomas (ed.) *A Wiser Century? Judicial Dispute Settlement, Disarmament and the Laws of War 100 Years after the Second Hague Peace Conference.* Duncker and Humblot, 89–105, 90.

[11] *Ibid.* [12] See Chapter 2.

more recently for both combatants and non-combatants through the prohibition, or abstention from use, of weapons that cause 'superfluous injury or unnecessary suffering'[13] or 'unacceptable harm' to civilians.[14] Such conventions challenge the *jus in bello* understanding that some suffering is 'necessary' or 'acceptable' for the achievement of a legitimate military objective – indeed, one of the early justifications for biological weapons was that death through the spread of disease was less awful than being wounded. The emphasis on the humanitarian impact of weapons and the associated lack of security for civilian populations has been a favoured strategy of civil society, especially since the end of the Cold War.

The third approach is to seek to reduce the likelihood of war through a focus on disarmament, rather than only on regulation of use of certain categories of weapons. Disarmament requires positive action; it is a broad enough concept to encompass the reduction of existing weapon stocks and prohibition of the development, production and stockpiling of further weapons. Disarmament campaigns conducted by peace movements from the nineteenth century onwards were based on the idea that arms races fuel wars and that reversing the momentum of arms build-ups could help to avoid wars. The more than a thousand women who formed the Women's International Congress in The Hague in April 1915 advocated 'universal disarmament' through international agreement and urged state control over the manufacture and traffic of arms. The Congress considered 'private profits accruing from the great armament factories [to be] a powerful hindrance to the abolition of war'.[15]

During the Cold War, disarmament was contrasted with arms control through emphasis on the elimination of entire categories of weapons as was achieved in the Biological Weapons Convention (1972) and the Chemical Weapons Convention (1989). Another disarmament approach is the call for weapons-free zones. The idea of nuclear-free zones was an important part of peace campaigns during the Cold War; many local authorities and some states such as New Zealand and the Baltic countries have declared themselves as nuclear-free zones. Of broader geographic scope are nuclear-free regions: the Treaty of Tlateloco (1967) applies to

[13] *Convention on Prohibitions or Restrictions on the Use of Certain Conventional Weapons Which May Be Deemed to Be Excessively Injurious or to Have Indiscriminate Effects*, Geneva, 10 October 1980, preamble.

[14] *Convention on Cluster Munitions*, Dublin, 30 May 2008, preamble.

[15] Women's International League for Peace and Freedom, RESOLUTIONS, 1st Congress, The Hague, the Netherlands, 1915, http://wilpf.org/wp-content/uploads/2012/08/WILPF_triennial_congress_1915.pdf

Latin American and Caribbean countries; the Treaty of Rarotonga (1985) to the South Pacific; the Bangkok Treaty (1995) to Southeast Asia; the Treaty of Pelindaba (1996) to Africa; the Treaty of Semipalatinsk (2006) to Central Asia. In addition the Antarctic Treaty (1959),[16] Outer Space Treaty (1967)[17] and Moon Treaty (1979)[18] all contain prohibitions on nuclear activities.

In the literature on weapons regulation, a distinction is often drawn between weapons of mass destruction and conventional weapons. The former term was first used by the Archbishop of York in response to the German bombing of Guernica on 26 April, 1937[19] when between 250 and 1,500 people were killed and many more injured. Nowadays, the expression 'weapons of mass destruction' is not defined in terms of massive destruction, even though some of these weapons can cause unimaginable destruction. Rather it refers to unconventional weapons – nuclear, radiological, chemical and biological. In fact, many so-called conventional weapons can cause mass destruction. Aeroplanes flying into inhabited buildings are a weapon of mass destruction. So too are the four million cluster munitions dropped by the Israelis in the last few days of the war with Lebanon in 2006. By and large both arms control and disarmament efforts have focussed on WMDs, although not exclusively.

The following sections address each of the three approaches in turn.

7.3 Arms Control

Arms control efforts primarily apply to nuclear weapons. The accumulation of nuclear weapons in the aftermath of the Second World War and during the Cold War has amassed sufficient capacity to destroy all

[16] *The Antarctic Treaty*, Washington, 1 December 1959, article V (1); 'Any nuclear explosions in Antarctica and the disposal there of radioactive waste material shall be prohibited'.

[17] *Treaty on Principles Governing the Activities of States in the Exploration and Use of Outer Space, Including the Moon and Other Celestial Bodies*, January 1967, article IV: 'States Parties to the Treaty undertake not to place in orbit around the Earth any objects carrying nuclear weapons or any other kinds of weapons of mass destruction, install such weapons on celestial bodies, or station such weapons in outer space in any other manner'.

[18] *Agreement Governing the Activities of States on the Moon and Other Celestial Bodies*, December 1979, article 3(3): 'States Parties shall not place in orbit around or other trajectory to or around the Moon objects carrying nuclear weapons or any other kinds of weapons of mass destruction or place or use such weapons on or in the Moon'.

[19] Cited Bentley, Michelle 2014. *Weapons of Mass Destruction and U.S. Foreign Policy*. Routledge, 30.

human beings. It is difficult to understand what possible military utility such weapons can possess. But perhaps by the same token their metaphorical significance cannot be underestimated; they represent a symbol of the absolutism of state sovereignty as well as, by analogy, extreme constructions of masculinity.[20] For example, India has stated its nuclear tests to be 'to prove that we are not eunuchs'.[21] The United Kingdom is described as 'punching above [its] weight'; having nuclear weapons is about joining an 'exclusive club', enhancing national pride, asserting independence and power.[22]

In what follows, we cover two forms of arms control – bilateral deals among the superpowers and multilateral efforts to prevent the spread of nuclear weapons through non-proliferation, the ban on testing and, more recently, what has come to be called counter-proliferation. There are, of course, other examples of arms control that are not discussed, for example, the Conventional Forces in Europe Treaty signed in 1990, but designed long before the end of the Cold War to maintain a military balance in Europe between the two Cold War blocs.

7.3.1 Bilateral Arms Control

The later Cold War policy of détente saw the negotiation of various bilateral treaties between the former Soviet Union and the United States. From 1969, the Strategic Arms Limitations Talks (SALT) were a way of managing and reducing the risks of the arms race. The 1972 Salt I Accords,[23] including the Anti-Ballistic Missile Treaty, reflected the recognition by both the United States and Soviet Union that the arms race lessened their security, while legitimising the logic of MAD.[24] These agreements were based on a literally mad logic. They presupposed an extraordinary faith in the rationality of states, and the aim was to

[20] Cohn, Carol 1987. 'Sex and Death in the Rational World of Defense Intellectuals', *Signs* 12(4): 687–718.

[21] India nationalist leader Bal Thackeray, cited Chacko, Priya 2012. *Indian Foreign Policy: The Politics of Postcolonial Identity from 1947 to 2004*. Routledge, 181.

[22] Johnson, Rebecca 2012. 'The NPT in 2010-2012: A Control Regime Trapped in Time', in Johnson, Rebecca, Caughey, Tim and Borrie, John (eds.). *Decline or Transform Nuclear Disarmament and Security beyond the NPT Review Process*. Acronym Institute for Disarmament Diplomacy, 3–34, 26.

[23] The *SALT II Treaty* was signed in Vienna in 1979 but was withdrawn from the Senate by President Carter in 1980, following the Soviet invasion of Afghanistan in December 1979.

[24] Gaddis, John 2005. *The Cold War: A New History*. Penguin Books, 200.

preserve the ability of both sides to destroy each other as a guarantee that this would not happen. The classic arms control process expressed an obsession with rationality, vulnerability and parity. Each side was allowed a small number of point defences around the capital and selected launch sites so as to protect the capacity both for decision-making and for a second strike in the event of an attack. Despite the fact that each side possessed sufficient nuclear capacity to destroy each other several times over, so that numbers were irrelevant, complex calculations of parity were incorporated into the SALT treaty. A veritable apparatus of officials and experts and subsequently verification and inspection mechanisms were caught up in the strange perverted rationality of this process.

Efforts by President Reagan to introduce the Strategic Defense Initiative (popularly known as Star Wars) threatened to derail the MAD premise of the SALT talks by upsetting the bilateral Anti-Ballistic Missile Treaty (ABM)[25] and, in theory, protecting the United States from nuclear attack. Eventually the ABM Treaty was repudiated by the second President Bush,[26] demonstrating a shift from the logic of MAD to an imaginary conception of invulnerability.

After the easing of Cold War tensions, in the 1980s and 1990s there was a trend towards further reductions in the existing nuclear arsenals. There have been a series of complicated bilateral negotiations commencing with the Strategic Arms Reduction Talks, originally between the Soviet Union and the United States and continued by the Russian Federation, which ratified the Strategic Arms Reduction Talks Treaty (START I) in 1994. The Treaty resulted in the reduction of the major part of the then existing strategic nuclear weapons. Further progress has not been straight-forward. START II did not enter into force, and negotiations for START III have never got underway.

However, when President Obama came to power, he announced a new disarmament approach, echoing calls from elder statesmen of the Cold War period,[27] for a 'world without nuclear weapons'. In his speech in

[25] *Treaty on the Limitation of Anti-Ballistic Missile Systems*, Moscow, 26 May 1972.

[26] On 13 December 2001, the United States gave notice of its withdrawal from the ABM Treaty, which became effective six months later.

[27] Known as the 'four horsemen of the nuclear apocalypse' the article by George Schulz, William Perry, Henry Kissinger and Sam Nunn in the *Wall Street Journal* of 30 January 2007 calling for a world free of nuclear weapons initiated a cascade of similar articles by former Cold War elder statesmen. Schulz, George *et. al.*, 'Commentary: Toward a Nuclear Free World', *Wall Street Journal*, (updated) 15 January 2008, www.wsj.com/articles/SB120036422673589947.

Prague on 5 April 2009, he promised to 'reduce the role of nuclear weapons in our national security strategy', to aggressively pursue ratification of the Comprehensive Test Ban Treaty (1996), to negotiate a treaty to end the production of fissile material and to strengthen the Treaty on the Non-Proliferation of Nuclear Weapons (1968; Non-Proliferation Treaty, NPT). The speech was greeted with enthusiasm and earned him the Nobel Peace Prize. But the end result was a return to a Cold War–style arms control. Both the US Nuclear Posture Review of 2010[28] and the NATO Strategic Concept[29] of the same year remained committed to the concept of nuclear deterrence and mutual vulnerability. The 2014 NATO Strategic Concept reiterated the core tasks of defence and deterrence as set out in 2010.

After the expiry of START I in 2009, NEW START[30] entered into force in 2010 to replace the 2002 Strategic Offensive Reductions Treaty (SORT). NEW START further reduces the limits on both strategic offensive arms from those permitted by START I and on operationally deployed warheads from those established under SORT. New verification and inspection mechanisms are also provided for. Predictability and stability are seen as core to security. Indeed, the START process has provided a new lease of life for the arms control apparatus, including career bureaucrats, the National Nuclear laboratories and their representatives in Congress, as well as various conservative think tanks like the Heritage Foundation and the American Enterprise Institute. Officials from the US Department of Defense have described the idea of a world free of nuclear weapons as 'rhetorical garnish'. Recent nuclear posturing by the Russian government even before the Ukraine crisis, including declarations, exercises, and overflights, and the deployment of nuclear missiles in Kaliningrad near the border with Lithuania and Poland, raises concern about the prospects of even limited arms control measures.[31]

28 U.S. Department of Defense, 'Nuclear Posture Review: 2010', www.defense.gov/News/Special-Reports/NPR.

29 NATO, '2010 Strategic Concept for the Defence and Security of the Members of [NATO]: Active Engagement, Modern Defence', www.nato.int/nato_static_fl2014/assets/pdf/pdf_publications/20120214_strategic-concept-2010-eng.pdf.

30 *Treaty between the United States of America and the Russian Federation on Measures for the Further Reduction and Limitation of Strategic Offensive Arms (New START)*, 8 April 2010.

31 See Durkalec, Jacek. 'Russia's Evolving Nuclear Strategy and What It Means for Europe' European Council for Foreign Relations, 6 July 2016, www.ecfr.eu/article/commentary_russias_evolving_nuclear_strategy_and_what_it_means_for_europe; www.theguardian.com/world/2016/oct/08/russia-confirms-deployment-of-nuclear-capable-missiles-to-kaliningrad.

7.3.2 Non-proliferation and Counter-proliferation

The idea of non-proliferation was introduced during the Cold War and was about preventing the spread of nuclear weapons to other states and entrenching the balance between nuclear and non-nuclear states. Counter-proliferation is more recent and is an integral part of the War on Terror. It starts from the assumption that it is no longer possible to assume the rationality of those who possess or might possess nuclear weapons. This was the argument of the second President Bush, who introduced the concept of counter-proliferation in the 2002 National Security Strategy.[32] Thus it is argued that suicide bombers and rogue leaders do not fear retaliation. Indeed, they might welcome retaliation since they do not care about human life: it would prove that they are involved in a war against the West. In these circumstances deterrence no longer works, and pro-active efforts are needed to prevent deadly technologies (not just nuclear technologies) coming into the hands of 'rogue' states or terrorists.

The preamble to the multilateral NPT (1968)[33] recognised the need 'to safeguard the security of peoples'. The then nuclear weapon states (United States, United Kingdom, Soviet Union, France and People's Republic of China) undertook not to transfer nuclear weapons or other nuclear explosive devices, and non-nuclear weapon states undertook not to receive such devices. The NPT is monitored and verified by the International Atomic Energy Agency (IAEA) and also provides for regular review conferences. In effect this treaty is a way of legitimating deterrence as a source of security through maintaining the possession of nuclear WMDs by a small number of powers while denying this right to other states, thereby contributing to 'strategic stability, the avoidance of global conflict and the maintenance of international peace and security'. Non-nuclear states were said to have benefitted through reliance on the nuclear states for their security, and through the Mutual Defence Agreements they entered into.[34] However, it has been argued that far from enhancing state security, the NPT in reality undermines security in that it

See also Spear, Joanna 2011. 'More Business as Usual? The Obama Administration and the Nuclear Posture Review', *Contemporary Security Policy* 32(1): 241–263.

32 The White House, 'National Security Strategy', 2002, www.state.gov/documents/organization/63562.pdf.

33 London, Moscow and Washington, 1 July 1968.

34 Letter dated 20 June 1995 from the Acting Legal Adviser to the Department of State, together with Written Statement of the Government of the United States of America, 20 June 1995, *Legality of the Threat or Use of Nuclear Weapons*, 1996 ICJ Reports 226, advisory opinion of 8 July 1996 (*Nuclear Weapons*). See Chapter 4.

has failed to strengthen its verification processes, has no provision for responding to noncompliance and does not deter withdrawal from the regime (as was announced by North Korea on 10 January 2003).[35]

However, article VI of the NPT also envisaged more than maintenance of the *status quo*. It requires nuclear weapon states to negotiate nuclear disarmament agreements, making it the 'only existing international treaty under which the major nuclear powers are legally committed to disarmament'.[36] The *travaux* show that article VI was an integral part of the NPT package, not just an 'add-on'.[37] Its importance to the objectives of the Treaty is indicated by its preamble, which spells out the 'intention to achieve at the earliest possible date the cessation of the nuclear arms race' and 'to undertake effective measures in the direction of nuclear disarmament'. Although this 'bargain' between nuclear and non-nuclear states is weak in that it imposes no timetable nor any sanctions for failure to comply, it was reinforced by the ICJ when it asserted that '[t]here exists an obligation to pursue in good faith and bring to a conclusion negotiations leading to nuclear disarmament in all its aspects under strict and effective control'.[38] The Court broadened the scope of article VI from being just a 'code of conduct' to involving an obligation of result, that is to conclude those negotiations.[39]

Although the NPT was extended indefinitely in 1995, the bargain is widely perceived as having been broken by the nuclear weapon states. In April 2014 the Republic of the Marshall Islands (RMI) filed an application in the ICJ against the nuclear weapon states, both parties and non-parties to the NPT. The RMI claimed that these states are in violation of the NPT article VI and/or customary international law through their failure to actively pursue good faith negotiations with respect to the cessation of the nuclear arms race and nuclear disarmament.[40] The Court

[35] Johnson, *op. cit.*

[36] Rauf, Tariq 1995. 'Nuclear Disarmament: Review of Article VI', in Simpson, John and Howlett, Darryl (eds.). *The Future of the Non-Proliferation Treaty*, 67.

[37] Firmage, Edwin Brown 1969. 'The Treaty on the Non-Proliferation of Nuclear Weapons', *American Journal of International Law* 63(4): 711–746, 716–721.

[38] *Nuclear Weapons, op. cit.*, para. 105(2)(F).

[39] Bosch, Miguel Marin 1999. 'The Non-Proliferation Treaty and Its Future', in Boisson de Chazournes, Laurence and Sands, Phillipe (eds.). *International Law, the International Court of Justice and Nuclear Weapons*. Cambridge University Press, 375–389.

[40] Republic of the Marshall Islands, Application Instituting Proceedings against the Republic of India; Application Instituting Proceedings against the Islamic Republic of Pakistan; Application Instituting Proceedings against the United Kingdom of Great Britain and Northern Ireland, ICJ, all on 24 April 2014.

was thus once again faced with the nuclear question, but as in previous cases it has failed to respond to the substantive issues at stake.[41]

Counter-proliferation has become prominent after 9/11. It involves an active policy of preventing both states and non-state actors deemed as irrational or inimical from acquiring WMD. In terms of states, the main targets are Iraq (before 2003), Iran and North Korea. In the latter cases, the US position has been endorsed by the UN Security Council (SC). In the case of Iran, the SC imposed sanctions in accordance with UN Charter, article 41, reviewed by a panel of experts and subject to the requirements of the IAEA,[42] and called upon Iran to become a party to the Comprehensive Nuclear Test Ban Treaty. This would not bring the Treaty into force as long as other states required to become parties fail to do so, including permanent members of the Security Council. An agreement was concluded with Iran in 2015, which will constrain its ability to develop nuclear weapons and has meant the end of sanctions.[43]

In response to the withdrawal of North Korea from the NPT and its conduct of nuclear tests, the SC has demanded that the state conduct no more tests, return to the NPT, abandon all WMDs and has imposed economic measures.[44] The NPT recognizes state sovereignty by providing that a state may withdraw 'if it decides that extraordinary events, related to the subject matter of this Treaty, have jeopardized the supreme interests of its country'.[45] The condition for withdrawal is phrased subjectively: the Treaty does not specify the consequences of an unwarranted withdrawal, nor does it authorise the SC to make this determination. In resolutions with respect to both Iran and North Korea the

41 On 5 October 2016 the ICJ dismissed the cases finding there was no dispute between the RMI and the respective respondent states, in the case of the United Kingdom by the President's casting vote; *Obligations concerning Negotiations relating to Cessation of the Nuclear Arms Race and to Nuclear Disarmament* (Marshall Islands v. United Kingdom). On other litigation before the ICJ on nuclear matters see further below.

42 E.g., UN SC Resolution 1929, 9 June 2010; UN SC Resolution 2105, 5 June 2013.

43 *Joint Comprehensive Plan of Action*, Vienna, 14 July 2015. UN SC Resolution 2231, 20 July 2015 provided for the termination of sanctions on receipt of an IAEA report confirming fulfilment of all conditions by Iran.

44 UN SC Resolution 1718, 14 October 2006; UN SC Resolution 2094, 7 March 2013 (in response to the nuclear test carried out on 12 February 2013); UN SC Resolution 2270, 2 March 2016 (in response to the test carried out on 6 January 2016).

45 The NPT article X (1) provides that '1. Each Party shall in exercising its national sovereignty have the right to withdraw from the Treaty if it decides that extraordinary events, related to the subject matter of this Treaty, have jeopardized the supreme interests of its country. It shall give notice of such withdrawal to all other Parties to the Treaty and to the United Nations Security Council three months in advance'.

Council has affirmed the importance of compliance with the NPT by all states. The SC has undoubtedly extended its chapter VII powers and while the nuclear weapon states fail to comply with NPT, article VI, has laid itself open to accusations of double-standards.

Along with the emphasis on preventing the acquisition of WMDs by so-called rogue states has been the preoccupation with the risk that terrorists might acquire such weapons, especially in the context of increasing amounts of enriched fissionable material that became unaccounted for after the break-up of the Soviet Union. Even though it is clear from 9/11 that terrorists do not need WMDs to cause large-scale destruction, and even though the use of WMDs may require a more complex infrastructure than is normally available to non-state actors, this preoccupation has been framed through further treaty-making and by SC actions under its mandate for the maintenance of international peace and security.

States have been unable to agree a comprehensive treaty on terrorism, or even a definition of terrorism.[46] Instead the approach has been the adoption of a slew of sectoral treaties, each criminalising specific defined acts (e.g., aerial hijacking, hostage seizure, threats to diplomatic staff) and setting out states' obligations with respect to their suppression. They also require international co-operation. The 2002 G-8 Global Partnership Against the Spread of Weapons and Materials of Mass Destruction, the 2003 Container Security Initiative, the 2002 Proliferation Security Initiative and the 2005 International Convention for the Suppression of Acts of Nuclear Terrorism[47] all come within this framework. The last Treaty requires states to criminalise and to make punishable by appropriate penalties acts relating to the unlawful possession or use of radioactive material or devices with the intent to cause death or serious bodily injury or serious damage to property or the environment; to establish

[46] The Appeal Chamber of the Lebanon Special Court has defined terrorism under customary international law as consisting of the following three key elements: (1) the perpetration of a criminal act (such as murder, kidnapping, hostage-taking, arson etc.), or threatening such an act; (2) the intent to spread fear among the population (which would generally entail the creation of public danger) or directly or indirectly coerce a national or international authority to take some action, or to refrain from taking it; (3) when the act involves a transnational element. Interlocutory Decision on the Applicable Law: Terrorism, Conspiracy, Homicide, Perpetration, Cumulative Charging, Feb. 16, 2011, Case No. STL-11-01/I, www.stl-tsl.org/x/file/TheRegistry/Library/CaseFiles/chambers/20110216_STL-11-01_R176bis_F0010_AC_Interlocutory_Decision_Filed_EN.pdf).

[47] *International Convention for the Suppression of Acts of Nuclear Terrorism*, 14 September 2005. The Treaty entered into force on 7 July 2007.

jurisdiction over such acts and to extradite or prosecute suspected offenders. The offences are deemed to be extraditable offences in any extradition treaty existing between states parties, and if there is no such treaty in force in any given case the Convention can serve as the basis for extradition. States must also take steps to render harmless any such material that comes within their possession or control following the commission of an offence under the Convention. That the Convention is directed at acts of non-state actors is made clear by provisions excluding 'the activities of armed forces during an armed conflict, as those terms are understood under international humanitarian law' and official acts of military forces of a state. The Convention expressly states that it does not address the legality of the threat or use of nuclear weapons.

States are free not to enter into treaties for any reason, but decisions of the SC are binding upon member states of the UN under article 25 of the Charter. The Council has used its UN Charter chapter VII powers in effect to bypass the WMD conventions to legislate against the proliferation of these weapons and their means of delivery to non-state actors.[48] SC Resolution 1540[49] decides upon an array of obligations upon states including legislating to prevent the proliferation of nuclear, chemical and biological weapons, and their means of delivery, and establishing domestic controls to prevent their illicit trafficking. The Resolution decides that none of the obligations it imposes conflict with those accepted under the NPT, Biological Weapons and Chemical Weapons Conventions. Security Council Resolution 1540 applies to all states, requires actions within the domestic jurisdiction of states and is proactive in that it seeks to prevent the proliferation of WMDs to unnamed terrorist groups.

The obsession with the acquisition of WMDs by so-called rogue states or by terrorist groups is central to the framing of the War on Terror and the way it echoes the idea of a grand contest of the Cold War years. At the same time, it diverts our gaze from the everyday experience of terror and counter-terror in new war situations.

[48] As an instance of Security Council legislation, UN SC Resolution 1540, 28 April 2014 follows UN SC Resolution 1373, 28 September 2001 adopted in the wake of 11 September 2001 which requires states to adopt a range of measures against the financing of terrorist acts; see further Chapter 2.

[49] 28 April 2004. UN SC Resolution 1540 has been followed by Resolutions 1673, 27 April 2006; 1810, 25 April 2008; 1977, 20 April 2011; 2055, 29 June 2012; see also SC Presidential Statement S/PRST/2014/7.

7.4 Humanitarian Regulation of Weapons

The humanitarian approach is part of the *jus in bello* tradition and has paralleled the development of international humanitarian law (IHL). What has been novel in the post–Cold War period is a whole series of new treaties and initiatives aimed at alleviating human suffering in 'new wars' that are often outside The Hague and Geneva frameworks and are the consequence of pressure from civil society. As critical scholars point out, there is considerable overlap between the humanitarian and the arms control approaches since IHL has been used to keep weapons out of the hands of states or non-state actors who might challenge the role of the dominant powers. Nevertheless, regulation of the means and methods of warfare has become an integral part of international humanitarian law. Despite weaknesses, it is unarguable that these treaties fill some legal gaps and make a significant contribution to the regulation of the possession and use of different conventional weapons, before, during and post-conflict.[50] With the landmines and cluster munitions treaties it is also possible to observe an overlap with disarmament.

In what follows, we start by outlining the efforts to regulate weapons within the IHL framework. We then describe some of the various novel approaches, including the treaties to ban landmines and cluster munitions, the Arms Trade Treaty and the significance of arms embargoes.

7.4.1 The Jus in Bello *Tradition*

The Declaration of St Petersburg in 1868[51] sought to alleviate as much as possible the 'calamities of war' and to this end declared the employment of arms that 'uselessly aggravate[d] the sufferings of disabled men', or made their death inevitable, to be 'contrary to the laws of humanity'. But this high-sounding sentiment was limited: it was only applicable to wars between 'civilized nations', by which those adopting the Declaration meant themselves. Conflicts involving colonial possessions or non-European states were not subject to such limitations, an example of how international law was used to justify colonisation and repressive actions against those deemed 'uncivilised'.[52] Further, the Declaration

50 Dörmann, Knut 2009. 'Conventional Disarmament: Nothing New on the Geneva Front?' in Giegerich (ed.), *op. cit.*, 143–166, 151.

51 *Declaration of St. Petersburg*, 29 November 1868.

52 Mazower, Mark 2006. 'An International Civilization? Empire, Internationalism, and the Crisis of the Mid-Twentieth Century', *International Affairs* 82(3):552–566.

sought only to relieve the suffering of fighting men, as was the case with the Geneva Conventions of 1864.

Thirty years later protections for civilians come into the international picture,[53] albeit in an extremely limited way. Tsar Nicholas II, who had become apprehensive about falling behind in the arms race, convened the 1899 Hague Peace Conference. The issue was not yet arms reduction so the focus of The Hague Conference was to limit the growth of armaments and military budgets. Delegates were unable to agree upon any binding treaty on the subject (as they did with respect to limiting recourse to war, and restrictions on its conduct), but instead, in a weak form of the principle of distinction, they adopted two Declarations with application to civilians: on the Launching of Projectiles and Explosives from Balloons, and on the Use of Bullets Which Expand or Flatten Easily in the Human Body. Another Declaration on the Use of Projectiles the Object of Which is the Diffusion of Asphyxiating or Deleterious Gases was again directed at alleviating the suffering of armies. It has been noted, however, that all three weapons were of 'dubious military value' and thus restrictions could be supported by 'delegates eager to demonstrate humanitarian motives but reluctant to compromise military interests'.[54] Further, the Declarations were binding only on 'contracting powers in case of war between two or more of them' and ceased to be so if joined in conflict by a non-contracting power. No progress was made at The Hague in 1899 on freezing military or naval spending. The issue was not included on the agenda of the Second Hague Peace Conference in 1907 and is not on the international agenda today, other than through the arguments of some human rights groups and other civil society advocacy. Such an approach to the regulation of weapons has been described as a 'utopian idea that never had a chance of entering the realm of practical politics'.[55]

In the carnage of World War I both deleterious gases and aerial warfare were used and, even though, strictly speaking, the types of armaments used were neither projectiles nor balloons, their use seemed to point to the failure of The Hague Peace Conference at restraining the excesses of war. Following limited provisions in the Treaty of Versailles,[56]

[53] General Orders No. 100 (Lieber Code), 24 April 1863; see Chapter 6.

[54] Jochnick, Chris and Normand, Roger 1994. 'The Legitimation of Violence: A Critical History of the Laws of War', *Harvard International Law Journal* 35: 49–90, 72.

[55] Neff, Stephen C. 2009. 'The Hague Peace Conferences and a Century of Further Struggles', in Giegerich (ed.), *op. cit.*, 59–87, 69.

[56] *The Treaty of Peace between the Allied and Associated Powers and Germany*, Versailles, 28 June 1919, article 8: 'The Members of the League recognise that the maintenance of

there were attempts to strengthen them. The 1925 Conference on supervision of the international trade in arms and ammunition adopted a Protocol against the use of poisonous gases,[57] which applied to all use of poisonous gases and to bacteriological and chemical forms of warfare. In contrast, The Hague Rules on Aerial Warfare adopted in 1923 effectively legitimised this form of warfare. In the inter-war years aerial bombardment became an instrument of terror against colonial uprisings, for example, in South West Africa (by South Africa), Iraq in 1923 (by the United Kingdom), Syria in 1925–1926 (by France) and elsewhere in the Middle East.[58] Likewise, Spain used poison gas against Rif Tribesmen in Morocco in 1920 and 1924, and Italy used mustard gas in the 1935–1936 war with Ethiopia.[59] The carpet bombing of cities in World War II was one of the ways the different sides showed that they recognised no limits to the 'suffering they were prepared to impose on the population of the enemy'.[60] Today, controversy centres on the legality or otherwise of target and precision bombing through the use of unmanned aerial vehicles,[61] not *per se* on the use of bombing.

As part of its responsibility for the maintenance of international peace and security, the UN Charter placed responsibility for formulating plans for the establishment of a system for the regulation of armaments on the SC, with the assistance of the Military Staff Committee.[62] The GA was also made competent to consider and make recommendations with respect to 'the principles governing disarmament and the regulation of

peace requires the reduction of national armaments to the lowest point consistent with national safety and the enforcement by common action of international obligations. ... The Members of the League agree that the manufacture by private enterprise of munitions and implements of war is open to grave objections'.

[57] *Protocol for the Prohibition of the Use of Asphyxiating, Poisonous or Other Gases, and of Bacteriological Methods of Warfare*, Geneva, 17 June 1925. The Protocol was separate from the Convention for the supervision of the international trade in arms, munitions and implements of war, which was adopted by the Conference but has never entered into force.

[58] 'Schemes of air control similar to that practiced in Mesopotamia were set up in the Palestine Mandate in 1922 and in the Aden Protectorate six years later. Bombers were active at various times against rioters in Egypt, tribesmen on the Frontier, pastoralists in the Southern Sudan and nomads in the Somali hinterland'. Omissi, David 1990. *Air Power and Colonial Control: The Royal Air Force 1919–1939*. Manchester University Press.

[59] See Balfour, Sebastian 2001. 'Secret Wars in Forgotten Africa', *Journal of Romance Studies* 1(3): 121–131.

[60] Hobsawm, Eric 1994. *The Age of Extremes*. Abacus, 391.

[61] See further Chapters 4 and 6.

[62] UN Charter, article 26.

armaments'.[63] In fact, the Military Staff Committee has never functioned, and while these provisions have not operated as intended, other actors within and outside the Organisation have played diverse roles and instituted new mechanisms.[64]

After World War II, there were further restrictions on the means and methods of conventional warfare within the *jus in bello* tradition. The framework Convention on Prohibitions or Restrictions on the Use of Certain Conventional Weapons Which May Be Deemed to be Excessively Injurious or to Have Indiscriminate Effects (CCW) was adopted as an annex to the 1949 Geneva Conventions. Three Protocols were annexed to the Convention: Protocol I prohibits the use of weapons which cause injury through non-detectable fragments; Protocol II (updated in 1996) prohibits or restricts the use of mines, booby traps and other devices; and Protocol III prohibits or restricts the use of incendiary weapons. States must accept two Protocols for the Convention to become binding upon them. These were the first international humanitarian law instruments since the beginning of the twentieth century, but in substance they added little to the general principles of international humanitarian law, notably the principle of distinction.[65] Further they applied only to international armed conflict (although the Convention was extended to non-international armed conflict by the Second Review Conference in 2001).[66] In general it was felt by critics of the Convention and Protocols that 'military considerations had been given much greater weight in the negotiations than relevant humanitarian concerns'.[67]

Two further Protocols have been subsequently adopted: Protocol IV (adopted in 1996) prohibits the use of blinding laser weapons – 'a landmark in international humanitarian law/arms control history because the prohibition was negotiated before the weapon had been deployed in battle';[68] and Protocol V (adopted in 2003) applies to the aftermath of conflict, requiring parties that have used explosive devices to assist in the clearing of unexploded ordinance, including providing information as to their use. At the Second Review Conference of the CCW

63 UN Charter, article 11.

64 Boulden, Jane and Thakur, Ramesh and Weiss, Thomas (eds.) 2009. *The United Nations and Nuclear Orders*. UN University, 7.

65 Dörmann, *op. cit.*, 146.

66 Protocol II was extended to non-international armed conflict in 1996.

67 Dörmann, *op. cit.*, 146.

68 *Ibid.*, 147.

there were moves towards a further Protocol on anti-vehicle mines. After the failure to reach agreement on the formal negotiation of such a protocol, in 2006 concern 'about the humanitarian impact of these weapons' motivated a number of states to adopt a soft law political Declaration on Anti-Vehicle Mines,[69] committing them to restrictive practices as a matter of national policy.

The use of some weapons, for example, incendiary weapons, is not entirely prohibited by international law, but restrictions on their use have been provided for by treaty, at least for states parties thereto. Protocol III to the CCW on the Use of Incendiary Weapons attempts to balance military necessity with humanitarian concerns for the protection of civilians. Making civilians the object of attack by such weapons is prohibited by the Protocol. But the situation where there is a military objective located within a concentration of civilians is less clear: civilians may not be the object of an attack from air-delivered incendiary weapons, but otherwise there is an exception where the 'military objective is clearly separated from the concentration of civilians and all feasible precautions are taken with a view to limiting the incendiary effects to the military objective'. What constitutes a 'feasible precaution' is to be determined with reference to all applicable circumstances, including both 'humanitarian and military considerations', with no indication of the priority between these often conflicting factors. 'Military considerations' is also a softer test than 'military necessity', itself determined by the military. The difficulties are illustrated by the use of white phosphorus by Israel (a non-party to Protocol III) in Lebanon in 2006 and in the ground phase of Operation Cast Lead in Gaza in 2009. White phosphorus is not proscribed and has valid uses in military operations, for instance, as an obscurant for screening troops from observation or enemy fire. It also causes deep, and sometimes untreatable, burns. In Gaza doctors reported cases of patients dying of wounds they believed they had successfully treated, only for complications to develop through deeper damage to tissue and organs than had earlier been detected. The UN Fact-Finding Mission to Gaza concluded that the repeated misuse of white phosphorus 'in and around areas dedicated to the health and safety of civilians' carried a substantial risk to health, noted that there are 'other screening and illuminating means which are free from the toxicities, volatilities and hazards that are inherent in the chemical white

[69] *Declaration on Anti-Vehicle Mines*, CCW/CONF.III/WP.16, 16 November 2006.

phosphorus' and recorded its belief that 'serious consideration' should be given to banning the use of white phosphorus as an obscurant.[70] Where the presence of civilians is foreseeable, weapons of this sort are contrary to the IHL principle of distinction, but explicit provisions would promote legal clarity.

7.4.2 The Landmines and Cluster Munitions Conventions

The Conventions on landmines (1997) and cluster munitions (2008) stemmed from civil society outrage about the indiscriminate and ongoing harm caused to civilians through the use of these weapons. The broader issues of insecurity are well summarised in the preamble to the Cluster Munitions Convention:

> cluster munitions remnants kill or maim civilians, including women and children, obstruct economic and social development, including through the loss of livelihood, impede post-conflict rehabilitation and reconstruction, delay or prevent the return of refugees and internally displaced persons, can negatively impact on national and international peace-building and humanitarian assistance efforts, and have other severe consequences that can persist for many years after use.[71]

These Conventions were negotiated outside both the UN Geneva Conference on Disarmament, the traditional forum for the negotiation of treaties on WMDs,[72] and the International Committee of the Red Cross. Instead a coalition of civil society organisations, international governmental organisations and like-minded states came together in the so-called 'Ottawa/Oslo' process.

The Landmines Convention was the first success story in this new approach to negotiation of weapons treaties[73] and the first treaty to ban a

[70] Report of the United Nations Fact-Finding Mission on the Gaza Conflict, UN A/HRC/12/48, 25 September 2009, paras. 886–901, 1924 ('UN Fact-Finding Mission on Gaza').

[71] Compare similar language in the *Convention on the Prohibition of the Use, Stockpiling, Production and Transfer of Anti-Personnel and on Their Destruction*, 18 September 1997 ('Landmines Convention'): 'Determined to put an end to the suffering and casualties caused by anti-personnel mines, that kill or maim hundreds of people every week, mostly innocent and defenceless civilians and especially children, obstruct economic development and reconstruction, inhibit the repatriation of refugees and internally displaced persons, and have other severe consequences for years after emplacement'.

[72] This body has been essentially inactive since 1996 as measures of legal regulation have been addressed elsewhere, as discussed below.

[73] Cameron, Maxwell, and Lawson, Robert and Tomlin, Brian (eds.) 1998. *To Walk without Fear: The Global Movement to Ban Landmines*. Oxford University Press.

weapon in widespread use. An anti-landmine campaign was initiated and progressed by numerous non-governmental organisations (NGOs), which formed in the early 1990s a global NGO coalition, the International Campaign to Ban Landmines (ICBL). The ICBL includes cluster munitions within its remit, and in 2003 the Cluster Munitions Coalition was also formed. The ICBL was supported by like-minded states, notably Canada, Austria and Norway, and more generally by the GA, which urged states 'to pursue vigorously an effective, legally binding international agreement to ban the use, stockpiling, production and transfer of anti-personnel landmines'.[74] The campaign was strengthened by the simplicity of its central humanitarian message, which was backed by data about the numbers and devastating effects of landmines.[75] That this was also an aspect of human security was especially promoted by the Canadian Minister of Foreign Affairs, Lloyd Axworthy.[76] The adoption in 1996 by the Geneva Disarmament Conference of the amended Protocol II to the CCW, which only added further restrictions to the use of landmines, booby traps and other devices, had disappointed those who sought nothing less than the outright prohibition of such devices. This objective was pursued through the diplomatic Ottawa process. The separateness of this process from that of the Conference on Disarmament was deliberate: the latter was perceived as slow and the requirement for unanimity (or at least consensus) as weakening text and allowing any single state (including a state that might have no intention of ever ratifying the treaty) to impede progress. Further, voting groups remained frozen within their Cold War alliances. In contrast the Ottawa process allowed for text to be adopted by a two-thirds majority if consensus could not be achieved, although ironically the prospect of a vote (which did not in fact occur) may have facilitated consensus.

The Landmines Convention was adopted in 1997 in Oslo. It calls for the non-use, possession or transfer of anti-personnel mines, and also for the destruction by parties of all stockpiled anti-personnel mines they own

[74] UN GA Resolution 51/45, 10 December 1996, S(1).

[75] In UN GA Resolution 51/45, *ibid.*, it was estimated that there are more than 110 million landmines in more than sixty countries; that an estimated two million new landmines are laid each year; and that landmines kill or maim hundreds of mostly innocent and defenceless civilians, especially children, every week, obstruct economic development and reconstruction, inhibit the repatriation of refugees and the return of internally displaced persons, and have other severe consequences for years after emplacement.

[76] Axworthy, Lloyd 1999. *Human Security: Safety for People in a Changing World.* Canadian Department of Foreign Affairs and Trade.

or possess. Uniquely at the time, the Convention requires those states parties that can do so to provide 'assistance for the care and rehabilitation, and social and economic reintegration, of mine victims and for mine awareness programs' (article 6). The reduction in deaths and injuries on the ground has been called the greatest achievement of the Landmines Convention.[77]

The success of the Landmines Convention spurred similar civil society efforts with respect to cluster munitions, again supported by like-minded states through the Ottawa/Oslo process. The Convention, adopted in May 2008 in Dublin and opened for signature in Oslo later that year, likewise calls for the non-use, possession or transfer of cluster munitions and requires the destruction of existing weapons, and clearance and destruction of cluster munitions remnants located in cluster munitions contaminated areas under a state party's jurisdiction or control. Provision for victim assistance is more detailed than in the Landmines Convention, requiring in accordance with international humanitarian and human rights law, 'age and gender-sensitive assistance, including medical care, rehabilitation and psychological support'.

Nevertheless in both Conventions, provision for compliance and enforcement is weak, essentially limited to consultation and cooperation between states parties. The NGO coalitions have taken up an important monitoring role, as well as promoting universal ratification. Even though key countries remain outside both Convention regimes, including the United States, Russia, China, Iran, North Korea, India and Pakistan, a number of the Arab states and Israel, the Conventions have undoubtedly done much to stigmatise these weapons and to change behaviours, even among non-party states.

International law is strengthened by a 'fluid and dynamic model' of law-making that can respond quickly to scientific understanding and public opinion.[78] While treaty negotiation must always involve states seeking to preserve their sovereign rights, the Ottawa/Oslo process demonstrates that strong coalitions – a strategic partnership between like-minded states, IGOs and NGOs – can 'work together to change international law more quickly and radically than traditional diplomacy'.[79] The

[77] Dörmann, *op. cit.*, 149.

[78] Lewis, Patricia and Thakur, Ramesh 2004. 'Arms Control, Disarmament and the United Nations', *Disarmament Forum* 1: 17–28, 26.

[79] Bleicher, Maurice 2000. 'The Ottawa Process: Nine Day Wonder or a New Model for Disarmament Negotiations?' *Disarmament Forum* 2: 69–86, 73.

involvement of civil society in drafting proposed texts may encourage a more flexible use of language and development of law-making techniques as those accustomed to working in different legal regimes bring their experience and expertise to this new enterprise. According to Thomas Nash, an active member of the campaign to ban cluster munitions: 'The unrelenting focus on the human impact helped the campaign to occupy the moral high ground, foster a sense of urgency and maintain pressure on delegates, it also kept the standard of ambition high during the negotiations, challenging others to reach the maximum humanitarian protection possible rather than lowering the bar in compromise'.[80]

The Landmines and Cluster Munitions Conventions demonstrate legal cross-fertilisation as they incorporate obligations and mechanisms drawn from human rights (e.g., state reporting, reparations for victims), disarmament (e.g., verification) and humanitarian law (e.g., humanitarian language, fact-finding). As well as these practical measures, the Ottawa/Oslo process also provides a symbolic link with international humanitarian and human rights law, underscoring the humanitarian objectives of these treaties by focusing on the unacceptable harms to individuals and the needs of victims rather than the strategic and militaristic thinking of non-proliferation and arms control regulation. This concentration on 'unacceptable harm' has been described as an 'astute innovation' in that it is both a political target and a benchmark for the determination of weapons that should be prohibited.[81] While characterising contemporary campaigns in disarmament, it can also be perceived as a return to the style of early humanitarian treaty negotiation that prevailed before the institutionalisation of multilateral processes through the UN.

7.4.3 The Regulation of Small Arms

Small arms are the weapons of choice in civil wars,[82] in terrorist attacks, in organised crime and gang warfare – in effect 'new wars'. Small arms

[80] Nash, Thomas 2012. 'Civil Society and Cluster Munitions: Building Blocks of a Global Campaign', in Kaldor, Mary, Moore, Henrietta and Selchow, Sabine (eds.). *Global Civil Society 2012: Ten Years of Critical Reflection*. Palgrave Macmillan,130.

[81] Borrie, John and Caughey, Tim 2012. 'How Are Humanitarian Approaches Relevant to Achieving Progress on Nuclear Disarmament?' in Johnson, Caughey and Borrie, *op. cit.*, 35–56.

[82] 'The weapon of choice for any self-respecting rebel movement is the Kalashnikov. ... it seldom goes wrong, needs little maintenance, and so can be entrusted to anyone who is pretty clueless'. Collier, Paul 2009. *Wars, Guns and Votes: Democracy in Dangerous Places*. HarperCollins, 114.

and weapons have been termed a 'worldwide scourge' by the UN Office for Disarmament Affairs. They are used in widespread violations of international humanitarian law and human rights, such as the right to life and bodily integrity, in preventing peaceful assembly and exercise of the right to freedom of expression, as has been seen in the protests and mounting violence in the Middle East since 2011. Their illicit circulation 'destabilizes communities, and impacts security and development in all regions of the world', aiding terrorism and illegal armed groups, and facilitating increasing levels of transnational organised crime with 'devastating humanitarian and socioeconomic consequences, including by impeding the provision of humanitarian assistance to victims of armed conflict, contributing to the displacement of civilians, and undermining sustainable development and poverty eradication efforts'.[83] Porous borders facilitate their ready transnational transfer and 'cheap guns on informal markets increase the risk of civil war'.[84]

The continued availability of small arms and weapons in what is termed post-conflict threatens local reconstruction and regional stability. For example, the UN Secretary-General has reported that 'small arms and light weapons in the wake of the Libya crisis has had a detrimental impact on an already precarious situation in the neighbouring Sahel region',[85] causing a surge in weapons trafficking, criminality, insurgencies and terrorist acts. They also contribute to the normalisation of violence with significant gendered consequences. Men and boys are the major possessors, users and victims of small arms and weapons and within many cultures possession of such arms sustains notions of masculinity and of being a 'real man'. This in turn contributes to the terrorising of women and children through wartime sexual and gendered violence and to domestic violence.[86] The special rapporteur on violence against women has reported that the proliferation of small arms, in conjunction with such factors as gangs, organised crime, drug dealing,

[83] Outcome Document, Programme of Action to Prevent, Combat and Eradicate the Illicit Trade in Small Arms and Light Weapons in All Its Aspects, A/CONF.192/2012/RC/CRP.3/Rev.3, June 2015, paras. 4 and 5.

[84] Collier, *op. cit.*, 119.

[85] Report of the Secretary-General, Assistance to States for Curbing the Illicit Traffic in Small Arms and Light Weapons and Collecting Them, A/67/176, 25 July 2012, para. 5.

[86] *The Convention on Preventing and Combating Violence against Women and Domestic Violence* (Istanbul Convention), 11 May 2011, article 51 requires an assessment of the lethality risk with respect to violence against women that takes into account the fact that perpetrators of acts of such violence possess or have access to firearms.

human and drug trafficking chains, has had a 'devastating impact' on women's lives, particularly in Mexico and Central America.[87]

Attempts at regulation of the illicit trade in and availability of small arms, both within specific locations and more generally, have been ongoing since the 1990s. Perspectives have shifted within the debates and their outcomes. At first, following the 1991 Gulf War, the influence of civil society actors meant that human rights and humanitarian issues were accorded significant weight. In this, Amnesty International played a lead role and supported by Nobel Laureates, in particular Óscar Arias, began lobbying and acting against the unregulated arms trade and its adverse impact on human security.[88] But these concerns were 'slowly eroded' by states seeking to ensure their sovereign rights of self-defence, non-intervention in internal affairs and their commercial interests.[89] With the emergence of the human security agenda, there has again been some counter-balance to the traditional national security agenda.

Civil society voices too have been divided. Opposition to the human rights and humanitarian lobbyists came from those committed to the right of individuals to possess arms, notably the American National Rifle Association. Critics on the left suggest that the focus on constraining small arms illicitly supplied to actors in 'new wars' has left the vast bulk of small arms untouched. Thus it is estimated by the Small Arms Survey that 'of the over 875 million firearms in circulation around the globe, 650 million (or 74 per cent) are in the hands of civilians, 270 million of these in the United States. A further 200 million (23 per cent) are held by state militaries and 26 million (3 per cent) by law enforcement officials around the world. Less than one million are held by insurgents'.[90] Reportedly, 87 per cent of the firearms seized by Mexican authorities originate in the United States. Efforts to regulate small arms are made within an international law framework ('outside') and therefore focus

[87] Manjoo, Rashida. Report of the Special Rapporteur on Violence against Women, Its Causes and Consequences, A/HRC/20/16, 23 May 2012, para. 66. The special rapporteur has also noted that 'in 2008 firearms were the most common weapon used by men to murder women. ... Women also suffer "hostile gun displays" as a form of intimate partner violence, by which abusive partners threaten to use guns against their victims' (para. 35).

[88] Mahmoud, Dina 2012. 'A Short Guide to the Arms Trade Treaty', Advocates for International Development.

[89] Farr, Vanessa and Myrttinen, Henri and Schnabel, Albrecht 2009. *Sexed Pistols: The Gendered Impact of Small Arms and Light Weapons*. United Nations University, 3.

[90] Quoted in Stavrinakis, Anna 2011. 'Small Arms Control and the Reproduction of Imperial Relations', *Contemporary Security Policy* 32: 193–213, 197.

upon trade and transfer. Yet as the statistics show, possession and access to such weapons (and their use) require linking domestic ('inside') regulation with 'outside' forms. In addition, it is argued that the focus on small arms completely neglects the production and trade in major weapons systems, which has risen substantially in recent years as licensing of major weapons has been relaxed.

In continuance of its agenda to combat organised crime, in 2001 the UN Office on Drugs and Crime completed the first legally binding instrument on small arms – the Protocol to the 2000 Convention on Transnational Organized Crime against the Illicit Manufacturing of and Trafficking in Firearms, Their Parts and Components and Ammunition.[91] This casts the issue within the framework of crime control, requiring states parties to criminalise the illegal manufacturing of, and trafficking in, firearms; to establish a licensing (or other authorisation) system to ensure legitimate manufacturing of, and trafficking in, firearms and also the marking and tracing of firearms. Importantly the Protocol includes ammunition and manufacturing, but excludes 'state-to-state transactions' and 'state transfers' that would prejudice 'the right of a State Party to take action in the interest of national security' (article 4).

Also in 2001, the UN Conference on Illicit Trade in Small Arms and Light Weapons was convened. Interests and policies brought to the Conference were shaped by earlier initiatives at the regional level.[92] Civil society was active prior to the Conference, with the formation of another umbrella NGO, the International Action Network on Small Arms, but in order to limit NGO influence, participation at the Conference was contested and access to formal negotiation sessions limited.[93] The Conference adopted a Programme of Action to prevent, combat and eradicate the illicit trade in small arms and light weapons in all its aspects.[94] The preamble references both the humanitarian needs for action, for instance, the reduction of human suffering and enhancement of respect

[91] The Protocol was adopted by UN GA Resolution 55/255, 2001.

[92] E.g., Bamako Declaration on an African Common Position on the Illicit Proliferation, Circulation and Trafficking of Small Arms and Light Weapons, 2000; European Union Programme for Preventing and Combating Illicit Trafficking in Conventional Arms, 1997; see Krause, Keith 2002. 'Multilateral Diplomacy, Norm Building, and UN Conferences: The Case of Small Arms and Light Weapons', *Global Governance* 8(2): 247–263, 254.

[93] *Ibid.*, 256.

[94] Report of the United Nations Conference on the Illicit Trade in Small Arms and Light Weapons in all its Aspects, A/CONF.192/15, 9-20 July 2001.

for the life and the dignity of the human person, (paragraphs 4–6) and a state's right 'to manufacture, import and retain small arms and light weapons for its self-defence and security needs, as well as for its capacity to participate in peacekeeping operations' (paragraph 10). The operative paragraphs do not mention states' human rights obligations; while they are encouraged 'to consider ratifying or acceding to international legal instruments against terrorism and transnational organized crime' the same is not said about human rights treaties. Although non-binding, states are required to report to the GA on their implementation of the Programme of Action.

Five years later in 2006, another discourse was engaged as a high-level diplomatic initiative led to the adoption of the Geneva Declaration on Armed Violence and Development.[95] This recognises the 'profoundly negative impact' of armed conflict on human development and on realisation of then applicable Millennium Development Goals.[96] Among other undertakings, the signatories (now more than 100 states) commit to action 'to deal effectively both with the supply of, and the demand for, small arms and light weapons' including implementation of the Programme of Action and 'promoting the development of further international instruments, including legally binding ones'.

The Arms Trade Treaty

The UN General Assembly in 2006 endorsed the negotiation of an arms trade treaty, to establish common international standards for the import, export and transfer of conventional arms.[97] Negotiations for a robust treaty were prolonged by continuing disagreement between states over such issues as the definition of small arms, the treaty's potential scope, the relevance of human rights and the relationship between 'illicit' trade and lawful transfer.[98] At the core of the debate are the familiar tensions between the weight to be given to alleviation of the humanitarian costs of small arms and weapons, states' obligations under international humanitarian and human rights law and the significance of these weapons for states' security and sovereignty. In July 2012 a draft treaty was negotiated,

[95] The Geneva Declaration on Armed Violence and Development, 7 June 2006, www.genevadeclaration.org/fileadmin/docs/GD-Declaration-091020-EN.pdf.

[96] UN GA Resolution 70/1, 25 September 2015: Transforming Our World: The 2030 Agenda for Sustainable Development (Sustainable Development Goals), A/Res/70/1, 2015. Article 16.4 requires significant reductions in illicit arms flows.

[97] UN GA Resolution 61/89, 6 December 2006.

[98] Krause, *op. cit.* ('Multilateral Diplomacy'), 247.

but agreement on the final text was postponed until March 2013. The UN Conference on the Arms Trade Treaty was unable to adopt the Treaty by consensus, so it was instead adopted on 2 April 2013 by an overwhelming majority vote of the GA.[99]

The Arms Trade Treaty first sets out the traditional core principles of state sovereignty: the right of states to self-defence; the peaceful settlement of disputes; the prohibition of the use of force in accordance with UN Charter, article 2 (4); the responsibility of states to regulate international trade in conventional arms; and respect for states' legitimate interests in acquiring conventional arms for self-defence and peacekeeping operations and in the production and transfer of small arms. But respecting and ensuring respect for international humanitarian law and human rights law are also key principles. Among the Treaty's specified objects are contributing to international (and regional) peace and security and the reduction of human suffering, (article 1), thus giving space to the concerns of human security.

The Landmines and Cluster Munitions Convention had humanitarian concerns at their heart; the Arms Trade Treaty goes further by bringing states' human rights obligations into the heart of weapons control. The Treaty regulates international trade in conventional arms, including small arms and light weapons, battle tanks, combat aircraft, attack helicopters and warships (article 2); states are encouraged to apply the Treaty 'to the broadest range of conventional arms' (article 5 (3)). It also applies to ammunition, weapons' parts and components (articles 3 and 4). In general states parties are required to establish national control mechanisms and are prohibited from authorising the transfer of such weapons where to do so would violate their obligations under Security Council resolutions, other relevant international obligations or where there is knowledge 'that the arms or items would be used in the commission of genocide, crimes against humanity, grave breaches of the Geneva Conventions of 1949, attacks directed against civilian objects or civilians . . . or other war crimes as defined by international agreements to which it is a Party' (article 6). State parties are also required to carry out a risk assessment as to the potential for the arms to be used to commit or facilitate a serious violation of IHL or human rights law, an act of terrorism or an offence of transnational organised crime. 'Transfer' is defined somewhat narrowly in article 2 (2), excluding, for instance,

[99] UN Doc. A/CONF.217/2013/L.3, 27 March 2013.

gifts such as in military aid. Where there is an 'over-riding risk of such acts' the export shall not be authorised (article 7). Further (and exceptionally) in undertaking this assessment states shall take into account the risk of such weapons 'being used to commit or facilitate serious acts of gender-based violence or serious acts of violence against women and children'[100] (article 7 (4)). States are also required to prevent the diversion of conventional weapons into the hands of illicit persons. The Arms Trade Treaty came into force on 24 December 2014, having received the requisite fifty ratifications.

In addition many of its obligations are tied to existing treaties and other international obligations. For instance, in accordance with common article 1 of the Geneva Conventions, states 'undertake to respect and to ensure respect for the ... Convention[s] in all circumstances'. This makes it clear that the Conventions do not apply only during international or non-international armed conflict, and the wording is wide enough to encompass commercial dealings. States, especially those that produce and export arms, should therefore take measures to ensure that exported weapons are not to be used in ways that violate their obligations under the Geneva Conventions.[101] Similarly, under human rights law, the right to life includes the positive obligation to prevent acts of mass violence causing arbitrary loss of life.[102] Positive obligations require the state to protect individuals 'not just against violations of Covenant rights by its agents, but also against acts committed by private persons or entities'. Regional treaties, the Committee on the Elimination of Discrimination against Women (CEDAW) and the regional human rights courts have all expressly asserted states' obligation to exercise due diligence to prevent and protect against gender-based violence.[103] More

[100] UN SC Resolution 2117, 26 September 2013, also recalls 'with concern' that 'the illicit transfer, destabilizing accumulation and misuse of small arms and light weapons fuel armed conflicts and have a wide range of negative human rights, humanitarian, development and socioeconomic consequences, in particular on the security of civilians in armed conflict, including the disproportionate impact on violence perpetrated against women and girls, and exacerbating sexual and gender-based violence and the recruitment and use of children by parties to armed conflict in violation of applicable international law'. UN SC Resolution 2220, 22 May 2015 expresses similar concern. See also UN HRC/Res/24/35, 8 October 2013.

[101] Dörmann, Knut, *op. cit.*, 165.

[102] UN HRC, ICCPR General Comment No. 6: The Right to Life (article 6), Sixteenth Session of the HRC, 30 April 1982.

[103] This is also consistent with UN SC Resolution 1325, October 2000, on women and peace and security.

directly, the CEDAW has noted the need for 'robust and effective regulation of the arms trade, in addition to appropriate control over the circulation of existing and often illicit conventional arms, including small arms, to prevent their use to commit or facilitate serious acts of gender-based violence' and has recommended that states 'address the gendered impact of international transfers of arms, especially small and illicit arms including through the ratification and implementation of the Arms Trade Treaty'.[104]

Failure by a state party to carry out the required risk assessment or to export arms despite indications of an over-riding risk of their being used in commission of the acts specified in article 6 would constitute breach of the Arms Trade Treaty. In addition there might be state responsibility for giving 'aid or assistance' in the commission of such acts under the International Law Commission (ILC) Articles on State Responsibility.[105] The ILC Commentary to article 16 affirms such responsibility if a state provides material aid to a another state that uses the aid to commit human rights violations. The ILC draws upon the GA's call to member states 'to refrain from supplying arms and other military assistance to countries found to be committing serious human rights abuses'. State responsibility for facilitating human rights abuses committed by another state must depend upon the facts in any given situation, particularly whether the aiding state 'was aware of and intended to facilitate the commission of the internationally wrongful conduct'. This is a high threshold standard, but given the data on the killings committed by small arms and weapons, such deaths must be regarded as foreseeable, thereby lending support to an argument that the obligation to prevent violations of the right to life requires restraints upon the transfer and circulation of small arms.

The Treaty has been widely greeted. UN Secretary-General Ban Ki-moon has called its adoption 'a victory for the world's people' as it 'will make it 'more difficult for deadly weapons to be diverted into the illicit

[104] Committee on the Elimination of Discrimination against Women, General Recommendation no. 30 on Women in Conflict Prevention, Conflict and Post-Conflict Situations, CEDAW/C/GC/30, 18 October 2013.

[105] International Law Commission, Responsibility of States for Internationally Wrongful Acts, UN GA Resolution 56/83, 12 December 2001, article 16 provides: 'A State which aids or assists another State in the commission of an internationally wrongful act by the latter is internationally responsible for doing so if: (*a*) that State does so with knowledge of the circumstances of the internationally wrongful act and (*b*) the act would be internationally wrongful if committed by that State.

market and it will help to keep warlords, pirates, terrorists, criminals and their like from acquiring deadly arms'.[106] Similarly Amnesty International heralded it as a 'lifesaving treaty with human rights protection at its core' that 'can prevent the flow of arms into countries where they will be used to commit atrocities'.[107] Amnesty International considers that the Treaty will be a 'powerful new tool' in efforts to prevent human rights abuses and violations of international humanitarian law, observing that for the first time in history states were obliged 'to consider international human rights and humanitarian law, as well as international criminal law, as a basis on which to decide whether an arms transfer across borders should go ahead'.[108] In addition there have been further efforts at regulation of small arms at the regional level, notably in Africa, arguably the continent where their lethality has been most destructive of security.[109]

Despite enthusiasm for the adoption of the Arms Trade Treaty, it has only weak enforcement measures. It has not been signed by Russia, China and India, and although the United States has signed the Treaty, it has not ratified it. For European and North American countries, the Treaty does not go further than existing mechanisms for controlling arms transfers adopted in national and EU legislation. One critical scholar, Anna Stavrianakis, suggests that the treaty could turn out to be a cover for the 'liberal militarism' of countries like the United States and the United Kingdom. She argues that the process of vetting exports may legitimise those exports that receive formal approval; 'the case by case risk assessment assumes that human rights are aberrations that can be ironed out rather than an organic component of support for elites and

[106] On the UN GA vote on the Arms Trade Treaty, 2 April 2013, www.un.org/disarmament/convarms/ArmsTrade/.

[107] Amnesty International, 'UN Puts Human Rights at Heart of Historic Arms Trade Treaty', 2 April 2013, www.amnesty.org.au/news/comments/31459/.

[108] Amnesty International, 'The Long Journey towards an Arms Trade Treaty', 5 June 2013, www.amnestyusa.org/news/news-item/the-long-journey-towards-an-arms-trade-treaty.

[109] *ECOWAS Convention on Small Arms and Light Weapons, Their Ammunition and Other Related Materials*, 2006; *Central African Convention for the Control of Small Arms and Light Weapons, their Ammunition, Parts and Components that can be used for their Manufacture, Repair and Assembly* (*'Kinshasa Convention'*) 2010; *The Nairobi Protocol for the Prevention, Control, and Reduction of Small Arms and Light Weapons in the Great Lakes Region and the Horn of Africa* (*'Nairobi Protocol'*), 2004. See further, Anning, Kwesi 2010. 'Understanding the Nexus between Human Security and Small Arms in Africa: The Case of Ghana', in Abass, Ademola (ed.). *Protecting Human Security in Africa*. Oxford University Press, chapter 4, 63.

authoritarian social relations'.[110] She provides the example of arms transfers to Egypt, where many licences for arms export have been revoked, but at the same time the UK government maintains that weapons such as semi-automatic pistols, assault rifles, sniper rifles, sub-machine guns and armoured personnel carriers can be regarded as 'crowd control goods'.[111] She also suggests that reference to human rights as well as IHL in the Treaty could mean that human rights, like IHL, become subservient to the concept of 'military necessity'. According to Stavriakanis, 'the very existence of a bureaucratic process that refers to human rights and IHL is taken as evidence that arms transfer practices do not violate human rights or IHL'.[112]

On the other hand those who favour the treaty suggest that, despite the lack of enforcement mechanisms, it offers an instrument to those who wish to uphold international norms and can use the treaty for 'naming and shaming'. For example, a legal opinion commissioned by three NGOs that were instrumental in bringing about the treaty (Saferworld, Oxfam and Amnesty International) has found that the UK government is acting in breach of its obligations arising under the United Kingdom's Consolidated Criteria on arms exports, the EU Common Position on Arms Exports and the Arms Trade Treaty by continuing to authorise transfers of weapons and related items to Saudi Arabia in a context in which Saudi Arabia is using those weapons to attack civilians in Yemen.[113]

Arms Embargoes

Since the end of the Cold War the Security Council has extended the threshold for recourse to its UN Charter chapter VII powers by recognising threats to international peace and security in a wider range of

[110] Stavrianakis, Anna 2016. 'Legitimizing Liberal Militarism: Politics, Law and War in the Arms Trade Treaty', *Third World Quarterly*, 37 (5): 840–865.

[111] *Ibid.* [112] *Ibid.*

[113] Sands, Phillippe, Clapham, Andrew, Ghrálaigh, Blinnení, *The lawfulness of the authorisation by the United Kingdom of weapons and related items for export to Saudi Arabia in the context of Saudi Arabia's military intervention in Yemen,* 11 December, 2015 Matrix Chambers, Gray's Inn, London. In September 2016 the Parliamentary Committee on Arms Exports Controls reported that it was 'highly likely' that that weapons sold to Saudi Arabia had been used in violation of international humanitarian and human rights laws, a claim denied by Foreign Secretary Boris Johnson; BBC News, 'MPs call for UK to halt arms sales to Saudi Arabia', 7 September 2016 at www.bbc.co.uk/news/uk-politics-37293426.

situations, including intra-state violence.[114] One response has been the attempted disarmament of people from all communities within a state through the imposition of a mandatory arms embargo for the purpose of establishing peace, stability and security. During the period 1945–90, there were only two mandatory embargoes imposed globally (Rhodesia and South Africa). Since then there have been two mandatory embargoes and twenty-seven cases of sanctions – mostly directed against conflicts in Africa.

Somalia is a case in point. The country has experienced a typical new war: ongoing violence of relatively low intensity since the 1980s that has mutated from civil war, through collapse of state institutions, clan factionalism and war lordism, to a 'globalised ideological conflict'.[115] Somalia epitomises contemporary forms of insecurity, 'characterized by small-scale engagements of limited duration, poorly disciplined and irregular forces armed with conventional infantry weapons, sustained by constant low-level flow of weapons and ammunition . . . and one of Africa's most acute humanitarian crises'.[116] There are high rates of violence against women, including by militias and gangs.[117]

Security Council Resolution 733 of 23 January 1992 was innovative, imposing a 'general and complete embargo on all deliveries of weapons and military equipment' to Somalia 'for the purposes of establishing peace and stability'. Successive resolutions have expanded the scope of the arms embargo, clarified its terms and improved and strengthened mechanisms for monitoring compliance and implementation. The embargo has now been in effect for over twenty years – the longest continuing SC-imposed sanctions regime. Throughout the period of sanctions, the Council has itemised very specific (humanitarian) exemptions and has required that exemptions be approved in advance by the Sanctions Committee on a case-by-case basis.

Insecurity persists with military actions between the Somali National Army and AMISOM on the one hand, and Al-Shabaab on the other,

[114] See Chapter 5.

[115] Bradbury, Mark and Healy, Sally 2010. 'Endless War: A Brief History of the Somali Conflict', in Bradbury, Mark and Healy, Sally. *Whose Peace Is It Anyway? Connecting Somali and International Peacemaking. Accord 21*, Conciliation Resources.

[116] Report of the Monitoring Group on Somalia pursuant to UN SC Resolution 1811, 10 December 2008, UN Doc. S/2008/769, Summary.

[117] Manjoo, Rashida. Report of the Special Rapporteur on Violence against Women, its Causes and Consequences, Mission to Somalia, UN Doc. A/HRC/20/16/Add. 3, 14 May 2012.

asymmetric and terrorist attacks by Al-Shabaab, piracy in the seas off Somalia, armed robbery, hostage taking and terrorism.[118] Requests for the arms embargo to be lifted to enable the Somali National Army to be better equipped to fight Al Shabaab have been responded to by its partial suspension with respect to weapons 'intended solely for the development of the Security Forces of the Federal Government of Somalia, to provide security for the Somali people'.[119]

Meanwhile, and despite the constant reiteration that states must refrain from any action in contravention of the arms embargo, there has been constant violation. For example, in 2008 the Monitoring Group noted that most of the serviceable weapons and almost all ammunition in the country had been delivered since 1992 and therefore in violation of the embargo.[120] In July 2012 the Monitoring Group reported that the pattern of arms embargo violations remained little changed, with arms markets in Yemen constituting the main source of arms for Somali non-state armed groups. In a lengthy Report it itemises the actions of non-compliant private corporations, states and international organisations, describing the last as 'a growing problem in Somalia over the past year' and expressing concern about the lack of co-operation from states.[121]

It is apparent that the long-term arms embargo has not provided security in Somalia, either through general application or when targeted at non-state actors. The Monitoring Group also reports on the high number of incidents of harm to civilians and of gender-based violence, including to children and especially to internally displaced persons in camps.[122] On the one hand it might be argued that violations of the arms embargo are the reason for the continued violence, while on the other it might be that such embargoes are simply not an effective way of regulating small arms and enhancing security. One problem is that neither an arms embargo nor an arms trade treaty prevents domestic manufacture of small

[118] UN SC Resolution 2297, 7 July 2016 expresses 'serious concern at the ongoing threat posed by Al Shabaab' and Al Shabaab continues to hold territory and extort revenue in Somalia, and causes loss of civilian life.

[119] UN SC Resolution 2142, 5 March 2014.

[120] Report of the Monitoring Group on Somalia pursuant to UN SC Resolution 1811, 10 December 2008, UN Doc. S/2008/769, 9.

[121] Letter dated 11 July 2012 from the Chair of the Security Council Committee Pursuant to Resolutions 751 (1992) and 1907 (2009) concerning Somalia and Eritrea addressed to the President of the Security Council, S/2012/544, 13 July 2012, Annex 5.5.

[122] See also Report of the Special Rapporteur on violence against women, its causes and consequences, Rashida Manjoo, Country visit to Somalia, UN Doc. A/HRC/20/16/ Add.3,14 May 2012, paras. 25–27.

arms and weapons. Another is that states and other bodies are reluctant to deny arms to those with whose position they agree. For example, the Monitoring Group found that Ethiopia, France, the Sudan, Turkey, the United Arab Emirates, the United Nations and the United States had all provided support to Somali security sector institutions without providing prior notice or obtaining advance authorisation from the Committee.[123] A third is that allowing weapons into the area for use by regional or international peacekeepers enhances the risk that they will be seized by warring factions. A fourth is that arms imported legally into a neighbouring state, not subject to an arms embargo, are likely to find their way across borders, 'and so the cheap guns slosh around the continent going to where there is currently demand'.[124] In light of the failure of arms embargoes mandated by the SC and binding upon states under UN Charter article 25,[125] it has to be questioned whether a treaty is likely to be more effective.

While availability of arms fosters violence, refusal to provide arms to those under attack can be seen as a failure of the Responsibility to Protect,[126] or even of the right to self-defence and self-determination. In 1991, in response to the unfolding violence in Yugoslavia as that state unravelled, 'for the purposes of establishing peace and stability in Yugoslavia' the SC imposed 'a general and complete embargo on all deliveries of weapons and military equipment'.[127] Bosnia-Herzegovina claimed before the ICJ that this embargo could not be applied to itself as that would impair the state's inherent right of individual or collective self-defence under UN Charter, article 51.[128] The Court did not make any order in this regard. On the basis of similar reasoning, despite the European Union arms embargo in November 2012, France advocated supplying arms to the Syrian opposition to enable 'defensive arms' to reach opposition fighters.[129] However, the

[123] *Ibid.*, para. 77. [124] Collier, *op. cit.*, 115–116.

[125] As stated by the international gun prohibition lobby group Control Arms: 'every one of the 13 United Nations arms embargoes imposed in the last decade has been systematically violated'. Cited in Kopel, David, Gallant, Paul and Eisen, Joanne D. 2010. 'The Arms Trade Treaty: Zimbabwe, the Democratic Republic of the Congo, and the Prospects for Arms Embargoes on Human Rights Violators', *Penn State Law Review* 114(3): 101–163, 103.

[126] See Chapter 4.

[127] UN SC Resolution 713, 25 September 1991, subsequently renewed in many resolutions.

[128] *Application of the Republic of Bosnia and Herzegovina, 20 March 1993, in Application of the Convention on the Prevention and Punishment of the Crime of Genocide* (Bosnia and Herzegovina v. Serbia and Montenegro), 2007 ICJ Reports, judgment of 26 February 2007.

[129] 'France to Push for Arming Syria's Opposition Coalition', *BBC News*, 15 November 2012, www.bbc.co.uk/news/world-middle-east-20340664.

legality of supplying weapons to opposition forces is controversial and unsubstantiated under the *jus ad bellum*, IHL or human rights law.[130] In the *Nicaragua* case the ICJ rejected the notion that it could constitute an 'armed attack' within the terms of UN Charter, article 51.[131] The ICJ asserted that 'the protection of human rights, a strictly humanitarian objective cannot be compatible ... with the training, arming and equipping of the Contras'.[132] Admittedly this was in 1986, and perhaps the development of and greater commitment to human rights law since then might make the position different today. But when the Court reiterated the principles of non-intervention in 2005 in *DRC v. Uganda*, after the enunciation of the Responsibility to Protect and its endorsement by the GA in the 2005 Summit Outcome Document, the Court did not indicate any exception with respect to human rights.[133] Neither the Outcome Document nor the SC thematic resolutions on the protection of civilians hint at any general support for the provision of weapons to rebels; indeed, they emphasise the importance of DDR programmes post-conflict, which is at odds with allowing for greater availability of weapons prior to this time.

In resisting the proposal to lift the EU arms embargo against the Syrian opposition, Austria argued that to do so would 'constitute a breach of international and EU law' and be contrary to the 'principle of non-intervention and non-use of force' laid down in the UN Charter. It added that if the weapons ended up in the hands of the al-Nusra Front, it would also violate SC resolutions on Al Qaeda,[134] given al-Nusra's stated affiliation. Tellingly Austria added that 'delivery of more weapons' would 'only spark an arms race' and pose a threat to UNDOF peacekeepers.[135] This reasoning is in line with the prohibitions against the transfer of arms

[130] Schmitt, Michael 2014. 'Legitimacy versus Legality Redux: Arming the Syrian Rebels', *Journal of National Security Law and Policy* 7: 139–159. Ruys, Tom 2014. 'Of Arms, Funding and 'Non-Lethal Assistance': Issues Surrounding Third-State Intervention in the Syrian Civil War', *Chinese Journal of International Law* 13: 13–53.

[131] *Military and Paramilitary Activities in and against Nicaragua* (Nicaragua v. United States of America), (Merits) 1986 ICJ Reports 14, judgment of 27 June 1986. See further Chapter 5.

[132] *Ibid.*, at para. 268.

[133] *Case Concerning the Armed Activities on the Territory of the Congo* (*DRC v. Uganda*) 2005 ICJ Reports 168, judgment of 19 December 2005, para. 164.

[134] E.g., UN SC Resolution 2083, 2012.

[135] Text available at Borger, Julian, 'The Austrian Position on Arms Embargo in Syria – Official Document', *The Guardian*, 15 May 2013, www.theguardian.com/world/julian-borger-global-security-blog/interactive/2013/may/15/austria-eu-syria-arms-embargo-pdf.

where there is a risk of violations of human rights and IHL, as discussed above. In the event the arms embargo was lifted in May 2013, but no EU state has supplied arms to the opposition, although non-lethal assistance and training has been supplied and European weapons have reached the rebels via other states.[136]

7.4.4 Regulation of Autonomous and Semi-Autonomous Weapons?

Advances in weapons technology ensure new dilemmas with respect to legal regulation. Unmanned Aerial Vehicles (UAVs) are now in use, notably for targeted killings and the legal challenges are discussed in Chapters 4 and 6. Some limited forms of autonomous weapons are already available,[137] while the potential development of 'fully autonomous weapons'[138] or 'lethal autonomous robotics'[139] (LAR or 'killer robots') where humans are 'out of the loop' poses further questions, including those of definition, of morality, of legal responsibility and accountability, of their probable detrimental impact on arms racing and of international peace and security. IHL must be applicable to the use of any weapon in armed conflict, and Protocol I to the Geneva Conventions, article 36 requires consideration of the compatibility of new weapons with the law.[140] What are already complex exercises in determining what constitutes lawful targeting in accordance with the

[136] www.theguardian.com/world/2016/jul/27/weapons-flowing-eastern-europe-middle-east-revealed-arms-trade-syria.

[137] 'Weapons systems with significant autonomy in the critical functions of selecting and attacking targets are already in use'. Report of the ICRC Expert Meeting on 'Autonomous Weapon Systems: Technical, Military, Legal and Humanitarian Aspects', 26–28 March 2014, Geneva: ICRC, 9 May 2014 ('ICRC Report').

[138] 'A weapon system that once activated can select and engage targets without further intervention by a human operator'. US Defence Policy, cited in *ibid.*

[139] '[R]obotic weapon systems that, once activated, can select and engage targets without further intervention by a human operator. The important element is that the robot has an autonomous "choice" regarding selection of a target and the use of lethal force'. Heyns, Christof, Report of the Special Rapporteur on Extrajudicial, Summary or Arbitrary Executions, UN Doc. A/HRC/23/47, 9 April 2013, para. 38.

[140] *Protocol Additional to the Geneva Conventions of 12 August 1949, and relating to the Protection of Victims of International Armed Conflicts (Additional Protocol I)*, 8 June 1977, article 36 states that 'In the study, development, acquisition or adoption of a new weapon, means or method of warfare, a High Contracting Party is under an obligation to determine whether its employment would, in some or all circumstances, be prohibited by this Protocol or by any other rule of international law applicable to the High Contracting Party'.

principles of distinction, proportionality and precaution are likely to be made even harder by the inclusion of autonomous weapons into the equation. The inherent asymmetry of military action without risking human costs for the user state emphasises a hierarchy of human lives at odds with the human rights principle of universality. The humanitarian imperative opens up the moral inquiry as to whether it can ever be acceptable to target and kill humans without human control; do the 'dictates of public conscience' allow for life and death decisions to be made by a machine? On the other hand, some argue that 'such technological advances – if kept within proper bounds – represent legitimate military advances, which could in some respects even help to make armed conflict more humane and save lives on all sides'.[141] Further, they have considerable military advantages by 'saving on human and financial resources, allowing for longer periods on station and withstanding other forces'. 'They can enhance the quality of life of soldiers of the user party: unmanned systems, especially robots, are increasingly developed to do the so-called dirty, dull and dangerous work'.[142]

The UN Human Rights Council special rapporteur on extrajudicial and arbitrary killings has called for national moratoria on 'the testing, production, assembly, transfer, acquisition, deployment and use of LARs until such time as an internationally agreed upon framework on the future of LARs has been established'.[143] For our purposes, the core issue is what form any international legal regulation of autonomous and/or semi-autonomous weapons should take: limitations on deployment and use or total prohibition? Should there be a ban on proliferation along arms control lines, creating a further inequality between have and have-not states? Without agreed international legal standards, states are free to determine their own policies, as has already been the case with respect to the United States and United Kingdom. The latter has stated that the 'operation of weapon systems will always be under human control' and that it is 'committed to using remotely piloted rather than highly automated systems as an absolute guarantee of oversight and authority for weapons release'. The United States has policy guidelines 'designed to minimize the probability and consequences of failures in autonomous and semi-autonomous weapons systems'; 'such systems shall be designed to allow commanders and operators to exercise appropriate levels of human judgment over the use of force'.[144] Are autonomous weapons

[141] Heyns, *op. cit.*, para. 31. [142] *Ibid.*, para. 51. [143] *Ibid.*, para. 113.
[144] The UK and US policies are cited in ICRC Report, *op. cit.*

best regulated through a humanitarian framework, or should there be an outright ban on these systems, that is to say a disarmament framework?

7.5 Disarmament

Both during the Cold War and subsequently, the disarmament approach has also been pursued especially in relation to so-called weapons of mass destruction, nuclear, biological and chemical weapons (although not all chemical and biological weapons cause mass destruction).

7.5.1 Biological and Chemical Weapons

Disarmament treaties have been agreed with respect to both biological and chemical weapons. The Biological Weapons Convention was agreed in 1972.[145] It prohibits the possession, development, production, stockpiling and acquisition of biological weapons and reinforces the rule on their non-use. Although parties to the Biological Weapons Convention also affirmed the 'objective of effective prohibition of chemical weapons' and undertook to negotiate in good faith to achieve this end, the Chemical Weapons Convention was not adopted until 1993. However, the twenty-year delay meant that this Convention was adopted after the end of the Cold War, and in the changed political environment it emerged as the 'most far-reaching multilateral disarmament treaty ever negotiated'.[146] Both treaties aim at the complete elimination of biological and chemical weapons and require the destruction of existing stockpiles of weapons.

The Biological Weapons Convention has minimal provisions for implementation and enforcement; it provides for consultation and co-operation and for a state party that has a complaint about breach by another state party to make a complaint to the SC, the only body with the competence to authorise intervention. The Chemical Weapons Convention establishes an implementing body, the Organisation for the Prohibition of Chemical Weapons (OPCW), introduces a verification regime including a 'challenge inspection' process, requires state reporting and makes provision for the holding of regular review conferences. In

[145] *Convention on the Prohibition of the Development, Production and Stockpiling of Bacteriological (Biological) and Toxin Weapons and on their Destruction*, London, Moscow and Washington, 10 April 1972.

[146] Burroughs, John. 'Requirements to Achieve Non-Proliferation and Disarmament', Article VI Forum, The Hague, 2 March 2005, footnote 9, www.middlepowers.org/docs/BurroughsSpeechA6F.pdf.

response to activities prohibited by the Convention, the Conference of States parties may recommend collective measures in conformity with international law and bring grave issues to the UN Security Council. Destruction of a state's chemical weapons is an expensive and onerous task, if undertaken with proper environmental standards, as is verification that this has been done. Certain states (Russia, United States and Libya) indicated that they could not eliminate all prohibited weapons within the required time frame, and extensions have been acquiesced in.

The effectiveness of the taboo against the use of chemical weapons was illustrated by global reactions to the chemical weapons attacks in Syria in August 2012 resulting in the SC's affirmation of the decision of the Executive Council of OPCW demanding the destruction of chemical weapons in Syria.[147] In August 2013 use of chemical weapons in a suburb of Damascus spurred demands in the West for military intervention, but that did not eventuate. In September 2013 the SC condemned any use of chemical weapons in Syria, welcomed Syria's accession to the Chemical Weapons Convention[148] and unanimously endorsed a Russian-US–negotiated agreement for the destruction of the chemical weapons,[149] for inspections by the OPCW and for UN Charter chapter VII measures in the event of non-compliance.[150] It also expressed 'its strong conviction' that individuals responsible for the use of chemical weapons should be held accountable.[151] The agreement and subsequent SC endorsement

[147] The Decision is annexed to UN SC Resolution 2118, 27 September 2013. The SC determined that 'the use of chemical weapons anywhere constitutes a threat to international peace and security' and that it would remain alert to the matter.

[148] For analysis of the legal issues arising see Jacobsson, Marie 2014. 'Syria and the Issue of Chemical Weapons: A Snapshot of a Legal Time-Frame, the United Nations Security Council Resolution 2118 (2013) and the OPCW Executive Council Decision' in Ebbesson, Jonas et al., *International Law and Changing Perceptions of Security*. Brill Nijhoff, chapter 10, 134.

[149] Framework for Elimination of Syrian Chemical Weapons, Annex to the letter dated 19 September 2013 from the Permanent Representatives of the Russian Federation and the United States of America to the United Nations addressed to the Secretary-General, UN Doc. A/68/398–S/2013/565, 24 September 2013.

[150] UN SC Resolution 2118, 27 September 2013.

[151] *The Rome Statute of the ICC*, article 8(2)(b) applies to weapons prohibited in an international armed conflict: (xvii) poison or poisoned weapons; (xviii) asphyxiating, poisonous or other gases and all analogous liquids, materials or devices; (xix) bullets which expand or flatten easily in the human body. An amendment adopted at the Review Conference in 2010 made these provisions applicable to non-international armed conflict (for those states accepting the amendment); Amendment to article 8 of the *Rome Statute of the International Criminal Court*, RC/Res. 5 (2010), Kampala, 2010. A proposal by Belgium for a further amendment adding to the list of prohibited

can be viewed within the framework of the Responsibility to Protect: a linkage instituted between the concept and the possibility of authorised military action being held out as a 'last resort' in the event of non-compliance with the demands for the dismantling of all chemical weapons in Syria. It is a sign of the continuing importance attached to the taboo against chemical warfare that it has been possible to pass a SC Resolution declaring that chemical weapons use anywhere constitutes a threat to international peace and security and establishing an investigative mechanism to identify 'individuals, entities, groups or Governments perpetrating, organizing, sponsoring or otherwise involved in the use of chemicals as weapons in Syria'.[152] This robust reaction to the use of chemical weapons, however, contrasts markedly with the absence of an effective international response to the continued killings and destruction in Syria by conventional weapons and small arms and indeed legitimated their use. In the words of Secretary-General Ban Ki-moon: 'A red light for one form of weapons does not mean a green light for others. This is not a license to kill with conventional weapons. All the violence must end. All the guns must fall silent'.[153] Yet it has not been possible to refer 'the situation' in Syria to the ICC for investigation of war crimes and crimes against humanity by different parties (for instance, the Assad regime, IS, Russia) even though the use of chemical weapons is counted as a war crime in the 1998 Rome Statute of the ICC. Further, human insecurity is exacerbated by displacement and regional instability accentuated by refugee flows, public health concerns through the spread of infectious diseases[154] and terrorist activities.[155]

weapons, including chemical weapons, cluster munitions and anti-personnel landmines, did not achieve consensus and has been referred to a Working Group; Clark, Roger 2010. 'Amendments to the Rome Statute of the International Criminal Court Considered at the First Review Conference on the Court, Kampala, 31 May–11 June 2010', *Goettingen Journal of International Law* 2(2): 689–711, 709–710.

152 UN SC Resolution 2235, 7 August 2015. The UN SC requested the SC to submit terms of reference for an Organization for the Prohibition of Chemical Weapons (OPCW)–UN Joint Investigative Mechanism to investigate and identify those involved in the use of chemicals as weapons, including chlorine, in Syria.

153 Secretary-General's remarks to the SC on the situation on Syria, New York, 27 September 2013, www.un.org/sg/statements/index.asp?nid=7165.

154 Letsch, Constanze. 'Syrian Crisis Fuelling Public Health Emergency, Doctors Warn', *The Guardian*, 1 November 2013, www.theguardian.com/world/2013/nov/01/syrian-crisis-public-health-emergency.

155 McDonnell, Patrick J. 'Turkey Is Alarmed by Extremist Militants in Syria Border Area', *Los Angeles Times*, 10 November 2013, www.latimes.com/world/la-fg-turkey-border-radicals-20131110,0,4858958.story#axzz2kSLD0dSt.

Questions of definition are also problematic and may also weaken the taboo on chemical weapons, for instance, the use of barrel bombs filled with chlorine in Syria. Although chlorine is not explicitly prohibited under the CWC, it does come under what is known as the General Purpose Criterion, which prohibits the use of any chemical whose toxicity is used for the purposes of warfare.[156] The Chemical Weapons Convention allows the use of chemical weapons such as tear gas, for purposes of law enforcement, including domestic riot control. This is consistent with human rights law; for instance, article 2 of the European Convention on Human Rights allows the use of force to quell a riot or insurrection,[157] although, as noted by the European Court of Human Rights (ECtHR), law enforcement officials should perform such operations in accordance with the (non-binding) Basic Principles on the Use of Force and Firearms by Law Enforcement Officials.[158] In a world where the line between war and law enforcement becomes fuzzy, notably in counter-terrorism operations, the scope of these provisions and the use of different weapons[159] becomes problematic. The ECtHR addressed some of these issues in a case brought against Russia by sixty-four survivors of the assault by the authorities on the Dubrovka theatre in 2002.[160] Terrorists had forcefully taken a large number of people hostage in the theatre and held them there for three days, amidst explosives and at gunpoint. Some hostages who sought to escape were killed by the

[156] In February 2015 the OPCW Executive Council expressed serious concern regarding the findings of the fact-finding mission that chlorine has been used as a weapon in the Syrian Arab Republic, 'the first ever documented instance of the use of toxic chemicals as weapons within the territory of a State Party to the CWC'; UN SC Resolution 2209, 6 March 2015. It subsequently noted 'that the use of any toxic chemical, such as chlorine, as a chemical weapon in the Syrian Arab Republic is a violation of resolution 2118'; UN SC Resolution 2235, 7 August 2015.

[157] The 'mere fact' of using tear-gas to dispel demonstrators does not violate ECHR, article 3; however, 'firing a tear-gas grenade along a direct, flat trajectory by means of a launcher' was held not to be an appropriate police action; *Abdullah Yasa and Others v. Turkey*, ECtHR application no. 44827/08, 16 July 2013.

[158] Adopted by the Eighth United Nations Congress on the Prevention of Crime and the Treatment of Offenders, Havana, Cuba, 27 August–7 September 1990.

[159] In *Anzhelo Georgiev and Others v. Bulgaria*, ECtHR application no. 51284/09, 30 September 2014, the ECtHR found on the facts of the particular case the use of electrical-discharge weapons in police operations to be disproportionate; among the factors considered was the intense pain and temporary incapacitation caused by these weapons.

[160] *Finogenov and Others v. Russia,* ECtHR applications nos. 18299/03 and 7311/03, 20 December 2011.

terrorists. In the early morning of 26 October, Russian security forces released an aerosol of fentanyl-type narcotics[161] into the main auditorium. The aerosol caused the terrorists to lose consciousness, during which time the special squad stormed the building. Most of the terrorists and suicide bombers were killed in the ensuing action; a large number of hostages also died, and others who were affected by the narcotic aerosol have suffered continuing serious health issues. The applicants to the European Court claimed violation of their right to life, while the Government averred that all their actions had been in accordance with national and international law relating to counter-terrorist operations. In particular '[t]he choice of means had been justified by the risks posed by the possible explosion of the bombs, which would have resulted in the death of all of the hostages' so that the use of gas was 'absolutely necessary' in the circumstances. The Court characterised the case as 'about the use of a dangerous substance ... by the authorities within a rescue operation which resulted in the death of many of those whom the authorities were trying to liberate and in mortal danger for many others'. It accepted that the decision to storm the building was compatible with the ECHR, article 2 in the circumstances. In response to the applicants' argument that the gas was a lethal weapon which was used indiscriminately against both terrorists and innocent hostages, the Court found that it 'was not in the circumstances a disproportionate measure, and, as such, did not breach article 2 of the Convention'. However, the subsequent rescue operation was inadequately conceived and carried out in various respects and thus constituted a breach of article 2.

7.5.2 *Efforts to Achieve Nuclear Disarmament*

Throughout the Cold War period non-traditional methods have been engaged by civil society movements opposed to nuclear weapons: local protests (CND marches), confrontation (Greenpeace and the sinking of the *Rainbow Warrior* in Auckland Harbour)[162] and global legal challenge (seeking of advisory opinions from the ICJ on the legality of

161 Robinson, Julian Perry, '"Incapacitating Chemical Agents" in Context: An Historical Overview of States' Policy' in ICRC Expert Meeting, '*Incapacitating Chemical Agents', Law Enforcement, Human Rights Law and Policy Perspectives*, Montreux, Switzerland, 24–26 April 2012.

162 Palmer, Geoffrey 1989. 'Settlement of International Disputes: The "Rainbow Warrior" Affair', *Commonwealth Law Bulletin* 15(2): 585–598.

nuclear weapons). More recently civil society success with the legal prohibition of landmines and cluster munitions has encouraged the call for an international ban on nuclear weapons, based on humanitarian arguments.

Early achievements of the anti-nuclear movement were associated with efforts to prohibit atmospheric or other testing of nuclear weapons through treaty and to challenge such testing through international litigation. After long years of discussion and negotiation, in 1963 the United States, United Kingdom and Soviet Union agreed the Partial Nuclear Test Ban Treaty,[163] prohibiting all testing of nuclear weapons except underground. France did not accept the Treaty and continued atmospheric nuclear testing in the Pacific. In the 1970s Australia and New Zealand (joined by Fiji) sought a declaration from the ICJ that this constituted a violation of their rights under international law. Behind their immediate claim was their fundamental difference with France with respect to the place of nuclear weapons and the testing of such weapons in the contemporary world. Environmental concerns were also becoming stronger by the 1970s. New Zealand and Australia had indicated that what they sought was termination of the testing. The French authorities (including from as high up as the President of the Republic) made a series of unilateral statements to the effect that atmospheric tests in the Pacific were to cease – at least for the time being. The Court considered that these statements constituted a legal undertaking, binding upon France and therefore declined to address the substantive question of the legality of such testing, thereby avoiding having to confront the nuclear powers, or to disappoint non-nuclear states. New Zealand responded to this non-decision by asserting that:

> New Zealand's concern about nuclear testing had never been confined to the particular case of the tests conducted by France – or indeed, to the question of testing in the atmosphere. It would continue to be the New Zealand government's aim to bring about the ending of all forms of nuclear weapons testing, by any country.[164]

[163] *Treaty Banning Nuclear Weapon Tests in the Atmosphere, in Outer Space and under Water*, Moscow, 5 August 1963.

[164] The Official Statement of the New Zealand Prime Minister, the Rt. Hon. W. E. Rowling, 21 December 1974; *Request for an Examination of the Situation in Accordance with Paragraph 63 of the Court's Judgment of 20 December 1974 in the Nuclear Tests* (*New Zealand v. France*) dissenting opinion of Judge *ad hoc*, Sir Geoffrey Palmer, 1995 ICJ Reports 288, 387, order of 22 September 1995, para. 19.

New Zealand's anti-nuclear policy generated further international controversies, for example, between itself, Australia and the United States with respect to the obligations incurred by the ANZUS Treaty and with France over the sinking in 1985 of the Greenpeace ship *Rainbow Warrior* in Auckland Harbour. An attempt to reactivate the case in 1995 when France proposed further nuclear testing, albeit underground, also failed. The ICJ found that the earlier case was exclusively about the continuation of atmospheric nuclear testing, while the 1995 situation raised questions relating to underground nuclear tests: essentially it was a different dispute for which the Court did not have jurisdiction.[165] Like the contemporaneous request for an advisory opinion from the ICJ, this litigation before the World Court publicised the concerns of the anti-nuclear states and lobbyists. However, the Court's determination that it lacked jurisdiction, coupled with the unsatisfactory conclusion to the question of the legality of the threat or use of nuclear weapons, as discussed below, disappointed those who sought legal certainty, including a number of states that sought to intervene in the Court's proceedings.[166] The Court's retreat to procedural formalism undermined its legitimacy and role in offering guidance on core questions of international security.[167]

Following the end of the Cold War there had been optimism for a comprehensive banning of nuclear testing. The Comprehensive Nuclear Test Ban Treaty was negotiated within the Conference on Disarmament and adopted for signature in 1996. The basic obligation is simple (although institutional arrangements are more complex): 'Each State Party undertakes not to carry out any nuclear weapon test explosion or any other nuclear explosion, and to prohibit and prevent any such nuclear explosion at any place under its jurisdiction or control'. In an attempt to bring states that have developed nuclear weapons outside the NPT (India, Pakistan, Israel) into the system, article XIV makes the coming into force of the Treaty contingent on ratification by all states listed in Annex II – forty-four states with nuclear capabilities. This has backfired by giving these states the power to prevent the Treaty from coming into force, which remains the case.

165 *Ibid.*, majority opinion.

166 Australia, Samoa, Solomon Islands, Marshall Islands, Federated States of Micronesia; *ibid.*, at para. 67.

167 Some commentators considered that such questions of individual conscience and morality were unsuited to legal determination; Koskenniemi, Martti, 'The Silence of Law/The Voice of Justice', in Boisson de Chazournes and Sands (eds.), *op. cit.*, 488–510.

Meanwhile civil society sought another way to achieve a definitive assertion of the illegality of the use of nuclear weapons in armed conflict, and more generally. In 1988 the International Association of Lawyers against Nuclear Arms was founded. The Association adopted in 1989 The Hague Declaration on the Illegality of Nuclear Weapons, which asserted that the threat or use of nuclear weapons constituted a war crime and a crime against humanity. The Association appealed to states members of the UN to seek a resolution from the GA asking the ICJ for an advisory opinion. In 1992 the World Court Project was formed which furthered lobbying for such a resolution. Success came in the form of two requests for advisory opinions from the Court. The first was sought by the World Health Assembly which asked whether 'the use of nuclear weapons by a State in war or other armed conflict [would] be a breach of its obligations under international law including the WHO Constitution'. This was followed by a broader question from the General Assembly as to the legality of the threat or use of nuclear weapons. The Court declined to answer the first request on the basis that the question asked was not within the scope of the WHO's activities.[168] With respect to the second, it analysed the legality of the threat and potential use of nuclear weapons from the perspective of multiple legal regimes: the *jus ad bellum*, *jus in bello*, international humanitarian law, human rights and environmental law. The majority advised that there is neither a treaty nor a rule of customary international law prohibiting the threat or use of nuclear weapons, and while accepting that such a use would generally be incompatible with international humanitarian law, it finally could not conclude definitively whether the threat or use of nuclear weapons would be lawful or unlawful in an 'extreme circumstance of self-defence, in which the very survival of a State would be at stake'. While refusing to answer the precise question, the formalistic reasoning placed state security as the highest priority. The retention – and potential use – of nuclear weapons is thus justified in terms of sovereign rights: 'the fundamental right of every State to survival' and the principle of deterrence. The majority opinion (7-7, with the President's casting vote)[169] was rejected by other judges who considered the Court had abdicated its judicial

[168] *Nuclear Weapons* case, *op. cit.*

[169] In the Declaration accompanying his casting vote, the President of the Court asserted that the Court's conclusion could not be interpreted as 'leaving the door ajar to recognition of the legality of the threat or use of nuclear weapons'. *Ibid.*, Declaration of President Bedjaoui, para. 11.

responsibility and some of whom expressly looked to the humanitarian consequences of nuclear weapons. For instance, Judge Weeramantry considered that such reasoning 'represents the very negation of the humanitarian concerns which underlie the structure of humanitarian law' and 'contradicts the fundamental principle of the dignity and worth of the human person on which all law depends'.[170]

In the mid-1990s the GA also called again for a convention on the prohibition of the use of nuclear weapons,[171] and the ICJ too affirmed the obligation on states to pursue in good faith – and to bring to a conclusion – negotiations on nuclear disarmament. In 1995 the GA requested the Conference on Disarmament to commence negotiations on a convention and to report to the Assembly on their results.[172] The Assembly stressed that banning the use of nuclear weapons would be an important step in a phased programme towards the complete (or ultimate) elimination of nuclear weapons, within a specified time framework. However, the Conference on Disarmament has been unable to undertake negotiations on this subject as called for by this and subsequent GA resolutions.

In 2008 UN Secretary-General put forward his five-point plan for a nuclear-free world, based on state commitments to existing or further treaties, strong verification measures and further research into verification, moratoria and dissemination of information from nuclear weapon states about their efforts in this regard.[173] The International Campaign to Abolish Nuclear Weapons (ICAN) seeks to bring into the mainstream of NPT discourse the concept of a treaty-based ban (not merely control) on nuclear weapons with 'humanitarian facts and arguments to transform debates around nuclear use and possession'.[174] This shifts the debate away from military utility and national strategic capability to one emphasising the effects of nuclear weapons on humans, a humanitarian dimension[175] that puts human security at the centre and also gives greater

[170] *Ibid.*, dissenting opinion of Judge Weeramantry, para. 433.

[171] The GA had called for a convention on the prohibition of nuclear weapons during the Cold War; UN GA Resolution 2164 (XXI), 5 December 1966; UN GA Res 2289 (XXII), 8 December 1967.

[172] Convention on the Prohibition of the Use of Nuclear Weapons, UN GA Resolution 50/ 71 E, 12 December 1995.

[173] Ki-moon, Ban, 'The United Nations and Security in a Nuclear-Weapon-Free World: The Secretary-General's Five Point Proposal on Nuclear Disarmament', 24 October 2008, www.un.org/disarmament/WMD/Nuclear/sg5point.shtml.

[174] Johnson, *op. cit.* [175] Borrie and Caughey, *op. cit.*

weight to the voices of non-nuclear states.[176] It also alters the burden of proof, bringing to the fore the concept of unacceptable harm and imposing the burden on the possessors of nuclear weapons 'to prove the[ir] continued legitimacy'[177] rather than demanding that opponents prove their illegality. The humanitarian discourse is strengthened by partnership between non-nuclear weapon states and civil society seeking to demystify and delegitimise nuclear weapons.[178] Support for this strategy is given by the Joint Statement of a number of like-minded states who in the preparatory committee for the 2015 NPT Review Conference have asserted that: 'All rules of international humanitarian law apply fully to nuclear weapons; those rules notably include the rules of distinction, proportionality and precaution, as well as the prohibition to cause superfluous injury or unnecessary suffering and the prohibition to cause widespread, severe and long-term damage to the environment'.[179] Further concurrence comes from the International Committee of the Red Cross, which in a 2011 resolution[180] emphasised 'the incalculable human suffering that can be expected to result from any use of nuclear weapons' and called upon those in the Red Cross movement to engage 'humanitarian diplomacy' in activities aimed at raising awareness 'among the public, scientists, health professionals and decision-makers of the catastrophic humanitarian consequences of any use of nuclear weapons, the international humanitarian law issues that arise from such use and the need for concrete actions leading to the prohibition of use and elimination of such weapons'.

There have been significant reductions in nuclear armaments (especially following the Intermediate Nuclear Forces Treaty and START I) and the establishment of nuclear-free zones within some regions and areas outside national jurisdiction, but the objectives of a comprehensive ban on nuclear testing and 'general and complete' nuclear disarmament have not been achieved. After considerable activity in the 1990s

176 Johnson, Caughey and Borrie (eds.), *op. cit.*

177 Borrie and Caughey, *op. cit.*

178 Johnson, *op. cit.*

179 First Session of the Preparatory Committee for the 2015 Review Conference of the Parties to the Treaty on the Non-Proliferation of Nuclear Weapons, Joint Statement on the Humanitarian Dimension of Nuclear Disarmament by Austria, Chile, Costa Rica, Denmark, Holy See, Egypt, Indonesia, Ireland, Malaysia, Mexico, New Zealand, Nigeria, Norway, Philippines, South Africa, Switzerland, 2 May 2012.

180 ICRC Council of Delegates 2011, 'Resolution 1, Working towards the Elimination of Nuclear Weapons', 26 November 2011, www.icrc.org/eng/resources/documents/resolution/council-delegates-resolution-1-2011.htm.

(following the end of the Cold War) there was a period of inactivity and set-backs. The use of nuclear weapons was not explicitly designated as a war crime[181] or crime against humanity in the 1998 Rome Statute of an International Criminal Court, despite attempts at its inclusion by some states (e.g., India, Mexico, Cuba, Sudan, Egypt, Bangladesh and Benin) and NGOs.[182] Subsequent attempts at amendment of the Statute to this effect have also been unsuccessful.

7.6 Conclusion

This chapter has argued that efforts to regulate weapons since the end of the Cold War have focused on arms control and on humanitarian approaches. The classic arms control logic, embedded in the geo-political assumptions of the Cold War and based on notions of numerical parity, assumptions of rationality and a belief in mutual vulnerability, has continued to animate bilateral negotiations between the United States and Russia about nuclear weapons as well as the continuing non-proliferation process. The new emphasis on counter-proliferation, linked with the War on Terror, has placed the spotlight on preventing the spread of WMD technologies to so-called rogue states and terrorist groups and is central to the framing of the War on Terror. Along with arms control has been a revival of humanitarian efforts to alleviate suffering in war through the prohibition or regulation of those weapons that are typically used in the new wars. The emphasis on protection is associated with ideas linked to Responsibility to Protect, while the concern with new wars makes this approach relevant for the Liberal Peace. New types of treaty-making involving coalitions of NGOs and like-minded states have led to the treaties to ban landmines and cluster munitions as well as to the Arms Trade Treaty of 2013.

Two features of the post–Cold War process of legislation and regulation are worth noting. One is the growing intrusiveness and transparency of various agreements and treaties, involving much more extensive mechanisms for verification, inspection and the adoption of domestic rules. Keith Krause talks about the shift from sovereignty to governmentality.[183] What is emerging is a deeply interconnected and increasingly

[181] However, the use of poisonous weapons and 'asphyxiating, poisonous or other gases, and all analogous liquids, materials or devices' are included as war crimes; *Rome Statute of the ICC*, article 8 (2)(b).

[182] Burroughs, *op. cit.*

[183] Krause, *op. cit.*

dense global governance regime for regulation, which both offers possibilities for an international rule of law and at the same time upholds existing hierarchies in increasingly powerful ways.

The other feature of this period is the role of civil society. Following in the footsteps of nineteenth-century peace activists and pacifists,[184] broad-based civil society movements comprising *inter alia* lawyers, doctors, philosophers, scientists, adherents to diverse religious beliefs, women's groups, student groups and trade unions have united in campaigns against certain weapons,[185] and to express the 'role of public conscience in furthering the principles of humanity'.[186] In some instances their message is a simple one based on the evident harm caused by, for instance, landmines; in others they are informed by modern research on the impact of, for instance, even limited nuclear exposure on life – the environment, climate, agriculture, food resources.[187] This has pitted civil society, in conjunction with 'like-minded' states motivated by humanitarian concerns that reject the over-riding demands of military objectives, against those who are unwilling to abandon the right of sovereign states to possess, acquire or develop such weapons as they deem necessary for their national security or some other stated legal purpose (such as developing nuclear energy for peaceful uses). The former have supplemented the traditional language of arms regulation with concepts and obligations drawn from human rights law.[188]

There are downsides, however, to the legal regulation of weapons. The negotiating process – and the aim of bringing as many states into the conventional regimes – works against strong language so that weapons treaties typically lack timelines, are not easily amended, and have weak

[184] Mazower, *op. cit.*

[185] E.g., 'Strong protests against nuclear weapons have come from learned societies, professional groups, religious denominations, women's organizations, political parties, student federations, trade unions, NGOs and practically every group in which public opinion is expressed. Hundreds of such groups exist across the world'. *Nuclear Weapons* case, *op. cit.* (per dissenting opinion of Judge Weeramantry, para. 533).

[186] *UN Convention on the Prohibition of the Use, Stockpiling, Production and Transfer of Anti-Personnel Mines and on their Destruction,* 1997 (Landmines Convention), preamble.

[187] Johnson, *op. cit.*, 27.

[188] In this they are supported by specialist human rights bodies; e.g., 'It is evident that the designing, testing, manufacture, possession and deployment of nuclear weapons are among the greatest threats to the right to life which confront mankind today'.; UN Human Rights Committee, ICCPR General Comment No. 14: Article 6 (Right to Life): Nuclear Weapons and the Right to Life, Twenty-third session of the HRC, 9 November 1984.

enforcement and verification processes. States may choose to remain outside the legal regime. Definitions are contested, may be deliberately ambiguous and legal loopholes remain; what does not fall within a legal prohibition is legitimised. Law may in fact be enabling rather than constraining. The right of states to national security and self-defence (the former subjectively determined and the scope of the latter contested as discussed in Chapter 4) further undermines the effective regulatory regimes for weapons. Where even mandatory arms embargoes and sanctions for violation of non-proliferation norms imposed by the SC are widely violated (including by the members of the Security Council themselves) and despite civil society efforts at enforcement, it is hard to assert the success of legal weapons regimes.

Despite civil society pressure on the nuclear front, the big lacuna in the post–Cold War period, has been disarmament as it relates both to nuclear weapons and to major conventional weapons that still constitute the vast bulk of military spending and that can cause immense destruction and suffering where used in 'new war' situations such as by Russia in Chechnya and Syria, Assad in Syria, Israel in Lebanon and Gaza, or Saudi Arabia in Yemen. These are hugely expensive and threatening weapons systems, and even where not actually used, they have considerable power of intimidation that is evident in 2016 in Crimea or eastern Ukraine or in Egypt and Saudi Arabia.

Critics suggest that the other side of the coin of humanitarian achievements is the neglect of disarmament and the pursuit of more precise and discriminate technologies for killing. We would argue that achievements in the humanitarian field are significant, but if they are to be sustained, they need to be complemented by greater efforts not only to address disarmament but also to unpack the cultures of the Geo-Politics and War on Terror models in which military arsenals and associated arms control measures are embedded.

PART IV

Jus Post Bellum

8

'Post-Conflict' and Governance

8.1 Introduction

Classic international law was based on the distinction between war and peace.[1] The prohibition of the use of force in international relations in UN Charter article 2(4) denoted the end of the theoretical distinction, although the fact of armed conflict continued, as recognised by the applicability of the Geneva Conventions to international and non-international armed conflict. In addition to the classic distinction between *jus ad bellum* and *jus in bello*,[2] a new terminology is emerging signifying a moment of social and legal change: a post-conflict instant, where transitional justice and state-building are pursued through what is becoming known as a *jus post bellum*.[3]

This tripartite categorisation has in fact a long ancestry,[4] and how victors act after a conflict is part of the just war tradition. According to several traditions a just victor had no additional rights over and above the *res*, the 'thing' for which the war was fought, the injury to be avenged. Thus the victor was supposed to act as a judge treating the defeated population fairly.[5]

[1] E.g., Oppenheim's classic treatise on international law comprised volume I: *Peace* (1905) and volume II: *War* (1906); the current edition is Jennings, Sir Robert and Watts, Sir Arthur (eds.) 1992. *Oppenheim's International Law, Volume I: Peace*. Longman, 9th ed.

[2] See Chapter 6.

[3] Carsten Stahn has argued that the period of transition from conflict to peace should be recognised as an 'autonomous legal space'; Stahn, Carsten 2007. "Jus ad bellum', 'jus in bello' ... 'jus post bellum'? Rethinking the Conception of the Law of Armed Force', *European Journal of International Law* 17(5): 921–943, 929 ('Jus ad bellum').

[4] Suarez, Francisco 1621. *Disputationes XIII*, discussed in the *Stanford Encyclopedia of Philosophy*, 12 July 2014, http://plato.stanford.edu/entries/suarez/; Chetail asserts that it was Immanuel Kant who systematised the tripartite notion through his analysis of going to war, during war and after war; Chetail, Vincent 2009. 'Introduction: Post-Conflict Peacebuilding – Ambiguity and Identity', in Chetail, Vincent (ed.). *Post-Conflict Peace-building: A Lexicon*. Oxford University Press, 1–33, 18–19.

[5] Thus according to Francisco Vitoria, the 'victorious party must think of himself as a judge. ... He must give satisfaction to the injured party as far as possible without causing

According to Hugo Grotius, *post bellum* law consisted of practical principles of war termination such as rules of surrender and interpretation of peace treaties, while for Immanuel Kant *post bellum* law (*Recht nach der Krieg*) involved substantive principles of justice such as the fairness of peace settlements, respect for the sovereignty of the defeated states and limits to the punishment of the people of the defeated states.[6] This classic *jus post bellum* applied to the traditional wars between states regulated by the laws of war, which were supposed to have a clear beginning, for instance, through a formal declaration of war, and ending, usually in the form of a victory/defeat, ceasefire, armistice and peace agreement(s).[7] The last may come years after the notional end of violence, as with the Peace Agreement with Japan following World War II,[8] or indeed may never materialise as in the case of the Korean War. Classic *post bellum* rules tended to refer to the period between the cessation of hostilities and a formal settlement.

In contrast, contemporary forms of political violence rarely exhibit such well-defined phases. Ceasefires are declared and broken, multiple processes of peacemaking commenced and some agreements reached, yet violence continues. Peace agreements do not hold amid recurring cycles of violence. International institutions are likely to be participants in peace processes through attempting to broker a peace deal in accordance with their own values and priorities and in mandating regional and/or international peacekeeping forces. Peace agreements and other international frameworks for post-conflict reconstruction are now about much more than establishing a ceasefire and ending conflict in that they have become a pivotal moment for determining the future constitutional and legal framework for a post-conflict zone. International and/or regional peacekeepers are frequently mandated to secure the terms of peace agreements and provide security. In practice peacekeepers may

utter ruination of the guilty commonwealth'. Quoted in Neff, Stephen 2008. 'Conflict Termination and Peacemaking in the Law of Nations: A Historical Perspective', in Stahn, Carsten and Kleffner, Jann K. (eds.). *Jus Post Bellum: Towards a Law of Transition from Conflict to Peace*. Asser Press,

6 See Stahn, Carsten 2008. '*Jus Post Bellum:* Mapping the Discipline(s)', in Stahn and Kleffner (eds.), *op. cit.*, 93–114.

7 On different ways of terminating conflict see Wallensteen, Peter and Sollenberg, Margareta 1997. 'Armed Conflicts, Conflict Termination and Peace Agreements: 1989–96', *Journal of Peace Research* 34(3): 339–358.

8 *Treaty of San Francisco*, 8 September 1951; there has been no peace agreement between the Soviet Union (Russian Federation) and Japan.

find themselves in situations of resumed fighting as the peace agreement collapses and a further round of peacemaking embarked upon. International and regional institutions are involved at the post-agreement stage too, at one extreme as a territorial administration (e.g., the United Nations Interim Administration in Kosovo, UNMIK,[9] and the United Nations Transitional Administration in East Timor, UNTAET)[10] or with a lighter touch through partnership with, and assistance (technical, legal, financial) to, local entities. The international financial institutions and donor agencies too will become active players instigating and following donor conferences. It is the web of external and internal obligations thus created and the actions of international, regional and local institutions and players that are argued to constitute the elements of a *jus post bellum*.

Unlike the *jus ad bellum*, the *jus post bellum* does not rest upon any founding principle of the UN Charter, nor has it been codified into international treaty law (in conjunction with customary international law) as with the *jus in bello*. It is rather being constructed by commentators by reference to diverse treaties, state and institutional practices, terms of peace agreements, resolutions and guidelines. It encompasses multiple international legal regimes, notably international humanitarian law, international human rights law and international criminal law, as discussed in earlier chapters. In addition elements of refugee law and principles relating to internally displaced persons, UN law (especially relating to peacekeeping), transitional justice and development law are especially pertinent.[11] The variable activities of humanitarian agencies are another relevant factor.[12] Thus the content is unsettled, and it is hard to assert either a determinative *post bellum* legal regime, or on whom any such obligations might rest.[13] Peace agreements are binding only on the

[9] Established in accordance with UN SC Resolution 1244, 10 June 1999.

[10] Established by UN SC Resolution 1272, 25 October 1999.

[11] Chetail adds other areas of international law including international economic law, the law of international organisations, of responsibility, of peaceful settlement of disputes, treaty law and the law of state succession; Chetail, *op. cit.*, 18.

[12] Holmes, John 2013.*The Politics of Humanity: The Reality of Relief Aid*. Head of Zeus.

[13] Chayes, Antonia. 'On Chapter VII ½ of the UN Charter', http://fletcher.tufts.edu/FILA/~/media/Fletcher/Microsites/Fila/PDFs/FILADiscussionPaperNo0111.pdf (military victory implies no legal obligation for reconstruction; there is at best only a moral imperative). But see also Verdirame, Guglielmo 2013. 'What to Make of *Jus Post Bellum*? A Response to Antonia Chayes', *European Journal of International Law* 24: 307–313, 311; Verdirame argues that 'an obligation to reconstruct . . . would rather signal a paradigm shift in the legal regulation of war: from a Grotian approach to a Kantian one'.

parties to them[14] and operate for the most part internally to the state in question. Other parties (for instance, peacekeepers, international agencies) may be subject to a range of normative standards set out in Security Council (SC) resolutions (although their provisions relating to post-conflict reconstruction are rarely in terms of legal obligation), rules of engagement, memoranda of understanding and agreements with the host state. This confused and fluid situation undermines legal clarity and determinacy.

Central to the emerging body of *post bellum* law is the assumption that the international community plays a critical role in post-conflict situations in constructing, implementing and being bound by the new or newly revived rules. This chapter focusses on the different arrangements or frameworks for the international presence in so-called post-conflict settings; the two following chapters deal with other aspects of *post bellum* law. We start this chapter by considering what is meant by *post bellum*. We then distinguish between three types of legal regimes pertaining to the international presence. The first, military occupation, derives from a very traditional view of conflict – occupation by state forces following military victory. In its present guise, it can be considered part of the War on Terror model, although claims can also be made that some instances of occupation seek legitimacy through upholding the Liberal Peace. The meaning of occupation has been transformed in the context of 'new wars'. The two other types of legal regime involving varying degrees of international or multilateral governance represent a late twentieth-century innovation; they can be considered as a manifestation of the Liberal Peace model, sometimes building upon humanitarian models of intervention and to be elaborated in the next chapter. Yet, as is the case more generally for the Liberal Peace model, innovation in forms of governance tend to be constrained by traditional assumptions about the nature of conflict, and, in particular, the notion of a clear dividing line between war and peace. All three types are regarded as temporary; they are not substitutes for eventual local exercise of authority but perceived as stepping stones towards that goal.[15] They all seek to maintain the security of the domestic population (although this is regarded as less

[14] On the problematic legal status of peace agreements see Bell, Christine 2006. 'Peace Agreements: Their Nature and Legal Status', *American Journal of International Law* 100 (2): 373–412.

[15] This is made explicit in various SC resolutions, e.g., UN SC Resolution 1244, 10 June 1999 (responsibility of UNMIK is promoting the establishment, pending a final settlement, of substantial autonomy and self-government in Kosovo); UN SC Resolution 1272, 25 October 1999 (UNTAET to 'support capacity-building for self-government'); UN SC

important than the security of those intervening), but are also top-down and militaristic in character.

8.2 *Jus Post Bellum:* What Constitutes Post-Conflict?

Just as the segue from violence associated with internal protest to non-international armed conflict is uncertain (see Chapter 6), so too is the conclusion of conflict. The Geneva Conventions and Additional Protocol I are applicable until 'the general close of military operations',[16] but this frequently does not conform with the termination of violence, which may continue albeit often in different forms. The formal end of conflict may be marked by defeat and conquest or by a negotiated agreement or settlement. With respect to the latter, data bases suggest that levels of violence can be at least as high after peace agreements as before.[17] As an instance of the former, President George W. Bush famously declared the end of 'major combat operations' in Iraq from the deck of the *USS Abraham Lincoln* on 1 May 2003. President Obama in May 2013 claimed that 'We ended the war in Iraq and brought 150,000 troops home'.[18] The figures belie these claims. As of December 2013 the Iraq Body Count records between 115,778 and 127,128 civilian deaths with more than 9,000 killed in 2013, ten years after the supposed end of conflict.[19] The numbers for population displacement are even more dramatic; some 4 million displaced from their homes in the period from 2003–2008 and a further million displaced during recent fighting with IS.[20] The insurgency in Iraq entailed higher coalition military fatalities in 2004 than in 2003 and did not go under 2003 levels until 2008.[21] Whether the reduced violence in 2008 was a result of US counter-insurgency tactics

Resolution 1483, 22 May 2003 (the Authority to work to create 'conditions in which the Iraqi people can freely determine their own political future').

[16] *Convention Relative to the Protection of Civilian Persons in Time of War*, Geneva, 12 August 1949, article 6 (*Geneva Convention IV*); *Protocol Additional to the Geneva Conventions of 12 August 1949, and relating to the Protection of Victims of International Armed Conflicts*, 8 June 1977, article 3 (b) (*Additional Protocol I*).

[17] Rigterink, Anouk 2015. 'Does Security Imply Safety: On the (Lack of) Correlation between Different Aspects of Security', *Stability Journal* 4(1): 1–21.

[18] Crook, John R. (ed.) 2013. 'President Obama Outlines Shifts in U.S. Counterterrorism Policy', *American Journal of International Law* 107: 674–679.

[19] Iraq Body Count website, www.iraqbodycount.org/.

[20] See, for example, UNHCR, 2014. *World at War: UNHCR Global Trends: Forced Displacement in 2014*, http://unhcr.org/556725e69.pdf.

[21] Coalition fatalities: 2003: 580; 2004: 906; 2005: 897; 2006: 873; 2007: 961; 2008: 322; Iraq Coalition Casualty Count website, www.icasualties.org/Iraq/.

and the 'surge' or other factors is debated,[22] but what is evident is the misleading designation of Iraq as 'post-conflict' in the second half of 2003. In 2016 with the military action against IS, including US airstrikes in Syria and operations by the Iraqi army, Shi'ia militias and Kurdish fighters, this is even more the case.[23]

As we have already argued, the concept of 'post-conflict' is especially problematic in the context of new wars. The many manifestations of post-conflict violence encompass criminality, gang warfare, insurgency and counter-insurgency, gendered violence and outbreaks of overt conflict. Porous borders allow for trafficking (drugs, arms, people) and continued cross-border violence.[24] The economic situation generally remains dire with high unemployment, extreme inequalities and lack of access to essential everyday services. The predatory political economy[25] of war continues unabated and is even exacerbated, not least by external flows of aid.[26]

A Council of Europe Report is illustrative. It details the situation in Kosovo following SC Resolution 1244, 10 June, which brought to an end the NATO bombing campaign and annexed the principles for agreement.[27] The Report describes the chaos in the summer of 1999 with thousands of Kosovars who had fled from Serbian repression and slaughter returning and the withdrawal of all military, police and paramilitary forces of the Federal Republic of Yugoslavia from Kosovo.

[22] Michael Cohen states: 'Since the frequency and intensity of violence abated just as the U.S. military was implementing a kinder, gentler, population-centric, COIN fighting strategy, well, surely that means that the adoption of COIN tactics was decisive – or so the surge narrative goes. But this is a dangerous and false myth that obscures a far more complicated reality'. Cohen, Michael 2010. 'The Myth of a Kinder, Gentler War', *World Policy Blog*, 22 June 2010, www.worldpolicy.org/blog/myth-kinder-gentler-war. See also Beebe, Shannon D. and Kaldor, Mary 2010. *The Ultimate Weapon Is No Weapon: Human Security and the New Rules of War and Peace*. Public Affairs, chapter 4.

[23] Civilian deaths from violence increased dramatically in 2014; Iraq Body Count reports 9,851 in 2013 and 20, 179 in 2014; in 2015 the number dropped from 2014 but remained high at 17, 511; Iraq Body Count website, www.iraqbodycount.org/database/.

[24] E.g., Cole, Peter 2013. 'Borderline Chaos? Stabilizing Libya's Periphery', in Wehrey, Frederic and Boukhars, Anouar (eds.). *Perilous Desert Insecurity in the Sahara*. Carnegie Endowment for International Peace, 35–59.

[25] See Chapter 1.

[26] De Waal, Alex 2015.*The Real Politics of the Horn of Africa: Money, War and the Business of Power*. Polity Press.

[27] Annex 1, Statement by the Chairman on the Conclusion of the Meeting of the G-8 Foreign Ministers held at the Petersburg Centre on 6 May 1999; Annex 2, Agreement on the Principles to Move Towards a Resolution of the Kosovo crisis.

'KFOR took quite some time to gain control of the situation'.[28] The Kosovo Liberation Army (KLA) moved to fill the vacuum, and in this critical period numerous crimes – killings, disappearances, rapes, destruction of property and looting – were committed against Kosovar Serbs and also against Kosovar Albanians suspected of having collaborated with the Serbs.[29] Human Rights Watch has documented the attacks that were committed at that time against the Roma community in Kosovo, which before the conflict was the largest in Europe. The Roma Mahala was destroyed through looting and burning and the inhabitants forcibly expelled, either fleeing from Kosovo or being located in camps where living conditions were reportedly appalling.[30] The border between Albania and Kosovo effectively disappeared. The Council of Europe Report further explains how during the conflict KLA factions and splinter groups had been able to establish, and run, organised criminal enterprises almost at will. These included detention facilities as 'elements of a well-established, co-ordinated and joined up network of unlawful activity', in which measures of 'punishment, intimidation and terror' were regularly carried out. Following the end of the conflict, secret detentions continued, captives were transported to Albania, including to 'a state-of–the-art reception centre for the organised crime of organ trafficking'.[31] Captives taken to this facility are 'victims of enforced disappearance' who have not been heard of since their abduction from Kosovo in the period immediately after 12 June 1999,[32] which is supposedly post-conflict. The Report suggests two reasons for the lack of accountability of top KLA personnel for criminal acts such as human trafficking, the sale of stolen motor vehicles and the sex trade; fear and violent intimidation of witnesses[33] and the unwillingness of the international community to tackle these

[28] Council of Europe, Committee on Legal Affairs and Human Rights, *Inhuman Treatment of People and Illicit Trafficking in Human Organs in Kosovo*, AS/Jur 46, 12 December 2010, Explanatory Memorandum, para. 4 ('Council of Europe' memo).

[29] *Ibid.*

[30] Human Rights Watch, '*Kosovo Poisoned by Lead: A Health and Human Rights Crisis in Mitrovica's Roma Camps*', June 2009, www.hrw.org/sites/default/files/reports/kosovo0609 webwcover_0.pdf.

[31] Council of Europe memo, *op. cit.*, para. 136. [32] *Ibid.*, para. 137.

[33] Witness intimidation was a major issue throughout the trial and retrial of KLA commanders for crimes against humanity and violations of the laws and customs of war. The ICTY noted the need for measures of protection of witnesses in the original trial and retrial in the case of *Prosecutor v. Ramush Haradinaj, Idriz Balaj, and Lahi Brahimaj*, 29 November 2012, IT-04–84bis-T, para. 12. During the retrial, the Court moved to an

crimes.[34] It concludes that 'The international actors chose to turn a blind eye to the war crimes of the KLA, placing a premium instead on achieving some sort of short-term stability'.[35] In 2014 the chief prosecutor of the Special Investigative Task Force established by the EU to pursue the allegations made in the Council of Europe Report made a statement to the effect that the Task Force largely agreed with the earlier Report, that there was a 'campaign of persecution' against the minority populations in Kosovo that 'effectively resulted in the ethnic cleansing of large portions of the Serb and Roma populations from Kosovo and that these crimes were not the acts of rogue individuals acting on their own accord, but rather that they were conducted in an organized fashion and were sanctioned by the KLA leadership'. With respect to trafficking in organs, the Task Force had not sufficient evidence for the laying of charges.[36] In August 2015 the Kosovo Parliament voted in favour of the establishment of a special court to be situated in The Hague for the trial of Kosovar Albanians accused of war crimes.[37]

Thus whether we are talking about the situation in Kosovo after the NATO bombing, the continued violence in Iraq and Libya, that in Afghanistan following the Bonn Agreement in December 2001 or in South Sudan following its independence in accordance with the Comprehensive Peace Agreement of 2005, or indeed many other examples of 'new wars', the distinctions between war and peace are increasingly blurred. In the context of the global spread of counter-terror operations states that are subject to targeted attacks by unmanned aerial vehicles, as discussed in Chapters 4 and 6,[38] are neither in a situation of conflict nor post-conflict in their relations with the United States. The applicability of the *jus ad bellum* and *jus in bello* are contested,[39] and the application of a *jus post bellum* regime must also be excluded.

Post-conflict is a particular misnomer for women. Women continue to face threats to their security, through gendered violence that is

undisclosed secret location in order to secure the testimony of a protected witness. The accused were all acquitted.

[34] Council of Europe memo, para. 69. [35] *Ibid.*, para. 7.

[36] 'In Kosovo, Signs of Organ Harvesting during War', *Reuters,* 29 July 2014, www.newsweek.com/kosovo-signs-organ-harvesting-during-war-261896.

[37] 'Kosovo Parliament Approves Special War Crimes Court', *BBC*, 4 August 2015, www.bbc.co.uk/news/world-europe-33770897.

[38] 'Beyond Afghanistan, we must define our effort not as a boundless "global war on terror," but rather as a series of persistent, targeted efforts to dismantle specific networks of violent extremists that threaten America'. Crook, *op. cit.*, 674.

[39] See Chapters 4 and 6.

committed in ways still connected to the conflict and its aftermath.[40] For instance, in 2006–2007 when sectarian violence was at its then highest in Iraq, 'women were kidnapped, raped and killed on an almost daily basis'.[41] Indeed, rape and other forms of sexual violence are major contributing factors to the fragility of post-conflict peace processes.[42] The description may shift from military violence to criminal violence, from the collapse of law and order or from wartime rape to domestic violence.[43] Research consistently shows high rates of domestic violence in the aftermath of conflict. For example, in 2001 in East Timor (i.e., during the period of UNTAET) 40 per cent of officially reported offences were violent crimes against women, and statistics suggest that most reported cases to the police involved domestic violence.[44] Such violence is associated with returning, often traumatised, men who themselves face social dislocation and unemployment, the pressures of the aftermath of conflict and the availability of arms. Violence has become normal to them throughout the conflict. It has been suggested that men defeated in conflict may seek to restore their dented sense of manhood but return to women who have experienced a new level of autonomy during the conflict. It is argued that post-conflict, men use violence to 'reinforce their hold on women; they compel women to comply because they need to re-establish or preserve control over wealth and resources and, above all, over women's productive and reproductive labour'.[45] The pervasive phenomenon of post-conflict violence against women thus has multiple explanations: normalisation of violence, extreme masculinities, changed gender roles, humiliation and stigma associated with sexual violence are just some of the experiences of conflict with long-term consequences.

[40] 'As research on women's security highlights, there are numerous obstacles in the post-conflict and transitional political environment to meaningful security for women'. Ní Aoláin, Fionnuala 2013. 'What Does Post Conflict Security Mean for Women?' in Tripp, Aili Mari and Marx Ferree, Myra and Ewig, Christina (eds.), *Gender, Violence and Human Security: Critical Feminist Perspectives*. NYU Press, 33–49, 33, 41.

[41] Puttick, Miriam 2015. *No Place to Turn: Violence against Women in the Iraq Conflict*. Minority Rights Group International.

[42] Manjoo, Rashida and McRaith, Calleigh 2011. 'Gender-Based Violence and Justice in Conflict and Post-Conflict Areas', *Cornell International Law Journal* 44: 11–31, 13.

[43] Although this statement takes no account of continued domestic violence in wartime.

[44] Charlesworth, Hilary and Wood, Mary 2002. 'Women and Human Rights in the Rebuilding of East Timor', *Nordic Journal of International Law* 71: 325–348, 331.

[45] Meintjes, Sheila, Pillay, Anu and Turshen, Meredith 2001. 'There Is No Aftermath for Women', in Meintjes, Sheila, Pillay, Anu and Turshen Meredith (eds.).*The Aftermath: Women in Post-Conflict Transformation*. Zed Books, 3–18, 13.

The destruction of communities in the conflict as well as a result of the economic devastation associated with both conflict and its aftermath also means the loss of social structures that might previously have offered a safety-net against such violence.

Violence 'post-conflict' restricts women's movement and their access to sites of reconstruction: employment, healthcare facilities and schools. In Iraq, girls were kept from attending school through fears for their safety.[46] The home thus becomes simultaneously a place of protection and of control. But women and girls who have no such protection (for instance, because they are displaced from their homes) or who are economically destitute are vulnerable to being exploited, for instance being trafficked or forced into prostitution.[47] In Afghanistan after the 2001 Bonn Agreement signified the formal end of conflict, Ritu Sharma, executive director of a Washington-based advocacy group, Women's Edge Coalition, commented that 'Afghan women are not doing as well as many want to believe. Lack of security and an increase in sexual violence against Afghan women have made it nearly impossible for them to get jobs or attend school'.[48] Traditional forms of violence – such as honour killings – may also increase. For example, in December 2012 the UN Mission in Afghanistan reported that:

> Incidents of violence against women still remain largely under-reported due to cultural restraints, social norms and taboos, customary and religious beliefs, discrimination against women that leads to wider acceptance of violence against women, fear of social stigma and exclusion, and at times threat to life. Those incidents that reach law enforcement and judicial authorities or receive public attention through the media due to their egregious nature represent the tip of the ice-berg of incidents of violence against women throughout the country.[49]

Continued violence may be discounted or minimised as private or criminal and, as such, unconnected to either the conflict or to efforts

[46] 'IRAQ: Number of Girls attending School Dropping, Say Analysts', *IRIN*, 29 October 2007, www.irinnews.org/report/75037/iraq-number-of-girls-attending-school-dropping-say-analysts.

[47] Puttick, *op. cit.*

[48] 'Afghan Women No Better Off: US Accused of Not Fulfilling Promises', *Chicago Tribune*, 23 September 2004, www.rawa.org/election-w.htm.

[49] United Nations Assistance Mission in Afghanistan 2012. *Still a Long Way to Go: Implementation of the Law on Elimination of Violence against Women in Afghanistan*, http://unama.unmissions.org/sites/default/files/evaw_still_a_long_way_to_go_11dec12_final.pdf.

for post-conflict reconstruction, for example, where the conflict has removed a regime notorious for its violent subordination of women and that objective was used as one of the justifications for war – as in Afghanistan. To acknowledge the many levels and forms of violence women now face would undermine still further any claims of a successful international intervention. But what has been very apparent is that even where claims for participation by some women in the post-conflict constitutional order have been legally approved through constitutional or other reforms, as in Afghanistan, Iraq and Timor Leste (due primarily to the leverage from women's groups mentioned earlier),[50] security for women as a whole has not been enhanced. Paradoxically, at the same time as the formal participation of women is increasing in some post-conflict settings through the implementation of at least some civil and political participatory rights, the security of the majority of women has been lessened as gendered violence has soared in the post-conflict environment.

'Post-conflict' violence can be variously labelled: insurgency, sectarian conflict, terrorism, domestic violence, crime or resistance. Whatever mode of governance is adopted, in most contemporary post-conflict situations, public security and quelling of such violence are of paramount concern, involving policing, law enforcement, counter-terrorism and counter-insurgency. Different personnel (military, civilian, security forces) and discourses are engaged and different legal regimes applicable.

So what does it mean to talk about post-conflict? Traditionally, post-conflict referred to the cessation of hostilities. Today, it appears to refer either to post-invasion, as in the cases of military occupation, or to what happens after a peace agreement or settlement has been signed; in both cases it has to do with the deployment of some form of international presence. But neither situation corresponds to the end of violence. The next section examines in more detail these forms of what is termed 'post-conflict' governance.

8.3 Military Occupation

Adam Roberts has distilled two main characteristics of military occupation: first, a formal system of external control by a force whose presence

[50] E.g., in 2003 Afghanistan ratified and Timor Leste acceded to the *Convention on the Elimination of All Forms of Discrimination against Women*, 1979, both in the aftermath of conflict.

is not sanctioned by international agreement (or local will) and, second, a conflict of nationality and interest between the inhabitants and those exercising power over them.[51] The state of occupation covers a range of political and ideological scenarios[52] as diverse as the post-war occupations of Germany and Japan following total surrender in 1945, the Soviet occupation of Afghanistan in the 1980s, the long-lasting Israeli occupation of the Occupied Palestinian Territory (OPT) and the short-lived Iraqi occupation of Kuwait in 1990–1991 and of the Coalition Provisional Authority (CPA) in Iraq in 2003–2004.

'Traditional' occupations such as those during and after World War II rest upon realist, geo-political assumptions – contestations of power and military dominance. By contrast, contemporary occupations have become entwined with the War on Terror so that repressive actions by the occupier are tolerated, even normalised, rather than challenged in accordance with international law. For instance, with the growing power of Al Qaeda–associated groups in the Sahel, the prospect that the occupied Western Sahara could be integrated into the criminal and terrorist networks in North Africa and the Sahel is a concern to the United States and its allies.[53] Fears of radical infiltration into the camps have been expressed.[54] As an ally in the War on Terror, violations of human rights and oppression by Morocco (the occupying power) are little challenged; for instance, in 2014 human rights abuses committed against Saharawi people in the occupied area led to a campaign for human rights monitoring to be incorporated into the mandate of the United Nations Mission for the Referendum in Western Sahara (MINURSO).[55] Morocco's objections were upheld, and no such mandate has been introduced by the SC, although this is now common in peacekeeping mandates.

[51] Roberts, Adam 1984. 'What Is a Military Occupation?' *British Yearbook of International Law* 55: 249–305.

[52] Adam Roberts found there to be a bewildering variety of circumstances and forms of occupation. *Ibid.*

[53] Wehrey and Boukhars (eds.), *op. cit.*, 180.

[54] Report of the Secretary-General to the Security Council, UN Doc. S/2015/246, 10 April 2015, para. 33.

[55] E.g., Human Rights Watch, 'Letter to Members of the UN Security Council: Extend MINURSO Mandate to Human Rights', 14 April 2014, www.hrw.org/news/2014/04/14/letter-members-un-security-counctil-extend-minurso-mandate-human-rights; UN Secretary-General Ban Ki-moon noted that *Frente Polisario* had sought this and noted that 'the end goal remains ... the sustained, independent and impartial monitoring of human rights, covering both the Territory and the camps'. Report of the Secretary-General to the Security Council, UN Doc. S/2014/258, 10 April 2014, para. 100.

Palestinian scholars have analysed the way a 'politics of fear' has been manipulated out of a reversal of the realities of power in occupation. The occupier has constructed fear of the occupied people as the 'other', as people seeking to harm the occupying forces or the population of the occupier and has used this fear as a justification for repressive policies, draconian emergency powers and violations of human rights.[56] In the OPT this politics of fear has been intensified by the designation of the occupied people as terrorists or potential terrorists. The determination by the International Court of Justice (ICJ) of the applicability of human rights obligations in the OPT [57] has been met by criticisms of the Court's failure to take into account this context for Israel's building of its security wall.[58]

In Iraq, following the military action in 2003 that was widely held to be illegal, the United States and United Kingdom needed the assistance of the international community in Iraq's reconstruction. They therefore sought the legitimacy of SC endorsement of their occupation. The Council noted their presence as the occupying CPA and mandated a UN presence to co-ordinate humanitarian and reconstruction activities during the period of occupation.[59] The tasks of the Secretary-General's Special Representative to Iraq explicitly included promotion of human rights.[60] The occupation – described as liberation and democratisation[61] by the United States[62] – was characterised by both expressed commitment to these values and, at the same time, by human rights violations on the ground, especially with respect to those suspected of being terrorists or insurgents,[63] exposing the tensions between the War on Terror and the Liberal Peace.

[56] Shalhoub-Kevorkian, Nadera 2011. 'Counter-Narratives of Palestinian Women', in Ennaji, Moha and Sadiqi, Fatima (eds.). *Gender and Violence in the Middle East*. Routledge.

[57] *Legal Consequences of the Construction of a Wall in the Occupied Palestinian Territory*, 2004 ICJ Reports 136, 9 July 2004 (the *Wall* case).

[58] E.g. 'But to reach that conclusion with regard to the wall as a whole without having before it or seeking to ascertain all relevant facts bearing directly on issues of Israel's legitimate right of self-defence, military necessity and security needs, given the repeated deadly terrorist attacks in and upon Israel proper coming from the Occupied Palestinian Territory to which Israel has been and continues to be subjected, cannot be justified as a matter of law'. *Ibid.*, Declaration Judge Buergenthal, paras. 240–241.

[59] UN SC Resolution 1483, 22 May 2003.

[60] UN SC Res 1483, 22 May 2003, para. 8(g).

[61] Whether a territory is regarded as occupied or liberated will often be subject to differing objective and subjective determinations.

[62] In accordance with the Iraq Liberation Act, 1998.

[63] E.g., see the facts of *Al-Skeini v. UK*, ECtHR GC application no. 55721/07, 7 July 2011 and *Al-Jedda v. the United Kingdom*, ECtHR GC application no. 27021/08, judgment 7 July 2011.

Jean Cohen points out that occupation law can be read both from a humanitarian perspective and from a realist/Schmittian perspective.[64] The humanitarian reading starts with the notion of 'belligerent occupation' as it was developed in the Lieber Code during the American Civil War. On this reading, belligerent occupation was considered a humanitarian advance on the earlier 'right of conquest',[65] which ascribed full sovereignty over conquered territory. It was seen as a step towards the humanisation of war because it was a way of restraining the excesses of conquest and occupation and protecting the civilian population; indeed, it can be seen as part of the growing emphasis during the nineteenth century on the distinction between combatant and civilian, discussed in Chapter 6. This humanitarian version was further expanded after World War II when legal measures were sought to prevent the kind of brutal experiences (including deportations, mass rapes, mass killings, forced prostitution, detention, forced labour) of Nazi, Japanese and Soviet occupations. On the other hand, the realist reading suggests that occupation law developed as a way of protecting state sovereignty rather than the civilian population. According to this version, the task of the occupiers is to preserve order and conserve the *status quo*. The introduction of rights-based approaches or a notion of 'transformative occupation', as discussed below, can alternatively be seen as a manifestation of the Liberal Peace, the humanitarian reading of occupation or as a form of imperialist interference.[66]

Military occupation is the one instance where IHL continues to be applicable despite the asserted termination of military operations.[67] Contemporary occupation law is constructed by The Hague Regulations, [68]

64 See Cohen, Jean L. 2006/7. 'The Role of International Law in Post-Conflict Constitution-Making: Towards a *Jus Post Bellum* for "Interim Occupations"', *New York Law School Review* 51, 520–527.

65 In the post–UN Charter era occupation cannot give rise to legal title: 'No territorial acquisition resulting from the threat or use of force shall be recognized as legal'; Declaration on Principles of International Law concerning Friendly Relations and Co-operation among States in Accordance with the Charter of the United Nations, UN GA Resolution 2625 (XXV), 24 October 1970.

66 The notion of 'imperial' presence in occupation in Iraq is illustrated by the title in a journalist's account: Chandrasekaran, Rajiv 2007. *Imperial Life in the Emerald City: Inside Baghdad's Green Zone*. Bloomsbury.

67 Geneva Convention IV, article 6 makes it clear that there is 'no intermediate period between what might be termed the invasion phase and the inauguration of a stable regime of occupation'. *ICRC Commentary on the Geneva Conventions of 12 August 1949, Volume IV*.

68 *Laws and Customs of War on Land* (Hague IV), 18 October 1907, Annex to the Convention.

the Fourth Geneva Convention (Geneva IV), articles 47–78 and Additional Protocol I (AP I), supplemented by soft law instruments and customary international law.[69] The legal regime does not create the status of occupation – exercise of power does this – but imposes constraints and obligations upon the occupier in an attempted mitigation of naked military power. It is both permissive (recognising the exercise of powers by the occupier) and prohibitive (constraining the exercise of those powers)[70] by providing for minimum humanitarian standards for the protection of civilians.

The legal regime of occupation allows the occupier to ensure the security of its military presence and administration while maintaining the legal *status quo*.[71] Occupying forces have tasks that are more akin to policing the civilian population than to military campaigns, including quelling public disorder, but counter-insurgent and counter-terrorist operations may involve greater coercive force.[72] Powers that occupying forces may seek to engage include arrest and detention, disbanding assemblies in public places and media censorship. Questions abound such as: how much force may an occupier use in seeking to neutralise those suspected of resisting the occupation and ensuring public order? How is legitimate resistance to occupation distinguished from insurgency or terrorist activity, especially in light of any lack of definitive definition of terrorism in international law? May the occupier detain indefinitely and without trial those deemed to constitute a threat to public order? Alongside ensuring public order are other questions relating to the powers and responsibilities of an occupier, particularly one that has displaced an oppressive regime. Can the occupier depart from the legislative *status quo* for the benefit of the occupants through, for instance, the introduction of human rights standards? Some answers to these questions may be found in the application of two legal regimes alongside international humanitarian law and which are said to have 'transformed'

[69] ICRC, Customary International Law Database, www.icrc.org/customary-ihl/eng/docs/home.

[70] Roberts, *op. cit.*

[71] Article 43 of *The Hague Regulations* requires an occupier to 'take all the measures in his power to restore, and ensure, as far as possible, public order and safety, while respecting, unless absolutely prevented, the laws in force in the country'.

[72] E.g., the US and UK operation against insurgents in Fallujah, November–December 2004. See Kaldor, Mary 2012. *New and Old Wars: Organised Violence in a Global Era*. Polity Press, 3rd ed., chapter 7.

occupation law:[73] SC resolution and human rights law. These are discussed below in the context of Iraq.

In Iraq occupation law was modified by SC resolution.[74] Resolution 1483 recognised the 'specific authorities, responsibilities, and obligations under applicable international law' of the United States and United Kingdom as occupying powers, denoted the 'Authority' (CPA). On the basis of this the CPA vested in itself all legislative, executive and judicial authority necessary to achieve its objectives and thereafter adopted over 100 Orders and Regulations that constituted a sweeping reorganisation of Iraqi society, which far exceeded the conservationist principles of IHL and provided for the preferred legal order of the invader and occupier. This has been characterised as 'a new model of multilateral occupation, which merged the structures of belligerent occupation with elements of peacemaking under [UN Charter] chapter VII, in order to facilitate reconstruction under the umbrella of collective security'.[75] The SC in effect provided for parallel legal regimes: traditional occupation law and Council-authorised action, allowing for far-reaching measures of economic and social reconstruction, but creating the possibility of conflict between them.

The moral justification for such transformative powers remains that of the Liberal Peace – the human rights, rule of law and democracy mantra – despite its displacement by the fact of occupation. These values, in conjunction with an intuition that those that have intervened in another state should in some way seek to repair some of the harms, provide the ethical underpinnings for pursuit of transformative post-conflict policies. In the words of Michael Walzer: 'The argument about endings is similar to the argument about risk: once we have acted in ways that have significant negative consequences for other people … we cannot just walk away'.[76] Nevertheless this approach subjects occupation to the security agenda and power politics of the SC, to its double standards and currently to the counter-terrorism priority of the United States. Nor does it sit well with the fact of military force, occupation and violations of human rights by those forces. Indeed, the main consequence of the invasion was to speed up the collapse of the Iraqi state, already greatly

[73] Roberts, Adam 2006. 'Transformative Military Occupation: Applying the Laws of War and Human Rights', *American Journal of International Law* 100: 580–622; Fox, Gregory 2008. *Humanitarian Occupation*. Cambridge University Press.

[74] UN SC Resolution 1483, 22 May 2003.

[75] Stahn, *op. cit.*, 929 ('Jus ad bellum').

[76] Walzer, Michael 2004. *Arguing about War*. Yale University Press, 20.

weakened by years of war and sanctions. Together with the decisions to dismantle the Iraqi army[77] and to dismiss all public servants who were members of the Ba'ath party,[78] this set the scene for the new war of insurgency and the subsequent new war framed as a sectarian conflict between Sunnis excluded from public life and Shias. The continued weakness of the Iraqi state and armed forces was further illustrated by the speed with which IS occupied parts of the country in 2014.

The second legal regime is that of human rights. In Chapter 6 we discuss the applicability of human rights to armed conflict; as a continuation of military force, the same questions arise with respect to occupation. By definition an occupying state is acting outside its own territory. Human rights lawyers have sought to hold occupiers, notably the United Kingdom through its status as a party to the European Convention on Human Rights (ECHR), to their human rights obligations so that the question whether human rights treaties apply extraterritorially in occupied territory has become subject to repeated litigation in national courts, regional human rights courts and the ICJ. The following section discusses some of the issues raised.

In its advisory opinion on the Israeli security wall, the ICJ considered that Israel as the occupying power was bound by – and was in violation of – both the relevant IHL (primarily The Hague Regulations and Geneva IV) and human rights treaties (the International Covenant on Civil and Political Rights, 1966 (ICCPR), the International Covenant on Economic, Social and Cultural Rights, 1966 (ICESCR), the Convention on the Rights of the Child, 1989).[79] The Court stated that 'while the jurisdiction of States is primarily territorial, it may sometimes be exercised outside the national territory. . . . It would seem natural that, even when such is the case, States parties to the Covenant should be bound to comply with its provisions'.[80] The Court did not spell out how compliance with the human rights Covenants was to be achieved nor did it explain their interaction with occupation law. In the case of *Armed Activities on the Territory of the Congo* the Court found Uganda in 1998 to be in military occupation of the border regions of eastern Congo that lasted until its withdrawal in 2003. During this time Ugandan soldiers had perpetrated mass killings of civilians, committed acts of torture and inhumane

[77] Coalition Provisional Authority Order Number 2: Dissolution of Entities, 23 May 2003.
[78] Coalition Provisional Authority Order Number 1: De-Ba`athification of Iraqi Society, 16 May 2003.
[79] *The Wall* case, *op. cit.* [80] *Ibid.*, para. 109.

treatment, and had destroyed villages and civilian dwellings. These acts constituted violations of the right to life and of the prohibition against torture and cruel, inhuman or degrading treatment under the ICCPR and African Charter on Human and Peoples' Rights (1981) as well as of IHL.[81] In neither the *Wall* nor the *Ugandan* case did the ICJ question the extraterritorial applicability of the relevant human rights treaties to protect civilians who had come under the occupiers' jurisdiction.

The European Court of Human Rights (ECtHR) was presented with similar questions arising out of the United Kingdom's occupation of Iraq as a member of the CPA from May 2003 until June 2004. The United Kingdom was responsible for the southern sector. The case of *Al Skeini* involved a number of test cases brought on behalf of Iraqi civilians who were killed by UK soldiers during this period of occupation in varying circumstances.[82] Their relatives sought an independent and impartial enquiry into the incidents that had led to the deaths in accordance with the procedural requirements of the ECHR, articles 2 (right to life) and 3 (prohibition of torture) and which are more stringent than investigative requirements under IHL.[83] In arguing against the applicability of the ECHR, the UK government relied on the earlier case of *Bankovic*[84] where the ECtHR had held that the Convention was not applicable to deaths caused by the NATO aerial bombing during the military action in the Kosovo conflict. In *Al-Skeini*, the UK House of Lords held that an Iraqi hotel receptionist, Baha Mousa, who had died as a result of brutality inflicted by British troops whilst being held in UK military custody in Iraq, comes within the jurisdictional requirement of article 1 of the ECHR[85] and that his relatives could therefore claim Convention rights.[86] However, this did not extend to other Iraqi civilians whose deaths did not occur in custody, instead being shot at a road block, or in house searches or caught in crossfire. The European Court dismissed

[81] *Armed Activities on the Territory of the Congo* (*Democratic Republic of the Congo v. Uganda*), 2005 ICJ Reports 168, judgment of 19 December 2005, para. 219.

[82] *Al-Skeini v. UK*, *op. cit.*

[83] UN SC Resolution 2286, 3 May 2016: Protection of Civilians, however, '*Strongly urges* States to conduct, in an independent manner, full, prompt, impartial and effective investigations . . . of international humanitarian law'.

[84] *Bankovic v. Belgium*, ECtHR GC appl. no. 52207/99, 12 December 2001. See Chapter 6.

[85] *ECHR* article 1 sets out the jurisdictional scope of the Convention; 'The High Contracting Parties shall secure to everyone within their jurisdiction the rights and freedoms defined in Section I of this Convention'.

[86] *R. on the Application of Mazin Jumaa Gatteh Al-Skeini v. Ministry of Defence*, [2007] UKHL 26, 13 June 2007.

this narrow understanding of the jurisdictional scope of the ECHR. It held that while jurisdiction under the Convention is primarily territorial, extraterritorial jurisdiction arises in two generalised situations. First is the exercise of effective control over a person ('state agent authority and control',[87] for example, through taking the person into military custody).[88] The second is through lawful, or unlawful, military action by which the state exercises effective control over an area outside its own territory ('effective control over an area') bringing all people in this territory within its jurisdiction and making the ECHR applicable. This was the case with occupation even though Iraq is outside the so-called legal space of the Convention. The Court acknowledged that the events occurred during a period of endemic crime and violence, with serious breakdowns in the civilian infrastructure, including the law enforcement and criminal justice systems. Nevertheless the Court considered that the procedural obligation under article 2 (to investigate deaths in suspicious circumstances) 'continues to apply in difficult security conditions, including in a context of armed conflict'.[89] In particular such investigation must be independent of the military chain of command. To dispense with this procedural obligation would render less effective the right to life. Human rights law offers more than IHL. In the words of a Judge in the UK Court of Appeal:

> What is known as international humanitarian law imposes a number of unexceptional moral precepts on occupying forces . . . but it imposes none of the positive human rights obligations that are inherent in the European Convention on Human Rights (ECHR). It is a far cry from the complacency of 'You must not kill but need not strive officiously to keep alive' to the obligation imposed . . . by the case law on Articles 1 and 2 of the

[87] State agent authority and control also applies in particular situations – 'to the acts of diplomatic and consular agents present on foreign territory; to circumstances where a Contracting State, through custom, treaty or agreement, exercises executive public powers or carries out judicial or executive functions on the territory of another State'. Summary of *Al-Skeini* in *Chagos Islanders v. UK*, ECtHR application no. 35622/04, 11 December 2012, para. 70.

[88] In *Hassan v. UK*, ECtHR application no. 29750/09, 16 September 2014, the Grand Chamber ECtHR found that such physical control extended from the time of the arrest of the person from his family home through to the time of his release from Camp Bucca. Although the Camp was formally under the control of the United States, 'the United Kingdom retained authority and control over all aspects of the detention relevant to the applicant's complaints' (para. 78).

[89] *Al-Skeini v. UK*, *op. cit.*, para. 164.

> ECHR ('the High Contracting parties shall secure to everyone within their jurisdiction [their] right to life').[90]

In *Al Skeini* the European Court was unsympathetic to the argument that the United Kingdom lacked the troops to make security effective in South Iraq – a warning to states that if they undertake military occupation, they must comply with their obligations towards the citizens. Indeed, in a subsequent case the Court found an Iraqi civilian who was killed at a vehicle check point to be within the jurisdiction of the Netherlands, although that country was not part of the occupying force.[91] However, it should also be noted that human rights law applies to all persons within the territory without distinction as to their activities (for instance, combatant or non-combatant) or the legality of their presence. Thus settlers in the OPT would be able to claim human rights protections against occupying forces.[92]

The UN Human Rights Committee has explained the underlying policy for holding occupying forces to their human rights obligations: 'It would be unconscionable to so interpret the responsibility under article 2 of the [ICCPR] as to permit a State party to perpetrate violations of the Covenant on the territory of another State, which violations it could not perpetrate on its own territory'.[93] While this policy is evidently welcome in terms of protection of civilians subject to occupation, there are also some concerns, which come from different perspectives. First, which rights are applicable? In *Bankovic* the European Court held that the Convention could not be 'divided and tailored' in accordance with the particular circumstances of the extraterritorial act. It was to be applied in its entirety or not at all. This caused the UK Government in *Al Skeini* to question how, and even whether, certain rights could be applied. Human rights guarantees are a form of social engineering, and for an occupying power to introduce, for instance, freedom of religion, or non-discrimination into a territory where it is not sovereign and only temporarily present can be seen as a form of imperialism. The Court was

[90] Lord Justice Brooke in *R on the Application of Mazin Mumaa Galteh Al-Skeini and Others v. The Secretary of State for Defence*, [2005] EWCA Civ 1609.

[91] *Jaloud v. The Netherlands*, ECtHR application no. 47708/08, 20 November 2014.

[92] Dinstein, Yoram 2009. *The International Law of Belligerent Occupation*. Cambridge University Press; Gross, Aeyal 2007. 'Human Proportions: Are Human Rights the Emperor's New Clothes of the International Law of Occupation?', *European Journal of International Law* 18:1–35.

[93] *Burgos Lopez v. Uruguay*, UN Human Rights Committee, Merits, 29 July 1981, 68, *International Law Reports*, 29.

again unsympathetic. In the words of one Judge: 'It ill behoves a State that imposed its military imperialism over another sovereign State without the frailest imprimatur from the international community, to resent the charge of having exported human rights imperialism to the vanquished enemy. It is like wearing with conceit your badge of international law banditry, but then recoiling in shock at being suspected of human rights promotion'.[94] Nevertheless it has now been accepted that the occupying state is not required to guarantee all Convention rights, but only those with respect to which the case has been brought, typically the right to life, to be free from torture and from arbitrary detention.[95] However, since the occupying powers introduced other far-reaching and structural changes in Iraq, for instance de-Ba'athification, changes to the penal code, liberalisation of trade and licensing laws, the Court's response to their anxieties about human rights innovation remains valid.

There are other concerns especially with respect to long-term occupation such as that in the OPT (Israeli occupation since 1967) and the Western Sahara (occupied by Morocco since 1975). The ICJ has determined the ICESCR to be applicable in the OPT.[96] On the one hand implementation of Covenant obligations carries with it the danger of entrenching the occupation and supporting an argument that facts on the ground have changed the position; on the other hand, if these human rights obligations are not complied with and delivery of economic and social rights denied, the hardships of occupation for the population are exacerbated.

From another perspective it has been argued that upholding human rights obligations upon military forces – bringing civilian standards into military activities – and enforcing them through litigation imposes excessive and dangerous limitations upon them. Critiques of the judicialisation of conflict (or 'legal siege' 'legal encirclement', 'judicial creep', 'lawfare'[97] or even 'emasculation'[98]) have been furthered by the decision in *Smith v. MOD* in June 2013.[99] The UK Supreme Court held that the

[94] *Al-Skeini v. UK, op. cit.*, concurring opinion of Judge Bonello, para. 37.

[95] '[T]he Court has now accepted that Convention rights can be "divided and tailored"' (see *Al-Skeini and Others, op. cit.*, paras. 136–137); *Hirsi Jamaa and Others v. Italy*, ECtHR GC, application no. 27765/09, 23 February 2012, para. 74.

[96] The *Wall* case, para. 112.

[97] See further Chapter 6.

[98] Hansen, Michelle 2007. 'Preventing the Emasculation of Warfare: Halting the Expansion of Human Rights Law into Armed Conflict', *Military Law Review* 94: 1–65. Note 17 explains Hansen's choice of the word 'emasculation'.

[99] *Smith and Others v. MOD*, [2013] UKSC 41, 19 June 2013, para. 55 per Lord Hope.

ECHR (through its incorporation by the Human Rights Act 1998) was applicable to protect the rights (including the right to life) of soldiers in active service in Iraq. Lord Hope cited the Parliamentary Assembly of the Council of Europe that 'members of the armed forces cannot be expected to respect humanitarian law and human rights in their operations unless respect for human rights is guaranteed within the army ranks'. The incidents in question occurred in March 2003 (during the armed conflict in Iraq) and in 2005 (after the end of the occupation when UK troops remained in Iraq as part of the multinational force)[100] and accordingly the case is not directly relevant to occupation. However, the holding that the 'jurisdiction of the United Kingdom under article 1 of the Convention extends to securing the protection of article 2 to members of the armed forces when they are serving outside its territory' was based on that in *Al Skeini* and is therefore likely to be equally applicable to occupation.

The implications of this judgment have been greeted with dismay by some. Lord Mance, dissenting in the Supreme Court, said:

> a soldier might, even during the war, [or military actions in an occupation] complain that his or her equipment or training was inadequate and that it would be a breach of the state's . . . duties under the Human Rights Convention even to order him or her to go into combat with it. If domestic legislation compelled this, then the soldier could seek relief in the Strasbourg court – maybe even interim relief prohibiting the further use or giving of orders to use the allegedly defective equipment.[101]

This would impede military decision-making and activity. Others have argued that it undermines the agility and flexibility of the armed forces and puts 'judges at the very heart of the tactical battle'.[102] 'Rather than promoting the ethos that wins wars, the armed forces will, in effect, be forced to focus efforts on preserving evidence'. Uncertainty generated by the possibility of litigation 'constrains the ability of commanders to react, undermining their cooperation with allies and affecting the combat capability of the Services. Together, these weaken the defence of the realm. In the longer run, they are also a mortal threat to the culture and ethos of the military – which, unlike troop numbers, cannot easily be

[100] The multinational force was now in Iraq 'at the request of the incoming Interim Government of Iraq'; UN SC Resolution 1546, 8 June 2004.

[101] *Smith and Others v. MOD*, *op. cit.*, para. 131 per Lord Mance, dissenting.

[102] Tugendhat, Thomas and Croft, Laura 2013. *The Fog of Law: An Introduction to the Legal Erosion of British Fighting Power*. Policy Exchange.

reversed'.[103] It makes wars unwinnable, so the argument goes, prolongs conflict and thus enhances insecurity.

8.4 International Territorial Administration

International control over divided, disputed or violent territory is not new.[104] For the most part, however, earlier international mandates or trusteeships were carried out on behalf of the League of Nations or the United Nations by states or groups of states. The first years of the twenty-first century saw the most extensive powers granted by the SC to an international administrative authority[105] – full executive power on a temporary basis in Cambodia (UNTAC),[106] eastern Slavonia (UNTAES)[107] Kosovo (UNMIK)[108] and East Timor (UNTAET).[109] This bestowal of power differs from occupation in that it has the institutional authority of the SC; it is in effect a form of international protectorate. Its purpose was to provide security to civilians in the aftermath of widespread and horrific violence, and to assist in institution building, restoration of services, as well as the broader political and social transition to self-government. UNTAC was the most extensive and expensive operation ever launched by the UN following the Paris Peace Accords in October 1991; it lasted 18 months from March 1992 to September 1993, and in practice its role was much more supervisory than was originally intended. UNTAES was established to supervise the integration and demilitarisation of three Serb-held areas (eastern Slavonia, Baranja and western Sirmium) into Croatia after the end of the war in Bosnia. It lasted two years, January 1996–1998, and is widely considered a success. UNTAET was short-lived as the former Portuguese colony of East Timor that had been invaded and annexed by Indonesia in 1975[110] gained

103 *Ibid.*

104 Wilde, Ralph 2008. *International Territorial Administration: How Trusteeship and the Civilizing Mission Never Went Away*. Oxford University Press; Stahn, Carsten 2008. *The Law and Practice of International Territorial Administration: Versailles to Iraq and Beyond*. Cambridge University Press.

105 For a fuller description of international territorial administrations, see Caplan, Richard 2002. *A New Trusteeship: The International Administration of War-torn Territories*. Adelphi Series.

106 UN SC Resolution 745, 28 February 1992.

107 UN SC Resolution 1037, 15 January 1996.

108 UN SC Resolution 1244, 10 June 1999.

109 UN SC Resolution 1272, 25 October 1999.

110 Chinkin, Christine 1999. 'East Timor: A Failure of Decolonisation', *Australian Year Book of International Law* 20: 35–54.

independence as Timor Leste in May 2002. UNTAET was replaced by the UN Mission of Support to East Timor (UNMISET). UNMIK has been longer lasting, and although 'the democratically elected leaders' of Kosovo declared independence on 17 February 2008, SC Resolution 1244 remains in effect.[111] This section therefore concentrates on UNMIK.

The Special Representative of the Secretary-General (SRSG) in Kosovo 'enjoy[s] the maximum civilian executive powers envisaged and vested in him by the Security Council in its resolution 1244 (1999)'.[112] This civil authority worked alongside the international security presence (KFOR), also mandated by SC Resolution 1244,[113] in effect combining peacekeeping and peacebuilding.[114] The first Regulation adopted by UNMIK asserted that 'All legislative and executive authority with respect to Kosovo, including the administration of the judiciary, is vested in UNMIK and is exercised by the Special Representative of the Secretary-General'.[115] UNMIK's post-conflict tasks were immense: it had to 'govern an entire province and re-establish a functioning public sector in the midst of substantial destruction, communal devastation, and the exodus of the former regime'.[116] While KFOR was responsible for military security, UNMIK's policing responsibility entailed providing security for people in Kosovo against criminal activities and to conduct effective investigations into crimes.[117] This was a considerable assignment; in the supposed post-conflict phase of June 1999 following the end of the NATO bombing and when UNMIK deployed, the crime rate was 'at its highest'. The SRSG reported that 'The security problem in Kosovo is largely a result of the absence of law and order institutions and

[111] On 9 December 2008, UNMIK's responsibility with regard to police and justice in Kosovo ended with the European Union Rule of Law Mission in Kosovo (EULEX) assuming full operational control in the area of the rule of law. Statement made by the President of the United Nations Security Council, UN Doc. S/PRST/2008/44, 26 November 2008.

[112] Report of the Secretary-General on the United Nations Interim Administration Mission in Kosovo, UN Doc S/1999/779, 12 July 1999, para. 44.

[113] The Security Council 'Decides on the deployment in Kosovo, under United Nations auspices, of international civil and security presences, with appropriate equipment and personnel as required'; UN SC Resolution 1244, 10 June 1999, para. 5.

[114] See Chapter 9.

[115] UNMIK/ Reg./1999/1, 25 July 1999, On the Authority of the Interim Administration in Kosovo.

[116] Marshall, David and Inglis, Shelley 2003. 'The Disempowerment of Human Rights-Based Justice in the United Nations Mission in Kosovo', *Harvard Human Rights Journal* 16: 95–146.

[117] *S.C. v. UNMIK*, Kosovo Human Rights Advisory Panel, 02/09, 6 December 2012.

agencies. Many crimes and injustices cannot be properly pursued. Criminal gangs competing for control of scarce resources are already exploiting this void'.[118] During the initial phase of its mission the international police force was slow to deploy leaving UNMIK without a functioning police apparatus or specialised personnel to investigate crimes. Further, UNMIK had no control over the recruitment of international police officers, who often had insufficient experience in investigating crimes with an inter-ethnic aspect in a post-conflict context, and were assigned to UNMIK for short periods undermining any continuity.

The absence of law and order also affected the economic situation. Despite rapid economic growth, largely due to the international presence, and a stable currency linked to the euro, reports on the situation some years after the end of the conflict stated that the economic situation of individuals and their families had continued to deteriorate. They explained that there was very little domestic production, mainly because of legal disputes about ownership, especially in relation to Kosovo's main resource, the Trebča mine, and telecoms. The main external source of income, apart from foreign assistance, was remittances from the diaspora (which declined after the financial crisis). Unemployment was very high; among young people around 60 per cent, and there were concerns about the break-up of patriarchal rural households owing to the fall in remittances on which such families were dependent.[119] Service provision remained uncertain, and, even in Pristina, neither electricity nor water supply was continuous. Up to 2008, the international community was jointly responsible for major public enterprises like water, electricity and telecoms through the Kosovo Trust Agency, which UNMIK established. There have been corruption charges in the case of electricity and telecoms, but they have never resulted in convictions. A major problem has been the impunity of UNMIK and KFOR personnel as well as the lack of access for civil society.[120] In 2016 socioeconomic problems continue. [121]

[118] *Ibid.*, para. 6.

[119] European Stability Initiative, *Cutting the Lifeline. Migration, Families and the Future of Kosovo*, 18 September 2006.

[120] Amnesty International *Kosovo (Serbia): The UN in Kosovo – A Legacy of Impunity*, 8 November 2006.

[121] In 2015 the dispute about ownership of the Trebča mine continued, as well as other property disputes. The Secretary-General noted that 'further and longer-term efforts should be undertaken to improve the socioeconomic conditions in Kosovo'; Report of the Secretary-General on the United Nations Interim Administration Mission in Kosovo, UN Doc. S/2015, 303, 27 April 2015.

An illustrative story dating back to the beginning of UNMIK concerns Rexhep Luci, Kosovo's leading urban planner who launched an initiative called 'Vision for Pristina 2000–2005' at a workshop in the Grand Hotel. He expressed his determination to tackle illegal construction, which was threatening the historic centre of Pristina and producing many ugly and unsafe buildings. Teams of municipal staff and students were dispatched across Pristina with cameras documenting more than 2,000 cases of illegal construction. On his way home after the workshop, Luci was shot and killed. His murder has never been solved, and, even though many regulations on construction have been issued both by UNMIK and by the Kosovo authorities, these have not been implemented, and illegal construction continues to be rampant.[122]

Some argue that the problem was the priority given to inter-ethnic issues rather than individual human rights. According to Albin Kurti, the former student leader:

> There are no people in Kosovo. There are only different ethnicities. Multi-ethnicity is the concept with which the lenses of the international community are built. What in modernity were 'tribes', in post-modernity are 'ethnicities'. Since the year 1999 onwards, the approach as well as the starting point was ethnic. UNMIK identified, like in a terra nullus: Albanians, Serbs, Roma, Turks, Egyptians, Bosniaks, and Ashkalis. Therefore, it started from ethnic belonging, not from what is common, what is universal among people – not from their need for freedom, dignity, jobs, qualitative education, healthcare and social insurance.[123]

The model of UNMIK was that of the Liberal Peace, discussed in the following chapter, established through multilateral mandate, committed to 'overseeing the development of provisional democratic self-governing institutions to ensure conditions for a peaceful and normal life for all inhabitants of Kosovo'[124] and 'protecting and promoting human rights'.[125] However, it operated, especially in the early years, in a heavily securitised environment, where local institutions had collapsed, where extreme violence continued, the population traumatised and policing inadequate as described above. It dealt primarily with the criminalised ethnic leaders rather than with those who might have constituted a basis

[122] The story is reported in *Utopian Visions: Governance Failures in Kosovo's Capital*, European Stability Initiative, Discussion Paper 8 June 2006.

[123] Quoted in 'Transitional Justice in Kosovo', 28 May 2008, www. Newkosovareport.com.

[124] UN SC Resolution 1244, 10 June 1999, para. 10. [125] *Ibid.*, para. 11(j).

for overcoming sectarianism. UNMIK's powers were essentially those of a sovereign state, but without the checks and balances of a democratic state. Commission of human rights violations, including by UNMIK personnel, followed, causing concern to human rights bodies and NGOs. In other words, international territorial administration does not resolve continuing societal tensions and often fails to meet the need for security in so-called post-conflict contexts.

8.5 Local Rule with International Presence

Peace agreements provide for a range of post-conflict governance models, for instance, a consociational model as in Bosnia,[126] a unitary model as in Afghanistan,[127] or a temporary constitutional arrangement pending a referendum for independence as in South Sudan.[128] In all such cases provision is made for temporary assistance to local institutions from internationals, falling short of an international territorial administration but with an extensive mandate for, *inter alia*, security sector reform, institution and capacity building, disarmament, demobilisation and reintegration (DDR), economic reconstruction in accordance with market principles and the holding of elections. Such international peace operations may comprise both a security and a civil presence and may engage multiple agencies.

The fiction is maintained of the territorial integrity and political independence (sovereignty) of the state and that the political solution, including the presence of internationals, is with consent. At the same time the international presence is justified on the basis that although there has been a peace agreement, the situation still constitutes a threat to international peace and security. For example, SC Resolution 1031, 15 December 1995, adopted the day after the signing of the Dayton Peace Agreement in Paris, affirms the territorial integrity of all states in the former Yugoslavia, 'welcomes' the agreement or invitation of the parties to the presence of the Organisation for Security and Co-operation in Europe (OSCE, to organise elections), the Office of the High

126 See further Chapter 9.

127 *The Agreement on Provisional Arrangements in Afghanistan Pending the Re-Establishment of Permanent Government Institutions*, Bonn, 5 December 2001 (*Bonn Agreement*).

128 *Comprehensive Peace Agreement, between the Government of Sudan and the SPLM/SPLA*, agreed 31 December 2004, signed 9 January 2005.

Commissioner for Human Rights (OHCHR) and other bodies (to monitor the human rights situation), notes the parties' invitation for the presence of a multinational implementation force and authorises member states 'to take all necessary measures' (to ensure compliance with Annex 1-A of the Peace Agreement) and, 'following the request of the parties', endorses the establishment of an Office of the High Representative (OHR), as the 'final authority' on the civilian implementation of the Agreement. Similarly SC Resolution 1383, adopted in the wake of the Bonn Agreement[129] after the military action in Afghanistan in 2001 by the coalition of the willing, reaffirmed the SC's 'strong commitment to the sovereignty, independence, territorial integrity and national unity of Afghanistan'.[130] A few weeks later the Council mandated an International Security Force (ISAF) to assist the Afghan interim government to maintain security in Kabul and its surrounding areas. In this instance the conjunction of the Liberal Peace (epitomised by the peace agreement) and the War on Terror was made explicit: '*Supporting* international efforts to root out terrorism'.[131] Nevertheless there was always a tension between ISAF that was primarily concerned with stability and the US command Operation Enduring Freedom that was preoccupied with the defeat of terrorism. This tension persisted even after the merger of the two commands.

The Dayton Peace Agreement was brokered by a US mediator, Richard Holbrooke,[132] supported by the United States, far from Bosnia and with no local civil society presence. In this instance leaders of one of the warring factions were excluded (the Bosnian Serbs) because of indictments issued against Karadžić by the International Criminal Tribunal for former Yugoslavia (ICTY). President Milošević from Serbia (himself subsequently indicted by the ICTY during the conflict in Kosovo) was deemed able to negotiate on their behalf. It epitomises a 'top-down' conclusion to a war and state-building, including detailed constitutional arrangements in a foreign language. In 1997 the Peace Implementation Council increased the OHR's powers so he could resist attempts to prevent the implementation of Dayton, allowing him to adopt binding decisions when local parties were unable or unwilling to act and to remove from office public officials who were in violation of their legal

[129] Bonn Agreement, *op. cit.* [130] UN SC Resolution 1383, 6 December 2001.

[131] UN SC Resolution 1386, 20 December 2001.

[132] For Holbrooke's account of the negotiations see Holbrooke, Richard 1999. *To End a War*. Modern Library.

commitments or acting contrary to Dayton, although, in practice, the extent to which these powers were used varied for different holders of the office.[133] The OHR is unaccountable for his actions, except to the Peace Implementation Council.[134]

Human rights are embedded in such peace agreements and are the responsibility of both the local and international authorities. For instance, the Dayton Agreement annexes a number of human rights treaties and incorporates the ECHR into domestic law.[135] A Human Rights Chamber was established as a part of the Bosnian Human Rights Commission and was vested with the authority to issue decisions binding upon both the Republika Srpska (RS) and the Federation of Bosnia and Herzegovina, as well the state authorities of Bosnia- Herzegovina.[136] However, the tension with the War on Terror has interfered with their implementation, and local courts became subject to the pressures imposed by international powers and their political imperatives. In the notorious case of *Boumediene* the United States suspected six men (five were Bosnian and Algerian dual nationals) of terrorist activities, including a feared attack on the US embassy in Sarajevo. The Bosnian government detained them in 2001, and while in pre-trial custody they were stripped of their Bosnian citizenship, although in some cases this was subsequently restored.[137] They were tried in the local competent court

[133] E.g., in *Dušan Berić and Others v. Bosnia and Herzegovina*, ECtHR application no. 36357/04 and others, decision on admissibility, 16 October 2007, the applicants complained that they had been dismissed by the High Representative from all their public and political party positions and been indefinitely barred from holding any such positions and from running for election. The Court found the applications inadmissible.

[134] European Commission for Democracy through Law (the Venice Commission), *Opinion on the Constitutional Situation in Bosnia and Herzegovina and the Powers of the High Representative*, adopted at the Sixty-Second Session of the Venice Commission, CDL-AD (2005) 004: 'The main concern is however that the High Representative does not act as an independent court and that there is no possibility of appeal'.

[135] The Bonn Agreement also requires 'the Interim Authority and the Emergency Loya Jirga [to] act in accordance with basic principles and provisions contained in international instruments on human rights and international humanitarian law to which Afghanistan is a party'. See Bonn Agreement, *op. cit.*

[136] The Chamber had eight international judges, elected by the Committee of Ministers of the Council of Europe, and six Bosnian judges. Its mandate expired on 31 December 2003. After January 2004 the Constitutional Court has jurisdiction over human rights matters.

[137] Bosnian citizenship was acquired by each of the men sometime after 1995, in some instances on the basis of forged or otherwise unreliable documents; see *Boumediene and Others v. Bosnia and Herzegovina*, ECtHR application no. 38703/2006, and others, 18 November 2008, para. 2.

but released for lack of evidence. Immediately on release in January 2002, they were turned over to US intelligence officials in Sarajevo and transported to Guantánamo. The Human Rights Chamber of Bosnia-Herzegovina (to which the men had filed applications) found multiple violations of the ECHR and explicitly ruled that the government must take all steps to prevent their forcible deportation. In 2006 the Human Rights Commission within the Constitutional Court of Bosnia and Herzegovina (the legal successor to the Human Rights Chamber) criticised the Bosnian authorities for taking a 'particularly passive attitude' towards the entire matter. Eventually, following a case in the US Supreme Court that detainees and foreign nationals had access to federal courts to assert *habeas corpus* rights,[138] a US District Court judge ordered five of the Bosnians to be released based on insufficient evidence following his review of their cases. In 2009 the United States released the men. Three were flown to Bosnia to reunite in 'protective custody' with their families.

The handover of the men by the Bosnian authorities to the United States was against international law and the legal structures put in place by the Dayton Peace Agreement, which were intended to enhance security in Bosnia. In the words of Amnesty International:

> the decision by the Bosnian authorities to hand the men over to US custody ignores the Human Rights Chamber's order and undermines respect for this institution as well as adherence to international human rights law as prescribed by the Dayton Agreement . . . the blatant flouting of an order by the Chamber in this case sets a dangerous precedent which may have far-reaching consequences for future adherence to applicable national and international law and implementation of the Chamber's decisions.[139]

A case before the ECtHR alleging violations of the Convention with respect to the Bosnian government's disregard of its obligations arising out of domestic judicial decisions and its failure to take all possible steps to protect their basic rights was found inadmissible; the Court concluded that 'Bosnia and Herzegovina can be considered to be taking all possible steps to the present date to protect the basic rights of the applicants, as required by the domestic decisions in issue'.[140] The High Representative

138 *Boumediene v. Bush*, 553 USSC 723 (2008).

139 Amnesty International, Public Statement, Bosnia-Herzegovina: Letter to the US Ambassador Regarding Six Algerian Men, 18 January 2002, AI Index EUR 63/003/2002 – News Service Nr. 11.

140 *Boumediene and Others v. Bosnia and Herzegovina, op. cit.*, para. 67.

in Bosnia at the time – Wolfgang Petritsch – reportedly stated that the US officials had told him they would remove their support for the international mission he was leading if Bosnia did not comply with their request.[141]

The *Boumediene* case shows how the presence of internationals and formally agreed human rights guarantees, regarded as essential to a *post bellum* reconstruction, may not provide security where the objectives of the War on Terror conflict with and undermine the objectives of post-conflict judicial institution building. But perhaps even more significant in the Bosnia case is the top-down character of the international presence and the way in which, for the most part, successive holders of the OHR went with the grain of ethnic politics –something which will be discussed at greater length in the next chapter. Reports of the OHR to the SC have painted a dispiriting picture of political power struggles taking precedence over the pressing needs of citizens, the leadership of the Republika Srpska openly and directly disputing and questioning the existence of the State of Bosnia and Herzegovina, advocating its dissolution, denying the occurrence of genocide in Srebrenica in 1995[142] and undermining the rule of law.[143] As discussed further in the following chapter, Bosnia remains in a situation of neither war nor peace.

8.6 Gender Relations and Post-Conflict Governance

All three models of post-conflict governance impact upon gender relations although the overall picture is little researched. The variety of forms of military occupation makes generalisations difficult with much depending on the context of the occupation and personal circumstances of women. It is noticeable that the Committee on Elimination of Discrimination against Women does not comment on the role of the

[141] Quoted (in French) in Perelman, Marc. 'Sarajevo-Guantanamo: Témoins à Charge Contre Washington', *Rue 89*, 27 November 2007, http://rue89.nouvelobs.com/2007/11/27/sarajevo-guantanamo-temoins-a-charge-contre-washington.

[142] E.g., Forty-Second Report of the High Representative for Bosnia and Herzegovina, UN Doc. S/2012/813, 6 November 2012, paras. 23, 49; in May 2014 the High Representative noted that there had been a 'notable rise' in such statements including in December 2013 a public statement from the RS President of independence as a national goal; Forty-Fifth Report of the High Representative for Bosnia and Herzegovina, 9 May 2014, paras. 19–22.

[143] Forty-Seventh Report of the High Representative for Implementation of the Peace Agreement on Bosnia and Herzegovina to the Secretary-General of the United Nations, 11 May 2015, part VI: 'Entrenching the Rule of Law'.

international actors in its concluding observations to states where there is a significant international presence. Studies tend to focus on particular aspects, for instance, the response to wartime violence and continued impunity or the incidence of trafficking, rather than provide an overview of women's lives under occupation or international administration. This section considers some particular aspects of gender relations and how they impact upon women living under occupation; women and peacekeepers is discussed in Chapter 9.

In all such instances women have at least three relationships to navigate: those with the occupier, with local elites and their personal relationships. These operate within what the former special rapporteur on violence against women has described in the context of the OPT as an 'integrated system of violence' constructed by the militarism, fear and humiliation of occupation and the patriarchy of the local society.[144] She adds that the tools of occupation weaken women's negotiating power to challenge the patriarchal gender contract that has in part become a defence mechanism to keep the society intact and is linked to preserving national identity, which is the over-riding goal of all occupied peoples.

Gender relations with the occupier are likely to intersect with discriminatory behaviours associated with race, ethnicity or religion, as occupiers perceive occupied peoples as inferior to themselves – after all the latter have been defeated and their state institutions collapsed. At the same time, and in a pattern dating back to colonial interactions, the occupiers may see themselves as 'civilising' and as protecting women from their men within their own communities. Thus occupiers and internationals may use the language of rights, modernisation and liberation, but this is 'problematic, not because it is a façade or a lie but because rights and liberty are defined by those who are in power: the state, the occupiers'.[145] Further, the occupier defines the historical narrative. For instance, the US project for Iraqi or Afghan women was as though invasion and occupation freed these women and allowed them to emerge as from 'under a shell'. It ignored their history such as that of Iraqi women who, like women in many territories, resisted earlier occupations or colonisation

[144] Ertürk, Yakin, Report of the Special Rapporteur on Violence against Women, Its Causes and Consequences, Mission to Occupied Palestinian Territory, UN Doc. E/CN.4/2005/72/Add.4, 2 February 2005. The mission was before the election of Hamas in Gaza and the economic blockade.

[145] Shalhoub-Kevorkian, Nadera 2011. 'Counter-Narratives of Palestinian Women', in Ennaji and Sadiqi (eds.) *op. cit.*, 29–60, 40.

and despotic rule. This denial of histories has local consequences, for instance, allowing other Arab states to stigmatise the endeavour to liberate Iraqi women as a task taken from the agenda of Western imperialism.[146] But, of course, the same was also true of Soviet attempts to force women's rights and gender equality on Afghanistan during their occupation between 1979 and 1989. When the Soviets withdrew women lost the advances the Soviets had promoted, and a backlash was deliberately instituted against women's rights: 'In their politicized Islamicized notion of Afghan culture, if the Soviets were un-Islamic and had supported women's rights, then women's rights and anyone who supported them must be un-Islamic. Thus to [the fundamentalist mujahedin] returning Afghan women to their "traditional" place would aid in the creation of an Islamic Afghanistan', paving the way for the extreme Taliban's denial of women's rights. But both the Soviets and the subsequent Islamic groups ignored earlier histories of women in Afghanistan.[147] Women's rights become caught between the politics and ideologies of the occupier and the liberation goals of the occupied – including those of occupied women.

The roles of women *vis-à-vis* their own people in occupation also depend upon the social and political status of women in the occupied territory prior to occupation. For instance, in the Western Sahara nomadic traditions gave women greater freedoms than in other societies where Islam is the prevailing religion: 'While men travelled women controlled household finances and ran the community'.[148] This has played out in occupation with women engaging as activists and leaders of resistance, in many instances dating back to active roles during the fighting prior to the ceasefire in 1991 and imprisonment and torture by the Moroccan authorities. Today it is reported that the majority of protesters in the regular street demonstrations against occupation are women, who facilitate communication between activists across cities and towns, organise protests, work in clandestine journalism and collaborate with international human rights bodies.

Demonstrations are a form of resistance in public spaces, but research on occupation has also highlighted the importance of the home as a place

[146] Al-Ali, Nadje and Pratt, Nicola 2010. *What Kind of Liberation? Women and the Occupation of Iraq*. University of California Press.

[147] Brodsky, Anne 2011. 'Violence against Afghan Women: Tradition, Religion, Conflict and War', in Ennaji and Fatima, *op. cit.*, 115–138, 124.

[148] Morris, Loveday. 'Women on Frontline in Struggle for Western Sahara', *The Guardian*, 16 July 2013, www.theguardian.com/world/2013/jul/16/women-western-sahara-independence-morroco.

of active resistance, which may provide some privacy from the occupying forces. This is the case in the Western Sahara, where activists meet in homes and in a merger of public and private life much of women's social life centres around resistance; children too are brought into this strategy. An interviewee in a rare research project into women in the Western Sahara stated that her 'children will play out in the street and tell me if there is a car outside, if police have walked by, or if strangers were walking by more than usual. This is how we know if it is safe to meet'.[149] Similarly, a Palestinian researcher has explained that 'for Palestinian women the home becomes a site not just of personal growth but a space of political resistance in which to confront the dehumanizing forces of racist and sexist oppression and make demands for historical justice and ... a source of empowerment'.[150] But the very importance of the home in the context of militaristic oppression makes especially damaging for women the policy of house destruction in the OPT, thereby adding a significant gender dimension to the practice. The home is thus a contested place in occupation. On the one hand it is a place of security from government intrusion; on the other hand the special rapporteur on violence against women reports that domestic violence increases before and during a forced eviction, and women have to shoulder the burden of rebuilding the home, comforting traumatised children and losing privacy through having to seek shelter in the homes of other people. Further, she reports that women with husbands told her that the dire economic situation and the pressures of occupation have made men more violent because they can no longer provide and protect – two essential attributes of masculinity in a patriarchal society. She describes women as the 'shock absorbers of the crises as targets of domestic violence'.[151] Women are, of course, also subject to violence and harassment at the hands of the occupiers including at checkpoints and in detention.

8.7 Conclusion

In all three types of post-conflict governance, it is possible to identify a tension between the idea of war and the idea of human rights. The Iraqi example shows the way in which human rights claims could potentially

[149] Vasquez, Erica 2014. 'Living under Occupation in the Western Sahara: Women, Resistance and Self-Determination'. *Georgetown Institute for Women, Peace and Security, Research Paper Series No. 6.*

[150] Shalhoub-Kevorkian, *op. cit.*, 56.

[151] Ertürk, *op. cit.*

disrupt more status quo oriented forms of occupation. In the case of Bosnia and Herzegovina, it is the other way around; a Liberal Peace model of governance with built-in commitments to human rights has been overridden both by the requirements of the War on Terror and the power relations and divisions entrenched in peace agreements. And in the Kosovo example, the lack of capacity and the ambiguous post-conflict settlement undermined the effectiveness of the international administration in maintaining security and order and thus human rights.

A range of problems characterise the new forms of international presence. Some have to do with the multiplicity of agencies and the lack of appropriate resources; some have to do with mind-sets and short-term outlooks of international personnel; and some have to do with intractability of the situations that they are supposed to address. These will be further elaborated in the next chapter, which deals with the tasks carried out by the international community. In terms of the legal regimes discussed in this chapter, the fundamental tension between war and human rights is an expression of the underlying assumption that war is a discrete episode according to which different rules apply, and that post war contexts are temporary and provisional and will be followed by peace or non-war. Our argument is that what is termed 'post-conflict' is defined as what comes after an invasion or a peace agreement that is usually associated with an international presence. But this bears very little relation to the distinction between war and peace.

9

The Liberal Peace: Peacemaking, Peacekeeping and Peacebuilding

9.1 Introduction

Since 1989, a new and large part of *post bellum* law has been based on what has come to be known as the Liberal Peace model comprising commitments to democracy, the rule of law and human rights.[1] The model is also associated with standard neo-liberal recipes designed for the introduction or expansion of a free market economy. It encompasses *inter alia* regimes for political power-sharing, capacity building, security sector reform, legal reform, accountability (trials or other processes for perpetrators of war crimes and other atrocities) and economic reconstruction. According to Duffield, 'the idea of the *liberal peace* ... combines and conflates "liberal" (as in contemporary liberal economic and political tenets) with "peace" (the present policy predilection toward conflict resolution and societal reconstruction)'.[2] Others offer a more empirical definition of the Liberal Peace as 'the dominant form of peacemaking and peacebuilding favoured by leading states, international organisations, and international financial institutions'.[3]

In recent years the Liberal Peace model has come under a spate of criticism.[4] While the evidence suggests that the Liberal Peace operations

[1] The Document of the Copenhagen Meeting of the Conference on the Human Dimension of the Conference for Security and Cooperation in Europe (CSCE), 1990, set out the commitment to these values: 'The participating States express their conviction that full respect for human rights and fundamental freedoms and the development of societies based on pluralistic democracy and the rule of law are prerequisites for progress in setting up the lasting order of peace, security, justice and co-operation that they seek to establish in Europe'.

[2] Duffield, Mark 2001. *Global Governance and the New Wars: The Merging of Development and Security*. Zed Books, 11.

[3] MacGinty, Roger 2010. 'Hybrid Peace: The Interaction between Top-down and Bottom-up Peace', *Security Dialogue* 41(4): 391–412.

[4] For an overview, see Newman, Edward, Paris, Roland and Richmond, Oliver P. 2009. *New Perspectives on Liberal Peacebuilding*. United Nations University; also Chandler, David 2006. *Empire in Denial: The Politics of State-building*. Pluto Press; Duffield, *op. cit.* (*Global Governance*).

have been associated with the ending of overt conflict, however defined, at least some of the time,[5] most so-called *post bellum* regimes are characterised by continuing high levels of violence (crime, insurgency, human rights violations, trafficking, domestic violence), by continued dominance of wartime leaders,[6] high unemployment and inequalities, corruption and lack of justice and the risk of relapse into war should the international presence withdraw.[7] Indeed, two 2015 reports commissioned by the United Nations Secretary-General draw attention to the shortcomings of the peacebuilding agenda.[8]

In this chapter, we argue that key components of the Liberal Peace, particularly peacemaking and peacekeeping, are based on old-fashioned assumptions about the nature of war. Indeed, the very term *jus post bellum* is misleading;[9] it presupposes a Clausewitzean war as a contest of wills, which can only be ended through victory, defeat or mutual compromises between opposing sides. Not only are the terms peacemaking, peacekeeping and peacebuilding[10] conceptually confused,[11] since there are no distinct phases of conflict, they overlap and merge in practice. But perhaps more importantly, Liberal Peace is based on the idea of compromise between those responsible for the violence in which it is assumed that the opposing 'sides' can be monitored/tamed through peacekeeping and that warring parties who are ready to agree to a

[5] See Andersen, Louise Riis and Engedal, Peter 2013. 'Blue Helmets and Grey Zones: Do UN Multidimensional Peace Operations Work?' *DIIS Report* 2013(29), Danish Institute for International Studies; Call, Charles T. 2008. 'Knowing Peace When You See It: Setting Standards for Peacebuilding Success', *Civil Wars* 10(2): 173–194.

[6] Zaum, Dominik 2012. 'Beyond the "Liberal Peace"', *Global Governance* 18: 121–132.

[7] Andersen and Engedal, *op. cit.*; Newman *et al.*, *op. cit.*

[8] *United Nations Peacebuilding Commission, Challenge of Sustaining Peace: Report of the Advisory Group of Experts on the Review of the Peacebuilding Architecture*, UN Doc. A/69/968–S/2015/490, 30 June 2015 ('*Report on Peacebuilding Architecture*'); United Nations, *Report of the High-Level Independent Panel on Peace Operations on Uniting our Strengths for Peace: Politics, Partnership and People*, UN Doc. A/70/95–S/2015/446, 17 June 2015 ('*Report of the High-Level Independent* Panel').

[9] See Chapter 8.

[10] The terms peacemaking, peacekeeping and peacebuilding were defined in the Report of the Secretary-General Pursuant to the Statement Adopted by the Summit Meeting of the Security Council on 31 January 1992, *An Agenda for Peace Preventive Diplomacy, Peacemaking and Peacekeeping*, UN Doc. A/47/277–S/24111, 17 June 1992 ('*An Agenda for Peace*'); and the *Supplement to an Agenda for Peace, Position Paper of the Secretary-General on the Occasion of the Fiftieth Anniversary of the United Nations*, UN Doc. A/50/60-S/1995/1, 3 January 1995 ('*Supplement to an Agenda for Peace*').

[11] 'Discussions of peace operations are notorious for their conceptual muddles'. Diehl, Paul 2008. *Peace Operations*. Polity, 3.

settlement will be amenable to the mantra of international peacemakers of a post-conflict society built around democracy, human rights, free markets and the rule of law.

Or to put it another way, there is a fundamental contradiction between the peacemaking and peacekeeping parts of the Liberal Peace agenda, which are largely based on traditional Clausewitzean thinking, and the peacebuilding part of the agenda, which tends to focus on state-building (law and order, democracy, market economy). Peacemaking and peacekeeping could be described in the language of earlier chapters as typical of 'outside' approaches, namely the use of military force and/or diplomacy, while peacebuilding is more akin to 'inside' approaches – the rule of law and politics, but with outside intervention.

We argue that the root of the problem is the nature of the power relations established both as a consequence of conflict and because of the centrality of the international presence. The weaknesses of the Liberal Peace model cannot only be laid at the door of those international personnel that are responsible for implementing the Liberal Peace. Rather it has to do with the confluence of the global and the local and the way in which outsiders feed into, distort or accommodate the restructuring of power relations that takes place during conflict. A particular expression of this problem is the peace agreement or settlement, which, we argue, entrenches the power relations established through violence. We suggest that peacekeeping is designed to uphold peace agreements and remains within the discourse of war and conflict, while peacebuilding, quite apart from any flaws in the design of policies, faces insurmountable obstacles posed by the framework of peace agreements and peacekeeping.

In developing this argument, we make use of the example of Bosnia, although we also cite others. If Bosnia between 1992 and 1995 was the archetypal example of a 'new war', it has also become the laboratory of the post-conflict peacebuilding agenda. Large amounts of resources, including a permanent international presence both military and civilian, have been devoted to the reform process, and this has been augmented by the lure of membership in the European Union. Indeed, according to one estimate Bosnia-Herzegovina received six times more aid per head than western Europeans received under the Marshall Plan.[12] Yet Bosnia

[12] Barakat, Sultan and Zyck, Steven A. 2009. 'The Evolution of Post-War Recovery', *Third World Quarterly* 30(6): 1069–1086.

remains a dysfunctional society where the legacy of the war continues to affect everyday life and the potential for reigniting violence is never far from the surface.[13] As one commentator reported on a visit to the country, nearly twenty years after the Dayton Peace Agreement[14] that formally brought an end to the war in Bosnia: '[The] public discourse filling the radio waves for almost two hours sounded like the country I was driving through had just exited a war the day before ... or was about to enter a new one the day after ... locked in a horrible limbo that was neither war or peace'.[15] In 2016, over twenty years after Dayton, the international presence remains. Poverty and unemployment are high with the ensuing social problems. Bosnia is even more divided. Intermarriage between the ethnic groups is said to be 'far less common that it was before the war, and children in Bosnia's two constituent entities ... are now growing up with minimal contact with each other'.[16] In the words of another commentator, security following Dayton has only been maintained by 'backing the bully on the block'.[17]

This chapter covers the three main elements of the Liberal Peace – peacemaking, peacekeeping and peacebuilding. In the section on peacemaking, we draw attention to the problems of peace agreements and the way they reflect an old war mentality. We also discuss why it is so difficult to establish more inclusive, more bottom-up and more long-term peace processes. In the section on peacekeeping, we describe and discuss the role of international peace operations in upholding peace agreements and the way they tend to be captured by a military discourse. And in the section on peacebuilding, we investigate the main components of peacebuilding – elections and legitimate political authority, law

[13] The Office of the High Representative (OHR) regularly reports to the UN SC that 'officials of the ruling SNSD party in Republika Srpska continued their longstanding practice of directly questioning and challenging the sovereignty and territorial integrity of Bosnia and Herzegovina'. 47th Report of the High Representative for Implementation of the Peace Agreement on Bosnia and Herzegovina to the Secretary-General of the United Nations', S/2015/300, 29 April 2015, para. 22.

[14] *General Framework Agreement for Peace for Bosnia and Herzegovina,* Dayton, initialed 21 November 1995, signed at Paris, 14 December 1995.

[15] Latal, Srecko 2014. 'Neither War nor Peace in Bosnia', *Balkan Insight,* 27 January 2014, www.balkaninsight.com/en/blog/neither-war-nor-peace-in-bosnia. See also Vulliamy, (ed.) 2012. *The War Is Dead, Long Live the War: Bosnia: The Reckoning.* Bodley Head.

[16] Borger, Julian. 'Bosnian War 20 Years on: Peace Holds but Conflict Continues to Haunt', *The Guardian*, 4 April 2012.

[17] Vulliamy, *op. cit.*, xxxiii.

and order and security sector reform, and regulating the economy in order to illustrate how international efforts are undermined, first and foremost, as a consequence of the centrality of top-down peace agreements.

9.2 Peacemaking

Peacemaking comprises the processes for resolving disputes under UN Charter chapter VI;[18] it largely applies to concluding peace agreements, aimed at ending violence between the warring parties. Some of the arguments also apply to peace settlements after an outside military intervention such as the Bonn Agreement in Afghanistan or United Nations Security Council Resolution 1244 after the NATO intervention into Kosovo, both of which privileged the role of some of the warring parties.[19]

9.2.1 Peace Agreements

Since the 1980s there has been a historic upsurge in the conclusion of peace agreements.[20] According to the peace agreements data base some 646 'documents which could lay claim to the name peace agreement' were signed addressing 102 conflicts in eighty-five jurisdictions between 1990 and 2007.[21] Many of these agreements fail. A widely touted figure is that 50 per cent of peace agreements fail within five years; that is to say, conflict recurs within five years. Paul Collier and Anke Hoeffler have estimated that there is a 39 per cent risk that peace will collapse within five years and a 32 per cent risk that it will collapse in the next five

[18] '*Peacemaking* is action to bring hostile parties to agreement, essentially through such peaceful means as those foreseen in Chapter VI of the Charter of the United Nations'. *Agenda for Peace*, *op. cit.*, para. 20; see also *Report of the Panel on United Nations Peace Operations*, UN Doc. A/55/305–S/2000/809, 21 August 2000 (*Brahimi Report*) para. 11: Peacemaking 'addresses conflicts in progress, attempting to bring them to a halt, using the tools of diplomacy and mediation'.

[19] E.g., the departure of Serbian military, police and paramilitary forces from Kosovo pursuant to UN SC Resolution 1244, 10 June 2010, benefitted the KLA.

[20] Stedman, Stephen John, Rothschild, Donald S. and Cousens, Elizabeth M. 2002. *Ending Civil Wars: The Implementation of Peace Agreements*. Lynne Rienner Publishers; Bell, Christine 2004. *Peace Agreements and Human Rights*. Oxford University Press.

[21] Bell, Christine 2008. *On the Law of Peace: Peace Agreements and the Lex Pacificatoria*. Oxford University Press; the Ulster Transitional Justice Institute data base, www.transitionaljustice.ulster.ac.uk/peace_agreements_database.html.

years.[22] Notorious cases are the outbreak of violence in Angola in 1993, in which 350,000 people died, and the genocide in Rwanda in 1994, in which some 800,000 died; both followed previous peace agreements.[23] Nevertheless, it can be argued that the success in sustaining peace agreements in perhaps 50 per cent of the cases explains the decline in the number of conflicts traced by the Uppsala Conflict Data Base during the 1990s and early 2000s.[24]

Today's peace agreements are very different from the peace treaties that were characteristic of 'old wars'. In old wars, peace treaties were signed between the warring parties where the parties were states or entities similar to states (e.g., representatives of Native Americans and other indigenous persons).[25] It was assumed that the warring parties had the will and capacity to implement the agreements. Peace treaties laid down the rules that were to be followed to prevent a future war. In particular, since wars were often fought over differing views of the international order and the relationships between states, peace treaties provided, at least in theory, a structural framework for international order. As scholars have noted, the history of international law is largely about peace treaties, based almost entirely on Great Power interests and responsibility.[26] Since old wars often ended with victory and defeat, those treaties embodied victor's justice and entrenched the post-war hierarchy of international relations. For instance, although the UN has long embraced almost universal membership, article 4 of the Charter specifies that it is open to 'peace loving States', a formulation that in 1945 excluded the Axis powers. Likewise, the composition of the UN Security Council (SC) reflects the perceived hierarchy of power of that period.

[22] Collier, Paul 2006. 'Post-Conflict Economic Recovery', A paper for the International Peace Academy, Department of Economics, Oxford University.

[23] *Angola Peace Accords*, 1 May 1991 signed between the Government of the People's Republic of Angola and the National Union for the Total Independence of Angola (UNITA); *Arusha Peace Agreement*, 4 August 1993, signed between the government of Rwanda and the then-rebel Rwandan Patriotic Front.

[24] The Uppsala Conflict Data Program shows a decline in conflict up to 2008: Uppsala Department of Peace and Conflict Research, Uppsala Conflict Data Program, www.pcr.uu.se/research/UCDP/ . The data are used by the World Bank, the Human Security Report and the Stockholm International Peace Research Institute. The most recent report suggests that 2015 was the most lethal year for conflict since the end of the Cold War.

[25] E.g., *Treaty of Waitangi* (*TeTiriti o Waitangi*), 1840, between representatives of the British Crown and Māori.

[26] Simpson, Gerry 2004. *Great Powers and Outlaw States*. Cambridge University Press.

It can be argued that too often peace processes seeking to reach agreement,[27] or at least a 'roadmap' to guide subsequent negotiations, represent old war thinking imposed on new war settings. Stedman says that in the 1980s, when the practice of contemporary peace agreements gathered pace, the main preoccupation was bringing the parties to the table. It was assumed that 'a contract between state and insurgent leaders would remain binding in the post-agreements phase'. There was also a tendency to conceive of conflict resolution in a linear fashion, where successful negotiation signalled an irreversible reduction in conflict'.[28] The new wars of the 1990s challenged these linear assumptions, with violence diminishing and again erupting in irregular patterns.

Peace agreements take the form of a legalistic document like a treaty,[29] but they often fail to represent prevailing norms of domestic or international law since they endorse unfair rules such as ethnic partition; in the attempt to stop the violence what they do is to establish rules designed to entrench the power of the warring parties, where these parties are not states but rather predatory and/or extremist networks. Another way to describe them is as mafia-type truces that are awarded a veneer of legality by international mediators, a legality that is furthered though adoption by the SC. If we understand new wars less as a contest of wills by well-organised hierarchical fighting groups and more as a kind of mutual enterprise among loosely organised networks that have an interest not in winning but in the economic and political gains to be achieved from fighting,[30] then 'successful' agreements translate the gains from violence into permanent positions of power, making possible continued predation and the ever present possibility of a return to war.

Bell argues that peace treaties are a mixture of international law and domestic constitutionalism.[31] On the one hand, they take the form of a treaty between collectivities and usually involve an important role for the international (or regional) community in mediation, supervision and implementation. On the other hand, they lay down the rules – even

[27] Ramcharan, Bertrand 2009. 'Peace Process', in Chetail, Vincent (ed.) 2009. *Post-Conflict Peacebuilding: A Lexicon*. Oxford University Press, 228–242.

[28] Stedman *et al., op. cit., 2*.

[29] For a discussion of the legal status of a peace agreement see Bell, Christine 2006. 'Peace Agreements: Their Nature and Legal Status', *American Journal of International Law* 100 (2): 373–412.

[30] Keen, David 2012. *Useful Enemies: When Waging Wars Is More Important than Winning Them*. Yale University Press.

[31] Bell, *op. cit.* (*On the Law of Peace*).

constitutional requirements – for how domestic politics are to be conducted and resources allocated. Yet unlike domestic constitutional settlements, these are not inclusive agreements, as we discuss below; they primarily include the warring parties since they are the groups that have to be persuaded to stop fighting. But in new wars, the warring parties frequently represent extremist positions that are often politically marginal in terms of society as a whole, and/or those seeking to maintain control over resources. As the Report of the Advisory Group on Peacebuilding Architecture put it: 'In many situations of relapse, the leaders around whom peace agreements were framed turned out to have no sense of mutual purpose with broader society beyond their narrow self and group interests'.[32] Indeed, the Report goes on to suggest that many problems stem from the 'often overwhelming focus of peace efforts on the protagonists or individuals who bear arms, diminishing the attention given to the rest of society'.[33]

As a consequence, the rules enshrined in peace agreements lay down certain guarantees of political power for the warring parties that may directly contradict the possibilities for a rule of law and therefore a sustainable peace. In the rule of law literature a distinction is drawn between rule of law and rule by law.[34] In rule by law situations, the rulers do not feel bound by the law in contrast to rule of law where everyone is subject to the law.[35] Essentially, peace agreements could be said to be documents where, for the most part, those representing and acting in the name of the international community endorse a rule by law – a situation in which the previous warring parties are not bound by the same rules as everyone else. What constitutes a successful peace agreement is

[32] *Report on Peacebuilding Architecture*, *op. cit.*, para. 85. [33] *Ibid.*, para. 86.

[34] Samuels, Kirsti 2006. 'Rule of Law Reform in Post-conflict Countries: Operational Initiatives and Lessons Learnt', in *Social Development Papers: Conflict Prevention and Reconstruction*, Paper No. 37. See also Rangelov, Iavor 2014. *Nationalism and the Rule of Law: Lessons from the Balkans and Beyond*. Cambridge University Press.

[35] The UN Secretary-General has defined the rule of law as 'a principle of governance in which all persons, institutions and entities, public and private, including the State itself, are accountable to laws that are publicly promulgated, equally enforced and independently adjudicated, and which are consistent with international human rights standards and norms'. Report of the Secretary-General, The Rule of Law and Transitional Justice in Conflict and Post-Conflict Societies, UN Doc. S/2004/616, 23 August 2004, para. 6. Rajagopal has, however, pointed to the political agenda of the rule of law arguing it has come to mean 'those institutions that are important for the creation and operation of an ideal-type free market and *nothing more*'. Rajagopal, Balakrishnan 2008. 'Invoking the Rule of Law in Post-Conflict Rebuilding: A Critical Examination', *William and Mary Law Review* 49: 1347–1376, 1363.

problematic; one evident criterion is not whether they lead to a rule of law but whether conflicts recur. But it is difficult to separate these two notions since the absence of a rule of law provides a context for the survival of predatory networks which may, from time to time, re-engage in war or at least some form of violence.

Bell analyses peace agreements as by and large comprising three main components: the cessation of hostilities; the disaggregation of power; and international supervision. She suggests that peace agreements can be characterised as a combination of 'power sharing and fuzzy [fluid, ambiguous or attenuated] sovereignty'.[36] It is the rules about disaggregation of power that build into peace agreements huge obstacles to effective or even democratic governance and a rule of law. Essentially this usually involves some kind of power sharing (for instance, between ethnic and/or religious groups) in relation to both politics and security. This power sharing may be based on electoral quotas, on territorial or functional divisions, for instance, the sharing out of ministerial portfolios. Thus the Dayton Peace Agreement established an immensely complicated administrative hierarchy and territorial division involving fourteen governments: a somewhat weak central state of Bosnia and Herzegovina; two Entities (Republika Srpska and the Federation of Bosnia and Herzegovina); within the Federation ten cantons; and an internationally administered district, Brčko. This complex system was designed to ensure that ethnic nationalists had natural territorial constituencies – the Serb entity and the separate Croat and Muslim cantons as well as two mixed cantons within the Federation.[37]

The Oslo Accords relating to the Israel-Palestine conflict are similarly complicated, involving territorial divisions and power sharing. Oslo I[38]

[36] Bell, *op. cit.*, 117, 381 (*On the Law of Peace*).

[37] To ensure that this arrangement was permanent, the House of Representatives for the State, based on election by the population, was balanced by the House of Peoples consisting of fifteen members (five from each of the three constituent peoples: Serb, Croat and Muslim/Bosniak). The Presidency of the state is also composed of three representatives, one from each of the constituent peoples. Only members of each of the ethnic groups could originally vote for their own ethnic representatives in the House of Peoples or the Presidency and each ethnicity could in principle exercise a veto right over any issue that it considers threatening to its 'vital interests'. The Constitutional Court has nine judges: four selected by the House of Representatives of the Federation, two from the National Assembly of RS and three selected by the ECtHR in consultation with the Presidency.

[38] *Declaration of Principles on Interim Self-Government Arrangements,* 13 September 1993.

was followed by Oslo II in 1995.[39] The Accords allowed for some degree of Palestinian self-government, but for implementation Oslo II divided Palestinian territory into three categories known as A, B and C. In Areas A, mostly Palestinian towns in the West Bank and Gaza, Palestinians were given control; in Areas B, civilian authority was ceded to the Palestinian Authority but Israel retained security control; and in Areas C (comprising 60 per cent of Palestinian territory including all Israeli settlements, the Jordan valley and all major roads and transportation routes) Israel retained full control. The result (exacerbated by the continued building of illegal settlements and roads connecting them) is a large number of disconnected enclaves making everyday life for Palestinians hugely difficult with long waits at numerous checkpoints to travel anywhere and establishing an emasculated and ultimately dysfunctional Palestinian Authority.[40] Essentially the Accords represent the codification of a continuing conflict, which benefit some elites on both sides, but which make the prospect of sustainable peace even more elusive.

Other agreements involve the sharing out of functional responsibilities. Thus the Good Friday Agreement or Belfast Agreement in Northern Ireland,[41] which actually comprises two agreements – one among the Northern Ireland political parties and one between Ireland and the United Kingdom – involves cross-community voting on certain issues, particularly security and justice, and a sharing out of ministerial portfolios. The Lomé Agreement of 1999,[42] which was supposed to bring an end to the conflict in Sierra Leone, also involved a sharing out of portfolios; in particular the rebel leader Foday Sankoh was offered the chairmanship of the Commission for the Management of Strategic Resources, National Reconstruction, and Development (article V), with the status of Vice President, answerable to the President. The Good Friday Agreement has lasted and has transformed the main armed groups into political parties; nevertheless the Agreement has also cemented the divisions constructed through the conflict between Protestant and Catholic communities, and

[39] *Israeli-Palestinian Negotiations: Interim Agreement on the West Bank and the Gaza Strip*, 28 September 1995.

[40] Israel withdrew from Gaza in 2005 but by imposing an economic blockade in 2007, as well as making frequent military incursions, Gaza has become effectively closed in a dangerous Islamist-controlled enclave. In 2014 a Palestinian Unity Government was agreed between Fatah and Hamas.

[41] *Good Friday Agreement*, Belfast, 10 April 1998.

[42] *Peace Agreement between the Government of Sierra Leone and the Revolutionary United Front of Sierra Leone*, Lomé, Togo, 7 July 1999 (the Lomé Peace Accord).

sporadic violence continues and could worsen after Brexit. In contrast, the Lomé Agreement broke down within six months; further extreme violence ensued, which only ended with the intervention by British troops in 2001.

The significance of international supervision is more ambiguous. In many peace agreements, for instance Dayton, it is the international community that insists on incorporating human rights provisions. In the case of Bosnia, the OHR intervened, often quite robustly, to strengthen the role of the state as opposed to the Entities or the Cantons and to ensure the implementation of human rights, including refugee return, property rights and judicial reform. On the other hand, the international community also tends to condone (and by implication uphold) the disaggregation of power either in order to preserve the agreement, which is seen as essential in preventing a recurrence of conflict, or because the international community itself is not solely motivated by humanitarian or peace concerns and takes into account geo-political considerations. Thus in the case of Israel and Palestine, the Quartet composed of the United Nations, the United States, the EU and Russia, which is tasked to take the peace process forward, is often more preoccupied with Israeli state security than with the individual security of Palestinians, or indeed of Israelis. In Afghanistan, the Bonn process, which was intended to establish a legitimate political authority for Afghanistan, was hijacked by warlords who had been former commanders. They were able to do this because the United States relied on their co-operation in continuing the hunt for Osama Bin Laden and pursuing the War on Terror.[43]

A good example of 'old war' assumptions about peace agreements is the critique put forward by Christopher McCrudden and Brendan O'Leary of the decision by the European Court of Human Rights (ECtHR) in 2009 that the Dayton Peace Agreement violated human rights.[44] Two Bosnian citizens – Dervo Sejdić, a Roma and Jacob Finci, a Jew – challenged the constitutional provisions that only persons declaring affiliation with one of the three 'constituent peoples' can stand for election to the House of the Peoples or the Presidency. The ECtHR declared in their favour by fourteen votes to three.[45]

[43] See Rangelov, Iavor and Theros, Marika 2012. 'Abuse of Power and Conflict Persistence in Afghanistan', *Conflict, Security and Development* 12(3): 227–248.

[44] McCrudden, Christopher and O'Leary, Brendan 2013. 'Courts and Consociations, or How Human Rights Courts May De-stabilize Power-Sharing Settlements', *European Journal of International Law* 24(2): 477–501.

[45] *Sejdić and Finci v. Bosnia and Herzegovina*, ECtHR GC, application nos. 27796/06 and 34836/06, 22 December 2009.

The most important argument made by McCrudden and O'Leary is that the Court 'essentially avoided considering whether achieving peace between the groups in conflict after a vicious civil war continued to be a legitimate purpose'.[46] They suggest that the Court should have taken more heed of the Bosnian government's position that the decision risked 'unravelling' the inter-ethnic bargain reached at Dayton and plunging Bosnia back into civil war. While they concede that there may be agents in the current Bosnian government who have disincentives to change the system, this argument is based on the implicit assumption that the Bosnian government, and indeed the local participants in the Dayton process, represent the Bosnian people, or at least their 'groups'. 'If the parties to negotiations cannot agree on difference-blind rules, it may not be because they are illiberal, or contemptuous of human rights provisions or lacking in knowledge of alternatives, but rather because they are existentially anxious about the future of their groups and see no reason to trust cosmopolitan rules to protect them from their equally anxious co-negotiators'.[47] In other words they assume that the war was a contest of wills representing large parts of Bosnian society.

But what if it is just the opposite? We know that the parties to the negotiations had undertaken ethnic cleansing and massive human rights violations. We know that the strict division into three constituent peoples was an outcome of the war; before the war some 25 per cent of the Bosnian population were intermarried and more Bosnians than anywhere else in the former Yugoslavia declared themselves as Yugoslavs. What if the various warring parties were rather marginal groups aiming to shore up their ethnic and economic positions? If this is the case, then perhaps the parties to the negotiations were existentially anxious about their own individual futures in a more liberal set of constitutional arrangements.

As a consequence of the Court's decision, the EU halted the ratification of the Stabilisation and Association Agreement (SAA) between Bosnia and Herzegovina and the EU, the precondition for membership, and insisted that amendments to the Constitution be adopted so as to comply with the ECtHR decision. In December 2014 the EU Council modified its position by no longer requiring the Constitution to be amended prior to the initiation of further steps towards EU accession. The European Court's decision must still be implemented, but this may be done later

[46] McCrudden and O'Leary, *op. cit.*, 491–492. [47] *Ibid.*, 493.

in the accession process. Nevertheless, the lack of a credible process for the harmonisation of the Constitution with the European Court of Human Rights decision of December 2009 in the *Sejdić and Finci* case remains, as of 2016, an issue of serious concern.[48]

The fundamental assumption made by McCrudden and O'Leary is that the war in Bosnia took the form of an 'old war' – a contest of wills between organised, coherent and legitimate groups. But if we understand the war instead as a sort of mutual enterprise in which predatory networks construct and maintain ethnic hatred through massive human rights violations as a means of gaining access to power, then the Dayton Agreement, far from being a mechanism to guarantee peace, has to be understood as a way of formalising the power of these predatory networks. Any human rights challenge, on this interpretation, is more likely to contribute to peace.

9.2.2 *Participation in Peace Agreements*

Peace processes are top-down affairs, negotiated through a team of international (or regional) mediators between the delegations from the warring parties, often at some place far removed from the conflict zone.[49] Other participants may be the representatives of 'contact groups' – states that have an interest in the conflict, consider they may contribute in some way to the process or seek to ensure that any agreement does not impinge upon their interests. Conspicuously absent in many instances are members of local communities.[50] In response to some of the problems described above, there have been moves to make the process and subsequent efforts at reconstruction more inclusive of civil society.[51] 'Local ownership' is considered valuable for a peace agreement and lends

[48] Quoted in Vettori, Emilio 2013. 'EU Conditionality on Nationality Sensitive Matters in Bosnia and Herzegovina: Promoting Democracy or Maintaining the Status Quo', *European Diversity and Autonomy Papers* 5, 23. See also European Commission, Press Release, Bosnia-Herzegovina. EU: Deep Disappointment on *Sejdić-Finci* implementation, 18 February 2014, http://europa.eu/rapid/press-release_MEMO-14-117_en.htm.

[49] International control of peace processes can also be viewed as neo-colonialism; Bhuta, Nehal 2010. 'New Modes and Orders: The Difficulties of a *Jus Post Bellum* of Constitutional Transformation', *University of Toronto Law Journal* 60(3): 799–854.

[50] Thania, Pfaffenholz and Kew, Darren and Wanis-St. John, Anthony 2006. 'Civil Society and Peace Negotiations: Why, Whether and How They Could Be Involved', *Oslo Forum* 6, 67–76.

[51] Report of the Secretary-General, *Peacebuilding in the Aftermath of Conflict*, UN Doc. A/69/399–S/2014/694, 23 September 2014, para. 27ff.

legitimacy to deliberations about the ensuing constitution. In the words of the Secretary-General '[w]here peacebuilding efforts are rooted in inclusive societal consultation and efforts to minimize exclusionary practices, they generate trust and legitimacy in the State and its institutions'. In contrast exclusion 'too often contributes to violent contestation for control of the State'.[52] Likewise the Report on Peacebuilding Architecture calls for 'inclusive national ownership. . . . This implies participation by community groups, women's platforms and representatives, young people, labour organisations, political parties, the private sector and national civil society including underrepresented groups'.[53]

The issues of inclusion have been especially raised in the context of recognising the importance of women participating in peace processes. UN SC Resolution 1325, adopted in 2000, urged member states 'to ensure increased representation of women at all decision-making levels . . . for the prevention, management, and resolution of conflict'. In addition, Resolution 1325 sought the inclusion of a gender perspective in the substantive contents of peace agreements.[54] In 2015 the SC again took up the issue, urging member states to 'ensure increased representation of women at all decision-making levels in national, regional and international institutions and mechanisms for the prevention, and resolution of conflict' and encouraged 'those supporting peace processes to facilitate women's meaningful inclusion in negotiating parties' delegations to peace talks'.[55]

In new wars, civil society groups, especially women, often play an active role. Those engaged in pro-democracy protests that in many cases precede the war[56] (e.g., Bosnia, Libya, Syria and Ukraine) frequently establish themselves as civil society groups during the war – providing humanitarian assistance, mediating among warring groups, protecting historic and cultural buildings, documenting war crimes and so on. Typically such groups describe themselves as being concerned with the public interest as opposed to private or sectarian interest.[57] The argument for including civil society groups has to do with understanding the importance of process. The traditional model of peace agreements is a

[52] *Ibid.*, para. 28. [53] *Report on Peacebuilding Architecture*, *op. cit.*, para. 34.

[54] UN SC Resolution 1325, para. 8: '*Calls on* all actors involved, when negotiating and implementing peace agreements, to adopt a gender perspective'.

[55] UN SC Resolution 2242, 13 October 2015, para. 1. [56] See Chapter 1.

[57] Kaldor, Mary and Theros, Marika 2011. *Building Afghan Peace from the Ground Up*. A Century Foundation Report, The Century Foundation.

linear model in which the sides agree to take part and the potential outlines of an agreement are already established before the talks begin. Civil society groups, and especially women's groups, are able to shift the dynamics[58] and change the conversation, seeking to emphasise the importance of everyday life and of shared societal interests. They can put a wider range of issues on the table, and they appeal to public conscience. They can help to identify 'a common ground between opposing views and visions; to re-frame either/or questions to more creative and inclusive approaches'.[59] Their background and activities during the conflict give them a much deeper understanding of its context than the external international negotiators and they are able to use that knowledge to challenge the positions of the warring parties in a way that is more difficult for the internationals. If peace agreements are about codifying power relations, then the presence of civil society groups can potentially shift the composition and accountability of power relations.

The role of women is particularly important. Indeed, the omission of women – and other local civil society groups – from formal negotiating roles in peace processes[60] further reinforces the power structures established during conflict and excludes them from contributing to planning for the future. Conflict is gendered, and women's experiences of conflict are different from those of men (and vary between women according to their own circumstances and the context of the conflict). It seems illogical to premise the possibilities of peace without taking into account the widest possible range of views, capabilities and lived-knowledge of the local situation. Women's participation rests upon pragmatic understandings about how best to move forward. As the Report on Peacebuilding Architecture puts it: 'Too often, no space is afforded for social conversations about the deep-seated causes of the conflict and the collective aspirations for building a more harmonious nation (a criticism particularly levelled from the perspective of women organizing for peace)'.[61] It is also a matter of justice and a simple application of women's equal right to

[58] UN Women 2015. *Preventing Conflict, Transforming Justice, Securing the Peace: A Global Study on the Implementation of Security Council Resolution 1325* ('Study on 1325'). New York, 42.

[59] Herbolzheimer, Kristian 2011. 'Muslim Women in Peace Processes: Reflections for Dialogue in Mindanao', *Conciliation Resources Discussion Paper*, 2.

[60] In other roles in peace processes, such as politicians, lawyers and diplomats, women also remain under-represented, but the gap is decreasing; *Ibid.*

[61] *Report on Peacebuilding Architecture*, *op. cit.*, para. 86.

participation under articles 7 and 8 of the 1979 Convention on Elimination of All Forms of Discrimination against Women.

Despite these advantages, the participation of civil society groups and of women is very low. One analysis suggests some level or form of civil society involvement in approximately one-third of peace processes.[62] For instance, Nelson has estimated that only some 34 per cent of eighty-three peace agreements after the end of the Cold War have included at least one civil society actor.[63] Nine years after Resolution 1325, the SC expressed its deep concern about the 'under-representation of women at all stages of peace processes, particularly the very low numbers of women in formal roles in mediation processes'.[64] UN Women reported in 2012 that out of thirty-one peace processes conducted between 1992 and 2011, women comprised '4 per cent of signatories, 2.4 per cent of chief mediators, 3.7 per cent of witnesses and 9 per cent of negotiators'.[65] In 2015 the Global Study on the implementation of Resolution 1325 found some improvement in participation, although it also described this progress as 'inching upwards'. The Study cited peace processes in Colombia and the Philippines as having included greater participation by women.[66]

There are many explanations for this lack of inclusivity. 'Local ownership' is difficult to achieve, and despite the Secretary-General's words, there is no necessary correlation between participation by local representatives and wider public acceptability.[67] Disadvantages to local representation must also be recognised; for instance, local representatives may be divided, co-opted or sidelined,[68] and there is a view, especially among practitioners, that inclusion of civil society complicates the process and makes agreement harder to achieve.[69] Civil society groups in general are

[62] Pfaffenholz, Thania 2014. 'Civil Society and Peace Negotiations: Beyond the Inclusion-Exclusion Dichotomy', *Negotiation Journal* 30: 69–91, 74.

[63] Nelson, Desiree 2012. 'Anchoring the Peace: Civil Society Actors in Peace Accords and Durable Peace'. *International Interactions* 38(2): 243–266.

[64] UN SC Resolution 1889, 5 October 2009.

[65] UN Women 2012. *Women's Participation in Peace Negotiations: Connections between Presence and Influence*. New York, 2nd ed.

[66] Report on 1325, *op. cit.*, 45.

[67] Hay, Emily 2014. 'International(ized) Constitutions and Peacebuilding', *Leiden Journal of International Law* 27: 141–168, 154. The author gives the example of the Eritrean Constitution, which was highly participatory in its drafting but widely ignored by the government.

[68] Pfaffenholz *et al., op. cit.*, 67.

[69] Jan Melisson, for example, writes that 'old school diplomats' are sceptical of what is known as public diplomacy involving civil society though they rarely say so publicly, and he suggests that they 'do have a case' where bilateral relationships with, say authoritarian

typically not considered relevant to ending the violence because they do not engage in violence or they have not been elected; they may be treated as idealistic but powerless, and gendered language is often used to describe them. In many instances women have a subordinate social status in the conflict zone, and there is a widely held perception that the subject matter of peace agreements is not 'women's business'.[70] The complexity of conflicts and processes, including their fragmentation and splintering, the unpredictability of follow-up steps, changing personnel and evolution of multiple agreements all work against the inclusion of civil society groups that simply have neither the time nor resources for such uncertain enterprises. Further, their security may be at risk. International mediator(s) may be unsympathetic or even obstructionist to the inclusion of women; where women formulate their concerns in 'track-two' processes, their insertion into the formal, 'track-one' process is likely to be dependent on the mediator's willingness to accept them.[71]

Where peace agreements are more inclusive, the evidence does suggest that they are more long-lasting. In a quantitative study, Desiree Nelson shows that the inclusion of civil society is correlated with the durability of peace agreements. If one takes into account the inclusion of political parties, and whether the state was previously non-democratic, that correlation is even stronger.[72] Similarly, the Global Study on Resolution 1325 reported in 2015 on empirical evidence that inclusion of women enhances the sustainability of peace agreements.[73]

One model for women's inclusion is that of the Darfur peace process (2004–2005) where women were represented in the formal peace panels and

states, leave 'relatively little room for enagagement with civil society'. Melissen, Jan. 2013, 'Public Diplomacy', chapter 24 in Cooper, Andrew P., Heine, Jorg, Thakur, Ramesh. *The Oxford Handbook of Modern Diplomacy*. Oxford University Press, 439.

70 Women interviewed about the Aceh peace negotiations said that 'in Aceh today most men and women think that it is not "a woman's business" to participate in discussions and decision making on issues related to society or politics'. Crisis Management Initiative 2006. *The Aceh Peace Process: Involvement of Women*.

71 An oft-cited example is the 'track-two' All-Party Burundi Women's Peace Conference held in July 2000, which produced a declaration with proposals for the final agreement. These were submitted to Mandela, the mediator, and many were incorporated into the comprehensive peace agreement; UN Women 2012, *op. cit.*, 10.

72 Nelson, *op. cit.*

73 '[I]n cases of women's participation and strong influence, an agreement was almost always reached. Furthermore, strong influence of women in negotiation processes also positively correlated with a greater likelihood of agreements being implemented'. Report on 1325, *op. cit.*, 41. See also Thania Paffenholz *et al.*, *Making Women Count Not Just Counting Women* (UN Women, 2016).

advisory groups to all panels in the process. In an illustration of the important role of the international or regional mediator in this regard, the mediator, Salim Ahmed Salim, publicly appealed for the increased participation of women in the parties' delegations. A group comprising fifteen Darfurian women from diverse social and professional backgrounds established a Gender Expert Support Team (GEST) with international support. The GEST was accepted as a semi-official body to assist the parties at the negotiations. It interacted directly with all official women delegates to develop a common position paper that reflected the needs and concerns of women.[74] These included 'wealth-sharing and land rights, affirmative action, physical security, women's participation in the DDR (disarmament, demobilisation and reintegration) process, and a gender-responsive reconciliation commission'. Some of these concerns found their way into the Darfur Peace Agreement.[75] The Liberian peace deal in 2003 was signed not only by the Government and two rebel groups but also eighteen political parties and several civil society organisations including the Inter-religious Council for Liberia and the Mano River Women Peace Network.[76]

In Syria women were active in the protests against Assad in 2011 that precipitated the conflict and have long sought to be part of the peace process. Earlier attempts at participation were unsuccessful. In December 2015 the UN Security Council endorsed a road map for a Syrian peace process, setting a timetable for international talks[77] and stressing that 'the Syrian people will decide the future of Syria'. Ban Ki-moon said that the 'parties must ensure the full and effective participation of women in intra-Syrian talks to be mediated by his Special Envoy'.[78] Staffan de Mistura, UN Special Envoy for Syria, has created a Syrian Women's Advisory Board 'after lobbying from the UK and other likeminded states'.[79] The Board of twelve representatives will meet regularly with De Mistura during the peace talks and, in the words of UN Women, will 'raise matters missing from the agenda, provide options, form consensus positions and make recommendations to assist peace talks, address key points of contention and offer creative solutions, propose gender-responsive perspectives and channel relevant civil society expertise'.[79a]

[74] Herbolzheimer, *op. cit.*, 5. [75] *Ibid.* [76] Nelson, *op. cit.*

[77] SC Resolution, 2254, 18 December 2015.

[78] 7588 meeting of the Security Council, SC/12171, 18 December 2015.

[79] Government Response to the Report of the House of Lords Sexual Violence in Conflict Committee (HL123), 30 June 2016, para. 68.

[79a] http://www.unwomen.org/en/news/stories/2016/2/ed-statement-on-syrian-womens-advisory-board.

UN Women welcomes this as a historic first, but some women's organisations have been less enthusiastic, noting that an advisory body is not the same as full participation in negotiations.

Greater participation in peace processes entails other changes in the way they are conducted. This encompasses the range of issues to be taken into account, the time period over which such processes are conducted and the levels of negotiation. As concerns issues, the examples of Darfur and Liberia suggest what might be included, given higher priority or addressed differently if attention is given to ensuring a gender or bottom-up perspective. First, the obligation to deliver economic, social and cultural rights, for example, the need for immediate access to appropriate health care services in the aftermath of conflict (especially where there has been widespread sexual violence), is rarely mentioned in peace agreements but such rights may be of higher immediate importance to women, and other civil society actors, than civil and political rights such as access to political participation in the reconstituted state institutions.[80] Indeed, delivery of and access to economic and social rights may be key to overcoming obstacles to such participation. Economic, social and cultural rights are often presented as issues of development not rights, and are put aside from peace processes for consideration at subsequent donor conferences (from which women and civil society groups may also be excluded). Second, the obligation to investigate and prosecute (or otherwise address) sexual and gender-based violence committed in armed conflict should be dealt with, as well as ongoing violence against women. Seeking accountability for conflict-based crimes and delivery of economic, social and cultural rights are inter-connected, since failure to ensure the latter may be a factor in preventing successful prosecution of crimes against women committed during the conflict. Transitional justice that neglects economic and social rights is a narrow perception of social justice.[81] Third, in light of the often changed demographics post-conflict there should be guarantees of legal rights and access to resources (including land) for widows and female-headed households. Fourth, women's participation in all post-conflict institutions and decision-making with respect to implementation of the peace agreement must be made explicit.

[80] Arbour, Louise 2007. 'Economic and Social Justice for Societies in Transition', *NYU Journal of International Law and Politics* 40: 1–27.

[81] *Ibid.* See also Rees, Madeleine and Chinkin, Christine 2016. 'Exposing the Gendered Myth of Post Conflict Transition: The Transformative Power of Economic and Social Rights', *NYU Journal of International Law and Politics* 48, 1211.

In sum, what is sought is women's *de iure* and *de facto* equality in state reconstruction. Women are too often perceived as a 'problem', along with other marginalised or problematised groups. This also places women as the responsibility of humanitarian agencies rather than as active players in power and wealth allocation.

Timing and the level of peace negotiations are also important. As the Report on Peacebuilding Architecture points out, peace operations are often conducted in haste. If there is to be proper participation and consultation of different groups in society and at different levels, this takes time. In many new wars, it is possible to identify safer areas or 'islands of civility' where local administrations or local civil society groups have been able to prevent violence or to negotiate cease fires. It is important to build on these achievements and to link top-down peace processes with local processes that may be achieved piece-meal. A non-linear more inclusive peace process is discussed further in Chapter 11.

Finally, it should be pointed out that it is of course not sufficient that women and civil society groups participate in decision-making roles in peace processes. Those who participate need to be competent in the wide range of relevant issues raised in peace processes, for example, technical, security and military issues, issues relating to resources, law and justice issues, landholding regimes, financial and budgetary issues, as well having expertise in gender analysis and an understanding of the relevant legal framework. They need to be able to translate their knowledge of the everyday into the language of negotiation in order to challenge the power relations of predatory networks that currently dominate top-down peace processes. They also need to be clear in their own priorities, demands and the means of achieving them. There may be support from international bodies, for instance, UN Women,[82] which must cover the selection of women participants, and long-term assistance must be based in local knowledge. Women delegates in negotiation teams do not necessarily speak for women or for civil society in general, but for the interests of their clan, party or group. The creation of an all-party political women's group speaking on behalf

[82] The UN SC has called upon 'donor countries to provide financial and technical assistance to women involved in peace processes, including training in mediation, advocacy, and technical areas of negotiation, as well as providing support and training to mediators and technical teams on the impact of women's participation and strategies for women's effective inclusion', UN SC Resolution 2242, 13 October 2015, para. 1.

of women, as in the comparatively short-lived Women's Coalition in Northern Ireland, is unusual and difficult to sustain.[83]

9.3 Peacekeeping

Former UN Secretary-General Boutros Boutros Ghali claimed that 'Peacekeeping can rightly be called the invention of the United Nations'.[84] However, what are now termed 'peace operations' have a long history that predates the UN Charter.[85] Since 1945 the concept of peacekeeping has further evolved over time, taking on different attributes and responses to changed circumstances in the international arena – decolonisation, the Cold War, détente, the end of the Cold War, the phenomena of failed and collapsed states and eruption of new wars characterised by nationalisms, ethnic divides and violent extremisms. It has been argued that the basic objective of peacekeeping has from the outset been to regulate and uphold the state-based system.[86] In other words, the fundamental aim of peacekeeping has been to uphold peace agreements, which are seen as a necessary condition for the stability of the state-based international system. However, since the end of the Cold War, in response to new wars, the mandate and functions of peace operations have greatly expanded. Traditionally peacekeeping was about keeping warring sides apart; now it is also about creating conditions for reconciliation and reconstruction and thus merges into peacebuilding. Starting with Cambodia, El Salvador, Mozambique and Namibia in the period 1989 to 1992, peace operations have been gradually enlarged to include security sector reform, DDR of former combatants, organising and monitoring elections, drafting constitutions, establishment of justice mechanisms and various economic stabilisation and development programmes – a package of measures that have come to be known as state-building, peacebuilding or nation-building. The role of peacekeepers has likewise changed commensurate with their enhanced activities, including most significantly providing security for returning displaced people, protection of civilians or providing security for elections. In other words,

[83] Cowell-Meyers, Kimberly 2014. 'The Social Movement as Political Party: The Northern Ireland Women's Coalition and the Campaign for Inclusion', *Perspectives on Politics* 12: 61–80.

[84] *Agenda for Peace, op. cit.*, para. 46.

[85] McQueen, Norrie 2006. *Peacekeeping and the International System*. Routledge, 23–42.

[86] *Ibid.*, 17.

a broad range of political, social and economic objectives have been explicitly made part of the peacekeeping narrative. The tools available for such complex peace operations are also now extensive.[87]

Nevertheless, the term peacekeeping and the focus on the use of military forces, even if peace operations now include police and other civilian experts still suggests that peacekeeping is predominantly about separating sides and preventing the eruption of conflict rather than about the more everyday 'inside' issues associated with peacebuilding. This is reflected in the language of civilian protection, which is part of a military discourse as opposed, for example, to the language of law and order or public security.

9.3.1 The Evolution of Peacekeeping

Peacekeeping was first used in the UN era in situations of interstate tension (Greece/Yugoslavia, 1947–1951; Palestine, commencing 1948; India/Pakistan over Kashmir, commencing 1949) On this assumption and following the establishment of the United Nations Emergency Force (UNEF) in 1956[88] 'to secure and supervise the cessation of hostilities' in the Suez Canal area, Dag Hammarskjold formulated the main criteria for peacekeeping: the consent of the host state, neutrality and non-use of force except in self-defence. These principles reflected a classic view of war as a contest of wills. At that time, the main role of peacekeeping was observing, monitoring and verifying the separation and/or withdrawal of forces and the control of heavy weaponry under the terms of ceasefire agreements. It was about keeping warring sides apart, not about upholding human rights, maintaining law and order or, more generally, protecting the civilian population. The hope was that by stabilising the situation peacekeeping might create and maintain a political space for evolving long-term solutions; on the other hand peacekeeping was also symbolic of the need for separation. In the Cold War environment of the time Hammarskjold excluded permanent members of the SC from

[87] They include special envoys and mediators; political missions, including peacebuilding missions; regional preventive diplomacy offices; observation missions, including both ceasefire and electoral missions; small, technical-specialist missions such as electoral support missions; multidisciplinary operations drawing on civilian, military and police personnel to support peace process implementation, as advance missions for planning. *Report of the High-level Independent Panel, op. cit.*, para. 18.

[88] UNEF was authorised by the UN GA under the Uniting for Peace Resolution; UN GA Resolution 998 (ES-I), 4 November 1956.

participation in peacekeeping.[89] These foundational assumptions were rapidly challenged in the Congo in 1960 where the United Nations Operation in the Congo (ONUC) found itself set between the state and the secessionists in Katanga.[90]

In the immediate euphoria of the 'New World Order', in 1992, UN Secretary-General Boutros Boutros Ghali explicated the differences between preventive diplomacy, peacekeeping, peacemaking and post-conflict peacebuilding.[91] He defined multilateral (or multidimensional) peacekeeping operations (the terminology that is now favoured) as involving the 'deployment of a United Nations presence in the field, hitherto with the consent of all the parties concerned, normally involving United Nations military and/or police personnel and frequently civilians as well. Peacekeeping is a technique that expands the possibilities for both the prevention of conflict and the making of peace'.[92] This is reflected in different timing of deployment of peacekeepers. It may be in a preventive capacity before overt violence breaks out (Macedonia),[93] during conflict with a primarily humanitarian and protective mandate (e.g., UNPROFOR in Bosnia, 1992–1995), following a ceasefire or other cessation of violence but remaining in place when conflict again erupts,[94] seeking to establish an environment conducive to further peace negotiations[95] or be deployed for the first time 'post-conflict' to support the settlement (e.g., KFOR in Kosovo in June 1999).

As well as articulating his Agenda for Peace, in 1992 Boutros Boutros Ghali also established the UN Department of Peacekeeping Operations (DPKO) to integrate and co-ordinate peacekeeping activities. Three years later, referring to Somalia and Bosnia, he noted that the 'classic' principles

[89] McQueen, *op. cit.*, 74–78.

[90] Diehl, *op. cit.*, 45, discussing the Congo operation as 'A Proto-Peacebuilding Operation'.

[91] *An Agenda for Peace op. cit.* [92] *Ibid.* para. 20.

[93] UN SC Resolution 983, 31 March 1995: recalling 'concern about possible developments which could undermine confidence and stability in the former Yugoslav Republic of Macedonia or threaten its territory . . . UNPROFOR within the former Yugoslav Republic of Macedonia shall be known as the United Nations Preventive Deployment Force (UNPREDEP)'.

[94] In Côte D'Ivoire, UN Peacekeepers became caught up in a non-international armed conflict and in effect directly participated in that conflict, taking sides as to who had won the election and allowing peacekeepers to become legitimate targets of violence; see Chapter 5.

[95] E.g., MINURSO (the United Nations Mission for the Referendum in Western Sahara) was established following a ceasefire to prepare the way for a referendum on the status of the Western Sahara; UN SC Resolution 690, 29 April 1991. The referendum has never taken place.

of consent and non-use of force could not work in the contexts of 'protecting humanitarian operations during continuing warfare, protecting civilian populations in designated safe areas and pressing the parties to achieve national reconciliation at a pace faster than they were ready to accept'. These situations required expanded mandates, for nothing is 'more dangerous for a peacekeeping operation than to ask it to use force when its existing composition, armament, logistic support and deployment deny it the capacity to do so'.[96] As Boutros Boutros Ghali reflected in his *Supplement to an Agenda for Peace*, the increased presence of peacekeepers in the early 1990s did not prevent the commission of atrocities. Peacekeepers were criticised for their inability – or unwillingness – to use force to protect civilian populations from murder and genocide.[97]

Following the failures of peacekeeping in the early 1990s – Somalia, Angola,[98] Rwanda and Srebrenica and the unauthorised enforcement action in Kosovo[99] – Kofi Annan commissioned detailed investigations into the institutional breakdowns of protection in Rwanda and Srebrenica and a third general review of UN peacekeeping (and other) activities. The chair of this last panel, Lakhdar Brahimi, reporting before the articulation of the Responsibility to Protect but after the first SC thematic resolution on protection of civilians,[100] reiterated the core principles of peacekeeping. But he also provided for 'robust' peacekeeping, arguing that '[i]mpartiality for United Nations operations must therefore mean adherence to the principles of the Charter: where one party to a peace agreement clearly and incontrovertibly is violating its terms, continued equal treatment of all parties by the United Nations can in the best case result in ineffectiveness and in the worst may amount to complicity with evil'.[101] Mandates must therefore be robust and rules of engagement allow peacekeepers to 'silence a source of deadly fire that is

[96] *Supplement to an Agenda for Peace*, *op. cit.*, para. 35.

[97] Criticism also came from within the UN; Report of the Secretary-General, *The Fall of Srebrenica*, UN Doc. A/54/549, 15 November 1999; *Report of the Independent Inquiry into the Actions of the United Nations during the 1994 Genocide in Rwanda*, UN Doc. S/1999/1257, 16 December 1999.

[98] 'In Angola, peacekeepers deployed to monitor a ceasefire and elections were utterly ill-prepared and ill-equipped to prevent and mitigate a sharp descent into the worst violence of that country's decade-old civil war'. Bellamy, Alex and Williams, Paul 2010. *Understanding Peacekeeping*. Polity Press, 2nd ed., 119.

[99] On Somalia, Rwanda and Srebrenica, see Chapter 5.

[100] UN SC Resolution 1265, 17 September 1999.

[101] *Brahimi Report*, *op. cit.*, Executive Summary.

directed at United Nations troops or at the people they are charged to protect'. Attackers must not be allowed to seize the initiative.[102]

The Brahimi Report included a slew of reform proposals, relating to enhanced decision-making at UN headquarters, clear and feasible mandates and adequate resources, capability for rapid deployment of forces when needed and effectiveness.[103] However, the departure from the traditional tenets of peacekeeping concerned some states.[104] And in keeping with this, only the same basic principles – consent, impartiality and non-use of force, except in self-defense and defense of the mandate – were reiterated; other 'success factors' were also extolled but not elevated to the level of principles: legitimacy, credibility and promotion of national and local ownership.[105] Without expressly articulating the point, the expectation was that peacekeeping forces should engender a culture of peace,[106] in place of one of war where these terms were defined conservatively. In 2013 the basic principles, without expansion, were reiterated by the SC in an enunciation of traditional peacekeeping missions and 'complex multi-dimensional operations'.[107] In 2015 the UN Secretary-General announced a further appraisal of peacekeeping by the appointment of a High Level Independent Panel on UN Peace Operations to determine how they could be made 'more effective, efficient and responsive in a changing world'.[108] The High-Level Panel reported in July 2015.[109] It stressed the primacy of politics, the need to be more field focused and people centred, as well as emphasising the importance of better integration of peace operations.[110]

Peacekeeping and related peace and security activities are also carried out by regional organisations,[111] either in conjunction with UN

102 *Ibid.*, para. 49.

103 This classification of recommendations in the Brahimi Report is that of Bellamy and Williams, *op. cit.*, 129–133.

104 *Ibid.*, 133.

105 UN Department of Peacekeeping Operations Department of Field Support 2008 (review 2010), United Nations Peacekeeping Operations Principles and Guidelines.

106 UN GA Resolution 52/13, 15 January 1998 (Culture of Peace), and UN GA Resolution 53/243, 6 October 1999, (Declaration and Programme of Action on a Culture of Peace) shortly preceded the *Brahimi Report*.

107 UN SC Resolution 2086, 21 January 2013.

108 Report of the Secretary-General, *The Future of United Nations Peace Operations: Implementation of the Recommendations of the High-Level Independent Panel on Peace Operations*, UN Doc. A/70/357–S/2015/682, 2 September 2015, para. 1.

109 *Report of the High-level Independent Panel*, *op. cit.*

110 *Ibid.*

111 UN Charter, chapter VIII allows for regional arrangements 'dealing with such matters relating to the maintenance of international peace and security as are appropriate for regional action'.

peacekeepers or alone. These include NATO, OSCE, EU, AU,[112] the OAS and sub-regional groupings such as ECOMOG (ECOWAS), the Southern African Development Community (SADC)[113] and the CIS, which undertakes missions in post-Soviet states.[114] The UN and regional organisations work through a range of different models. In some instances the involvement of the regional organisation may be little more than a cloak for the enforcement activities of a single state. Coleman has argued that the state in question seeks to legitimate what might otherwise be regarded as wrongful intervention (or even aggression) by the state by presenting it as the peacekeeping operations of the organisation.[115] Of course, regional organisations have their own constitutive arrangements with which such exercises should, but do not always, comply.

The trend of regional – and individual – involvement in peace operations has been encouraged by UN bodies since the end of the Cold War, both as a matter of resources and for the regional commitment and expertise. The 2015 High Level Panel Report on Peace Operations also stressed the growing significance for the UN of partnerships with states and regional organisations.[116] Brahimi had emphasised that resources must match the mandate, in particular where it includes the protection of civilians who accordingly have raised expectations. Recourse to regional organisations is one way of attempting to achieve this.[117] So too is some form of joint peacekeeping operation between the UN and a regional body, although this risks diverse or overlapping mandates, priorities and lack of hierarchical authority or control. Individual states also enter into

[112] For a detailed account of the African Peace and Security Architecture see Abass, Ademola 2010. 'African Peace and Security Architecture and Protection of Human Security', in Abass, Ademola (ed.). *Protecting Human Security in Africa*. Oxford University Press, 247–283, 247.

[113] Interventions ostensibly as peacekeeping missions were carried out under the auspices of SADC in the DRC by Zimbabwe and Angola. On interventions by ECOWAS and SADC and their compatibility with the UN Charter and with the consent of the governments subject to intervention see De Wet, Erica 2014. 'The Evolving Role of ECOWAS and SADC in Peace Operations: A Challenge to the United Nations Security Council in Matters of Peace and Security', *Leiden Journal of International Law* 27(2): 353–369, and in Lesotho by South Africa and Botswana; Coleman, Katharina 2007. *International Organisations and Peace Enforcement: The Politics of Legitimacy*. Cambridge University Press, chapter 5.

[114] Konstantin Korkelia, 'The CIS Peace-keeping Operations in the Context of International Legal Order', Final Report at www.nato.int/acad/fellow/97-99/korkelia.pdf.

[115] Coleman, Katharina, *op. cit.* chapter 2.

[116] *Report of the Independent High-Level Panel*, *op. cit.*, paras. 53–58.

[117] *Brahimi Report*, *op. cit.*, para. 63.

peacekeeping, either singly or in conjunction with other states. For instance, following violence in South Ossetia in 1991–1992, Georgia and Russia entered into the Sochi Agreement providing for Joint Peacekeeping Forces there.[118] Peacekeeping by a single state can contribute to friction and further violence; Georgia subsequently argued that the Agreement gave legitimacy to Russia's military presence in South Ossetia and allowed Russian control in the area.[119]

At the time of writing, some 85,000 UN troops are engaged in complex and dangerous UN operations worldwide;[120] there are now 106,000 combined military and police personnel, and more than 19,000 civilian staff in peacekeeping operations,[121] in many instances under UN Charter chapter VII mandates (or combined chapter VI and VII mandates) and engaging in activities that move from or combine the peacekeeping/peace enforcement line described by Boutros Boutros Ghali.[122] Despite these numbers, many missions operate at below full strength. The presence of UN peacekeeping forces in a state is legally determined by SC mandate, within which they must operate. The legal relationship with the host government is determined by a Status of Forces Agreement (SOFA)[123] and with troop contributing countries by a memorandum of understanding. Forces operate in accordance with their Rules of Engagement tailored to the specific mission mandate. Within the framework of the basic principles of peacekeeping, peacekeeping forces have wide-ranging mandates and functions, ranging from 'traditional peacekeeping missions, which primarily monitor ceasefire to

118 *Agreement on the Principles of Settlement of the Georgian-Ossetian Conflict*, Sochi, 24 June 1992.

119 *Application of the International Convention on the Elimination of All Forms of Racial Discrimination* (*Georgia v. Russian Federation*), ICJ, Written memorial of Georgia, 2 September 2009, para. 4.15 ff.

120 Peacekeeping Fact Sheet, 31 August 2015. www.un.org/en/peacekeeping/resources/statistics/factsheet.shtml.

121 *Report of the High-Level Independent Panel*, *op. cit.*, para. 20.

122 'The logic of peacekeeping flows from political and military premises that are quite distinct from those of enforcement; and the dynamics of the latter are incompatible with the political process that peacekeeping is intended to facilitate'. *Supplement to an Agenda for Peace*, *op. cit.*, para. 35.

123 The Secretary-General issued a Model SOFA in 1990, although this is often subjected to changes in mission-specific SOFAs; 'UN Peacekeeping and The Model Status of Forces Agreement', background paper prepared for experts' workshop, hosted by the New Zealand High Commission in London, UK, 26 August 2010, www.essex.ac.uk/plrp/documents/default.aspx.

complex multidimensional operations, which seek to undertake peacebuilding tasks and address root causes of conflict'.[124]

A crucial question is the timing and process of departure of the international bodies, whether present as peacekeepers or with a more extensive mandate for territorial administration. Premature departure may spur a relapse into violence[125] (although the presence of internationals does not guarantee the discontinuance of violence), but longevity may foster dependence and an unsustainable stability; it can also contribute to polarisation and hostility. Gendered forms of insecurity should also be a factor in determining when military forces should withdraw. For instance, increased sexual violence against women and against men and boys has been reported in Afghanistan in 2013. 'Perpetrator profiles include police and military commanders, former warlords, tribal leaders and non -State armed groups'.[126] Former British Prime Minister David Cameron's assessment of 'mission accomplished'[127] does not take account of these realities. Karima Bennoune has argued that many women she interviewed in field work in Afghanistan view the departure of US, UK and other forces in 2014 with concern for their security, fearing violent attacks by the Taliban on girls' schools and in other areas of public life.[128] Women's security – touted as a justification for intervention – may be too easily negotiated away in light of other political imperatives. Such action is contrary to the Committee on the Elimination of Discrimination against Women's recommendation that states parties 'Reject all forms of rollbacks in women's rights protections in order to appease non-State actors such as terrorists, private individuals or armed groups'.[129] Domestic political pressures, including an unwillingness to continue to supply resources, may urge withdrawal, while lack of agreement in the SC may prolong the mandate. In Bosnia the international presence remains in place, pending the achievement of the objectives and conditions

[124] UN SC Resolution 2086, 21 January 2013 (on UN peacekeeping operations).

[125] E.g., UNMIL left Liberia in 1997 only for a renewal of the civil war in 1999.

[126] Report of the Secretary-General, *Conflict Related Sexual Violence*, UN Doc. S/2014/181, 13 March 2014, para. 12.

[127] Mason, Rowena. 'Mission Accomplished in Afghanistan, Declares David Cameron', *The Guardian*, 16 December 2013, www.theguardian.com/uk-news/2013/dec/16/afghanistan-mission-accomplished-david-cameron.

[128] Bennoune, Karima. 'A Peace of Her', paper presented at Wisconsin Journal of International Law Symposium: Creation of International Law: Exploring the International Law Components of Peace, April 2014.

[129] Committee on the Elimination of Discrimination against Women, General Recommendation No. 30, on Women in Conflict Prevention, Conflict and Post-Conflict Situations, UN Doc. CEDAW/C/GC/30, 18 October 2013, para. 17.

for closure. In Kosovo too UNMIK remains in place, although it has been much scaled down following the Declaration of independence in February 2008. Other peacekeeping missions, for instance, UNFICYP,[130] have become apparently permanent presences, and their presence may substitute for effective peacemaking.

9.3.2 Peacekeeping and the Protection of Civilians

In new wars, battles between opposing forces are rather rare, and the main violence is directed against civilians.[131] The traditional job of separating forces or maintaining peace agreements where the warring parties are the main signatories is not so difficult for peacekeepers. The problems arise in relation to the protection of civilians, which is central to contemporary mandates.

The tragedies of Rwanda and Srebrenica have drawn attention to the failure of peacekeeping forces to prevent genocide even where they are present. The inability of peacekeepers to prevent continued eruptions of violence directed against civilians following a ceasefire or peace agreement is hugely problematic. In Bosnia, the handover of Serb suburbs of Sarajevo in 1996 to the multi-ethnic canton of Sarajevo under the terms of the Dayton Peace Agreement led to the expulsion of large numbers of Serbs in full view of international forces. In Kosovo, the arrival of international troops in June 1999 was accompanied by widespread reverse ethnic cleansing – revenge attacks on Serbs, other minorities and Kosovar Albanians believed to have been Serb sympathizers, which the international forces did little to prevent or investigate. Indeed, these events were repeated five years later in March 2004 when three days of rioting by extremist Albanian nationalists resulted in the torching of Serb Orthodox churches and houses and the displacement of several thousand Serbs despite the presence of KFOR and the newly established Kosovo Police Service (KPS).[132] In Haiti in 1994 during the American-led

[130] The United Nations Peacekeeping Force in Cyprus was first mandated in 1964 following violence between the Greek Cypriot and Turkish Cypriot communities in the island.

[131] See generally, Office for the Coordination of Humanitarian Affairs, Security Council norms and practice on the Protection of Civilians in Armed Conflict, OCHA Policy and Studies Series, 008, May 2014.

[132] See Bieber, Florian. 'Policing the Peace after Yugoslavia: Police Reform between External Imposition and Domestic Reform', in *GRIPS Policy Research Center Discussion Paper*: 10-07, January 2010; Human Rights Advisory Panel, *S.C. v. UNMIK*, Case No. 02/09, 6 December 2012.

intervention to restore the democratically elected government, Haitian army units beat up civilians gathered to welcome the US forces while American soldiers stood passively by.[133] And it is possible to enumerate many similar examples in other supposedly post-conflict situations.

In response to these challenges, most mandates now emphasise the protection of civilians. In 2013 the extensive protective responsibilities of UN peacekeepers were summarised by the UN Security Council.[134] Peacekeepers:

(f) *Help* to establish the necessary security conditions to *facilitate* delivery of humanitarian assistance, taking into account the special needs of refugees, IDPs, women, children, elderly and disabled people, and to create conditions necessary for voluntary, safe, dignified and sustainable return of refugees and IDPs;
(g) *Contribute* towards agreed international efforts to protect human rights including through monitoring and prevention and support national governments' efforts to promote and protect human rights, within its capacities and resources and according to its mandate throughout the life cycle of a Mission;
(h) *Protect* civilians, particularly those under imminent threat of physical violence, in conformity with paragraph 16 of its resolution 1674 (2006), within missions' zones of operation and taking into account their capacities and resources, and *support* the efforts of the host authorities in protection of civilians from violence, including all forms of sexual- and gender-based violence, and in this regard, *help* in building and reforming security sector institutions of the host country that are able to sustainably and consistently protect civilians, while recognizing that protection of civilians is the primary responsibility of the host country.

The language of protection of civilians is drawn from the classic *in bello* discourse. As elaborated in Chapter 6, the language presupposes a war in which the main violence is between the warring parties and civilians are caught in the cross-fire. The principles of peacekeeping – consent, neutrality and non-use of force – stem from this history, but they are difficult to apply in the context of new wars. Consent refers to host state consent,

[133] Stromseth, Jane and Wippman, David and Brooks, Rosa 2006. *Can Might Make Rights? Building the Rule of Law after Military Interventions*. Cambridge University Press.
[134] UN SC Resolution 2086, 21 January 2013 (on UN peacekeeping operations).

but what does consent mean when the host government has been constructed on the basis of a peace agreement, where the various parties to the conflict have been incorporated into the government? It is easy enough to agree to traditional peacekeeping functions like separating hostile forces when this is in the interests of the parties to the agreement. It is much more difficult to undertake tasks designed to improve the security of the population when the warring parties continue their predatory behaviour. Does consent allow for the arrest of soldiers or police of the host government when they commit violent acts against civilians?[135] Likewise, what does neutrality mean if one side is committing human rights violations? And, as argued above, how can the non-use of force be reconciled with the need to protect civilians from violent threats? Contrariwise, the use of military force may militate against the reduction of violence; use of force against those attacking civilians may put civilians at greater risk of retaliatory attacks and turn the local population against the peacekeepers.[136]

There have been efforts to modify the language and introduce practices more in line with human rights than war. In 2013, for example, the Secretary-General launched the Human Rights Up Front initiative. The programme aims to integrate human rights throughout UN operations and to ensure that the protection of civilians is a system-wide core responsibility – from prevention of conflict through peacekeeping and peacebuilding. The aim is to prevent violations and thus the 'cycles of violence and long-term animosities, presenting serious obstacles to the social cohesion needed to restore peace and security'.[137] Where violations do occur the focus must be on protection of civilians. The initiative was central to the UN response to the relapse into violent conflict in the Central African Republic and South Sudan, but human rights violations to civilians continue to take place on a large scale.[138]

The problems of protecting civilians that have been faced by UN peacekeepers are manifold. An independent report on the protection of

[135] See Wills, Siobhan 2009. *Protecting Civilians: The Obligations of Peacekeepers*. Oxford University Press, 83.

[136] Marks, Joshua 2007. 'The Pitfalls of Action and Inaction: Civilian Protection in MONUC's Peacekeeping Operations', *African Security Review* 16: 67–80, 77.

[137] Report of the Secretary-General, *Peacebuilding in the Aftermath of Conflict*, UN Doc. A/69/399–S/2014/694, 23 September 2014, para. 20.

[138] UN SC Resolution 2301, 26 July 2016, condemns in the CAR 'the multiple violations of international humanitarian law and the widespread human rights violations and abuses,' On South Sudan see UN SC Resolution 2304, 12 August 2016, below.

civilians in UN operations undertaken for the United Nations found that there is still insufficient clarity of mandates, lack of planning, training and preparation, and lack of appropriate structures, resources and tools despite the perseverance of 'many dedicated and creative individuals'.[139]

The first problem is the inadequacy of resources. Recent reports on peace operations and peacebuilding emphasise the huge gap between mandates and consequent expectations, on the one hand, and allocated resources, on the other. How can a limited number of peacekeepers protect potentially large numbers of civilians? In Bosnia, it was estimated that 35,000 troops would be required to protect the safe havens announced by the United Nations in 1992; in the end only 7,500 troops were deployed.[140] With respect to the AU force in Darfur it was asked: 'How much protection could a small fledgling military deployment offer "within resources and capability" in a region the size of France?'[141] The first priority in the mandate for MONUSCO (United Nations Organization Mission in the Democratic Republic of the Congo) is 'to ensure the effective protection of civilians, including humanitarian personnel and human rights defenders, under imminent threat of physical violence, in particular violence emanating from any of the parties engaged in the conflict'.[142] But as the Under-Secretary-General for Peacekeeping Operations has said: 'The recommended force size of over 6,000 troops is far too small to present a credible military deterrent, if challenged, while it is perhaps too large to be perceived as a symbolic presence. The risks are tremendous'.[143]

A second problem is interpretation of mandates and rules of engagement. In performing protective responsibilities, the crucial question for peacekeepers is whether they can legally use force (or be at fault for not

[139] Holt, Victoria and Taylor, Glenn 2009. 'Protecting Civilians in the Context of UN Peace Operations', Independent Study Commissioned by UNOCHA and DPKO, 8.

[140] See Kaldor, Mary 2012. *New and Old Wars: Organized Violence in a Global Era*. Polity, 3rd ed., chapter 3.

[141] Holt, Victoria K. and Berkman, Tobias C. '*The Impossible Mandate? Military Preparedness, the Responsibility to Protect and Modern Peace Operations*. Henry L. Stimson Center, September 2006, Introduction.

[142] UN SC Resolution 1925, 28 May 2010. The resolution first 'Emphasizes that the Government ... bears primary responsibility for security, peacebuilding and development in the country, and encourages the Government ... to remain fully committed to protecting the population through the establishment of professional and sustainable security forces'.

[143] Cited in Marks, *op. cit.*, 67.

doing so) and the extent of any such force.[144] The answer rests upon interpretation of their mandate. SC mandates are politically negotiated by diplomats in New York, far from the realities of the prevailing violence,[145] driven by the need to secure consensus and with different priorities and often in language that is ambiguous and equivocal. While missions learn from each other and continuity of practice is furthered through personnel moving from one mission to another, individual missions have differently worded mandates (which also may be restructured as events unfold), but in all cases their interpretation and execution will depend upon those responsible for operations, who have to make decisions on the ground in shifting circumstances and in accordance with the resources made available. Peacekeepers must also comply with the applicable Status of Forces Agreement and Rules of Engagement. They may not all be familiar with the language in which these are written and command and control structures may also be unclear. The Brahimi report warned that the 'compromises required to build consensus can be made at the expense of specificity, and the resulting ambiguity can have serious consequences in the field'.[146] The wording cited above is from a thematic resolution of the SC (Resolution 2086), not a country-specific mandate, but nevertheless lacks clarity. In Chapter 5 we drew attention to the gap between the broad mandate under UN Charter chapter VII given to UNPROFOR in Bosnia-Herzegovina and the much more limited Rules of Engagement.

An innovation in the case of the DRC was the SC's decision in March 2013 to bring together peacekeeping and *jus ad bellum* authorisation of coercive action through the extension of the mandate of the UN mission, MONUSCO. Noting the 'recurring cycles of conflict and persistent violence by armed groups, both Congolese and foreign', the SC decided to include an '"Intervention Brigade" with the responsibility of neutralizing armed groups . . . and the objective of contributing to reducing the threat posed by armed groups to state authority and civilian security in eastern DRC'.[147] In November 2013 the defeat and surrender of the

[144] This is sometimes spelled out in the relevant resolution, for example, 'MONUC is authorized to use all necessary means, . . . may use cordon and search tactics to prevent attacks on civilians and disrupt the military capability of illegal armed groups that continue to use violence in those areas'. UN SC Resolution 1592, 30 March 2005, para. 7. Nevertheless this wording still does not clarify the level of appropriate force.

[145] It has also been argued that failing to take account of or misreading local conditions can impact upon the success or failure of the mission; MacQueen, *op. cit.*

[146] *Brahimi Report*, *op. cit.*, para. 56.

[147] UN SC Resolution 2098, 28 March 2013.

leading rebel group in the eastern DRC, M23, was reported, although the contribution of the UN Intervention Brigade to this is unclear since it operated together with the Congolese army.[148] The brigade has been much less successful in targeting the LRA or the Democratic Forces for the Liberation of Rwanda.[149] This mandate blurs the line between peacekeeping and peace enforcement (military action) but was stipulated to be on an exceptional basis and 'without creating a precedent or any prejudice to the agreed principles of peacekeeping'.

A third problem is the relation to the host government. Some mission-specific mandates include reminders of the primary responsibility of governments for the protection of civilians and require peacekeepers to act 'without prejudice' to that responsibility. What is the peacekeepers' task where the national government is not making efforts to protect civilians from violence, but is in fact committing those acts of violence? What are the implications when UN forces act in conjunction with local forces, providing them with assistance, money or logistical support, such as food and transport to armies or police, and they are then responsible for the commission of abuses and human rights violations?

For example, it transpired that joint military operations between the DRC peacekeeping force, MONUSCO, in eastern Congo and the Congolese army was being undermined by human rights abuses by army personnel. 'Some of the U.N.-backed Congolese troops had engaged in rape, murder and pillage'.[150] The initial response was to screen Congolese army units and to remove army officers with a record of human rights abuses. This was followed by the introduction in 2013 of a system-wide policy, the 'Human Rights Due Diligence Policy on U.N. support to non-U.N. security forces',[151] in an attempt to limit such harms and enhance compliance with IHL and human rights law. In essence the policy requires that no UN entity should support, train or finance, even

148 'DR Congo's M23 Rebel Chief Sultani Makenga 'surrenders', *BBC News*, 7 November 2013, www.bbc.co.uk/news/world-africa-24849814.

149 Caryannis, Tatiana and Pangburn, Aaron. 'Lessons from AU-UN Cooperation in Peace Operations in the Democratic Republic of Congo (DRC)' in Appendix B, World Peace Foundation, *African Politics: African Peace*, 2016.

150 Bolopion, Philippe. 'Can the UN Help Itself from Underwriting Human Rights Abuses?' *Human Rights Watch*, 24 July 2012, www.hrw.org/news/2012/07/24/can-un-help-itself-underwriting-human-rights-abuses.

151 Report of the Secretary-General on the Work of the Organization, UNGA OR A/67/1, 8 August 2012, para. 58; Human Rights Due Diligence Policy on United Nations Support to Non-United Nations Security Forces, UN Doc. A/67/775–S/2013/110, 5 March 2013, Annex.

indirectly, any army or police force likely to engage in serious human rights violations. An assessment is required prior to offering support of the risk of the recipient committing grave violations of IHL, human rights or refugee law, and UN support is prohibited 'where there are substantial grounds for believing there is a real risk of the receiving entities' committing such violations and 'where the relevant authorities fail to take the necessary corrective or mitigating measures'.[152] It sets out in some detail the elements that comprise the due diligence standard, including definitions, a framework for implementation, procedures for monitoring the recipient's compliance with international legal standards, operational measures and allocation of responsibility. The policy has been well-received, for instance, by the UN High Commissioner on Human Rights,[153] but practical and ethical problems of implementation have also been identified, not least that upon occasion if the UN refuses to work with certain forces there is no other entity available to assist civilians: 'In Somalia, if it refuses to finance AMISOM, no one will be left to fight Islamic insurgents and the country could descend into even worse chaos'.[154]

A fourth challenge is the security of UN personnel. Because sending governments are often anxious about the effects on public opinion of casualties, security arrangements for peacekeepers are usually much greater than the arrangements for the security of the population they are supposed to protect, thereby further weakening credibility. Lightly armed peacekeepers may not be able to defend themselves against a determined attack (as was the case of the Belgian peacekeepers in Rwanda at the outset of the 1994 genocide, and the Pakistani peacekeepers in Mogadishu on 5 June 1993), let alone protect the beleaguered population. Increasingly UN personnel are based in fortified areas and travel around in protected vehicles creating a profound divide between the international and the local and limiting the understanding of

[152] 'Human Rights Due Diligence Policy on U.N. Support to Non-U.N. Security Forces', UN Doc. A/67/775–S/2013/110, 5 March 2013.

[153] 'The [Due Diligence Policy] is an example of the UN taking its responsibilities seriously in this regard. It seeks to ensure that the Organization does not provide support to security forces involved in serious human rights violations, and acts to reduce the risk of violations'. Statement by Navanethem Pillay, High Commissioner for Human Rights, at the Open Debate of the Security Council on Protection of Civilians in Armed Conflicts, 25 June 2012, www.ohchr.org/EN/NewsEvents/Pages/DisplayNews.aspx?NewsID=12280&LangID=E.

[154] Bolopion, *op. cit.*

international forces about what is happening on the ground. Andersson and Weigand have vividly described the way in which risk aversion has weakened the capacity of UN missions in Mali and Afghanistan and also undermined their reputation and legitimacy.[155]

A fifth challenge is the military nature of peacekeeping forces. Many military forces have increasingly come to emphasise stabilisation and constabulary roles alongside their traditional war fighting roles, although the latter still tends to take precedence in planning and training. Moreover, stabilisation and constabulary duties are generally understood in military terms. Yet the protection of civilians often requires capacities and/or capabilities that are more akin to policing or indeed wider issues of governance relating to the construction and preservation of norms and upholding the rule of law. In partial recognition of this problem, international civilian police as well as lawyers have increasingly been deployed to conflict-affected areas, especially in the Balkans, even though it has turned out to be extremely difficult to recruit sufficient numbers who are sufficiently qualified and experienced to respond adequately to the levels of violence and disorder characteristic of the insecurity in a post-conflict environment. Further, the capacity of international forces to undertake such roles is limited. They are foreigners and lack the linguistic skills and local knowledge that law and order efforts require. The local law and order infrastructure is often very weak or non-existent. In Kosovo, for example, KFOR took on the role of policing and began to arrest dozens of individuals, but because there were no functioning courts or adequate prisons, no uniform standard of arrest and, indeed no agreement on the legal code, KFOR 'undercut its own rule of law message'.[156]

Understanding civilian protection in military terms also fails to take account of the adverse impact of militarism and military activities on women, including those undertaken by peacekeepers, as discussed in Chapter 10.

And a sixth problem is the fragmentation and incoherence of many peace operations. For example, one of the listed tasks of protection, facilitation of delivery of humanitarian assistance,[157] is the domain of the Office for the Coordination of Humanitarian Affairs (OCHA), which must work with DPKO, other agencies, local groups, humanitarian

[155] Andersson, Ruben and Weigand, Florian 2015. 'Intervention at Risk: The Vicious Cycle of Distance and Danger in Mali and Afghanistan', *Journal of Intervention and Statebuilding* 9(4): 519–541.

[156] Stromseth *et al.*, *op. cit.*, 172.

[157] See Chapter 5.

NGOs and peacekeepers on the ground. This cannot be described as a 'system' but rather 'a collection of organizations and groups which have, over the years, been morally impelled to alleviate the world's misery'.[158] The establishment of the Peacebuilding Commission in 2005 was supposed to integrate the various organisations that are involved in Peace Operations; yet as the Report on Peacebuilding Architecture has made clear, it has merely added to the fragmentation of missions. If we take into account the UN's partners such as states and regional organisations, the problem is multiplied.

Finally, it is noticeable that the resolutions relating to the protection of civilians, including those relating to the protection of children and women in armed conflict, as discussed in Chapter 5, make little reference to participation by the civilian population in question.[159] Resolution 1894 (protection of civilians in armed conflict) does request the Secretary-General to ensure local communities are informed about the mission and stresses the importance of consultation and co-operation between the UN, the ICRC and other organisations but not with local civil society movements.[160] Resolution 2122 (women, peace and security) goes somewhat further by recognising that it is important that the Council interacts with civil society, especially women's organisations, and it commits to 'ensuring that its periodic field visits to conflict areas include interactive meetings with local women and women's organizations in the field'. This greater openness has been continued in Resolution 2242, which reiterates the Council's intention to ensure its missions 'take into account gender considerations and the rights of women, including through consultation with local and international women's groups' and to invite civil society to brief it on country-specific situations.[161] Despite these moves towards a more collaborative engagement with civil society, the concept is of 'top-down' protection, and the capabilities of civilians (especially women and children) with respect to their own protection and security are barely recognised.

All the dilemmas discussed above have become starkly apparent in South Sudan, and attempts to resolve them have highlighted the need for further responses. In December 2013 thousands of people fleeing the outbreak of extreme ethnic and political violence sought shelter and

[158] Holmes, John 2013. *The Politics of Humanity: The Reality of Relief Aid*. Head of Zeus, 3.

[159] The same is also true of the Responsibility to Protect; see Chapter 5.

[160] UN SC Resolution 1894, 11 November 2009.

[161] UN SC Resolution 2242, 13 October 2015.

protection with the UN Mission in South Sudan (UNMISS).[162] This has evolved into what are termed 'protection of civilian sites' – a form of protection arguably unprecedented in UN peacekeeping history.[163] Humanitarian aid organisations such as Médecins Sans Frontières have exceptionally delivered assistance within the drastically overcrowded UN compound despite their usual policy of remaining distant from the armed forces.[164] UNMISS was established in July 2011 on the independence of South Sudan with the mandate *inter alia* to protect 'civilians under imminent threat of physical violence' and was authorised 'to use all necessary means, within the limits of its capacity and in the areas where its units are deployed, to carry out its protection mandate in particular when the Government of the Republic of South Sudan is not providing such security'.[165] Its mandate now encompasses deterring violence against civilians through proactive deployment and active patrolling in the protection sites, in short to 'maintain public safety and security of and within UNMISS protection of civilians sites'. This also requires 'regular interaction with civilians' and working in high-risk areas with humanitarian, human rights and development organisations, in such localities as schools, places of worship, hospitals and oil installations.[166] Other tasks include monitoring and investigating violations of human rights and IHL, and ensuring proper coordination with the Technical and Verification bodies. But how much force does 'all necessary means' to perform this mandate entail? Further the 'extensive resources' needed at the protection of civilians sites limits protection that can be offered elsewhere.[167] Other decisions facing UNMISS are how to respond to criminal acts carried out within the camps; peacekeeping missions do not have powers of arrest or to establish an independent criminal justice system.[168] The usual response is to hand a detained person to the government, but in this instance there are concerns that this would offend against the principle of non-

[162] By January 2014 this amounted to some 80,000 civilians. Mamiya, Ralph 2014. 'Legal Challenges for UN Peacekeepers Protecting Civilians in South Sudan', *ASIL Insights* 18 (26).

[163] Lilly, Damian, 2014. 'Protection of Civilians Sites: A New Type of Displacement Settlement?' *Humanitarian Exchange Magazine* 62.

[164] Mamiya, *op. cit.* [165] UN SC Resolution 1996, 8 July 2011.

[166] UN SC Resolution 2241, 9 October 2015; UN SC Resolution 2304, 12 August 2016.

[167] UN SC Resolution 2304, 12 August 2016.

[168] Such executive power may be authorised as is the case under UN SC Resolution 1244, 10 June 1999 with respect to the UN Interim Mission in Kosovo.

refoulement.[169] Further, what law would apply? Guidelines have been developed to address questions of legal applicability and more generally for managing the situation, allocating responsibilities and facilitating coordination with humanitarian agencies[170] but inevitably they have been formulated on an *ad hoc* basis to situations as they have arisen. Recent research shows how people in the protection sites do find their own solutions; in particular chiefs' courts are operating in the sites and, while these do help to preserve social order and reduce violence, they also purvey norms that reproduce gender and generational inequalities.[171]

Despite this extensive mandate, violence and insecurity prevail,[172] with an especially violent episode in July 2016 when three days of intense fighting saw multiple civilian deaths and severe sexual violence, including within or nearby UNMISS headquarters and the protection of civilian sites nearby. Crimes were committed by both Government security forces and rebel forces. Peacekeepers were also attacked and two were killed and others injured. There was widespread damage to UN buildings and the protection of civilian sites. An independent inquiry into the violence found that lack of preparedness, ineffective command and control, and a risk-averse culture among peacekeepers meant that UNMISS did not respond effectively to protect civilians, including from sexual violence and human rights violations.[173] Secretary-General Ban Ki-moon announced the dismissal of the force commander and that he would introduce further measures to enhance civilian protection, including through greater accountability of uniformed and civilian personnel.[174]

169 Mamiya, *op. cit.* 170 *Ibid.*

171 Ibreck, Rachel and Pendeleton, Naomi 2016. 'Customary Protection? Chiefs' Courts as Public Authority in UN Protection of Civilian Sites in South Sudan', *Justice and Security Research Programme Paper 34,* September 2016.

172 UN SC Resolution 2304, 12 August 2016, strongly condemns in South Sudan: 'all human rights violations and abuses and violations of international humanitarian law, including those involving extrajudicial killings, ethnically targeted violence, rape and other forms of sexual and gender-based violence, recruitment and use of children, enforced disappearances, arbitrary arrests and detention, violence aimed at spreading terror among the civilian population, targeting of members of civil society, and attacks on schools, places of worship, hospitals, and United Nations and associated personnel, by all parties'.

173 Executive Summary of the Independent Special Investigation into the violence which occurred in Juba in 2016 and UNMISS response at www.un.org/News/dh/infocus/sudan/Public_Executive_Summary_on_the_Special_Investigation_Report_1_Nov_2016.pdf.

174 'South Sudan: Ban to Put in Place Measures to Improve UN Mission's Ability to Protect Civilians', at www.un.org/apps/news/story.asp?NewsID=55448#.WBjEtPkrKUk.

However, inadequate resources and the complexity of the tasks – and dangers – facing peacekeepers mean that, despite detailed and wide-ranging mandates, civilian protection in new wars remains severely limited.

9.3.3 Gender Breakdown of Peacekeeping Forces

In 2000 SC Resolution 1325 on women and peace and security urged the Secretary-General to 'to seek to expand the role and contribution of women in United Nations field-based operations, and especially among military observers, civilian police, human rights and humanitarian personnel'. In 2013 the Council again encouraged 'troop- and police-contributing countries to increase the percentage of women military and police in deployments to United Nations peacekeeping operations'.[175] The reality is thin. In 1993 women made up approximately 1 per cent of deployed uniformed personnel. In 2015 the figure is 3 per cent of women in UN missions, and the Global Study on SC Resolution 1325 notes that most of these are support staff and that the figure was the same as in 2011.[176] All-female UN police units have been deployed around the world, for instance, in Liberia, Haiti and the DRC with the reported advantage of creating safer spaces for women.[177]

Does it matter if women are included in peacekeeping forces or international civilian police forces? The UN argues that women's presence 'helps reduce conflict and confrontation', gives women and children a greater sense of security, improves access and support for local women and makes peacekeepers 'more approachable' to local women.[178] In reality there is insufficient data for any empirical evidence to measure the success or effectiveness of the inclusion of more women in peacekeeping operations,[179] including whether this would reduce the incidence of sexual exploitation and abuse by peacekeepers. The Global Study, however, notes that no single woman peacekeeper has been accused of sexual exploitation or abuse while on mission.[180] Practical outcomes of

[175] UN SC Res 2122, 18 October 2013. [176] Study on 1325, *op. cit.*, 139.
[177] GENDER: Women UN Peacekeepers – More Needed' at www.irinnews.org/report/89194.
[178] *Ibid.*
[179] The UN SC has recognised 'the need for timely information and analysis on the impact of armed conflict on women and girls, the role of women in peacebuilding and the gender dimensions of peace processes'; UN SC Resolution 2122, 18 October 2013.
[180] Study on 1325, 141.

the greater participation by women might include the empowering of women in the host community; addressing the specific needs of women former combatants during the DDR process; allowing searches of female areas and houses (such searches by male military personnel contributed to local tensions in Iraq and Afghanistan); interviewing women survivors of sexual violence in order to facilitate access to legal, health and other services; or mentoring female cadets at police and military academies. Enhancing the participation of women in UN peacekeeping operations (and in senior roles) would also be in conformity with the Convention on the Elimination of All Forms of Discrimination against Women, 1979, article 8.[181] More importantly perhaps, a gendered perspective could counter the linear and binary conception of conflict that underpins peacekeeping efforts. Tarya Varynen points out that UN efforts to increase women's participation in peacekeeping are rooted in modern assumptions about the role of expertise and rationality as well as the notion that gender equals women and that women are differentiated from men. Without a rethinking of the nature of conflict as 'zones of ambiguity' and the ways in which gender roles are constructed and perpetuated in such zones, any numerical increase in the participation of women may not make much difference. Given the gendered nature of war and conflict and the way that conflict is constructed on the basis of gender relations, it can be argued that countering some of the gender asymmetries of conflict could also weaken the very way that war and conflict are constructed. A gendered perspective would thus require a rethinking of the role of peacekeeping more in keeping with the everyday reality of 'new wars'.[182]

9.4 Peacebuilding

The peacebuilding component of the *jus post bellum* is composed of a package of measures aimed at avoiding recurrence of conflict through developing democracy and a rule of law as well as a market economy that are variously described as peacebuilding, state-building, nation-building

[181] 'States Parties shall take all appropriate measures to ensure to women, on equal terms with men and without any discrimination, the opportunity to represent their Governments at the international level and to participate in the work of international organizations'. *Convention on the Elimination of All Forms of Discrimination against Women*, 18 December 1979, article 8.

[182] Varynen, Tarya 2004. 'Gender and Peace Operations: The Confines of Modernity', *International Peacekeeping* 11(1): 125–142.

or reconstruction. As is evident from the previous sections it is hard to separate peacebuilding from peacemaking and peacekeeping; the tasks often go hand in hand. Peacebuilding, in UN parlance, is no longer understood narrowly as activities undertaken in the immediate aftermath of conflict, but looks to long-term sustainable stability and security through three priority principles: inclusivity, institution-building and sustained international support and mutual accountability.[183] Multiple players are engaged in international peacebuilding bodies: military and civilian, specialists in humanitarian, human rights and development work, public and private financial institutions and donors, intergovernmental and non-governmental institutions. Overlapping mandates, different priorities and lack of hierarchical authority or control can undermine efforts.[184]

In 2005, in response to the recognised need for a 'coordinated, coherent and integrated approach to post-conflict peacebuilding and reconciliation with a view to achieving sustainable peace' and, as one of the two institutional reforms accepted by it, the General Assembly (GA) decided to establish a Peacebuilding Commission (PBC).[185] This was achieved through concurrent resolutions of the GA[186] and SC,[187] thereby seeking to 'fill an institutional gap between the work of the Security Council (which addresses threats to international peace and security) and the Economic and Social Council (which addresses issues of human development)'.[188] As a central part of the UN peacebuilding architecture,[189] the Peacebuilding Commission is mandated to 'bring together all relevant actors to marshal resources and to advise on and propose integrated strategies for post-conflict peacebuilding and recovery'. Its role is thus

[183] Report of the Secretary-General, *Peacebuilding in the Aftermath of Conflict*, UN Doc. A/69/399–S/2014/694, 23 September 2014, para. 4.

[184] For instance, in Kosovo ICTY investigators had the first responsibility for the exhumation of mass graves. However, their concern with securing evidence for potential prosecution of war crimes and crimes against humanity at times conflicted with the identification of bodies, the interests of local families and the humanitarian goals of UNMIK.

[185] UN GA Resolution 60/1, 24 October 2005, World Summit Outcome, para. 97.

[186] UN GA Resolution 60/180, 20 December 2005, The Peacebuilding Commission.

[187] UN SC Resolution 1645, 20 December 2005.

[188] Jenkins, Rob 2008. 'The UN Peacebuilding Commission and the Dissemination of International Norms', *Crisis States Working Papers Series No. 2, LSE Destin,* Working Paper No. 38.

[189] The other institutional bodies are the Peacebuilding Fund and Peacebuilding Support Office.

primarily advice and coordination with respect to reconstruction and sustainable development in the states it has included in its agenda (currently Burundi, the Central African Republic, Guinea, Guinea-Bissau, Liberia and Sierra Leone).

It has been argued that to be effective, peacebuilding 'requires a human security perspective' which denotes a 'bottom-up' process giving 'concrete expression to the ideas of "local ownership" and community and civil society engagement in these processes'.[190] As a UN institution the PBC is evidently 'top-down', but it is encouraged to 'to consult with civil society, nongovernmental organizations, including women's organizations, and the private sector engaged in peacebuilding activities'. Despite apparent acceptance of this position, it has been noted that in practice the inclusion of women in the development of strategic thinking and policy development in the PBC is limited, and 'dependent on the lobbying of dedicated norm entrepreneurs among member states, UN bureaucrats and nongovernmental organizations'.[191] The PBC has since adopted a Declaration on Women's economic empowerment for peacebuilding.[192] The Declaration recognises the 'critical role' of women in working towards economic recovery and, in language reminiscent of Security Council Resolution 1325 (2000), urges relevant bodies to improve women's participation in the various peace processes and to recognise the importance of creating post-conflict conditions that 'generate decent jobs for women, nurture their business skills, encourage them to join the workforce, and deliver the financial services that these women need, both in the formal and informal sectors'. Enhancing women's economic independence is important step for their 'full development and advancement',[193] but it is noticeable that the Declaration is not cast in terms of women's rights, but rather in those of post-conflict market oriented economic growth.[194]

Despite the presence of external forces, in the post–UN Charter era the fiction is maintained of the territorial integrity of the state and the goal of

[190] Office of the Special Adviser on Africa, Report: *Human Security and Peacebuilding in Africa: The Need for an Inclusive Approach*, December 2009, www.un.org/africa/osaa/reports/human_security_peacebuilding_africa.pdf.

[191] Tryggestad, Torunn L. 2010. 'The UN Peacebuilding Commission and Gender: A Case of Norm Reinforcement', *International Peacekeeping* 17(2): 159–171.

[192] UN Peacebuilding Commission, PBC/7/OC/3, 26 September 2013.

[193] *Convention on the Elimination of All Forms of Discrimination against Women,* 1979, article 3.

[194] See generally Claire, Duncanson 2016. *Gender and Peacebuilding*, Polity Press.

governance in accordance with internal will. However, this goal is necessarily constrained both by the international presence and by the nature of any peace agreement or post-conflict political settlement. In what follows we outline some of the various components of peacebuilding and try to show how these are often weakened, undermined or subverted as a consequence of these constraints.

Elections and Legitimate Political Authority

It is widely agreed that the basis of a lasting peace has to be a legitimate political authority.[195] Compliance with a rule of law depends on trust and the belief that public authority guarantees a rule of law. In a democracy, legitimate political authority is equated with the state and the means of establishing its legitimacy tends to be through 'free and fair' elections. The Brahimi Report saw such elections as underpinning efforts to strengthen governance institutions, requiring civil society support and a culture of respect for human rights.[196] Very often, elections are considered the precondition for an exit strategy for the international community determining the moment when a locally based legitimate political authority is established, able to take over the role of the international presence. Within the expert community of peacebuilders, there are debates about the timing and sequencing of elections, the pros and cons of different electoral systems, and the best mechanisms for management, monitoring and dispute resolution.[197] While these issues are highly pertinent in specific situations, the broader question is how far elections in conflict-affected areas do in practice underpin the construction of legitimate political authority.

Thad Dunning suggests that elections can be viewed either as an alternative to violence or as a complement.[198] It can be argued that where war is conceived in traditional terms as a political contest involving legitimate

[195] See World Development Report 2011. *Conflict, Security and Devlopment*. World Bank; see also DFID and UKaid 2010. *Building Peaceful States and Societies: A DFID Practice Paper*. DFID.

[196] *Brahimi Report, op. cit.*, para. 38.

[197] See, for example, Reilly, Ben 2003. 'Democratic Validation', in Darby, John and McGinty, Roger (eds.). *Contemporary Peacemaking: Conflict, Violence and Peace Processes*. Palgrave Macmillan, 174–183; IDEA. *Electoral System Design: The New International IDEA Handbook*, www.idea.int/publications/esd/upload/ESD_Handb_low.pdf; Brancati, Dawn, and Snyder, Jack L. 2011. 'Rushing to the Polls: The Causes of Premature Post-Conflict Elections', *Journal of Conflict Resolution* 55(3): 469–492.

[198] Dunning, Thad, 2011. 'Fighting and Voting: Violent Conflict and Electoral Politics', *Journal of Conflict Resolution* 55(3): 327–339.

grievances, it is possible to conceive of elections as a continuation of the contest, an alternative way of deciding differences of opinion. In this instance, elections can be understood as a substitute for violence and thereby establishing the basis of legitimate authority.[199] But if war is understood less as a political contest and more as mutual enterprise for achieving political power, then violence can easily be viewed as a mechanism for winning elections, in other words, elections are a complement to violence, and the legitimacy of authority so established is highly dubious.[200]

Violence as a tool for winning elections is a phenomenon that is often to be found during and following contemporary wars. A typical tactic in 'new wars' is establishing control through the expulsion of those who challenge that control – dissidents, peoples of other ethnicities or religion depending on the form of control. In both Croatia and Bosnia-Herzegovina, ethnic cleansing was a way to ensure electoral majorities for the HDZ and the SDS (the Croat and Serb nationalist parties, respectively) in specific areas. A similar pattern can be observed in Iraq where displacement in Baghdad during the civil war of 2006–2008 established a chequer board of safe Shi'ia and Sunni constituencies. And there are plenty of other examples. In an extraordinary piece of investigative research, Abbey Steele shows how the Colombian military and right-wing para-military during the 1990s undertook what became known as 'political cleansing' in the town of Apartado, where they used electoral data to expel people in leftist neighbourhoods, thereby changing the political composition of the town.[201] As one priest noted, it was a 'perverse policy of "draining the sea". It was barbaric'.[202] Others have shown similar patterns in Gujarat, where Hindu-Muslim violence made possible swings to the Hindu nationalist party, the Bharatia Janata party (BJP), in 2002 – a 'particularly brutal form of campaign expenditure'[203] – and in Kenya's Rift Valley during the 1990s.[204] In other words, tactics of

199 This is very much the argument of Chantal Mouffe who takes a Schmittian view of domestic struggle and the need to hold elections as a way of determining the outcome of the struggle. See Mouffe, C. 1999. *The Challenge of Carl Schmitt.* Verso

200 Elections in low income ethnically divided countries enhance the risk of politically organised violence; Collier, Paul 2009. *Wars, Guns and Votes: Democracy in Dangerous Places.* HarperCollins.

201 Steele, Abbey 2011. 'Electing Displacement: Political Cleansing in Apartado, Colombia', *Journal of Conflict Resolution* 55(3): 423–445.

202 *Ibid.*, 437. 203 Dunning, *op. cit.*, 333.

204 Klopp, Jacqueline M. 2001. '"Ethic Clashes" and Winning Elections: The Case of Kenya's Electoral Despotism', *Canadian Journal of African Affairs* 35(3): 473–517.

this kind, which are widespread in contemporary wars and their aftermath, constitute a kind of violent gerrymandering.

Where peace agreements or political settlements have been signed that confirm the results of this type of violence, elections do not express the voice of the people; rather they serve to entrench the *status quo*. They 'legitimise' the power relations established during wartime and recognised in political settlements rather than create a basis for the provision of public goods as demanded by the population. In other words, they enable the warring parties to sustain their positions and, if necessary, use violence to retain the political composition of their constituencies, thereby posing a long-term obstacle to peacebuilding. As Barnet Rubin puts it in relation to Afghanistan: 'The election of representatives ... [is supposed to be] a means to the accountable provision of public services by the state. If the state is incapable of providing those public services, elections can lead to kleptocracy rather than democracy'.[205]

The case of Bosnia and Herzegovina is an excellent example. Since 1995, there have been general elections every two years up to 2002 and every four years thereafter, not to mention municipal and cantonal elections. Because of the ways in which rules, procedures, quotas and constituency boundaries reflect what was agreed at Dayton, elections are normally won by the nationalist parties. On two occasions, in 2002 and 2010, a non-nationalist party, the SDP (although its members are predominantly Bosniak), gained the largest number of seats, but because of the complexity of the institutional arrangements and because it lacked an overall majority, it was unable to overcome the strait jacket of ethnic politics. 'In sum', says Robert Belloni, 'elections empowered nationalist parties, made the reversal of ethnic cleansing more difficult and complicated plans for the departure of international peace-builders from the country'.[206]

Security Sector Reform and Law and Order

The first Special Representative of the UN Secretary-General to Kosovo, Bernard Kouchner, argued that the main 'lesson from Kosovo' is the need

[205] Quoted in Sisk, Timothy. 'Pathways of the Political: Electoral Processes after Civil War', in Paris, Roland and Sisk, Timothy (eds.). *The Dilemmas of Statebuilding*. Routledge, 196–224.

[206] Belloni, Robert 2004. 'Peacebuilding and Consociational Electoral Engineering in Bosnia and Herzegovina', *International Peacekeeping* 11(2): 334–353.

for an immediate 'Law and Order' kit.[207] Alongside the adaptation of international forces has been the effort to transfer responsibility for security to local forces. Although there are a few cases where international programmes for disarmament and demobilisation have been deemed successful, most notably in Sierra Leone, in general the aim has to been to absorb fighting units into the army and police forces and to reform and restructure these services. The consequence has been extremely high levels of security spending in all post-conflict situations. In Bosnia in 1998, expenditure on security services (including international forces) was 130 per cent of Bosnian GDP, of which around 20 per cent of GDP was spent on Bosnian security forces and about 6 per cent was spent on the Bosnian military.[208] In Iraq by 2011, some $24.5 billion had been spent on rebuilding the security forces. There were some 933,000 people in the security services spread between the Ministry of Defence, the Ministry of Interior and the Prime Minister's counter-terrorism force; Iraq had become the biggest military spender as a share of GDP in the world.[209] Yet in 2014 these forces melted away in the face of the threat from IS (although in 2016 they were more militarily successful). A further problem has been the way in which SSR incentivizes armed groups because they can gain in money and rank by being part of an SSR programme.[210]

The results of these efforts have in most cases been disappointing. In general most explanations have to do with the need to be more holistic and to address norms as well as technical capacity-building. Thus Stromseth argues that the emphasis on the police has often neglected other aspects of the justice system, such as courts and prisons, as well as basic economic and social services that are preconditions for law and order. She points out, for example, that after the US-led invasion of Haiti, considerable progress was said to have been made in vetting and training

[207] Quoted in Stromseth *et al., op. cit.*, 173.

[208] Kaldor, Mary 2003. 'Security Structures in Bosnia Herzegovina', in Cawthra, Gavin and Luckham, Robin. *Governing Insecurity: Democratic Control of Military and Security Establishments in Transitional Democracies*. Zed Books, 205–231.

[209] Dodge, Toby 2012. *From War to a New Authoritarianism*. International Institute for Strategic Studies, Routledge.

[210] In DRC, Baaz and Verrewijen offer several examples of examples of leaders being welcomed back into the FARDC with higher ranks and better deployments as a consequence of SSR clauses in peace negotiations. See Baaz, M. E. and Verweijen, J. 2013. 'The Volatility of a Half-Cooked Bouillabaisse: Rebel-Military Integration and Conflict Dynamics in the Eastern DRC', *African Affairs* 112 (449): 563–582.

the Haitian police, but these achievements were undermined by the corruption and lack of capacity of the judiciary.[211] She and other scholars also argue that insufficient attention is paid to culture and norm construction and that the international community has failed to engage civil society organisations and grassroots actors.[212]

These explanations are undoubtedly important; excessively securitised societies are rarely safe societies. But perhaps the biggest failure is cognitive; the continuing tendency to perceive conflict in terms of a contest of wills with a clear ending. In particular, what is neglected are two aspects of post-conflict settings that are actually built into peace agreements. First is the continuing role of the warring parties. Security sector reform does not work either because there are continuing parallel structures within the security services, for instance, in Iraq and Afghanistan, where 'transition' processes have been undertaken in haste as part of an exit strategy for the intervening forces. Or they do not work because, even where the security services have been effectively purged, they are subject to political interference and are used as the tools of those whose political positions have been entrenched in peace agreements or, in the case of Iraq, through the priorities of the international presence. Second is the tendency to impose a Western model of security when the Western model itself is in need of reform. Thus, for example, Western armies are designed primarily for 'classic' European wars. Where the problem is no longer war between states but instead war within and across states, what is the function of armies? If their role is to integrate the various armed factions, do they not require a purpose other than the defence of external borders? If they are trained for an internal combat role, might that not interfere with stabilisation efforts? This problem became acute in Palestine after the Oslo agreements, where in addition

[211] According to Stromseth: 'Although enormous initial progress was made in vetting and training the Haitian National Police during the United Mission following Jean-Bertrand Aristide's return to power, other parts of the justice system did not receive the same degree of assistance or pressure for reform. As a result, corrupt judges could be bribed to release suspects and bad governance generally undermined the larger political system in which police operated. Large numbers of pre-trial detainees languished for months or years in squalid prisons without legal process. Little was done, moreover, to address the widespread suspicion that law is a vehicle for control rather than of justice'. Stromseth, *op. cit.*, 1454.

[212] See also Carothers, Thomas 2009. 'Rule of Law Temptations', *The Fletcher Forum of World Affairs* 33(1): 49–61. Golub, Stephen 2003. 'Beyond Rule of Law Orthodoxy: The Legal Empowerment Alternative', *Carnegie Endowment for Peace, Working Paper* No. 41.

to the Palestinian civilian police, which had a long history and had formerly been the only Palestinian security service, outside countries, especially the United States and Iran, trained a number of combat services accountable to different factions within the Palestinian Authority that ended up fighting each other.[213]

Police reform in Bosnia exemplifies the fundamental dilemma. In Bosnia, there have been a number of police missions – the United Nations International Police Task Force (IPTF) from 1996 to 2002, which at its peak numbered 1,800 officers; the European Police Mission (EUPM), which succeeded the IPTF; and the West European Union mission to Mostar from 1994 to 1996 designed to unify the police forces in Mostar. These missions, especially the IPTF, have been relatively successful in reducing the numbers in the police force (which had been artificially inflated by the inclusion of various militias) and weeding out some human rights offenders, but the process has been criticised for being partial and undertaken in haste; there remain some war criminals in the police, and decertified police in an unprecedented co-operation have protested the process.[214] The reforms also led to increased minority representation in the police, with the aim of reassuring returnees, even though the process has been much slower than anticipated and minority police officers are often relegated to desk positions. But the fundamental problem is that police remain under the control of the former warring parties because they are accountable to ethnically administered institutions, and it is the former warring parties that are primarily responsible for predatory behaviour. It is true that everyday security has improved, and it is also the case that the police, by and large, no longer directly engage in human rights violations; nevertheless, they often fail to react when human rights violations are committed, especially where this relates to ethnic discrimination.[215]

[213] Jan Faber, Mient, and Kaldor, Mary 2009. 'The Deterioration of Human Security in Palestine', in Martin, Mary and Kaldor, Mary (eds.). *The European Union and Human Security: External Interventions and Missions*. Routledge, 95–111.

[214] Collantes-Celador, Gemma 2013. 'Civil Society and the Bosnian Police Certification Process: Challenging "the Guardians"', in Bojicic-Dzelilovic, Vesna and Kostovicova, Denisa and Ker-Lindsay, James (eds.). *Civil Society and Transitions in the Western Balkans*. Palgrave Macmillan, chapter 10.

[215] See Collantes-Celador, Gemma 2006. 'Police Reform: Peacebuilding through 'Democratic Policing'?' *International Peacekeeping* 12(3): 364–376; Collantes-Celador, Gemma 2009. 'Becoming "European" through Police Reform: A Successful Strategy in Bosnia and Herzegovina?' *Crime, Law and Social Change* 51(2): 231–242.

In addition to police reform, Bosnia has been exemplary in post-conflict judicial reform, including the dismissal of all judges, who then had to go through a vetting process before being rehired, and court restructuring.[216] Nevertheless the judiciary 'is still embedded in a restrictive social and political fabric'.[217] Especially in the RS, the judiciary 'cannot take on the political leadership. Police drag their feet or lose evidence, witnesses fail to appear, judges acquit on technicalities'.[218] For example, the RS Prime Minister Milorad Dodik was successfully able to manipulate the system by threatening a referendum on the independence of the RS and ratcheting up the risk of renewed conflict so as to avoid charges of corruption, misuse of office and fraud.[219]

In other words, the example of Bosnia shows the way in which political elites legitimised through an international sponsored peace agreement are able to obstruct law and order reforms as well as security sector reforms. Even where the international community pushes for these reforms, as in Bosnia, it often ends up compromising in order to retain the peace agreement. In other places, as in Palestine, 'old war' understandings of the security sector may actually contribute to insecurity.

Regulating the Economy

In 'new wars', formal economies tend to collapse. There are dramatic falls in GDP, especially in manufacturing, as well as through taxation, and big increases in unemployment. Human capital is destroyed through death and displacement, especially of the highly skilled. The provision of basic services like water and electricity is often non-existent or intermittent, while the provision of other public goods like health and education are greatly weakened. This is almost completely the opposite of what happened in 'old wars' where the state mobilised the whole economy for the war effort, increasing employment and taxation, as well as social services. Of course, there were disruptions to non-military production, destruction of physical infrastructure and black market activities. But because of higher levels of taxation, and indeed higher levels of political

216 See Pimentel, David 2008. 'Restructuring the Courts: In Search of Basic Principles for the Judiciary of Post-War Bosnia and Herzegovina', *Chicago Journal of International Law* 9 (1): 107–111.

217 International Crisis Group 2011. 'Bosnia What Does Republika Srpska Want?' *ICG Europe Report* No. 214.

218 *Ibid.*

219 Kaldor, Mary, 'How Peace Agreements Undermine the Rule of Law', *Global Policy,* Volume 7, Issue 2 May 2016, pages 146–155

legitimacy, these could be dealt with rapidly after the wars. Old war economies were also largely self-sufficient and autarkic. By contrast, 'new war' economies are open economies, heavily dependent on imports of weapons and food.

In 'new wars', the formal economy is replaced by what Andreas describes as the 'clandestine' political economy of war. Many of the Serb paramilitaries who carried out the worst atrocities in Bosnia were formed out of criminal gangs and were rewarded by looting. The bigger and more important paramilitaries seized valuable goods – homes, appliances, small businesses, jewellery and money – while the smaller paramilitaries and local militia 'stripped the wires out of the walls and dismantled windows and door frames'.[220] On the Bosniak side, Sarajevo was initially defended by criminal gangs who teamed up with the police; as one former commander put it, there was a 'thin line between patriotism and criminality and some didn't see the difference as real'.[221] The black market became the source of basic necessities. Checkpoints were used to manipulate prices, and smuggling of all kinds (people, cigarettes, weapons) was rife. Humanitarian agencies were 'taxed' and were used as a cover for smuggling.

Similar descriptions can be found of the political economy of other 'new wars'. In particular smuggling in valuable commodities – oil (Iraq and Angola) diamonds (Sierra Leone, Liberia, Angola), drugs (Afghanistan and Colombia) and antiquities (Iraq and Syria) – has been critical especially in resource-rich areas. Because of the importance of generating foreign exchange, the clandestine economy is increasingly integrated into the wider regressive global economy. In Somalia, Syria and other places, hostage taking and seeking large monetary ransoms has become a significant source of income.[222] This has set government refusals to pay money to terrorists or pirates against humanitarian demands by families for payment. It has also led to friction between states that allegedly pay for the release of hostages and those that do not.

[220] Andreas, Peter 2004. 'The Clandestine Political Economy of War and Peace in Bosnia', *International Studies Quarterly* 48: 29–52, 35.

[221] *Ibid.*, 37.

[222] The Special Representative of the Secretary-General on Sexual Violence in Armed Conflict has reported that in one month ISIL extorted $850,000 for the release of 200 abducted Yezidi and in 2014 ransom money to the Yezidis amounted to between $35 million and $45 million; Report of the Secretary-General on the threat posed by ISIL (Da'esh) to international peace and security and the range of United Nations efforts in support of Member States in countering the threat, UN Doc. S/2016/92, 29 January 2016.

It is worth noting that the effects of sanctions are often very similar. Comprehensive sanctions were imposed on what was then Yugoslavia in May 1992. They may be regarded as having been effective; the formal economy contracted dramatically in 1992 and 1993. But the sanctions led to state-sanctioned smuggling not only in Serbia and Montenegro but all over the region.[223] When sanctions were eventually lifted, smugglers turned to other activities:

> Out of the deals to link Serbian intelligence to professional smugglers emerged new networks dealing in stolen cars, cigarettes, arms, illegal aliens and heroin that were the scourge of Europe. Government functionaries who had begun smuggling to prop up the regime continued to smuggle to prop up their own bank accounts.[224]

Something similar happened in Iraq as has been revealed in the investigations into the Oil for Food programme and also more recently in Syria.[225]

In the immediate aftermath of a peace agreement or an international intervention, there are usually donors' conferences and proposals for a 'Marshall Plan' to kick start reconstruction on the model of World War II when generous economic assistance stimulated rapid recovery and indeed growth. Bakarat and Zyck have shown that economic assistance in contemporary conflict-affected countries is actually much larger than was the Marshall Plan.[226] But economic assistance in 'new war' settings tends to be much less effective than it was after World War II. International intervention triggers short-term economic growth as a range of activities are required to service the international presence – housing, restaurants and bars, transportation and so on. But it is much less effective at generating legitimate ways of making a living and self-

[223] Andreas, Peter 2005. 'Consequences of Sanctions: Embargo Busting and Its Legacy', *International Studies Quarterly* 49(2): 335–360; Bojicic, Vesna and Dyker, David 1993. 'Sanctions on Serbia: Sledgehammer or Scalpel?' Sussex European Institute, Working Paper No. 1.

[224] Andreas, *op. cit.*, 348 ('Consequences of Sanctions').

[225] Volcker, Paul and Goldstone, Richard and Pieth, Mark 2005. *Independent Inquiry into the United Nations Oil-for-Food Programme: Manipulation of the Oil-for Food Programme by the Iraqi Regime*, www.iic-offp.org; Turkmani, Rim, Ali K. Ali, Kaldor, Mary and Bojicic-Dzelilovic, Vesna 2015. 'Countering the Logic of the War Economy in Syria: Evidence from Three Local Areas', London School of Economics, 30 July 2015; at www.securityintransition.org/wp-content/uploads/2015/08/Countering-war-economy-Syria2.pdf.

[226] Barakat and Zyck, *op. cit.*

sustaining economic development. This is partly because of the way aid is absorbed through layers of subcontracting; in a review of four hundred projects in Afghanistan, Ghani and Lockhart found that up to 70 per cent of the funding had been spent on internal costs 'for international salaries, white land cruisers, satellite communications, and specially chartered airlines'.[227] It is also partly because of the way the international presence distorts local salary scales as skilled personnel like civil servants, doctors, teachers, university professors, engineers or lawyers can earn more as drivers and interpreters for international agencies. But this is by no means the whole story.

Critics of the Liberal Peace often, with some reason, charge that the problem is the standard neo-liberal recipe involving macro-economic stabilisation, trade liberalisation and privatisation.[228] The strategy focusses on stability of the currency and on economic growth but does not take into account key post-conflict issues such as employment, social welfare and poverty. Neo-liberalism, like new wars, is a good way to dismantle planned economies and especially old-fashioned uncompetitive industries. In theory, the neo-liberal model stimulates growth through the development of a legitimate private sector. But in countries where the legitimate economy is already massively weakened, neo-liberalism tends to mean cuts to all kinds of state activities such as basic services and the rise of criminal activities as the only way to make a living. In particular, aid and reform policies are easily subverted by the predatory networks established during the war. Since the warring parties transform themselves into political and business leaders and businessmen, they are often in control of contracting, privatisation, and regulation. Gustiozzi, for example, traces the way that former commanders from the Soviet period have gradually emerged as warlords and entrepreneurs in Afghanistan, enriching themselves through land grabs, property and illicit activities like drugs, as well as contracts with the international agencies.[229]

227 Ghani, Ashraf and Lockhart, Clare 2007. 'Writing the History of the Future: Securing Stability through Peace Agreements', *Journal of Intervention and Statebuilding* 1(3): 275–306, 293.

228 E.g., Chimni notes the need for the 'post-conflict' state to comply with IMF and World Bank prescriptions whereby it continues to be repressive and its resources privatised. This also limits the possibility of local participation or of a reconstruction agenda taking account of their needs; Chimni, B. S. 2004. 'International Institutions Today: An Imperial Global State in the Making', *European Journal of International Law* 15: 1–37, 16.

229 Giustozzi, Antonio 2011. 'War and Peace Economies of Afghanistan's Strongmen', *International Peacekeeping* 14(1): 75–89.

As has been the case with law and order, these difficulties are increasingly recognised by the international community. There has been a growing emphasis on the importance of establishing a legal framework for economic activity, including property rights, privatisation, enforcement of contracts, competition rules, dispute resolution and arbitration, banking supervision and so on. However these efforts to introduce commercial law are often stalled. Again, Bosnia represents an illuminating example, even though the restoration of property rights has been one of the more successful planks of international policy. Annual reports on the Stabilisation and Accession Process (SAP) show that Bosnia has been slow to advance sales of state-owned property and that there exist significant barriers to private sector development. There are weaknesses in banking sector supervision, competition rules and anti-trust legislation.[230] Initially, the various ethnic elites obstructed the privatisation of state-controlled enterprises that had dominated the Bosnian economy because they were under their political control and were therefore a source of predation. When privatisation did get under way in the mid-2000s, enterprises largely came under the control of companies linked to the ethnic elites. This 'ethnic privatisation' helps to explain why investment is so low and why it has been so difficult to generate new sources of employment and growth.[231]

In other words, international policies aimed at establishing a market economy often fail to contribute to economic reconstruction, aimed at building legitimate livelihoods as an alternative to the criminalised war economy. As long as predatory networks remain in power, international policies, especially those framed in market terms, tend to feed into and strengthen the activities of these networks rather constructing an alternative. This is why establishing a legal framework is so important, but it is also why attempts to establish such a framework are usually undermined.

[230] See Bojicic-Dzelilovic, Vesna and Kostovicova, Denisa 2013. 'Europeanization and Conflict Networks: Private Sector Development in Post-conflict Bosnia-Herzegovina', *East European Politics* 29(2): 19–35.

[231] See Pugh, Michael 2005. 'Transformation in the Political Economy of Bosnia since Dayton', *International Peacekeeping* 12(3): 448–462; Donais, Timothy 2002. 'The Politics of Privatization in Post-Dayton Bosnia', *Southeast European Politics* 3(1): 3–19; Venugopal, Rajesh 2011. 'Privatisation, Private Sector Development and Horizontal Inequalities in Post-Conflict Countries', in Langer, Arnim, Stewart, Frances and Venugopal, Rajesh (eds.). *Horizontal Inequalities and Post-Conflict Development: Conflict, Inequality and Ethnicity*. Palgrave Macmillan, chapter 5.

Because the predatory local economy is interconnected to the global economy, some of the more successful efforts to address the problems have involved regulation at a global level. Thus the Kimberly process for the certification of diamonds, pushed by NGOs such as Global Witness, contributed to the weakening of the war economies in Sierra Leone and Liberia, while control of Diaspora funding may have been a significant factor in the ending of the war in Sri Lanka.

9.5 Conclusion

Explanations for the shortcomings of the Liberal Peace model tend to fall into two camps. Supporters of the Liberal Peace tend to explain the failures in terms of mistakes in policy or in the execution of policy, for example, emphasis on liberalisation rather than institutionalisation,[232] or short-termism and incoherence of missions. Critics of the Liberal Peace charge that the whole project is flawed since externally assisted top-down peacebuilding or state-building is not possible and merely represents a form of neo-imperialism.[233]

We have argued in this chapter that the various mistakes in policy or the execution of policy noted by supporters of the Liberal Peace have to be understood in systemic terms as a consequence of the way that power relations are restructured in new wars. This restructuring of power relations tends to be confirmed and codified in peace agreements, upheld by peacekeeping and often further entrenched in elections and attempts to introduce markets. It therefore presents big obstacles to the restoration (or establishment) of normal life and the establishment of a rule of law, whether we are talking about everyday security or legitimate economic activity. As Donais puts it: 'If domestic political elites are both indispensable partners and primary impediments in rule of law implementation, precisely how should international actors proceed in their engagement with such actors?'[234] The problem of the Liberal Peace, say Newman, Paris and Richmond, is that it 'tends to mediate – from the top-down –

232 Paris, Roland 2004. *At War's End: Building Peace after Civil Conflict*. Cambridge University Press.

233 Chandler, *op. cit.*; Richmond, Oliver P. 2009. 'A Post-Liberal Peace: Eirenism and the Everyday', *Review of International Studies* 35(3): 557–580; Duffield, Mark and Hewitt, Vernon (eds.) 2013. *Empire, Development and Colonialism: The Past in the Present*. James Curry.

234 Donais, Timothy 2013. 'Power Politics and the Rule of Law in Post-Dayton Bosnia', *Studies in Social Justice* 7(2): 189–210, 202.

between local powerbrokers, who are often politically extremist or exclusionary, and ignores grassroots community actors who are potentially more inclusive and moderate'.[235]

This is not just a problem of local power relations, leaving aside the global networked character of many conflict parties. When international actors argue that stopping violence is only possible through political compromise this may not only be because of the top-down old war lens through which they view conflict, it may also chime better with dominant international geo-political thinking. Or, to put it another way, the persistence of the old war discourse, which profoundly shapes the nature of peace agreements, the character of peacekeeping and the difficulties of peacebuilding, is not just about the old-fashioned assumptions of international leaders, it is also deeply embedded in power relations at an international level having to do both with geo-politics and neo-liberal economic assumptions. And, as we have shown, both peacemaking and peacekeeping are highly gendered, also making it difficult to address the asymmetric gendered nature of new wars.

Radical critics like Mark Duffield, David Chandler or Oliver Richmond are right to point to the way power relations are represented in the 'liberal peace complex' or the Liberal Peace discourse.[236] Indeed, they could be described as 'empire' in a Foucauldian sense. But the word 'empire' does have normative connotations and implies that such power is bad. Power is a necessary condition for emancipation as well as oppression. The global is imbricated in the local and cannot be undone; rather it has to be rethought in emancipatory terms. This chapter has also pointed to trends towards adapting peacekeeping for human-centred purposes as well as efforts to emphasise human rights in peacebuilding albeit somewhat straitened alongside the more dominant preoccupations of stabilisation as well as geo-political, neo-liberal and counter-terror imperatives. It is also the case that civil society groups at local levels (and not only grassroots community actors) press for more emancipatory and just policies and processes. It is in the tension between these different approaches that constructive openings might be identified.

[235] Newman, Edward and Paris, Roland and Richmond, Oliver P. 2009. 'Introduction', in Newman *et al.*, *op. cit.*

[236] Chandler, *op. cit.*; Duffield, *op. cit.* (*Global Governance*); Richmond, *op. cit.* ('A Post-Liberal Peace').

10

Justice and Accountability

10.1 Introduction

It could be argued that some of the problems of the Liberal Peace can be redressed through effective justice and accountability mechanisms. The former warring parties comprise networks that often conflate extremist ideologies and criminality; justice mechanisms that remove those who committed the worst war-time crimes and those who continue to commit economic predations or to violate human rights would be a way of weakening entrenched power relations established through war and confirmed in peace settlements. Certainly, this is a widely held view among civil society groups, who often argue that impunity for those who committed crimes during the conflict and who continue to act in predatory ways represents the major obstacle to reconstruction and a rule of law.[1] Likewise the lack of accountability of international personnel – peacekeepers, members of civilian missions – in conflict-affected situations is a gap in constructing democracy and may also allow international personnel to accept and even endorse the *status quo*.

It is in the area of justice and accountability mechanisms that global civil society has been especially active from the nineteenth- and early twentieth-century campaigns for a permanent international court of justice[2] to the establishment of the *ad hoc* criminal tribunals for the former Yugoslavia and Rwanda, and, above all, the permanent International Criminal Court. At the national level too, civil society has been instrumental in pursuing accountability through universal jurisdiction[3] and in challenging legal obstacles that enhance impunity. In some

[1] Kaldor, Mary and Theros, Marika 2011. *Building Afghan Peace from the Ground Up.* A Century Foundation Report, Century Foundation.

[2] See Chapters 2 and 3.

[3] Universal jurisdiction allows for the prosecution and trial of those accused of especially heinous crimes, regardless of any link between accused and the place of trial based upon territoriality or nationality of the accused or victim.

instances where there have been no formal state-sponsored processes, civil society efforts have turned to peoples' tribunals, that is, asserting accountability before a public audience.[4] However, in recent years, the War on Terror and the resurgence of geo-politics have reduced the possibilities for effective civil society action, and this has allowed for the reversion to 'old war' thinking.

In this chapter we argue that the lack of accountability for perpetrators of atrocities, including international personnel, can be explained primarily in terms of the dominance of 'old war' assumptions, whether this is because of the Liberal Peace belief that stability can be achieved through compromise among the warring parties, or because of the priorities of international power relations. It develops this argument through two aspects of justice and accountability: what has become known as transitional justice as it affects conflict situations and the accountability of international personnel.

10.2 Transitional Justice

International criminal law is largely founded upon international humanitarian law and human rights law,[5] notably through the concept of what has become known as transitional justice.[6] This primarily refers to the process of dealing with past crimes after the end of war, dictatorship and oppressive societies as a means of enabling the society to move forward. Criminal trials and truth and reconciliation processes as aspects of transitional justice have generated a huge literature and contested views about most aspects of their operation. As Rangelov and Teitel put it:

> the legal phenomenology that characterizes modern periods of political flux could be seen as giving rise to a transitional paradigm. While the modalities of justice-seeking during transformative periods may appear diverse – retributive, reparatory, bureaucratic, constitutional, and

[4] Byrnes, Andrew and Simm, Gabrielle 2013. 'Peoples' Tribunals, International Law and the Use of Force', *University of New South Wales Law Journal* 36(2): 711–744; Chinkin, Christine and Rangelov, Iavor 2011. 'A Bottom-Up Approach to Redressing Past Violations of Human Rights', in Kostovicova, Denisa and Glasius, Marlies (eds.). *Bottom-Up Politics: An Agency Approach to Globalization*. Palgrave Macmillan, 112–126.

[5] This analysis omits reference to the first designated international crime – piracy, which states accepted could be tried in the courts of any state detaining the pirate; Simpson, Gerry 2007. *Law, War & Crime: War Crimes, Trials and the Reinvention of International Law*. Polity Press.

[6] Teitel, Ruti 1999. *Transitional Justice*. Oxford University Press.

> historical, across plural legal responses, there are distinctive processes associated with political change. Across legal categories, a paradigm of law emerges that is best understood as a form of 'transitional jurisprudence'. At its core are the questions of what is deemed fair and just in these extraordinary political circumstances, and how is this determined from the perspective of the transitional position.[7]

Ruti Teitel suggests that there have been three phases of transitional justice.[8] The first phase was after World War II with the Nuremberg and Tokyo Courts, which mainly focussed on criminal prosecutions for crimes against peace (the crime of aggression) and war crimes, and a series of cases in national courts in Europe,[9] which also prosecuted crimes against humanity,[10] that is to say, responsibility for the Holocaust.[11] The second phase followed the fall of military dictatorships in Latin America and communist regimes in Eastern Europe as well, of course, as the end of apartheid and majority rule in South Africa. In Latin America and South Africa, the emphasis was on restorative models, including truth and reconciliation processes. The tension between punishment and amnesty led many countries to forgo prosecutions in favour of alternative methods of truth-seeking and accountability.[12] In Eastern

[7] Rangelov, Iavor and Teitel, Ruti 2014 'Transitional Justice' in Kaldor, Mary and Rangelov, Iavor. *Handbook of Global Security* Blackwell.

[8] Teitel, Ruti 2003. 'Transitional Justice Genealogy', *Harvard Human Rights Journal* 16: 69–94.

[9] The United Nations War Crimes Commission Project at the School of Oriental and African Studies in London is exploring the archival material relating to previously little known war crimes trials in national jurisdictions; Plesch, Dan and Sa'Couto, Susana and Lasco, Chante 2014. 'The Relevance of the United Nations War Crimes Commission to the Prosecution of Sexual and Gender-Based Crimes Today', *Criminal Law Forum* 25: 349–381. See also Linton, Suzanne (ed.) 2013. *Hong Kong's War Crimes Trials.* Oxford University Press.

[10] Crimes against humanity were included within the jurisdiction of both the *Agreement for the Prosecution and Punishment of the Major War Criminals of the European Axis*, and *Charter of the International Military Tribunal*, London, 8 August 1945 (Nuremburg) and the *International Military Tribunal for the Far East Charter*, Tokyo, 19 January 1946 (IMTFE). Crimes related to the Holocaust were prosecuted as 'persecution on political, racial or religious grounds in execution of or in connection with any crime within the jurisdiction of the Tribunal'.

[11] Rangelov, Iavor 2014. *Nationalism and the Rule of Law.* Cambridge University Press.

[12] For different views on the acceptability of this trade-off see *Azanian Peoples Organization (AZAPO) v. President of the Republic of South Africa and Others* (CCT17/96) [1996] ZACC 16; 1996 (8) BCLR 1015; 1996 (4) SA 672, 25 July 1996, (Truth and Reconciliation Commission in South Africa compatible with the Constitution) and *Case of Barrios Altos v. Peru*, IACtHR, 14 March 2001, Merits, (amnesty incompatible with the Inter-American Convention on Human Rights).

Europe, the emphasis was on what became known as lustration, a term which referred to the 'disqualification of a former elite, of the secret police and their informers, or of civil servants from holding political office under the new regime'.[13]

The third and most recent phase is, Teitel argues, a global phase of 'tribunalisation'[14] or criminalisation[15] through implementation of 'a process and machinery ... for adjudicating human rights',[16] and it has to do primarily with crimes committed in new wars. This phase criminalises conflict by providing for individual criminal responsibility, which avoids collective punishment of the civilian population. However, it is also argued that it allows for the 'bad apple argument', the idea that abuses are committed only by 'rogue' individuals against the command framework.

This phase marked the establishment, first, of the *ad hoc* International Criminal Tribunals for the former Yugoslavia (ICTY)[17] and Rwanda (ICTR),[18] and then the Rome Statute of 1998, which established the permanent International Criminal Court (ICC), which was set up when the Statute entered into force in 2002.[19] As well as the international judicial mechanisms, and as the *ad hoc* international criminal tribunals are nearing their conclusion, there has been an increase in domestic trials of individuals responsible for war crimes and crimes against humanity. In addition is the establishment of what are known as 'hybrid' courts in which transitional justice bodies have been entrenched with local justice systems, but with extra international personnel. Hybrid courts include the Special Court of Sierra Leone, set up by the Government of Sierra

13 The term *lustration* derives from the Latin term for purifying sacrifice that followed the quinquennial census in Rome; Chesterman, Simon 2005. *You, the People: the United Nations, Transitional Administration, and State-Building.* Oxford University Press, 72.

14 Judith Shklar called the recourse to rules and judicial institutions 'tribunality', which must be assessed alongside other ways of doing politics: fairness, justice, compromise, power, religious truth, military values, friendship, charity or Marxism; Shklar, Judith 1964. *Legalism: Law, Morals and Political Trials.* Harvard University Press; see Simpson, *op. cit.* (*Law, War and Crime*), 25.

15 Meron, Theodor 1998. 'Is International Law Moving towards Criminalization?' *European Journal of International Law* 9: 18–31.

16 Teitel, *op. cit.* ('Transitional Justice Geneology'), 83, 93.

17 UN SC Resolution 827, 25 May 1993, Statute of the International Criminal Tribunal for the former Yugoslavia (ICTY).

18 UN SC Resolution 955, 8 November 1994, Statute of the International Criminal Tribunal for Rwanda (ICTR).

19 *Rome Statute of the International Criminal Court,* UN Doc. A/CONF.183/9, 17 July 1998 (ICC). The Statute entered into force on 1 July 2002.

Leone and the UN,[20] the Court of Bosnia and Herzegovina, which includes a war crimes chamber, the Special Panels for Serious Crimes established by the UN Transitional Administration in East Timor (UNTAET), special panels established by the United Nations Interim Administration Mission in Kosovo (UNMIK) and subsequently the EU Rule of Law mission (EULEX) and the Extraordinary Chambers in the Courts in Cambodia. Despite intensive civil society involvement, the establishment of these bodies has been 'top-down' through Security Council (SC) resolution, or by international agreement between states, or between states and the UN. In Kosovo in 2015 a further twist has been the demand from the EU for the creation of a special tribunal to try cases against members of the Kosovo Liberation Army (KLA) arising out of the allegations of crimes committed during conflict made in a Council of Europe report, leading to ongoing further investigations.[21]

Increasingly the idea is that the international courts focus on prosecutions of high-level officials (and charged through principles such as command or superior responsibility[22] and joint criminal enterprise[23]) while middle and lower level offenders are dealt with in hybrid and local courts, as well as through truth and reconciliation commissions, or other locally based processes such as the *Gacaca* process in Rwanda.[24] Jurisdiction under the Rome Statute is based on the notion of 'positive complementarity', that the ICC can exercise its jurisdiction only if the local state is 'unable or unwilling' (ICC Statute, article 17 (1) (a)) to do so, thereby implying active encouragement to domestication of international criminal law and the handover of cases to local courts.

The emergence of international judicialisation was in a sense meant to offer an authoritative symbol of international determination to ensure compliance with international law, including by the most powerful.[25] It is

[20] *Agreement between the United Nations and the Government of Sierra Leone pursuant to Security Council Resolution 1315*, 14 August 2000.

[21] The EU Special Investigations Task Force was set up to conduct a fair and independent criminal investigation into the war crime and organised crime allegations made in the Report of the Council of Europe Parliamentary Assembly, Committee on Legal Affairs and Human Rights, 'Inhuman Treatment of People and Illicit Trafficking in Human Organs in Kosovo', Doc. 12462, 7 January 2011 ('Dick Marty Report'); Parliamentary Assembly, Resolution 1782, 25 January 2011; see Chapter 8.

[22] E.g., *Rome Statute of the ICC, op. cit.*, article 28.

[23] E.g., *ibid.*, article 25 (d).

[24] Drumbl, Mark 2007. *Atrocity, Punishment, and International Law*. Cambridge University Press, chapter 4, especially 85–98 on *Gacaca* courts in Rwanda.

[25] *The Rome Statute of the ICC, op. cit.*, article 27 provides that 'This Statute shall apply equally to all persons without any distinction based on official capacity. In particular,

a peace project since 'such grave crimes threaten the peace, security and well-being of the world'.[26] The preamble of the Rome Statute states that the aim of the ICC is to put an 'end to impunity' for the perpetrators of the 'most serious crimes of international concern' and to contribute to their prevention. International criminal law thus also derives from the goal of ensuring accountability by denoting individual responsibility enforced through acceptance of universal jurisdiction for the commission of heinous crimes that threaten the international community at large, not just the immediate victim. The first such designated crimes were piracy and slavery,[27] and subsequently the category was extended to war crimes, crimes against humanity and genocide.[28] The essence of the concept of crimes against humanity is the unacceptable dehumanisation of individuals, and that of genocide is the right to existence of groups based on their national, ethnic, racial or religious identity.[29] Genocide is a crime whether committed in peace or war,[30] and under the ICC Statute, article 7, crimes against humanity no longer need to be linked to armed conflict but are 'committed as part of a widespread or systematic attack directed against any civilian population, with knowledge of the attack'. Such inhuman behaviour is the very essence of 'new wars'.

Yet despite this dramatic increase in justice mechanisms and associated normative advances, the record in dealing with the kind of predatory networks described in Chapter 1 has been discouraging. The goal of universal jurisdiction for such crimes has not been realised. At the national level there still remains little evidence that the idea of universal jurisdiction has become an accepted principle of customary international law.[31] Trials in national courts tend therefore to be of nationals accused

official capacity as a Head of State or Government, a member of a Government or parliament, an elected representative or a government official shall in no case exempt a person from criminal responsibility under this Statute, nor shall it, in and of itself, constitute a ground for reduction of sentence'.

26 The *Rome Statute of the ICC, op. cit.*, preamble.

27 Simpson, *op. cit.* (*Law, War and Crime*).

28 Other crimes such as trafficking (e.g., human, drug and arms) have not been explicitly brought within the jurisdiction of the international criminal tribunals and specific acts of terror (e.g., hijacking, hostage taking etc.) are defined and criminalised under a number of separate treaties.

29 *The Convention on the Prevention and Punishment of the Crime of Genocide*, UN GA Resolution 260 (III), 9 December 1948, article II ('*Genocide Convention*').

30 *Ibid.*, article I.

31 Wuerth, Ingrid 2012. 'Pinochet's Legacy Reassessed', *American Journal of International Law* 106(4): 731–737.

of such crimes or concerning crimes committed in that territory. At the international level the *ad hoc* criminal tribunals have limited temporal and territorial jurisdiction, and the ICC's jurisdiction depends upon the relevant state (of place of commission of the offence, or nationality of the alleged offender) having consented through becoming a party to the Statute,[32] although the SC can refer 'a situation' to the ICC without state consent;[33] this is the case with Sudan with respect to the situation in Darfur[34] and Libya with respect to events in 2011.[35] Members of a fighting group whose degree of organisation does not bring them within Common Article 3 of the Geneva Conventions or Additional Protocol II[36] may thus be liable for the commission of crimes against humanity and, if jurisdiction is established, could potentially be indicted by the ICC.

More importantly perhaps, international enforcement mechanisms are weak and criminal prosecutions are few and face many obstacles, including within domestic jurisdictions. Some of the reasons are practical – the limited capacity of international courts; the time and effort required to acquire credible evidence;[37] the difficulty of arresting indicted offenders. The length of the processes gives a public platform to people who dissent from the narrative of objective criminal justice and espouse extremist ideas such as former President of Serbia Milošević. But despite these practicalities, we argue that the primary reasons for the discouraging poverty of prosecutions are political. On the one hand, a growing humanitarian consciousness, often articulated by civil society groups, has opened the way for the growth of judicial mechanisms. On the other hand, geo-political, statist and 'old war' considerations have often turned out to trump justice.

[32] *Rome Statute of the ICC, op. cit.*, article 12. [33] *Ibid.*, article 13 (b).

[34] The situation in Darfur was referred to the ICC by UN SC Resolution 1593, 31 March 2005.

[35] The situation in Libya was referred to the ICC by UN SC Resolution 1970, 26 February 2011, para. 4.

[36] See Chapter 6.

[37] The UK Government has prepared, disseminated and provided training on the International Protocol on the Documentation and Investigation of Sexual Violence in Conflict: Basic Standards of Best Practice on the Documentation of Sexual Violence as a Crime under International Law, London, July 2014, in an effort to increase prosecutions of these crimes; see also Guidelines for Investigating Conflict-related Sexual and Gender-Based Violence against Men and Boys, Institute for International Criminal Investigations, The Hague, 29 February 2016, www.gov.uk/government/uploads/system/uploads/attachment_data/file/546569/PSVI_training_-_violence_against_men_and_boys.pdf.

Peace versus Justice

One set of reasons why prosecutions have stalled is the concern that these will interfere with peace processes.[38] This is a central debate among scholars concerned with transitional justice. Again, this depends very much on the interpretation of 'conflict'. For those who see conflict as a contest of wills among organised groups with legitimate grievances, reaching a negotiated compromise is the only way to end a conflict other than through victory or defeat, even if this means that amnesties have to be offered for crimes committed during the war. For those who understand conflict more as a mutual enterprise in which the warring parties have deliberately eschewed non-violent forms of conflict resolution because they have more to gain from violence, then addressing their crimes is a precondition for peace. Of course, reality is much more messy and conflicts may be mixtures of both contests of will and mutual enterprises. Some kind of agreement may be necessary to halt the worst of the violence and to establish conditions in which the power restructuring that took place during the war can begin to be addressed.

The evidence on whether prosecutions interfere with peace processes is mixed. There have been cases where amnesties allowed a renewal of fighting, for example, the first peace agreement with Savimbi in Angola (1994) and the Lomé Agreement in Sierra Leone (1999).[39] When the Dayton Agreement[40] was being negotiated, the international negotiators proposed amnesties for draft dodgers and deserters, while the Bosnian politicians favoured amnesty for illegal commerce, tax evasion and illegal use of humanitarian aid (sic!).[41] Richard Goldstone (then ICTY

[38] *The Rome Statute of the ICC* allows the UN SC to request the Court to defer investigation or proceedings for twelve months. It is generally recognised that this exceptional power was 'intended to deal with situations where peace negotiations were at a delicate stage and might be compromised by the simultaneous continuation of international criminal prosecutions'. Okowa, Pheobe 2014. 'The Security Council, the African Union and the International Criminal Court', in Ebbesson *et al.* (eds.). *International Law and Changing Perceptions of Security*. Brill/Nijhoff, 234.

[39] However, the SCSL Appeals Chamber decided that amnesties granted under the Lomé Peace Agreement did not prevent prosecution; *Prosecutor v. Morris Kallon and Brima Buzzy Kamara*, SCSL-2004-15-AR72(E) and SCSL-2004-16-AR72(E) (Decision on Challenge to Jurisdiction: Lomé Accord Amnesty (Appeals Chamber, 13 March 2004) ('Lomé Decision').

[40] *General Framework Agreement for Peace for Bosnia and Herzegovina,* Dayton, initialed 21 November 1995, signed at Paris, 14 December 1995.

[41] Andreas, Peter 2004. 'The Clandestine Political Economy of War and Peace in Bosnia', *International Studies Quarterly* 48: 29–52.

prosecutor) noted that 'astute politicians and commentators' were concerned that the ICTY's work was 'retarding' the peace process.[42] However, this same work was also valued as an 'instrument of policy', as it allowed indicted persons, notably Karadzić and Mladić, to be excluded from the Dayton process but not, of course, Milošević who was only later indicted.[43] In the end Dayton did include, at international insistence, a pledge by the parties to cooperate with the ICTY,[44] as well as the exclusion of indicted fugitives from positions of authority. However, as it turned out, international agencies such as the OSCE in Bosnia did not insist on the latter provision when it came to elections.[45] Many peace agreements include some mix of amnesties and commitments to accountability whether through convictions or truth and reconciliation commissions.[46]

There are also cases where it is claimed that referral to the ICC actually hastened the end of hostilities. For example, in 2004, the Government of Uganda referred the situation in the North of the country where a rebel group, the Lord's Resistance Army (LRA), had abducted tens of thousands of people and engaged in a pattern of 'brutalization of civilians'.[47] In response, the Government had herded more than a million people into squalid and insecure camps. Critics suggested 'that international prosecutions would undermine fragile local peace initiatives; would prolong the conflict by obliterating the LRA's incentive to negotiate; and would make displaced Northern Ugandans even more vulnerable'.[48] There was also an argument that the ICC represented Western justice (despite the presence of 148 states at the Rome Conference and numerous NGOs)

[42] Goldstone, Richard 1995–1996. 'Justice as a Tool for Peacemaking: Truth Commissions and International Criminal Tribunals', *NYU Journal of Law and Politics* 28: 485–503, 488.

[43] Holbrooke, Richard 1999. *To End a War*. Random House, rev. ed., 190.

[44] *General Framework Agreement for Peace for Bosnia and Herzegovina, op. cit.*, article IX.

[45] In a case brought to the European Court of Human Rights the applicants claimed that being removed from public and political party positions and prohibited from holding such positions or running for election to such positions violated their rights under the European Convention on Human Rights. The Court found the case inadmissible; *Dusan Beric et al. v. Bosnia and Herzegovina*, ECtHR application no. 36357/04 and others, 16 October 2007.

[46] UN SC Resolution 1820, 19 June 2008 'stresses the need for the exclusion of sexual violence crimes from amnesty provisions in the context of conflict resolution processes'.

[47] Situation in Uganda, Warrant of Arrest for Joseph Kony, issued on 8 July 2005, as amended on 27 September 2005, ICC-02/04-01/05, 27 September 2005.

[48] Grono, Nick and O'Brien, Adam 2008. 'Justice in Conflict? The ICC and Peace Processes', in Waddell, Nicholas and Clark, Phil 2008. *Courting Conflict? Justice, Peace and the ICC in Africa*. Royal African Society, 13–20, 15.

and an approach more sensitive to local culture and tradition would be much more effective. In fact, the opposite happened. The Cessation of Hostilities Agreement that was signed in 2006 removed most of the LRA combatants from Northern Uganda, even though LRA activity has continued in South Sudan and eastern Democratic Republic of Congo (DRC). Hundreds of thousands of civilians began to be resettled. While referral to the ICC is not considered to be the main reason for the Agreement, Grono and O'Brien argue that it contributed in significant ways: by making the LRA leadership nervous, by raising the stakes for Sudan, which supplied weapons, training and transportation to the rebels, by raising international and regional awareness and support for the peace process. Because of referral to the ICC, moreover, the Agreement has 'embedded accountability and victims' interests in the structure of the peace process'.[49] The Agreement was followed by the June 2007 Agreement on Accountability and Reconciliation, and its Annex, signed in February 2008, created a national framework for transitional justice. On the other hand, Kony and his commanders have stated that they will not do a peace deal unless the charges are dropped. But does this matter once a cessation of hostilities agreement has been signed?

A preferable approach may be to marginalise rebels rather than elevate them through talks with international mediators. In cases where political and criminal violence are blurred and where the parties have an interest in violence itself as a way to mobilise extremist ideologies and to extract resources, justice mechanisms serve to marginalise those with an interest in protracted conflict, thereby enhancing prospects for peace. Brutal dictators like Bashir in Sudan, Gaddafi in Libya or Assad in Syria are never likely to leave power voluntarily, so the issue is how indictment might affect the loyalty of those upon whom they depend to remain in power.

States versus Civil Society

A second and perhaps more important reason for the difficulty in using justice mechanisms to address distorted power relations is the ambiguous role of states in the judicial process. Five of the situations so far referred to the ICC have been referred by states: Uganda, DRC, Central African Republic I and II, Mali and Côte d'Ivoire. In these cases, it is argued that despite the supposed impartiality of the Court, indictments and

[49] *Ibid.*, 16.

prosecutions have tended to be one-sided against the rebels, in part, because the Court needs the co-operation of the government. Thus despite the success of referral in Uganda in contributing to a ceasefire, there have been no cases commenced against alleged offenders on the Government side. In the DRC, the ICC has so far focused on Ituri province and arrested several Ituri militia leaders, including Thomas Lubanga, who was the first person to be convicted by the ICC, but there have been no indictments of Government personnel. It is also argued, that since Ituri has probably the best functioning judiciary in the DRC, these cases could have been brought locally.[50] The ICTR and the Special Court of Sierra Leone have been similarly criticised for one-sidedness, although the latter has prosecuted three members of the Civil Defense Forces, which fought for the Government.[51] In the case of Darfur, it was the SC that referred the situation to the ICC after a very public campaign in the United States to intervene to stop genocide. Among those indicted is the President of Sudan, Omar Bashir, who responded by expelling all aid agencies from Darfur and whose indictment was opposed by most other Arab and African heads of state.

Where civil society plays an active role, the local legitimacy of international prosecutions does seem to be greater. This is the case in Kenya where it was civil society groups (and the Commission of the African Union (AU)) that pressed the prosecutor to initiate an investigation into the situation following the post-electoral violence in late 2007 and early 2008. Following the first *proprio motu* investigation,[52] indictments were issued, including against the now President Kenyatta and Deputy President Ruto.[53] Nevertheless, in May 2013 the AU adopted a resolution calling for the cases to be referred back to Kenya for proceedings to be heard in the national courts;[54] the ICC resisted this position, but the charges against Kenyatta were withdrawn in 2015 and the case against Ruto and Arap Sang terminated in April 2016.

[50] Clark, Phil 2008. 'Law, Politics, and Pragmatism: The ICC and Case Selection in Uganda and the Democratic Republic of Congo', in Waddel and Clark, *op. cit.*, 37–46.

[51] *Prosecutor v. Fofana and Kondewa* (CDF Case), SCSL-04-14, 28 May 2008. The third indictee, Sam Hinga Norman, died before the close of the proceedings, and the case against him was closed.

[52] *Rome Statute of the ICC, op. cit.*, article 15(1).

[53] *The Prosecutor v. Uhuru Muigai Kenyatta*, ICC-01/09-02/11; *The Prosecutor v. William Samoei Ruto and Joshua Arap Sang*, ICC-01/09-11/11.

[54] The decision was adopted at the 21st Ordinary Session of the Summit of the African Union (AU), Addis Ababa, Ethiopia, 26–27 May 2013.

In the Balkans, civil society groups have played an active role. They pressed the EU to make the handover of indicted criminals part of its conditionality for membership. In Bosnia, significant groups include the Sarajevo Research and Documentation Centre, that has collected statistics on war victims, and the Association for Truth and Reconciliation, led by Jakob Finci, that has campaigned for a Truth and Reconciliation Commission. The main grassroots organisations are victims and veterans associations. Particularly important has been the Women of Srebrenica. They succeeded, with support from the NGO sector and from the then High Representative, Paddy Ashdown, in pressurising the Government of the Republika Srpska (RS) into establishing the Srebrenica Commission, which led to an apology from the Government of the RS. They have also submitted many cases to the War Crimes Chamber. Perhaps their most significant victory was two cases brought before the Dutch courts against the Dutch forces that were supposedly defending the safe area when the massacre took place.[55] Other victims' [victims'] associations include those supporting victims of sexual violence, who have brought cases in foreign courts, and the associations of the families of missing persons who succeeded in pushing through the Law on the Missing.[56]

Perhaps the most hopeful initiative in the Balkans is the proposal to establish a Regional Commission for Establishing the Facts about War Crimes and Other Serious Human Rights Violations in Former Yugoslavia (RECOM). RECOM arose in direct response to the perceived weaknesses of trials as a transitional justice instrument and the need for a bottom-up and regional approach. The Coalition for RECOM has held extensive civil society consultations all over the region, and the petition to establish RECOM attracted half a million signatures. It is credited with generating a moderating effect on regional-level debates.[57] While progress remains precarious on persuading the governments in the region to begin negotiations for establishing a regional commission, civil society has been building up the documentation. The most significant documentation efforts are the Kosovo Human Losses Database and Kosovo Memory Book, a joint project of the Humanitarian

[55] See below discussion under immunity of international personnel.

[56] Rangelov Iavor, and Theros, Marika 2007. 'Maintaining the Process in Bosnia and Herzegovina: Coherence and Complementarity of EU Institutions and Civil Society in the Field of Transitional Justice', Working Group on Development and Peace (FriEnt) Bonn.

[57] See Bojiči--Dželilović, Vesna, Kostovicova, Denisa, and Randazzo, Elisa 2016. 'EU in the Western Balkans', LSE, Security in Transition Working Paper.

Law Center in Belgrade and Pristina to document the death or disappearance of every casualty of the Kosovo conflict from 1998 to 2001, and an initiative of civil society groups from the Federation and RS to document wartime human rights abuses at camps and detention sites in Bosnia.

Double Standards

A widespread criticism, not without some basis, is that the various international transitional justice mechanisms are compromised by power considerations and double standards. Early criticism that the *ad hoc* international criminal tribunals were processing primarily the unimportant 'small fry' have been largely dispelled by the highly public arrests of Vojislav Šešelj, the leader of the Serbian radical party, Radovan Karadžić, the former leader of Republika Srpska (RS), and Ratjko Mladić, the general accused of responsibility for the Srebrenica genocide. These cases have extended the life of the ICTY[58] and represent a further achievement in institutionalising humanitarian norms. However, violent situations in the Balkans and Africa[59] have been referred to international tribunals, whereas there have been no such referrals with respect to American or British actions, such as their behaviour in Kosovo, Iraq or Afghanistan, including, for example, the use of depleted uranium, aerial bombing and drones, or the treatment of so-called illegal combatants. The Prosecutor of the ICTY determined that no personnel from NATO would be prosecuted following the Kosovo military action,[60] although the jurisdiction of the ICTY was wide enough to include it. One commentator has noted that 'the Report left many by no means convinced of the integrity of the process'.[61] It is hard not to conclude that there was an unwillingness to prosecute NATO personnel given their role in capturing suspects in the Balkans, as the NATO spokesperson Jamie Shea reminded the Court. Robert Cryer concludes that the 'extent to which the ICTY relied

58 In 2010 the UN SC adopted the Statute of the International Residual Mechanism for Criminal Tribunals as 'a small, temporary and efficient structure' to carry out essential functions of the Tribunals as they complete their work; UN SC Resolution 1966, 22 December 2010.

59 Mutua, Makau W. 1997. 'Never Again: Questioning the Yugoslav and Rwanda Tribunals', *Temple International and Comparative Law Review* 11: 167–187.

60 Final Report to the Prosecutor by the Committee established to Review the NATO Bombing Campaign against the Federal Republic of Yugoslavia, 8 June 2000, 38 *International Legal Materials* (2000) 1257.

61 Cryer, Robert 2005. *Prosecuting International Crimes Selectivity and the International Criminal Law Regime*. Cambridge University Press, 214 ff.

on NATO states for evidence and obtaining indictees was clearly being used by Shea to influence the Prosecutor'.[62] One aspect of the behaviour of American and British forces relates to the legality of their military actions, especially in Kosovo (1999) and Iraq (2003).[63] However, and although crimes against peace were predominant at Nuremburg and Tokyo, the crime of aggression is not yet subject to the ICC's jurisdiction. A definition of aggression[64] was accepted by the Review Conference in 2010, but under the terms negotiated it will not come within the Court's jurisdiction until after 1 January 2017 when a decision is to be made by states parties to activate the jurisdiction.[65]

Many situations from around the globe have by 2016 been communicated to the ICC and are subject to preliminary examination, including Afghanistan, Burundi, Colombia, Gabon, Guinea, Iraq/UK,[66] Nigeria, Palestine, Ukraine, but until early 2016[67] the ICC had only proceeded to investigation in cases arising from violence in Africa (Uganda, Central African Republic, DRC, Côte D'Ivoire, Kenya and Mali). Both cases referred by the SC have also arisen out of situations in Africa (Darfur and Libya). In the words of William Schabas, 'Why prosecute post-election violence in Kenya [on the prosecutor's powers][68] or recruitment of child soldiers in the Congo, but not murder and torture of prisoners in Iraq or illegal settlements in the West Bank?'[69] In May 2013 Comoros

62 *Ibid.*, 215. 63 See Chapters 4 and 5.

64 The accepted definition follows that of UN GA Resolution 3314 (XXIX), 14 December 1974.

65 *Rome Statute of the ICC*, article 5 and article 8 *bis*, agreed Kampala, 11 June 2010.

66 The United Kingdom is a party to the *Rome Statute*. The European Center for Constitutional and Human Rights (ECCHR) and Public Interest Lawyers (PIL, now defunct), submitted on 10 January 2014 a communication to the Office of the Prosecutor of the International Criminal Court, 'The Responsibility of UK Officials for War Crimes Involving Systematic Detainee Abuse in Iraq from 2003–2008'. On 4 July 2016 the Office of the Prosecutor confirmed that it is conducting a preliminary examination with respect to the Situation in Iraq; //www.icc-cpi.int//Pages/item.aspx?name=160704-otp-stat.

67 In January 2016 the prosecutor was authorised to open *proprio motu* investigation in Georgia (with respect to South Ossetia); ICC-01/15.

68 Under the *Rome Statute of the ICC*, article 15. Admittedly the Commission of Inquiry into Post-Election Violence ('Waki Commission') set up by the African Union Panel of Eminent African Personalities recommended an investigation by the ICC; International Centre for Transitional Justice 2008. 'The Kenyan Commission of Inquiry into Post-Election Violence', www.ictj.org/sites/default/files/ICTJ-Kenya-Dialogue-Inquiry-2008-English.pdf. Full report available at www.kenyalaw.org/Downloads/Reports/Commission_of_Inquiry_into_Post_Election_Violence.pdf.

69 Cited, Dersso, Solomon. 'The International Criminal Court's Africa Problem', *Al Jazeera*, 11 June 2013, www.aljazeera.com/indepth/opinion/2013/06/201369851918549.html.

referred the situation 'with respect to the 31 May 2010 Israeli raid on the Humanitarian Aid Flotilla bound for Gaza Strip'.[70] The Prosecutor announced the conclusion of the preliminary investigation and that it would not be proceeded with as any cases 'likely arising from an investigation into this incident would not be of "sufficient gravity" to justify further action by the ICC'. The Pre-Trial Chamber has asked the Prosecutor to reconsider this decision, a position upheld by the Appeal Chamber.[71] It must also be remembered that many of the African cases have been submitted by the governments in question. However, a good example of the way that selectivity is shaped by geo-politics is the way that Libya was referred by the SC to the ICC in 2011, when Western governments were keen to intervene militarily and did so shortly after the referral. [72] The result was the overthrowing of the Gaddafi government. In contrast the Syrian situation has not been referred to the ICC, despite the fact that war crimes and crimes against humanity have been committed on a large scale,[73] including the use of chemical weapons, which is explicitly mentioned as a war crime in the Rome Statute.[74] A SC resolution for referral was defeated by Russia and China's negative votes.[75]

Although more than two-thirds of the members of the African Union are parties to the Rome Statute, African hostility to the ICC continues. African leaders are questioning the Court's fairness and are failing to cooperate, as, for instance, when the government of South Africa allowed Bashir to leave the country in June 2015 in the face of an international

[70] Although Israel is not a party to the *Rome Statute*, the situation with respect to the Humanitarian Aid Flotilla bound for the Gaza Strip occurred on a vessel flying the flag of Comoros, thereby allowing for the claim of jurisdiction based on the territory of the commission of the offence. Comoros is a party to the *Rome Statute.*

[71] 'ICC Pre-Trial Chamber I requests Prosecutor to reconsider decision not to investigate situation referred by Union of Comoros', *ICC Press Release*, ICC-CPI-20150716-PR1133, 16 July 2015; on 6 November 2015, the Appeals Chamber dismissed the Prosecutor's appeal against the decision of Pre-Trial Chamber I requesting the Prosecutor to reconsider the decision.

[72] UN SC Resolution 1970, 26 February 2011 (referral to the ICC); UN SC Resolution 1973, 17 March 2011 (authorising 'all necessary measures ... to protect civilians and civilian populated areas under threat of attack'). See Chapter 5.

[73] The Reports of the UN Human Rights Council, Independent International Commission of Inquiry on the Syrian Arab Republic, established August 2011, record many instances of violations of human rights and international humanitarian law.

[74] *Rome Statute of the ICC, op. cit.*, article 8 (b)(xviii)(xx).

[75] 'Referral of Syria to International Criminal Court Fails as Negative Votes Prevent Security Council from Adopting Draft Resolution', *UN Press Release*, 22 May 2014, www.un.org/press/en/2014/sc11407.doc.htm. The United States supported the resolution.

arrest warrant and a Pretorian court order for his arrest. [76] Among other concerns are that there is a bias against African states and a failure to protect witnesses from Africa. Some also suggest that that the Court imposes a Western conception of justice.[77] In late 2016 three African states – Burundi, South Africa and the Gambia – announced their departure from the Court.[78] Proposals for a regional African international criminal court have progressed to the drafting of a protocol that would add criminal jurisdiction over genocide, war crimes and crimes against humanity (and other crimes such as terrorism, corruption and piracy) to the jurisdiction of the African Court of Justice and Human Rights: 'All that now remains is for the AU Assembly to formally adopt the draft protocol'.[79] In line with the view that cases concerning African leaders should be tried in Africa, in 2006 the African Union ordered Senegal to try former Chadian dictator Hissène Habré for crimes against humanity. After much delay, in February 2013 Senegal opened criminal proceedings in an especially constituted court in Senegal ('Extraordinary Chambers') and in May 2016 Habré was convicted of crimes against humanity, war crimes and torture, including rape and sexual violence.[80] This significant move for accountability within Africa is ground-breaking as it is the first time a country's former leader has been tried by the courts of another country.

International versus Local

Critics of international justice often suggest that international conceptions of justice do not chime with local culture and norms.[81] Local justice is favoured by critics of international justice as it is 'generally believed to

[76] Other African countries (Malawi, Chad, Sudan, DRC) had likewise failed to arrest Bashir when he was on the state's territory.

[77] This underlies much of the criticism made at the Tokyo war crimes trials by the dissenting Indian Judge Pal; Takeshi, Nakajima 2011. 'Justice Pal (India)', in Tanaka, Yuki, McCormick, Tim and Simpson, Gerry (eds.). *Beyond Victor's Justice? The Tokyo War Crimes Trial Revisited.* Martinus Nijhoff, chapter 10, 127.

[78] 'Gambia Is Latest African Nation to Quit International Criminal Court', *The Guardian,* 26 October 2016. *Rome Statute of the ICC, op. cit.,* article 127 provides for withdrawal, which takes effect twelve months after written notification.

[79] du Plessis, Max and Maluwa, Tiyanjana and O'Reilly, Annie. 'Africa and the International Criminal Court', *Chatham House,* July 2013, www.chathamhouse.org/publications/papers/view/193415.

[80] Human Rights Watch, 'The Trial of Hissène Habré', www.hrw.org/tag/hissene-habre.

[81] Laban, Alexander 2011. *Transitional Justice: Global Mechanisms and Local Realities after Genocide and Mass Violence.* Rutgers University Press.

be able to improve justice seeking processes by reflecting the justice needs of the groups that were most affected by the injustices'.[82] Justice in local courts is either with respect to territorial crimes, crimes allegedly committed by the nationals of the country in question, or through exercise of universal jurisdiction against the nationals of another country.[83] With respect to the former, the *Gacaca* Courts in Rwanda, which tried thousands of *genocidaires*, drawing on local traditions, is often held up as a good model although there are also many criticisms.[84] In another example, in Uganda critics of international justice have proposed that local rituals such as *mato oput* ('drinking the bitter root') or *gomo tang* ('bending the spear')[85] should be used instead.[86] Similarly in Afghanistan, some international agencies advocate the use of Shari'a law or tribal justice mechanisms as a way of filling the justice gap. What this somewhat romantic view of local culture fails to take into account is the way that local justice can be subverted by local power brokers[87] and that tradition has been reinvented as a consequence of wars. For instance, in Uganda, the LRA has been adept at making use of supposedly traditional ceremonies as a way of binding its members to it, often in vicious ways. In Afghanistan, which has been the location of violent conflict now for more than thirty years, two-thirds of the population have been uprooted, and new, often brutal leaders thrown up through violence reclaim extremist versions of tradition. A study by the Afghan Human Rights Commission based on two hundred focus groups across Afghanistan showed a yearning for a more universal conception of justice, and this was seen as being intrinsically linked to the removal of predatory networks. 'Many Afghans, for instance, have made it clear that their trust in

[82] Bonora, Caterina 2014. 'Opening Up or Closing the Historical Dialogue: The Role of Civil Society in Promoting the Debate about the Past', *Dialogues on Historical Justice and Memory Network Working Paper Series* No. 4.

[83] A celebrated trial of this sort is *Attorney-General of the Government of Israel v. Eichmann*, (1961) 36 ILR 5, District Court of Jerusalem.

[84] For a balanced account see Clark, Phil 2010. *The Gacaca Courts, Post-Genocide Justice and Reconciliation in Rwanda: Justice without Lawyers*. Cambridge University Press.

[85] *Mato oput*, for example, 'involved the killer and the family of the bereaved drinking a concoction of the blood of sacrificed sheep and a bitter root to indicate that their dispute had been resolved, following agreement and compensation'. Allen, Tim 2008. 'Ritual (Ab)use? Problems with Traditional Justice in Northern Uganda', in Waddell and Clark, *op. cit.*, 47–54, 48.

[86] *Ibid.*

[87] Allen, Tim 2006. *Trial Justice: The International Criminal Court and the Lord's Resistance Army*. Zed Books.

justice and government institutions depends on removing serious abusers from positions of power and that they view this as essential for, not contrary to, security and long term stability'.[88] Further, informal justice systems are often 'highly problematic' with respect to prosecuting and punishing appropriately crimes of sexual and gender-based violence as they 'tend to be dominated by older men and maintaining social harmony is often prioritised over [women's and other] victims' rights'.[89]

In the long term, international criminal law must be domesticated to be effective,[90] and in many places the existence of international justice mechanisms has spawned demands for prosecution at local levels, even if this has not occurred on the scale or as effectively as many of the promoters of justice had hoped. In some cases the international courts have actively promoted local justice, something that is in the remit of the ICC through the principle of complementarity. The Sierra Leone Special Court can be singled out for its contribution to local justice. Activities included the training of lawyers; other benefits were 'the experience gained by Sierra Leonean investigators, lawyers and other personnel participating in the Court and social capacity building more broadly by creative outreach to Sierra Leone's population', including the establishment of 'Accountability Now' clubs at schools and universities, community dialogue and support for NGOs.[91] The winding-down of the ICTY has precipitated the shift of trials for war crimes and crimes against humanity in the Balkans to national jurisdictions,[92] and significant local cases have been brought against war criminals in Serbia and Croatia as well as in the State court of Bosnia[93] (but not in the RS).

[88] Cited in Stromseth, Jane and Wippman, David and Brooks, Rosa 2006. *Can Might Make Rights? Building the Rule of Law after Military Interventions*. Cambridge University Press, 258.

[89] International Alert 2014. 'Rethinking Gender in Peacebuilding', http://international-alert.org/sites/default/files/Gender_RethinkingGenderPeacebuilding_EN_2014.pdf.

[90] 'The question of place has hovered over the war crimes field since its inception'. Simpson, *op. cit.* (*Law, War and Crime*), 30.

[91] Stromseth, Jane 2008. 'Post-Conflict Rule of Law Building: The Need for a Multi-Layered, Synergistic Approach', *William and Mary Law Review* 49(4): 1443–1471, 1466.

[92] UN SC Resolution 1534, 26 March 2004 called upon the Prosecutors of the ICTY and ICTR to review the case loads to determine which cases should be transferred to competent national jurisdictions. UN SC Resolution 1966, 22 December 2010 established the International Residual Mechanism for International Criminal Tribunals to carry out essential functions of the ICTY and ICTR after completion of their mandates.

[93] The Court of Bosnia and Herzegovina (State Court), Criminal Division has jurisdiction over war crimes; it can also transfer less sensitive and complex cases to the competent Entity court. International judges sit on the State Court.

In Kosovo, as with the other Balkan states, there has been a mix of international and local forms of judicialisation. Yet the prosecution of war crimes has been limited and 'there is a common perception . . . that the majority of persons suspected of committing war crimes during the conflict have not been held accountable'.[94] International involvement includes the ICTY, UNMIK and EULEX. Complaints brought before the Human Rights Advisory Panel (HRAP) established by UNMIK with respect to persons who disappeared or were killed in the period after June 1999 demonstrate a consistent failure by UNMIK to investigate them adequately. The Panel has noted that the shortcomings and deficiencies in investigations into killings, abductions and disappearances 'exemplify a pattern of perfunctory and unproductive investigations conducted by the UNMIK Police into killings and disappearances in Kosovo'.[95] An OSCE report came to a similar conclusion: 'there has been a systemic failure to adjudicate war crimes cases. From the beginning, prioritizing war crimes cases has been frequently the focus of public discourse, but it has been a priority in name only. Sufficient resources have never been allocated to this goal'.[96] More generally, where there has been ethnic conflict there may be concerns that trials will be brought only against those of a different ethnicity; this was the case, for example, in Bosnia in the immediate post-Dayton period.[97] Since 2008, responsibility for war crimes investigation in Kosovo lies with EULEX, the European law and order mission, whose mandate requires it to 'ensure that cases of war crimes . . . and other serious crimes are properly investigated, prosecuted, adjudicated and enforced, according to the applicable law, including, where appropriate, by international investigators, prosecutors and judges jointly with Kosovo investigators, prosecutors and judges or independently'.[98] The appointment of international judges may alleviate ethnic bias, but their task is unclear: is it to ensure fair trials in individual cases

[94] OSCE mission in Kosovo 2010. 'Kosovo's War Crimes Trials: An Assessment Ten Years On 1999–2009' May 2010, 8.

[95] E.g., *Radomir Pantović v. UNMIK*, HRAP Case No. 239/09, 13 May 2015.

[96] OSCE Mission in Kosovo 2010. 'Kosovo's War Crimes Trials: An Assessment Ten Years On: 1999–2009' May 2010.

[97] This was the reason for the Rome Agreement signed in 1996, which established the 'Rules of the Road' whereby domestic courts could only issue arrest warrants after the case had been reviewed by the ICTY. See Moratti, Massimo and Sabic-El-Rayess, Amra 2009. *Transitional Justice and DDR: The Case of Bosnia and Herzegovina*, International Center for Transitional Justice Research Unit.

[98] Council Joint Action 2008/124/CFSP, 4 February 2008, on the European Rule of Law Mission in Kosovo, article 3 (d).

or to assist in training of local judges? Further they do not know the local law, and as they are subject to rotation, individuals are likely to move on just as they gain expertise. They are not subject to any of the conditions relating to tenure, accountability and discipline applicable to local judges. International judges of themselves will not ensure fairness or create legitimacy.[99]

Convictions in local courts are often against vocal opposition from extremist groups. Thus, for example, when a court in Rijeka indicted Croatian General Mirko Norac for war crimes against Serb civilians, a rally of some 150,000 people (war veterans and right-wing political groups) was held in Split chanting 'We are all Mirko Norac' and 'Hands off our Holy War'. A much smaller counter-demonstration was held in Zagreb under the slogan 'Our voice for the rule of law'.[100]

From a different and opposing perspective, trials in local courts may exhibit differing standards and processes not necessarily accepted by Western commentators. In Kosovo, for example, the judicial system had collapsed, and even after some time there were 'specific, ongoing problems within the Kosovo judiciary, including poor management of cases, executive interference, judicial bias and intimidation of judges'.[101] Or local justice may be perceived as vengeance. For instance, the UN Human Rights Council special rapporteur on extrajudicial, summary or arbitrary executions identified three ways in which the trial in Iraq of Saddam Hussein for crimes against humanity violated international human rights standards: there were serious irregularities in the trial proceedings denying the right to a fair hearing; the Government 'engaged in an unseemly and evidently politically motivated effort to expedite the

[99] In *Maktouf and Damjanovic v. Bosnia and Herzegovina*, ECtHR GC application no. 2312/08. 34179/08, 18 July 2013, the Government argued that international judges in the state courts lacked independence because they were appointed by the Office of the High Representative. The Grand Chamber found that the appointment of the international members 'was indeed motivated by a desire, *inter alia,* to reinforce the appearance of independence of the State Court's war crimes chambers (in view of remaining ethnic bias and animosity in the population at large in the post-war period) and to restore public confidence in the domestic judicial system' and that 'Although they were appointed by the High Representative, the Court finds no reason to question that the international members of the State Court were independent of that institution'; paras. 50–52.

[100] Rangelov, Iavor and Teitel, Ruti 2014. 'Transitional Justice', in Kaldor, Mary and Rangelov, Iavor (eds.). *Handbook on Global Security Policy*. Wiley-Blackwell, 338–352, 176.

[101] Everly, Rebecca 2007. 'Reviewing Governmental Acts of the United Nations in Kosovo', *German Law Journal* 8: 21–38, 31.

execution by denying time for a meaningful appeal and by closing off every avenue to review the punishment'; and the humiliating and mocking manner in which the execution was carried out violated the right not to be subjected to cruel, inhuman or degrading punishment.[102]

The ICC may have to determine the suitability of a national jurisdiction, in effect to judge it. The situation in Libya was referred to the ICC by the SC in February 2011[103] and indictments issued against Muammar Gaddafi, his son, Saif Al-Islam Gaddafi, and Abdullah Al-Senussi. Following the fall of the Gaddafi government (and death of Muammar Gaddafi), the successor Libyan government sought to have the trials of Al-Islam Gaddafi and Abdullah Al-Senussi held in Libya and appealed to the ICC against the admissibility of the case.[104] It argued that the national judicial system was actively investigating Gaddafi for his alleged criminal acts and that substantial resources were being directed towards this end. Libya also argued that the trial would be in accordance with international human rights standards. The ICC Pre-Trial Chamber, with which the Appeal Chamber agreed, acknowledged that 'the principle of complementarity expresses a preference for national investigations and prosecutions but does not relieve a State, in general, from substantiating all requirements set forth by the law when seeking to successfully challenge the admissibility of a case'. It determined that Libya had not adequately demonstrated that 'the Libyan and the ICC investigations cover the same conduct and that Libya is able genuinely to carry out an investigation against Mr Gaddafi'.[105] The Chamber reminded Libya of its obligation to surrender him. In contrast, the Pre-Trial Chamber has determined the case of Abdullah Al-Senussi to be inadmissible since there were proceedings before the competent authorities in Libya and that Libya was deemed willing and able genuinely to carry out such investigation. The Appeal Chamber has upheld

[102] 'UN Human Rights Expert Deplores Saddam's Trial and Execution; Calls for Legal Overhaul', *UN News Centre*, 4 January 2007, www.un.org/apps/news/story.asp?NewsID=21155&; similarly Human Rights Watch characterised the trial as flawed with 'serious administrative, procedural and substantive legal defects', see 'Saddam trial flawed and unsound', BBC News, 20 November 2006, http://news.bbc.co.uk/1/hi/world/middle_east/6163938.stm.

[103] UN SC Resolution 1970, 26 February 2011.

[104] Situation in Libya, *Prosecutor v. Saif Al-Gaddafi and Abdullah Al-Senussi*, Decision on the admissibility of the case against Saif Al-Gaddafi, ICC-01/11-01/11, 31 May 2013.

[105] *The Prosecutor v. Saif Al-Islam Gaddafi*, ICC-01/11-01/11, 21 May 2014.

this decision. In July 2015 a court in Tripoli pronounced guilty verdicts and the death sentence on both men.

The detention and trial of Saif Al-Gaddafi and Al-Senussi took place in a complex security situation in which sectarian violence continues. Senussi's defence lawyer, Ben Emmerson QC, has described the trial as dominated by 'extreme fear, insecurity and intimidation ... every one of his basic rights to a fair trial and due process have been completely ignored'.[106] The case raises the question of whom the criminal proceedings are for: the Libyan people, the victors against the Gaddafi regime or the international community? Undoubtedly, the Gaddafi regime committed terrible crimes, but in the context of the current pervasive insecurity, do these trials offer the possibility of ending impunity? It can be asked why the ICC needs the case against Saif Al-Islam Gaddafi when it ruled the case against Abdullah Al-Senussi inadmissible and thus legitimately held in Libya, despite the shortcomings of the trial. Is the ICC trying to demonstrate its superiority (despite the principle of complementarity) or is it genuinely attempting to guarantee a fair trial? It has been argued that the AU considers that the SC's referral of the Libya situation 'was not the act of an impartial and independent body acting in the interest of the Libyan people but a morally compromised organisation acting in the pursuit of political self-interest, with the sole agenda of securing regime change'.[107] So can the trials be construed as a means of retribution against the Gaddafi family rather than a commitment to the rule of law? Another factor is that the death penalty is not possible under the ICC Statute[108] but remains a possibility in Libya. Can criminal proceedings against the members of former oppressive regimes serve the security of the population, or is international criminal justice a pawn in the geopolitics of post-conflict?

Root Causes

Finally an important argument put forward by critics of the Liberal Peace is that transitional justice fails to deal with the continuing structural or 'root causes' of the abuses. Those who emphasise root causes generally

[106] Stephen, Chris. 'Gaddafi's Son Saif Al-Islam Sentenced to Death by Court in Libya', *The Guardian*, 29 July 2015, www.theguardian.com/world/2015/jul/28/saif-al-islam-sentenced-death-by-court-in-libya-gaddafi-son.

[107] Roberts, Hugh. 'Who Said Gaddafi Had to Go?' *London Review of Books* 33(22): 8–18, 11 cited in Ebbesson *et al.*, *op. cit.*, 233.

[108] *Rome Statute of the ICC, op. cit.*, article 77.

focus on socio-economic issues,[109] for instance, unemployment, poverty, inequalities including horizontal inequalities, corruption, repression and social exclusion.[110] Paul Gready, for example, has criticised the South African Truth and Reconciliation Commission for a 'narrow and impoverished conception of justice'[111]. By focusing on political violence, civil and political rights abuses and the past to a greater extent than criminal or social violence, socio-economic rights and the present, the transitional justice tool-kit does little to challenge, for example, the impacts of neo-liberal economics and/or rising levels of violent crime and punitive response to such crime. Limits are placed on structural change in new democracies, and within these limits the danger is that the marginalised are remarginalised. 'Holistic understandings of transitional justice too rarely extend to a critique of these other facets of globalization that profoundly shape transitional realities'.[112] It is proposed therefore that transitional justice mechanisms should also extend to economic and social rights and that failure to do so contributes to widespread disappointment with the process.[113]

At the same time, it can be argued that effective transitional justice is a necessary condition for the construction of a legitimate economy that could provide the basis for addressing these deep-seated structural problems. Those who commit war crimes are, by and large, those who gain from the predatory war economy which they helped to build at the most acute phases of conflict. Putting peace and stability before transitional justice will not make it easier to deal with these problems. On the contrary, unless there are mechanisms of accountability for those who committed the most egregious crimes it will not be possible to build a fairer economy and society. Of course, the inclusion of economic crimes, say, pillage, could be important but even the prosecution of civil and political crimes could be highly relevant in socio-economic terms. The concept of transformative justice as discussed below is relevant here.

[109] See, for example, Stewart, Frances. 'The Root Causes of Conflict: Some Conclusions', Queen Elizabeth House Working Paper 16.

[110] For a summary of these critiques, see Miller, Zinaida 2013. 'Review Essay: (Re)Distributing Justice', *International Journal of Transitional Justice* 2013, 1–11.

[111] Gready, Paul 2010. *The Era of Transitional Justice: The Aftermath of the Truth and Reconciliation Commission in South Africa and Beyond*, Routledge, 9.

[112] *Ibid.*, 8.

[113] Rees, Madeleine and Chinkin, Christine 2016. 'Exposing the Gendered Myth of Post Conflict Transition: The Transformative Power of Economic and Social Rights', *New York University J Int'l L and Politics* 48, 1211. See Chapter 9.

The Weakening of Judicialisation

Perhaps the most important reason for the patchy record of justice mechanisms is the priority given to geo-political considerations. There are many instances. A classic case is Afghanistan. Despite a growing consensus about the way in which the warlords undermine political legitimacy through wide-scale corruption and violence,[114] and therefore Western efforts to restore security, and although (or perhaps because) many of the warlords hold contracts with the United States and several are American citizens, there has been no attempt to bring any of them to justice. This can perhaps be explained in terms of the support they provide to the United States and particularly the CIA in counter-terror operations.[115] But even in less obvious cases, power considerations may explain why justice mechanisms have not been fully applied and the rule of law thwarted. For instance, the HRAP in Kosovo questioned whether there was an unwillingness on the part of UNMIK to risk the instability that would have erupted if there had been serious investigations into the activities of the KLA in the aftermath of the conflict.[116] In addition, revelation of crimes committed by KLA members would have challenged the NATO narrative of a successful military action against the Serb oppressors and violators of human rights in Kosovo.

Similar concerns have been raised in the context of the international criminal tribunals. During negotiations the United States sought unsuccessfully to subject prosecutions before the ICC to the authority of the SC and subsequently used its position to shield American forces from prosecution.[117] The ICTY and ICTR were created pursuant to SC resolution as a political response to the violence in those countries. The former ICTR prosecutor Carla del Ponte has indicated that she was unable to bring to trial members of the Rwanda Patriotic Front (now the Rwandan government) for crimes committed during the genocide.[118]

[114] Chayes, Sarah 2015. *Thieves of State: Why Corruption Threatens Global Security.* W. W. Norton and Co.

[115] Rangelov, Iavor and Theros, Marika 2012. 'Abuse of Power and Conflict Persistence in Afghanistan', *Conflict, Security and Development* 12(3): 227–248.

[116] '[T]he Panel fears that such inaction indicates certain reluctance on the part of UNMIK Police to pursue the investigations when there were indications of ethnically motivated violence pointing towards persons associated with the KLA'. *Janković v. UNMIK*, HRAP, no. 249/09, opinion of 16 October 2014, para. 108.

[117] UN SC Resolution 1422, 12 July 2002. The United States used its veto power to renew immunity in 2003 but has not done so since then.

[118] del Ponte, Carla and Sudetic, Chuck 2009. *Madame Prosecutor: Confronting Humanity's Worst Criminals and the Culture of Impunity: A Memoir.* Other Press; Erlinder, Peter

While it may be argued that genocide against the Tutsis was far worse than anything the present government has committed, such one-sidedness undermines the credibility of the criminal justice process.

A series of high-level acquittals in the last few years at the ICTY including of Franko Simatović and Jovica Stanišić[119] (leaders of some of the most vicious Serb militias during the wars in former Yugoslavia) and Ante Gotovina and Mladen Markać[120] (leaders of Croat operations against Serbs in Krajina) have deeply disappointed victims; they have also weakened the legitimacy of international justice, and of the ICTY in particular, in some people's eyes and through the example they offer to local courts. There are two main legal justifications for the acquittals. One is that the judges have abandoned the principle used in earlier cases of 'joint criminal enterprise', and the other is the interpretation of the concept of 'aiding and abetting'. In the past the argument was that these operations were organised and coordinated, but now it is necessary to prove that the leaders specifically directed the operations, which turns out to require a high burden of proof; the accused Stanišić's statement that 'we'll exterminate them completely'[121] was apparently insufficiently precise to constitute the requisite intention to carry out the alleged crimes.

A shift in jurisprudence that puts into question earlier convictions undermines the legitimacy of the institution. This is underscored by the dissenting opinion of Judge Carmel Agius[122] in the case of *Gotovina* and in an unprecedented e-mail letter from the Danish Judge, Frederik Harhoof.[123] In asking what lessons can be learned, Judge Harhoof comments that the 'military establishment in leading states (such as United States and Israel) felt that the courts in practice were getting too close to the military commanders' responsibilities'. He also reports 'rumours' of external pressure being brought to certain Judges of the Tribunal and in turn of those Judges pressuring their colleagues.

'The Rwanda War Crimes Cover up', *Global Research*, 7 April 2014, www.globalresearch.ca/the-rwanda-war-crimes-coverup/15037.

119 *Prosecutor v. Jovica Stanišić, Franko Simatović*, IT-03-69-T, 30 May 2013, vol. II.

120 *Prosecutor v. Gotovina et al. 'Operation Storm'*, IT-06–90-A, 16 November 2012.

121 Shapiro, Michael J. 2015. *War Crimes, Atrocity and Justice*. Polity Press, 40.

122 Judge Carmel Agius stated: 'I wish to register my disagreement with the approach taken by the Majority throughout the Appeal Judgement, and to distance myself from that approach'; *Prosecutor v. Ante Gotovina and Mladen Markać*, IT-06–90-A, 16 November 2012.

123 'ICTY Judge Frederik Harhoff's email to 56 Contacts', 6 June 2013, www.bt.dk/sites/default/files-dk/node-files/511/6/6511917-letter-english.pdf.

Despite these implications of outside political pressures, the point is rather that lawyers (and politicians) fear the all-embracing character of the notion of joint criminal enterprise, which in theory at least could involve a wide number of possible offenders, including those who arm and train warring parties from the outside. From a humanitarian perspective, widening the net might well be desirable, but from a geopolitical perspective this raises all sorts of risks. All the same, acquittals on technical grounds such as the level of the accused's intent may cause victims to feel that they were disbelieved and undermines confidence in the criminal process. As one victim who spent years in the detention camp at Omarska put it: 'You cannot admit that these people founded the forces that committed the mass war crimes over a period of four years and then conclude it is not their fault'.[124]

Nevertheless there are some grounds for optimism. On 15 December 2015, the Appeals Chamber ordered a retrial of Franko Simatović and Jovica Stanišić, stating that the Trial Chamber 'had erred in law in finding that it was not established that Stanišić and Simatović shared the intent to further the common criminal purpose'.[125] In its opinion, the Appeal Chamber referred both to the basis for liability in a joint criminal enterprise and in 'aiding and abetting'.

Acquittals in criminal trials have been matched by the failure of the ICJ to hold that genocide was committed in Bosnia (with the exception of the killings in Srebrenica in 1995).[126] In the words of the Vice President of the Court, Judge Al-Khasawneh (dissenting): 'If the only objective was to move the Muslim population, and the Court is willing to assume that

[124] Holligan, Anna. 'ICTY Hague Court in Turmoil amid Claims of Manipulation', *BBC*, 13 June 2013, www.bbc.co.uk/news/world-europe-22941857.

[125] www.icty.org/en/press/appeals-chamber-orders-retrial-jovica-stani%C5%A1i%C4%87-and-franko-simatovi%C4%87.

[126] *Application of the Convention on the Prevention and Punishment of the Crime of Genocide* (Bosnia and Herzegovina v. Serbia and Montenegro), 2007 ICJ Reports, judgment of 26 February 2007, para. 376: The Court concluded that 'save in the case of Srebrenica – the Applicant has not established that any of the widespread and serious atrocities, complained of as constituting violations of article II, paragraphs (a) to (e), of the Genocide Convention, were accompanied by the necessary specific intent (*dolus specialis*) on the part of the perpetrators. It also finds that the Applicant has not established the existence of that intent on the part of the Respondent, either on the basis of a concerted plan, or on the basis that the events reviewed above reveal a consistent pattern of conduct which could only point to the existence of such intent'. The Court also found no violation of the Genocide Convention by either Croatia or Serbia in *Application of the Convention on the Prevention and Punishment of the Crime of Genocide* (Croatia v. Serbia), 2015 ICJ Reports, judgment of 3 February 2015.

the Bosnian Serbs did only that which is strictly necessary in order to achieve this objective, then what to make of the mass murder?'[127] One wonders whether Bosnian Muslims consider the ICTY or ICJ to have delivered a legitimate verdict on the Bosnian conflict.[128]

In Bosnia, these developments have been compounded by a misinterpretation of a decision of the European Court of Human Rights (ECtHR).[129] In *Maktouf and Damjanović v. Bosnia and Herzegovina*[130] the ECtHR found a violation of the principle of non-retroactivity with respect to the application of the 2003 Criminal Code of Bosnia to war crimes committed in 1992 and 1993, rather than the then applicable (and in some respects more lenient) 1976 Criminal Code of the former Yugoslavia. The ECtHR found that this related to sentencing not conviction. Nevertheless the Constitutional Court of Bosnia and Herzegovina interpreted this to apply to a broader range of cases, leading to the release pending retrial of a number of persons convicted of war crimes and genocide, including 'convicted genocide offenders in the Srebrenica case where perpetrators had received more than 30 years imprisonment for taking part in the execution of more than a thousand persons and persons convicted of serious war crimes against civilians with more than 20 persons killed'.[131] This premature release has been disturbing to victims and witnesses of their crimes, including women subjected to crimes of sexual violence, and has been criticised by various regional bodies.[132] According to one of the Srebrenica relatives, 'I feel like a victim

[127] *Ibid.*, para. 41 (Judge Al-Khasawneh dissenting).

[128] These concerns are heightened by claims that certain documents were excluded from the ICTY hearings in the trial of Milošević and were thus not brought to the attention of the ICJ. Florence Hartmann, spokesperson for Carla del Ponte, the prosecutor, was convicted for contempt of court for knowingly disclosing such documents in a book, *Paix et Châtiment* and an article, 'Vital Genocide Documents Concealed'. Her appeal was dismissed; IT-02-54-R77.5-A, 19 July 2011.

[129] Forty-fourth Report of the High Representative for Bosnia and Herzegovina, 8 November 2013, paras. 65–68 ('Forty-fourth Report').

[130] *Case of Maktouf and Damjanović v. Bosnia and Herzegovina*, ECtHR GC application nos. 2312/08 and 34179/08, 18 July 2013.

[131] Forty-fourth Report, *op. cit.*, para. 74.

[132] 'The EU, the OSCE and the Office of the High Representative, the top international official in Bosnia, all said . . . that the state court's decision. . . to free the war criminals was a worrying development that must be addressed urgently'; Balkan Transitional Justice, 'Bosnian War Criminals' Release Sparks International Concern', 20 November 2013, www.balkaninsight.com/en/article/internationals-concerned-with-bosnian-legal-problems.

again. I don't know where the released criminals now are. They could be standing behind my back as we speak'.[133]

Women and Transitional Justice

Transitional justice mechanisms pose particular dilemmas for women.[134] There are at least two 'abusive paradigms' that women in oppressive regimes must navigate: 'one ethnic, racial, religious or political, and the other patriarchal'.[135] The danger is that transitional justice mechanisms look only at one paradigm and ignore that of gender. The CEDAW Committee has concluded that, in general, processes have failed to address the gendered dimensions of conflict. Further 'For most women, post-conflict justice priorities should not be limited to ending violations of civil and political rights but should include violations of all rights including economic, social and cultural rights'.[136] Over the past two decades most attention has been on securing accountability for crimes of sexual violence.[137] The statutes for the various international criminal tribunals have brought crimes of sexual and gender-based violence within their jurisdiction as war crimes and crimes against humanity; some jurisprudence has been developed and convictions secured with respect to rape and crimes of sexual violence against women and men.[138] The Rome Statute of the ICC has provisions for

[133] 'Bosnia Frees Srebrenica Convicts over Legal Error', *BBC*, 19 November 2013, www.bbc.com/news/world-europe-25007858.

[134] Bell, Christine and O'Rourke, Catherine 2007. 'Does Feminism Need a Theory of Transitional Justice? An Introductory Essay', *International Journal of Transitional Justice* 1: 23–44.

[135] Gray, David and Levin, Benjamin 2012. 'Feminist Perspectives on Extraordinary Justice', in Fineman, Martha and Zinsstag, Estelle (eds.). *Conflict and Transitional Justice: Feminist Approaches*. Intersentia, 63–88.

[136] Committee on the Elimination of Discrimination against Women, General Recommendation No. 30 on Women in Conflict Prevention, Conflict and Post-Conflict Situations, UN Doc. CEDAW/C/GC 30, 18 October 2013, para. 76 ('General Recommendation No. 30'); Chinkin, Christine 2009. 'The Protection of Economic, Social and Cultural Rights Post-Conflict', paper series commissioned by the UN Office of the High Commissioner for Human Rights, www.ohchr.org/Documents/Issues/Women/WRGS/Paper_Protection_ESCR.pdf.

[137] This was the motivation for the Preventing Sexual Violence in Conflict Initiative of the United Kingdom Government, co-founded by then Foreign Secretary William Hague and Angelina Jolie Pitt in 2012; www.gov.uk/government/policies/sexual-violence-in-conflict.

[138] A valuable reflection about lessons learned in prosecuting crimes of sexual violence is contained in Brammertz, Serge and Jarvis, Michelle (eds.) 2016. *Prosecuting Conflict-Related Sexual Violence at the ICTY*. Oxford University Press.

victim protection and participation.[139] The Security Council through its resolutions on Women, Peace and Security has emphasised the importance of sexual violence as a tactic of war and of accountability through criminal processes.[140] Yet although there has been mass perpetration of crimes of sexual violence, there have been very few prosecutions, trials and convictions. The rules of criminal procedure tend to undermine the narratives of victims and survivors, protective measures have been limited and definitions of core crimes disputed. Local courts or traditional processes may be the only realistic option, but they may too be problematic for women: the CEDAW Committee has noted that 'given that the processes and decisions of these mechanisms may discriminate against women, it is critical to carefully consider their role in facilitating access to justice for women, such as defining the type of violations that they will be addressing and the possibility to challenge their decisions in the formal justice system', although the latter too may reinforce discriminatory practices and stereotypes prevalent before the conflict.[141]

The consequences of proceedings before customary courts may deny women justice. The Special Representative of the Secretary-General on Sexual Violence in Armed Conflict has reported that customary courts in South Sudan often require rape victims to marry the perpetrator as a form of settlement; similarly in 'north-east Nigeria and in Somalia, "restitution" through marriage is widely accepted by victims' families in order to avoid "shame"'. She concludes that such 'measures not only fail to provide deterrence, but also deny the victim a future, effectively sentencing her to repeated rape'.[142] Even if convictions result in appropriate sentences, they cannot alone provide the types of remedies needed,

[139] *Rome Statute of the ICC, op. cit.*, article 68.

[140] E.g., UN SC Resolution 1820, 19 June 2008 calls upon 'Member States to comply with their obligations for prosecuting persons responsible for such acts, to ensure that all victims of sexual violence, particularly women and girls, have equal protection under the law and equal access to justice, and stresses the importance of ending impunity for such acts as part of a comprehensive approach to seeking sustainable peace, justice, truth, and national reconciliation'. UN SC Resolution 2122, 18 October 2013 calls upon Member States 'to comply with their relevant obligations to end to impunity and to thoroughly investigate and prosecute persons responsible for war crimes, genocide, crimes against humanity or other serious violations of international humanitarian law'.

[141] General Recommendation No. 30, *op. cit.*, para. 80.

[142] Report of the Secretary-General on conflict-related sexual violence, UN Doc. S/2016/361, 20 April 2016, para. 10.

and focus on criminal trials deflects attention from other gendered harms experienced in conflict and continuing inequalities.

What is needed – and not just with respect to prosecution of crimes against women – is a concept of justice that is not solely about transitional justice but one that combines it with restorative justice. Restorative justice seeks to place the needs of victims at the centre, as one step towards restoring peace to communities.[143] It is therefore a 'legitimate concern of the international community',[144] not just of the particular individuals. Judge Cançado Trindade of the ICJ has remarked on how '[r] estorative justice grows in importance in cases of grave and systematic violations of human rights, of the integrity of human beings'; he was referring to torture, but the same is true of many crimes committed against women in conflict, including sexual and gender-based violence. It can be crucial in enabling victims 'to find bearable to keep on relating with fellow human beings, and, ultimately, to keep on living in this world'.[145] This in some ways reflects the thinking behind local processes such as the *Gacaca* trials described above.

Truth and reconciliation processes provide space for narratives of the conflict away from the adversarial processes of trials. They may offer amnesties for perpetrators where the facts of the offences have been acknowledged and their recommendations – if implemented – may provide a basis for social reform. Truth and reconciliation commissions have not always included a gender analysis, nor taken into account structural inequalities and the way in which women experience harms in conflict. For instance, transitional justice mechanisms invariably focus on violations of civil and political rights which discounts 'the ways in which women and girls often do not enjoy the conditions that make the exercise of civil and political rights possible . . . or their disproportionate experience of socio-economic rights violations'.[146] Some TRC processes

[143] Handbook on Justice for Victims on the Use and Application of the United Nations Declaration of Basic Principles of Justice for Victims of Crime and Abuse of Power, UN Doc. E/CN.15/1998/CRP.4/add.1, 17 April 1998, 52.

[144] *Questions Relating to the Obligation to Prosecute or Extradite* (Belgium v. Senegal), 2012 ICJ Reports, 20 July 2012; Separate Opinion of Judge Cançado Trindade, para. 169.

[145] *Ibid.*, para. 172.

[146] *Preventing Conflict, Transforming Justice Securing the Peace, A Global Study on the Implementation of United Nations Security Council Resolution 1325*, October 2015 ('Study on 1325'), 110.

such as those in Peru,[147] Timor-Leste and Liberia have taken into account the harms committed against women and integrated a gender perspective.[148] The Sierra Leone Truth and Reconciliation Commission recommended a number of measures for the purposes of transforming the place of women and girls in the cultural life of the country, including free healthcare, educational support, skills training, provision of housing, symbolic reparations and urgent reparations for those in greatest need of an effective outcome (for example, victims of sexual violence or widows). The Report led to three pieces of legislation on gender inequality issues, as well as a public apology for a failure to protect women during the armed conflict and promises to prevent the recurrence of such wrongs.[149] However, full implementation of recommendations may not always follow the closing of a truth and reconciliation process: 'the best designed truth commission will have little impact, however, if there is no political will to implement its recommendations'.[150]

Women often face financial hardship following conflict. Although victims of conflict, they may be ineligible for pensions paid to combatants; welfare programmes may be limited by neo-liberal programmes for economic reconstruction, and economic and social rights are rarely incorporated into post-conflict reconstruction.[151] As victims of crime they may be able to receive reparations. Criminal prosecutions result in punishment for convicted offenders, but in an innovative provision the ICC Statute allows for reparations, including restitution, compensation and rehabilitation.[152] In the *Lubanga* case the Appeal Chamber has set out the applicable principles for payment of reparations, including that a gender-sensitive approach must be taken throughout.[153]

[147] In *Miguel Castro-Castro Prison v. Peru,* IACtHR, 25 November 2006, Merits, Reparations and Costs, the Inter-American Court referenced the chapter of the Truth and Reconciliation Commission specifically on sexual violence against women (para. 206).

[148] Study on 1325, *op. cit.*, 111.

[149] For a summary see UN Secretary-General, *Guidance Note of the Secretary General: Reparations for Conflict-Related Sexual Violence*, June 2014, 9.

[150] Study on 1325, *op. cit.*, 111.

[151] Arbour, Louise 2007. 'Economic and Social Justice for Societies in Transition', *NYU Journal of International Law and Politics* 40: 1–27.

[152] *Rome Statute of the ICC, op. cit.*, article 75. Since 2008 the Trust Fund for Victims has provided support to over 110,000 victims; Study on 1325, *op. cit.*, 103.

[153] *Prosecutor v. Thomas Lubanga Dyilo*, ICC-01/04-01/06 AC, 3 March 2015. See also Rubio-Marin, Ruth (ed.) 2009. *The Gender of Reparations: Unsettling Sexual Hierarchies While Redressing Human Rights Violations*. Cambridge University Press; Declaration on Women's and Girls' Right to a Remedy and Reparation, Nairobi, 2007, www.fidh.org/IMG/pdf/NAIROBI_DECLARATIONeng.pdf.

Human rights bodies too have considered the transformative potential of reparations, in particular those payable by the state for its failure to comply with the obligation of due diligence to ensure the prevention, protection and punishment for acts of violence against women. The special rapporteur on violence against women has noted that states need to be 'involved more concretely in overall societal transformation to address structural and systemic gender inequality and discrimination'.[154] Thus the obligation in respect of remedies cannot be just about returning women to the situation they were in before the violence, but should strive to have a transformative potential. This implies that remedies should aspire, to the extent possible, to subvert instead of reinforce pre-existing patterns of cross-cutting structural subordination, gender hierarchies, systemic marginalisation and structural inequalities that may be at the root cause of the violence that women experience.[155] Reparations need to be both individually assessed and directed towards societal transformation. The CEDAW Committee in its inquiry into the hundreds of women killed and tortured in Mexico (a situation not unlike a conflict zone) had taken a similar approach. It argued for 'a global and integrated response, a strategy aimed at transforming existing sociocultural patterns, especially with regard to eradicating the notion that gender violence is inevitable'.[156] Again in the words of the special rapporteur on violence against women: 'A gender-sensitive reparations programme should seize this opportunity to advance, as part of the venture of constructing a new and more inclusive democratic order, a society that overcomes the systemic subordination of women'.[157]

10.3 Immunity of International Personnel

In all the models of post-conflict governance described in Chapter 8, although international personnel are subject to local law they can claim

[154] Manjoo, Rashida, Report of the Special Rapporteur on Violence against Women, its Causes and Consequences, UN Doc. A/HRC/23/49, 14 May 2013, para. 71.

[155] *Ibid.*, para. 75.

[156] Report on Mexico produced by the Committee on the Elimination of Discrimination against Women under article 8 of the Optional Protocol to the Convention, and reply from the Government of Mexico, CEDAW/C/2005/OP8/Mexico, 27 January 2005, (Mexico Inquiry), paras. 159 and 287; see also *González et al. ('Cotton Field') v. Mexico*, IACtHR Series C No. 205, 16 November, Preliminary Objection, Merits, Reparations, and Costs, para. 450.

[157] Manjoo, *op. cit.*, para. 62.

immunity from the jurisdiction of the host state. In the case of UN personnel this is pursuant to the UN Charter, article 105 and the 1946 Convention,[158] given local effect by Regulation,[159] or by the relevant Status of Forces Agreement (SOFA). The US/UK Coalition Provisional Authority in Iraq in 2003–2004 also adopted Regulations guaranteeing immunity to all of their personnel, including independent contractors.[160] Although the UN Secretary-General may waive immunity 'where, in his opinion, the immunity would impede the course of justice and can be waived without prejudice to the interests of the United Nations',[161] in practice he does not often do so. Peacekeepers and internationals in the territory as part of the post-conflict programme are in a position to commit human rights and other abuses; their immunity undermines the legitimacy of their position.

This impunity gap has been challenged in the European Court of Human Rights. The first attempt was to impute harm done by peacekeepers to the troop-contributing state. In *Behrami v. France*[162] children in Kosovo playing with an undetonated cluster bomb unit were injured and a child was killed when one went off. The claim was that the international security force in Kosovo, KFOR, had not carried out its duty of 'supervising de-mining until the international civil presence can, as appropriate, take over responsibility for this task' and that the death constituted a violation of the right to life under the European Convention on Human Rights (ECHR), article 2. As non-state entities neither the UN nor KFOR can be a respondent before the European Court, so the case was brought against France in whose area of responsibility the events occurred.[163] The Grand Chamber of the European Court determined that the SC retained ultimate authority and control over KFOR's operations within the framework of the UN Charter, chapter VII. Accordingly

[158] *Convention on the Privileges and Immunities of the United Nations*, New York, 13 February 1946.

[159] E.g., UNMIK Regulation 2000/47, On the Status Privileges and Immunities of KFOR and UNMIK and their Personnel in Kosovo, 18 August 2000.

[160] Coalition Provisional Authority (CPA) Order 17, 17 June 2003; revised CPA Order 17, 27 June 2004.

[161] *Convention on the Privileges and Immunities of the United Nations*, New York, 13 February 1946, section 20.

[162] *Behrami v. France*, ECtHR GC application no. 71412/01, 31 May 2007.

[163] In the companion case of *Saramati v. France, Germany and Norway*, ECtHR GC application no. 78166/01, 31 May 2007, the complaint was of extra-judicial detention by UNMIK and KFOR and lack of access to the courts contrary to the ECHR, articles 5 and 6.

KFOR's actions were attributable to the UN and not to the individual states that were carrying out the SC mandate, even in the areas where specific sectors of operations had been designated to a lead country.[164] The Court found that it was not competent to consider the compatibility with the Convention of actions attributable to the UN. It should also be remembered that KFOR is made up of NATO troops, responsible for the dropping of the cluster bombs in Kosovo in the first place.

The consequence was to leave those injured through the acts of KFOR, mandated by the SC, without an enforceable legal remedy, despite the human rights commitments of the European contributing states. Troop contributing governments, parties to the European Convention on Human Rights, had argued that requiring their compliance with the Convention would undermine the coherence, unity and comprehensive structure of a UN mission. The Grand Chamber agreed:

> Since operations established by UNSC Resolutions under Chapter VII of the UN Charter are fundamental to the mission of the UN to secure international peace and security and since they rely for their effectiveness on support from member states, the Convention cannot be interpreted in a manner which would subject the acts and omissions of Contracting Parties which are covered by UNSC Resolutions and occur prior to or in the course of such missions, to the scrutiny of the Court. To do so would be to interfere with the fulfilment of the UN's key mission in this field including, as argued by certain parties, with the effective conduct of its operations. It would also be tantamount to imposing conditions on the implementation of a UNSC Resolution which were not provided for in the text of the Resolution itself.[165]

However, states routinely enter international organisations with a slew of differing legal obligations and entitlements; states have entered into different treaties;[166] multinational forces operate under diverse rules of engagement and their members come from different social, cultural and military backgrounds. It seems somewhat disingenuous for troop-contributing states to be concerned about multiple varied obligations in this context.

In a subsequent case, *Al Jedda v. the United Kingdom*, the Grand Chamber denied that the troops in question were peacekeepers under

[164] The decision has been much criticised; see, e.g., Mujezinović Larsen, Kjetil 2008. 'Attribution of Conduct in Peace Operations: The "Ultimate Authority and Control" Test', *European Journal of International Law* 19(3): 509–531.

[165] *Behrami* and *Saramati*, *op. cit.*, para. 149.

[166] One significant difference between NATO states is that the United States is not a party to the ECHR.

the authority of the UN, identifying them instead as members of the UK occupying forces in Iraq. The context was the detention without trial of a dual Iraqi/UK citizen in Iraq, for what the United Kingdom asserted was for imperative reasons of security.[167] The Court was unwilling to allow the United Kingdom to evade its responsibilities as occupying power by equating the position in Iraq (unauthorised invasion followed by military occupation, which was recognised but not mandated by the Security Council)[168] to that in Kosovo where the international security presence (KFOR) and the international civilian presence (UNMIK) had both been mandated by SC Resolution 1244. Accordingly acts of the UK forces were attributable to the state, not to the UN. At least in the context of the facts in Iraq, the gap in responsibility opened by *Behrami* was closed.

Another attempt to redress the gap in accountability of peacekeepers was to claim that immunity violates the right of access to courts under ECHR, article 6. As discussed above, the Mothers of Srebrenica is a foundation created to bring proceedings on behalf of the relatives of persons killed in and around Srebrenica in 1995 against the Dutch peacekeepers, contributing troops to UNPROFOR, who had failed to protect the victims of genocide. The Supreme Court of the Netherlands held 'that immunity belongs to the United Nations regardless of the seriousness of the allegations'. The ECtHR rejected the application finding that according immunity to the UN 'served a legitimate purpose and was not disproportionate' and thus did not constitute a violation of ECHR, article 6.[169] The Court also declined to consider whether the UN Secretary-General was under any moral or legal obligation to waive the UN's immunity. The legitimate purpose of UN immunity is to ensure 'the proper functioning' of the Organisation 'free from unilateral interference by individual governments'. As suggested above, such functioning is also impaired by the loss of legitimacy incurred when the UN fails to live up to its own commitment to human rights.

Two further cases that have been brought before the Dutch courts have come to a somewhat different and potentially ground-breaking conclusion. One was brought by Hasan Nuhanović, who had been a translator for Dutch troops, and whose father and brother were killed, together with

[167] *Al Jedda v. United Kingdom*, ECtHR GC application no. 27021/08, 7 July 2011, para. 80. See Chapter 8 for discussion of a different aspect of this case.

[168] UN SC Resolution 1483, 22 May 2003, preamble.

[169] *Stichting Mothers of Srebrenica and Others v. The Netherlands*, ECtHR application no. 65542/12, 27 June 2013.

the family of Rizo Mustafić, an electrician who was also killed after they were forced by Dutch peacekeepers to leave the 'safe area'. In this case the Supreme Court of the Netherlands found that the Dutch Government was liable for the three deaths. In the second case brought by the Mothers of Srebrenica, the Dutch Court found the Government partially responsible for the deaths of residents in the safe area of Srebrenica but only established liability with respect to those three hundred people who had sought refuge in the UN base at Potočari and were forced off the base by Dutch soldiers.[170]

10.3.1 Accountability of Peacekeepers

Peacekeepers are deployed to unstable and violent places, where they too often themselves become the targets of attack. Their weapons, supplies and equipment may be prized by the protagonists of violence and feed into the political economy of war. Peacekeeping failure to protect the population undermines credibility and loses the goodwill of the population.[171] Worse is when that credibility is undermined by the abuses they themselves commit. These include sexual abuse (violence) and exploitation, including of children, harassment, involvement in human trafficking and cruel and degrading treatment of civilians. Such crimes have been well documented, notably by the media and human rights NGOs. Concern about the involvement of UN peacekeepers (and humanitarian workers) in sexual exploitation and trafficking became widespread during the 1990s, especially in the context of Bosnia and Kosovo, and in the early years of the twenty-first century in the context of West Africa[172] and the DRC. But such abuses go back to early missions such as ONUC in the Congo in the 1960s[173] and in Cambodia and Somalia[174] in the early 1990s. Institutional legitimacy also depends on the behaviour of

170 See Nettelfield, Laura J. 'States Heed the Warning: Srebrenica's Survivors Make International Legal History', *Open Democracy*, 22 July 2014, www.opendemocracy.net/can-europe-make-it/lara-j-nettelfield/states-heed-warning-srebrenica%E2%80%99s-survivors-make-international.

171 See Chapter 9.

172 UN GA Resolution 57/306, 15 April 2003, Investigation into Sexual Exploitation of Refugees by Aid Workers in West Africa.

173 Van den Haag, Ernest 1962. *The War in Katanga: The United Nations in Congo, Report of a Mission*. American Committee for Aid to Katanga Freedom Fighters, 10.

174 Razack, Sherene 2004. *Dark Threats and White Knights: The Somalia Affair, Peacekeeping, and the New Imperialism*. University of Toronto Press, provides a vivid analysis of the implicit racism in the criminal abuse of Somalis by Canadian peacekeepers.

peacekeepers in local spaces, and damage may be caused through omission, negligence or misfortune rather than criminal or abusive acts. Marsha Henry gives examples of peacekeepers apparently asleep on duty.[175] In Kosovo, disappearances occurred after the deployment of KFOR (the international security force) and UNMIK (the civilian administration). Relatives of disappeared persons have given accounts of abductions taking place in the presence of KFOR troops, or being immediately reported to the authorities, but without any positive response. An especially egregious example of harm is the severe outbreak of cholera in Haiti following the deployment of additional peacekeepers in the aftermath of the earthquake in January 2010.[176] Concerns that the source of the cholera was peacekeepers from a cholera-afflicted country led the UN Secretary-General to set up an Independent Panel to investigate. The Panel concluded that the introduction and spread of the epidemic was due to a number of connecting factors and 'was not the fault of, or deliberate action of, a group or individual'. It made a number of recommendations for preventive measures for further UN missions to follow.

Peacekeepers are subject to the national laws 'by which military personnel remain bound throughout the operation' and to whatever rules of engagement may be determined by the relevant SOFA. After some debate as to whether UN peacekeepers are bound by international humanitarian law (IHL) (the UN is not and cannot be a High Contracting Party to the Geneva Conventions) the Secretary-General clarified that this is the case in a Bulletin in 1999.[177] The first paragraph states that IHL applies 'to United Nations forces when in situations of armed conflict they are actively engaged therein as combatants, to the extent and for the duration of their engagement. They are accordingly applicable in enforcement actions or in peacekeeping operations when the use of force is permitted in self-defence'. However, in practice, peacekeepers, like other international personnel, have immunity from the jurisdiction of the national courts. If acts fall within the definitions of crimes within the ICC Statute,

175 Henry, Marsha 2007. 'Gender, Security and Development', *Conflict, Security and Development* 7(1): 61–84.

176 'The outbreak subsequently claimed over 4,500 lives, sickened almost 300,000 people, and continues to cause infections and deaths in Haiti'. Final Report of the Independent Panel of Experts on the Cholera Outbreak in Haiti, 4 May 2011, www.un.org/News/dh/infocus/haiti/UN-cholera-report-final.pdf.

177 United Nations, Secretary-General's Bulletin: Observance by United Nations Forces of International Humanitarian Law, ST/SGB/1999/13, 6 August 1999.

the situation could be subject to the Court's jurisdiction.[178] Third-party claims for compensation for 'personal injury, illness or death, and for property loss or damage (including non-consensual use of premises) resulting from or attributable to the activities of members of peacekeeping operations' may be made against the Organisation.[179] However, liability is not engaged for harms arising out of 'operational necessity', compensation is not payable for non-economic loss such as pain and suffering or moral anguish and claims must generally be brought within six months of the harm, or of discovery of the harm.

The UN refused payment of any compensation for the cholera outbreak in Haiti.[180] However following a report from the UN special rapporteur on extreme poverty and human rights, Professor Philip Alston,[181] the UN adopted a 'new approach' in that instance. It has established a Haiti Cholera Response Multi-Partner Trust Fund, seeking to raise $400 million a year to support efforts for the elimination of cholera and to develop a framework for providing material assistance to Haitians most affected by the 2010 outbreak. However, while 'warmly welcoming' this initiative, the special rapporteur points out that the UN has accepted only moral, not legal, responsibility and its immunity from suit remains intact.[182]

In practice peacekeepers are rarely subject to domestic discipline for abuse. Where there are disciplinary measures, soft penalties may not reflect the severity of the abuse or its consequences to the mission. To take one example, three Pakistani officers in the UN mission in Haiti were court-martialed in a case involving the repeated rape of a 14-year-old boy. The fact that the officers were reportedly held accountable and were flown home to face a year in jail and a loss of their military benefits represents progress on one level. In years past, they might have just been sent home. On the other hand, no information surfaced on the charges,

[178] *Rome Statute of the ICC, op. cit.*, article 27 denies immunity based on 'official capacity'. However, jurisdiction of the Court still must be established.

[179] UN GA Resolution 52/247, 17 July 1998, Third-Party Liability: Temporal and Financial Limitations.

[180] 'Haiti Cholera Victims' Compensation Claims 'Not Receivable' under Immunities and Privileges Convention, United Nations Tells Their Representatives', UN Doc. SG/SM/14828, 21 February 2013.

[181] Special Rapporteur on Extreme Poverty and Human Rights, UN Doc. A/71/367, 26 August 2016.

[182] Alston however notes that by failing to accept legal responsibility the UN jeopardises its immunity 'by encouraging arguments calling for it to be reconsidered by national courts'. *Ibid.*

the sentences or compensation for the boy. And the sentence for repeated rape of a minor hardly reflects the gravity of the crime.[183]

There is an inherent power imbalance between international peacekeepers and local populations, exacerbated by the disruption of social and economic structures caused by conflict followed by an influx of military and civilian personnel, well paid in comparison with the local population. Trivialisation of abuses and lack of accountability create a climate of impunity and destroy the credibility and legitimacy of the mission, thereby weakening its ability to provide security. Such crimes make a mockery of attempts to assert the priority of human rights and the rule of law as the basis for post-conflict reconstruction. Training of local police and security forces on whom responsibility will fall after the termination of the mission is also undermined by the commission of crimes by the internationally mandated peacekeeping forces. The impunity of the latter creates a significant gap in the 'post-conflict' security framework.

The UN has attempted to reduce the incidence of offences through monitoring and other measures. In 2003, Secretary-General Kofi Annan introduced standards under the United Nations Staff Regulations and Rules which asserted sexual exploitation and abuse to constitute 'serious misconduct' and grounds for summary dismissal. Further, any sexual activity involving those under eighteen is prohibited and 'sexual relationships between United Nations staff and beneficiaries of assistance … strongly discouraged'.[184] In 2005 he commissioned an investigative report (the Zeid Report) when 'it became clear that the measures currently in place to address sexual exploitation and abuse in peacekeeping operations were manifestly inadequate and that a fundamental change in approach was needed'. This Report discussed the incidence of sexual exploitation by peacekeepers, its context, problems of ensuring accountability and made recommendations. It too emphasised that '[t]he illdiscipline engendered by sexual exploitation and abuse also degrades the effectiveness of the peacekeeping operation, especially in times of crisis'.[185] Following the Report, the code of conduct has evolved into the

183 Bolopion, Philippe. 'Can the UN Help Itself from Underwriting Human Rights Abuses?' *Human Rights Watch*, 24 July 2012, www.hrw.org/news/2012/07/24/can-un-help-itself-underwriting-human-rights-abuses.

184 Secretary-General's Bulletin: Special Measures for Protection from Sexual Exploitation and Sexual Abuse, UN Doc. ST/SGB/2003/13, 9 October 2003.

185 Special Adviser to the Secretary-General, Prince Zeid, 'A Comprehensive Strategy to Eliminate Future Sexual Exploitation and Abuse in UN Peacekeeping Operations', UN Doc. A/59/710, 24 March 2005.

so-called 'zero tolerance' policy now incorporated into the mandate of all peacekeeping missions and affirmed in SC resolutions relating to women, peace and security.[186] Other measures are also urged on troop-contributing states, for instance, strategies to raise awareness, disciplinary measures and screening of recruits to peacekeeping missions, increasing the number of women peacekeepers and the development of further guidelines. The development of institutional posts (e.g., gender advisers in peacekeeping forces and women protection advisors) and training for peacekeepers were also recommended.

In 2013 it was noted that allegations of sexual abuse involving peacekeeping personnel had dropped 19 per cent from 74 in 2011 to 60 in 2012.[187] As noted by the EU representative, however, one case is too many, and under-reporting remains an unknown factor. The zero tolerance policy has also been criticised for perpetuating gender stereotypes, presenting almost all sex as coercive, ignoring the realities of agency and survival, and characterising peacekeepers as sexual predators.[188] Security Council Resolution 2242 (2015) on women, peace and security welcomes the Secretary-General's commitment 'to bring to public light misconduct by United Nations personnel', and his 'decision that all countries repeatedly listed in the annexes of his reports on Children and Armed Conflict and Sexual Violence in Conflict are prohibited from participating in United Nations peacekeeping operations'.[189] These measures, however, fall short of removing the immunity from jurisdiction peacekeeping personnel currently enjoy.

[186] The Women, Peace and Security agenda commenced with UN SC Resolution 1325, October 2000. Subsequent resolutions are UN SC Resolution 1820, 19 June 2008; UN SC Resolution 1888, 30 September 2009; UN SC Resolution 1889, 5 October 2009; UN SC Resolution 1960, 16 December 2010; UN SC Resolution 2106, 24 June 2013; UN SC Resolution 2122, 18 October 2013; UN SC Resolution 2242, 13 October 2015.

[187] UN GA, Fifth Committee, 'Reviewing Reports on Peacekeeping Operations, Fifth Committee Hails Progress Towards Zero Tolerance of Sexual Abuse by United Nations Personnel', 14 May 2013, www.un.org/News/Press/docs/2013/gaab4065.doc.htm.

[188] Simic, Olivera. 'Distinguishing between Exploitative and Non-Exploitative Sex involving UN Peacekeepers: The Wrongs of "Zero Tolerance"', *Norwegian Peacebuilding Resource Centre*, Expert Analysis November 2013, http://peacebuilding.no/var/ezflow_site/storage/original/application/18283244a25599f4883ec5e6ea0d255d.pdf.

[189] See also UN SC Resolution 2272, 11 March 2016, which provides for a number of responses, including the repatriation of an entire police or military unit where 'there is credible evidence of widespread or systemic sexual exploitation and abuse by that unit', and for replacement of units where appropriate investigative steps have not been taken, or perpetrators not held accountable.

The Global Study on women, peace and security cited this situation as the 'major controversy' that brings the UN into disrepute and recommended discussion about the setting up of an International Tribunal for Sexual Exploitation and Abuse by UN peacekeepers and staff in the field.[190]

The problems of imputability and accountability have been heightened by outsourcing, or 'sub-contract peacekeeping', whereby the SC authorises another body or state to carry out peacekeeping functions, as discussed above. The United States, for instance, outsources its commitment to supply peacekeepers, or civilian security personnel (UN police) to multinational corporations, which hire people on contract from all over the world. In such a scenario to whom is wrongful behaviour attributable – the state, the private contractor or the UN? And where therefore is the accountability? Such contracted persons are not agents of the state, as is the case with military personnel, and are not subject even to the developing codes of conduct appertaining to military personnel. They may be covered by immunity under a Status of Forces Agreement.[191] It may be possible to bring actions against the company in its place of registration, but such actions are likely to relate to terms of employment and may not cover human rights abuses against the supposedly protected population.[192]

Enhancing accountability appears problematic in face of the resistance to weakening immunity. One response is the establishment of some form of external monitoring system, as has been done with respect to the UN executive presence in Kosovo, as discussed below. However, the actions of KFOR are excluded from the jurisdiction of the Human Rights Advisory Panel, and there is, at present, no alternative mechanism.

[190] Study on 1325, *op. cit.*, 17. A United Kingdom House of Lords, Select Committee, report recommended a new tribunal 'light' to ensure peacekeeper accountability for sexual abuse and exploitation; House of Lords Select Committee on Sexual Violence in Armed Conflict, *Sexual Violence in Armed Conflict: A War Crime*, HL Paper 123, 12 April, 2016, para. 475.

[191] E.g., the Status of Forces Agreement between the United Nations and the Government of the Republic of South Sudan concerning the United Nations Mission in South Sudan, 2011, articles 3 and 15.

[192] The film *Whistleblower* illustrates the lack of accountability for UN peacekeepers involved in trafficking in post-Dayton Bosnia. Mentioned in Vulliamy, Ed., 'Has the UN Learned Lessons of Bosnian Sex Slavery Revealed in Rachel Weisz Film?' *The Guardian,* 15 January 2012, www.theguardian.com/world/2012/jan/15/bosnia-sex-trafficking-whistleblower.

10.3.2 *The UNMIK Human Rights Advisory Panel*

In the context of Kosovo the UN has taken the first steps towards an accountability mechanism. In the exercise of its powers as a 'surrogate' state, UNMIK carried out such actions as detentions without judicial decision or control, releasing people from detention contrary to the decisions of international judges and prosecutors, and removal of persons from the electoral list.[193] In addition UNMIK police failed to adequately investigate the many complaints it received of persons murdered or abducted in the aftermath of the conflict. Commentators concluded in 2003 (four years after the end of conflict) that in ensuring respect for human rights within the territory, 'both in legal institutions and the populace at large' UNMIK had failed, and failed so profoundly 'that it puts at risk the transition as a whole'.[194] The main human rights issue was lack of personal security, notably for the non-Albanian population – Serbs, Roma and other minorities – and in the northern predominantly Serb areas for Albanians.[195] In particular, UNMIK had apparently been taken by surprise by the major eruption of violence on 17 March 2004, which had resulted in deaths, injuries, displacement and destruction of houses, churches and monasteries and had not been able to contain the violence or maintain order.

Various external bodies expressed disquiet about UNMIK's non-compliance with international human rights. For instance, the UN Human Rights Committee concluded that 'human rights concerns are often not sufficiently attended to in the programmes of UNMIK'.[196] UNMIK responded by setting up the Human Rights Advisory Panel in 2006,[197] the first UN accountability mechanism of this sort with respect

[193] Ombudsperson Institution in Kosovo, Second Annual Report: 2001–2002, 10 July 2002.

[194] Marshall, David and Inglis, Shelley 2003. 'The Disempowerment of Human Rights-Based Justice in the United Nations Mission in Kosovo', *Harvard Human Rights Journal* 16: 95–146, 96.

[195] Venice Commission (European Commission for Democracy through Law), Opinion no. 280/2004 on Human Rights in Kosovo: Possible Establishment of Review Mechanisms, Venice, 8–9 October 2004, para. 29; Marshall and Inglis, *ibid.*, 106.

[196] UN Human Rights Committee, Consideration of Country Report: United Nations Interim Administration Mission in Kosovo (Initial Report), UN Doc. CCPR/C/UNK/CO/1, 14 August 2006.

[197] United Nations Interim Administration Mission in Kosovo, UNMIK Regulation No. 2006/12, On the Establishment of the Human Rights Advisory Panel, 23 March 2006, www.unmikonline.org/hrap/Documents%20HRAP/Regulations%20Eng/RE2006_12.pdf.

to a mission in the field.[198] The model was the individual communications procedure available before some UN human rights treaty bodies whereby individuals can complain of violation of listed human rights treaties by UNMIK. If the Panel determines there to have been a breach, it can make recommendations. However, the Panel has limited jurisdiction as it can only hear claims with respect to events after 23 April 2005, nearly six years after SC Resolution 1244 and only with respect to UNMIK, thereby excluding KFOR from its scrutiny.[199] It was established without effective consultations with the local population; consultative mechanisms with the local legal community were set up but without the immediate and substantial resources needed to support them and make them operationally effective.[200] Further it was seen by some observers as institutionally too close to UNMIK.

Does the HRAP provide a model that might have precedential value for further UN accountability mechanisms, enhancing compliance by UN missions with human rights and thus enhancing security? The Panel received more than five hundred complaints, more than had been anticipated, primarily with respect to the failure by UNMIK Police to investigate deaths and disappearances, issues arising out of displacement from property and claims to the proceeds of the privatisation of previously socially-owned enterprises. Most are from the non-Albanian population of Kosovo who have been subjected to various forms of hardship and abuse following the withdrawal of Serbia from Kosovo in June 1999. Especially in the immediate aftermath, they had their houses in Kosovo destroyed, looted and taken over by Albanians, lost their jobs and could not find further employment, in a situation of high unemployment. Many feel that UNMIK has offered them inadequate protection or has failed to make the relevant institutions, such as courts, available to or effective for them. The complaints provide an account of the post-conflict situation where ethnicity is core and of transition from socialism. They also paint a vivid picture of the issues that cause distress and insecurity 'post-conflict' and where the international presence offers inadequate protection.

198 The ombudsperson institution, as established in both Kosovo and East Timor while under UN territorial administration allowed for individual complaints.

199 Further restrictions on the Panel's operations were imposed by Administrative Direction 2009/1, 17 October 2009. Implementing UNMIK Regulation No. 2006/12 on the Establishment of the Human Rights Advisory Panel.

200 Miller, Anthony 2004–5. 'UNMIK: Lessons from the Early Institution-Building Phase', *New England Law Review* 39: 9–24, 12.

The HRAP applied international human rights standards (primarily through reference to the jurisprudence of the European Convention on Human Rights) to UNMIK and in many instances found that these have not been satisfied. In the context of UNMIK's failure to adequately investigate disappearances and deaths in accordance with the procedural obligation of the ECHR, article 2, its opinions have been lauded as 'landmark decision[s] by an international expert body in the difficult process of holding international organizations, including the United Nations accountable for human rights violations'.[201] But it must also be asked whether a human rights mechanism is an appropriate way to enhance security post-conflict and whether the administrator's distinct tasks of ensuring security, bringing perpetrators of atrocities to account, and accountability for failure to do so are compatible. For instance, seeking witnesses of ethnic violence may create fear and insecurity where there are insufficient protective measures, perpetrators are known and may still be in the vicinity. KFOR's immediate task (and subsequently that of UNMIK) was to achieve stability in Kosovo; rigorous investigations of disappearances, especially when the perpetrators were reported by relatives of the victims to be 'Albanians' or 'persons wearing KLA insignia', could generate further violence. As in Bosnia, overall security and stability may be maintained by selective enforcement, whereas the main objective of a human rights mechanism is to enhance official compliance with human rights standards. Victims want something different. In cases of disappearance they want to know what happened to their relative, where the body can be located and how the person died. This was not the function of the Panel, which was not a fact-finding body. It could only determine whether UNMIK had complied with its obligation to investigate or whether it should have done more. Further, even though the Panel recommended non-pecuniary compensatory remedies in many instances and pecuniary compensation for non-pecuniary damage, such recommendations were advisory and not binding. The UN generally only pays for material not non-pecuniary damage, such as pain and suffering or moral anguish, and no payments have been made. The issue of reparations goes to the heart of whether the UN is serious about accountability for its own human rights violations. As noted by the Panel in its Final Report: 'the UN's legitimacy and credibility is undermined

[201] Novak, Manfred 2013. 'Enforced Disappearance in Kosovo: Human Rights Advisory Panel Holds UNMIK Responsible', *European Human Rights Law Review* 3: 275–283, 282.

where there is no legal accountability. Further, the human rights system as a whole is weakened when it can be observed that the UN, one of the main guardians of the world's human rights system, is itself failing to live up to the obligations it has promoted.'[202] Of course, for the families there is almost bound to be disappointment and frustration with the outcome.

Is the experiment of a UN accountability mechanism likely to be repeated? Kosovo presented an exceptional set of circumstances, including its location in Europe, the role played by NATO in the war and the powers conferred on UNMIK. No similar institution was established by UNTAET in East Timor (although there was an ombudsperson and East Timor gained its independence before the Kosovo Panel was established). A similar Panel has been set up with respect to the EULEX rule of law mission that took over many of UNMIK's functions in Kosovo from the end of 2008,[203] although EULEX has a much more limited mandate than UNMIK. If there is any future UN territorial administration, it would be important to analyse the problems faced by the Panel, and by UNMIK in complying with its human rights standards. It should also be considered whether a similar model might serve for UN peacekeepers and other tasks undertaken by the UN. However, the Panel represents some recognition of the need for accountability of UN bodies, and it would be hard to retreat on at least an assumption of accountability for any such institution.

10.4 Conclusion

The establishment of accountability mechanisms raises the important question of who should be made accountable and for what. Individual accountability may constitute a more effective form of inducing compliance and of enforcement than sanctions for collective guilt, if applied in broader, more consistent and effective ways. Nevertheless the reality that only a fraction of those involved in the commission of atrocities are likely to be subject to prosecution challenges the legitimacy of those trials that

[202] The HRAP completed its case load in June 2016. Human Rights Advisory Panel, *The Human Rights Advisory Panel History and Legacy Kosovo, 2007–2016*, Final Report, 30 June 2016, para. 279; www.unmikonline.org/PublishingImages/2016/HRAP%20Final%20Report/HRAP%20Final%20Report%20(final%20version%2030%20June%202016).pdf.

[203] Human Rights Review Panel, established 29 October 2009; Council Joint Action 2008/124/CFSP of 4 February 2008 on the European Union Rule of Law Mission in Kosovo.

do take place. This is one of the reasons why international trials should focus on the 'most serious crimes of concern to the international community' (Preamble, Rome Statute of the ICC), but there may be disagreement as to which these are, or who are the most significant accused.

The increase in international judicialisation was an outcome of the post–Cold War moment when the opportunities for international co-operation and greater attentiveness to human rights opened up. That moment appears to have come to an end, and the possibilities for humanitarian perspectives are closing in again, as is reflected in the criticisms of the ICC and, in broader terms, the failure to tackle impunity for international crimes in Syria or Ukraine. Neither state is a party to the Rome Statute; nor is Russia. Local human rights bodies and NGOs have documented crimes, but in 2016 the geo-political situation makes the establishment of any international or hybrid tribunal with jurisdiction unlikely. But the very existence of the international court and, indeed other accountability mechanisms, is a reminder of those possibilities. As Rangelov and Teitel put it: 'The *ad hoc* international criminal tribunals and the ICC, in particular, have become evident sites of the new global politics of contestation between multiple actors, including states as well as multilaterals, NGO's, victims groups, corporations, individuals and peoples'.[204]

What has come to be known as *post bellum* law comprises a range of activities, including legal authority for the presence and role of international personnel; growing numbers of peace agreements ratified by the international community; mandates and rules of engagement for peacekeeping forces; hybrid legal arrangements for peacebuilding; and a range of emerging mechanisms for justice and accountability. What we have tried to show in Part IV of the book is the ever-present tension that runs through all these different phenomena between a war-based conception of law and a rights-based conception of law. This tension is both global and local. At a global level it is the tension between geo-politics and human rights, or the way in which geo-political considerations and/or the War on Terror interfere with humanitarian and rights-based objectives. At a local level it has to do with the tension between a traditional view of peace as the end of a contest of wills in which the warring parties are treated as winners and a peace based on the security of individuals.

[204] Rangelov and Teitel, *op. cit.*, 164.

PART V

The Way Forward

11

Second-Generation Human Security

11.1 Introduction

Second-generation human security is about a practical strategy in difficult places. First-generation human security marked the emergence of an idea in the aftermath of the Cold War – an idea that was shaped by the experience of conflict in the 1990s and was able to take root because of the greater international consensus of that period. Even though the concept continues to be mainstreamed in international institutions like the UN, the European Union and the African Union and indeed could be considered one strand of the Liberal Peace, its implementation and its discursive resonance have been marginalised by the War on Terror and the resurgence of Geo-Politics.

We argue for the relevance of a second-generation Human Security model in a new and dangerous global context where all other models have proved inadequate. The Liberal Peace model has had some success in halting overt conflict, but, as we elaborated in Chapter 9, the top-down approach to peacemaking has ended up entrenching the power relations established through war and thus contributing to continuing violations of human rights, economic predation and virtual conflict. Military interventions in the name of the War on Terror (Iraq, Afghanistan and Syria) or Geo-Politics (Georgia and Ukraine) have a much worse record; far from causing violence to cease, they have tended to fuel the mutual enterprise that constitutes a new war. And those military interventions in the name of humanitarianism or the Responsibility to Protect (Kosovo, Libya and Côte d'Ivoire) may well have succeeded in avoiding or reversing immediate humanitarian catastrophes, but they also involved violence and have empowered violent actors that are associated with continuing polarisation, instability and disorder.

At the time of writing conflicts in places such as Syria, Iraq, Libya, Yemen, Sudan, South Sudan, Mali and Democratic Republic of Congo (DRC) exhibit only too vividly the new war logic of persistence and spread[1] and the inadequacy of existing international approaches. Moreover, the migrant crisis and the increase in terrorist attacks, including in what are supposed to be stable parts of the world, have made it impossible to ignore these catastrophes in more unstable neighbourhoods. Second generation human security is a rights-based approach to peacemaking and intervention that is both top-down and bottom-up, both international and local, and that requires extensive political, economic, legal and security tools. Instead of a single top-down peace agreement, second generation human security involves a hybrid process of peacemaking, whereby talks from above complement and harmonise with talks at local and regional levels aimed at individual, community and gender security rather than (or possibly as well as) a grand overall solution, and where localised cease-fires combined with political, social and economic initiatives expand secure areas. Instead of a focus on military intervention (especially air strikes), second-generation human security might involve the deployment of an international presence to work with local personnel that could include, according to context, aid agencies, security forces (police, peacekeepers, even on occasion military), conflict mediators and human rights monitors as requested and negotiated at local levels. Hence second generation human security is a complex ambitious approach that requires considerable long-term commitment of resources, political will and learning. But it may be the only way to address the deteriorating interconnected spiral of new wars.

The chapter starts with an outline of the evolution of the concept of human security and the debates about its meanings. It pays particular attention to the gender aspects of human security. It then describes the shifting context in which ideas about human security have been manifested and the ways in which the idea has become increasingly marginalised. The chapter then discusses the burgeoning of radical critiques of human security during the last decade and argues that these can be construed as representing the discursive achievement of the War on Terror, even though the debates about what it is to be human, the meaning of security and the use of the idea of biopower all have potential to substantiate our understanding of human security. It concludes by pointing to the ways a reconstructed second generation human security can build on these insights and contribute to what might be described as a post-liberal peace.

[1] See Chapter 1.

11.2 The Evolution of the Concept of Human Security

The story of human security usually starts with the UN Development Programme (UNDP) *Human Development Report* of 1994.[2] Yet the ideas and practices that came together under the umbrella of the term 'human security' had a much longer trajectory. Indeed, the reiteration of 'freedom from want' and 'freedom from fear' in the UN Secretary-General's 2005 follow-up to the Millennium Summit[3] is a deliberate echo of President Franklin Roosevelt's Four Freedoms address in 1941[4] and the preamble to the 1948 Universal Declaration of Human Rights (UDHR).[5] Even earlier, Jane Addams, a member of the American delegation to the Women's Peace Congress in The Hague in 1915 and the 1931 winner of the Nobel Peace prize, wrote in 1922 of 'two of men's earliest instincts ... the first might be called security from attack, the second security from starvation'.[6] David Bosold suggests that the first actual use of the term human security was by Nils Bohr in 1945 when he said that 'active atomic materials' represent a 'perpetual menace to human security'.[7] As it developed during the last decades of the Cold War, the concept can be said to have emerged from two strands of thinking that became increasingly salient in this period.

One strand of thinking had to do with disarmament and development. It was expressed through concern with the burden of the East-West arms race and the idea that resources devoted to the amassing of arms could be better directed towards solving social problems such as

[2] For a 'Prehistory' of human security see MacFarlane, Neil and Khong, Yuen Foong 2006. *Human Security and the UN: A Critical History*. Indiana University Press, chapter 1; for more detail on human security see Kaldor, Mary 2007. *Human Security: Reflections on Globalization and Intervention*. Polity; Beebe, Shannon and Kaldor, Mary 2010. *The Ultimate Weapon Is No Weapon: Human Security and the New Rules of War and Peace*. Public Affairs.

[3] Report of the Secretary-General, *In Larger Freedom: Towards Development, Security and Human Rights for all*, UN Doc. A/59/2005, 21 March 2005 ('In Larger Freedom').

[4] 87 Cong. Rec. 44 (1941).

[5] UN GA Res 217A (III), 10 December 1948: 'the advent of a world in which human beings shall enjoy freedom of speech and belief and freedom from fear and want has been proclaimed as the highest aspiration of the common people'.

[6] Addams, Jane 2002. *Peace and Bread in Time of War*. UI Press, Reissue Ed., 116, cited Sharp, Ingrid 2015. 'The Women's Peace Congress of 1915 and the Envisioning of Women's Rights as Human Rights', paper given at a conference at the Mile End institute on Women, Peace and Transitional Activism, March 2015.

[7] Bosold, David 2011. 'Development of the Human Security Field: A Critical Examination'. in Chandler, David and Hynek, Nik (eds.). *Critical Perspectives on Human Security: Rethinking Emancipation and Power in International Relations*. Routledge, 28–42, 30.

those of poverty and disease. This preoccupation was the subject of a series of reports undertaken by the United Nations as well as a number of independent commissions that all tried to broaden the concept of security and provide a blueprint for human survival.[8] The term human security was used a year before the 1994 Report in the press release for UNDP's 1993 *Human Development Report*, which was primarily about people's participation. The press release drew attention to 'new concepts of human security that stress security of the people not just nations and territory. This means accelerated disarmament using defence cuts to boost development. It also means a new role for the United Nations, increasingly intervening to provide human security in areas such as the former Yugoslavia and in Somalia, where people are fighting within countries rather than between countries'.[9] The 1993 Report itself stressed that 'we have to redefine our concept of security, as security for people, not security for land'.[10]

For UNDP the emphasis was on material security, even though it insisted on the link between freedom from fear and freedom from want. The 1994 Report lists seven types of security (economic, food, health, environmental, personal, community and political), of which only one, 'personal security', referred to physical safety from violence. There was an underlying assumption that deprivation is the main cause of war and, through development, the problem of war and violence could be solved. This understanding of human security is evident in the writing of Mahboob ul Haq, special advisor and 'chief architect' of the UNDP Report, who is credited with the concept of human security:

> Two major issues dominated the creative period of international rethinking during and just after the Second World War. One was to avoid a catastrophic war. The other was to avoid another economic depression and to ensure universal economic and social well-being. The first preoccupation was with military security, the second with human security – and the link between the two was never forgotten. Unfortunately, with the

[8] E.g., Independent Commission on International Development Issues (Brandt Commission), *North-South* (1980) and *Common Crisis* (1983); Independent Commission on Disarmament and Security Issues, *Common Security: A Blueprint for Survival* (1982) ('Palme Report'); World Commission on Environment and Development, *Our Common Future* (1987) ('Brundtland Report'); The South Commission, *The Challenge of the South* (1990) ('Nyerere Report').

[9] Quoted in Bosold, *op. cit.*, 32.

[10] United Nations Development Program 1993. *Human Development Report: 1993*. Oxford University Press, Foreword.

> start of the Cold War between the superpowers, the first component often dominated the second.[11]

This version of human security has been followed through by UNDP with a series of human security reports focusing on different regions and countries and is also widely used within the broader UN system. Ten years later, in May 2004, a Human Security Unit was established within the Office for the Coordination of Humanitarian Affairs (OCHA) to administer the Japanese-funded United Nations Trust Fund for Human Security and to mainstream human security within UN activities. The fund has undertaken a series of human security projects that largely but not exclusively focus on material insecurity. A human security advisor to the Secretary-General was appointed in 2010 who is responsible for regular reporting on the implementation of human security. And in 2012, the UN General Assembly 'for the first time ... agreed on a common understanding of human security'.[12]

The second strand of thinking drew on the growing influence of human rights in international affairs and the link that came to be made between security and human rights. The UN Human Rights Covenants,[13] adopted in 1966 and which came into force in 1976, gave legal weight to and furthered the emerging human rights movement, particularly in Eastern Europe and Latin America.[14] Within the former, a key moment was the Helsinki Agreement of 1975,[15] which ushered in a period of East-West détente. The three baskets of Helsinki (security, economic and social co-operation and human rights) essentially constituted a human security concept even though the term was not used at the time. This human rights focus became especially influential in both Canada and Australia where innovative foreign ministers (Lloyd Axworthy and Gareth Evans) pioneered the idea of human security. Writing in 1994, Gareth Evans argued:

11 Quoted in Bosold, *op. cit.*, 34.

12 Takasu, Yukio 2014. 'Japan and Networked Human Security', in Martin, Mary and Owen, Taylor 2014. *Routledge Handbook of Human Security*. Routledge, 239–250, 246.

13 International Covenant on Civil and Political Rights (ICCPR)and International Covenant on Economic, Social and Cultural Rights (ICESCR), both of 16 December 1966.

14 The historic origins of human rights and when they emerged as influential in international relations is debated. See, for example, Moyn, Samuel 2011. *The Last Utopia: Human Rights in History*. Belknap Press; for a rejoinder to this view see Alston, Philip 2013. 'Does the Past Matter? On the Origins of Human Rights', *Harvard Law Review* 126 (7): 2043–2081.

15 *Final Act of the 1st CSCE Summit of Heads of State or Government* (Helsinki Final Act), 1 August 1975.

> Two approaches seem particularly worthy of further exploration. The first is to develop the notion that 'security' as it appeared in the Charter is as much about the protection of individuals as it is about the defense of the territorial integrity of states. . . . A second approach, which could either stand alone, or be seen as reinforcing the 'human security' reading just described, would pursue to its logical limits the international community's obligations under the UN Charter, to protect basic human rights bearing in mind that the most basic human rights of all, that of life, is violated on a very large scale in intra-state conflicts.[16]

Indeed, the historical trajectory of human security tracks to some extent that of human rights. Human rights were, of course, formally espoused by the General Assembly as early as 1948 with the adoption of the UDHR, but Cold War politics impeded the negotiation of the UN Covenants and their eventual coming into force until 1976, the year following the Helsinki Agreement. The end of the Cold War allowed the affirmation at the 1993 Vienna World Conference on Human Rights that 'human rights are universal, indivisible and interdependent and interrelated' and their protection the 'first responsibility of Governments' and a 'priority objective' of the United Nations.[17] They 'contribute to the stability and well-being necessary for peaceful and friendly relations among nations, and to improved conditions for peace and security'.[18] This strong statement thus coincided with the articulation of human security in 1993–1994. While it is accepted that human rights and human security are complementary concepts and 'mutually reinforcing',[19] their relationship remains controversial.[20] Both, however, can be seen as part of the post–Cold War 'New World Order', which, while short-lived, in some respects continues to have resonance.

The quote from Gareth Evans above highlights another factor – the post–Cold War prevalence of new wars and the high levels of violence associated with such wars. The policy high point of the human rights strand of human security thinking may be the work of the International Commission on Intervention and State Sovereignty (ICISS), established by the Canadian government and chaired by Gareth Evans and

[16] Quoted in Bosold, *op. cit.*, 36.

[17] Vienna Declaration and Programme of Action, UN Doc. A/CONF.157/23, 12 July 1993, I, paras. 1, 4 and 5.

[18] *Ibid.*, para. 6.

[19] Commission on Human Security 2003. *Human Security Now.*' New York.

[20] von Tigerstrom, Barbara 2007. *Human Security and International Law.* Hart Publishing, 38–43.

Mahmoud Sahnoun, and which developed the concept of the Responsibility to Protect as a principled response to such violence.[21] As explained in Chapter 5, the concept of the Responsibility to Protect was adopted in the report on UN reform by the UN Secretary-General's High Level Panel on Threats, Challenges and Change, *A More Secure World: Our Shared Responsibility* and was approved by the UN General Assembly in the World Summit Outcome document of 2005.[22]

The former UN Secretary-General, Ban Ki-moon, has emphasised that the Responsibility to Protect is not the same as 'its conceptual cousin' human security; the latter is broader and in the words of the Secretary-General 'posits that policy should take into account the security of people, not just of States, across the whole range of possible threats'.[23] This distinction is repeated in the definition of human security agreed by consensus by the GA in 2012, in compliance with the undertaking in 2005 to discuss and define the concept.[24] The Secretary-General cautioned against a concrete legal definition which 'would be counter-productive since the notion is both an operational and policy framework'.[25] In 2012 the GA described, rather than defined, human security in broad terms as 'identifying and addressing widespread and cross-cutting challenges to the survival, livelihood and dignity' of people.[26] It does not entail the threat or use of force or coercion, and does not replace, but complements, state security. However, the GA also made it clear that human security is a political concept that does not entail any legal obligations for states; the Secretary-General too had noted that the Responsibility to Protect is more embedded in international law than is human security.[27] The GA's definition thus

[21] Report of the International Commission on Intervention and State Sovereignty 2001. *The Responsibility to Protect.* Ottawa: International Development Research Centre ('ICISS Report').

[22] UN GA Resolution 60/1, 24 October 2005, paras. 138–140 (*2005 World Summit Outcome*).

[23] Ban Ki-moon, 'Responsible Sovereignty: International Cooperation for a Changed World', Berlin, 15 July 2008, UN Doc. SG/SM/11701.

[24] *2005 World Summit Outcome,* para. 143.

[25] Report of the Secretary-General, *Follow-up to General Assembly Resolution 64/291 on Human Security,* UN Doc. A/66/763, 5 April 2012, para. 14.

[26] UN GA Resolution 66/290, 25 October 2012.

[27] 'The concept of Responsibility to Protect is more firmly anchored in current international law than the two related concepts' of humanitarian intervention and human security; Ban Ki-moon, 'Responsible Sovereignty: International Cooperation for a Changed World', Berlin, 15 July 2008, UN Doc. SG/SM/11701.

maintains the distinction between human rights as legal entitlements incurring state obligations, compliance with which is monitored through a range of mechanisms and processes[28] and human security – lacking normative language – as a policy consideration that reflects unwillingness on the part of states to undertake further legal commitments.[29] It is also noteworthy that the resolution was adopted at the time when the lack of collective action in Syria, either in terms of Responsibility to Protect, or more broadly to uphold the human security of the Syrian people caught up in the violence and suffering widespread violations of human rights, first became controversial.

11.3 The Scope of Human Security

11.3.1 The Broad versus Narrow Interpretation of Human Security

The evolutionary story of human security reveals lack of agreement about its scope and application. In particular the two strands of thinking – focus on material insecurity or on physical insecurity – have sparked a debate about whether it should be understood narrowly (physical security), or more broadly (encompassing material security). The idea that human security is primarily about the right to physical security is reflected in the Human Security Reports and Briefs produced at Simon Fraser University in Canada, which analyse trends in armed conflict. The Human Security Report Project defines human security as 'the combination of threats associated with war, genocide, and the displacement of populations. At a minimum, human security means freedom from violence and from the fear of violence'.[30] This language evidently echoes that of the Responsibility to Protect. A broader version is the regional approach adopted by the Organisation of American States (OAS) in its Declaration to promote security in the Americas.[31] The 'multidimensional' concept of security favoured in this instrument affirms the basis and purpose of security to be 'the protection of human beings'. Accordingly 'conditions for human security are improved

[28] See Chapter 3.

[29] A GA resolution is not of itself legally binding but rather a form of 'soft' law.

[30] Human Security Report Project, *Human Security Backgrounder*, www.hsrgroup.org/press-room/human-security-backgrounder.aspx.

[31] OAS, Declaration on Security in the Americas, adopted at the 3rd Plenary Session, Mexico City, 28 October 2003, www.oas.org/en/sms/docs/DECLARATION%20SECURITY%20AMERICAS%20REV%201%20-%2028%20OCT%202003%20CE00339.pdf.

through full respect for people's dignity, human rights, and fundamental freedoms, as well as the promotion of social and economic development, social inclusion, and education and the fight against poverty, disease, and hunger'. Africa too has seen support for a broad version that 'goes beyond military considerations'. The Organisation for African Unity (OAU) adopted in 1999 an approach to security 'that must be construed in terms of the security of the individual citizen to live in peace with access to basic necessities of life while fully participating in the affairs of his/her society in freedom and enjoying all fundamental human rights'.[32]

Those who favour the broad version have argued that the narrow version is too concentrated on military intervention, while those who favour the narrow version have argued that the broad version is indistinguishable from development and covers too much ground to be analytically useful.[33] It is argued that the lack of specificity in the concept allows it to be all things to all people making operational content elusive. Keith Krause has suggested that the 'broad version of human security is ultimately nothing more than a shopping list; it involves slapping the label on a wide range of issues that have no necessary link and, at a certain point, human security becomes a loose synonym for "bad things can happen."'[34] Indeed, since the problems that might be addressed under a rubric of human security have generally already been recognised, what advantage is gained by combining them under a new label? Moreover, it is also argued the broad version risks 'securitising' development.[35] Still another view is that there are three understandings of human security: a 'narrow view' that is based in natural rights and the rule of law, anchored in human rights, also understood narrowly as civil and political rights; a humanitarian approach that sees it as the basis for responding to war crimes, crimes against humanity and genocide; and a

32 Conference on Security, Stability, Development and Cooperation in Africa (CSSDCA), Kampala, 1991, adopted by the OAU in 1999; see generally Abass, Ademola 2010. *Protecting Human Security in Africa*. Oxford University Press.

33 Roland, Paris, 2001. 'Human Security: Paradigm Shift or Hot Air?' *International Security* 26(2): 87–102.

34 Krause, Keith 2004. 'Is Human Security "More than Just a Good Idea"?' in Brzoska, Michael and Croll, Peter J. (eds.). *Promoting Security: But How and For Whom? Contributions to BICC's Ten-Year Anniversary Conference*, Bonn International Centre for Convention Brief No. 30, 43–46, 44.

35 'Securitising Development or Developing Security?' *ODI blog*, 10 July 2005, www.odi.org/comment/4092-securitising-development-developing-security.

broad approach that links human security with the global economy, development and globalisation.[36]

The debate about the broad versus narrow version was to some extent reconciled by the 2003 Report of the Commission on Human Security, *Human Security Now Protecting and Empowering People,* co-chaired by Sadako Ogata and Amartya Sen. The Commission was established at the initiative of the Japanese government at the Millennium Summit, but reported after the terrorist attacks of 11 September 2001, which had focused attention on the 'whole range of threats that require our urgent, collective and more determined response'.[37] The Report developed what has become known as the 'threshold' approach to human security.[38] In the Commission's view human security was to:

> protect the vital core of all human lives in ways that enhance human freedoms and human fulfilment. Human security means protecting fundamental freedoms – freedoms that are the essence of life. It means protecting people from critical (severe) and pervasive (widespread) threats and situations. It means using processes that build on people's strengths and aspirations. It means creating political, social, environmental, economic, military and cultural systems that together give people the building blocks of survival, livelihood and dignity.[39]

This notion of the 'vital core of all human lives' implied that human security comprises both human rights and human development, but is simultaneously concerned with what Amartya Sen called the 'downside risks'.[40] The GA in 2012 also reiterated that 'all individuals are entitled to freedom from fear and freedom from want . . . and to fully develop their human potential' and recognised the 'interlinkages between peace, development and human rights'.[41]

[36] Oberleitner, Gerd 2005. 'Porcupines in Love: The Intricate Convergence of Human Rights and Human Security', *European Human Rights Law Review*, 588–606.

[37] UN GA Resolution 60/1, 24 October 2005, para. 69.

[38] Owen, Taylor 2004. 'Human Security – Conflict, Critique and Consensus: Colloquium Remarks and a Proposal for a Threshold-Based Definition', *Security Dialogue* 35(3): 373–387.

[39] *Human Security Now, op. cit.*

[40] Sen has asserted that 'a reasoned concentration on the downside risks of human lives, rather than on the overall expansion of effective freedom in general (contrasting with the broader objective of the promotion of "human development") is an element that must underpin human security'; Sen, Amartya 2002. 'Basic Education and Human Security', Kolkata, www.hegoa.ehu.es/dossierra/seguridad/Basic_education_and_human_security.pdf.

[41] UN GA Resolution 66/290, 25 October 2012.

Another aspect of human security emphasised by Sadako Ogata and the Japanese version of human security is that of individual empowerment[42] linked to the bottom-up character of human security. According to the Japanese Ministry of Foreign Affairs:

> In addition to protection by the state and the international community, it is necessary for the international community to put the focus on individuals and endeavour to empower people and societies through co-operation by countries, international organisations, non-governmental organisations (NGOs) and civil society so that people can live self-sufficient lives. This is the thinking behind 'human security'.[43]

Yukio Takasu, the UN Special Advisor on human security, considered the most important contribution made by the Ogata-Sen Commission to be the 'emphasis it placed on empowerment as on protection'.[44] The 2012 GA definition, however, does not refer to empowerment,[45] but does stress national ownership and that human security 'requires greater collaboration and partnership among Governments, international and regional organisations and civil society'.

The Report of the Commission also emphasised the particular situation in Africa where human security is 'most fragile'.[46] Threats to human security in Africa have been described as implying conditions of inhumanity that no longer prevail in other parts of the world and which make even the most basic form of existence unattainable for millions of people. They encompass such dehumanising conditions as:

> violent conflicts, pandemic[s], ... proliferation of arms and small weapons, endless streams of refugees and internally displaced peoples, forced labour, exponential violence against women, the 'curse' of natural resources, environmental degradation, abject poverty, corruption, the lack of basic health care, terrorism, and the rape of constitutionalism and the rule of law.[47]

42 *Human Security Now*, *op. cit.*: 'Empowerment enables people to develop their potential and become full participants in decision-making'.

43 Quoted in Bosold, *op. cit.*, 37.

44 Takasu, *op. cit.*, 242.

45 In contrast the UN SC Resolutions on Women and Peace and Security stress (but do not define) women's empowerment, as does the full title of UN Women, the United Nations Entity for Gender Equality and the Empowerment of Women, created by UN GA Resolution 64/289, 2 July 2010.

46 United Nations Office of the Special Adviser on Africa (OSAA) 2005. *Human Security in Africa*.

47 Abass, *op. cit.*, 10.

The complexity of the challenges to human security underlines the need for inclusive, multisectoral responses involving regional, local and community bodies and individuals, as well as the international.

11.3.2 The Barcelona Version

Another regional analysis of human security, also formulated in the period 2003–2004, is that of the Study Group on Europe's Security Capabilities (later renamed the Human Security Study Group). The Study Group was assembled at a 'critical moment for the European Union'.[48] The lack of any coherent and concerted response to violence on the continent, or any common defence policy, had been exposed by the war in Bosnia, the United States had just published its controversial 2002 National Security Strategy[49] and the EU its first security strategy in December 2003, and the new Constitution for the Union was adopted in June 2004. The Study Group adopted the term 'human security' to describe its distinctive approach, and its first report to Javier Solana, then High Representative for Common Foreign and Security Policy within the European Union, presented in Barcelona in September 2004, was entitled 'A Human Security Doctrine for Europe'. The version of human security put forward by the Study Group had its roots in the experience of the Helsinki process in Europe but could not be construed as the 'narrow version' of human security, nor was it the same as the Responsibility to Protect, or the approach of the UNDP. Rather it added a new component to the definition of human security. As well as the usual elements of human security – focus on the individual as opposed to the state and on the link between 'freedom from fear' and 'freedom from want' – it put particular emphasis on the link between human security and law and the blurring of the difference between internal and external security.

Human security, according to the Human Security Study Group, is about the kind of security that individuals expect in rights-based law-governed societies where law is based on an implicit social contract among individuals, and between individuals and the state. Fundamental to law-governed societies is the assumption of equality before the law. In a law-governed national society it is assumed that the state will protect

[48] The Barcelona Report of the Study Group on Europe's Security Capabilities, 'A Human Security Doctrine for Europe', Barcelona 2004, Foreword ('*The Barcelona Report*').

[49] See Chapter 4.

individuals from existential threats and that emergency services – among others, ambulances, firefighters, police – are part of state provision. In many such societies human rights are enshrined in national constitutions and/or national legislation, in accordance with international law. Admittedly, especially in Western societies such as the United States and United Kingdom, civil and political rights are accorded greater weight than social and economic rights in law and practice even though all such rights are inter-related and interdependent, as was affirmed by the World Conference on Human Rights at Vienna.[50] In the approach of the Study Group, human security is about extending individual rights beyond domestic borders and about developing a capacity at a regional or global level to provide those kinds of emergency services to be deployed in situations where states either lack capacity or are themselves the violators of rights. What this means is that national security cannot be assured unilaterally, that security in any part of the world depends on a global or human security system. Thus instead of defending borders against external attack (or those seeking to enter), the security capabilities of states are designed to contribute to global emergency services.

Unlike earlier enunciations of human security, the *Barcelona Report*, and its follow-up, the *Madrid Report*,[51] focussed on implementation and on recommending the kind of capabilities required to operationalise this understanding of human security. It was proposed to establish human security forces composed of both military and civilian officers under civilian control and with substantial participation of women. This coming together of military and civilians for human security is only possible if they both conform to certain principles, which guide the way they are used and operate. These principles are:

- *The primacy of human rights.* The primacy of human rights is what distinguishes the human security approach from traditional military approaches to intervention. What this principle means is that the primary goal of intervention is to protect civilians rather than to defeat an adversary. Of course. sometimes it is necessary to try to capture or even defeat those responsible for the violence but it has to be seen as a means to an end, civilian protection, rather than

[50] Declaration and Programme of Action, World Conference on Human Rights, Vienna, 25 June 1993, *op cit.*, I, 5.

[51] The Madrid Report of the Human Security Study Group. 'A European Way of Security', Madrid, 2007.

the other way round. Since the objective is civilian protection not military necessity, so-called collateral damage is unacceptable.[52] At the same time, the application of this principle to saving lives that are directly under threat from other parties may require a greater readiness to use force and to risk the lives of soldiers or aid workers, denoting a shift in the balance between force protection and civilian protection. Human rights must include economic and social rights; rights such as those to shelter, access to education and health care, are to be respected and protected even in the midst of conflict and its aftermath.

- *Legitimate political authority.* Human security can only be guaranteed by a rule of law that depends on the existence of legitimate institutions that gain the trust of the population and have some enforcement capacity. This applies both to physical security, where the rule of law and access to a well-functioning system of justice are essential,[53] and to material security, where increasing legitimate employment or providing infrastructure and public services require effective state policies. Legitimate political authority does not necessarily need to mean a state; it could consist of local government, a city, for example, or regional or international political arrangements such as a transitional administration. Since state failure is often the primary cause of conflict, the reasons for state failure have to be taken into account in reconstructing legitimate political authority. Measures like justice and security sector reform, disarmament, demobilisation and reintegration (DDR), extension of authority and public service reform are all critical for the establishment of legitimate political authority,[54] at the local as well as the national level, as is the involvement of civil society in political debate and decision-making.

This principle explicitly recognises the limitations on what global emergency services can achieve, often little more than a humanitarian band aid. The aim of a human security operation is to stabilise the situation so that a local space can be created for a peaceful political

[52] See Chapter 6.

[53] In a landmark decision the Inter-American Court of Human Rights recognised that it is not sufficient for the state to have an adequate legal framework for it must operate within an effective system; *Velasquez Rodrigues v. Honduras*, IACtHR (Ser. C) No. 4, 29 July 1988.

[54] See Wulf, Herbert 2005. 'The Challenges of Re-Establishing a Public Monopoly of Violence', in Glasius, Marlies and Kaldor, Mary (eds.). *A Human Security Doctrine for Europe: Project; Principles; Practicalities.* Routledge, 20–40.

process rather than to win through military means alone. It is the political process that is critical.[55]

- *Effective multilateralism.* This is related to legitimacy and distinguishes a human security approach from unilateralism and neo-colonialism. Human security means a commitment to work with others, with international or regional institutions, creating or complying with existing common rules and norms and solving problems through rules and co-operation, as well as with individual states, regional actors and NGOs. It also means a co-ordinated and rational division of tasks and agreeing the appropriate means to resolve conflict and build peace. It is also closely related to international law and the need to operate within an international legal framework. In the current 'strategic complexes' with layers of contractors and numerous agencies, and an internal logic of competition, this may turn out to be one of the biggest obstacles to the implementation of human security.
- *The bottom-up approach.* Notions of 'partnership', 'local ownership' and 'participation' are already key concepts in development policy, while the military often refer to the 'ground truth' or to knowledge of the 'human terrain'. Decisions about the kind of security and development policies to be adopted, whether or not to intervene with military forces or through various forms of conditionality, and how, will only work if they take account of the most basic needs identified by the people who are affected by violence and insecurity. This is not just a moral issue; it is also a matter of effectiveness. People who live in zones of insecurity are the only ones able to sustain long-term security. There is a tendency among outsiders to focus on those who carry guns, for instance, as participants in peace processes.[56] Yet those who carry guns may often be those with a long-term interest in insecurity. Thus communication, consultation and dialogue with local stakeholders are essential tools for human security, not simply to win hearts and minds, nor even to gain knowledge and understanding, but to empower those who will have to be responsible for security in the

[55] The High Level Panel on Peace Operations took a similar view: 'Lasting peace is achieved not through military and technical engagements, but through political solutions. Political solutions should always guide the design and deployment of UN peace operations.' *Report of the High-Level Independent Panel on Peace Operations on Uniting our Strengths for Peace: Politics, Partnership and People*, UN Doc. A/70/95–S/2015/446, 17 June 2015 ('*Report of the High-Level Independent* Panel'), Executive Summary.

[56] See Chapter 9.

long run. The participation of teachers, doctors, tribal leaders, religious leaders and young people[57] are all critical for both understanding and operationalising human security. Particularly important, in this context, is the role of women.

- *Regional focus*. The tendency to focus attention on areas that are defined in terms of statehood has often meant that relatively simple ways of preventing the spread of violence are neglected. Time and again, foreign policy analysts have been taken by surprise when, after considerable attention had been given to one conflict, another conflict would seemingly spring up out of the blue in a neighbouring state. For example, the war in Sierra Leone could not be resolved without also addressing the causes of conflict in Liberia. Violence in Afghanistan can only be contained and managed if the neighbouring states, especially Pakistan, are involved. The violence that erupted in northern Mali in 2012 cannot be disaggregated from that in Libya from before and after the overthrow of Gaddafi, troops returning from Libya to Chad and Mali, the long-running dispute about the status of Moroccan-controlled Western Sahara, and criminal networks operating in the Sahel.[58]
- *Clear Civilian Command*. Human security operations are civilian, not military; hence civilians are in command. This means that the military must operate in support of law and order and under rules of engagement that are more similar to those of police work than to the rules of armed combat. Everyone needs to know who is in charge, and leaders must be able to communicate politically with local people as well as people in the sending countries.

Fundamental to all these principles is a change of mindset. Human security is about the equality of all human beings. This sounds obvious, but, as discussed in Chapter 9, in war zones local civilians are not treated by intervening forces as though they were equal in importance to civilians back home nor, indeed, to the forces themselves.

[57] UN SC Resolution 2250, 9 December 2015 recognises that 'youth should actively be engaged in shaping lasting peace and contributing to justice and reconciliation, and that a large youth population presents a unique demographic dividend that can contribute to lasting peace and economic prosperity if inclusive policies are in place . . . Urges Member States to consider ways to increase inclusive representation of youth in decision-making at all levels in local, national, regional and international institutions and mechanisms for the prevention and resolution of conflict'.

[58] Wehrey, Frederic and Boukhars, Anouar (eds.). *Perilous Desert Insecurity in the Sahara*. Carnegie Endowment for International Peace; Integrated Strategy for the Sahel Region, UN Doc. S/2015/866, 12 November 2015.

11.4 Human Security and Gender

Despite their many variants and emphases, the understandings of human security discussed above, with the exception of that of the Human Security Study Group, share a gender-neutral and gender-blind assumption of what constitutes insecurity and thus human security. [59] Further, the Human Security Study Group's focus on women as key players in a 'bottom-up' approach to intervention is based on the valuable insights and advice women may have to offer;[60] it does not identify women as a referent of security, the ways women experience insecurity differently from men, based on their gender, or how the discourse and hierarchies of security are themselves gendered.[61] The concept of 'human' is undifferentiated, and there is a presumed essentialism to humanity.[62] This assumption of universalism is the basis of human rights; in the words of the UDHR, 'All human beings are born free and equal in dignity and rights'. Accordingly 'all people are equal before the law and are entitled without any discrimination to the equal protection of the law'.[63] However, such gender blindness obscures the realities of human rights violations committed against both women and men because of their gender, in particular forms of gender-based violence.[64] Achievement of substantive equality requires gender analysis, exposing the impact of gender on enjoyment of rights and adapting policies and practices accordingly. The same is true with respect to human security: 'history has shown that women's experience of insecurity is fundamentally different than that of men'.[65] Inclusion of gender also allows for linkages to be made between

[59] See generally Tripp, Aili Mari, Ferree, Myra Marx and Ewig, Christina (eds.) 2013. *Gender, Violence and Human Security: Critical Feminist Perspectives*. NYU Press; Detraz, Nicole 2012. *International Security and Gender*. Polity Press, chapter 5, 'Human Security and Gender'.

[60] *The Barcelona Report*, *op. cit.*, 18.

[61] Hudson, Natalie 2009. *Gender, Human Security and the United Nations: Security Language as a Political Framework for Women*. Routledge Critical Security Studies, 34.

[62] Hudson, Heidi 2005. '"Doing Security" as though Humans Matter: Gender and the Politics of Human Security', *Security Dialogue* 36(2): 155–174, 157.

[63] ICCPR, *op. cit.*, article 26.

[64] E.g., *Council of Europe Convention on Combating and Preventing Violence against Women and Domestic Violence*, 11 May 2011, CETS, 2010, article 3(d): '"gender-based violence against women" shall mean violence that is directed against a woman because she is a woman or that affects women disproportionately'.

[65] Jolly, Richard and Basu Ray, Deepayan 2006. *The Human Security Framework and National Human Development Reports: A Review of Experiences and Current Debates*. UNDP, 5.

forms of insecurity, such as between domestic violence and armed conflict,[66] or between militarisation and violence against women.[67] Accordingly the enjoyment 'of survival, livelihood and dignity of people in response to current and emerging threats' requires different considerations for some groups than for others, and this needs to be taken into account in determining appropriate policies and practices to enhance their human security.

The construction of social and gender roles, sexuality and gender identity, bears on all social relations, including forms of political violence. Violence and conflict are also deeply gendered.[68] Conflict is about a violent distribution of power where 'culturally and historically specific understandings of gender as a power relationship are reproduced'(and produced); thus 'human security is gendered because it is imbued with gendered power relations'.[69] Crises of violence – political upheaval,[70] armed conflict – are not phenomena apart from normal underlying gender-based violence; rather there is an effect of 'layered violence', whereby pre-existing violence is exploded, exposing those targeted to 'deeper and greater threats of harm and insecurity'.[71] The special rapporteur on violence against women has explained that gender-related killings, including those that occur in armed conflict, are not isolated, unexpected incidents, but are rooted in structural inequalities which require taking into account the political, social and economic context in which they occur.[72]

[66] Tripp, Aili Mari 2013, 'Towards a Gender Perspective on Human Security', in Tripp *et al.*, *op. cit.*, 3–32, 15.

[67] Enloe, Cynthia 1989. *Bananas, Beaches and Bases: Making Feminist Sense of International Politics.* Pandora Press; Detraz, Nicole 2012. *International Security and Gender.* Polity, chapter 2, 'Gendered Militarization and Militarism'.

[68] Goldstein, Joshua 2001. *War and Gender: How Gender Shapes the War System and Vice Versa.* Cambridge University Press.

[69] Tripp, *op. cit.*, 16 (*'Towards a Gender Perspective'*).

[70] Women's security is impacted upon in other 'situations of concern': 'internal disturbances, protracted and low intensity civil strife, political strife, ethnic and communal violence, states of emergency and suppression of mass uprisings, war against terrorism and organized crime'. Committee on the Elimination of Discrimination against Women (CEDAW), General Recommendation No. 30 on Women in Conflict Prevention, Conflict and Post-Conflict Situations, CEDAW/C/GC/30, 18 October 2013, para. 4 ('General Recommendation No. 30').

[71] Aoláin, Fionnuala 2011. 'Women, Vulnerability and Humanitarian Emergencies', *Michigan Journal of Gender and Law* 18: 1–23, 12.

[72] Manjoo, Rashida, Report of the Special Rapporteur on Violence against Women, Its Causes and Consequences, UN Doc. A/HRC/23/49, 14 May 2013, para. 52.

Gender relations are not just about women and men, but also about sexual and gender identities. The Office of the High Commissioner for Human Rights (OHCHR) has identified forms of homophobic and transphobic violence and noted that people perceived as LGBTI 'may be targets of more organized abuse, including by religious extremists, paramilitary groups, neo-Nazis and extreme nationalists'.[73] The predatory set of relationships that use political violence to acquire and maintain positions of power and which characterises [characterises] new wars is often associated with the gender-based and sexual violence that is integral to ethnic cleansing, although focus on ethnicity may render invisible the gendered dimensions of this violence.[74]

Gender analysis requires recognition of how we all lead gendered lives and how our other identities – our age, class, health, sexuality and so on – all intersect with our gender.[75] For instance, men and women detainees are especially vulnerable to sexual violence; men and women who experience war-related violence are often also poor, from minority populations, or of different religion from their attackers, or are 'othered' in some way. The widespread and multiple killings, disappearances and torture of women in Ciudad Juárez, Mexico, over many years illustrates these combined signifiers of insecurity: the CEDAW Committee noted that 'the social and cultural environment that constructed women as poor, vulnerable and insignificant facilitated human rights abuses'.[76] While this violence occurred outside the conventional understanding of war, it demonstrates the insecurity faced by women in situations of structural inequalities and marginalisation. Age is another identity factor that intersects with gender. The first completed trial before the International

[73] Report of the UNOHCHR, Discriminatory Laws and Practices and Acts of Violence against Individuals Based on their Sexual Orientation and Gender Identity, UN Doc. A/HRC/19/41, 17 November 2011, para. 21. UN SC Resolution 2242, 13 October 2015, Women and Peace and Security, recognises that women and girls are 'directly targeted by terrorist groups, and *express[es]deep concern* that acts of sexual and gender-based violence are known to be part of the strategic objectives and ideology of certain terrorist groups.'

[74] Gray, David and Levin, Benjamin 2012. 'Feminist Perspectives on Extraordinary Justice', in Fineman, Martha and Zinsstag, Estelle (eds.). *Conflict and Transitional Justice: Feminist Approaches*, 63–88.

[75] International Alert, 'Rethinking Gender in Peacebuilding', March 2014, http://international-alert.org/sites/default/files/Gender_RethinkingGenderPeacebuilding_EN_2014.pdf.

[76] Report on Mexico produced by the Committee on the Elimination of Discrimination against Women under article 8 of the Optional Protocol to the Convention, and reply from the Government of Mexico, CEDAW, UN Doc. CEDAW/C/2005/OP.8/MEXICO, January 2005.

Criminal Court (ICC) concerned child soldiers, both girls and boys. The gendered dimensions of enlisting and conscripting children were put forward by the prosecution in its opening: 'young boys were instructed to rape . . . girl soldiers were the daily victims of rape by the commanders. Girl soldiers ... were used as cooks and fighters, cleaners and spies, scouts and sexual slaves'.[77] Yet in the judgment against Lubanga such gendered analysis was lost, except in the separate and dissenting, in part, opinion of Judge Odio Benito.[78]

Gender is often – wrongly – equated with women rather than understood as relational. However, the previous invisibility of women, for instance, in war crimes trials,[79] and more generally the failure to recognise gender-based violence against women as structural and systemic has generated significant research and normative development over the past decades. The UN Security Council (SC) resolutions on Women and Peace and Security[80] are one manifestation of this, as are developments in international criminal law. There has, however, been dissent both with respect to levels of gender-based violence against women in armed conflict and the desirability of such focus.[81] With respect to the former, the 2012 Human Security Project Report argues that the level of sexual violence against women in war-affected countries is exaggerated and that generalisations are drawn from victims' accounts in a relatively small number of the worst affected states. In contrast the special rapporteur of the UN Secretary-General on sexual violence in armed conflict reported that in 2011 there were 'several new and ongoing armed conflicts where sexual violence was widespread';[82] in 2016 she noted that for every reported rape in conflict some ten to twenty are not reported so

[77] Moreno-Ocampo, Luis 2010. 'Keynote Address Interdisciplinary Colloquium Sexual Violence as International Crime: Interdisciplinary Approaches to Evidence', *Law and Social Inquiry* 35(4): 839–846.

[78] *Situation in the Democratic Republic of the Congo in the case of Prosecutor v. Thomas Lubanga Dyilo*, ICC-01/04-01/06, 14 March 2012.

[79] Such crimes were charged in war crimes trials following World War II undertaken under the auspices of the UN War Crimes Commission; Plesch, Dan and Sacouto, Susana and Lasco, Chante 2014. 'The Relevance of the United Nations War Crimes Commission to the Prosecution of Sexual and Gender-based Crimes Today', *Criminal Law Forum* 25: 345–381.

[80] See Chapters 5 and 9.

[81] E.g., Chinkin, Christine 2014. 'Gender and Human Rights', in Clapham, Andrew and Gaeta, Paola (eds.). *The Oxford Handbook of International Law in Armed Conflict*. Oxford University Press, 675–699, 693–699.

[82] UN Secretary-General, *Conflict-Related Sexual Violence*, UN Doc. A/66/657–S/2012/33, 23 February 2012, para. 15.

that figures do not represent the magnitude of the problem.[83] Even if the highly publicised accounts are the exceptions from which generalisations should not be drawn, they represent serious gendered incidents of insecurity. The argument is made in the Human Security Project Report that exaggeration of the incidence of sexual violence against women in armed conflict obscures the high level of gendered violence, including sexual abuse, committed against men in armed conflict,[84] as well as of domestic violence, both of which thus remain less visible and without response. Sexual violence against men remains under-reported, stigmatised, often unrecognised as a crime and thus inadequately addressed.[85] The particular ways men experience gender and sexual violence committed against them in armed conflict, its impact on their lives, how this contributes to further and ongoing insecurity and appropriate responses requires a good deal more research and consideration. So too does understanding how multiple forms of violence against women, whether or not occurring in and connected to conflict, is a further gendered form of insecurity.[86]

It might be asked why it matters that understandings of human security fail to take account of the gendered dimensions of insecurity. There are at least two responses. First, a narrative of human security that fails to take account of how gender constructs peoples' everyday experiences and to link them to broader local, regional and global political processes and structures is an inadequate account of human security, diminishes its scope and inhibits proper policy consideration. Gender analysis of human security requires consideration of different forms of insecurity and the interaction between human security and each of power, global inequalities and agency.[87] Such analysis opens up a wider range of transformative possibilities: 'it also enables a sharper focus on

[83] UN Secretary-General, *Conflict-Related Sexual Violence,* UN Doc. S/2016/361, 20 April 2016, para. 7.

[84] UN SC Resolution 2106, 24 June 2013, on Women Peace and Security notes that sexual violence in armed conflict also affects men and boys.

[85] Report of the Secretary-General, *Conflict Related Sexual Violence*, UN Doc. S/2014/181, 13 March 2014, para. 7.

[86] 'Violence against women seriously violates and impairs or nullifies the enjoyment by women of their human rights, in particular their fundamental rights to life, security, freedom, dignity and physical and emotional integrity, and that it therefore cannot be ignored by governments'. Explanatory Report to the Council of Europe Convention on Preventing and Combating Violence against Women and Domestic Violence, 2011, para. 26.

[87] Tripp, *op. cit.*

groups of people who are particularly vulnerable, as well as those whose attitudes and practices most need to be changed and those most [or least] amenable to change'.[88] This requires bringing men – as men – into the analysis,[89] and understanding how masculinities are constructed by social and cultural norms so as to normalise men's engagement in violence, for instance, by seeing themselves as the 'protector', and not admitting to vulnerability. This in turn necessitates understanding and seeking to redress the consequences for men who have been made vulnerable, as through the commission of sexual violence against them. It also requires a shift in the mind-set that accepts the inevitability of constructed binaries:[90] men as violent and women as victims; men as warmongers and women as peacemakers (promoted in many ways by the SC resolutions on women, peace and security); men as protectors and women as protected. It has been reported that social expectations with respect to 'violent masculinities' influence the behaviours of those working on promoting peace, leading them to discount, or regard with suspicion, the attempts of men who reject such stereotypes and promote a model of 'peaceful masculinity'. Such men may find their own masculinity and sexual orientation questioned; what is needed is to examine more openly the roles of men and of women in 'reproducing expectations of violent male behaviour'.[91]

A second reason for a gendered understanding of human security is instrumental. It has been argued that 'there is a correlation between the increased prevalence of gender-based violence and discrimination and outbreak of conflict'[92] and, further, that there is a causal relationship between the treatment of women by a society and thus the security of women within the society and the level of security/insecurity of the state.[93] In the words of Kofi Anan: 'there is no policy more effective in promoting development, health and education than the empowerment of women and girls. And we would venture that no policy is more important in preventing conflict, or in achieving reconciliation after a conflict

[88] International Alert, *op. cit.*

[89] SC Resolution 2106, 24 June 2013, on women, peace and security affirms the importance of 'enlistment of men and boys in the effort to combat all forms of violence against women are central to long-term efforts to prevent sexual violence in armed conflict and post-conflict situations'.

[90] See also Chapter 6 (*jus in bello*).

[91] International Alert, *op. cit.*

[92] General Recommendation No. 30, *op. cit.*, para. 29.

[93] Hudson, Valerie *et al.* (eds.) 2012. *Sex and World Peace*. Columbia University Press, chapter 4.

has ended'.[94] This last has been little researched and can be debated in essentialist and other terms, but it is suggested that what research has been carried out sustains such conclusions. For instance, empirical work by Mary Caprioli suggests both that 'higher levels of gender equality make a state less likely to threaten display or use force' and that 'states with higher levels of gender equality are less likely to experience domestic conflict'.[95] Such work – while still in its initial stages – suggests promotion of gender equality 'goes far beyond the issue of social justice and has important consequences for international [and human] security'. In the words of Potts and Hayden:

> [O]ne way to reduce the risk of violence is to empower women and maximise their role in society. This is perhaps the most profound insight to come from taking an evolutionary perspective on war: empowering women reduces the risk of violent conduct ... women's role in reducing the risk of war is borne out by rigorous study and historical experience. ... Contemporary Western nations have a great opportunity to make the world more secure and reduce terrorism by doing everything they can to empower women who live in countries where they currently enjoy few choices and wield little or no political power.[96]

The relationship between gender security and the generation of political violence within and between states requires much further exploration and research, but even a suggestion that there is such a relationship warrants being taken seriously and being factored into accounts of human security.[97]

11.5 Shifting Contexts and Manifestations of Human Security

In the 1990s the concept of human security was being formulated against the backdrop of an eruption of violent conflicts, for instance, those in the Balkans and Africa (including Somalia, Sudan, Rwanda, Uganda and DRC), which defied ready categorisation as international or non-international armed conflict.[98] There was a dramatic growth in Liberal

[94] Message of the Secretary-General, International Women's Day, 8 March 2006, www.un.org/events/women/iwd/2006/message.html.

[95] Hudson, Valerie *et al.*, *op. cit.*, 101–102.

[96] Potts, Malcolm and Hayden, Thomas 2008. *Sex and War: How Biology Explains Warfare and Terrorism and Offers a Path to a Safer World.* Benbella Books, 118.

[97] It can be suggested that the feminist foreign policy advanced by Sweden in 2015 is implicitly grounded in such concerns: www.government.se/government-policy/feminist-foreign-policy.

[98] See Chapter 6.

Peace interventionism, through UN and regional peacemaking, peacekeeping and peacebuilding as described in Chapter 9. Many proposals of the 1990s more directly associated with ideas about human security came out of the experience both of international agencies operating in difficult situations and from locally based peace and human rights groups, with links to the broader peace and human rights community. In particular, as discussed in Chapter 5, the war in Bosnia became the focus of an often agonised public debate in Europe and the United States about how international intervention could protect people from ethnic cleansing and massive violations of human rights.[99]

Proposals at this time emanating from the insecurity experienced by people in different parts of the world included:

- Safe havens, no-fly zones or humanitarian corridors aimed at the direct protection of civilians (e.g., northern Iraq, 1991; Bosnia-Herzegovina, 1992–1995);
- New formal justice mechanisms in relation to war crimes and crimes against humanity – including in the case of Bosnia their establishment and operation while the war was still continuing; other transitional justice mechanisms such as Truth and Reconciliation Commissions and Commissions of Inquiry;
- Ways to control forms of finance for war through transparency and accountability mechanisms, especially for valuable resources like diamonds or oil (e.g., Kimberly Process Certification Scheme, set up in 2003 to prevent the trade in diamonds that fund conflict; the Extractive Industries Transparency Initiative of the UK Government which seeks transparency by publication and verification of company payments and government revenues from oil, gas and mining);[100]
- In legal terms, peacekeepers being mandated without the consent of the state in question (Somalia, 1992) and the transformation of their role from separating warring sides to protection of civilians and promoting individual security;[101]
- Substantive changes in international law such as the evolution of crimes against humanity decoupled from conflict thus applicable to

[99] See Kaldor, Mary 2001. 'A Decade of Humanitarian Intervention: 1991–2000', in Anheier, Helmut and Glasius, Marlies and Kaldor, Mary (eds.). *Global Civil Society 2001*. Oxford University Press, chapter 5.

[100] Alao, Abiodun 2010. 'Natural Resource Management and Human Security in Africa', in Abass (ed.), *op. cit.*, 102–121, 115.

[101] See Chapter 9.

> widespread or systematic violence against a civilian population in an international armed conflict, non-international armed conflict or violence not recognised as conflict.[102]

Innovations of this kind potentially constituted a radical change in the nature of international intervention in situations of violence, which can be sharply distinguished from classic military intervention, especially air strikes, even though some such interventions involved military personnel. The mandated tasks of military personnel where they were deployed came to include civilian protection, dampening down violence and the arrest of war criminals rather than defeating enemies and winning. Of course, for the most part, such interventions have not been sufficiently robust, well supported, or have even avoided some such tasks because of fears of causing further violence as was explained in Chapter 9. Nevertheless they represented the building blocks of a possible human security approach in crisis zones.

The story of human security in the early 2000s, after the experience of Kosovo and subsequently the wars in Iraq and Afghanistan, was much more mixed and indeed contradictory. This was a period when the idea of human security was spreading rapidly in academic and policy circles. Thus many feminist scholars embraced the concept as an alternative to the patriarchal statist approach[103] because of its bottom-up character,[104] which creates 'a security space in which gendered insecurities can be recognised and addressed'.[105] Likewise, it was taken up by those interested in its emancipatory potential such as the so-called Welsh School of critical security studies.[106]

It was also a period that witnessed the institutionalisation of the human security concept through the incorporation of some elements of its building blocks into institutional practice. The progress of the concept through the United Nations after the Sen-Ogata Commission, with the establishment of the UN Trust Fund for Human Security, the

[102] The decoupling of crimes against humanity from armed conflict is apparent in the *Rome Statute of the ICC*, 1998, article 7 (1) in contrast to the Statute of the International Tribunal for the former Yugoslavia, 1993, article 5.

[103] Hamber, Brandon *et al.* 2006. 'Discourses in Transition: Reimagining Women's Security', *International Relations* 20(4): 489–502.

[104] Tickner, Ann J. 2001. *Gendering World Politics: Issues and Approaches in the Post-Cold War Era*. Columbia University Press.

[105] Fox, Mary-Jane 2004. 'Girl Soldiers: Human Security and Gendered Insecurity', *Security Dialogue* 35(4): 465–479.

[106] See Booth, Ken 2007. *Theory of World Security*. Cambridge University Press.

appointment of a Special Advisor for Human Security, regular reports from the Secretary-General on Human Security from 2010 onwards and the UN General Assembly resolution of 2012 have already been mentioned. Other developments within the UN have also been credited to the human security concept; these include the appointment of Special Representatives for the Prevention of Genocide and Mass Atrocities, for Children and Armed Conflict, and for Gender Issues and Advancement of Women.[107] These developments were paralleled by more informal groupings. Thus the Human Security Network was founded by Canada and Norway in 1998, with the aim of informally influencing the international security agenda.[108] The network promoted a wide array of initiatives including the International Criminal Court (ICC),[109] the Land Mines Treaty,[110] various measures to do with civilian protection especially of children in armed conflict, the regulation of small arms, and trade in conflict commodities. It also sponsored the ICISS that formulated the Responsibility to Protect and regular Human Security reports published by Simon Fraser University. According to Lloyd Axworthy, who was Canadian Foreign Minister and perhaps the key actor in promoting human security, the Ottawa process, which led to the Landmines Treaty, was the:

> beginning of a network of like-minded actors as a burgeoning new tool in world affairs. It was this collusion of events – the shift in focus to protecting civilians, along with the great aggregation of civil society efforts that demonstrated how in this interconnected world, our own security is not only increasingly indivisible from our neighbours but that individual human suffering is an irrevocable universal concern.[111]

The Human Security Network also led to the establishment of the Friends of Human Security whose focus was mainstreaming human security within the UN as well as a focus on human security by individual members of the network, especially Japan and Switzerland, which established a Human Security Division.

[107] See Newman, Edward 2014. 'The United Nations and Human Security: between Pluralism and Solidarism', in Martin and Owen, *op. cit.*, 225–238.

[108] Members included Austria, Canada (until 2009), Chile, Costa Rica, Greece, Ireland, Jordan, Mali, the Netherlands (until 2007), Norway, Slovenia, South Africa (observer), Switzerland, and Thailand; see www.hpcrresearch.org/research/human-security-network

[109] See Chapter 10. [110] See Chapter 7.

[111] Axworthy, Lloyd 2014. 'Human Security in the R2P era', in Martin and Owen, *op. cit.*, 149–158, 151.

Human Security was also taken up by regional institutions, especially the European Union and the African Union. The European Security Strategy was issued in December 2003 after the deep divisions within the Union over the March 2003 invasion and occupation of Iraq. As Javier Solana, who was then the High Representative for Foreign Common and Security Affairs, explains, it was an attempt to establish a distinctive posture that could command consensus within the Union and operate autonomously.[112] The Strategy did not explicitly mention human security but was in line with human security precepts. The Human Security Study Group, according to Solana, acted as a ginger group and articulated the principles that guided the dramatic increase in external missions (some twenty by 2010). The term was adopted in the Report on the Implementation of the European Security Strategy in December 2008 and by the Commissioner for External Relations (RELEX), Benito Ferrerro-Waldener; it missed by only seven votes being adopted by the European Parliament. Further, many Common Security and Defence Policy (CSDP) missions were designed around human security precepts. These included the use of human rights monitors,[113] 'town hall'-type consultations[114] and, in the case of the anti-piracy mission, the introduction of fishing licences for fishing off the Somali coast.[115]

Human Security was central to the establishment of the African Union in May 2001. The focus of its predecessor, the OAU, was state sovereignty. Human Security was promoted by the Kampala movement, an initiative of civil society groups that met in Kampala in the early 1990s, and by newly emerging African elites including Nelson Mandela and Salim Ahmed Salim, the Tanzanian Secretary General of the OAU, who were interested in promoting pan-Africanism. A key role was played by the newly established Peace and Security Council and by the African Citizens Directorate.[116] Although Japan has been a champion of human

[112] Solana, Javier 2014. 'The European Union and Human Security: The Making of a Global Security Actor', in Martin and Owen *op. cit.*, 251–259.

[113] Schulze, Kirsten 2009. 'The AMM and the Transition from Conflict to Peace in Aceh, 2005–2006', in Martin, Mary and Kaldor, Mary (eds.). *The European Union and Human Security: External Interventions and Missions.* Routledge, chapter 1.

[114] Martin, Mary 2009, 'Crossing Boundaries: The European Union Monitoring Mission to Georgia', in Martin and Kaldor, *op. cit.*, chapter 7.

[115] Kaldor interview with Rear Admiral Robert Tarrant, Operational Commander, European Union Naval Force Somalia Operation Atalanta.

[116] Tieku, Thomas Kwasi 2014. 'The Pan-Africanization of Human Security', in Martin and Owen, *op. cit.*, 260–271.

security, other Asian states, for instance, members of ASEAN, have found the concept challenging to their state-centred notion of security. Nevertheless the language of human security has been engaged,[117] and some consideration of the approach been entered into within ASEAN, especially in the aftermath of the Asian financial crisis.[118]

At the same time as these positive developments, however, this was also the period in which the concept of human security came under sustained attack by radical critics, as discussed in the next section. It became increasingly marginalised, especially within the UN, despite continued lip service, the appointment of a Special Advisor and the GA resolution. The Human Security network was hollowed out after Canada abandoned the concept so vehemently that the term human security was banished by the Canadian government.[119] The EU also became less active after 2010, and the role of human security in the AU lost momentum. According to Thomas Tieku, human security has turned from being 'a darling idea to almost a taboo subject in the corridors of the AU'.[120]

In part this marginalisation can be explained in terms of the contested and fuzzy character of the concept itself. As Martin and Owen point out, it suffers from overlaps with human rights and human development as well as conceptual overstretch – being applied to everything and thus perhaps to nothing. According to Lakhdar Brahimi in an interview: 'I don't use the term human security because I don't know exactly what I mean and I worry that someone will come up and contradict me'.[121]

But perhaps more importantly, the 'normalisation' of the War on Terror and the reversion to Geo-Politics have blunted and side-lined the distinctiveness of a human security approach and muffled those voices advocating it. The reaction by Western states and others to the attacks on the World Trade Towers and the Pentagon in 2001 was a

[117] E.g., 'It is very, very important that all of us would accept and understand this very, very important concept, shifting from purely exclusively state security to the human person'; message from the Secretary-General of ASEAN, H. E. Dr. Surin Pitsuwan, for the 'Realizing Human Security in Asia' Symposium at the University of Tokyo, 23 February 2010, www.asean.org/resources/2012-02-10-08-47-56/speeches-statements-of-the-former-secretaries-general-of-asean/item/message-from-the-secretary-general-of-asean-he-dr-surin-pitsuwan-for-the-realizing-human-security-in-asia-symposium-at-the-university-of-tokyo.

[118] Nishikawa, Yukiko 2010. *Human Security in South East Asia*. Routledge.

[119] See Martin, Mary and Owen, Taylor 2010. 'The Second Generation of Human Security: Lessons from the UN and EU Experience', *International Affairs* 86(1): 211–224.

[120] Tieku, *op. cit.*, 260.

[121] Quoted in Martin and Owen, 215 ('The Second Generation of Human Security').

national security reaction. They were treated as an attack by a foreign power on the United States that demanded a military response.[122] A human security approach would have treated what happened as a humanitarian catastrophe and focussed on the needs of the victims, methods of preventing any repetition,[123] and efforts to arrest those responsible. As it turned out, the national security response led to the wars in Afghanistan (2001) and subsequently Iraq (2003), both classic military interventions against a state enemy.

Because the language of the Liberal Peace and humanitarianism was deployed in both these interventions, the legitimacy of the concept and the institutions associated with the concept were weakened. After the invasion and occupation of Iraq in 2003 the UN itself became a target even though the SC had refused a second resolution authorising the invasion. Interestingly, the United States' subsequent counter-insurgency campaigns in both Iraq and Afghanistan incorporated the concept of 'population security'[124] that has many similarities with human security; but population security was a means to an end – identifying and killing insurgents or terrorists – not an end in itself. In effect, the wars reduced humanitarian space and securitised international institutions. In Baghdad and Kabul and now Bamako, Juba and Tripoli, the international presence is sealed up into walled enclaves venturing out only in armoured cars and undermining the possibility of everyday communication that is a basic prerequisite for human security.[125]

More generally, the counter-terror measures introduced world-wide have led to new forms of regulation, surveillance and control over a range of development actors.[126] For instance, in the Horn of Africa and elsewhere the demands of counter-terror overwhelmed earlier human security approaches. It led to the 'securitisation' of aid in that development

[122] See Chapter 4.

[123] This was indeed the primary focus of UN SC Resolution 1373, 28 September 2001, which decided on steps that states were to take to 'prevent and suppress the financing of terrorist acts'.

[124] United States Army and Marine Corps 2006. *Counter Insurgency*. Field Manual 3–24.

[125] Andersson, Ruben and Weigand, Florian 2015. 'Intervention at Risk: The Vicious Cycle of Distance and Danger in Mali and Afghanistan', *Journal of Intervention and Statebuilding* 9(4): 519–541.

[126] See Howell, Jude and Lind, Jeremy 2009. *Civil Society under Strain: Counter-Terrorism Policy, Civil Society and Aid Post-9/11*. Kumarian Press.

functions increasingly came under the purview of security agencies (the Pentagon, the intelligence agencies, US Africom and others).[127]

The War on Terror polarised the public debate between those in favour of classic military intervention and those against all forms of intervention. In particular, it pulled apart the humanitarian community. Some who had favoured liberal interventionism joined the 'warrior' camp. Others, like the veteran war correspondent David Rieff, became disillusioned and cynical about humanitarian intervention and joined the anti-interventionist camp. This polarisation is reflected in the radical critiques of human security. Those such as ourselves who remain largely in the human rights movement argue that humanitarian intervention is different from war and has to be conducted appropriately. We acknowledge that this stance has little public resonance nowadays, except perhaps among civil society groups inside war zones as in Afghanistan and Syria, but hope that the arguments put forward in this book will reactivate interest.

So while the momentum of the 1990s carried the idea of human security through to the international institutions during the early 2000s, by the end of the decade any public support for a human security model of intervention seemed to have virtually disappeared. In 2016 the continued use of drones by the Obama administration for targeted killings, the refusal to deploy ground troops or peacekeepers, and reliance on airstrikes against IS in Iraq and Syria and against others elsewhere all militate against a human security perspective. The response to the terrorist attacks in Paris in November 2015 was again in the language of war[128] and led to increased spending on weapons, surveillance and security apparatus. The policies of the Trump administration are also inimical to human security.

11.6 The Critiques of Human Security

Most of the radical critiques of human security have to do with its rapid acceptance by institutions. On one reading, this represents a move away from national-based security doctrines. On another reading, however, it constitutes co-option allowing the term to be used to legitimise classic military power by Western states. According to Ryerson Christie:

[127] Duffield, Mark and Waddell, Nicholas 2006. 'Securing Humans in a Dangerous World', *International Politics* 43(1): 1–23.

[128] 'Paris Attacks 'an Act of War', says Francois Hollande', *BBC*, 14 November 2015, www.bbc.co.uk/news/world-europe-34821110.

> Advocates [of human security] have chosen to ignore the hidden dangers of engaging in a discourse of sovereignty that has been embraced by the policy community. Far from challenging traditional security practices, human security narratives and practices have demonstrated the resilience of traditional actors who, while incorporating some new policy communities (such as development workers) into security practices, have dominated the interpretation and enactment of human-centred security.[129]

According to Booth, human security has taken on 'the image of the velvet glove on the iron hand of hard power'.[130] The rapid acceptance by institutions also opens up a gap between discourse and practice. Newman argues that there is a fundamental contradiction between the pluralist character of the United Nations (composed of states) and solidarist implications of human security (people centred).[131] In other words, adoption of the concept risks not only co-option but also raising expectations that are beyond the institution's capacity to fulfil.[132]

The critiques of human security largely arise from this contradiction between mainstream acceptance and critical aspiration. They are drawn from feminist and constructivist scholarship as well from the theoretical work of Michel Foucault, Giorgio Agamben and Carl Schmitt. As Suvi Alt points out,[133] these various sources of criticism are often lumped together in confusing and misleading ways. In what follows, we attempt to outline different lines of argument taken from different sets of critiques.

What It Is to Be Human

The first set of arguments has to do with what it is to be human. Feminist scholars point out, not necessarily critically, that humans cannot be conceived of as autonomous individuals. They are social beings intimately connected through networks of social relationships. Fiona Robinson draws attention to the importance of incorporating the ethics of care into concepts of human security and of situating such approaches in real lived

129 Christie, Ryerson 2014. 'The Siren Song of Human Security', in Martin and Owen, *op. cit.*, 94–108, 94.

130 Booth, *op. cit.*, 324.

131 Newman, *op. cit.* ('The United Nations and Human Security').

132 Jolly, Richard and Basu Ray, Deepayan 2006. *The Human Security Framework and National Human Development Reports: A Review of Experiences and Current Debates.* UNDP, 8.

133 Alt, Suvi 2011. 'Problematizing Life under Biopower: A Foucauldian versus an Agambenite critique of Human Security', in Chandler and Hynek, *op. cit.*, 144–156.

experience: 'feminist ontology reveals the extent to which the continuity of life and a sense of security in people's day-to-day lives are impossible without relations of care and responsibility'.[134] Thus human security has to encompass attentiveness, responsibility and responsiveness to the needs of others, and a rethinking of the relation between private and public spheres. Robinson notes that the tendency of human security to focus on state discourses, 'international law and the macropicture of global governance' inhibits such thinking.[135]

The argument about autonomous individuals is also taken up by those who put forward the proposition, drawing on Agamben, that human security reduces human beings to 'bare life'. Similar to the feminist standpoint, the argument is that human security neglects 'the cultural context within which the individual realises his/her self-consciousness' and produces a 'de-historicized and deracinated individual'.[136] For Agamben, '['bare life'] bare life' refers to the simple fact of living (taken from the Greek term Zoë) and is contrasted with the social, cultural human being; bare life reached its apogee in the concentration camps.[137] Judith Butler too finds that 'there are "subjects" who are not quite recognizable as subjects, and there are "lives" that are not quite – or, indeed, are never – recognized as lives'.[138] She too sees the prison camp as a place where lives are stripped bare: 'The lives of those at Guantanamo do not count as the kind of "human lives" protected by human rights'.[139] These examples show how bare life equates with the dehumanisation of some people – terrorists, enemy combatants, migrants – making a hierarchy of humanness that impacts upon how violence is perpetuated including through means that are not 'human' such as robots and drones. Human security, it is argued, fails to recognise the culturally contested and embedded nature of individual identities. Humanitarian emergencies, similarly 'strips people of their history, culture and identity'.[140] The implication is that human security entrenches systems of power, reduces people to victims and depletes the possibility of human agency.

[134] Robinson, Fiona 2011. *The Ethics of Care: A Feminist Approach to Human Security.* Temple University Press, 44.

[135] *Ibid.*, 50.

[136] Shani, Giorgio 2011. 'Securitizing "Bare Life": Critical Perspectives on Human Security Discourse', in Chandler and Hynek, *op. cit.*, 56–68, 57.

[137] Giorgio, Agamben 1998. *Homo Sacer: Sovereign Power and Bare Life.* Stanford University Press.

[138] Butler, Judith 2009. *Frames of War: When Is Life Grievable?* Verso, 4.

[139] *Ibid.*, 58.

[140] Alt, *op. cit.*, 146.

In this vein, for example, the essentialism of 'human' – not allowing for differentiation between people – has fostered the idea of 'the most vulnerable' into UN resolutions and practice, which tends to paint people (and some more than others) as victims needing to be 'rescued' by the international community. It does not identify either the ways in which different people have different security needs, nor the ways in which people act to enhance their own security through their agency and empowerment.

While the importance of the everyday and of the cultural contexts cannot be over-emphasised, it is also important not to romanticise the local and the everyday. As feminists are only too aware, the family is often a site of insecurity, as is the local community.[141] Moreover what is regarded as 'local' is frequently globally connected. Local warlords, jihadists, drug and diamond smugglers are often integrated into global networks. The 'bottom-up' principle of human security involves alliances of care among local citizens seeking outside help to escape the nexus of violence in which they are caught. In other words the blurring of public and private also involves a blurring of local and global.

Securitisation

The idea of 'securitisation' developed by the Copenhagen School is that by calling something a security issue, it does something and justifies various responses.[142] It is assumed that this is negative. However, what it does and what it justifies, depends on how the term 'security' is understood.

One meaning of security is safety or, as Fiona Robinson points out, free of care.[143] This is the sense in which it was used by those who formulated the original version of human security. For them calling something a security issue highlighted its importance, for instance, development as a security issue. Understood in this way, the significance of securitisation is rather trivial, and the charge that the broad vision of

[141] The first report of the special rapporteur on violence against women identified sites of violence such as in the family, the community and perpetrated or condoned by the state; Coomaraswamy, Radhika. *Preliminary Report Submitted by the Special Rapporteur on Violence against Women, Its Causes and Consequences, in Accordance with UN Commission on Human Rights Resolution 1994/45,* UN Doc. E/CN.4/1995/42, 22 November 1994.

[142] Buzan, Barry and Wæver, Ole and de Wilde, Jaap 1998. *Security: A New Framework for Analysis*. Lynne Rienner.

[143] Robinson, *op. cit.*

security 'securitises' development is not serious; indeed, to securitise in this sense may have positive consequences, as the originators of the concept of human security believed.

The second meaning of security is the identification with security services (the police, the military, intelligence services, border controls). In this sense, securitisation refers to the way in which security services expand their remit and budgets to cover fields formerly addressed by other agencies such as social services, immigration or development agencies. For instance, the 2002 National Security Strategy of the United States linked poverty and security, arguing that poverty may render a weak state vulnerable to terrorist networks and drug cartels within its borders. If poverty is recast as a security threat, responses may be militarised: '[p]overty alleviation – through the Millennium Development Goals [since 2015 the Sustainable Development Goals], for example – becomes a means of addressing a security threat, as opposed to a set of tools required either because of moral duties or because of a broad-brushed development strategy'. The implication is that military intervention to secure development goals (as defined by the intervener) would be legitimate and perhaps even lawful.[144]

Securitisation of human rights, and its effect on extensive counter-terror measures (and vice versa), is especially problematic. Alongside other human rights treaties the ICCPR affirms the right to security: 'Everyone has the right to liberty and security of person'.[145] There has been little analysis by the Human Rights Committee or regional human rights courts as to what this right entails, and it is often elided with the first part of the sentence – the right to liberty.[146] It has also been suggested that it might be viewed as a 'meta-right', 'the legitimating principle upon which all fundamental rights are grounded'.[147] The danger arises when such a conception is called upon in a political climate of securitisation and when the liberty of some is curtailed in the name of

[144] Rajagopal, Balakrishnan 2008. 'Invoking the Rule of Law in Post-Conflict Rebuilding: A Critical Examination', *William and Mary Law Review* 49: 1347–1376, 1370.

[145] ICCPR, article 9; see also the European Convention for the Protection of Human Rights and Fundamental Freedoms (ECHR), 1950, article 5; Inter-American Convention on Human Rights, 1969 (IACHR), article 7; African Charter on Human and Peoples' Rights, article 6.

[146] Lazarus, Liora 2007. 'Mapping the Right to Security', in Goold, Benjamin and Lazarus, Liora (eds.). *Security and Human Rights*. Hart Publishing, 325–346, 333–334.

[147] *Ibid.*, 328.

security for others.[148] This is well illustrated by the case of *Al Jedda v. United Kingdom*.[149]

Mr Al Jedda is an Iraqi/UK dual national who was detained by UK forces in Iraq in October 2004, suspected of membership of a terrorist group. No charges were brought against him. His detention was preventive, based on 'imperative reasons of security'. The UK government claimed the detention to be in accordance with the SC resolution authorising the use of 'all necessary measures to contribute to the maintenance of security and stability in Iraq'.[150] Accordingly, claims that Mr Al Jedda's detention without charge or trial set his right to liberty (and security) under ECHR article 5[151] against the SC's primary responsibility for the maintenance of international security, and, in this context, security in Iraq and the right to security of others in Iraq. The European Court of Human Rights Grand Chamber (to which the case was referred) avoided a direct conflict between the SC and the European Convention on Human Rights,[152] but the case illustrates well the danger that a 'right to security [or a mandate to ensure security] can inadvertently legitimise security measures that encroach upon those values it has now displaced'.[153] The response, Lazarus argues, is to ensure that an autonomous right to security is 'narrowly and rigorously construed' with a corollary state duty 'to develop structures and institutions' that are capable of responding to and minimising 'critical and pervasive threats to human security'.[154] Of course, the UK government did not define what sort of security justifies violations of human rights; was it national or human security, or that of the UK forces in Iraq?

148 Gearty, Conor 2013. *Liberty and Security*. Polity Press.

149 *Al Jedda v. the United Kingdom*, ECtHR GC application no. 27021/08, 7 July 2011. For other aspects of the case see Chapters 8 and 10.

150 UN SC Resolution 1546, 8 June 2004.

151 The ECHR is mainly incorporated into UK law by the Human Rights Act 1998. In the UK courts, Al Jedda's claim was under the Human Rights Act.

152 In a subsequent case the ECtHR found Switzerland to be in violation of the ECHR, article 6 (access to court) through its failure to provide for meaningful judicial review of the actions of the SC Sanctions Committee in listing the applicants for targeted sanctions. However, the Court again avoided finding a direct conflict between the security actions taken by the SC and human rights but that 'the Security Council is required to perform its tasks while fully respecting and promoting human rights . . . To sum up, the Court takes the view that paragraph 23 of Resolution 1483 (2003) cannot be understood as precluding any judicial scrutiny of the measures taken to implement it.' *Al-Dulimi and Montana Management Inc. v. Switzerland*, ECtHR GC, application no. 5809/08, 21 June 2016, especially paras. 145–149.

153 Lazarus, *op. cit.*, 328. 154 *Ibid.*, 329.

But it is the third meaning of security that preoccupies the critics of human security. This is the understanding of security as having to do with a supreme emergency, which is intrinsically linked to sovereign power. In this sense securitisation is defined as the 'speech act of labelling an issue a "security Issue" [which] removes it from the realm of normal day-to-day politics casting it as an "existential threat" and justifying extreme measures'.[155] Sovereignty, from a Schmittian perspective, is about the ability to decide what is an 'existential threat'. Carl Schmitt's famous dictum 'Sovereign is he who decides on the exception'[156] means that the ability to act is revealed at moments of crisis or emergency when normal laws can be suspended. Thus the US Patriot Act of 26 October 2001 and the subsequent 'Military Order' issued by President Bush on 13 November 2001 gave the President far-reaching powers to suspend the rule of law and, in particular, permitted the indefinite detention and trial of non-citizens suspected of involvement in terrorism. Similarly, President Hollande declared a national state of emergency following the attacks in Paris in November 2015, which was extended by the National Assembly. Effectively, these responses establish a 'state of exception'; indeed, Agamben argues that a state of exception has become a normality for contemporary states.[157]

Critics of human security suggest that if sovereignty is constructed through the exception, then human security represents a way of establishing global sovereign power. The ICISS argued that the Responsibility to Protect applies in 'cases of violence which so genuinely "shock the conscience of mankind" or which present such a clear and present danger to international security, that they require coercive intervention'.[158] According to Doucet and Larrinaga, '[i]n this the concept of human security plays a central role in identifying and defining those extreme and exceptional circumstances that not only set the conditions for the suspension of the law but also for its refounding in the language of new

155 Robinson, *op. cit.*, 42.

156 Schmitt, Carl 1985. *Political Theology*. Schwabb, George (trans.), University of Chicago Press, 1.

157 Agamben, Giorgio 2005. *State of Exception*. University of Chicago Press. Israel has been in a state of emergency since its creation in 1948; see Human Rights Committee, Concluding Observations on the Fourth Periodic Report of Israel, UN Doc. CCPR/C/ISR/CO/4, 21 November 2014, para. 10.

158 Quoted in Doucet, Marc and De Larrinaga, Miguel 2011. 'Human Security and the Securing of Human Life: Tracing Global Sovereign and Biopolitical Rule', in Chandler and Hynek, *op. cit.*, 129–143, 139.

international norms on intervention'.[159] A similar argument is put forward by Anne Orford in relation to the Responsibility to Protect.[160]

Even if it were the case that international institutions had the capacity to act decisively in emergencies and were not constrained by their member states and by lack of resources, this reading of sovereignty is at variance with that required by a human security approach. Human security blurs the inside and outside. Sovereignty, from a human security perspective, is constructed through a social contract negotiated at national levels but supplemented by negotiations in the international arena on which the international rules are based. Any human security intervention has to operate within the framework of rules just as is the case for emergency services in domestic settings. This is what makes a human security intervention different from a military intervention. The rules of war do represent a suspension of 'normal' laws, as do derogations from human rights treaties.[161] This cannot be the case for human security.

The sovereignty argument is linked to the idea that human security reduces human beings to 'bare life'. It is also linked to Schmitt's critique of wars for humanity.[162] Writing during World War Two, on the German side, Schmitt argued that wars for humanity treat the enemy as non-human and justify extreme and brutal methods. But a human security intervention is not a war; in a war, the enemy is collective. If human security is viewed as human rights-based international law enforcement, rather than war, then there are no collective enemies, but there may be individual criminals whose lives and rights also have to be respected.

Biopower

The third set of arguments has to do with the Foucauldian idea that human security and the strategic complexes it has spawned constitutes a form of biopower. Biopower refers to the form of power that focusses on

[159] *Ibid.*

[160] Orford, Anne 2012. 'In Praise of Description', *Leiden Journal of International Law* 25(3): 609–625.

[161] Derogation to some rights are allowed, for instance, by ICCPR, article 4 and the ECHR, article 15.

[162] 'To confiscate the word humanity, to invoke and monopolize such a term probably has certain incalculable effects, such as denying the enemy the quality of being human and declaring him to be an outlaw of humanity; and a war can thereby be driven to the most extreme inhumanity'. Schmitt, *op. cit.*, 54.

the population rather than territory. It has to do with technologies of health and welfare rather than with disciplinary technologies; it is about the 'power to make live' rather than the 'right to kill'. Mark Duffield who pioneered this Foucauldian critique suggests that biopower can be regarded as a social mechanism used to maintain stability in what he describes as the uninsured part of the world – a way to maintain the quarantine of rich countries and salve their consciences. The strategic complexes of human security constitute a new paraphernalia of international intervention – a technology of power that preserves the submission of conflict-ridden parts of the world to an unequal world order.[163]

But to describe human security as a global extension of biopower is not necessarily a critique of human security. As Alt points out, while the concept of 'bare life' offers a bleak prospect of human agency, for Foucault the possibility of resistance is always present. Not only do people govern themselves through various techniques of the self, but also life is not 'inescapably integrated into techniques of governance; it escapes constantly'.[164] 'Whereas a Foucauldian perspective would see human security as a perspective that is constantly being reshaped, an Agambenite perspective would claim that it cannot be reshaped'.[165]

Of course, human security is about power. Power is intrinsically linked to notions of security and the question concerns which notions of security. The normative question is not about power but about the dominant paradigm (what Foucault would describe as *dipositif*) within which power is exercised; what sort of practices and ideas are entailed? In other words, to suggest that human security is a form of biopower is a research strategy rather than a normative standpoint. What is then required is an empirical dissection of the way that power functions.

The Duffield argument that human security is a way of quarantining the insured world is relevant, of course, whether or not the term biopower is applied. Similar arguments relate to the way in which human security 'pathologises' what are known as weak states[166] and entrenches existing power inequalities by focussing on the individual rather than on structural inequalities.[167] It is worth noting that ideas of human security

[163] Duffield, Mark 2001. *Global Governance and the New Wars: The Merging of Development and Security*. Zed Books.

[164] Alt, *op. cit.*, 152. [165] *Ibid.*, 153.

[166] McCormack, Tara 2011. 'The Limits to Emancipation in the Human Security Framework', in Chandler and Hynek, *op. cit.*, 99–113.

[167] Newman, Edward 2004. 'The "New Wars" Debate: A Historical Perspective Is Needed', *Security Dialogue* 35(2): 173–189.

have coincided with the dominance of neo-liberal economic policies; it can be argued that human security complements neo-liberalism because it offers the sort of minimum safety net that neo-liberalism requires. The question is whether such approaches actually constitute obstacles to structural change. We must ask whether they are a way of postponing change, or whether by offering an alternative set of norms they contribute to further pressure for change; whether people are being helped whatever the consequences, whether such help sustains existing inequalities of wealth and power or whether it represents a challenge to such structural inequalities.

11.7 Reconstructing Human Security

The critiques of human security offer a bleak future. They offer no alternative for protecting and empowering people in faraway places. The implication of the critiques is that all forms of state-based (or international community) international intervention are harmful and we should only be concerned about human security in a domestic context. Yet in our globalised world, the local is imbued with the global; the rejection of all types of intervention amounts to the application of *laissez-faire* in the political arena alongside dominant *laissez-faire* economics.

The Human Security model needs to be reconstructed as a strategy of resistance – as an alternative to the War on Terror not as its adjunct (or apologia). In contrast to the top-down character of the Responsibility to Protect (which is about the right of outside powers to intervene), the Human Security model needs to be understood as the right to be protected. The value of the critiques is that they offer some pointers as to how this might be accomplished. First, human security has to understand the human as gendered, contextual and social. It has to be a strategy that emanates from the context rather than imposed from above. Secondly, human security does have to be about the extension of rights-based international law but that process is also contextual. Law can be used as an instrument of resistance by local groups trying to reduce violence and to enhance the safety of their own communities, and it is only through such pressure that international tendencies to override law can be constrained. International intervention must be about assisting local people on their terms with respect to their priorities, not imposing geo-political or counter-terror strategies. And thirdly, we need a micro- and granular empirical picture of the variety of international interventions in practice, what Duffield calls the 'strategic complexes of global governance' to identify nodal points of resistance.[168]

Second-generation human security, as Martin and Owen argue, is not about widening versus narrowing but about deepening the concept.[169] It is about how to respond to the crises of our time, including especially new wars. The Barcelona version of human security needs to be updated and complemented by some of the ideas relating to hybrid or post-liberal peace, which bring together bottom-up and top-down approaches.[170] It should be stressed that the idea of hybrid peace is an empirical description rather than a normative project. All interventions necessarily involve complex interactions at all levels. The 'international' tends to refer to the messy conglomeration of international agencies involved in particular interventions while the local, according to Richmond and Mitchell, refers to a 'territorialized space . . . in this sense, the local is not to be essentialized or parochialized; it refers to a space, that is, in a sense, transversal, transnational and even global, or at least a feature of most human societies'.[171] In other words, interventions are about the blurring of the inside/ outside distinction and reconceptualisng some of the dominant binaries that underpin conventional liberal thinking. Richmond and Mitchell suggest that hybridisation is about 'the way in which local actors respond to resist and ultimately reshape peace initiatives through interactions with international actors and institutions'.[172] This formulation is perhaps too passive. International actors (those representing other states, international institutions and agencies) possess monetary resources and some capacity for force, but local actors possess contextual knowledge, through which they do not merely respond or resist but also manipulate and indeed precipitate international action. MacGinty talks about the

168 Duffield, *op. cit.* (*Global Governance and the New Wars*).

169 Martin and Owen, *op. cit.*

170 Some of these arguments were included in a new report from the Human Security Study Group in 2016 entitled *From Hybrid Peace to Human Security: Rethinking EU Strategy towards Conflict: The Berlin Report of the Human Security Study Group*. The report was an input in to the review of the EU's Global Strategy undertaken by Federica Mogherini, the High Representative for Common Foreign and Security Policy. The final report advocates a human security approach to conflict. See *A Global Strategy on Foreign and Security Policy of the European Union*, June 2016.

171 Richmond, Oliver P. and Mitchell, Audra 2012. 'Chapter 1: Introduction – Towards a Post-liberal Peace: Exploring Hybridity via Everyday Forms of Resistance, Agency and Autonomy', in Richmond, Oliver P. and Mitchell, Audra. *Hybrid Forms of Peace: From Everyday Agency to Post-Liberalism*. Palgrave, 1–38, 11.

172 *Ibid.*, 9.

'interaction of already hybridised actors and structures. Although these actors and structures may be labelled as "local", "indigenous", "liberal" "exogenous" or "international" it is useful to see them as composites, or amalgamations resulting from long-term processes of social negotiation and adaptation'.[173]

Different interactions have different consequences. American policy in Afghanistan, for example, was much more shaped by the alliances with the so-called warlords than is ever officially acknowledged. A reconstructed human security strategy would build on a granular analysis of local contexts in order to identify those interactions that are more conducive to individual and community well-being, that is to say, human security. It would be a multi-scalar approach involving global, regional, national and local levels of policy and decision-making that would be connected and harmonised and that would eschew standard recipes. In the following sections, we sketch some elements of this approach and how they differ from the Liberal Peace.

Political

New wars take place where states are weak or failing, where governments lack legitimacy. Central to any effort to dismantle the mutual enterprise of war is the establishment of an inclusive political settlement. IS, for example, can be regarded as a symptom – a response to the sectarian behaviour of the Iraqi government and the collapse and abuse of state authority in parts of Syria. Even if IS is militarily defeated, a similar phenomenon is likely to emerge unless inclusive governments in the area which is now Syria and Iraq are established. And this also applies at local levels. IS has not been able to move into areas where local authorities command respect and support.[174] Involving civil society in political discussions at all levels is a prerequisite for the establishment of inclusive political authority. By civil society, we do not mean NGOs; rather we mean civilians or active citizens, including women, youth groups, faith groups, who are not involved in fighting and who are concerned about the public interest and who offer a political alternative to sectarian identities. In Bosnia, Syria, Libya and Ukraine, the pro-democracy protest movements did not morph into military rebellion even though this is

[173] MacGinty, Roger 2010. 'Hybrid Peace: The Interaction between Top-down and Bottom-up Peace', *Security Dialogue* 41(4): 391–412, 398.

[174] Turkmani, Rim 2015. 'ISIL, JAN and the War Economy in Syria', *Security in Transition,* www.securityintransition.org/projects/syrias-war-economy-new-research/.

the standard narrative. Rather the rebels were recruited from often poor unemployed young men, while those, often more educated, who took part in the protests transformed themselves into civil society groups, providing humanitarian assistance, mediating between different groups, monitoring human rights abuses and engaging social media. It is these people that need to be involved in political discussions and negotiations at all levels.

Unlike the Liberal Peace model, an inclusive political settlement is not something that can be achieved through a single overarching peace agreement (or set of agreements) as we have argued in Chapter 9; such an agreement is only possible if it entrenches the political power of the warring parties and in a context of new wars, this does not end violence. The political track needs to be viewed as a process, which not only reflects on the possible nature of a political solution but widens participation and includes specific issues concerning security, economic and social conditions, gender and justice that might help to alleviate human suffering, counter the logic of new wars and provide a basis for the construction of an inclusive political settlement in the future.

Of course, the Liberal Peace is similarly focussed on the importance of state-building. Where this post-Liberal Peace approach differs is its focus on inclusive political settlements that draw attention to politics as opposed to technical aspects of state-building, to political processes as opposed to the single top-down agreement and to different levels of authority (municipalities, governorates, regional and international arrangements) rather than the focus on the state.

Security

New wars are fragmented – some locations experience high levels of violence while others are relatively secure – what Faber and Dekker call security zones.[175] Some areas provide exclusive security for specific groups and/or are dominated by 'strong (heavily armed) men' or particular factions. IS, for example, does introduce state-like behaviour in the areas it controls establishing a monopoly of violence, introducing draconian laws and judgments and implementing them in brutal ways, but this does impose a sort of security for those locals who are not targets.[176] Other localities negotiate localised ceasefires and try to

[175] Faber, Mient Jan and Dekker Martin 2014. 'Human Security from Below', in Martin and Owen, *op. cit.*, chapter 9.

[176] Turkmani, *op. cit.*

establish inclusive local administrations; it is possible to identify many such examples in Syria and Libya.[177] The 'bottom-up' determination of these areas differentiates them from UN-designated 'safe areas'.[178] A hybrid peacebuilding strategy would aim at strengthening those security zones that are more conducive to the construction of inclusive authority, through international presence, assistance with mediation, monitoring and the equal provision of public goods, particularly economic and social rights.[179] Some steps have been taken in this direction by the *ad hoc* creation of 'Protection of Civilian Sites' in South Sudan,[180] but their emergency establishment means they are basic and, as discussed in Chapter 9, some unresolved problems remain and violence is still prevalent.

This approach would also involve rethinking of peacekeeping. Human security personnel would have the task of dampening down violence, defending people and property, and, where possible, arresting rather than killing those responsible for criminal acts. Such personnel must be trained in various skills, including those currently associated with military, police, humanitarian aid, healthcare, or development expertise. They would need to be located on the ground able to assist or mediate in the negotiation and monitoring of local ceasefires and together with local counterparts help to reconstruct legitimate forms of governance and to provide public services at local levels, including justice and social services. This bringing together of 'top-down' and 'bottom-up'

[177] Turkmani, Rim *et al.* (eds.) 2014. 'Hungry for Peace: Positives and Pitfalls of Local Truces and Ceasefires in Syria', *Security in Transition*, www.securityintransition.org/publications/hungry-for-peace-positives-and-pitfalls-of-local-truces-and-ceasefires-in-syria/; Megerisi, Terek and Toaldo, Mattia 2015. 'Action Points for Europe after the Libya Deal', *European Council on Foreign Relations*, www.ecfr.eu/article/commentary_action_points_for_europe_after_the_libya_deal3093.

[178] Judge Cançado Trindade refers to the protection provisionally ordered by the ICJ to both territory and the people within a demilitarized zone, bringing together '*territory, people and human values*, well in keeping with the *jus gentium* of our times'. In *Application of the Convention on the Prevention and Punishment of the Crime of Genocide* (*Croatia v. Serbia*) Merits, 2015 ICJ Reports 3, 3 February 2015, dissenting opinion Judge Cançado Trindade, para. 71, referring to *Request for Interpretation of the Judgment of 15 June 1962 in the Case concerning the Temple of Preah Vihear Request for Interpretation of the Judgment of 15 June 1962 (Cambodia v. Thailand)*, Request for the Indication of Provisional Measures, 2011 ICJ Reports 537, individual opinion Judge Cançado Trindade, para. 64.

[179] Arbour, Louise 2007. 'Economic and Social Justice for Societies in Transition', *NYU Journal of International Law and Politics* 40: 1–27.

[180] See Chapter 9.

approaches would also help to provide a bulwark against further take-overs by armed groups. Something of this sort in purely security terms was undertaken by General Petreaus in Baghdad in 2007–2008, and this led to a dramatic fall in violence. However, it was never followed through at national or international levels, which contributed to the deterioration of the situation.

A 'Human Security Response Force', as recommended by the Human Security Study Group, could be a possible model for the provision of such support. The Study Group's proposal was for a European force that would bring together military and civilian capabilities, although the idea could be extended to other regions. It suggested that the Force should comprise '15,000 men and women, of whom at least one third would be civilian (police, human rights monitors, development and humanitarian specialists, administrators, etc.). [It]would be drawn from dedicated troops and civilian capabilities already made available by member states as well as a proposed "Human Security Volunteer Service"'. The safety of those who are in combat areas must be a priority for any such force and assistance include essential services, rations, medical assistance and security. Trained experts on response to sexual violence in armed conflict such as the teams created by the UN and by the United Kingdom as part of its Preventing Sexual Violence in Conflict Initiative could also be integrated into a Human Security Response Force. Reliable provision of necessities, including immediate healthcare following sexual abuse, would reduce the flow of people from the conflict zone. Lessons learned from this emergency response to a life-threatening situation should be developed and integrated with broader objectives such as those suggested by the Study Group.

A practical example of co-operation encompassing the use of force and criminal enforcement has been action to tackle piracy in the Indian Ocean off Somalia. Multiple pirate attacks in the area caused a serious threat to human security,[181] destabilised the regional economy and posed serious threats to shipping and maritime commerce. Existing rules of international law presented obstacles to tackling the violence, including coastal state sovereignty over the territorial seas and legal dilemmas of jurisdiction, the human rights of accused persons, extradition, as well as

[181] '[S]ince 12 December 2008 (a period of two years), pirates have held close to 1,900 people and 105 vessels, off the coast of Somalia'. Report of the Special Adviser to the Secretary-General on Legal Issues Related to Piracy off the Coast of Somalia, UN Doc. S/2011/30, 25 January 2011, para. 29 (Lang Report).

those of political will. After some measures had already commenced, in 2011 a detailed report argued for the international community to take 'exceptional measures commensurate with the seriousness of the situation and the rapid implementation it calls for'[182] and made a number of far-reaching proposals encompassing *inter alia* legal (national and international law), political, economic, development, correctional, security and monitoring measures. Responses to the piracy included the SC authorising in 2008 'states and regional organisations that have the capacity to do so' to enter the territorial sea to repress piracy by all necessary means.[183] A number of states, notably Kenya, exercised universal jurisdiction over pirates detained and arrested through such co-operation. In sum, 'counter-piracy efforts of States, regions, organizations, the maritime industry, the private sector, think tanks, and civil society'[184] combined to reduce the number of pirate attacks. Without going into detail about this action, the anti-piracy campaign shows on the one hand how international rules can be adapted and co-operative action be relatively speedily entered upon in exceptional situations. Unity between the permanent members of the SC allowed for unprecedented military action, involving multiple states and leading to law enforcement. On the other hand, the proposal for a special court exercising extraterritorial jurisdiction for the trial of Somali pirates was not sufficiently supported.[185] While authorising enforcement action the SC was cautious; the 2008 authorising resolution was explicitly not to 'affect the rights or obligations or responsibilities of Member States under international law . . . with respect to any other situation' and was not to 'be considered as establishing customary international law'. Further it allowed intrusions into Somalia's territorial seas 'only following the receipt of the 20 November letter conveying the consent of the TFG'.[186]

Where this approach goes beyond the Liberal Peace is the understanding that security depends on trust in authority rather than on a security apparatus. Where security forces are deployed this is linked to the construction of inclusive political settlements; moreover such forces are likely to be neither classic peacekeepers nor classic military forces but tailored to a local context, constructed and acting more like police forces in rights-based societies.

[182] Lang Report, para. 77. [183] UN SC Resolution 1846, 2 December 2008.
[184] UN SC Resolution 2184, 12 November 2014.
[185] Lang Report, para. 116 (Proposal 25).
[186] The Transitional Federal Government in Somalia.

Economic and Social

Political and security aspects cannot be disentangled from economic and social phenomena. New wars constitute a new set of social relations shaped by the predatory economy which necessarily incentivises violence and draws, especially, unemployed young men into its ambit. Every area has a specific and different combination of predatory activities – extortion and kidnapping, smuggling and trafficking of various types, 'taxation' of humanitarian assistance. It is possible to identify concrete proposals for addressing the war economy and promoting legitimate livelihoods so as to reduce the incentives for war, but these proposals are different in different areas and can only be identified through analysis and communication at local levels, particularly with civil society. Such proposals might include international pressure to lift sieges, the provision of diesel oil (large parts of Syria are dependent on IS to acquire diesel and it is the high costs of diesel and not merely war and destruction that has damaged the legitimate economy), the international control of borders, or the regulation of trade in small arms, diamonds or antiquities. Often the warring parties make agreements about economic issues – the exchange of water for electricity, for example, between IS and the Government in Syria; such agreements should be leveraged to assist individuals and their communities.

It is probably in the economic arena that this approach most differs from that of the Liberal Peace. The Liberal Peace is associated with standard neo-liberal recipes. In so-called post-conflict situations, the focus is macro-economic stabilisation, liberalisation and privatisation. While these situations often experience rapid economic growth associated with the provision of aid and the international presence, they also tend to be characterised by deepening inequality, high levels of unemployment, increased corruption,[187] especially linked to privatisation and state contracting, and consequently, the continuation and perhaps spread of the predatory war economy. An alternative approach would both tackle some of the worst aspects of the war economy in very specific and tailored ways, but, at the same time, focus on legitimate livelihoods, as well as public works and equal access to and delivery of economic and social rights. Of course, in a corrupt, war economy context such initiatives are very difficult. Economic and social policy has to be viewed as

[187] Chayes, Sarah 2015. *Thieves of State: Why Corruption Threatens Global Security*. W. W. Norton & Company.

part of a symbiotic process of constructing an inclusive political settlement; such policies help to create space for alternative more inclusive politics, and, by the same token, they are difficult to introduce without effective and transparent public authority.

Gender

New wars are the site of the construction and continuation of harsh and unequal gender relations. They establish an extreme and unstable form of masculinity that becomes part of the logic of new wars because it can be only sustained in conditions of disorder and violence.[188] Participation of women in peace processes and the inclusion of gender-related issues such as accountability for sexual violence and the provision of health and education especially for women are ways to counter the gender construction in new wars and, by so doing, the logic of new wars.

While the Liberal Peace also insists on the importance of attention to gender issues, this tends to be viewed as an 'add-on' or a 'good thing to do' rather than a necessary approach for deconstructing extremist ideologies and the predatory war economy;[189] it is thus a method of dealing with armed conflict.

Justice and Accountability

Throughout this book, we have stressed the importance of accountability at all levels of society. Dealing with the criminalised networks responsible for new wars is very difficult, perhaps impossible, through military responses. Addressing impunity is the only way to establish a rule of law. Establishing legitimate authorities at all levels, including the international, is impossible without formal methods of accountability.

The justice element also represents a very important departure from the Liberal Peace model. Because the peace agreement is so central to that model, justice tends to be downplayed. There is a real dilemma of peace and justice within a Liberal Peace framework since effective justice mechanisms might well involve the arrest of the very people required to conclude a peace agreement. A post–Liberal Peace approach would presuppose war as a mutual enterprise and would involve an inclusive process of peacemaking that would marginalise the warring parties. In

[188] Chinkin, Christine and Kaldor, Mary 2013. 'Gender and New Wars', *Journal of International Affairs* 67(1): 167–187.

[189] For analysis of the impact of neo-liberal economics on gender-based violence see True, Jacqui 2012. *The Political Economy of Violence against Women*. Oxford University Press.

such a situation effective justice mechanisms, the arrest and trial of war criminals for example would be positively beneficial. Likewise because the Liberal Peace model is top-down, the accountability of international personnel has low priority – but in a hybrid post-liberal situation, accountability is critical to generate the kind of trust required to establish secure areas.

11.8 Conclusion

We have tried in this chapter to unpack the meaning of second-generation human security. We have outlined the contours of a post–Liberal Peace that builds on the experience of the Liberal Peace model and is guided by human security principles. In other words, we recognise that the Liberal Peace has involved a large-scale learning process for the international community; our aim is to take this further and contribute to a much needed post–Liberal Peace strategy that takes into account the mistakes, failures and shortcomings of the Liberal Peace, as well as its successes. Our emphasis is on understanding the logic of new wars in specific contexts instead of starting from generalisable old war assumptions.

The Human Security model that we propose requires a coordinated and long-term international response that determines priorities, allocates responsibility and budget and is backed by substantial resources. The longer that such efforts are put off, the more difficult and expensive it will be in the long run. Responses like air strikes seem to be the easier option, but they are not necessarily either cheap or effective. They will prolong the global new war for decades to come. Perhaps the explanation is not short sightedness or an anachronistic belief in old war tactics; rather it may suit specific economic and political interests of the dominant powers.

The interest in human security from the 1990s onwards was predicated on the assumption that both its broad and narrow versions were assured in societies where the rule of law prevailed. The War on Terror and, in 2016, Brexit and the rise of Trump have called that assumption into question. Human insecurity has crossed borders and is continuing to do so as exemplified by the increase in human migration and the tragic difficulties that migrants confront, the spread of corruption, ethnic, religious and racial polarisations and reversals of women's advancement contribute to human insecurity both 'inside' and 'outside' – a 'global new war'. The ideas and practical implementation of second generation human security, will we believe be all the more important everywhere.

12

What Does Human Security Require of International Law?

12.1 Introduction: The Aim of the Book

Throughout this book we have attempted two separate but inter-related tasks: to analyse the application of international law in situations of 'new wars' and to identify different models of security through which the international legal regulation of the use of force might be assessed. We labelled these the Geo-Politics, War on Terror, Responsibility to Protect, Liberal Peace and Human Security models. These tasks were undertaken in an attempt to change the conversation at the international level and to shift the global debate from the current priority accorded to Geo-Politics and the War on Terror to humanitarian concerns, thus establishing the conceptual basis for a second-generation Human Security model.

Our starting point was to highlight the central place of security in international law as a discipline. In the post–World War II era the UN Charter highlighted two principles: national state security and the security of the collectivity of states through the objective of the maintenance of international peace and security. International law upholds the sanctity of state borders and the 'containment' of external threats through the prohibition on the use of force in international relations (UN Charter, article 2 (4)), the self-defence exception (article 51) and Security Council–authorised collective action (articles 39–42). This puts the security of the political construct of the state at centre stage, the integrity of borders, without attention to the security of those who are within the borders, who seek to cross borders or operate across borders. Collective security puts the maintenance of the international *status quo* – the global regime of sovereign and equal states – at centre stage. These security regimes are further supported by the obligation for the peaceful settlement of disputes (article 2(3) and chapter VI). Despite its concentration on state sovereignty, the UN Charter simultaneously opened the door for the international protection of human rights and fundamental freedoms (articles 1 (3), 55 and 56) and thus for the security and integrity of the human person. In Chapter 11 we show how in the 1990s the idea of human rights was one of the key drivers in the widening of the concept of security to encompass that of human security – security with people at the core rather than states – and, despite critiques, the importance of a rights-based approach that cuts across structural power biases and is inclusive.[1]

Our central argument is that a visible and credible commitment to human security needs to be assured by international law. Indeed, human security entails a law-based rather than a war-based approach to security. This argument, however, confronts the core dilemma that is addressed throughout the book's chapters: how can a state-based system of international law, designed to uphold state sovereignty and non-intervention in the internal affairs of other states, operate to uphold a people-based concept of security?[2] The aim of this concluding chapter is to sketch out what human security requires of international law. What is, or could be, the law upon which human security derives its legitimacy?

12.2 International Law as a Contested Discipline

After outlining our argument and the conceptual framework upon which it is based in Part I (Chapters 1, 2 and 3), Parts II (Chapters 4 and 5), III (Chapters 6 and 7) and IV (Chapters 8, 9 and 10) describe in some detail the international legal regimes of the *jus ad bellum*, *jus in bello* and *jus post bellum* before concluding with the way forward (Chapters 11 and 12). Parts II, III and IV illuminate the multiple tensions and contested claims that reduce the effectiveness of international law to achieve its goals of achieving national and collective security, or indeed human security, while Chapter 3 recognised the essential weakness of international law compliance, implementation and enforcement.

These tensions include:

- Tension between different understandings of self-defence, when it is applicable and its limits (Chapter 4)

[1] There are, of course, many aspects of insecurity, including food insecurity, economic insecurity, insecurity engendered by climate change, gender insecurity etc. However, the book focuses on physical insecurity from extreme violence, although it insists that all these forms of security are inter-related.

[2] von Tigerstrom, Barbara 2007. *Human Security and International Law*. Hart Publishing.

- Tension between humanitarian motives for responding to gross atrocities in other states and the military methods for responding to those atrocities (Chapter 5)
- Tension between an international legal framework for the regulation of force that was designed in a former era and which assumed that conflict would be between states and which is inadequate for the regulation of 'new wars' (Chapter 6)
- Tension between the objectives and methodologies of extreme violence engaged by those fighting in new wars (ethnic cleansing; targeting of civilians; sexual violence; terrorist tactics) and the fundamental principles of international humanitarian law (IHL) – distinction, precautionary and military necessity (Chapter 6)
- Tension between the different approaches to regulation of the instruments of conflict: arms control (continued production, possession and transfer of weapons, with some states favoured over others); disarmament (illegality of production, possession and transfer of weapons); and humanitarianism based upon their inhumane consequences (Chapter 7)
- Tension between what is termed 'protection of civilians in armed conflict' (and separate groups defined by their vulnerabilities, notably children and women) in the different legal regimes and the military means by which such protection is sought (Chapters 5, 6 and 9)
- Tension between so-called 'post-conflict' and the realities of continuing violence
- Tension between the goals of the Liberal Peace and the realities of peace processes where negotiations are held between those with guns (the warring parties) who maintain an interest in enduring conflict as a mutual enterprise (Chapter 9)
- Tension between protecting civilians through military means or through law enforcement, and between upholding ceasefires (peacekeeping) and post-conflict reconstruction (civilian administration, civilian police and peacekeepers) in different post-conflict scenarios (Chapters 8 and 9)
- Tensions between the objective of securing accountability through international criminal justice and peace agreements or geo-politics (Chapter 10)

These and other tensions have been stimulated by the arguments and practice of some states, especially since the end of the Cold War, that have sought to stretch or expand international law to further protect state-based security.[3] These have to some extent been balanced by other arguments and practices (sometimes by the same states) that have similarly stretched international law to enhance human security.[4] These two opposing tracks and the differing histories, language, ethos, objectives and structures of the legal regimes have fuelled further legal debates, such as those about: the relationship between international humanitarian and human rights law and whether non-state actors are subject to these legal regimes (see Chapter 6); whether human rights claims can challenge Security Council decisions with respect to security (Chapter 11); and whether international legal texts should be interpreted narrowly so as to preserve their textual integrity or more purposively to respond to particular crises, particularly with respect to self-defence and other supposed exceptions to the UN Charter's prohibition against the use of force (Chapters 4 and 5), but which appear unprincipled and self-serving.

The legalisation and judicialisation of international affairs discussed in Chapters 3 and 10 have not resolved these contested areas. Indeed, legalisation has promoted legal definitions and technicalities allowing for fine distinctions which have little meaning for those facing insecurity on the ground (e.g., what constitutes a 'war crime', 'combatant', 'person directly participating in hostilities', 'armed attack', 'in accordance with the mandate', 'refugee', 'trafficked person', 'victim', 'genocide' and many other terms brought into legal texts). Legalisation also exposes omissions allowing for the presumed legality of actions not expressly prohibited.[5] Judicialisation has sometimes seemed to give rise only to fora for semantic debates around the meanings to be given to these definitions (or omissions) that are far removed from the violence of conflict. Legal regimes also construct opposing binaries such as war and peace; state and non-state; international and non-international armed conflict; internal unrest and non-international armed conflict; self-defence and aggression; international territorial administration and military occupation; conflict and post-conflict; counter-terrorism and extra-judicial killing; intervention and non-intervention; humanitarian

[3] See especially Chapter 4. [4] See Chapter 5; Tigerstrom, *op. cit.*

[5] Despite inroads, the dictum of the *Lotus* case that '[t]he rules of law binding upon States therefore emanate from their own free will' (*The Case of the S.S. Lotus* (France v. Turkey), PCIJ (Ser. A) No. 10, 18, 7 September 1927) retains its force today so that states still argue that what is not prohibited by or included within treaty or customary international law is excluded from international legal regulation. Arguments presented in the *Legality of the Threat or Use of Nuclear Weapons*, 1996 ICJ Reports 226, advisory opinion, 8 July 1996 ('*Nuclear Weapons*') well illustrate the point.

intervention and illegal intervention; just and unjust war; authorised and unauthorised military action; liberation and occupation. Such binaries reinforce hierarchical value systems and extra-legal assumptions of legitimacy. The use of force associated with our models is bolstered by other binaries: good and evil; modern and mediaeval; action and inaction; protector and protected. In sum they illustrate the tension between international law as 'apology' for the designs of the leading powers and the 'utopia' of human wellbeing and security.[6]

But we also have to recognise that many of these laws and the assumptions upon which they are based emerged as a response to classic 'old wars'. International law has a tendency to address the wars that have just passed. The 1949 Geneva Conventions followed World War II, and the 1977 Additional Protocols were an attempt to redress their shortcomings in light of the colonial wars of national liberation. These laws were not designed to address the 'new wars', of the late twentieth and early twenty-first centuries, in, *inter alia*, Africa, the Balkans, the Middle East, Central Asia and the Caucasus. As explained in Chapter 1, battles in new wars are rare and most violence is deliberately targeted at and inflicted on civilians, often with extreme cruelty, often involving the spread of terror through mass murder, rape and mutilation. Population displacement is a typical feature of such wars. Civilian populations flee within and across borders and networks of armed groups operate across porous borders, including traffickers and those who engage in the methods of terror. This makes the IHL distinctions between international and non-international armed conflict unworkable and calls into question further legal categorisations such as law enforcement by states (policing within states, although this may involve human rights violations but also through coercive methods abroad), 'protest' or 'abuses' by non-state actors and 'conflict' between armed combatants. 'New wars' also blur the distinction between public and private, since the violence involves regular state armed forces as well as paramilitary groups, warlords, mercenaries, terrorists and organised criminal groups. This distinction has been further broken down by the claims of IS to a caliphate – a form of statehood – forcibly collapsing existing state boundaries and exercising some of the accoutrements of statehood. 'New wars' spawn an abnormal political economy, in which most income-generating activity, ranging from diaspora support, to trafficking of various kinds, to looting and

[6] Koskenniemi, Martti 2005. *From Apology to Utopia: The Structure of Legal Argument.* Cambridge University Press, Reissued Ed.

pillage, depends on violence and coercion. The distinction between crime – subject to domestic law – and violent conflict – subject to these diverse international law regimes – becomes empirically difficult to identify and thus to implement.

Further, where there have been acclaimed proposals for legal reform, progress has been uncertain. For instance, the Responsibility to Protect remains a policy rather than legal concept and is open to critiques of hegemonic power and excessive reliance on military means (see Chapter 5); humanitarian successes in the adoption of the Landmines and Cluster Munitions Conventions have not led to a nuclear disarmament convention or for limitations on highly destructive conventional weapons (see Chapter 7). Despite innovations in individual criminal accountability for atrocities understood as international crimes, geo-political realities and legal technicalities have undermined their success (see Chapter 10). Progressive legal reform finds it hard to shake off the legacies of earlier law.[7]

What these tensions and inadequacies point to is the inability of an international legal system developed in a different world to provide effective and principled regulation of the complex new wars of the early twenty-first century and thus the need for a profound rethinking of some of the precepts of international law. But we must also recognise the political reality that state decision-makers, whether acting unilaterally, through defence alliances or within international or regional institutions, remain too often entrenched in 'old war' mentalities, even when addressing new security issues. The security models described in Chapter 1 elucidate this. The Geo-Political and War on Terror models centre on state security and classic war methods of addressing it. The Liberal Peace model assumes that the components of security lie in negotiating only with and for the warring factions, giving them territorial competence based on ethnicity (e.g., the Balkans, South Sudan, Kosovo, Iraq). This model tends to freeze the territorial gains made in 'new wars' but does not end the human rights violations that continue to be committed after an agreement has been signed and may also lead to further violence (South Sudan, DRC, Libya, Iraq) or to spill over into the wider region, including maritime regions (Somalia, Iraq, Syria, Libya, Mali), or the risk

[7] E.g., Louise Chappell has shown how despite progressive gender language in the *Rome Statute of the International Criminal Court*, judges, prosecutors and states persist in the legacies of past rules and practices; Chappell, Louise 2016. *The Politics of Gender Justice at the International Criminal Court*. Oxford University Press.

of renewed war. The Humanitarian Intervention/Responsibility to Protect model[8] has been distorted so that the pillar for military support has become the primary focus rather than merely the final one of last resort. It is also open to abuse on geo-political grounds and is framed within the World War II power structures of the SC. Besides it is now largely ignored.

We argue that the security challenges of new wars – including various forms of extremism and terrorism – require a shift in mind-set that is commensurate with a human security approach. The idea of a global extension of the rule of law was considered by realists as idealistic, and we recognise that we may face the same accusation. But we believe that our argument is based on the reality that war methods do not work. The military victory over the Taliban in Afghanistan in 2001 has proved to be non-sustainable; the defeat of Saddam Hussein in Iraq in 2003 was followed by Islamist insurgency and sectarian conflict; the temporary end of sectarian conflict and the defeat of Al Qaeda in Iraq did not prevent the rise of IS. Regime change in Libya has seen the eruption of armed groups and militias, and the porosity of the country's borders has allowed fighters and weapons to move from Libya to Mali and thousands of migrants from Eritrea, Somalia and Ethiopia and elsewhere to cross into the country, seeking access to the Mediterranean Sea and thence to Europe. Military peace operations are dangerous and limited in what they can achieve where there is no peace to keep, peacekeepers are targeted and killed and their supplies stolen to feed the war economy. It is unlikely that military action can inflict long-lasting defeat on IS or other terrorist networks and it provides an argument (however illegitimate) for recruitment; in late 2016 despite airstrikes in Iraq and Syria, terrorist attacks continue – including in Paris, Beirut, Nigeria, Kenya, Tunisia, Mali, Brussels, Istanbul, the United States and elsewhere. Nor do classic peace approaches, based on diplomacy between warring parties, fare much better. Peace agreements like Dayton (Bosnia) or Minsk (Ukraine) halt the territorial expansion of warring parties but do not stop the violence, criminality and human rights violations that such groups inflict. Security in Bosnia, Kosovo or eastern Ukraine is not assured. Another reality is that of globalisation, which has enhanced inequality in power structures through its operation in a neo-liberal economic framework. We argue that these realities must be taken into account in asking whether the

[8] In Chapter 5 we clarify the difference between the two concepts; see further Thakur, Ramesh 2016. 'The Responsibility to Protect at 15', *International Affairs* 92: 415–434, 418.

legal regimes can be developed and applied so as to provide a principled and sound basis for the regulation of threats to human security.

Moreover, considerations of law do not take place in a vacuum; moral and ethical questions also abound. For instance, can it be right to use the classic methods of war-fighting that also involve massive violations of human rights? Can it be right to inflict violations of human rights when the aim is to prevent them? Should the moral equivalence between those fighting in self-defence and those resorting to terrorist tactics be maintained, or does abandoning it involve a destructive disregard for the rule of law? We argue that the only ethical starting point must be the security of human persons, a law-based in place of a war-based approach. We agree with the reasons Vaughan Lowe has suggested for favouring a crime paradigm over a war paradigm: there is a risk that by calling, for example, terrorism 'war' a group of perceived 'enemy nationals' is created along religious and race lines, creating societal schisms; and that fundamentally '[t]errorism is completely antithetical to the rule of law; and *all* States should be free, and indeed obliged, to cooperate in its repression. For that, the appropriate framework is that of international criminal cooperation'.[9] This interpretation can also be applied to the various forms of political violence we have categorised as 'new wars'. We argue that without a human security approach, the world is likely to witness a return to naked power and violent exchanges with extremists and terrorists in which civilians are the major victims through collateral damage from military air strikes, revenge attacks, hostage taking and continued pursuit of terrorist methods. Thus ours is a practical rather than idealistic strategy.

The next section provides an overview of the main implications of the previous chapters for human security as a basis for further reflections as to how some of the principles and institutions of international law might be rethought.

12.3 Overview of Conclusions Relevant to Human Security

In Chapter 2 we argued that sovereignty is about the boundary between inside (the domestic sphere) and outside (the international arena). Historically, the 'outside' was largely characterised by war and diplomacy, while the 'inside' was the realm of politics, law and policing. Sovereignty

[9] Cited in Brown, Rory 2011. *Fighting Monsters: British-American War-Making and Law-Making*. Hart Publishing, 68.

always depended on mutual recognition in the international sphere –a recognition that was based on certain agreed rules, especially those relating to waging war that provided the basis for international law. We suggest that perhaps the most profound change in sovereignty that has taken place since the end of World War II is a change in the rules relating to the authority to use force. Modern concepts of sovereignty are usually associated with the Peace of Westphalia; what that peace signaled was the end of religious and private authority to use force – a shift from religious to state authority. We argue that the prohibition of the international use of force in the UN Charter signaled an equally momentous shift from national to international authority to use force.

We are not suggesting that this shift means the end of state sovereignty. While states remain the legal repositories for sovereignty, security is no longer the exclusive domain of the state. In Chapter 2, we outlined different scenarios of world order associated with different models of security. In the Human Security model, new layers of political authority complement and balance the role of states; what has come to be known as global governance comprises interconnected networks involving international and regional institutions, local and municipal forms of government, as well as states. International relations (between states) are embedded in a complex array of transnational (across borders) and cosmopolitan (among individuals and societies) relations. Human security both derives from existing elements of such an emerging world order and, at the same time, offers a key legitimation for further shifts in the composition of power. We would argue that this scenario for world order is best aligned with or is the best way of managing the process known as globalisation that is in part made possible by the phasing out of relations between states that were earlier fundamentally shaped by 'old war'.

'New wars', terrorism and violent extremisms are expressions of the blurring of outside and inside. Yet our language has not caught up with these emerging phenomena. Had the terrible events of 9/11 been conducted by the armed forces of another state, President Bush's depiction of the events as war might have been appropriate. Had they been conducted by American criminals with no links to abroad, they would have been treated as a domestic issue, and the response would have been domestic law enforcement. The attacks in Paris on 13 November 2015 were conducted by French and Belgian citizens, but their links with IS allowed the French President to treat them as an international phenomenon and declared France to be at war. Yet is there not something in between a domestic crime and a war? These were crimes of the deepest gravity, and they were framed in political terms. Is there not a category of global crimes, crimes against humanity or genocide, for example, that offers a language that allows for a response that is more akin to domestic law enforcement but derives its legitimacy from international law, that itself is becoming more like domestic law?

Our main proposition is that human security based on the primacy of human rights offers a framework for addressing the blurring boundary between inside and outside. The core of the rethinking that is required is that war must be recognised as illegitimate, a human catastrophe involving a massive violation of human rights and 'new wars' as crimes against humanity. This requires perceiving conflict not as a social or political phenomenon the legitimacy of which is bolstered by a power-based collective decision, a separate legal regime (IHL), by being regarded as in some sense 'just', or as rendered humane by the application of human rights law. What this might mean for international law can be inferred from our treatment of the different aspects of the law relating to the use of force in Parts II, III and IV of this book.

In Part II relating to the *jus ad bellum* we discuss what this might mean for justifications of the use of force. The only explicit exception to the prohibition of the use of force in the UN Charter is self-defence and arguments that humanitarian intervention constitutes another legal exception depend upon interpretation and customary international law.[10] Self-defence is the main argument for the legal use of force in the War on Terror and Geo-Politics models. In Chapter 4, we show how the concept has been stretched by being applied to attacks by non-state actors, through claims of anticipatory (and even pre-emptive) self-defence, that the state subject to military intervention is 'unable or unwilling' to take action against terrorists on its territory, and through woolly interpretations of the concepts of necessity and proportionality.

Self-defence is based on defence of the state, but may represent a human catastrophe to individuals, such as those in Afghanistan or Iraq where military interventions were justified in terms of self-defence. The same is true for individuals caught up in the War on Terror, for instance, in Pakistan where drone attacks have caused civilian casualties. From a human security perspective, it can be asked what it means to talk about self-defence of a state. In the International Court of Justice (ICJ) advisory opinion on the *Legality of the Threat or Use of Nuclear Weapons*, the

[10] See Chapter 5.

Court was unable to determine definitely (on the President's casting vote) that their use would be illegal in circumstances in which 'the very survival of a State would be at stake'.[11] But what does survival of the state mean? And does a lesser, non-nuclear attack, say, terrorist action, constitute an existential threat making self-defence 'necessary'? Who or what is the state? Are we talking about defence of its borders, territory and cities, nationals of the state[12] or those who reside on its territory? Or are we talking about something more abstract – a way of life, a social contract, order or freedom, a state apparatus? The problem with most of these definitions is that all of them, even territory, have become fuzzy in the context of globalisation and the development of cyberspace; there are so many interconnections, so much dispersal of regulatory frameworks, so much cultural mixing or pooling of sovereignty that it is difficult to justify the use of force on grounds such as protecting these often abstract notions. On the other hand, if we are referring to the residents or citizens of the state, is not an armed attack the same as a massive violation of human rights – a global crime? And in this case, we are surely talking about something akin to humanitarian intervention, an upscaling of the individual's undisputed rights to self-defence, or the right of a third party to come to the defence of an individual. In other words, if human security entails a reconceptualisation of war as a massive violation of human rights, then an armed attack also has to be reconceptualised in these terms. The implications of such a reconceptualisation are far reaching. If we argue for understanding self-defence as an upscaling of individual self-defence, then we have to ask whether the use of military force is warranted, and in those extreme circumstances where this is judged to be the case, whether rules of engagement based on existing 'laws of war' are appropriate.

We also need to take into consideration what happens when human rights are supposedly put at the core, as discussed in Chapter 5. The actual practice of humanitarian intervention or of the Responsibility to Protect has been profoundly contradictory. It has been characterised either by inaction as in the cases of the Rwandan genocide, the fall of Srebrenica, or in response to Saudi air strikes in Yemen, or by excessive reliance on classic military force as in Somalia (1992–1993), Kosovo (1999), Libya (2011) and Côte d'Ivoire (2011). In both Kosovo and Libya,

[11] *Nuclear Weapons* para. 105, E.

[12] Rescue of nationals abroad has been a claimed basis for the use of force, extended by Israel to the rescue of Jewish people at the airport in Entebbe in 1976; see Chapter 5.

NATO relied exclusively on air strikes. Similarly the military response to IS has been through airstrikes, in support of local ground forces (Kurdish Peshmerga in both Syria and Iraq, Shi'ia militias and the Iraqi army in Iraq, and, in Syria, armed rebel groups, although the latter are mainly fighting Assad). It is difficult to stop massive human rights violations on the ground through air strikes, which may indeed provoke further abuses (as in Kosovo in March–April 1999). Interventions are readily transformed into a conflict in which air strikes support local militias and the goal may become regime change rather than preventing human rights violations (the KLA in Kosovo, the Libyan rebels). Even though air strikes are more precise now than they were in 1999 in Kosovo and far fewer civilians die directly as a result of collateral damage, and even though they may destroy vehicles and weapons that can be used to attack civilians as in Libya, civilians die because of faulty intelligence, human error and subsequent fighting, as well as through the location of targeted armed fighters in civilian areas, the difficulty of distinguishing civilians from combatants, and the use by the armed fighters of human shields. Moreover, the end result is the empowerment of armed groups and destruction of infrastructure and services with serious consequences for civilian wellbeing, long term stability and human security.

In Chapter 5, we argue that the problem is the contradiction and confusion between goals and means, between *jus ad bellum* and *jus in bello*. The focus in contemporary debates on humanitarian intervention, which since 2001 has been frequently articulated as the Responsibility to Protect, has been on the responsibility of – in practice the United States and its allies – [13] to intervene with military force rather than on the rights of individual human beings to be protected. Hence there is always a tension between 'responsibility' towards individuals and the use of military power to reinforce national interests and status. The Human Security model is about the right to be protected, and this means that any human security intervention has to be different from war. We make the argument that the rules of engagement governing an intervention in the name of human security must be different from those that tend to be considered appropriate for war fighting. A human security operation is a civilian operation rather than a military operation, that is to say, it is more like an inside intervention (policing and other emergency

[13] Interventions by Western states tend to overshadow those by other states, including regional states such as those acting under ECOWAS or the African Union (AU). See Chapter 5.

responses) than an outside intervention (war fighting) with correspondingly appropriate rules of engagement. But what are those rules?

The third part of the book is about the rules governing how war is fought, *Jus in Bello.* The problem with existing rules, the subject of Chapter 6, is that while they were supposed to relieve human suffering, they also helped to construct war as a legitimate activity.[14] The fact that soldiers fight and kill within a set of prescribed rules is what makes them different from murderers. Ironically, even when the rules are disregarded, their existence frames debates and assumes the 'rightness' of conflict fought within their parameters. This difficulty is particularly relevant in the case of 'new wars'. Both the Russian and Syrian air strikes in Syria and Saudi air strikes in Yemen have demonstrated blatant disregard for humanitarian principles, with deliberate attacks on hospitals and, possibly, humanitarian convoys; yet both governments claim to be acting within a legal framework. In the case of Saudi Arabia the use of British equipment is justified in terms of having gone through arms export procedures and the claim that a Saudi-led enquiry into several bombing incidents showed that there was 'no clear breach' of international humanitarian law.[15] The post–World War II period has witnessed the emergence of two other bodies of law relating to the use of force – human rights law and international criminal law. Our argument in Chapter 6 is not that IHL should be rejected, but rather that it needs to be complemented by human rights law, which has at its heart the dignity of all human beings, and international criminal law, which at least in theory increases the accountability of those who use force.

In effect, we are saying that human security might necessitate the use of force in situations of humanitarian emergency, but under much tighter rules of engagement, which are aimed at minimising all loss of life, with a defensive focus on individuals on the ground and involving, where possible, the arrest rather than killing of those responsible for human rights violations as well as enhanced accountability. In Chapter 11, we outline some of the ways in which this might be done through the construction of human security forces that are civilian led and include an appropriate mix of civilian and military skills, and men and women, and through techniques, such as safe zones, humanitarian corridors or no

[14] See Chapter 6.

[15] See Patrick Wintour, 'Boris Johnson Defends UK Arms Sales to Saudi Arabia', *The Guardian,* 5 September 2016, www.theguardian.com/world/2016/sep/05/mps-to-urge-ban-on-uk-arms-sales-to-saudi-arabia.

fly zones, combined with political and economic support designed to assist the construction of legitimate political authority and legitimate economic activity at local levels.

Human Security also has implications for the regulation of weapons. In Chapter 7, we outline three different approaches to weapons law – arms control, which has largely been about managing the geo-political competition among the Cold War Great Powers, exemplified in the bilateral SALT and START Treaties to limit nuclear weapons and the Non-Proliferation Treaty,[16] that aimed to prevent the spread of nuclear weapons; the humanitarian approach in which efforts have been made within the IHL framework to prohibit or refrain from use of weapons that cause 'superfluous injury or unnecessary suffering'[17] or 'unacceptable harm' to civilians';[18] and the disarmament approach, which aims to eliminate whole categories of weapons, such as chemical and biological weapons, or to establish weapons-free zones. Disarmament is based on the assumption that the way to end war is to prohibit the means of fighting wars. It is in the field of weapons law that the greatest gains have been made in response to 'new wars' with treaties that ban land mines and cluster munitions as well as the 2013 Arms Trade Treaty. These initiatives have been criticised for focusing on the actors in 'new wars' while neglecting conventional military arsenals and weapons of mass destruction. We take the view that they do constitute a contribution to human security, but they need to be complemented by much broader disarmament efforts – a weapons of mass destruction–free zone in the Middle East and a convention on nuclear disarmament, for example – as well as greater attention to the control of weapons in domestic contexts, such as gun laws in the United States, and on legal arms trading.

And in the penultimate part of the book we address the growing body of what has come to be framed as *jus post bellum*. However, just as there is a blurring between the two former regimes (especially with respect to protection of civilians), so too is there between those two regimes and the use of force in the *jus post bellum*. What we refer to as the Liberal Peace constitutes an emerging model whereby international institutions play a

[16] *Treaty on the Non-Proliferation of Nuclear Weapons*, London, Moscow, Washington, 1 July 1968.

[17] *Convention on Prohibitions or Restrictions on the Use of Certain Conventional Weapons which may be deemed to be Excessively Injurious or to Have Indiscriminate Effects*, Geneva, 10 October 1980, preamble.

[18] *Convention on Cluster Munitions*, Dublin, 30 May 2008, preamble.

key role in bringing the warring parties together in order to bring an end to the violence and a substantial international or regional presence, including peacekeepers, is deployed in order to uphold any agreement and to engage in state-building and reconstruction. We argue in Chapter 9 that the Liberal Peace model is based on 'old war' assumptions. It presupposes that war consists of a contest of wills in which the different sides have legitimate grievances that can be resolved through talks and power-sharing, and that wars have clear beginnings and endings so that peace agreements can be framed as traditional peace treaties. The problem is that where armed violence/conflict takes the form not of a contest of wills but of a sort of mutual enterprise in which various predatory groups mobilise sectarian ideologies and/or engage in a range of war-related revenue-raising activities, such peacemaking processes may help to limit the violence between the warring parties (which is only a small part of the violence in new wars), but at the same time, they entrench and legitimise the various armed groups, thus undermining human security. This explains the widespread failure of international state-building activities and the difficulty of distinguishing conflict and post-conflict. While peace processes involving such groups may be necessary to stop the worst violence, we argue that the downsides need to be offset by greater inclusivity, especially of civil society and women, more incrementalism, more attention to locally driven efforts and by enhanced mechanisms for justice and accountability. It is true that human rights are given at least some rhetorical attention in the Liberal Peace, are incorporated into peace agreements and often made central to internal constitutional arrangements, but this rarely extends to the full canon of human rights or to the incorporation of economic and social rights. At the same time, the top-down peace agreement tends to prioritise anachronistic notions of stability over justice and involve power-sharing arrangements that are often incompatible with respect for human rights, as the *Sedjić-Finci* case before the European Court of Human Rights (ECtHR) has shown.[19]

Unlike in earlier wars, peace agreements do not necessarily mean the end of conflict. Rather they are moments that tend to legitimise an international presence. Following peace agreements, contemporary peacekeeping mandates give a high place to protection of civilians, although as discussed in Chapter 9, the operational practicalities are rarely made explicit and may be overwhelming. Further, we argue that

[19] See Chapter 9.

this confuses military activity and law enforcement. Such mandates must be performed in accordance with human rights standards. The introduction in 2013 of the 'Human Rights Due Diligence Policy on U.N. Support to Non-U.N. Security Forces'[20] and the Human Rights Up Front initiative of the Secretary-General, also in 2013, both recognise the importance of incorporating human rights into peacekeeping operations. There is no reason why similar creativity should not be part of any intervention force, including those for humanitarian goals.

Nor does an international presence prevent the persistence of the predatory political economy; black market profiteering, trafficking and organised crime, coupled with high unemployment and lack of services and resources, all contribute to inequalities and vulnerability to crime. The international presence – military or civilian – in fact distorts the economy. It may contribute to short-term stability through the creation of jobs and associated services, but the introduction of standard neo-liberal recipes such as privatisation and liberalisation that are predicated on a legitimate market can become tools of predation in the hands of the new criminalised elites. Economic aid is easily channelled into the continuation of an exploitative and deeply unequal war economy, and international jobs distort salary scales. The international presence institutionalises the causes of conflict, disempowers those who would be the drivers of change and either freezes an intolerable *status quo* (Bosnia, Kosovo, Ukraine)[21] and/or sets the scene for the next round of protest and conflict.

At the same time, as we show in Chapter 10, while justice and accountability are largely dismissed in the War on Terror and Geo-politics models, they have an uneasy place within the Liberal Peace model. Given that new wars deliberately target civilians, one aim of post-conflict Liberal Peace is accountability, yet this is too often discounted because those that target civilians are the partners in the Liberal Peace. The creation of international criminal tribunals was motivated by civil society and 'like-minded' states. However, as we argue in Chapter 10, their potential for increasing justice and accountability has been undermined by their jurisdictional limitations and the geo-political interests of

[20] Report of the Secretary-General on the Work of the Organization, UN Doc. A/67/1, 8 August 2012, para. 58; Human Rights Due Diligence Policy on United Nations support to non-United Nations Security Forces, UN Doc. A/67/775–S/2013/110, 5 March 2013, Annex.

[21] OSCE monitors are deployed in eastern Ukraine.

the Great Powers, which explains why the situation in Syria has not been referred to the ICC by the SC. The double standards of international justice mechanisms, in which there have been no prosecutions pertaining to Western interventions, such as in Kosovo, Libya or Iraq and the politicisation of the courts themselves are perceived as further obstacles to even-handed justice. Moreover the mechanisms for accountability of international peacekeeping personnel for abuses committed during Liberal Peace interventions are extremely weak, lack transparency and are rarely applied by troop-contributing countries.

The implications of this analysis is that the Human Security model requires a different type of peace process that is both top-down and bottom-up, that includes women and civil society, and that is spread over time, as we spelled out in Chapter 11. Any international presence needs to be civilian-led and any use of force more similar to law enforcement than war fighting. And justice and accountability are critical components of a Human Security model.

So what kind of measures might be required to bring the international regime into greater alignment with the Human Security model? In what follows we reflect, first, about what human security might mean for the gap between legality and legitimacy introduced in Chapter 1, and identify some further developments that point the way to the rethinking of some of the premises of the state-based international legal regime required by human security. Some would require recasting basic tenets of international law and thus commitment to structural legal change, as well as to the essential political commitment to implementation of change. Others require little more than legal reform, although political will to undertake such reform and to give it effect are, of course, always essential. In addition we need to take account of the extra-legal aspects that drive conflict and undermine peace.[22]

12.4 Closing the Gap between Legality and Legitimacy?

Our argument for human security understood as a law-based approach to security rests on the reality that war methods are not working: 'All armies ever say is: "Reason has failed"'.[23] Reliance upon political dialogue

[22] Marks, Susan 2011. 'Human Rights and Root Causes', *Modern Law Review* 74: 57–78; Pahuja, Sundhya 2011. *Decolonising International Law: Development, Economic Growth and the Politics of Universality*. Cambridge University Press.

[23] Orr, Deborah. 'I Pity ISIS Supporters: To Be Hard-Hearted Is Their Ideology, Not Ours', *The Guardian*, 28 November 2015, 35.

grounded in law is of course not new – the theme 'peace through law' has engaged the attention of states and international legal scholars for over a century.[24] International law is not static but is dynamic and based upon 'living instruments'.[25] What is important is that change is not simply happenstance and dependent only upon the interests of the powerful. As we have identified throughout the book, there have been many such attempts, especially in the furtherance of the War on Terror and in a regression to Geo-Politics. But there have also been other changes in the substance, processes and institutions of international law that have in a variety of ways served to reduce the grip of the state-based system. They stem from the ideas underpinning the pillars of the UN relating to development, peace and human rights and are the foundation blocks for 'humanity's law'.[26] In brief, these ideas derive from diplomatic negotiation (the Martens clause),[27] the insights of some Judges of the ICJ (for instance, Sir Hersh Lauterpacht[28] and Judge Alvarez[29] in the early days of the Court, Judge Weeramantry[30] in the 1990s and Judge Cançado Trindade[31] today) and the inputs of intellectuals, civil society activists and political lobbyists. The impulses of humanity (although admittedly these cannot always be easily disentangled from other, more political,

[24] Chimni, B. S. 2015. 'Peace through Law: Lessons from 1914', *London Review of International Law* 3(2): 245–265.

[25] Human rights treaties in particular have been described as 'living instruments whose interpretation must consider the changes over time and present-day conditions'. *Gomez Paquiyauri Brothers v. Peru*, IACtHR, Series C, No. 110, 8 July 2004, para. 165; see also *Loizidou v. Turkey* (Preliminary Objections), ECtHR application no. 15318/89, 23 March 1995, para. 71; Committee on the Elimination of Discrimination against Women, General Recommendation No. 28 on the Core Obligations of States Parties under article 2 of the Convention on the Elimination of All Forms of Discrimination against Women, CEDAW/C2010/47/GC2, 19 October 2010, para. 2 (a 'dynamic instrument').

[26] Teitel, Ruti 2011. *Humanity's Law*. Oxford University Press. [27] See Chapter 6.

[28] Lauterpacht, Hersch 1950. *International Law and Human Rights*. F. A. Praeger.

[29] Judge Alvarez expounded the 'new international law', the law of 'social interdependence' and social justice; e.g., *Corfu Channel* (United Kingdom of Great Britain and Northern Ireland v. Albania) (Merits) ICJ Reports 4, 40, 9 April 1949, per individual opinion Judge Alvarez.

[30] *Nuclear Weapons, op. cit.*, per dissenting opinion Judge Weeramantry.

[31] Most recently in *Application of the Convention on the Prevention and Punishment of the Crime of Genocide* (Croatia v. Serbia) (Merits), 2015 ICJ Reports 3, 3 February 2015, per dissenting opinion Judge Cancado Trindade, paras. 65–84. Judge Trindade asserts that 'the fundamental principle of humanity has indeed met therein with full judicial recognition . . . the primacy of the principle of humanity is identified with the very end or ultimate goal of the Law, of the whole legal order, both national and international, in recognizing the inalienability of all rights inherent to the human person'.

motivations) have led to treaty-based, customary law, institutional and jurisprudential developments that have been well elucidated by Ruti Teitel[32] and will not be repeated here.

But as we have shown in this book, this is a process in progress; further shifts in international law and practice can be identified, which should not be seen as isolated changes but as trends towards a reinterpretation of international law that is coherent, internally consistent and thus legitimate. Indeed, proposing international law as a 'new topos for contemporary peacemaking, peacekeeping and peacebuilding and overall for human security is an alternative way to construct a world order – through an interdisciplinary approach that effectively bridges conflict resolution and public international law beyond state-entrapped typologies'.[33]

The extent to which any legal regime can be constructed and implemented depends on the extent to which it can command widespread legitimacy among people as well as states. The assumption that underpins this exercise is that a Human Security model is more likely to command legitimacy than the partial conceptions of legitimacy implied by the other security models discussed in this book. Thus Geo-Politics is based on a national conception of legitimacy; the War on Terror derives its legitimacy from the idea of United States' exceptionalism, the associated claim to global hegemony and the repulsion at and fears generated by terrorist attacks; and Responsibility to Protect and Liberal Peace, while universalist in intention, are too top-down and open to imperialist abuse to mobilise popular support. We have argued that the construction of legitimate authority, at all levels – local, national, regional and international – is the only practical answer to 'new wars'. Intervention at any level is only effective if it is seen to be legitimate. And by the same token, the legitimacy of any intervention rests to a large degree on its effectiveness. Our argument is that Human Security, based on the primacy of human rights, is the model most in tune with a more globalised world in which the sharp distinction between outside ways of organising society and inside ways is no longer as relevant. The political position of Donald Trump, and of those who favour British exit from the European Union, signals a return to nationalism and xenophobia that cannot produce either national or human security in the contemporary interconnected context. Hence the aim of this exercise is to close the gap between legality

[32] Teitel, Ruti, *op. cit.*

[33] Sarigiannidis, Miltiadis 2007. 'Legal Discourses on Peacemaking/Peacekeeping/Peacebuilding', *International Journal* LXII(3): 519–538, 525.

and legitimacy by shifting the legal regime so that it is closer to a human centred form of legitimacy rather than reverting to self-defeating national conceptions.

A starting point is to outline some of the key principles. First, the discussion in this book has shown how the three distinct legal regimes that regulate political violence (*jus ad bellum, jus in bello and jus post bellum*) overlap and are inter-related. This suggests that a *co-ordinated, comprehensive and holistic approach* would best serve human security. We argue that this has a temporal element in that pre-conflict, conflict and post-conflict are not distinct phases and do not progress in a linear fashion. It has a functional element in the bringing together, *inter alia,* of military and civilian capabilities, human rights monitors, humanitarian assistance and gender expertise. And, of course, it has a legal element in that it seeks ways of dealing with the various inconsistencies, dilemmas and contradictions of different legal regimes. There is also a layered requirement in seeking co-ordination and engagement between top-down and bottom-up, but insisting that the priorities and agenda must be set by the latter.

It should also be pointed out that a genuinely comprehensive approach to human rights law requires an equal commitment to economic and social rights as rights (not welfare, benefits, needs or services)[34] and as integral to transitional justice and reconstruction. As we discuss in Chapter 10, transitional justice is too often limited by its focus on 'large-scale past abuses', [abuses',] understood as violations of civil and political rights – arbitrary deprivation of life and liberty, torture – and typically fails to recognise the need also to address the gross violations of economic, social and cultural rights associated with conflict and indeed pre-conflict. Inequalities in the distribution of economic and social rights across social, political, religious, ethnic and gender divides often constitute part of what are known as root causes of conflict and its extreme, related violence, including sexual violence. Without the empowerment

[34] This is presaged by the preambles to the International Covenant on Civil and Political Rights and International Covenant on Economic, Social and Cultural Rights, 1966: 'Recognizing that, ... the ideal of free human beings enjoying civil and political freedom and freedom from fear and want can only be achieved if conditions are created whereby everyone may enjoy his civil and political rights, as well as his economic, social and cultural rights' (ICCPR); 'Recognizing that, ... the ideal of free human beings enjoying freedom from fear and want can only be achieved if conditions are created whereby everyone may enjoy his economic, social and cultural rights, as well as his civil and political rights' (ICESCR).

provided by equal access to and delivery of economic and social rights through national legal frameworks, in accordance with international standards, the prospects for social or transformative justice are severely curtailed and the prospects of human security undermined. For instance, without access to their economic and social entitlements, survivors of and witnesses to wartime atrocities are less likely to be able participate in transitional justice programmes – court proceedings or truth commissions – thereby denying access to justice and sustaining perpetrator impunity. The same is true for meaningful participation in peace processes and in the political, institutional and social structures for reconstruction; such participation would be a luxury for those lacking adequate food, shelter and employment. Equal access to economic and social rights allows for economic redistribution and decreases inequalities. In short, denial of economic and social rights reduces access to justice and accountability and undermines the realisation of participatory democracy and the sought-after stability and national, collective and human security.

Second is the need for *inclusivity* in all relevant processes and programmes, not only with respect to peace processes and post-conflict reconstruction but also to political and policy-making in general and at all levels.[35] In particular it requires support for and insistence upon active participation by civil society and especially women, more specifically local women who have knowledge of what is needed at the community level to manage and end conflict and who are well prepared to participate throughout the multiple ups and downs of peace processes and their implementation. We know from research that the input of local women relating to basic issues with respect to how society is organised, how needs can be met and what steps must be taken to achieve those goals and how they can be effectively followed though during reconstruction is key to sustainable peace.[36] Assistance therefore should focus on developing participatory/negotiating skills, in framing demands and agendas out of their – not other peoples' – objectives. This is not to romanticise the local nor to assert that local demands should always take priority; rather it is an argument for ensuring that those who are ultimately responsible

[35] With respect to women's participation see UN Committee on the Elimination of Discrimination against Women (CEDAW) 1997, General Recommendation No. 23: Political and Public Life, UN Doc. A/52/38, on women in public life.

[36] See Chapter 9.

for their own security are involved in design and implementation, as well as acquiring the evidence base necessary for effective policymaking.

Third, participation is reinforced by goals of *co-operation, good neighbourliness and regional dialogue.* The Security Council has also incorporated these concepts into country-specific peace operation mandates,[37] which must be inclusive of local civil society actors, defined as those concerned about the public as opposed to private or sectarian interests. New, regular fora for broad participation at all levels might be considered. A proposal of this sort was made by International Women's Congress in 1915: 'a permanent International Conference holding regular meetings in which women should take part' for 'practical proposals for further International Cooperation among the States'. Accordingly the Conference should appoint a 'permanent Council of Conciliation and Investigation for the settlement of international differences arising from economic competition, expanding commerce, increasing population and changes in social and political standards'.[38] Such a recommendation warrants reconsideration today.

Taking these principles into account, a further step is to consider some concrete measures, reforms or innovations that could contribute to the development of the kind of legal regime consistent with a Human Security model. These suggestions are somewhat *ad hoc* – some are more significant than others, some are easier to introduce than others, some are obvious, others less so.

Jurisdiction and Responsibility

Jurisdiction and responsibility are key aspects of state sovereignty with both outside and inside implications. Under international law a state is responsible for the commission of an internationally wrongful act – breach of a treaty or customary international law – that is attributable to it.[39] But this is constraining in a world where internationally wrongful acts, notably gross violations of human rights and international humanitarian law, are also committed by both international institutions and

[37] E.g., 'recalling the importance of the principles of good-neighbourliness, non-interference and regional cooperation;' in UN SC Resolution 2062, 26 July 2012 (Côte d'Ivoire); UN SC Resolution 2091, 14 February 2013 (Sudan).

[38] Resolutions adopted by the International Congress of Women, The Hague, the Netherlands, 1 May 1915, Resolution 11(b), http://womhist.alexanderstreet.com/hague/doc1.htm.

[39] International Law Commission, Responsibility of States for Internationally Wrongful Acts, UN GA Resolution 56/83, 12 December 2001, Annex, article 1.

private (non-state) bodies such as private military companies, armed groups, militias, criminals and individuals. There have been some transformative changes through extension of the territorial reach of responsibility,[40] though reconceptualisation of state responsibility to encompass the acts of non-state actors and through a wider allocation of direct responsibility among other such actors. Nevertheless these fall short of a comprehensive theory of responsibility for the commission of all atrocities.

With respect to the former, states have been made legally responsible for the illegal acts of non-state actors through the application of the principle of due diligence. In another manifestation of a national of a state being regarded as in some sense commensurate with the state,[41] the concept of due diligence was engaged to hold a state responsible to another state for a wrongful act committed against a national of that other state. Since 1989[42] the concept of due diligence has been regularly extended to make states responsible for their failure to have in place and to give effect to structures and institutions for the investigation and prosecution of and provision of redress for the wrongful acts committed by non-state actors. This reasoning has particular resonance in the context of human rights guarantees and is founded upon the state's obligation to protect and respect, as well as to fulfil, human rights. It has had particular application in the context of forced disappearances, violence against women and to the acts of business enterprises.[43] It represents a significant reconceptualisation of the principle of responsibility, collapses the distinction between public and private acts and opens the way to further extensions of the duty of due diligence. Nevertheless the practical application of the principle is limited

[40] E.g., the extraterritorial application of human rights treaties; see Chapter 6.

[41] Another example of this is the extension of the principle of self-defence to the rescue of nationals abroad; see Chapter 4.

[42] The concept of due diligence to cover liability for the acts of non-state actors was enunciated in the landmark case of *Velasquez Rodrigues v. Honduras*, IACtHR, Series C, No. 4, 29 July 1988, para. 172: 'An illegal act which violates human rights [or other internationally wrongful act] and which is initially not directly imputable to a State (e.g., because it is the act of a private person or because the person responsible has not been identified) can lead to international responsibility of the State, not because of the act itself, but because of the lack of due diligence to prevent the violation or to respond to it.'

[43] Special Representative of the Secretary-General on the Issue of Human Rights and Transnational Corporations and other Business Enterprises, 'Guiding Principles on Business and Human Rights: Implementing the United Nations 'Protect, Respect and Remedy' Framework', UN Doc. A/HRC/17/31, Annex; endorsed by UN HRC Resolution 17/4, 16 June 2011.

where a government has only limited (or no) control over territory or peoples supposedly subject to its authority.[44]

Imposition of direct responsibility upon non-state actors is the second way of extending the concept of responsibility. International treaties and customary international law impose obligations upon states. There is a growing expectation that there should be a shift away from the state-centric concept of responsibility so that non-state actors too would, or at least should, be bound by international law. This has been accepted with respect to international organisations, including possible accession to human rights treaties.[45] It has also been put forward with respect to other legal, non-state, persons, at least with respect to the security of the human person. For instance, the Special Representative of the Secretary-General on the issue of human rights and transnational corporations and other business enterprises, John Ruggie, asserted the 'Foundational Principle' that 'Business enterprises should respect human rights. This means that they should avoid infringing on the human rights of others and should address adverse human rights impacts with which they are involved'.[46] Common article 3 of the Geneva Conventions and Additional Protocol II are explicit, albeit limited, exceptions to the principle that only states incur obligations under treaties in that they are applicable to all parties coming within their scope in a non-international armed conflict, although the legal basis for this position is unclear. Further, the voluntary acceptance by some non-state armed groups of these obligations is accepted and institutions such as the Human Rights Council and SC have assumed such groups to be bound by these rules, even without such express acceptance.[47] Consequences of this allocation of responsibility include targeted sanctions,[48]

44 Whether state responsibility is engaged by 'effective' or 'overall' control over non-state actors has been the subject of much debate and judicial consideration; see *Application of the Convention on the Prevention and Punishment of the Crime of Genocide* (Bosnia and Herzegovina v. Serbia and Montenegro), 2007 ICJ Reports, judgment of 26 February 2007, 43, paras. 396–407.

45 The *Convention on the Rights of Persons with Disabilities,* 13 December 2006, article 42 provides that the Convention is 'open for signature by all States and by regional integration organizations'.

46 Guiding Principles on Business and Human Rights: Implementing the United Nations 'Protect, Respect and Remedy' Framework, endorsed by Human Rights Council Resolution 17/4, 16 June 2011.

47 See Chapter 6.

48 UN SC Resolution 1267, 15 October 1999 (sanctions against the Taliban and Osama Bin Laden and his associates) was instrumental in the move to targeted sanctions against individuals.

becoming subject to international investigation by commissions of inquiry or fact-finding missions and, of course, individual criminal responsibility for the commission of an international crime. However, a significant omission remains the failure to address the criminal responsibility of a collectivity, such as an armed militia except through command responsibility or joint criminal enterprise.[49] A further extension of responsibility in this regard would be a significant additional step.

But this gives rise to questions of jurisdiction. Under international law a major obstacle to holding a sovereign state accountable before the ICJ for the commission of an international wrong is the requirement of consent.[50] But adjudication against states has been widened through provision for incurred consent through institutional membership, for instance, of the regional human rights systems, or economic associations such as the World Trade Organisation. The willingness by states to accept the jurisdiction of such courts shows that the requirement of consent need not be an insurmountable barrier, although the failure of the permanent members of the SC (with the exception of the United Kingdom) to accept the compulsory jurisdiction of the ICJ[51] and the absence of the United States, Russia and China from the ICC also shows resistance by powerful players.

Individual criminal responsibility requires a forum for the prosecution of those accused of international crimes, either an international (or hybrid) tribunal or through state courts. As discussed in Chapter 10, the effectiveness of international criminal tribunals has been undermined by geopolitics, by an unwillingness by some states to allow their own nationals to be subject to their jurisdiction and by flaws in the process of criminal justice. In any event, the principle of complementarity in the Rome Statute of the ICC and the principle that only the most serious crimes should be subject to international adjudication means that domestic courts are the primary place for the prosecution of international crimes. This depends upon a state being able and willing to exercise jurisdiction. However, states guard jealously their sovereign right to exclusive jurisdiction within their territory comprising legislative, executive and judicial competence. Enforcement jurisdiction under domestic law is most readily based on territoriality (the criminal act was committed within the territory) and nationality (the act is committed by

[49] *Rome Statute of the International Criminal Court*, 1998, article 25 (3) (aiding and abetting, joint criminal purpose) and article 28 (command or superior authority).

[50] *Statute of the ICJ*, 1945, article 36.

[51] The so-called optional clause; *ibid.*, article 36 (2).

a national of the state); these heads of jurisdiction are repeated in the ICC.[52] Unless there has been a change of regime (as in Rwanda, Libya and Iraq) states are generally not prepared to prosecute atrocities committed on their territory or by their nationals, and the record for the holding of such trials is poor. Where such trials do take place, they may be many years later,[53] and may represent revenge rather than justice. Failure to hold domestic trials necessitates finding other states willing to do so but other heads of jurisdiction are more contested. Universal jurisdiction – allowing for prosecution of a crime without any nexus between the offender, the place of commission or even the nationality of the victims – is an attempt to ensure that crimes do not fail to be prosecuted because of lack of jurisdiction. This is provided for only in a limited way under international treaties, for instance, grave breaches of the Geneva Conventions, or the requirement to exercise jurisdiction or extradite an alleged offender found on the territory under a slew of anti-terrorist conventions. Universal jurisdiction, argued for by civil society groups, has not become entrenched in domestic law; at the domestic level, the prospect of a more extensive acceptance of universal jurisdiction[54] as the basis for the trial of gross violations of human rights that seemed possible following the Pinochet litigation[55] has receded,[56] and the US Supreme Court has reduced the potential of civil claims under the Alien Tort Statute of 1789.[57] Universal jurisdiction can be criticised as a form of judicial imperialism, and states seeking to exercise it have been subjected to pressure to withdraw.

A further obstacle is the possibility of claims of immunity. The current state of the law relating to immunity from jurisdiction for gross violations of human rights or international humanitarian law lacks clarity. On the one hand, the *Pinochet* case appeared to debunk the certainty of immunity

[52] *Rome Statute of the International Criminal Court,* 1998, article 12.

[53] E.g., the controversial International Crimes Tribunal was established as a domestic court in Bangladesh in 2009 with respect to crimes committed in the conflict of 1971 which led to the independence of Bangladesh; the Extraordinary Chambers in the Courts of Cambodia were established pursuant to an Agreement in 2003 between the UN and the Government of Cambodia for the prosecution of crimes committed by the Khmer Rouge between 1975 and 1979.

[54] E.g., *The Princeton Principles on Universal Jurisdiction.* Princeton University, Program in Law and Public Affairs, 2001.

[55] *Regina v. Bow Street Metropolitan Stipendiary Magistrate, ex parte Pinochet Ugarte* (Amnesty International Intervening), [2000] AC 151.

[56] Wuerth, Ingrid 2012. 'Pinochet's Legacy Reassessed', *American Journal of International Law* 106: 731–768.

[57] *Kiobel v. Royal Dutch Petroleum Co.,* 569 US, 17 April 2013.

for a former head of state, and the Rome Statute allows for ICC jurisdiction over people with such status;[58] the ICJ has clarified that a former head of state can be extradited for trial[59] but has also held that an incumbent Minister of Foreign Affairs was entitled to immunity;[60] the European Court of Human Rights has determined that allowing for immunity does not deny the victims' right of access to court.[61] UN peacekeepers enjoy immunity from the local courts of the territory in which they are deployed.

Despite the centrality of state sovereignty this brief account demonstrates that there have been inroads into the classic international law doctrines of responsibility and jurisdiction; extensions to both doctrines in order to enhance legal accountability show the tools are there. But there remain obstacles and lacunae, and the lack of any international forum with jurisdiction for the trial of those accused of crimes against humanity in Syria exposes these. Some omissions might be addressed by the conclusion of further treaties; for instance, the fact that the Rome Statute does not allow for immunity for heads of state shows that immunity need not be permanent and can be discounted by treaty. An amendment would be required to the Rome Statute to allow for the prosecution of corporate entities or collectivities. Another possibility is the creation of further *ad hoc*, specialist tribunals such as that pushed for by the EU and now agreed by the Kosovo Assembly for the trial of war crimes committed there. In the case of Syria the veto has prevented any referral to the ICC by the SC and also makes unlikely any *ad hoc* tribunal. Would it be possible for the GA to establish such a body if there was the required number of supporting states? The GA is able to create subsidiary bodies and also has residual competence with respect to international peace and security, as exercised in the Uniting for Peace resolution.[62] After all, the competence of the SC to establish the ICTY was not a foregone conclusion and was unsuccessfully challenged in the first case brought before it.[63] Proposals for other, different tribunals, have also been put forward, for instance, a tribunal for the

[58] *Rome Statute of the International Criminal Court*, 1998, article 12.

[59] *Questions relating to the Obligation to Prosecute or Extradite* (Belgium *v.* Senegal), 2012 ICJ Reports, judgment of 20 July 2012, 422.

[60] *Arrest Warrant of 11 April 2000* (Democratic Republic of Congo *v.* Belgium), 2002 ICJ Reports, judgment of 14 February 2002, 3.

[61] *Stichting Mothers of Srebrenica and Others v. The Netherlands*, ECtHR application no. 65542/12, 27 June 2013.

[62] UN GA Resolution 377 (V), 3 November 1950.

[63] *Prosecutor v. Dusko Tadic, Decision on the Defence Motion for Interlocutory Appeal on Jurisdiction*, ICTY AC, 2 October 1995.

prosecution of peacekeepers for sexual abuse and exploitation, or greater official recognition of the importance of Peoples' Tribunals.[64]

Institutional Change

Those who recognise the need for greater international support for human rights often advocate for the reform of the political power structures, notably the SC to increase its representativeness and transparency and for mechanisms to be introduced to ensure its accountability.[65] Human security requires that 'right authority' for the use of force should rest not with states but at an international level. While core reform of the SC has not taken place,[66] the Council itself has undertaken some moves in this direction, for instance, in the inclusion of an ombudsperson into the sanctions regime.[67] In October 2015, SC Resolution 2242 on women, peace and security indicated perhaps a greater willingness on the part of the SC to allow for greater openness and accept civil society voices within its domain. The Resolution provides for an Informal Experts Group on women, peace and security to integrate women's concerns across all country-specific situations on the SC's agenda and for an intention to invite civil society, including women's organisations, to brief the Council in country-specific considerations and relevant thematic areas. Further, it recognises the relevance of gender considerations with respect to sanctions and the need for gender expertise on the sanctions committees, and encourages the inclusion of civil society groups as participants in relevant meetings (including donor conferences).[68] These are admittedly small steps but nevertheless contrast with the impermeability of the SC of only

[64] Byrnes, Andrew and Simm, Gabrielle 2013. 'Peoples' Tribunals, International Law and the Use of Force', *University of New South Wales Law Journal* 36(2): 711–742.

[65] Dervis, Kemal and Özer, Ceren 2005. *A Better Globalization: Legitimacy, Governance, and Reform*. Center for Global Development, Brookings Institution Press.

[66] In the Millennium Declaration 'all States resolved to intensify their efforts "to achieve a comprehensive reform of the Security Council in all its aspects"', UN GA Resolution 55/2, 8 September 2000, para. 30. *In Larger Freedom: Towards Development, Security and Human Rights for All*, UN Doc. A/59/2005, 21 March 2005, para. 168. Kofi Annan supported the proposals for reform made by the High-level Panel on Threats, Challenges and Change, UN Doc. A/59/565, and set out two options, which were not adopted.

[67] See Chapters 2 and 3.

[68] UN SC Resolution 2242, 13 October 2015: 'encourages the meaningful participation of civil society organizations at international and regional peace and security meetings, as appropriate, including donor conferences to help ensure gender considerations are integrated in the development, prioritization, coordination, and implementation of policies and programmes, and encourages the hosts of such meetings to give due consideration to facilitating a cross representation of civil society participants'.

a few decades ago. These means of allowing access to the Council by some civil society representatives have followed from the first opening provided by the Arria formula[69] and point the way for further transformation. However, the implementation record of the women, peace and security resolutions since the ground-breaking Resolution 1325 in 2000 has not been impressive,[70] and these provisions need to be made operational and extended into other contexts. Who determines which civil society groups are included and on what criteria will also be crucial. While not directly related to the SC, the mobilisation of civil society to have a voice in the nominations for election of the Secretary-General in 2016 was a further example of the engagement of civil society and a rejection of the state (P5) grip on the choice of person to fill this key position.[71] While the ICJ has apparently closed the door to review of SC action, other bodies – domestic courts, human rights courts, the European Court of Justice – 'have now begun to question national implementing measures, particularly in the context of counter-terrorism'.[72] Such a trend may lead to pressure for further changes in the procedures of the SC.

It is perhaps unrealistic to look to international institutions for radical change. They are after all the creation of states for the pursuit of state objectives, and it has been argued that their embrace of neo-liberalism is at odds with any alternative agendas from those advanced by the major powers.[73] In the first decade of the twenty-first century some change appeared possible through then UN Secretary-General Kofi Annan's proposals for UN reforms. However, those finally accepted were not as far-sweeping as he had hoped but did include the creation of two new institutions. The Human Rights Council as a direct subsidiary of the GA was a response to the politicisation of the now defunct Commission on Human Rights and the Peace-Building Commission was to advance the Liberal Peace Agenda by providing a focal point for all stakeholders in

69 'Arria-Formula Meetings', are informal gatherings of the Security Council. See UN Security Council, '"Arria-Formula" Meetings,' *UN Security Council Working Methods Handbook*, www.un.org/en/sc/about/methods/arriaformula.

70 UN Women 2015. *Preventing Conflict, Transforming Justice, Securing the Peace.* A Global Study on the Implementation of Security Council Resolution 1325. New York ('Study on 1325').

71 Institute for Global Policy 2014. '1 for 7 Billion Find the Best UN Leader', www.worldfederalistscanada.org/mondial-dec14-1for7.pdf.

72 Gowlland-Debbas, Vera 2011. 'The Security Council and Issues of Responsibility under International Law', *Hague Recueil des Cours* 353: 185–444, 189, 393.

73 Chimni, B. S. 2004. 'International Institutions Today: An Imperial Global State in the Making', *European Journal of International Law* 15: 1–37.

peacebuilding. In 2010 these were followed by the UN body for Gender Equality and Women's Empowerment (UN Women). While all three institutions offer transformative potential with respect to the enhancement of human security, they also continue the trend towards compartmentalisation and specialisation. Martti Koskenniemi has noted that the purpose of specialisation 'the creation of special regimes of knowledge and expertise' is to achieve change in the international legal arena. He observes that "[i]f such regimes are bold in ambition, and able to rely on the support of some powerful sector of the political world, then they may succeed in changing the general bias in the law'.[74]

There are some signs of the requisite boldness. For instance, the Human Rights Council indicated its unwillingness to accept membership of non-human rights–friendly states through its expulsion of Libya in 2011. It has extended its remit through the mandating of a slew of fact-finding missions including those to Syria, Guinea and North Korea. Its process of peer review of human rights compliance – the Universal Periodic Review – opens the door to extending human rights monitoring and challenging states on such issues as arms trading. Its special rapporteurs have broadened the scope of human rights thinking; for instance, the special rapporteurs on counter-terrorism and human rights and summary execution and extra-judicial killings have challenged the military narrative on targeted killings.[75] However, transformative possibilities have also been undermined on the one hand by geo-political interests and on the other by bureaucracy, managerialism and lack of resources. For instance, the inability or unwillingness to cast aside geo-political considerations is illustrated by the 2015 appointment of Saudi Arabia to the Presidency of the Human Rights Council. While human rights institutions sought improved monitoring of the UN human rights treaties through reform of the treaty bodies, state resistance has meant that the agreed measures are weak and geared primarily towards cost-saving.[76] Human rights in its institutional form appears as little more than a ritual lacking substance.[77]

[74] Koskenniemi, Martti 2009. 'The Politics of International Law – 20 Years Later', *European Journal of International Law* 20: 7–19, 9.

[75] See Chapters 4 and 6.

[76] UN GA Resolution 68/268, 9 April 2014: Strengthening and Enhancing the Effective Functioning of the Human Rights Treaty Body System.

[77] Ritual regulation perceived as 'as formal participation in a system of regulation, while losing sight of its substantive goals'. Charlesworth, Hilary and Larking, Emma (eds.) 2015. *Human Rights and the Universal Periodic Review: Rituals and Ritualism*. Cambridge University Press.

UN Women is undoubtedly a significant development of the structures of global governance and provides a focal point for analysis of women's lives at the international level.[78] However, despite this consolidation, issues relating to women's security are still dispersed across various bodies; the women, peace and security agenda through the SC and the special representative on sexual violence in conflict (with the ensuing securitisation of the agenda); condemnation of discrimination against women and promotion of women's human rights through the Convention on the Elimination of All Forms of Discrimination against Women and its monitoring committee; combating violence against women across the GA, Human Rights Council and special rapporteur on violence against women, CEDAW, UN Women and multiple special agencies; gender equality and women's empowerment through development, policy change and action on the ground through UN Women. In addition the Sustainable Development Goals, Goal 5, to 'achieve gender equality, empower women and girls' covers diverse areas, including prohibition of discrimination, violence against women, health and reproductive rights, access to economic resources, land and property, but does not offer any understanding of transformative, or even substantive, equality[79] and is not directly linked to human rights. Nor is empowerment explained (e.g., whether it encompasses social, economic or political empowerment) or its transformative potential developed. This spread of institutional mandates facilitates broad attention but risks duplication of programmes and policies, dilution of resources and insufficient coherence. Strong and concerted leadership by UN Women might remedy this, but it still leaves the human rights agenda (CEDAW) institutionally apart from the security agenda (the SC) and the development agenda (SDGs). The same problems of complexity, overlaps, institutional gaps and indeed contradictory programming characterises many other fields of UN endeavour particularly in the field of development and humanitarianism. There needs to be creative thinking that goes beyond institutional tinkering. One bold proposal for vertical reform is that put forward by Richard Falk for a UN parliament

[78] For the creation of UN Women and critique see Charlesworth, Hilary and Chinkin, Christine 2013. 'The New United Nations "Gender Architecture": A Room with a View?' *Max Planck Yearbook of United Nations Law* 17: 1–60.

[79] Chinkin, Christine, Freeman, Marsha and Rudolf, Beate (eds.) 2012. *The UN Convention on the Elimination of All Forms of Discrimination against Women: A Commentary.* Oxford University Press, chapter 2.

or assembly.[80] Another is for what might be termed an international think tank under the aegis of the UN Secretary-General and accountable to the SC that has a responsibility to consider all aspects of major questions relating to the use of force.

Finally, more attention needs to be directed at the role of regional security and international financial institutions. While NATO remains the archetypal geo-political institution, emphasising collective defence of borders and the role of the military, other organisations such as the EU and the AU, both of which include human security in their official commitments, and the OSCE, based on the Helsinki principles, could play an enhanced role, through improved capabilities and greater political direction. The obligations of the International Financial Institutions (and their member states) need to be scrutinised to ensure that their programmes and policies do not further instability and insecurity.

Civil Society: Law Making and Monitoring

Looking to international institutions for the enhancement of human security entails a top-down approach. Civil society access to and influence upon international institutions has undoubtedly increased throughout the lifetime of the UN. However, international institutions remain state-based; states are the gatekeepers that control attendance, participation and influence. How can international law encompass a more 'bottom-up' character, and where are the openings to allow for this? One possibility is through participation in international law-making that goes beyond lobbying and driving legal reform through coalition building between NGOs and between NGOs and like-minded states.[81]

Especially relevant to regulation of new wars, Anthea Roberts and Sandesh Sivakumaran have pointed to the 'anomaly' of state-made international law seeking to regulate the behaviour of all sides in a non-international armed conflict.[82] Jan Klabbers acknowledges that imposing obligations under IHL upon non-state actors 'require[s] a

[80] Falk, Richard 2006. 'Reforming the United Nations: Global Civil Society Perspectives and Initiatives', in Glasius, Marlies, Kaldor, Mary and Anheier, Helmut (eds.), *Global Civil Society 2005–6*. Sage.

[81] Boyle, Alan and Chinkin, Christine 2007. *The Making of International Law*. Oxford University Press, chapter 2.

[82] Roberts, Anthea and Sivakumaran, Sandesh 2012. 'Lawmaking by Nonstate Actors: Engaging Armed Groups in the Creation of International Humanitarian Law', *Yale Journal of International Law* 37: 108–153.

justification of sorts, if only for the sake of legitimacy'.[83] States are, of course, likely to jealously preserve their control over law-making and also to resist the legitimacy that allowing even a small role to non-state actors in this regard might invoke. But allowing this for at least some non-state actors[84] might also create some ownership of the rules and thus a push, even if minimal, towards compliance. Some suggest that non-state actors might also include armed groups and that where such groups have voluntarily accepted or agreed to international rules there appears to have been a positive effect on behaviour.[85] This might also extend to states fighting non-state groups through a notion of reciprocity that is missing where the latter have made no such gesture.[86] This approach mainly has relevance in classic civil wars involving a contest of will between organised rebels and the regimes; typically in new wars, the armed groups deliberately violate the rules and their inclusion in rule-making could have the contrary consequence of legitimating their behaviour.

As regards to non-violent groups, Isabelle Gunning argued over two decades ago for the practice of NGOs to be accorded weight for the determination of customary international law.[87] This suggestion has not had traction, but the input of civil society through intense lobbying and negotiation into various instruments of soft law and the contribution of such instruments to the formation of customary international law is an opening in this direction, albeit limited. While we also acknowledge

83 Klabbers, Jan 2003. '(I Can't Get No) Recognition: Subjects Doctrine and the Emergence of Non-State Actors', in Petman, Jarna and Klabbers, Jan (eds.) *Nordic Cosmopolitanism: Essays in International Law for Martti Koskenniemi*. Brill, 351–369, 354–355 cited *ibid.*, 122.

84 Roberts and Sivakumaran suggest those armed groups 'that are parties to noninternational armed conflicts and meet the definitional requirement of organization, such as the Fuerzas Armadas Revolucionarias de Colombia (Revolutionary Armed Forces of Colombia) (FARC) of Colombia, the Liberation Tigers of Tamil Eelam (LTTE) of Sri Lanka, and the Sudan People's Liberation Movement/Army (SPLM/A) of Sudan'. This would exclude terrorist networks; Roberts and Sivakumaran, *op. cit.*, 126.

85 Ibid.

86 In fact, 'the traditional, statist approach to the doctrine of sources is [already] descriptively outdated', for instance, through law-making capacities of international institutions (*ibid.*, 128). Roberts and Sivakumaran suggest that non-state-armed groups be allowed to formally accept existing obligations and to undertake new ones through unilateral declarations, bilateral or trilateral 'hybrid' treaties or through strategies for participation in multilateral treaty negotiations and becoming parties thereto, although there would have to be caution about whether this might legitimate their use of force.

87 Gunning, Isabelle 1991. 'Modernizing Customary International Law: The Challenge of Human Rights', *Virginia Journal of International Law* 31: 211–247.

concerns of Western dominance and non-democratic pressure, we argue that at the least widespread protest by civil society should be counted as practice; why should non-acquiescence by civil society be given less weight than that of states? Credible fact-finding reports by civil society have been admitted in international tribunals, and it seems somewhat perverse that they might not be regarded as practice.

Philip Alston and Bruno Simma argued, also some decades ago, for greater weight to be accorded to general principles of law. More recently, Judge Cançado Trindade has regretted in the context of the Genocide Convention what he calls the atomisation by the ICJ of customary international law and treaty law; he calls for them to be seen together instead of being regarded separately. The glue that allows for this is general principles of law, in particular the general principle of humanity: 'The atomized approach of the Court, furthermore, fails to recognize the great importance for both conventional and customary international law of the general principles of law, and in particular of the principle of humanity'.[88] General principles are to Judge Trindade not just a glue but a process which, when given greater attention, 'brings us closer to the domain of superior [higher] *human values*, to be safeguarded, not sufficiently worked upon in international case law and doctrine. It is, ultimately, those principles that inform and conform the applicable norms, and ultimately any legal system'.[89]

NGOs play a significant role in monitoring compliance with states' treaty obligations, especially in the contexts of human rights, IHL, international criminal law and weapons law, through collecting and collating documentation and evidence, providing argument through amicus briefs and interventions and supporting test cases. Allowing some limited access by individuals to institutions was started under the League of Nations through petitioning to the Mandate Commission.[90] History has shown that whenever there is such an opening it is used and states are forced to accept such unwelcome intrusion, which typically evolves beyond their imaginings.[91] Litigation against states in national or international courts

[88] Croatia v. Serbia, *op. cit.*, per dissenting opinion Judge Cançado Trindade, para. 513.

[89] *Request for Interpretation of the Judgment of 15 June 1962 in the Case concerning the Temple of Preah Vihear* (Cambodia v. Thailand) (Merits), 2013 ICJ Reports 281, 11 November 2013, per separate opinion Judge Cançado Trindade, para. 42.

[90] Pedersen, Susan 2015. *The Guardians: The League of Nations and the Crisis of Empire.* Oxford University Press.

[91] Simpson, Brian 2001. *Human Rights and the End of Empire: Britain and the Genesis of the European Convention.* Oxford University Press.

highlights the potential of international law as a form of resistance to state control and has been a significant consequence of the military interventions in Afghanistan and Iraq.[92] Is international law a legitimate instrument of resistance, or is 'lawfare' unreasonably restrictive of military action or defence policy? The ongoing challenge to the legality of nuclear weapons through the ICJ, most recently by the Marshall Islands[93] seeking to hold states with nuclear weapons to the obligations of the Non-Proliferation Treaty, article VI, starkly poses this question.[94] While to date the outcomes have not been those desired by non-nuclear weapon states or the civil society supporting them, such challenges keep the issue alive and emphasise the reluctance expressed through law to allow the possession of nuclear weapons to continue.[95]

Access to Justice/Transformative Justice

Human security requires the protection of law meaning that national jurisdictions must ensure access to justice for all victims of violence. Enhancing the rule of law and access to justice have been recognised as central to the realisation of human rights, transformative justice and hence human security. Some forward-looking recommendations have been made, in particular with respect to removing obstacles to access to justice for women. For instance, the Global Study on women, peace and security made specific recommendations for enhancing women's full participation in truth and reconciliation processes: quotas for women's leadership,[96] introducing measures for the protection of victims and witnesses, compensation for time and travel, childcare costs and facilities, the use of local languages and innovative ways of running proceedings to overcome obstacles.[97] The

[92] See Chapters 6 and 8.

[93] Republic of the Marshall Islands, Application Instituting Proceedings against the Republic of India; Application Instituting Proceedings against the Islamic Republic of Pakistan; Application Instituting Proceedings against the United Kingdom of Great Britain and Northern Ireland, ICJ, all on 24 April 2014.

[94] See Chapter 7.

[95] The ICJ determined that it would not proceed to the merits in the cases brought by the Marshall Islands as there was no dispute between that state and, respectively, the United Kingdom, India or Pakistan; see, e.g., *Obligations concerning Negotiations relating to Cessation of the Nuclear Arms Race and to Nuclear Disarmament* (Marshall Islands *v.* United Kingdom), judgment of 5 October 2016.

[96] This is in accordance with the Convention on the Elimination of All Forms of Discrimination against Women, 1979, article 4 (a). The usefulness of quotas in situations other than political participation is often overlooked.

[97] Study on 1325, 111.

CEDAW Committee too has made far-reaching recommendations with respect to access to justice, especially with regards to the role of civil society. It recommends, for instance, that states 'cooperate with civil society and community-based organizations to develop sustainable mechanisms to support women's access to justice and encourage non-governmental organizations and civil society entities to take part in litigation on women's rights'. It also recognises the need for an enhanced knowledge base, recommending 'qualitative studies and critical gender analysis in collaboration with civil society organizations as well as academic institutions of all justice systems in order to highlight practices, procedures and jurisprudence that promote or limit women's full access to justice'.[98] Transformative justice, of course, has to be part of a broader societal transformation.

It has been a long-accepted principle of international law that a state that commits an international wrong must make reparation.[99] More recently reparations have become part of transitional justice and their transformative potential explored. For instance, victims are entitled to reparations from convicted persons under the Rome Statute of the ICC,[100] which also set up a Trust Fund for the benefit of victims. This operates independently of convictions and to date has distributed support to more than 110,000 victims of crimes, including tens of thousands of survivors of sexual and gender-based violence through physical and psychological rehabilitation and material support.[101] This contrasts both with the lack of convictions before that Court for sexual violence by 2015[102] and with the unwillingness of the UN to pay compensation for moral (non-material) damages in third-party claims cases.[103] While earlier human rights treaties included the right to a remedy, the Convention on the Rights of Persons with Disabilities spells out what this entails: states parties to take all appropriate measures to promote

[98] CEDAW, General Recommendation on Women's Access to Justice, C/GC/33, 23 July 2015.

[99] *Chorzow Factory Case* (Germany v. Poland), PCIJ Series A, No. 17, 13 September 1928.

[100] *Rome Statute of the International Criminal Court,* 1998, article 75.

[101] Study on 1325, *op. cit.,* 103.

[102] The ICC has spelled out the importance of a gender inclusive approach in assessing the reparations to be paid to victims and that victims of sexual violence could benefit from assistance provided. However, in the *Lubanga* case since he was not convicted for crimes of sexual violence, these could not be included in the concept of harm; *The Prosecutor v. Thomas Lubanga Dyilo,* Decision establishing the principles and procedures to be applied to reparations, ICC-01/04-01/06, 7 August 2012.

[103] UN GA Resolution 52/247, 17 July 1998.

the physical, cognitive and psychological recovery, rehabilitation and social reintegration of persons with disabilities in an environment that fosters the health, welfare, self-respect, dignity and autonomy of the person and takes into account gender- and age-specific needs'.[104] Such an approach to reparations post-conflict would be transformative and preventive as a key to breaking the cycle of violence and is core to a comprehensive approach.[105] The InterAmerican Court of Human Rights and the special rapporteur on violence against women have both asserted the importance of reparations as transformative, as a mechanism for redistributive justice, which should target structural disadvantage and vulnerability – both for individuals and for communities.[106] They offer the opportunity to redress 'pre-existing inequalities, injustices, prejudices and biases or other societal perceptions and practices that enabled violations to occur, including discrimination against [minorities, ethnic groups] women and girls'.[107] Appropriate collective measures to an affected community include memorials, provision of education and health facilities for an affected community, accountability, public apology.[108] Again the participation of local civil society is crucial for determination of local needs and of women and girls, for without their input post-conflict initiatives are more likely to reflect men's experience of violence and their concerns, priorities and needs regarding redress. Guarantees of non-repetition have been argued to be especially transformative, for they require states to confront gender inequality as an underlying structural cause of the violence and insecurity and the necessary legal and institutional reforms and changed mindsets to redress this. A comprehensive approach thus should address seriously reparations.

[104] *The Convention on the Rights of Persons with Disabilities,* 13 December 2006, article 16.

[105] See Office of the UN High Commissioner for Human Rights 2008. *Rule-of-Law Tools for Post-Conflict States: Reparations Programmes*. United Nations.

[106] '[R]reparations must be designed to change this situation [structural discrimination], so that their effect is not only of restitution, but also of rectification. In this regard, reestablishment of the same structural context of violence and discrimination is not acceptable'. *Case of Gonzáles et al. ('Cotton Field') v. Mexico*, IACtHR, judgment of 16 November 2009, para. 450.

[107] Manjoo, Rashida, Report of the Special Rapporteur on Violence against Women, UN Doc. A/HRC/14/22, 19 April 2012, 2.

[108] Contreras-Garduño, Diana and Rombouts, Sebastiaan 2010. 'Collective Reparations for Indigenous Communities Before the Inter-American Court of Human Rights', *Utrecht Journal of International and European Law* 27(72): 4–17.

Summary

These are some of the changes that could be concretely pursued on the basis of a narrative that focusses on the safety of people whoever and wherever they are – New York, London, Bangui, Madrid, Kabul, Goma, Ramadi, Raqqa or Aleppo, Gaza or Tel Aviv, or in the middle of the Mediterranean. Evidently, implementation of the Human Security model would require a very big allocation of resources, a far-reaching reform of global security capabilities, and a transformation in power structures, involving more effective international and regional institutions as well as greater participation of civil society, local authorities and women. What we suggest is that there are already pointers in this direction in recent legal innovations and that it is possible to find additional mechanisms, some modest and some more ambitious, that would push this direction further and contribute to a change of mind-set.

12.5 Conclusion

We are not unaware of and do not ignore the 'dark side' of international law. Critical legal theorists have pointed to the role international law plays in protecting the interests of the powerful, perpetuating bias, sustaining inequalities between and within states,[109] legitimating violence and economic and sexual exploitation. The book has demonstrated the particular ways in which international law – dominated by the powerful – has been stretched by the War on Terror and the reversion to Geo-Politics, and how it has absorbed the Liberal Peace and human rights agenda and co-opted them for its own ends. We accept that it is a flawed system in substance and application and it could become even more so in what is being described as a post-truth world. In light of these realities can it be regarded as an appropriate tool for upholding human security, including the security of those made most vulnerable by the current system?[110] Should the structural biases of international law justify its being discounted, or should it be complied with in the hope of reform from within?[111] This last question is ironically the

[109] Chimni, *op. cit.* ('Peace through Law').

[110] E.g., Kennedy, David 2004. *The Dark Sides of Virtue: Reassessing International Humanitarianism*. Princeton University Press.

[111] In the context of feminist engagement with international law see Kouvo, Sari and Pearson, Zoe (eds.) 2011. *Feminist Perspectives on Contemporary International Law: Between Resistance and Compliance*. Hart Publishing.

same for both powerful states that view international law as excessively constraining and those marginalised by it.

At the beginning of this book, we suggested that law is best understood as a discourse that accommodates both the interests of ruling elites as well as widely agreed norms. Law provides, at one and the same time, a legitimation of the powerful and a tool for resistance of the weak. This is true of both domestic and international law. The difference between the two regimes is that because of the density of agreed procedures and enforcement mechanisms as well as greater transparency and accountability and more coherent (although often also polarised) public debate, norms may be more important at domestic levels, at any rate in rights-based societies. But international law also has transformative potential that needs to be harnessed and used for resistance – either through litigation that challenges the dominant paradigm, or through identifying practical sites of change – civil society, spaces for the operation of human security, zones of civility – combining these with the transformative potential offered by theoretical approaches such as feminism or critical security studies.

We believe that international law must be at the heart of human security and national standards must be in accordance with it. The components of international law upon which human security is constructed – Human Rights Law, International Criminal Law, IHL, Refugee Law, principles with respect to Internally Displaced Persons, what we might call a new law of peace – are, however, compartmentalised and fragmented. We need to work to ensure that they are integrated through a common theme of putting individuals at the fore and not allow human security to be co-opted to support other agendas, for instance, those of Geo-Politics and the War on Terror.

Finally human security cannot be compartmentalised away from other agendas, for instance, those of the Sustainable Development goals, of climate change or of migration flows. All these indicate that the self-reinforcing economic, social, environmental and cultural aspects of conflict are more deep-seated than can be addressed in localised peace negotiations; that alongside the local context are other causative factors that are entrenched in the international system, including issues of gender, in particular gendered power relations, the constructs of masculinities and femininities shaped and perpetuated by conflict, patriarchy, militarism and violence, the political economy of war, the impact of neo-liberalism and corporate imperatives or various forms of racism and xenophobia. All are inter-linked and impact on how the conflict affected societies are structured and managed. We recognise, of course, that implementation and enforcement remain intractable; what we have attempted throughout this book is to offer insights into the issues raised by the regulation of extreme political violence and some practical approaches. Ultimately these rest on political will.

INDEX

www.ingramcontent.com/pod-product-compliance
Lightning Source LLC
Chambersburg PA
CBHW060336210525
27036CB00003B/241
9781107171213